# Handbook of Digital Forensics and Investigation

# Handbook of Digital Forensics and Investigation

Edited by

**Eoghan Casey**

With contributions from

**Cory Altheide**
**Christopher Daywalt**
**Andrea de Donno**
**Dario Forte**
**James O. Holley**
**Andy Johnston**
**Ronald van der Knijff**
**Anthony Kokocinski**
**Paul H. Luehr**
**Terrance Maguire**
**Ryan D. Pittman**
**Curtis W. Rose**
**Joseph J. Schwerha IV**
**Dave Shaver**
**Jessica Reust Smith**

AMSTERDAM • BOSTON • HEIDELBERG • LONDON
NEW YORK • OXFORD • PARIS • SAN DIEGO
SAN FRANCISCO • SINGAPORE • SYDNEY • TOKYO

Academic Press is an imprint of Elsevier

Elsevier Academic Press
30 Corporate Drive, Suite 400, Burlington, MA 01803, USA
525 B Street, Suite 1900, San Diego, California 92101-4495, USA
84 Theobald's Road, London WC1X 8RR, UK

This book is printed on acid-free paper. ∞

Permissions may be sought directly from Elsevier's Science & Technology Rights Department in Oxford, UK: phone: (+44) 1865 843830, fax: (+44) 1865 853333, E-mail: permissions@ elsevier.co.uk. You may also complete your request on-line via the Elsevier homepage (http://elsevier.com), by selecting "Customer Support" and then "Obtaining Permissions."

**Library of Congress Cataloging-in-Publication Data**
Application Submitted

**British Library Cataloguing in Publication Data**
A catalogue record for this book is available from the British Library

ISBN 13: 978-0-12-374267-4

For all information on all Elsevier Academic Press publications
visit our Web site at www.elsevierdirect.com

Printed in the United States of America

09 10 9 8 7 6 5 4 3 2 1

*To Genevieve, Roisin and Hesper*

# Contents

Contributors . . . . . . . . . . . . . . . . . . . . . . . . . . . . . . . . . . . . . . ix
Foreword . . . . . . . . . . . . . . . . . . . . . . . . . . . . . . . . . . . . . . . . . . xi
About the Authors . . . . . . . . . . . . . . . . . . . . . . . . . . . . . . . . . . .xv
Acknowledgements . . . . . . . . . . . . . . . . . . . . . . . . . . . . . . . xxiii

**CHAPTER 1**   Introduction . . . . . . . . . . . . . . . . . . . . . . . . . . . . . . . . . . . . . 1
    *Eoghan Casey*

## Part 1     Investigative Methodology

**CHAPTER 2**   Forensic Analysis . . . . . . . . . . . . . . . . . . . . . . . . . . . . . . . 21
    *Eoghan Casey and Curtis W. Rose*

**CHAPTER 3**   Electronic Discovery . . . . . . . . . . . . . . . . . . . . . . . . . . . . 63
    *James O. Holley, Paul H. Luehr, Jessica Reust Smith,*
    *and Joseph J. Schwerha IV*

**CHAPTER 4**   Intrusion Investigation . . . . . . . . . . . . . . . . . . . . . . . . . 135
    *Eoghan Casey, Christopher Daywalt, and Andy Johnston*

## Part 2     Technology

**CHAPTER 5**   Windows Forensic Analysis . . . . . . . . . . . . . . . . . . . . . 209
    *Ryan D. Pittman and Dave Shaver*

**CHAPTER 6**   UNIX Forensic Analysis . . . . . . . . . . . . . . . . . . . . . . . . 301
    *Cory Altheide and Eoghan Casey*

**CHAPTER 7**   Macintosh Forensic Analysis . . . . . . . . . . . . . . . . . . . 353
    *Anthony Kokocinski*

**CHAPTER 8**   Embedded Systems Analysis . . . . . . . . . . . . . . . . . . . 383
    *Ronald van der Knijff*

**CHAPTER 9**    Network Investigations.................................437
*Eoghan Casey, Christopher Daywalt, Andy Johnston,
and Terrance Maguire*

**CHAPTER 10**  Mobile Network Investigations .....................517
*Dario Forte and Andrea de Donno*

Index  ..............................................................................559

# Contributors

**Eoghan Casey**   cmdLabs, Baltimore, MD

**Curtis W. Rose**   Curtis W. Rose & Associates, Laurel, MD

**Cory Altheide**   Mandiant Highlands Ranch, CO

**James O. Holley**   Ernst & Young LLP, New York, NY

**Paul H. Luehr**   Stroz Friedberg, Minneapolis, MN

**Jessica Reust Smith**   Stroz Friedberg, Washington, DC

**Joseph J. Schwerha IV**   TraceEvidence, Charleroi, PA

**Christopher Daywalt**   cmdLabs, Baltimore, MD

**Andy Johnston**   University of Maryland, Baltimore County, Baltimore, MD

**Ryan D. Pittman**   U.S. Army CCIU, Fort Belvoir, VA

**Dave Shaver**   U.S. Army, Woodbridge, VA

**Anthony Kokocinski**   CSC, Chicago, IL

**Ronald van der Knijff**   Netherlands Forensic Institute, Den Haag, The Netherlands

**Terrance Maguire**   cmdLabs, Baltimore, MD

**Dario Forte**   DFLabs, Crema (CR), Italy

**Andrea de Donno**   Lepta Milano (MI), Italy

# Foreword

Everywhere around you, you can find a digital storage device within arm's reach. We have "Electronic Attention Deficit Disorder:" our concentration being pulled from one device to another.

You use a mobile device where you make your phone calls, send text messages, post on Twitter, all while surfing the web. You use a computer to communicate, pay bills, order groceries, or even watch television. You probably also use one or more of the following devices on a daily basis: GPS, video game system, eReader, MP3 player, digital video recorder, or more.

For better or worse, our lives—our personal/private data—are recorded on these devices moment-by-moment. As a result, we are seeing the rise in crimes, civil litigation cases, and computer security incidents that exploit your data found on these devices. This Handbook is a powerful resource for investigating these cases and analyzing evidence on computers, networks, mobile devices and other embedded systems.

The demand for digital forensic professionals to analyze these devices has increased due to the sheer number of cases that organizations now face. Major incidents such as TJX, Heartland, and Hannaford may have drawn the most media attention, but attacks against small, medium, and large businesses that include data breaches, fund transfers, and intellectual property theft are no longer rare. And these security breaches are costing organizations millions of dollars. For the digital forensic investigator, he or she must be able to effectively respond, investigate, and ultimately answer difficult questions. As criminal cases continue collecting a subject's or victim's cell phone, computer, and other electronic devices to solve a crime, and as civil lawsuits introduce electronically stored evidence, the investigator's role is crucial.

For all of us, the digital forensic profession grows more challenging. We no longer analyze just a desktop system for evidence. In many cases, we examine an enterprise network with more than 1,000 nodes, a mobile device, or even a portable game system. The skills and the knowledge required to meet the increasing demands placed on a digital forensic investigator today are immense. That is why this Handbook helps us all. It sets the mark for an in-depth examination of the diversity that encompasses today's digital forensic field.

Digital Forensics is undergoing a transition from a perceived ad hoc field into a scientific one that requires detailed analysis combined with a variety of sound and proven methods. One of the main themes that struck me while reading this Handbook is the strong case made for why a scientific foundation is crucial to analyze a case successfully. The Handbook is organized by the old and new disciplines in the digital forensic field where the new breakthroughs are occurring daily. From network and mobile device forensics to traditional forensics using the latest techniques against UNIX, Apple Macintosh, and Microsoft Windows operating systems, this Handbook offers details that are extremely cutting edge and provides new approaches to digital based investigations—from data theft breaches to intellectual property theft. I particularly enjoy the sections that provide detailed explanations in straightforward terms; they offer good ideas that I hope to use in my own forensic reports.

When I first picked up the Handbook, I was impressed with the depth and scope of expertise of the assembled author team. Many led the investigations noted above and those that made national headlines in the past ten years. If you had the ability to truly call a digital forensic "A-Team" together to help with a case, these authors would comprise the majority of that team. We are fortunate that they bring their hard-core practical experiences to each and every chapter.

It is clear that this Handbook will become a must read for new and seasoned investigators alike.

I urge you to read and understand the principles presented in the following pages. True scientific analyses that use the techniques presented here will allow you to solve your cases. I hope you enjoy the Handbook as much as I have. My hat is off to the authors for their continued contributions to the digital forensic field and for coming together to produce this Handbook.

**Rob Lee**
*Director, MANDIANT, Inc.*
*Digital Forensic Curriculum Lead and Faculty Fellow, The SANS Institute*

## BIO:

Rob Lee is a Director for MANDIANT (http://www.mandiant.com), a leading provider of information security consulting services and software to Fortune 500 organizations and the U.S. Government. Rob is also the Curriculum Lead for Digital Forensic Training at the SANS Institute (http://forensics.sans.org).

Rob has more than 13 years experience in computer forensics, vulnerability and exploit discovery, intrusion detection/prevention, and incident response. After graduating from the U.S. Air Force Academy, he served in the U.S. Air Force as a founding member of the 609th Information Warfare Squadron, the first U.S. military operational unit focused on Information Operations. Later, he served as a member of the Air Force Office of Special Investigations where he conducted computer crime investigations, incident response, and computer forensics. Prior to joining MANDIANT, Rob worked directly with a variety of U.S. government agencies in the law enforcement, Department of Defense, and intelligence communities. He provided the technical lead for a vulnerability discovery and exploit development team, ran a cyber forensics branch, and led a computer forensic and security software development team. Rob is coauthor of the bestselling book, *Know Your Enemy, 2nd Edition,* and was named "Digital Forensic Examiner of the Year" by the Forensic 4Cast 2009 Awards. Rob holds a bachelor's degree from the U.S. Air Force Academy and his MBA from Georgetown University.

# About the Authors

## Eoghan Casey

Eoghan Casey is founding partner of cmdLabs, author of the foundational book *Digital Evidence and Computer Crime*, and coauthor of *Malware Forensics*. For over a decade, he has dedicated himself to advancing the practice of incident response and digital forensics. He helps client organizations handle security breaches and analyzes digital evidence in a wide range of investigations, including network intrusions with international scope. He has testified in civil and criminal cases, and has submitted expert reports and prepared trial exhibits for computer forensic and cyber-crime cases.

As a Director of Digital Forensics and Investigations at Stroz Friedberg, he maintained an active docket of cases and co-managed the firm's technical operations in the areas of computer forensics, cyber-crime response, incident response, and electronic discovery. He also spearheaded Stroz Friedberg's external and in-house forensic training programs as Director of Training. Eoghan has performed thousands of forensic acquisitions and examinations, including Windows, UNIX, and Macintosh systems, Enterprise servers, smart phones, cell phones, network logs, backup tapes, and database systems. He also has extensive information security experience, as an Information Security Officer at Yale University and in subsequent consulting work. He has performed vulnerability assessments, deployed and maintained intrusion detection systems, firewalls and public key infrastructures, and developed policies, procedures, and educational programs for a variety of organizations.

Eoghan holds a B.S. in Mechanical Engineering from the University of California at Berkeley, and an M.A. in Educational Communication and Technology from New York University. He conducts research and teaches graduate students at Johns Hopkins University Information Security Institute, and is Editor-in-Chief of *Digital Investigation: The International Journal of Digital Forensics and Incident Response*.

## Cory Altheide

Cory Altheide has been performing forensics and incident response for eight years. He has responded to numerous incidents for a variety of clients and is constantly seeking to improve the methodologies in use in the incident response field. Mr. Altheide is currently a principal consultant at Mandiant, an information security consulting firm that works with the Fortune 500, the defense industrial base and the banks of the world to secure their networks and combat cyber-crime.

Prior to joining Mandiant, Mr. Altheide worked at IBM, Google and the National Nuclear Security Administration (NNSA). Mr. Altheide has authored several papers for the computer forensics journal *Digital Investigation* and co-authored *UNIX and Linux Forensic Analysis* (2008). Additionally, Mr. Altheide is a recurring member of the program committe of the Digital Forensics Research Workshop (DFRWS).

## Christopher Daywalt

Christopher Daywalt is a founding partner of cmdLabs, and has considerable experience conducting digital investigations within large enterprises and handling security incidents involving persistent information security threats. He is dedicated to providing consistent, quality work that directly addresses the needs of organizations that experience information security events.

Before working at cmdLabs, Chris was an instructor and course developer at the Defense Cyber Investigations Training Academy, where he authored and delivered instruction in digital forensics and investigation to Federal law enforcement and counter intelligence agents. While there he produced advanced material in specific areas such as live network investigation, Windows and Linux intrusion investigation, log analysis and network exploitation techniques. During this work he frequently served as the lead for development and delivery.

Prior to that, he worked as an incident handler in the CSC Computer Investigations and Incident Response group, where he performed investigation, containment and remediation of enterprise-scale security incidents for large corporations. Through these endeavors he gained experience responding to a variety of events, including massive PCI/PII data breaches at corporate retailers and persistent intrusions into government-related organizations. Chris also worked as a global security architect at CSC, conducting assessment and design of security technologies and architectures for deployment in enterprise information systems.

Chris earned his bachelor's degree from UMBC, and holds an MS in Network Security from Capitol College.

## Andrea de Donno

Andrea De Donno was born in Milan, Italy in 1975. His education focused on science. After a brief stint with the Carabinieri, in 1998 he began working for one of the major intelligence firms, providing technical investigation services and technology to the Italian Military Operations Units. In 2002, he became Managing Director of the company, increasing the company's revenues and expanding it throughout Italy with the creation of new Operations Centers. That same year, he was also named Managing Director of an Italian consulting firm offering specialized risk analysis and risk management services to medium and large companies.

## Dario Forte

Dario Forte, former police detective and founder and CEO of DFLabs has worked in information security since 1992. He has been involved in numerous international conferences on information warfare, including the RSA Conference, Digital Forensic Research Workshops, the Computer Security Institute, the U.S. Department of Defense Cybercrime Conference, and the U.S. Department of Homeland Security (New York Electronic Crimes Task Force). He was also the keynote speaker at the Black Hat conference in Las Vegas. Mr. Forte is Associate Professor at UAT and Adjunct Faculty at University of Milano, Crema Research Center. With more than 50 papers and book chapters written for the most important scientific publishers worldwide, he provides security consulting, incident response and forensics services to several government agencies and global private companies.

## James O. Holley

James Holley leads a team of computer forensics and electronic evidence discovery professionals in the New York Metropolitan Area providing a wide range of dispute resolution services to clients, including Computer Forensics, Forensic Text and Data Analytics, Electronic Discovery/Discovery Response Services, and Electronic Records Management/Legal Hold services.

With Ernst & Young for ten years, James is the technology leader for their U.S. Computer Forensics team. He also leads EY's New York office of Forensic Technology and Discovery Services, a specialty practice in Fraud Investigation and Dispute Services. James has provided expert testimony in deposition and trial and has testified in arbitration proceedings.

Prior to joining EY, James spent nearly ten years as a federal agent with the U.S. Air Force Office of Special Investigations. As a special agent, he gained experience conducting general criminal investigations prior to beginning a career in counterintelligence. He spent six years as an AFOSI counterintelligence case officer planning, developing and executing offensive counterintelligence operations and teaching new case officers. In his final assignment, he was an AFOSI computer crime investigator focused on integrating computer forensics and incident response capabilities into counterintelligence operations.

James holds a bachelors' degree from the United States Air Force Academy, a Master's of Science in Computer Science from James Madison University, and is a Certified Computer Examiner (CCE).

## Andy Johnston

Andy Johnston has been a software developer, scientific programmer, and a Unix system administrator in various capacities since 1981. For the last ten years, he was worked as IT security coordinator for the University of Maryland, Baltimore County specializing in network intrusion detection, anti-malware computer forensics, and forensic log analysis.

## Ronald van der Knijff

Ronald van der Knijff received his B.Sc. degree in electrical engineering in 1991 from the Rijswijk Institute of Technology. After performing military service as a Signal Officer he obtained his M.Sc. degree in Information Technology in 1996 from the Eindhoven University of Technology. Since then he works at the Digital Technology and Biometrics department of the Netherlands Forensic Institute as a forensic scientist.

He is responsible for the embedded systems group and is also court-appointed expert witness in this area. He is author of the (outdated) cards4labs and TULP software and founder of the TULP2G framework. He is a visiting lecturer on 'Cards & IT' at the Dutch Police Academy, a visiting lecturer on 'Smart Cards and Biometrics' at the Masters Program 'Information Technology' of TiasNimbas Business School and a visiting lecturer on 'Mobile and Embedded Device Forensics' at the Master's in 'Artificial Intelligence' of the University in Amsterdam (UvA).

## Anthony Kokocinski

Anthony Kokocinski started his forensic career working for the Illinois Attorney General directly out of college. His passion for Macintosh computers quickly led him to research and continue work on this from the number of "it's a Mac, you do it" cases that came across his desk. During this tenure he began to work with the Macintosh Electronic Search and Seizure Course for the RCMP's Canadien Police College. When he became tired of the very well traveled roads in Illinois he fell in with CSC on a government contract for the DoD. One of the many duties there was to design the first Macintosh Forensics Examinations course. This became very popular for both the DoD as well as Federal Law Enforcement. He takes great credit and pleasure of having converted over half of the on-staff instructors at DCITA to the Macintosh. After leaving the DoD he can now be found residing happily in the finest city in the world (Chicago), where he is still doing security design, implementation, and testing as well as litigation support for CSC and their clients. He can usually be seen regularly at conferences talking at least once about Macintosh related topics.

## Paul H. Luehr, Esq.

Paul Luehr is Managing Director and General Counsel of Stroz Friedberg, a technical consulting firm. Mr. Luehr specializes in complex e-discovery, computer forensics, data breaches, and consumer protection issues. He is a former federal cybercrimes prosecutor and FTC Assistant Director who worked on matters ranging from national Internet fraud to the post-9/11 investigation of terrorist Zacarias Moussaoui. Mr. Luehr has lectured before the National Academy of Sciences, the FBI Academy, the U.S. Justice Department, and has traveled abroad as a U.S. State Department Speaker on e-commerce and cybercrime. He is a graduate of Harvard University and the UCLA School of Law.

## Terrance Maguire

Terrance Maguire is a partner at cmdLabs, conducting cyber-crime investigations, including those involving network intrusions, insider attacks, anonymous and harassing e-mails, data destruction, electronic discovery and mobile devices. He has nearly 20 years of experience in physical and digital forensic investigations, has developed and led training programs in varied areas of law enforcement and digital evidence, and has experience implementing counter-intelligence intrusion detection programs.

Before working at cmdLabs, Terry was Assistant Director of Digital Forensics at Stroz Friedberg, where he was responsible for casework, lab management, and internal training efforts. His prior experience includes senior-level Forensic Computer Analyst the U.S. State Department, where he was responsible for conducting analysis on digital evidence. As a cyber operations specialist for the Department of Defense, he implemented network surveillance, network packet analysis, wireless surveys, and intrusion detection. In addition, at the Defense Computer Investigations Training Program (DCITP), Terry developed and presented a broad range of instruction to federal law enforcement on topics such as computer search and seizure, incident response, digital evidence, computer forensic examinations, and intrusion investigations.

Earlier in his investigative career, as a forensic detective with the Chesterfield County Police Department in Virginia, Terry collected, evaluated, and processed evidence from crime scenes, prepared comprehensive case reports, and trained department personnel in forensic techniques. Subsequently, as a Forensic Scientist for the Virginia Division of Forensic Science, he conducted bloodstain pattern analysis in criminal cases and testified in court as an expert witness, and he was the Principal Instructor at the Forensic Science Academy.

Terry is a professorial lecturer at the George Washington University where he teaches graduate-level courses focusing on incident response and computer intrusion investigations involving network-based attacks. He received an M.S. in Communication Technology from Strayer University and a B.S. in Chemistry from James Madison University. He is qualified as an ASCLD/LAB inspector in digital evidence, and is a member of the Virginia Forensic Science Academy Alumni Association.

## Ryan D. Pittman

Ryan Pittman is currently a Criminal Investigator (1811) for the U.S. Army Criminal Investigation Command's Computer Crime Investigative Unit (CCIU) near Washington, DC, continuing a career of more than 12 years in law enforcement and forensic science. Special Agent Pittman previously served as a Digital Forensic Examiner for Stroz Freidberg, LLC; a Master Instructor for Guidance Software, Inc.; a Senior Forensic Analyst for Sytex, Inc.; and a Computer Crime Coordinator (as an active duty soldier) for the U.S. Army Criminal Investigation Command. He is currently a Ph.D. candidate with Northcentral University, after receiving his Master of Forensic Sciences from National University, his Master of Science in Management in Information Systems Security from Colorado Technical University, and his Bachelor of Science in Criminal Justice from the University of Maryland University College. Special Agent Pittman has taught for George Washington University, University of Maryland University College, and Central Texas College, among others, and has been invited to teach or speak about incident response, digital investigations, and computer forensics on five continents.

## Curtis W. Rose

Curtis W. Rose is the President and founder of Curtis W. Rose & Associates LLC, a specialized services company which provides computer forensics, expert testimony, litigation support, computer intrusion response and training to commercial and government clients. Mr. Rose is an industry-recognized expert in computer security with over 20 years' experience in investigations, computer forensics, technical and information security. Mr. Rose was also a founding member of the Mandiant Corporation, where he served as the Vice President of Research, Chief Technology Officer, and led technical teams which conducted research & development, computer intrusion investigations, forensic examinations, and provided technical support to criminal investigations and civil litigation.  Prior to joining Mandiant, Mr. Rose was the Director of Investigations and Forensics, and Principal Forensic Scientist, for The Sytex Group, Inc. where he helped develop and manage the company's investigations, incident response and forensics programs.  Prior to joining Sytex, Mr. Rose was a Senior Counterintelligence Special Agent with the United States Army's Military Intelligence Branch where he specialized in technical investigations and computer forensics.

## Dave Shaver

Dave Shaver is currently serving as a Criminal Investigator (1811) for the U.S. Army Criminal Investigation Command's Computer Crime Investigative Unit (CCIU) near Washington DC, continuing a career of more than 13 years in law enforcement and forensic science. He is a graduate of Ohio University, with a Bachelor of Arts degree in sociology/criminology. Dave is a frequent presenter at national and international events, sharing his research and experiences in incident response and network intrusion investigations, and has been intimately involved in the development of incident response and investigation tools and practices that are in wide-spread use by the digital forensic community.

## Joseph J. Schwerha IV

Joseph J. Schwerha IV is a professor, prosecutor and private attorney. Mr. Schwerha has the unique experience of having served in both the private and public sectors for several years. As an Associate Professor within the Department of Business and Economics at California University of Pennsylvania, he is responsible for instruction on all aspects of business law, as well as for development of new curriculum in the areas of privacy, cybercrime and information law. While not teaching, Mr. Schwerha primarily splits his time between his law firm, Schwerha & Associates (a boutique law firm concentrating in the areas of privacy, information security and electronic discovery law), and Trace Evidence, LLC. (his computer forensics and e-discovery consulting business).

Mr. Schwerha holds a Juris Doctor from the University of Pittsburgh, as well as both a Bachelors' and Masters' of Science from Carnegie Mellon University. He has published numerous articles in various publications, including law reviews.

## Jessica Reust Smith

Jessica Reust Smith is the Assistant Director of Digital Forensics at Stroz Friedberg's Washington, DC office, where she conducts digital forensic acquisitions and analyses on media pertinent to civil, criminal and regulatory matters, internal investigations and computer incident response efforts. Ms. Smith also assists with the strategic development of Stroz Friedberg's e-discovery methodologies and is responsible for supervising and performing the preservation, processing and production of data for complex, global electronic discovery projects. Ms. Smith has a Master of Forensic Sciences and Master of Arts in Computer Fraud Investigation from George Washington University, and a Bachelor of Science and Bachelor of Arts from the University of Queensland in Brisbane, Australia.

# Acknowledgements

## Eoghan Casey

Working with the contributing authors on this Handbook has been a deep honor and learning experience. Thanks to all involved for their commitment to advancing the field of digital forensics and investigation, and their willingness to share their knowledge. I have deepest gratitude for Christopher Daywalt for being smarter, better, faster, and repeatedly rescuing this book by lifting us over seemingly insurmountable hurdles. Thanks for the tireless support and patience of Liz Brown, Renske van Dijk, Nikki Levy, and everyone else at Elsevier who worked on bringing this book to print. Special thanks to Genevieve, Roisin and Hesper for their infinite love and reminding me what is important in life.

## Cory Altheide

There are a lot of people I owe a debt of gratitude with regards to Linux & UNIX forensics. First and foremost among these people is Brian Carrier – without the Sleuthkit we'd still be using stone knives and bearskins to examine any non-Windows file systems. I'd like to thank Eoghan Casey for encouraging me to share my knowledge with the community, first through Digital Investigation, then the Digital Forensics Research Workshop, and most recently this handbook. Thanks go to Rob Lee for his continued advice and support over the years, and to Andy Rosen for being the vanguard of our industry as well as a good friend. An enormous amount of gratitude goes to Avery Brewing for Mephistopheles Stout, Dogfish Head for Theobroma, and New Belgium for La Folie. Finally, to my incredible wife Jamie and my two amazing daughters for always reminding me why it is I do what I do – I love you.

## Chris Daywalt

I would like to thank Eoghan Casey for the opportunity to make my modest contribution to this excellent text.

### Dario Forte

I want to personally thank Eoghan Casey for his incredible patience and support during the whole chapter preparation. He was incredibly active and kind, also helping me and my co-author Andrea de Donno since the first moment. I dedicate this work to my daughter Nicole, my wife Kseniya, my mother Marisa and my sister Daniela. The contribution to this book will not help me to change my Ferrari, but will surely make me a better author.

### James O. Holley

I appreciate Eoghan for reaching out to me to ask me to contribute to this book and Ernst & Young for approving my participation. Books do not happen without some sacrifice from the authors and their families. Thank you Stacy, Jacob, Audra and Jenna for letting me take nights and weekends away from you to write. I also acknowledge the tremendous work of the other contributing authors of the electronic discovery chapter. They clearly have a wealth of experience in this area.

### Andy Johnston

I would like to acknowledge the continued support and patience of Eoghan Casey. Eoghan is, as my father used to say, "a gentleman and a scholar."

### Anthony Kokocinski

I would like to thank the following people for assisting in creation of the many iterations of Macintosh forensic courses I've worked on: Gord Beatty, France Thibodeau, Thane Erickson, Erinn Soule, Al Evans, and of course Jim May. I would also like to thank both Jesica and Marissa for their part during my very intensive research bouts during the past eight years. I would like to thank the following real or imaginary influences in no particular order: Johnny, the Dead Presidents and all other inhabitants of the Frat House, past and present of bfist, tmag20, Libby, Miko, Bill, Lisa, Ken, and lastly, Taft. I would like to issue a special thank you to all of my family, most of whom do not understand a thing I say about computers. Lastly I would like to thank Eoghan Casey for the opportunity to work with him in many endeavors.

### Paul H. Luehr, Esq.

I'd like to thank my wife Kathy, my children Maddy, Julia, and Nathan, and my colleagues at Stroz Friedberg for their encouragement, time, and support. I'd also like to thank Eoghan Casey for inviting me to join this worthy endeavor.

## Terrance Maguire

Thanks to my kids, Patrick, Morgan, Nicole and Collin, for showing me on a daily basis no matter what else I do you guys will always be the best thing I have ever done. Thanks to Chris Daywalt and Eoghan Casey, my colleagues and "partners in computer crime", for providing me company at the Brewer's Art. And thanks to my hero, a dentist in Wilmington Delaware, who taught me everything I ever needed to know about life.

## Ryan D. Pittman

Personally, this is for my Grandfather, Dr. Robert Renard, who is my model for living a fulfilling life, and for my wife and wonderful sons, who represent all that is good and contenting in my world. Professionally, for Dave Shaver, a great friend, archetypal mentor, and long-time collaborator; for Eoghan Casey, for being a true soul, opening this door (and many others), and being the nicest Jedi in our field; for Jamey Tubbs, a loyal friend and the reason I got my first break; for Bob Weitershausen, thanks for taking a chance on an unknown; for Lance Mueller, whose work continues to remind me everyday how much I have left to learn; for Dr. Larry Kurtz, who continues to inspire my professional and academic achievement; for Jon Evans, who forced me out of my Linux-less existence; for the other brilliant men and women in our field, like Harlan Carvey, Jesse Kornblum, and Brian Carrier, who constantly answer forensic questions I never even knew I had; and for CID Agents everywhere, working way too hard, in way too much danger, for way too little money or recognition.

## Curtis W. Rose

I would like to thank Federal Bureau of Investigation Special Agents Mike and Gail Gneckow; Wendy Olson and Traci Whelan, Assistants United States Attorney; Thomas Moss, United States Attorney for the District of Idaho, as well as all the other incredibly dedicated and hard working professionals involved in the capture, investigation and prosecution of Joseph Edward Duncan III.

## Dave Shaver

I would like to take a moment to thank my parents for giving me my first HP-UX computer in the late 1980s and always teaching me to find out the answers. Thanks to my wife for her patience and understanding. Brent Pack, who taught me Linux is almost as cool as UNIX; David House, who demonstrated the proper method for blowing up computers; Scott Stein, who taught me that a Mac computer is actually pretty damn cool; Ryan Pittman, who taught me that some hot sauces are actually quite hot and painful; Troy Asmus, who taught me that anything could be disassembled if you have a big enough hammer; Mark Diaz, who was always there to point out my errors ("Dave, your lug nuts are loose") and finally, a warm "thank you" to all the Usual Suspects, and to my fellow CID Agents who get the job done despite having to work long hours with little pay, not enough support and too much red tape.

### Jessica Reust Smith

I would like to thank my colleagues and friends for your encouragement, assistance and willingness to share your knowledge. Thanks to my mother and father, for your love, guidance and support. And thanks to my husband Taylor, for all the above and much more.

### Ronald van der Knijff

I would like to thank the people within the Dutch government supporting forensic embedded system analysis, and all the people from law enforcement organizations willing to share knowledge. Thanks also to my colleagues for reviewing the embedded systems analysis chapter.

# CHAPTER 1

# Introduction

Eoghan Casey

Computers and networks have become so ubiquitous in our society, such an integral part of our daily lives, that any investigation or legal dispute will likely involve some form of digital evidence. Crimes like child exploitation, fraud, drug trafficking, terrorism, and homicide usually involve computers to some degree (see Chapter 2, "Forensic Analysis"). Electronic discovery has become so common in civil disputes that countries are updating their legal guidelines to address digital evidence (see Chapter 3, "Electronic Discovery"). Investigations of intrusions into corporate and government IT systems rely heavily on digital evidence, and are becoming more challenging as offenders become more adept at covering their tracks (see Chapter 4, "Intrusion Investigation").

Media reports at the time of this writing clearly demonstrate the wide diversity of cases that involve digital evidence:

- The University of California at Berkeley notified students and alumni that an intruder had gained unauthorized access to a database containing medical records of over 160,000 individuals.

- Members of an international child exploitation enterprise were sentenced for participating in an illegal organization that utilized Internet newsgroups to traffic in illegal images and videos depicting prepubescent children, including toddlers, engaged in various sexual and sadistic acts.

- David Goldenberg, an executive of AMX Corp, pled guilty to gaining unauthorized access to and stealing sensitive business information from the e-mail systems of a marketing firm that was working for a competitor, Crestron Electronics.

## CONTENTS

Forensic Soundness ........... 3

Forensic Analysis Fundamentals ..... 5

Crime Reconstruction .. 13

Networks and the Internet ....... 15

Conclusions ....... 16

References ......... 16

1

- The FBI is investigating a security breach of Virginia Prescription Monitoring Program (VPMP) computer systems. The data thief placed a ransom message on the VPMP web site, demanding payment of $10 million for the return of 8 million patient records and 35.5 million prescriptions.

- Computers seized during military operations in Iraq contained details about enemy operations.

Criminals are becoming more aware of digital forensic and investigation capabilities, and are making more sophisticated use of computers and networks to commit their crimes. Some are even developing "anti-forensic" methods and tools specifically designed to conceal their activities and destroy digital evidence, and generally undermine digital investigators. The integration of strong encryption into operating systems is also creating challenges for forensic examiners, potentially preventing us from recovering any digital evidence from a computer (Casey & Stellatos, 2008).

Over the past few years, practitioners and researchers have made significant advances in digital forensics. Our understanding of technology has improved and we have gained the necessary experiences to further refine our practices. We have overcome major technical challenges, giving practitioners greater access to digital evidence. New forensic techniques and tools are being created to support forensic acquisition of volatile data, inspection of remote systems, and analysis of network traffic. Detailed technical coverage of forensic analysis of Windows, Unix, and Macintosh systems is provided in Chapters 5, 6, and 7, respectively.

These advances bring with them great promise, and place new demands on digital forensics and investigations, changing the terrain of the field and causing new practices to evolve, including forensic analysis of embedded systems (Chapter 8), enterprise networks (Chapter 9), and mobile telecommunications systems (Chapter 10). The recent advances and some of the current challenges were recognized in the 2009 National Academy of Sciences report:

> Digital evidence has undergone a rapid maturation process. This discipline did not start in forensic laboratories. Instead, computers taken as evidence were studied by police officers and detectives who had some interest or expertise in computers. Over the past 10 years, this process has become more routine and subject to the rigors and expectations of other fields of forensic science. Three holdover challenges remain: (1) the digital evidence community does not have an agreed certification program or list of qualifications for digital forensic examiners; (2) some agencies still treat the examination of digital evidence as an investigative rather than a forensic activity; and (3) there is wide variability in and uncertainty about the education, experience, and training of those practicing this discipline. (National Academy of Sciences, 2009)

All of these advancements and challenges bring us to the underlying motivations of this work; to improve technical knowledge, standards of practice, and research in digital forensics and investigation. Furthermore, by presenting state-of-the-art practices and tools alongside the real-world challenges that practitioners are facing in the field and limitations of forensic tools, the Handbook hopes to inspire future research and development in areas of greatest need. As far and quickly as this discipline has progressed, we continue to face major challenges in the future.

## FORENSIC SOUNDNESS

As the field of digital forensics evolved from primarily dealing with hard drives to include any and all types of computer systems, one of the most fundamental challenges has been updating the generally accepted practices. There is an ongoing effort to balance the need to extract the most useful digital evidence as efficiently as possible, and the desire to acquire a pristine copy of all available data without altering anything in the process. In many situations involving new technology, particularly when dealing with volatile data in computer memory, mobile devices, and other embedded systems it is not feasible to extract valuable evidence without altering the original in some manner. Similarly, when dealing with digital evidence distributed across many computer systems, it may not be feasible to preserve everything.

In modern digital investigations, practitioners must deal with growing numbers of computer systems in a single investigation, particularly in criminal investigations of organized groups, electronic discovery of major corporations, and intrusion investigations of international scope. In such large-scale digital investigations, it is necessary to examine hundreds or thousands of computers as well as network-level logs for related evidence, making it infeasible to create forensic duplicates of every system.

Existing best practice guidelines are becoming untenable even in law enforcement digital forensic laboratories where growing caseloads and limited resources are combining to create a crisis. To address this issue, the latest edition of *The Good Practice Guide for Computer-Based Electronic Evidence* from the UK's Association of Chief Police Officers has been updated to include preservation of data from live systems, as discussed in Chapter 3 (ACPO, 2008). As the quantity of digital evidence grows and case backlogs mount, we are moving away from the resource intensive approach of creating a forensic duplicate and conducting an in-depth forensic examination of every item. A tiered approach to digital forensic examinations is being used to promptly identify items of greatest evidentiary value and produce actionable results, reserving in-depth forensic analysis for particular situations (Casey, 2009).

At the same time, there have been developments in preserving and utilizing more volatile data that can be useful in a digital investigation. Memory in computer systems can include passwords, encrypted volumes that are locked when the computer is turned off, and running programs that a suspect or computer intruder is using. Developments in memory forensics, mobile device forensics, and network forensics enable practitioners to acquire a forensic duplicate of full memory contents and extract meaningful information. The DFRWS2005 Forensic Challenge (www.dfrws.org) sparked developments in analysis of physical memory on Microsoft Windows systems, leading to ongoing advances in tools for extracting useful information from Windows, Unix, and Macintosh operating systems. Techniques have even been developed to recover data from random access memory chips after a computer has been turned off (Halderman, 2008). Forensic acquisition and analysis of physical memory from mobile devices has gained more attention recently and is covered in Chapter 8, "Embedded Systems Analysis." As shown in Chapter 9, "Network Investigation," memory forensics has been extended to Cisco network devices.

We can expect continued advancement in both our ability to deal with large-scale digital investigations and to extract more information from individual systems. Whether we acquire a selection of logical files from a system or the full contents, we must keep in mind the overarching forensic principles. The purpose of a forensically sound authentication process is to support identification and authentication of evidence. In lay terms, this means that the evidence is what you claim and has not been altered or substituted since collection. Documentation is a crucial component of forensic soundness. Functionally, this process involves documenting unique characteristics of the evidence, like device IDs and MD5 hashes of acquired data, and showing continuous possession and control throughout its lifetime. Therefore, it is necessary not only to record details about the collection process, but also every time it is transported or transferred and who was responsible.

> From a forensic standpoint, the acquisition process should change the original evidence as little as possible and any changes should be documented and assessed in the context of the final analytical results. Provided the acquisition process preserves a complete and accurate representation of the original data, and its authenticity and integrity can be validated, it is generally considered forensically sound. Imposing a paradigm of 'preserve everything but change nothing' is impractical and doing so can create undue doubt in the results of a digital evidence analysis, with questions that have no relation to the merits of the conclusions. (Casey, 2007)

Considerations of forensic soundness do not end with acquisition of data. When analyzing and producing findings from digital evidence, forensic practitioners need to follow a process that is reliable and repeatable. Again, documentation is a critical component, enabling others to evaluate findings.

To appreciate the importance of forensic soundness, it is instructive to consider concrete problems that can arise from improper processing of digital evidence, and that can undermine a case as well as the underlying credibility of the forensic practitioner. Some worst-case scenarios resulting from sufficiently large breaks in chain of custody include misidentification of evidence, contamination of evidence, and loss of evidence or pertinent elements (e.g., metadata). In one case, evidence was collected from several identical computer systems, but the collection process was not thoroughly documented, making it very difficult to determine which evidence came from which system.

Forensic acquisition failures include destruction of original evidence by overwriting media with zeros, saving no data in "acquired" files that actually contained evidence on original media, and updating metadata to the current date. The most common forensic examination failures are misinterpretations of data, either by a tool or person. Provided forensic practitioners are careful to preserve the selected digital evidence completely and accurately, document the process thoroughly, and check their work objectively for possible errors or omissions, these kinds of failures can be avoided or overcome.

## FORENSIC ANALYSIS FUNDAMENTALS

Although practitioners must know how to obtain data using forensic tools, this alone is not sufficient. We must also have a solid understanding of how the underlying technology works, how the data are arranged, and how the tool interprets and displays the information. In addition, we require a comprehensive understanding of how to apply the scientific method to the output of our tools, closely analyzing available data for useful characteristics and possible flaws, comparing evidence with known samples to extract more information, and performing experiments to better understand the context of evidence. Forensic analysis forms the heart of this Handbook, providing useful tips for interpreting digital evidence, and conveying lessons learned from our collective experience. Whenever feasible, we provide examples of common misinterpretations and pitfalls to help digital investigators avoid repeating the same mistakes.

This section lays the groundwork for effective forensic analysis, providing an overview of the scientific method and the most common analysis techniques.

### Scientific Method

Forensic examiners are neutral finders of fact, not advocates for one side over the other. The scientific method is one of the most powerful tools available to forensic examiners in fulfilling our responsibility to provide accurate evidence relating to an investigation in an objective manner. The scientific method begins with gathering facts, and forming a hypothesis based on the available evidence. However, we must be ever cognizant of the possibility that our observations or analyses are incorrect. Therefore, to assess the veracity of our hypothesis, we need not only to seek supporting evidence but also to consider alternate possibilities. The process of trying to disprove our own hypothesis involves performing experiments to test our underlying assumptions and gain a better understanding of the digital traces we are analyzing. For instance, when examining metadata embedded in a specific file type, it is important to perform tests involving that file type to explore the relationships between common actions and associated application metadata. When forensic examiners are provided with an alternative explanation offered by the defendant, they have a duty to test such defense claims thoroughly. However, there is no ethical requirement that forensic examiners fully investigate any or all potential defenses; to do so is generally impractical.

The remainder of this section describes common pitfalls and analysis techniques to help forensic examiners implement the scientific method and achieve correct results.

## Data Abstraction Layers

At its basest level, digital evidence exists in a physical medium such as a magnetic disk, a copper wire, or a radio signal in the air. Forensic examiners rarely scrutinize the physical medium and instead use computers to translate the data into a form that humans can interpret. For instance, magnetic fields are translated into sectors, which are grouped into clusters in a file system, which in turn are organized logically into files and folders. Therefore, forensic examiners rarely see the actual data but only a representation, and we must keep in mind that each layer of abstraction can introduce error or information loss.

Forensic examination tools add yet another layer of abstraction on top of those inherent in the evidentiary data. As with any software, forensic examination tools have bugs. To complicate matters, developers of forensic examination tools may have an incomplete understanding of the systems being analyzed. A common problem in forensic examination tools is incomplete or incorrect interpretation of file systems as shown in Figure 1.1.

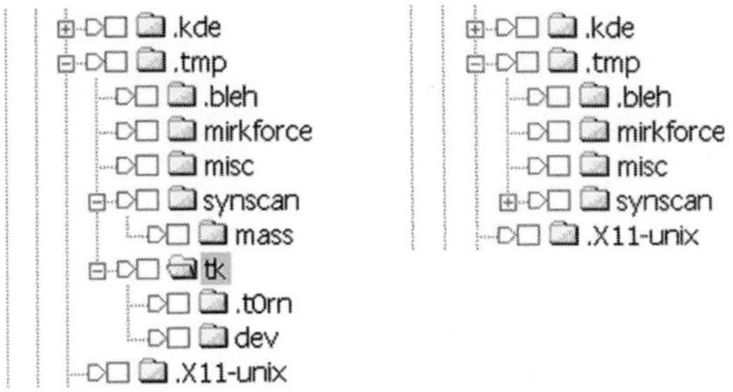

To mitigate the risk of errors caused by data translation, forensic practitioners need to validate findings using multiple tools, verifying that they interpret the data consistently. In addition, when feasible, forensic examiners should validate important findings by examining data at a lower level of abstraction to ensure that their forensic tools are not missing something important.

**FIGURE 1.1**

A folder named tk contained important evidence related to a computer intrusion investigation. The tk folder is visible using a newer version of a digital evidence examination tool (left) but not an older version containing a bug (right). (Casey, 2005)

Errors in data translation aside, it is a good practice to examine digital evidence at both the physical and logical layers of abstraction because each can provide additional useful information. Take a Windows Mobile handheld device as an example of the value of examining data at both the physical and logical levels. An examination of the full contents of the device's physical memory, as detailed in Chapter 8, "Embedded Systems Analysis," can reveal deleted items that are not accessible in files on the device, as shown in Figure 1.2.

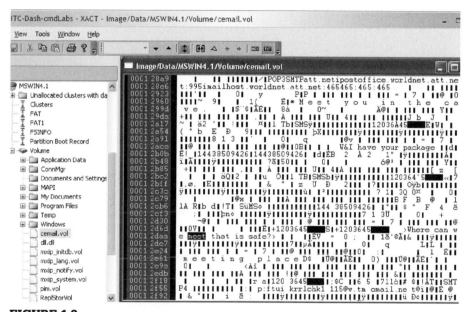

**FIGURE 1.2**
Physical acquisition of Windows Mobile using XACT.

On the other hand, examining a Windows Mobile device from a logical perspective enables the examiner to determine which data were stored in text messages versus the Memo application, and under which category the items were stored. For instance, Figure 1.3 shows the same information as Figure 1.2, with associated metadata, including the name of the folder of each message.

Take forensic examination of file systems as another example of the benefits of examining data at both the logical and physical levels. When instructed to search for child pornography on a computer, an inexperienced examiner might search at the file system (logical) level for files with a .GIF or .JPG extension. In some cases this may be sufficient to locate enough pornographic images to reach resolution. However, in most cases, this approach will fail to uncover all the available evidence. It is a simple matter to change a file extension from .JPG to .DOC or conceal images in some other manner, thus foiling a search based exclusively on this characteristic. Also, some

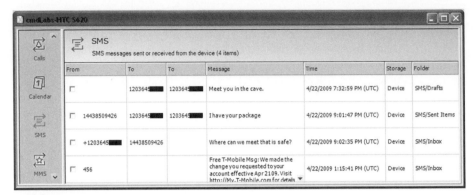

**FIGURE 1.3**
Logical acquisition of Windows Mobile device using .XRY.

relevant files might be deleted but still resident in unallocated space. Therefore, it is usually desirable to search every sector of the physical disk for certain file types using file carving techniques presented in Chapter 2, "Forensic Analysis."

## PRACTITIONER'S TIP: VARIATIONS IN HEADER SIGNATURE

As media formats evolve, their characteristics may change requiring forensic examiners to make adjustments to our processes and tools. For instance, when searching for JPG images, some file carving tools search for two header signatures: JFIF (hexadecimal \xff\xd8\xff\xe0) and Exif (\xff\xd8\xff\xe1). However, the two bytes following the 0xff d8 JPG header signature are an application marker that can vary depending on the implementation. For instance, the header signature \xff\xd8\xff\xe3 is associated with stereoscopic JPG files and commonly is found in graphics files on Samsung cell phones. Some photos on Samsung phones have been observed with the header signature \xff\xd8\xff\xdb, which relates to the quantization table in JPG files (Mansell, 2009). Therefore, using a tool that relies on only the more common signatures to recover photos from a Samsung phone would miss the majority of files. To avoid this type of situation, practitioners should check the header signature of files of the same type that are active on the phone or that are created using a test device.

This is not to say that searching at the physical level is always preferable. Searching for keywords at the physical level has one major limitation—if a file is fragmented, with portions in nonadjacent segments, keyword searches may give inaccurate results. Fortunately, most forensic examination tools can search each sector of the drive and are simultaneously aware of the logical arrangement of the data, giving the examiner the best of both worlds.

## PRACTITIONER'S TIP: PROXIMITY SEARCHING

When two apparently related pieces of information are found near one another on storage media, forensic examiners may need to perform additional forensic examination to determine whether they are, in fact, related. For instance, keyword searches that look for two words near each other will often return hits that associate two unrelated items. Even when a forensic tool displays both pieces of information as part of a single item, closer inspection may reveal that the tool is mistaken. In one case, a forensic tool displayed what appeared to be a web-based e-mail message but turned out to be an erroneous representation of two unrelated fragments of data on the hard disk.

## Evidence Dynamics

One of the perpetual challenges that commonly introduces error into forensic analysis is *evidence dynamics*. Evidence dynamics is any influence that changes, relocates, obscures, or obliterates evidence, regardless of intent, between the time evidence is transferred and the time the case is adjudicated (Chism & Turvey, 2000). Forensic examiners will rarely have an opportunity to examine a digital crime scene in its original state and should therefore expect some anomalies. Common causes of evidence dynamics in digital investigations are provided next, with illustrative examples.

- *System administrators*: In an attempt to be helpful, system administrators may perform actions on the computer that inadvertently obliterates patterns and adds artifact-evidence to the scene.
- *Forensic examiners*: A practitioner handling a computer system may, by accident or necessity, change, relocate, obscure, or obliterate evidence.
- *Offender covering behavior*: The perpetrator of a crime deletes evidence from a hard drive.
- *Victim actions*: The victim of a crime deletes e-mails in distress or to avoid embarrassment.
- *Secondary transfer*: Someone uses the computer after the crime is committed, innocently altering or destroying evidence.
- *Witnesses*: A system administrator deletes suspicious accounts that have been added by an intruder hoping to prevent further unauthorized access.
- *Nature/weather*: Damage to storage media caused by exposure to natural elements like mud, blood, water, or fire.
- *Decomposition*: A tape containing evidence decays over time, eventually becoming unreadable.

Evidence dynamics creates investigative and legal challenges, making it more difficult to determine what occurred and making it more difficult to prove that the evidence is authentic and reliable. Additionally, any conclusions that a forensic examiner reaches without the knowledge of how the evidence may have changed will be open to criticism in court, may misdirect an investigation, and may even be completely incorrect.

## Comparison and Identity of Source

Digital forensic examiners may be called upon to compare items to determine if they came from the same source. As part of a cyberextortion investigation, forensic examiners were asked to determine whether the ransom e-mails were sent from the suspect's computer. In an intellectual property dispute, the court needed to know whether the allegedly infringing computer program was derived from the plaintiff's work. In one case, digital investigators were asked to determine which printer was used to print sensitive documents in an effort to determine who had leaked the information to news media. To answer these kinds of questions, we compare the items, characteristic by characteristic, until we are satisfied that they are sufficiently alike to conclude that they are related to one another, or sufficiently dissimilar to be unrelated.

A piece of evidence can be related to a source in a number of ways (note that these relationships are not mutually exclusive):

1. Production: The source produced the evidence. The composition of the evidence is important here because any feature of the evidence may be related to the source. For example, the digital file that was sent by the Bind Torture Kill (BTK) serial killer to a television station contained data that had been embedded by the computer used to create the document,

leading investigators to a computer in the church where Dennis Rader was council president. Computers also have physical properties that can be embedded in the digital evidence they produce. The electronics in every digital camera has unique properties that specialized forensic analysts can utilize to link digital photographs to a specific device (Geradts et al., 2005; Fridrich et al., 2005). Production considerations are applicable when dealing with evidence sent through a network in addition to evidence created on a computer. For instance, e-mail headers are created as a message, which is passed through Message Transfer Agents.

2. Segment: The source is split into parts and parts of the whole are scattered. Fragments of digital evidence might be scattered on a disk or on a network. When a fragment of digital evidence is found at a crime scene, the challenge is to link it to its source.

## FROM THE CASE FILE

In a homicide case that hinged on DNA evidence, the crime lab was unable to locate the original digital files containing the DNA analysis results. A comprehensive search of the crime lab revealed that the files of interest had been on a Macintosh computer that had been reformatted. Forensic examination of data in unallocated space revealed fragments of thousands of files associated with DNA analysis from many different cases. To find fragments associated with the specific files of interest, it was necessary to develop a customized search algorithm based on the unique format of the files containing data associated with DNA analysis. After fragments of the files of interest were recovered, it was necessary to validate that they were put back together correctly. Viewing the data with DNA analysis software used in the crime lab indicated that the recovered fragments had been reconstituted correctly to form intact files. However, further review by subject matter experts revealed that some data were missing from the files. With this information forensic examiners were able to locate the missing data, which had not been documented in the file format specification, and complet the recovery of the files.

3. Alteration: The source is an agent or process that alters or modifies the evidence. In the physical world, when a crowbar is used to force something open, it leaves a unique impression on the altered object. A similar phenomenon occurs in the digital realm when an intruder exploits a vulnerability in an application or operating system— the exploit program leaves impressions on the altered system. The difference in the digital realm is that an exploit program can be copied and distributed to many offenders, and the toolmark that each program creates can be identical and can be erased by the cautious intruder.

4. Location: The source is a point in space. Determining where digital evidence came from is an obvious consideration that has already been alluded to in the context of creating spatial reconstruction. However, it is not always a trivial matter to determine where digital evidence originated. This consideration becomes more important as we move away from

the examination of standalone computers toward the examination of networks. For instance, determining the geographic location of a source of evidence transmitted over a network can be as simple as looking at the source IP address. However, if this source IP address is falsified, it becomes more difficult to find the actual source of the evidence.

## PRACTITIONER'S TIP: EMBEDDED GEOLOCATION INFORMATION

Modern mobile devices have the capability to embed Global Positioning System (GPS) location information in digital photographs. The following information extracted from a photograph taken using a G1 smart phone shows when and where the picture was taken.

```
Make:                    HTC

Model:                   T-Mobile G1

DateTimeOriginal:        2009:05:30   14:42:38

DateTimeDigitized:       2009:05:30   14:42:38

GPSLatitudeRef:          N

GPSLatitude:             39 deg 16' 0.000"

GPSLongitudeRef:         W

GPSLongitude:            76 deg 36' 0.000"

GPSDateStamp:            1911:12:18
```

As more computer systems incorporate GPS, we are finding more location-based information that could be useful in a digital investigation.

Of course, differences will often exist between apparently similar items, whether it is a different date-time stamp of a file, slightly different data in a document, or a difference between cookie file entries from the same web site.

It follows then that total agreement between evidence and exemplar is not to be expected; some differences will be seen even if the objects are from the same source or the product of the same process. It is experience that guides the forensic scientist in distinguishing between a truly significant difference and a difference that is likely to have occurred as an expression of natural variation.

But forensic scientists universally hold that in a comparison process, differences between evidence and exemplar should be explicable. There should be some rational basis to explain away the differences that are observed, or else this value of the match is significantly diminished. (Thornton, 1997)

The concept of a *significant difference* is important because it can be just such a difference that distinguishes an object from all other similar objects (i.e., an individuating characteristic that connects the digital evidence to a specific system or person).

# CRIME RECONSTRUCTION

Because every investigation is different, it is difficult to create standard operating procedures to cover every aspect of in-depth forensic analysis of digital evidence. Therefore, it is important to have a methodical approach to organizing and analyzing the large amounts of data that are typical when computers and networks are involved. Forensic science in general, and crime reconstruction specifically, provides such a methodology.

Crime reconstruction is the process of gaining a more complete understanding of a crime using available evidence. We use evidence to sequence events, determine locations, establish direction or establish the time and duration of actions. Some of the clues that are utilized in these determinations are *relational*, that is, where an object is in relation to the other objects and how they interact or relate to each other. Other clues are *functional*, the way something works or how it was used, or *temporal*, things based on the passage of time (Chisum, 1999). For example, when investigating a homicide perpetrated by an unknown offender, investigators try to determine how and when the victim was killed, as well as where the victim was and who the victim had contact with prior to the time of death. This reconstruction process often leads to the proverbial "smoking gun"—compelling evidence implicating a specific individual.

## FROM THE CASE FILE: TRACKING A KILLER

In late December 2005, 27-year-old Josie Phyllis Brown was reported missing in Baltimore. Digital evidence led investigators to a 22-year-old college student, John Gaumer. Brown met Gaumer on the Internet site MySpace.com and arranged to meet him for a date (Associated Press, 2006). On the night of her disappearance, Brown's mobile telephone records showed that she talked to Gaumer before meeting with him, and police placed her telephone many miles from where he claimed to have left her that night. After the web of evidence converged on Gaumer in February 2006, he led police to her body and admitted to beating Brown to death after their date.

Gaumer used the Internet extensively to communicate and meet potential dates. Part of the evidence against him was a digital recording of "thumping noises, shouting and brief bursts of a woman's muffled screams" apparently created when Gaumer's mobile phone inadvertently dialed Brown's (McMenamin, 2007). In his confession to police, Gaumer stated that he removed her nose, jaw, teeth, and most of her fingertips in an attempt to thwart identification of her body, and that he later sent an e-mail to her account to make it appear that he did not know she was dead.

In a civil dispute, such as theft of trade secrets, the goal of e-discovery may be to uncover communications or documents showing that particular individuals knowingly accessed the data of concern during a particular period.

As another example, when handling a computer intrusion, we strive to determine how and when the attackers gained unauthorized access, and which computers were involved.

## Relational Analysis

A full relational analysis can include the geographic location of people and computers, as well as any communication/transaction that occurred between them. In a major fraud investigation involving thousands of people and computers, creating a detailed relational analysis—where each party was located and how they interacted—can reveal a crucial relationship. Similarly, in a network intrusion investigation, it can be useful to generate a diagram of which computers contacted the victim system, or to create a list of IP-to-IP connections and sort them by quantity of data transferred, as detailed in Chapter 9, "Network Analysis."

## Functional Analysis

Forensic examiners perform a functional analysis to determine how a particular system or application works and how it was configured at the time of the crime. It is sometimes necessary to determine how a computer system or program works to gain a better understanding of a crime or a piece of digital evidence. If a compromised web server was configured to allow connections from only a small range of IP addresses or user accounts, this limits the number of machines or user accounts that could have been used to break into the web server.

Malware analysis is another example of functional analysis that is common in intrusion investigations, but this process is beyond the scope of this Handbook and has its own dedicated text (Malin et al., 2008).

## Temporal Analysis

One of the most common forms of temporal analysis is creating a timeline to gain a clearer overview of events relating to a crime and to help investigators identify patterns and gaps, potentially leading to other sources of evidence. There are other approaches to analyzing temporal data, such as plotting them in a histogram to find periods of highest activity.

### PRACTITIONER'S TIP: ATTENTION TO DETAIL

When dealing with digital data, forensic practitioners must pay close attention to details. Misreading 03:15 and 3:15 PM will impact a temporal reconstruction and misreading 232.23.22.1 as 23.223.22.1 will impact a relational reconstruction. When performing temporal analysis, any discrepancies such as system clock inaccuracies and different time zones must be taken into account. Such seemingly minor mistakes can completely misdirect an investigation. In a number of cases, including child exploitation and intrusion investigations, dates and IP addresses were transcribed incorrectly when drafting search warrants. These simple transcription errors led to the wrong person being implicated until the error was corrected.

# NETWORKS AND THE INTERNET

Beyond the basic requirement to collect evidence in a way that preserves its integrity and authenticity, there are a number of practical challenges that investigators can expect when dealing with networks.

One of the most significant challenges of investigating criminal activity involving networks is obtaining all the evidence. Several factors generally contribute to this challenge. First, the distributed nature of networks results in a distribution of crime scenes creating practical and jurisdictional problems. For instance, in most cases it may not be possible to collect evidence from computers located in China. Even when international or interstate procedures are in place to facilitate digital evidence exchange, the procedures are complex and only practical for serious crimes. Second, because digital data on networked systems are easily deleted or changed, it is necessary to collect and preserve them as quickly as possible. Network traffic exists for only a split second. Information stored in volatile computer memory may exist for only a few hours. Because of their volume, log files may be retained for only a few days. Furthermore, if they have the skill and opportunity, criminals will destroy or modify evidence to protect themselves.

A third contributing factor is the wide range of technical expertise that is required when networks are involved in a crime. Because every network is different, combining different technologies in unique ways, no single individual is equipped to deal with every situation. Therefore, it is often necessary to find individuals who are familiar with a given technology before evidence can be collected. A fourth contributing factor is the great volume of data that are often involved in an investigation involving computer systems. Searching for useful evidence in vast amounts of digital data can be like finding a needle in a haystack.

In the ideal case, when most of the digital evidence is available to investigators, another significant challenge arises when it is necessary to associate an individual with specific activity on a computer or network. Even when offenders make no effort to conceal their identity, they can claim that they were not responsible. Given the minor amount of effort required to conceal one's identity on the Internet, criminals usually take some action to thwart apprehension. This concealment behavior may be as simple as using a library computer. Additionally, there are many services that provide varying degrees of anonymity on the Internet, making the task even harder. Encryption presents the ultimate challenge, making it difficult or impossible for investigators to analyze evidence that has already been found, collected, documented, and preserved.

This book addresses these challenges by providing a methodology for investigating criminal activities on networks, delving into common sources of evidence on networks and their practical use in an investigation.

## CONCLUSIONS

With great achievements come great responsibilities. Digital forensics has progressed rapidly but much more is required, including developing more sophisticated techniques for acquiring and analyzing digital evidence, increasing scientific rigor in our work, and professionalizing the field. This Handbook aims to contribute to the advancement of the field by expanding knowledge in the major specializations in digital forensics and improving our ability to locate and utilize digital evidence on computers, networks, and embedded systems.

Specifically, the Investigative Methodology section of the Handbook provides expert guidance in the three main areas of practice: forensic analysis, electronic discovery, and intrusion investigation. The Technology section is extended and updated to reflect the state of the art in each area of specialization. The main areas of focus in the Technology section are forensic analysis of Windows, Unix, Macintosh, and embedded systems (including cellular telephones and other mobile devices), and investigations involving networks (including enterprise environments and mobile telecommunications technology).

## REFERENCES

Association of Chief Police Officers (ACPO). (2008). *The Good Practice Guide for Computer-Based Electronic Evidence* (4th ed.). Available online at www.7safe.com/electronic_evidence/

Breeuwsma, M. F. (2006). Forensic imaging of embedded systems using JTAG (boundary-scan). *Journal of Digital Investigation, 3*(1), 32–42.

Brunker, M., & Sullivan, B. (2000). *CD Universe evidence compromised*. MSNBC. Available online at http://stacks.msnbc.com/news/417406.asp

Bryson, C. & Anderson, M. R. (2001). *Shadow data*. NTI. Available online at www.forensics-intl.com/art15.html

Casey, E. (2005). Digital evidence and computer crime. In R. Byard, T. Corey, & C. Henderson (Eds.), *The encyclopedia of forensic and legal medicine*. Elsevier.

Casey, E. (2007). What does "forensically sound" really mean? *Journal of Digital Investigation, 5*(1).

Casey, E. (2009). Justice delayed. *Journal of Forensic Science*.

Dreyfus, S. (2000). *The idiot savants' guide to rubberhose*. Available online at http://iq.org/~proff/rubberhose.org/current/src/doc/maruguide/t1.html

*File slack defined*. (2000). NTI. Available online at www.forensics-intl.com/def6.html

Halderman, J. A., Schoen, S. D., Heninger, N., Clarkson, W., Paul, W., Calandrino, J. A., et al. (2008). Lest we remember: Cold boot attacks on encryption keys. In *Proc. 17th USENIX security symposium (Sec '08)*. San Jose, Calif. Available online at http://citp.princeton.edu/memory/

IACIS. (2000). *Forensic Examination Procedures*. Available online at www.cops.org/forensic_examination_procedures.htm

Malin, C., Casey, E., & Aquilina, J. (2008). *Malware forensics*. Syngress.

Mansell, K. (2009). How big is the iceberg. *Mobile Forensics World 09*.

McMenamin, J. (2007). Gaumer convicted of rape, murder: Prosecutors seeking death penalty for UMBC student, who met victim online. *Baltimore Sun*.

National Academy of Sciences. (2009). *Strengthening Forensic Science in the United States: A Path Forward*, 5–41. Available online at www.nap.edu/catalog.php?record_id=12589

SWGDE. (1999). *Digital Evidence: Standards and Principles*. Available online at www.fbi.gov/hq/lab/fsc/backissu/april2000/swgde.htm

Thornton, J. (1997). The general assumptions and rationale of forensic identification. In D. L. Faigman, D. H. Kaye, M. J. Saks, & J. Sanders (Eds.), *Modern scientific evidence: The law and science of expert testimony (Vol. 2)*. St. Paul: West Publishing Co.

*Transcript of Proceedings*. (1999). *US v. Wen Ho Lee*. Available online at www.abqjournal.com/news/leetran.htm

U.S. DOJ. (2001). *Searching and Seizing Computers and Obtaining Electronic Evidence in Criminal Investigations*. Available online at www.cybercrime.gov/s&smanual2002.htm

*U.S. v. Hanssen*. pp. 70. Available online at http://news.findlaw.com/cnn/docs/hanssen/hanssenaff022001.pdf

*U.S. v. Carey*. Available online at http://laws.findlaw.com/10th/983077.html

*U.S. v. Upham*.

*U.S. v. Gray*.

Villano, M. (2001). Computer Forensics: IT autopsy. *CIO Magazine*. Available online at www.cio.com/article/30022/Computer_Forensics_IT_Autopsy

Wigler, R. D. (1999). *U.S. District Court, District of New Jersey court order*. Available online at www.epic.org/crypto/breakin/order.pdf

# 1 PART

# Investigative Methodology

# CHAPTER 2

# Forensic Analysis

Eoghan Casey and Curtis W. Rose

## INTRODUCTION

The information stored and created on computers is a double-edged sword from a forensic perspective, providing compelling evidence in a wide variety of investigations but also introducing complexity that can trip up even experienced practitioners. Digital evidence can be used to answer fundamental questions relating to a crime, including what happened when (sequencing), who interacted with whom (linkage), the origination of a particular item (evaluation of source), and who was responsible (attribution). At the same time, the complexity of computer systems requires appreciation that individual pieces of digital evidence may have multiple interpretations, and corroborating information may be vital to reaching a correct conclusion. To make the most of digital evidence, forensic practitioners need to understand, and make regular use of, the scientific method. The scientific method applied in conjunction with digital forensics methodologies and techniques enables us to adapt to differing circumstances and requirements, and to ensure that conclusions reached are solidly based in fact. Familiarity with the limitations of forensic analysis of digital evidence will help investigators and attorneys apprehend modern criminals and exculpate the innocent.

The forensic analysis process involves taking factual observations from available evidence, forming and testing possible explanations for what caused the evidence, and ultimately developing deeper understanding of a particular item of evidence or the crime as a whole. Put another way, elements of digital forensic analysis include separating particular items for individual study, determining their significance, and considering how they relate to

## CONTENTS

Introduction.......21

Applying the Scientific Method to Digital Forensics ...........23

Uses of Digital Forensic Analysis.............26

Data Gathering and Observation........32

Hypothesis Formation ..........48

Evaluating Hypotheses .......48

Conclusions and Reporting...........56

Summary ...........61

References.........62

This chapter extends Eoghan Casey's *Reconstructing Digital Evidence* in Crime Reconstruction (Chisum W. J. & Turvey B).

the entire corpus of evidence. This process often involves experimentation and research, and may lead to additional information that must be synthesized into the overall process. For instance, analysis can suggest additional keywords that forensic practitioners use to find additional information that adds to the analysis process. As such, the process is cyclic, requiring multiple passes through the hypothesis formation and testing phases until a solid conclusion is reached.

In the simple case of an incriminating file on a hard drive, analysis of the contents and metadata of the file can reveal how the file came to be on the hard drive and can uncover distinctive characteristics to search all available media for related artifacts and file fragments. As another example, forensic analysis of SMS messages on a murder victim's mobile device may lead digital investigators to a prime suspect. Then, by obtaining usage details for the suspect's cell phone and analyzing the timing, location, and content of both the victim's and suspect's mobile devices immediately prior to the offense, digital investigators can place the suspect at the crime scene.

## FROM THE CASE FILES: CELL PHONE EVIDENCE

In late December 2005, 27-year-old Josie Phyllis Brown was reported missing in Baltimore. Digital evidence led investigators to a 22-year-old college student John Gaumer. Brown and Gaumer met on the Internet site MySpace.com, and arranged to meet for a date. On the night of her disappearance, Brown's mobile telephone records showed that she had talked to Gaumer before meeting with him, and police placed her telephone many miles from where he claimed to have left her that night. After the web of evidence converged on Gaumer in February 2006, he led police to her body and admitted to beating Brown to death after their date. Gaumer used the Internet extensively to communicate and meet potential dates. Part of the evidence against him was a digital recording of "thumping noises, shouting and brief bursts of a woman's muffled screams" apparently created when Gaumer's mobile phone inadvertently dialed Brown's. In his confession to police, Gaumer stated that he removed her nose, jaw, teeth, and most of her fingertips in an attempt to thwart identification of her body, and that he later sent an e-mail to her account to make it appear that he did not know she was dead (McMenamin, 2007).

More generally, forensic analysis involves objectively and critically assessing digital evidence to gain an understanding of and reach conclusions about the crime. This process can involve evaluating the source of digital objects, exploring unfamiliar file formats to extract usable information, developing timelines to identify sequences and patterns in time of events, performing functional analysis to ascertain what was possible and impossible, and relational analysis to determine the relationships and interaction between components of a crime. In essence, forensic analysts attempt to answer the fundamental questions in an investigation of what happened, where, when, how, who was involved, and why. In addition, forensic analysts may be directed to address specific questions relevant to the investigation, or to develop a list of other potential sources of evidence like e-mail accounts and removable storage media.

## PRACTITIONER'S TIP: THINKING OUTSIDE THE BOX

Although forensic protocols can help provide a standardized process, and keyword searches can help focus on important items and minimize the dataset, many digital investigations will require the forensic practitioner to explore the cybertrail, apply the scientific method, seek peer review, reach a conclusion, express an opinion, and prepare for expert testimony and presentation in a court of law. New versions of operating systems, software applications, and hardware platforms are constantly being released, including new generations of mobile devices. As such, it is clear that digital forensics is an ongoing and evolving scientific discipline. Procedures and protocols are not intended to limit a forensic analyst, but rather act as guidelines to help ensure consistency. Forensic analysts may detect and pursue something of relevance that even the most comprehensive protocol may not have anticipated.

This chapter focuses on important aspects of analyzing digital evidence to help investigators reconstruct an offense and assess the strength of their conclusions. By focusing on the use of digital evidence to reconstruct actions taken in furtherance of a crime, this chapter demonstrates how digital evidence that is properly interpreted can be used to apprehend offenders, gain insight into their intent, assess alibis and statements, authenticate documents, and much more. It is assumed that evidence has been preserved in a forensically sound manner. For background and technical coverage of how forensic science is applied to computers and networks, see Casey (2004).

A fictional digital forensic investigation scenario is used throughout this chapter to demonstrate key points. The scenario background is as follows.

## INVESTIGATIVE SCENARIO
## Part 1: Background

A suspected domestic terrorist code named "Roman" was observed purchasing explosive materials and investigators believe that he is involved in planning an attack in Baltimore, Maryland. We have been asked to perform a forensic analysis of his laptop to determine the target of the attack and information that may lead to the identification of others involved in the terrorist plot. This is purely a fictional case scenario developed for instructional purposes.

## APPLYING THE SCIENTIFIC METHOD TO DIGITAL FORENSICS

Forensic analysis of digital evidence depends on the case context and largely relies on the knowledge, experience, expertise, thoroughness, and in some cases the curiosity of the practitioner performing the work. Although every forensic analysis will have differing aspects based on the dataset, objectives, resources, and other factors, the underlying process remains fundamentally the same.

1. **Gather information and make observations**. This phase is sometime referred to as forensic examination, and involves verifying the integrity and authenticity of the evidence, performing a survey of all evidence to determine how to proceed most effectively, and doing some preprocessing to salvage deleted data, handle special files, filter out irrelevant data, and extract embedded metadata. This phase may include keyword searching to focus on certain items, and a preliminary review of system configuration and usage. This phase need not be limited to digital evidence, and can be augmented by interviews, witness statements, and other materials or intelligence.

2. **Form a hypothesis to explain observations**. While forensic practitioners are gathering information about the crime under investigation, we develop possible explanations for what we are seeing in the digital evidence. Although such conjecture is often influenced by the knowledge and experience of a forensic practitioner, we must guard against preconceived notions that are based on personal prejudice rather than facts.

3. **Evaluate the hypothesis**. Various predictions will flow naturally from any hypothesis (if the hypothesis is true, then we would expect to find X in the evidence), and it is our job as forensic practitioners to determine whether such expectations are borne out by the evidence. The success of a forensic analysis hinges on how thoroughly an initial hypothesis is attacked. Therefore, it is crucial to consider other plausible explanations and include tests that attempt to disprove the hypothesis (if the hypothesis is false, then we would expect to find Y). If experiments and observations do not support the initial hypothesis, we revise our hypothesis and perform further tests.

4. **Draw conclusions and communicate findings**. Once a likely explanation of events relating to a crime has been established, forensic practitioners must convey their work to decision makers.

Observe that the scientific method is cyclic, potentially requiring forensic analysts to repeat these steps until a conclusion can be made. If experiments disprove the initial hypothesis, a new one must be formed and evaluated. Even when some experiments support the hypothesis, new information often emerges that must be considered and tested to determine whether the hypothesis still holds.

## SCIENTIFIC METHOD

There are variations in how the scientific method is described but the overall principles and goals are the same: to reach an objective conclusion in a repeatable manner. The terminology used in this book is not intended to be definitive or exclusive, and is provided simply to demonstrate how the scientific method is applied to digital forensic analysis.

The scientific method provides the final bulwark against incorrect conclusions. Simply trying to validate a theory increases the chance of error—the tendency is for the analysis to be skewed in favor of the hypothesis. This is why the most effective investigators suppress their personal biases and hunches, and seek evidence and perform experiments to disprove their working theory. Experimentation is actually a natural part of analyzing digital evidence. Given the variety and complexity of hardware and software, it is not feasible for a forensic analyst to know everything about every software and hardware configuration. As a result it is often necessary to perform controlled experiments to learn more about a given computer system or program. For instance, one approach is to pose the questions, "Was it possible to perform a given action using the subject computer, and if so, what evidence of this action is left behind on the system?" Suppositions about what digital evidence reveals in a particular case may be tested by restoring a duplicate copy of a subject system onto similar hardware, effectively creating a clone that can be operated to study the effects of various actions. Similarly, it may be necessary to perform experiments on a certain computer program to distinguish between actions that are automated by the program versus those performed by a user action.

## PRACTITIONER'S TIP: DOCUMENTATION, DOCUMENTATION, DOCUMENTATION

Documentation is a critical part of each step—note every action you take and any changes that result from your actions. The aim is not only to give others an understanding of what occurred but also to enable others to reproduce your results. In cases involving a large number of computers, it is common practice to develop a review protocol for multiple forensic practitioners to follow. This type of protocol describes the sequence of steps each individual should perform and what output is expected, thus increasing the chances that consistent results will be obtained from all systems. Maintaining a record of your work and findings also helps avoid the unenviable position of remembering that you found something interesting but not being able to find it again. Therefore, during the forensic analysis process, it is advisable to extract key findings and organize these items in a folder (either digital or physical) to make it easier to reference them when reviewing the case, writing a report, or testifying in court.

Keep in mind that there is uncertainty in all observations, and every opinion rendered by a forensic practitioner has a statistical basis. Although the scientific method is designed to uncover the truth, we generally have only a limited amount of information about what occurred at a digital crime scene. Therefore, it is important that forensic practitioners qualify the results of their analysis to clearly convey what level of confidence we have in a certain conclusion. The C-Scale (Certainty Scale) provides a method for conveying certainty when referring to digital evidence and to qualify conclusions appropriately (Casey, 2002). Some forensic practitioners use a less formal system of degrees of likelihood that can be used in both the affirmative and negative sense: (1) almost definitely, (2) most probably, (3) probably, (4) very possibly, and (5) possibly.

## Tool Validation

One of the critical elements of the entire forensic analysis process hinges on practitioners' knowledge of the capabilities, limitations, and restrictions of their tools.

It is not feasible to calibrate digital forensic tools in the same way as equipment for analyzing DNA and other scientific evidence, because there are too many variables; each case has different data structures to interpret and unique problems to solve. The next best option is to test tools using a known data set to ensure that they can perform basic functions correctly like read partition tables and files systems, recover deleted files, and find keywords. The Computer Forensic Tool Testing group at the National Institute of Standards and Technology (www.cftt. nist.gov/) is conducting thorough tests of certain features of major forensic tools. However, there are more tools and capabilities than any one group can test, and forensic analysts generally are advised to perform some validation themselves of the specific tools and features on which they rely in their work.

The Digital (Computer) Forensics Tool Testing images project (http://dftt. sourceforge.net/) provides a limited test set for this purpose, and the Computer Forensic Reference Data Sets project (www.cfreds.nist.gov/) has forensic images that can be useful for tool testing. In addition to validating the basic functionality of forensic tools, some organizations develop their own test data with features that they commonly encounter in cases like Microsoft Office documents, Lotus Notes and Outlook e-mail, unsearchable PDF files, and foreign language characters. In special cases, it may be necessary to create a particular exemplar file containing known data, and check to see that the tool interprets and displays the information of interest correctly.

Even after performing a basic validation of a particular tool, experienced forensic analysts take a "trust but verify" approach to important findings. In some circumstances the validation process may be as straightforward as viewing data in a hex viewer, and in other situations it may be necessary to repeat the analysis using another forensic tool to ensure the same results are obtained. Most C programmers do not have one single book on their shelf as a reference guide. If they specialize in C programming, over time they have probably amassed a small reference library of books covering various aspects of the language. No single book covers every possible aspect of the C programming language; similarly, no single digital forensic utility provides the capabilities of performing every possible element of an analysis. Reliance on a single application platform will significantly hinder the review and subsequent analysis of digital evidence.

## USES OF DIGITAL FORENSIC ANALYSIS

Forensic analysis of digital evidence can play a significant role in a wide range of cases, in some cases leading investigators to the culprit. Some examples of this and other uses of digital forensics are provided here as context for the technical materials in this chapter and book as a whole.

## Attribution

Digital forensic analysis can play a direct role in identifying and apprehending offenders, helping investigators establish linkages between people and their online activities. In the Bind Torture Kill (BTK) serial killer case, forensic analysis of a floppy diskette that was sent to a television station by the offender led investigators to the church where Dennis Rader was council president. However, attributing computer activities to a particular individual can be challenging. For instance, logs showing that a particular Internet account was used to commit a crime do not prove that the owner of that account was responsible since someone else could have used the individual's account. Even when dealing with a specific computer and a known suspect, some investigative and forensic steps may be required to place the person at the keyboard and confirm that the activities on the computer were most likely those of the suspect. For instance, personal communications and access to online banking/e-commerce accounts can make it difficult for the person to deny responsibility for the illegal activities on the computer around the same time. Alternate sources of information like credit card purchase records, key card access logs, or CCTV footage may confirm the person in the vicinity during the time in question. When combined with traditional investigative techniques, digital evidence can provide the necessary clues to track down criminals.

### FROM THE CASE FILES: APPREHENDING A SERIAL KILLER

A lead developed during a serial homicide investigation in St. Louis when a reporter received a paper letter from the killer. The letter contained a map of a specific area with a handwritten X to indicate where another body could be found. After investigators found a skeleton in that area, they inspected the letter more closely for ways to link it to the killer. The FBI determined that the map in the letter was from Expedia.com and immediately contacted administrators of the site to determine if there was any useful digital evidence. The web server logs on Expedia.com showed only one IP address (65.227.106.78) had accessed the map around May 21, the date the letter was postmarked. The ISP responsible for this IP address was able to provide the account information and telephone number that had been used to make the connection in question. Both the dialup account and telephone number used to make this connection belonged to Maury Travis (Robinson, 2002).

In short, the act of downloading the online map that was included in the letter left traces on the Expedia web server, on Travis's ISP, and on his personal computer. Investigators arrested Travis and found incriminating evidence in his home, including a torture chamber and a videotape of himself torturing and raping a number of women, and apparently strangling one victim. Travis committed suicide while in custody and the full extent of his crimes may never be known.

Using evidence from multiple independent sources to corroborate each other and develop an accurate picture of events can help develop a strong association between an individual and computer activities. This type of reconstruction can involve traditional investigative techniques, such as stakeouts.

## FROM THE CASE FILES: PHYSICAL AND DIGITAL SURVEILLANCE

A man accused of possessing child pornography argued that all evidence found in his home should be suppressed because investigators had not provided sufficient probable cause in their search warrant to conclude that it was in fact he, and not an imposter, who was using his Internet account to traffic in child pornography (*U.S. v. Grant*, 2000). During their investigation into an online child exploitation group, investigators determined that one member of the group had connected to the Internet using a dialup account registered to Grant. Upon further investigation, they found that Grant also had a high-speed Internet connection from his home that was used as an FTP server—the type of file-transfer server required for membership in the child exploitation group.

Coincidentally, while tapping a telephone not associated with Grant in relation to another child pornography case, investigators observed that one of the participants in a secret online chat room was connected via Grant's dialup account. Contemporaneous surveillance of the defendant's home revealed that his and his wife's cars were both parked outside their residence at the time. The court felt that there was enough corroborating evidence to establish a solid circumstantial connection between the defendant and the crime to support probable cause for the search warrant.

Attributing a crime to an individual becomes even more difficult when a crime is committed via an open wireless access point or from a publicly accessible computer, such as at an Internet cafe or public library terminal. In one extortion case, investigators followed the main suspects and observed one of them use a library computer from which incriminating e-mails had been sent (Howell, 2004; Khamsi, 2005).

### Assessing Alibis and Statements

Offenders and victims may mislead investigators intentionally or inadvertently, claiming that something occurred or that they were somewhere at a particular time. By cross-referencing such information with the digital traces left behind by a person's activities, digital evidence may be found to support or refute a statement or alibi. In one homicide investigation, the prime suspect claimed that he was out of town at the time of the crime. Although his computer suffered from a Y2K bug that rendered most of the date-time stamps on his computer useless, e-mail messages sent and received by the suspect showed that he was at home when the murder occurred, contrary to his original statement. Caught in a lie, the suspect admitted to the crime.

## FROM THE CASE FILES: CELL PHONE LOCATION

Data relating to mobile telephones were instrumental in the conviction of Ian Huntley for the murder of Holly Wells and Jessica Chapman in the United Kingdom. The last communication from Jessica's mobile phone was sent to a cell tower several miles away in Burwell rather than a local tower in Soham (BBC, 2003). The police provided the mobile telephone specialist with a map of the route they thought the girls would have taken, and the specialist determined that the only place on that route where the phone could have connected to the cell tower in Burwell was from inside or just outside Huntley's house (Summers, 2003). In addition, Huntley's alibi was that he was with his friend Maxine Carr on the night the girls went missing but Carr's mobile phone records indicated that she was out of town at the time.

Investigators should not rely on one piece of digital evidence when examining an alibi—they should look for an associated cybertrail. On many computers it requires minimal skills to change the clock or the creation time of a file. Also, people can program a computer to perform an action, like sending an e-mail message, at a specific time. In many cases, scheduling events does not require any programming skill—it is a simple feature of the operating system. Similarly, IP addresses can be changed and concealed, allowing individuals to pretend that they are connected to a network from another location. In addition, the location information associated with mobile telephones is not exact and does not place an individual at a specific place. As noted earlier, it can also be difficult to prove who was using the mobile telephone at a specific time, particularly when telephones or SIM cards are shared among members of a group or family.

## Determining Intent

An individual's computer use can reveal innermost thoughts at a particular moment in time. Clear evidence of intent such as an offender's diary or planning of an offense may be found on a computer.

### FROM THE CASE FILE: *UNITED STATES v. DUNCAN*

Joseph Edward Duncan III pled guilty in December 2007 to 10 federal counts including murder, torture, and kidnapping. During a forensic review of his laptop, a forensic analyst identified what initially appeared to be an unused tab "Sheet 2" in an encrypted Excel spreadsheet named `Book1.xls`. Further analysis revealed the contents of this spreadsheet, which showed a mathematically weighted decision matrix that Duncan had generated to calculate the risks associated with taking certain actions relating to his crimes. During the capital sentencing hearing, this spreadsheet was introduced as Government Exhibit 59, and was used as the foundation for proving that the defendant acted with substantial planning and premeditation. In August 2008, Duncan was sentenced to death.

In three separate cases, Internet searches on suspects' computers revealed their intent to commit murder:

- Neil Entwistle was sentence to life in prison for killing his wife and baby daughter. Internet history on his computer included a Google search "how to kill with a knife."

- William Guthrie was convicted in 2000 and sentenced to life in prison for killing his wife, who was found drowned in a bathtub with a toxic level of the prescription drug Temazepam in her body. Guthrie lost multiple appeals to exclude Internet searches for "household accidents," "bathtub accidents," and various prescription drugs, including Temazepam.

- Prosecutors upgraded the charge against Robert Durall from second-degree to first-degree murder based on Internet searches found on his computer with key words including "kill + spouse," "accidental + deaths," "smothering," and "murder" (Johnson, 2000).

Forensic analysis of computers can reveal other behavior that can be very useful for determining intent. For instance, evidence of clock tampering may enable a forensic practitioner to conclude that the computer owner intentionally backdated a digital document. As another example, the use of disk cleaning or encryption programs on a computer can be used to demonstrate a computer owner's conscious decision to destroy or conceal incriminating digital evidence. However, these same actions may have innocent explanations and must be considered in context before reaching a definitive conclusion.

## Evaluation of Source

As introduced in the previous chapter, forensic analysts are commonly asked to provide some insight into the origins of a particular item of digital evidence. As detailed in Chapter 1, a piece of evidence may have been: 1) produced by the source; 2) a segment of the source; 3) altered by the source; 4) a point in space.

In addition to determining the origin of an e-mail message using IP addresses, different file formats have characteristics that may be associated with their source. As shown earlier, Microsoft Office documents contain embedded information, such as printer names, directory locations, names of authors, and creation/modification date-time stamps, that can be useful for determining their source.

### PRACTITIONER'S TIP: USEFUL CHARACTERISTICS OF EVIDENCE

A class characteristic is a general feature shared with similar items such as Kodak digital cameras that embed the make and model names in the photographs they take. An individual characteristic is a unique feature specific to a particular thing, place, person, or action. For example, a scratch on a camera lens that appears in photographs it takes, a distinct monument in the background of a photograph, or the defendant's face appearing in a photograph are all individual characteristics that may help investigators associate the photograph with its source—that is, a particular camera, location, or person.

Comparing an item of evidence to an exemplar can reveal investigatively useful class characteristics or even individual characteristics.

These embedded characteristics can be used to associate a piece of evidence with a specific computer. Earlier versions of Microsoft Office also embedded a unique identifier in files, called a Globally Unique Identifier (GUID), which can be used to identify the computer that was used to create a given document (Leach & Salz, 1998). More subtle evaluations of source involve the association of data fragments with a particular originating file, or determining if a given computer was used to alter a piece of evidence.

When a suspect's computer contains photographs relating to a crime, it may not be safe to assume that the suspect created those photographs. It is possible that the files were copied from another system or downloaded from the Internet. Forensic analysis of the photographs may be necessary to extract class characteristics that are consistent with the suspect's digital camera or flatbed scanner. The scanner may have a scratch or flaw that appears in the photographs, or the files may contain information that was embedded by the digital camera such as the make and model of the camera, and the date and time the photograph was taken. This embedded metadata could be used to demonstrate that a photograph was likely taken using a suspect's camera rather than downloaded from the Internet. This is particularly important during investigations involving child pornography because it is desirable to locate the original victims and protect them from further abuse. There is a body of research that concentrates on identifying the specific camera that was used to take a given photograph (Alles et al., 2009; Kurosawa et al., 2009).

## Digital Document Authentication

The author of a document and the date it was created can be significant. It is relatively straightforward to change a computer's clock to give the impression that a contract or suicide note was created on an earlier date. Such staging can make it more difficult to determine who wrote a document and when it was created. However, there are various approaches that forensic analysts can use to authenticate a digital document.

Forensic analysts can use date-time stamps on files and in log files to determine the provenance of a document such as a suicide note even when the digital crime scene is staged. For instance, it is possible to detect staging and document falsification by looking for chronological inconsistencies in log files and file date-time stamps. Nuances in the way computers maintain different date-time stamps can help forensic analysts reconstruct aspects of the creation and modification of a document. In addition, certain types of files, such as Microsoft Word, contain embedded metadata that can be useful for authenticating a document as detailed in Chapter 5, "Windows Forensic Analysis." This embedded metadata may include the last printed date and the last 10 filenames and authors.

### FROM THE CASE FILES: AN HONEST MISTAKE

A man was accused of backdating a document to cover up alleged environmental violations. Forensic analysis of his computer and e-mail, as well as the e-mail of his attorney, all combined to show that the document had not been fabricated. They had simply used a prior document as a template and had forgotten to update the date typed at the top of the page.

The arrangement of data on storage media (a.k.a. digital stratigraphy) can provide supporting evidence in this kind of forensic analysis. For instance, when a forensic analyst finds a questioned document that was purportedly created in January 2005 lying on top of a deleted document that was created in April 2005, staging should be suspected since the newer file should not be overwritten by an older one. Although the usefulness of digital stratigraphy for document authentication can be undermined by some disk optimization programs that reposition data on a hard drive, it can also be aided by the process. In one case, the suspect defragmented his hard drive prior to fabricating a document. The forensic analyst determined that the defragmentation process had been executed in 2003, causing all data on the disk to be reorganized onto a particular portion of the disk. The questioned documents that were purportedly created in 1999 were the only files on the system that were not neatly arranged in this area of the disk, which added weight to the conclusion that the questioned documents actually were created after the defragmentation process had been executed in 2003 (Friedberg, 2003).

## DATA GATHERING AND OBSERVATION

After verifying the integrity of the digital evidence, forensic practitioners perform an initial survey to gain an overview of the entire body of evidence, including capacity, partitions (including identification and reconstruction of deleted partitions), allocated and unallocated space, and encryption. Then the evidence is preprocessed to salvage deleted data, and translate and filter as needed to expose the most useful information and eliminate irrelevant data. Organization is an implicit part of this phase, resulting in a reduced set of data grouped into logical categories like e-mail, documents, Internet history, reconstructed web pages, Instant Messaging chat logs, logon records, and network logs.

The decision to eliminate or retain certain data for forensic analysis may be based on external data attributes like MD5 values used to identify known child pornography or to exclude known operating system and application files. It may also be possible to narrow the focus to a particular time period or to certain types of digital evidence relevant to the case. However, keep in mind that offenders might have concealed evidence, so care must be taken when filtering data. Something as simple as video segments having their extensions changed from `.MOV` to `.EXE` could result in an unwary examiner inadvertently filtering out incriminating evidence. Therefore, it is advisable to identify file extension/signature mismatches and process them separately to determine what data they contain. There is even greater risk of missing important evidence when encryption or steganography are used to hide incriminating evidence within other files.

### FROM THE CASE FILES: *UNITED STATES v. DUNCAN*

One of the home computers of convicted serial killer Joseph Edward Duncan III contained an encrypted PGPdisk container named `Readme.txt`. A limited cursory inspection of the dataset may have missed this simple attempt by the suspect to hide data, but a review of signature mismatches immediately brought this item to the attention of the examiner.

Depending on the forensic software utilized, certain data such as encrypted files, unusual archive compression, or Lotus Notes e-mail may need to be extracted for specialized processing. A simple example is a suspected compromised server where log files are archived as `.tar.gz` or `.bz2`. If the examiner's software does not automatically expand such files, they would need to be preprocessed prior to searching for a suspect IP address. This issue is covered further in the section "Special Files" later in this chapter.

---

## PRACTITIONER'S TIP: LIMITED RESOURCES

Many digital forensic laboratories have limited resources and are suffering from a backlog of cases. To deal with this problem and ensure that evidence is processed in a timely manner, some labs have adopted a tiered strategy for performing forensic processing, with three levels: (1) triage forensic inspection, (2) survey forensic examination, and (3) in-depth forensic analysis (Casey et al., 2009). If the triage forensic inspection reveals that the computer contains potentially relevant digital evidence, the computer can be assigned to a more experienced forensic practitioner for further levels of processing. Specialized tools are being developed to automate routine aspects for each level of processing. The FBI uses a preview tool called ImageScan to review all graphics files on a computer quickly without altering the original evidence. The Ontario Provincial Police developed a tool called C4P for a similar purpose (www.e-crime.on.ca). Triage-Lab is another tool used to automate triage forensic inspections of computers in various kinds of investigations (www.adfsolutions.com). In addition to keyword searching and other capabilities, triage tools like these can automatically identify previously unknown child pornographic images by utilizing image analysis technology, rather than just relying on MD5 hashes of known images.

The success of this approach depends on the laboratory establishing consistent methodologies for each level, and thresholds to guide the decision for use of different levels of forensic processing. In addition, proper training is needed to ensure that those performing the work at any level are not blinkered by protocols and procedures, and that they will recognize important evidence or indicators that require further forensic analysis. The use of encryption and data hiding can render cursory inspections and keyword searches of evidentiary media effectively useless.

---

## Salvaging Deleted Data

An important aspect of the forensic analysis process is to salvage all data from storage media and convert unreadable data into a readable form. Although data can be hidden on a drive in many ways and it is not feasible to look for all of them in all cases, examiners should be able to identify the major sources of data or at least be able to recognize large amounts of missing data. For instance, if the combined size of all visible partitions on a drive is much smaller than the capacity of the drive, this may be an indication that a partition is not being detected. Similarly, if a large amount of data cannot be classified or there are many files of a known type that are unusually large, this may be an indication that some form of data hiding or encryption is being used. The following sections cover the main areas on storage media where useful data may be found.

### Deleted Files and Folders

Criminals often take steps to conceal their crimes, and deleted data can often contain the most incriminating digital evidence. Therefore, one of the most fruitful data salvaging processes is to recover files and folders that have been deleted. When dealing with FAT or NTFS file systems, most tools can recover deleted files but not all can recover deleted folders that are no longer referenced by the file system. It is useful to know if and how different tools recover and present information about deleted files and folders.

Notably, automated file and folder recovery tools make assumptions that are not always correct. For instance, when recovering deleted files, many tools take the starting cluster and file size from a folder entry, and assign the next free clusters to the file sequentially. The underlying assumption in this process breaks down when the starting cluster of one deleted file is followed by free clusters that belonged to a different deleted file. So, automated tools can generate correct or incorrect results depending on the assumptions they make and the particular situation. Furthermore, if two deleted directory entries point to the same cluster, it can take some effort to determine which filename and associated date-time stamps referenced that cluster most recently. Some automated file recovery tools distinguish between directory entries that have been deleted versus those that have been deleted and overwritten. However, care must be taken not to assume that files with newer date-time stamps accessed the associated clusters more recently. There are sufficient nuances to file date-time stamps that an apparently newer file could be created before the apparently old one.

Figure 2.1 provides an example of an apparently recoverable deleted file. Closer inspection of the data that is displayed for this file reveals that it is not the actual original contents of the file.

These problems are compounded when more aggressive salvaging techniques are used. Some forensic analysis tools have a powerful feature that scours a disk for deleted folders on FAT and NTFS systems. For instance, X-Ways provides a "Thorough" salvaging capability and EnCase has a "Recover Folders" feature. The resulting salvaged file system information may enable forensic analysts to recovered data that was associated with deleted files that are no longer referenced by the current file system. However, different implementations of this salvaging process can lead to inconsistent results between different tools, or even different versions of the same tool. Many existing forensic tools combine salvaged file system details with the existing file system, and this mixing of two separate file system states often leads to more conflicts of the type described in the previous section. The conflicts arise when a new file has reused the clusters that were previously allocated to a salvaged file. To guard against mistakes and misinterpretations, it is critically important that forensic analysts conceptually separate these two system states, thinking of the salvaged file system information as separate and overlaid on top of the existing file systems.

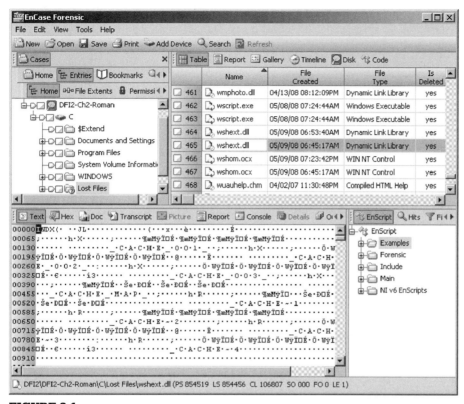

**FIGURE 2.1**
Example of incorrect data in recoverable deleted file.

For the simplest conflicts, both the current and salvaged file system have file system metadata pointing to same area on disk, generally providing forensic analysts with sufficient information to resolve the conflict. More difficult conflicts arise when the space allocated to a salvaged file has been overwritten by newer data but file system details about the newer file are not recoverable. In this situation, the diligent forensic analyst will determine that the file content is not consistent with the salvaged file system details. This inconsistency may be as simple as a salvaged Microsoft Word document pointing to an area of the disk that contains a JPEG graphics file. However, some inconsistencies are more difficult to detect, and require a more thorough comparison between the recovered data and the salvaged file system information. In more complicated situations, multiple salvaged filenames point to the same area of the disk, creating additional levels of complexity when trying to reconstruct activities on a computer system. Therefore, forensic analysts must take additional steps to determine whether the data that appears to have been allocated to a salvaged file in fact was recovered properly and accurately.

## FROM THE CASE FILES: DISAMBIGUATION OF DELETED FILES

This example clearly illustrates the potential problems of deleted file recovery in an Internet child pornography case.

> ...a JPG file was recovered from cluster 195,018 and two file entries were found pointing to it. The first of these indicated that a file named tn_pbb0915.jpg was written to this cluster at 22:16:06.30 on 10th October 2001 and it was 3051 bytes in length. The second entry however, indicated that a file named 3e.jpg had been written to the cluster at 00:24:08.75 on 14th January 2002 and it was 6497 bytes in length. The fact that the drive had been defragmented meant that it was not possible to make the simple assumption that the recovered JPG data was the later file. Even without defragmentation, ascribing the image to the later file entry was still weak because as both file entries were marked as deleted, it was a distinct possibility that the image data had been written after the 14th January 2002 and its attendant file entry had been lost. However, research into the internal structure of JPG files revealed that it is possible to calculate the original length of the file in bytes. The recovered data indicated an original file length of 6497 bytes, providing a much stronger inferential link to the second file entry. (Bates, 2002)

When a few deleted files or folders are critical to a case, forensic analysts should examine them closely for inconsistencies, and seek corroborating evidence from other areas of the computer system or connected networks. The same caveats apply to deleted items in physical memory of computers and mobile devices. Forensic tools are emerging that capture the full contents of memory from various devices and attempt to reconstruct the data structures containing files, processes, call logs, SMS messages, and other information. Given the variety of data structures, mistakes may be made when parsing physical memory dumps and attempting to recover deleted items.

Documentation relating to this recovery process, such as an inventory of the recovered files and a description of how they were salvaged, should be maintained to enable others to assess what was recovered. Given the variations between tools and the potential for error, it is advisable to compare the results from one tool using another. Such a comparison can be made by comparing the inventories of undeleted files from both tools for any differences.

### File Carving

Recall that, on storage media, the space that is available to store new data is called unallocated space. This area on a disk is important from an investigative standpoint because it often contains significant amounts of data from deleted files.

File carving tools like Foremost, Scalpel, DataLifter, and PhotoRec scour unallocated space for characteristics of certain file types in an effort to salvage deleted files. This salvaging process generally produces a large percentage of incomplete and corrupt files, because file carving tools rarely know the size of the original files, and the deleted files may be fragmented or partially overwritten. If the approximate size of the original files is known, forensic analysts can adjust a parameter in file carving tools to set the maximum size of the salvaged files to increase the number of successfully salvaged files. When specific files are of interest, like deleted NT Event Logs, file carving tools can be customized with the associated file signature to salvage these file types (Murphey, 2007).

---

**PRACTITIONER'S TIP: DIFFERENT TOOLS VIEW UNALLOCATED SPACE DIFFERENTLY**

Although most tools for examining storage media have the ability to extract unallocated space for separate processing, their approaches are not necessarily consistent. For instance, when EnCase recovers deleted files, it no longer considers the associated data to be in unallocated space whereas some other tools do, effectively accounting for the data twice. For instance, on the hard drive used in the investigative scenario for this chapter, the amount of unallocated space reported by EnCase is 16,606,420,992 bytes whereas other forensic tools like X-Ways report it as 16,607,297,536 bytes. The difference of 876,544 bytes does not correspond directly to the amount of data in recover-able deleted files. In some circumstances, having a forensic tool like EnCase recategorize recovered data may reduce the amount of redundant data through which a forensic practitioner has to wade. However, failure to realize that this recategorization has occurred can caused forensic practitioners to reach incorrect conclusions. For instance, as noted in the previous section, there is a chance that some unallocated clusters may be assigned to the incorrect file. It can be more effective to carve files out of unallocated space utilizing a tool that takes a stricter definition of unallocated space. If the undelete and file carving processes produce the same files, these duplicates can be eliminated.

---

Some forensic utilities break large files such as unallocated and swap space into smaller pieces to facilitate processing such as file carving and indexing. If an examiner exports and processes these segments of unallocated space individually with standalone file carving utilities, it is possible that, depending on where the boundaries are, portions of salvaged items may be missing.

Keep in mind that most file carving methods work on the assumption that a file is stored in contiguous clusters. The advantage of performing file carving on extracted unallocated space rather than on a full forensic image is that the data on disk may not have been arranged in consecutive clusters but may become consecutive when extracted into a single file. Also keep in mind that files salvaged using this technique do not have file names or date-time stamps associated with them so the examiner needs to assign them names in a systematic way.

Researchers are developing more sophisticated techniques to salvage fragmented deleted files in response to DFRWS Forensic Challenges (www.dfrws.org). Currently, these advanced salvaging methods work for only certain file types like PDF and ZIP files (Cohen, 2007).

## Handling Special Files

There are certain files that will not be immediately accessible to keyword searching. In addition to encrypted and password protected files, certain file formats store text in binary or proprietary formats. These "special" files include compressed archives, encoded attachments in e-mail messages, and encrypted and password protected files.

Another very common example is Adobe PDF documents that have been "secured" to prevent extraction of text, and TIFF fax documents. Keyword searches on these of course will be useless. If there is a large quantity of such unsearchable files that are relevant to a case, more than can be reviewed manually, the typical approach is to use optical character recognition (OCR) to convert them to text, thus rendering them searchable. Attention must be paid to ensure that mistakes are not introduced by the OCR process.

A criminal investigation may center around kickbacks on contracts, and forensic analysts may focus their attention on Microsoft Office documents and other files that are keyword searchable. However, the smoking gun evidence may actually be in TIFF e-mail attachments, JPG items in "My Scans," or received fax items. An effective identification and preprocessing procedure process will identify such items whereas just performing keyword would fail.

## PRACTITIONER'S TIP: UNCOMPRESSING FILES

Provided compressed files are not password protected or corrupted, they can be uncompressed with relative ease. However, there are many varieties of compression, and if your forensic tool does support a particular kind that you encounter, you can export the files, uncompress them using a specialized utility for that purpose, and add the uncompressed files to the case.

## PRACTITIONER'S TIP: DELETED E-MAIL FRAGMENTS

Be aware that Outlook e-mail is stored on disk using a simple form of encoding. Therefore, when searching for deleted e-mail associated with a particular address, forensic analysts select the appropriate decoding mechanism. EnCase provides this in a "code page" called "Outlook encryption" to search for such encoded e-mail addresses and text.

MIME encoding adds an additional layer of encoding to e-mail attachments. An alternate approach to searching for e-mail messages is to use a tool that understands the specific file format and makes it accessible for keyword searching. FTK can interpret and index an Outlook PST file as shown in Figure 2.2, giving forensic analysts efficient access to e-mail messages and many attachments. EnCase can also interpret some of these proprietary formats using the View File Structure feature. An added advantage of using this type of specialized tool is that they support analysis of metadata within e-mail. For instance, a search can be restricted to a date range of interest. When using such specialized tools for processing digital evidence, it is important to understand their inner workings in order to avoid mistakes and misinterpretations. For instance, exporting items found in e-mail using certain tools may not preserve the parent–child relationship between messages and attachments, which can be important in certain situations. Common examples of the pitfalls of processing e-mail are covered in Chapter 3, "Electronic Discovery," with a specific example relating to dtSearch.

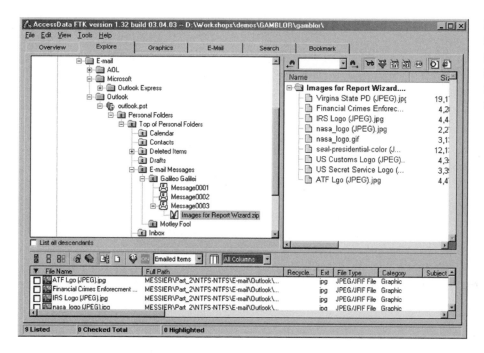

**FIGURE 2.2**

FTK used to extract e-mail messages and the contents of attachments such as images in a Zip archive shown here.

Another approach to viewing proprietary formats, such as America Online (AOL) or Lotus Notes, is to restore them to a disk and view them via the native client application. In some cases it is possible to recover messages that have been deleted but have not been purged from e-mail containers.

When special files are corrupt, it may be possible to repair the damage using specially designed utilities. For example, EasyRecovery Professional from Ontrack can repair a variety of file types from Windows systems including Outlook files and Zip archives. On UNIX systems, there are tools for repairing a more limited set of files such as tarfix and fixcpio.

### Encryption and Steganography

Encryption can present a significant challenge for digital forensic practitioners, particularly full disk encryption (Casey & Stellatos, 2008). Even when full disk encryption is not used or can be circumvented, additional effort is required to salvage data from password protected or encrypted files (Casey, 2002). When dealing with individually protected files, it is sometimes possible to use a hexadecimal editor like WinHex to simply remove the password within a file. There are also specialized tools that can bypass or recover passwords of various files. Currently, the most powerful and versatile tools for salvaging password protected and encrypted data are PRTK and DNA from AccessData. The Password Recovery Toolkit can recover passwords from many file types and is useful for dealing with encrypted data. Also, it is possible for a DNA network to try every key in less time by combining the power of several computers. Distributed Network Attack (DNA) can brute-force 40-bit encryption of certain file types including Adobe Acrobat and Microsoft Word and Excel. Using a cluster of approximately 100 off-the-shelf desktop computers and the necessary software, it is possible to try every possible 40-bit key in five days. Rainbow tables can be used to accelerate the password guessing process. Some vendors also have hardware decryption platforms based on implementation of field programmable gate arrays that can increase the speed of brute force attacks.

When strong encryption is used such as BestCrypt, PGP, or Windows Encrypting File System, a brute-force approach to guessing the encryption key is generally infeasible. In such cases, it may be possible to locate unencrypted versions of data in unallocated space, swap files, and other areas of the system. For instance, printer spool files on Windows and UNIX systems can contain data from files that have been deleted or encrypted. Alternatively, it may be possible to obtain an alternate decryption key. For instance some encryption programs advise users to create a recovery disk in case they forget their password. When EFS is used, Windows automatically assigns an encryption recovery agent that can decrypt messages when the original encryption key is unavailable (Microsoft, 1999). In Windows 2000, the built-in administrator account is the default recovery agent (an organization can override the default by assigning a domainwide recovery agent provided the system is part of the organization's Windows 2000 domain).

Notably, prior to Windows XP, EFS private keys were weakly protected and it was possible to gain access to encrypted data by replacing the associated NT logon password with a known value using a tool like ntpasswd and logging into a bootable/virtualized clone of the system with the new password.

When investigating a child exploitation case, it is advisable to be on the lookout for other forms of data concealment such as steganography. Forensic analysts can make educated guesses to identify files containing hidden data—the presence of steganography software and uncharacteristically large files should motivate examiners to treat these as special files that require additional processing. In such cases, it may be possible to salvage the hidden data by opening the files using the steganography software and providing a password that was obtained during the investigation. More sophisticated techniques are available for detecting hidden data. Even if encryption or steganography cannot be bypassed, documenting which files are concealing data can help an investigator, attorney, or trier-of-fact determine the intent of the defendant.

## Extracting Embedded Metadata

The purpose of this step is to harvest additional metadata relating to the files of interest to support further analysis. As noted at the beginning of this chapter, embedded metadata can answer a variety of questions regarding a document, including its provenance and authenticity. Embedded metadata can also help generate important leads, pointing to other sources of digital evidence on the system or Internet. As described in Chapter 1, photographs taken by digital cameras can contain details such as the make and model of the camera, the date and time the picture was taken (according to the camera's clock), and with some models the GPS coordinates of the camera when the photograph was taken. The data in such photographs found on a computer or on the Internet can be compared with those of a digital camera seized in the defendant's home to determine if they are consistent, helping to establish a link.

## INVESTIGATIVE SCENARIO
## Part 2: Embedded Metadata

Review of the EXIF header data in 24 digital photographs copied into the folder C\Documents and Settings\ Roman\My Documents\My Pictures\Valentines Day

on the subject system on February 15, 2009, indicate they were digitized utilizing a Nikon Coolpix P4 camera as shown in Figure 2.3.

**FIGURE 2.3**

EXIF data extracted from a digital photograph using JPEGsnoop.

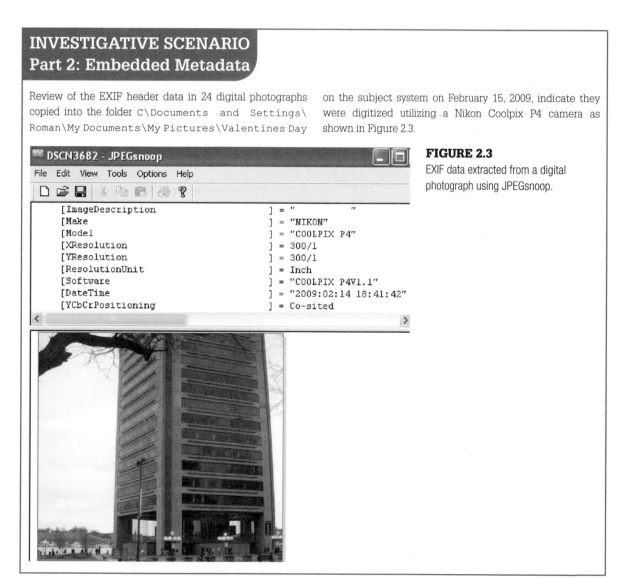

*(Continued)*

There are many other sources of metadata that can be useful in digital investigations, as detailed in the technology-specific chapters later in this Handbook. The experience and judgment of the examiner must be exercised to determine what data might be available and which might be useful to the investigation.

### Overview of System Configuration and Usage

After preprocessing the evidence, an initial review is performed to document information about the users of the system (e.g., user accounts, e-mail accounts, IM accounts), and configuration information like time zone, network, and wireless settings. Forensic practitioners look for items of interest in typical user storage areas (My Documents, e-mail), nontraditional or unusual storage areas (intruder storage of files in Recycle Bin, concealed files and directories, renamed file extensions, etc.), along with traditional areas of forensic interest including the Registry and log files. As part of this review process, forensic analysts try to establish an initial overview of user activities on the computer, including recent files accessed, Internet browsing history, and device connection information.

An analyst traditionally breaks down and associates activity with a specific user, and may need to repeat this process for every user account. In addition to logical document review and file system activity, this may include processing of the Internet history (Internet Explorer, Firefox, Safari, etc.), Registry (ntuser. dat), and file permissions.

*(Continued)*

## INVESTIGATIVE SCENARIO—CONT'D

files (SAM/System) from the subject computer as input, the administrator account password was determined to be L1b3r4t0r.

### User Folders of Potential Interest

Photographs of Baltimore World Trade Center office building taken on February 14, 2009 from multiple angles were found on the suspect's system. In addition, on February 15, 2009 at 2:45 PM, the folder C\Documents and Settings\Roman\My Documents\Garmin was created as shown in Figure 2.4.

The document named Funds.ods shown in Figure 2.4 was created on May 23, 2009 in the My Documents folder and requires further analysis (to be continued…).

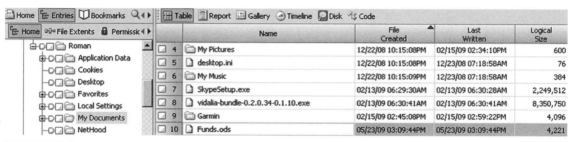

**FIGURE 2.4**

Contents of My Documents on subject system.

A review of all installed and uninstalled applications may provide significant information. For example, installed "covert" communications (steg), privacy software (Tor), specialized applications to destroy data (e.g., BCWipe or Evidence Eliminator), or transfer mechanisms (e.g., Winsock FTP, peer-to-peer) may dictate a much more detailed analysis in an attempt to document user activity associated with such utilities. Installed applications may also provide insight as the user's knowledge level. An example would be existence and use of hexadecimal editors, "patch" files, and low-level programming utilities such as Microsoft Assembler along with user generated source code. Specialized user generated material such as source code may require review by an expert.

## FROM THE CASE FILES: SUSPICIOUS SOFTWARE

In one case, a software development company released a large number of employees two months prior to a major product release. Two weeks prior to release, all source code and code repositories were mysteriously deleted, and unfortunately the tape backup was one month old. During a forensic analysis of one of the company's servers, a simple UNIX script was found that logged into each corporate server as root and executed an rm * to delete all files. In another case, during an initial incident response, the examiner responding to the suspect's work area noticed several items of concern. First, the user had a workstation with specialized password "crack" software connected via a serial cable to the company's PBX phone system. Not only had the user cracked the admin password, forensic analysis confirmed later by the suspect's confession determined he had created a logic bomb that would have deleted all phone system information. This company's lifeblood was the phone system, and the destruction/reconstruction of this material would easily have represented several million in losses.

In addition to review of applications, an examiner typically performs an antivirus and malware scan. Knowing which, if any, virus programs and/or malware or remote access tools are present may be an important aspect of the case. For example, forensic analysis of malware may be necessary when a defendant uses the "Trojan defense," claiming that all incriminating material on his computer is attributable to a remote intruder who compromised the system using a remote administration tool (a.k.a. Trojan horse program). Assessing the capabilities of malware found on the system may reveal that it could not have been used to place the incriminating files on the computer, and analyzing activities on the computer around the time in question may support the conclusion that the defendant was using the computer when the incriminating files were placed on the system.

## INVESTIGATIVE SCENARIO
### Part 4: Program Files of Potential Interest

Based on file system creation date-time stamps, the folder `C:\Program Files\Mozilla Firefox` was created on December 22, 2008 at 10:20 PM. This web browser maintains a history of URLs accessed and other useful information. On February 13, 2009, an installation file for Skype was created in the folder `C:\Documents and Settings\Roman\My Documents\` folder, and the file `Vidalia-bundle-02.0.34-0.1.10.exe` was created in the same folder minutes later. This bundle included The Onion Router (TOR), an application that utilizes a network of virtual tunnels to help improve privacy and security, and Vidalia, a graphic user interface to TOR. Both Skype and Vidalia/TOR were installed on the system on February 13, 2009.

Evidence of the existence of the file wiping utility Jetico BCWipe was detected on the subject system; however, there is no indication of recent use to overwrite data on the system. The folder `C:\Program Files\Jetico\BCWipe` was created and last accessed on December 22, 2008 at 10:22 PM, however, this folder contained no files. A reference to `E:\BCWIPE3.EXE` was found in pagefile.sys, suggesting the source of the application was a 60GB Western Digital USB drive that was connected approximately two minutes earlier as indicated by the `setupapi.log` file. At the time of acquisition, the subject system had no Prefetch folder. However, a reference to `BCWIPE3.exe-3484E676.pf` was found in unallocated space along with references to `\Documents and Settings\Roman\Local Settings\Temp\~BCWIPE3.TMP`.

Regarding the "Funds.ods" file mentioned in the previous part of this scenario, the file extension ".ods" is associated with OpenOffice, which was not installed on the subject system. The fact that Open Office was not installed is exactly the type of thing an analyst should catch, leading to further analysis as to how the document came to be on the system. The file is actually stored as a zip archive that includes and embedded file named `meta.xml` that contains metadata associated with the spreadsheet. Subsequent analysis of the `meta.xml` indicated it was created online at http://spreadsheets.google.com as detailed later in this chapter.

Once elements of a user's activity are processed, the examiner can identify significant elements for reporting or further analysis. An example would be the user executed Google searches on "deletion utilities", followed by "prevent undeleted", with subsequent download and execution of such a utility to delete several company confidential documents the day of her previously unannounced resignation, but only after she connected a USB thumb drive, reviewed the confidential documents, performed a `File->Save As` to save them to the thumb drive.

# INVESTIGATIVE SCENARIO
## Part 5: User Activities of Potential Relevance

Potentially relevant user activities on the subject system from the investigative scenario are summarized here.

### Removable Media Summary

On February 15, 2009 between 2:34 PM and 2:40 PM, the file `setupapi.log` indicated a USB Device identified as `garmin__nuvi` was successfully installed. On February 15, 2009 between 2:36 PM and 2:38 PM, 24 files, named `DSCN3680.JPG` through `DSCN3703.JPG` (with no number gaps in the naming scheme) were created in the `C\ Documents and Settings\Roman\My Documents\ My Pictures\Valentines Day` folder.

### Internet Access Summary

Web browsing activities were reconstructed from Firefox and Internet Explorer web browser history, along with search hits in unallocated space for "url:", "http://", "https://", and "file://".

On February 15, 2009 at 2:45 PM, Firefox was used to access the account bmoreagent@hushmail.com, which is a free privacy-enhanced web-based e-mail service. Five minutes later, at 2:50 PM, the user executed a Google search for "check ip address". Subsequently the user accessed http://whatismy-ipaddress.com with a web page title of Lookup IP, Hide IP, Change IP, Trace IP and more…. The act of checking which IP address is visible on the Internet indicates that the user had some knowledge of computers and the Internet, and how to conceal the IP address of a computer on the Internet. This may have been an attempt to confirm that TOR was functioning correctly to conceal the user's source IP address.

On March 19, 2009 at 12:32 PM, Firefox was used to execute a Google search for "World Trade Center Baltimore building plans" with subsequent access to the file www.marylandports.com/opsalert/eBroadcast/2008/HPPwtc2008.pdf. Subsequently, at 1:18 PM, Internet Explorer and file system activity reflect access to the web page Account is Now Active at www.gunbroker.com. The content of this page in conjunction with an earlier redirect page suggests the user received a Gunbroker.com account activation e-mail at bmoreagent@hushmail.me. After logging into the Gunbroker.com web site, the user accessed the auction web page for a specific weapon: www.gunbroker.com/Auction/ViewItem.asp?Item=125130891, (SIGARMS, P229, 9MM, NIGHT SIGHTS, 13RD, 2 MAGS). The user then viewed a listing of auctions for semi-automatic guns—the reconstructed web page is displayed in Figure 2.5.

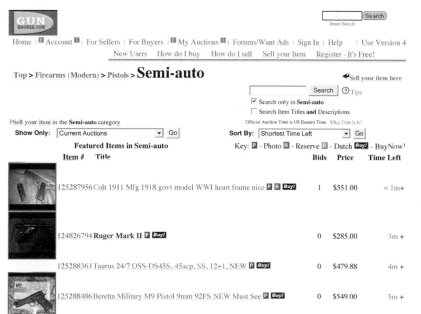

**FIGURE 2.5**

Part of a web page from the suspect's computer showing auctions of semi-automatic pistols on Gunbroker.com.

*(Continued)*

## INVESTIGATIVE SCENARIO—CONT'D

On March 19, 2009 at 1:19 PM, the user accessed a web page on Gunbroker.com to "Ask Seller A Question—Send Mail to User" for the specific auction item 125288486.

On March 20, 2009 at 12:00 PM, a Firefox 3 Bookmark was created concerning a Google search for "undetectable bomb". Checking Mozilla Firefox in a virtualized clone of the subject system confirmed recent entries, as shown in Figure 2.6.

Based on the keyword "undetectable bomb", additional analysis was performed of the unallocated areas of the system, resulting in additional items that may represent either web pages viewed or searches conducted by the user of the system. Examples included liquid-explosives, Baltimore building design plans office, Baltimore city building records, and Baltimore building planning records. No date/time structures were identified with these records.

On May 23, 2009, between approximately 2:59 PM and 3:20 PM, the user created the Gmail account bmoreagent@gmail.com. A total of six `CreateAccount[x].htm` files created during this process reflected several hidden values, some of which are visible in the reconstructed web page shown in Figure 2.7. The multiple `CreateAccount[x].htm` files were caused by several attempts to set the password. The most recent entered password was DFIChapter2.

On May 23, 2009 at 3:04 PM, the file `C:\Documents and Settings\Roman\My Documents\My Pictures\ValentinesDay\DSCN3682.JPG` was Last Accessed and was sent as an e-mail attachment via Outlook Express. This e-mail is shown in Figure 2.8.

**FIGURE 2.6**

Remnant of web search for "undetectable bomb".

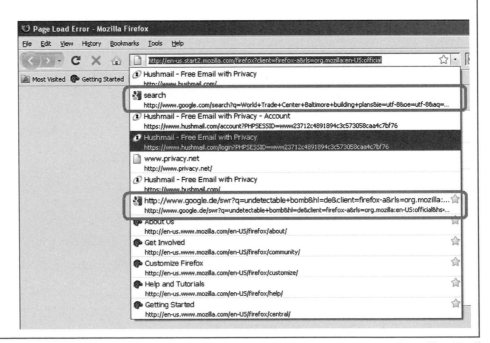

*(Continued)*

# INVESTIGATIVE SCENARIO—CONT'D

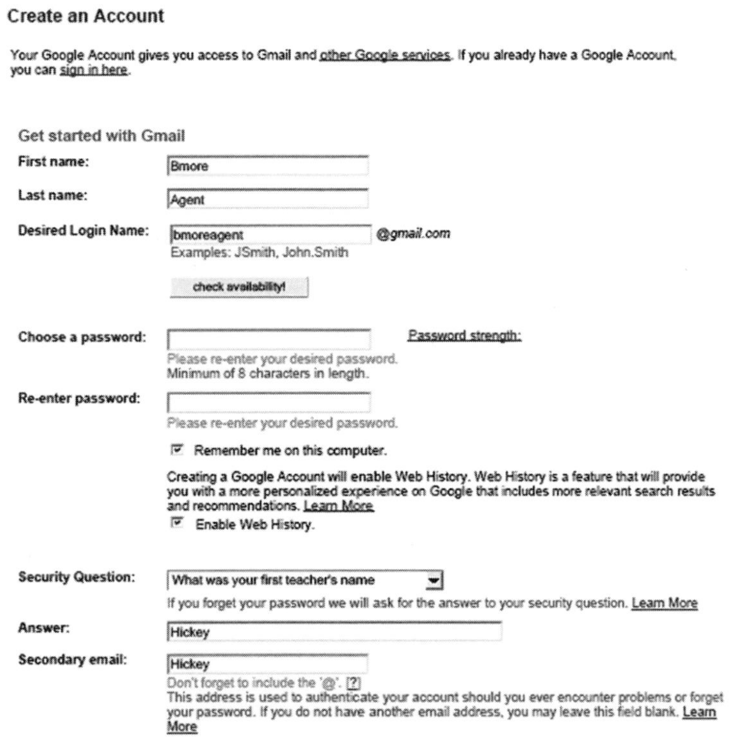

### Create an Account

Your Google Account gives you access to Gmail and other Google services. If you already have a Google Account, you can sign in here.

Get started with Gmail

| | |
|---|---|
| First name: | Bmore |
| Last name: | Agent |
| Desired Login Name: | bmoreagent        @gmail.com |

Examples: JSmith, John.Smith

[ check availability! ]

| | |
|---|---|
| Choose a password: | _____    Password strength: |

Please re-enter your desired password.
Minimum of 8 characters in length.

| | |
|---|---|
| Re-enter password: | _____ |

Please re-enter your desired password.

☑ Remember me on this computer.

Creating a Google Account will enable Web History. Web History is a feature that will provide you with a more personalized experience on Google that includes more relevant search results and recommendations. Learn More

☑ Enable Web History.

| | |
|---|---|
| Security Question: | What was your first teacher's name    ▼ |

If you forget your password we will ask for the answer to your security question. Learn More

| | |
|---|---|
| Answer: | Hickey |
| Secondary email: | Hickey |

Don't forget to include the '@'. [?]
This address is used to authenticate your account should you ever encounter problems or forget your password. If you do not have another email address, you may leave this field blank. Learn More

**FIGURE 2.7**

Reconstructed Gmail account setup page.

| | |
|---|---|
| **From:** | Bmore Agent <bmoreagent@gmail.com> |
| **To:** | 526177@gmail.com |
| **Subject:** | Visual |
| **Sent:** | Sat, 23 May 2009 15:04:26 -0400 |

[-- Mime Part , Type: image/jpeg; name="DSCN3682.JPG", Disp: attachment; filename="DSCN3682.JPG", Size: 1MB --]

**FIGURE 2.8**

E-mail message sent with digital photograph attached.

| | |
|---|---|
| **Mime-version:** | 1.0 |
| **Received:** | by 10.114.134.14 with HTTP; Sat, 23 May 2009 12:04:26 -0700 (PDT) |
| **Delivered-to:** | bmoreagent@gmail.com |
| **Message-id:** | <e82fcf1f0905231204q69e8fef3q6e4b2b5640ed3a20@mail.gmail.com> |
| **From:** | Bmore Agent <bmoreagent@gmail.com> |
| **Content-type:** | multipart/mixed; boundary=00163646bfd6c495fb046a990baa |

# HYPOTHESIS FORMATION

A hypothesis is an informed supposition to explain the observations in the data gathering phase of a forensic analysis. Even if it is difficult to come up with a hypothesis initially or this initial hypothesis is wrong, it is important to pick a place to start. The process of testing a hypothesis objectively will invariably improve a forensic analyst's understanding of the evidence, leading to continuous refinements of the hypothesis until a rational conclusion is reached.

There may be many individual hypotheses relating to different aspects of an offense, each of which must be verified independently. In a child exploitation investigation, the forensic analyst might think that incriminating photographs were produced using the suspect's digital camera and then transferred on the suspect's computer. The forensic analyst would have to test the two hypotheses that (1) the photographs were taken using a specific camera and (2) the photographs were transferred from that camera onto the suspect's computer. In an intellectual property theft investigation, the forensic analyst might think that the stolen files were copied from the suspect's computer onto removable media and then deleted from the suspect's computer. The forensic analyst would have to test the two hypotheses that (1) the stolen files were copied onto removable media and (2) they were subsequently deleted.

One of the most common mistakes that forensic analysts make when coming up with a hypothesis is to let themselves be influenced by prejudice. For instance, by starting with an assumption of guilt, a forensic analysis is already biased. An effective approach to mitigate this risk is to reverse the hypothesis. Using the child exploitation example in the previous paragraph, the hypotheses to be tested could be (1) the photographs were not taken using the specific camera and (2) the photographs were not transferred from that camera onto the suspect's computer. To test these hypotheses, a forensic analyst might look for evidence that the photographs were taken by someone else and downloaded from the Internet. When there is no evidence to support this explanation, or any other reasonable alternate explanation for the presence of the incriminating photographs on the suspect's system, and analysis of the camera, photographs, and computer all indicate that the photographs came from the camera onto the computer, this is a much stronger result.

# EVALUATING HYPOTHESES

Forensic practitioners are regularly presented with questions that require relatively straightforward analysis of the evidence. For instance, in order to determine whether incriminating files were downloaded from the Internet or copied onto the system from removable media, a forensic analyst might test the download speed of the subject system versus transfer rates of files copied from a CD,

DVD, or removable mass storage device. Running controlled tests with a specific set of files using similar or exact computer and network setup may show that files were copied from a DVD in 60 seconds, from a USB device in 30 seconds, and downloaded via the Internet in 10 seconds. Based on a series of such tests combined with other evidence on the system, a forensic analyst may be able to express an opinion that the incriminating files were downloaded onto the system from the Internet.

In addition, forensic practitioners may encounter files that are not directly processed by their forensic suite, and research fails to identify any utility to facilitate review. In such cases the forensic analyst may need to improvise, perform experiments, and develop their own analysis methods and techniques, guided the entire time by the scientific method.

## FROM THE CASE FILE: DISPROVING WITNESS STATEMENTS

In one case, the offender claimed that he could not remember the password protecting his encryption key because he had changed it recently. By experimenting with the same encryption program on a test system, the forensic analyst observed that changing the password updated the last modified date of the file containing the encryption key. An examination of the file containing the suspect's encryption key indicated that it had not been altered recently as the suspect claimed. Faced with this information, the suspect admitted that he had lied about changing the password.

Forensic practitioners may have to navigate various challenges and uncharted territory as part of their analysis. Evidence dynamics can make crime reconstruction using digital data more difficult, as described in Chapter 1. In some cases, the direct evidence may not be present but the forensic practitioner may be able to identify "forensic residue" or "intrusion residue." These are traces left by user actions or intruder actions, such as the execution of software that may no longer be present on the computer; however, such traces or residue can be used to determine what occurred. This is analogous to a poison that dissipates and is no longer detectable in a victim's body, but the result of the poison is the body's creation of some type of residue such as a specific chemical, protein, or enzyme that is detected in the victim's body. Despite the absence of the poison (which may exist in the body for only a short period of time, like a malicious binary that securely deletes itself after two weeks), the residue or the side effect of its use would be the forensic residue that allows a forensic pathologist to determine that that particular poison was used.

### Interpretation of Digital Evidence

Every observation and measurement has some degree of uncertainly, and it is a forensic practitioner's job to get as close to the truth as possible. There are some common pitfalls of which forensic analysts must be aware in order to avoid reaching the wrong conclusions.

## FROM THE CASE FILES: FORENSIC RESIDUE

A user noticed that an unauthorized $30,000 transfer from her account had occurred. No malware was identified on the system; however, the examiner documented intrusion residue of a buffer overflow by examining Dr. Watson log files. The log entry also provided the name of a suspicious binary, and a corresponding file system entry was identified that documented creation of a suspected piece of malware; however, it was deleted and unrecoverable. The malicious software was no longer on the system; however, the forensic and intrusion residue in this instance was an entry in the Dr. Watson log showing the existence and execution of the malware.

In this case, the forensic residue gave the examiner a starting point that not only facilitated the review, but revealed additional related evidence that might have otherwise gone unnoticed. Although the executable was no longer on the system, Prefetch files confirmed that the suspected piece of malware had been executed on the subject system. Correlating the user's web browsing history confirmed the source of compromise, and subsequent analysis allowed the examiner to identify a suspicious .INI file in the Windows\system32 folder. This file was determined to be a keystroke log file; and as the file was constantly changing, System Restore points were created. Subsequent forensic analysis of the reconstructed keystroke log files from System Restore points confirmed the username and password for the bank account in fact were compromised due to keystroke logging software on the user's system. Subsequent capture and analysis of the malicious software via a link obtained from the user's Internet Explorer history confirmed an embedded IP address (confirmed by the companies' firewall logs) where the log files were transferred to Eastern Europe via port 80. In many such cases, the forensic residue may provide the critical (and potentially otherwise unavailable) evidence.

As noted in Chapter 1, forensic analysts generally see only a representation of the actual digital evidence they are reviewing. The raw data is translated through multiple layers of abstraction that can misrepresent the underlying data or miss important details. Figure 2.9 shows file system information extracted from a physical memory dump of a Motorola Z3 mobile device using XACT. The JPG file in the "picture" folder selected on the left has been associated with non-JPG data shown on the right. Furthermore, a manual examination of the device shows that there are additional digital photographs in this folder that are not displayed using the forensic tool.

Some of the most detrimental errors and omissions occur when forensic tools incorrectly parse file system structures, because this information forms the foundation for many aspects of forensic analysis.

As another example of misinterpretations introduced by forensic software, some tools attempt to reconstruct remnants of web-based e-mail messages from unallocated space. This process can result in erroneous combinations of data fragments, giving the impression that someone sent a message that never existed. To avoid reaching conclusions or making false accusations based on incorrect information, it is necessary to verify important findings at a low level to confirm they exist and are being accurately represented by the forensic tool.

In addition, forensic analysts must consider the possibility that critical file date-time stamps may have been altered or are inaccurate. In a number of cases, mistakes in forensic analysis have arisen from differences in time zones and daylight savings.

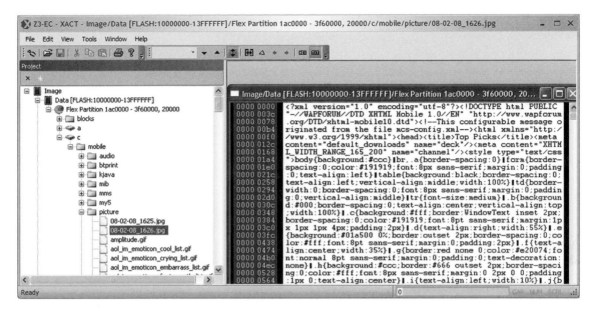

**FIGURE 2.9**
Memory contents from a Motorola Z3 cell phone viewed using XACT shows incorrect data associated with a digital photograph.

## FROM THE CASE FILES: IN THE WRONG TIME ZONE

In one child abuse case, an expert hired by the defense to examine the defendant's computer concluded that it had been used to access the Internet during the first six hours after it was in seized by police. The expert's report indicated that there was substantial evidence of the defendant's computer being altered while it was in police custody, including access to Hotmail login pages and a possible child pornography site. It transpired that the defense expert had not taken the difference in time zones into account when converting the date-time stamps in the Internet Explorer `index.dat` files (Foster, 2004).

In another case involving time zone complications, the suspect flew from Chelyabinsk to Seattle. While in Seattle, the suspect accessed remote hosts on the Internet from the laptop he brought with him before he and his associate were apprehended. The suspect challenged some of the data; having conducted his own review of the dataset, he believed it indicated he was framed by the undercover agents for some of the activity on the system when in fact he simply had failed to take into account the time zone difference. Once presented with the findings of an independent forensic analysis performed as a result of his complaint, he immediately recognized his fundamental mistake.

Digital evidence should always be interpreted in context. When reviewing the image content of web browser cache folders, it is a common mistake to take the existence of the images as something of more value then they may actually represent. In one case, an inexperienced forensic practitioner noticed several "terrorist related" images. This information was submitted in an affidavit and utilized to support requests for additional search warrants. Unfortunately, the forensic practitioner did not take into account the context of the images. They were all Temporary Internet Files associated with access to CNN.com.

## INVESTIGATIVE SCENARIO
## Part 6: Interpretation of Web Browsing Artifacts

Following are some images from the Internet Explorer cache. Knowing that the individual has reviewed weapons sites, conducted searches on terms such as liquid explosives and undetectable bombs, one might see the image of the Coast Guard ship and make an assumption that the user may also be interested in targeting it. Also, the images of Central America and Canada may cause the belief that the user was looking at map points in these areas as shown in Figure 2.10.

By reviewing the user's Internet history, we know the user visited Google Maps and entered coordinates. By recreating the web page from the cache contents as shown in Figure 2.11, or conducting a test on an operationally authorized computer to recreate the circumstances, an analyst will recognize that the image of the Coast Guard ship was displayed automatically.

No Internet history from Internet Explorer or Firefox revealed any specific user access to the image of the Coast Guard ship. Furthermore, the map images of Canada and Central America that looked potentially valuable were simply the result of accessing the default http://maps.google.com web page, which loaded various map segments.

| 1198716[1].jpg | 455957[1].jpg | 1937313[2].jpg | thumb[1].jpg | thumb[10].jpg | v=w2[1]2.png |
| v=w2[2].png | v=w2[1].png | v=w2[4].png | v=w2[5].png | v=w2[5]1.png | v=w2[7].png |

**FIGURE 2.10**
Graphics files in the Temporary Internet Cache.

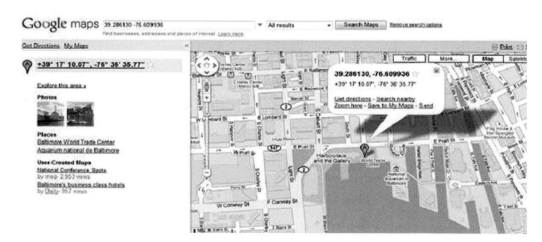

**FIGURE 2.11**
Reconstructed web page.

As another example, the mere presence of an incriminating file on a person's computer may not be sufficient to demonstrate guilt. Forensic analysis may reveal strong evidence that the file was placed on the system by a virus, intruder, or via a web browser vulnerability without the user's knowledge. An analysis of the file, its location, security vulnerabilities, artifacts of system usage, and other contextual clues may help determine how a file came to be on a given system.

Similarly a file with a creation date that is after its last modified date may be incorrectly interpreted as evidence that the system clock was backdated. In fact, the last written date of a file does not necessarily imply that the file was modified on the computer where it is found. Copying a file onto a computer from removable media or another system on a network may not change the last written date, resulting in a file with a modified date prior to its creation date.

## PRACTITIONER'S TIP: RECONSTRUCTING WEB PAGES

Another common process is to recreate web pages visited by the user of the computer. As images and cache content are frequently deleted, there is potential to manually recreate a web page that depicts incorrect information. An example might be a web page with content that was deleted previously, which included files named image01.jpg and image02.jpg. Another web page visited more recently, which happens to be stored in the same Internet Explorer history folder, may reference the exact same filenames. If the previous web page was recoverable and reconstructed (and the previous image files overwritten), reconstruction of the page may very well include images that were not associated with that actual page. Presented as fact without proper qualification, this information could be misleading. Considering that most forensic workstations are not connected to the Internet, and assuming that the content then was the same as it is now, it may be possible to reconstruct a page utilizing a workstation connected to the Internet, but there are many concerns with this process as well. In many cases, online resources like the Internet Archives (www.archive.org) have been utilized to help confirm the previous existence and general type of content of web sites.

There are many other nuances to digital evidence caused by the intricacies of computer operations that can cause confusion or misinterpretation, and the same holds true for networks. The Internet Protocol (IP) address in an e mail header may lead investigators to a particular computer, but this does not necessarily establish that the owner of that computer sent the message. Given the minor amount of effort required to conceal one's identity on the Internet, criminals usually take some action to thwart apprehension. This may be as simple as using a library computer or as sophisticated as inserting someone else's IP address into the e-mail header, requiring investigators to take additional steps to identify the culprit.

To mitigate the risks of evidence being missed or misinterpreted, experienced forensic analysts employ a variety of techniques, including comparing the results of multiple tools, validating important findings through contextual reviews and low level examination, and analyzing corroborating evidence for inconsistencies. For instance, when dealing with date-time stamps of files, look out for inconsistencies in other related, independent sources of information processed during the data gathering phase like embedded metadata, Internet history, and Registry entries. Also, as discussed in Chapter 9, "Network Analysis," it may be possible to correlate date-time stamps relating to downloaded files with network logs, thus not only validating the findings but also helping to reconstruct the cybertrail leading from a crime scene back to the offender.

## PRACTITIONER'S TIP: STUDYING A DIGITAL CLONE

An effective approach to verifying that you are interpreting particular digital evidence correctly is to create a digital clone of the subject system and inspect the evidence as it is seen through the device itself. For instance, booting a forensic duplicate of a computer through utilities such as LiveView may allow you to view important details in their native context. In one case, this type of functional analysis revealed that the desktop of the defendant's computer had a specialized theme with a skull and crossbones icon for My Computer and a Swastika for the Recycle Bin icon. In some cases, specialized applications and associated files (e.g., CAD/CAM files) on the subject system may prevent native review of files on the forensic workstation, in which case a LiveView session may provide a review capability otherwise unavailable. The same concept applies to mobile devices by viewing acquired evidence in a software emulator, or restoring it onto a test device of the same make, model, and firmware.

## Exploring Unfamiliar File Formats

Because of the rapid development of new software applications and updates to existing programs, digital forensic analysts are frequently faced with new file types. In some instances, the purpose of the file may be deduced from its context and the content may be readily interpreted.

## INVESTIGATIVE SCENARIO
## Part 7: Forensic Analysis of SatNav Artifact

On February 15, 2009 at 2:58 PM, the file `GarminDevice.xml` was created, which included text indicating the device was a Garmin nuvi, model 3386111263 with registration and unlock codes XYZABC and MLJ6XYZABC, respectively. Around the same time, the file `current.gpx` was created, which included XML text entries documenting the following stored GPS locations:

- Home, Residence, PhoneNumber 14105554523, wpt lat=39.29544, lon=-76.612045
- Meet Spot, Residence, PhoneNumber 14105554523, wpt lat=39.289761, lon=-76.612222
- Target (annotated with a blue Flag Symbol), wpt lat=39.286130, lon=-76.609936

On February 15, 2009 at 3:00 PM, the user accessed file `C:/Documents and Settings/Roman/My Documents/Garmin/gpx/current.gpx`. This may indicate that the user was aware of and specifically accessed this file. This is supported by use of the Target coordinates in subsequent communications described later in this chapter.

In the unknown areas, an examiner may need to review all possible associated files, filtered by relevant dates/times, and develop his or her own processes to facilitate review. An example of this from the investigative scenario developed for this chapter is recognizing that some Skype usage information on the suspect's system was stored in the SQLite database main.db, which appeared to map all of the Skype chatsync subfolders that contain data associated with various Skype activities as described further, next. Although a strings command obtained some of the information from the main.db SQLList database file, more usable information was obtained after export by utilizing the SQLite command-line program (www.sqlite.org/download.html) as shown here.

```
Sqlite3.exe main.db
>.tables
Accounts      ChatMembers    Conversations   Participants
Alerts        Chats          DbMeta          SMSes
CallMembers   ContactGroups  LegacyMessages  Transfers
Calls         Contacts       Messages        Voicemails
```

Inspection of these tables will help identify which .DAT files contain relevant data. However, an initial forensic analysis can focus on extraction and review of the material. Example commands for processing the Messages, Transfers, and Calls tables are as follows:

```
Sqlite>.mode csv
sqlite> .output Messages.csv;
sqlite> select * from Messages;
sqlite> .output transfers.csv
sqlite> select * from Transfers;
sqlite> .output Calls.csv;
sqlite> select * from Calls;
```

Date-time stamps are exported as Unix numeric values in UTC that can be converted using a utility like DCode (www.digital-detective.co.uk/) or Perl command line:

```
perl -e "print scalar(gmtime(1243102641))"
Sat May 23 18:17:21 2009
```

Knowledge of SQLite can also be useful for analyzing the use of Firefox and Google, and may provide access to deleted records (Pereira, 2008).

Even when a file appears to be in a familiar format, it can contain information that requires deeper analysis. In one case, forensic analysis incorrectly concluded that a Microsoft Excel spreadsheet contained no data of interest, not realizing that the default Sheet2 and Sheet3 contained additional data. Keep in mind that printing spreadsheets, which is a common form of production for

## INVESTIGATIVE SCENARIO
## Part 8: Skype Chat Log

Skype was used on the subject system for phone calls and Instant Messaging. The last dialed number listed in the Skype `config.xml` file was 18775425299, which is associated with Night Galaxy, Inc. (www.nightvisionplanet.com), specializing in night vision equipment. In addition, a call was made to 1-866-727-1401, which is associated with the gun sale web site One Click Shooting (www.oneclickshooting.com).

On May 23, 2009 at 2:17 PM, the user engaged in Skype chat with user js-526177 (John Smith) between 2:17 and 2:26 PM. The session was reconstructed from the associated Skype database files using information generated from queries of the `main.db` SQLite database shown in Table 2.1.

Another approach to examining this type of information, and validating the completeness and accuracy of the data, is to use virtualization to boot a clone of the subject system and access it as the user would. In this scenario, the Skype chat log was viewed in a virtualized functional reconstruction of the suspect's system as shown in Figure 2.12.

During the Skype chat, on May 23, 2009 at 2:21 PM, the user again accessed the file `C:/Documents and Settings/Roman/My Documents/Garmin/gpx/current.gpx`.

The Skype configuration file `shared.xml` contained the text `<ContraProbeResults>`**12.167.154.29:**57921 `</contraProbe Results>`, which is registered with the Emerging Technology Center, 1101 E 33rd St, Baltimore, MD 21218. This information indicates that the suspect connected to the Internet from this location, providing investigators with a potential lead for further information.

review, does not automatically print all sheets unless the application is specifically instructed to print the entire worksheet.

In more complicated situations, when the purpose and meaning of a file is unknown, it may be necessary to perform experiments with the software that created the file. By running the program through controlled tests and observing the effects on the file in question, it may be possible to figure out how to extract usable information from the evidentiary file and/or associated application memory.

## CONCLUSIONS AND REPORTING

The most brilliant forensic analysis can be for naught if it is not communicated clearly to decision makers such as attorneys, members of a jury, or executives in a company. In addition to providing the factual basis for all conclusions, it is advisable to summarize key results at the beginning and clearly restate them at the end of a presentation or report. This approach will provide busy, less technical decision makers with the most critical information they need up front, rather than burying them in technical details.

When communicating the results of forensics analysis, let the evidence speak for itself as much as possible, and do not leap to conclusions. Every conclusion should be solidly supported by the evidence in sufficient detail to enable another forensic analyst to repeat the analysis. Since there is always more that

**Table 2.1** Skype Chat Log Extracted from `main.db` File Using SQLite Tool

| Unix Numeric Value | Date/Time (Converted) | User | Name | Message |
|---|---|---|---|---|
| 1243102641 | Sat, 23 May 2009 14:17:21 -0400 | bmoreagent | bmoreagent | Bmore agent here |
| 1243102672 | Sat, 23 May 2009 14:17:52 -0400 | js-526177 | John Smith | Operational status? |
| 1243102695 | Sat, 23 May 2009 14:18:15 -0400 | bmoreagent | bmoreagent | Target selected and all plans in place. |
| 1243102741 | Sat, 23 May 2009 14:19:01 -0400 | js-526177 | John Smith | Please e-mail the target confirmation details to 526177@gmail.com. This account won't be checked again after today. |
| 1243102812 | Sat, 23 May 2009 14:20:12 -0400 | bmoreagent | bmoreagent | Will do. All that is needed for execution is final approval and funding. |
| 1243102980 | Sat, 23 May 2009 14:23:00 -0400 | bmoreagent | bmoreagent | Here is a photograph of target location (coordinates lat ="39.286130" lon ="-76.609936") |
| 1243103004 | Sat, 23 May 2009 14:23:24 -0400 | bmoreagent | bmoreagent | sent file &quot;DSCN3684.JPG&quot;<files alt=""><file size="1641245" index="0">DSCN3684.JPG</file></files> |
| 1243103084 | Sat, 23 May 2009 14:24:44 -0400 | js-526177 | John Smith | Action authorized and approved. Western Union code 170236723-00348. Use the ID card we previously coordinated. Also, you'll need to provide the password "Be3Ready2Serve" to pickup the cash. |
| 1243103190 | Sat, 23 May 2009 14:26:30 -0400 | js-526177 | John Smith | Received image. Target acknowledged. |

**FIGURE 2.12**

Skype chat log viewed in a virtualized functional reconstruction of the subject system.

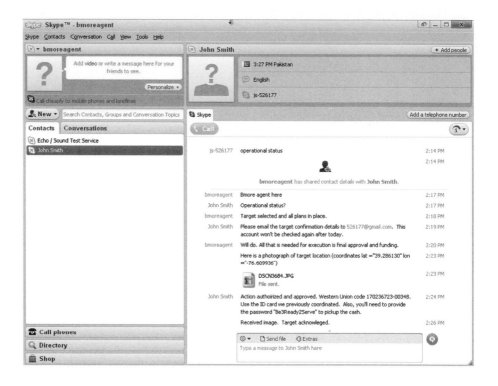

## INVESTIGATIVE SCENARIO
## Part 9: Google Document

On May 23, 2009 at 3:09 PM, the user Roman accessed http://spreadsheets.google.com, resulting in the creation of a `ccc[1].htm` Temporary Internet File, which referenced Funds. At this time, the file `C:\Documents and Settings\Roman\My Documents\Funds.ods` was created, last written, and last accessed.

The `Funds.ods` file actually was stored as a Zip archive, and extraction and review of the embedded `meta.xml` component identified the generator as Google Spreadsheets. Further inspection of the document statistic metadata revealed the Number of Sheets as 3, and Number of Cells as 5. The review of the document statistical information helped confirm there were no "hidden" cells such as white text on white background buried somewhere in the document (e.g., BB:1000). The content of the document was as follows:

Sheet1    "Funds Confirmed"
Sheet2    "Western Union code    170236723-00348"
Sheet3    "Password              Be3Ready2Serve"

Note that the information was divided between multiple worksheets within the file, so looking at only the first one would result in missed information.

**FIGURE 2.13**
Timeline of events relating to the investigative scenario developed for this chapter, organized chronologically using Microsoft Excel.

| | A | B | C |
|---|---|---|---|
| 1 | Date/Time | Entry | Source |
| 2 | | | |
| 3 | 02/16/13 02:34 PM | A USB Device identified as "garmin__nuvi" was successfully installed (2:34~2:40PM) | Setupapi.log & Filesystem |
| 4 | 02/16/13 02:36 PM | A total of 24 images (DSCN3680.JPG ~ DCN3703.JPG) were stored at My Pictures\Valentines Day folder. Taken with a Nikon Coolpix P4 camera between 2:36:22PM and 2:38:40PM. EXIF header information indicates these pictures were digitized between 6:41PM and 6:56PM on February 14, 2009. | File System & EXIF Header Information |
| 5 | 02/16/13 02:45 PM | The folder ...\Roman\My Documents\Garmin was created. | File System |
| 6 | 02/16/13 02:40 PM | Hushmail – Free Email with Privacy - bmoreagent@hushmail.com | Firefox 3 Internet History |
| 7 | 02/16/13 02:50 PM | Google search for "check ip address". Subsequent access to http://whatismyipaddress.com "Lookup IP, Hide IP, Change IP, Trace IP and more…" | Firefox 3 Internet History |
| 8 | 02/16/13 03:00 PM | User accessed file C:/Documents and Settings/Roman/My Documents/Garmin/gpx/current.gpx | IE History & "Recent" Links |
| 9 | | | |
| 10 | 03/20/13 12:32 PM | Google search for "Word Trade Center Baltimore building plans". Subsequent access to http://www.marylandports.com/opsalert/eBroadcast/2008/HPPwtc2008.pdf. | Firefox 3 Internet History |
| 11 | 03/20/13 01:12 PM | Accessed a Hushmail web page. Welcome to Hushmail Account (bmoreagent@hushmail.me). | File System |
| 12 | 03/20/13 01:18 PM | Accessed www.gunbroker.com web page "Account is Now Active". | File System & IE History |
| 13 | 03/20/13 01:18 PM | Accessed http://www.gunbroker.com/Auction/ViewItem.asp?Item=125130891 (SIGARMS, P229, 9MM, NIGHT SIGHTS, 13RD ,2 MAGS). | File System |
| 14 | 03/20/13 01:19 PM | Accessed http://www.gunbroker.com/Auction/Browse.asp?Cat=3026 (Browsed Pistols->Semi-Auto) | File System |
| 15 | 03/20/13 01:19 PM | Accessed web page to Ask Seller A Question - Send Mail to User (http://www.gunbroker.com/Auction/SendMailToUserForm.asp?User=398499&Item=1252884862 b67f14c) bmoreagent@hushmail.me, oneclickshooting.com Item 125288486. | File System |
| 16 | | | |
| 17 | 03/21/13 12:00 PM | Bookmark Created: http://www.google.de/swr?q=undetectable+bomb&hl=de&client=firefox-a&rls=org.mozilla:en-US:official&hs=WiN&swrnum=53600 | Firefox 3 Internet History |
| 18 | | | |
| 19 | 05/24/13 02:17 PM | User engaged in Skype chat with user js-526177 (John Smith) between 2:17 and 2:26PM. | File System and main.db |
| 20 | 05/24/13 02:21 PM | User again accessed file C:/Documents and Settings/Roman/My Documents/Garmin/gpx/current.gpx. | IE History & File System |
| 21 | 05/24/13 02:22 PM | User accessed http://login.live.com, Sign In page | IE History |
| 22 | 05/24/13 02:22 PM | User executed an initial failed Google Search ("we could not understand") on lat ="39.286130" lon ="-76.609936" | File System & IE History |

can be done in a digital forensic analysis, it is prudent to leave room for further analysis by making a statement to the effect of "Further review and analysis of any of this information is available upon request."

Forensic analysts often generate a timeline of key findings to help them identify patterns and organize findings to provide a useful summary for litigators. This timeline can be in a tabular or visual form. Figure 2.13 shows a portion of the timeline in a spreadsheet created for the investigative scenario developed for this chapter.

The forensic analyst may also generate a link analysis and association matrix to provide decision makers with a better understanding of important events and interactions between people involved in a crime. For example, Figure 2.14 provides a simple link diagram.

Some link analysis tools can import e-mail and other digital data to help investigators identify patterns and relationships. In some circumstances, it is also appropriate to summarize potential leads and other sources of evidence that may help investigators develop their case.

**FIGURE 2.14**

Link diagram of fictional murder showing communications between prime suspects with time progressing from left to right.

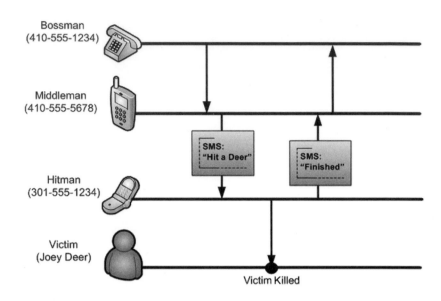

## INVESTIGATIVE SCENARIO
## Part 10: Summary of Forensic Analysis

The seized computer contained minimal and selective use, with relevant activity ranging from approximately February 13, 2009 to May 24, 2009. A timeline of important events is provided in Figure 2.15.

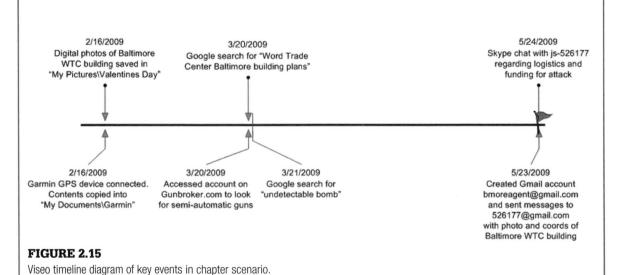

**FIGURE 2.15**

Viseo timeline diagram of key events in chapter scenario.

*(Continued)*

## INVESTIGATIVE SCENARIO—CONT'D

The user implemented privacy protection utilities like TOR, and there is further evidence of use of the "wiping" utility BCWipe. Neither BCWipe nor sanitization of Firefox 3 web browsing history was executed immediately prior to acquisition, indicating that the user of the laptop may not have had an opportunity, desire, or knowledge to destroy the data prior to its seizure by the investigative agency.

User activity on the system was extremely limited, possibly indicating a special-use system. However user Internet history revealed activity related to the review of weapons, and searches such as "liquid explosives" and "undetectable bomb". Combined with research of the Baltimore Inner Harbor and World Trade Center building, an analyst may reach the conclusion that the user was involved in some aspect of a potential domestic terrorist plot.

Numerous potential investigative leads were developed during the limited forensic analysis. Many of these findings would not have been found using simple keyword searches that unfortunately dictate many forensic analyses. Examples include reconstruction of Skype chats, critical Firefox 3 activity, and embedded data in files associated with a GPS device containing the user's Home coordinates and a Skype XML file with IP address assigned to the computer, leading to another location used by the suspect. Furthermore, forensic analysis of Internet activity combined with document metadata from the file `meta.xml` contained within the `Funds.odb` Open Office file enabled the examiner to confirm the `Funds.odb` spreadsheet document was generated online at http://spreadsheets.google.com.

At the beginning of this chapter, we mentioned that our task in the scenario was to determine the target of the attack and identify information that may lead to the identification of others involved in this terrorist cell.

Forensic analysis revealed that a user of the subject computer used privacy protection software, visited weapons related web sites, called night vision device vendors using Skype, conducted searches on terms such as "liquid explosives" and undetectable bomb", researched the Baltimore Inner Harbor World Trade Center, utilized various e-mail accounts, and engaged in a Skype communication where an image of the WTC was exchanged, a funds transfer was discussed, the target was acknowledged, and final authorization for the operation was confirmed.

Additionally, the forensic analysis identified several additional potential sources of evidence: the USB devices connected to the subject system, the user's and John Smith's Skype accounts, Hushmail account, Gmail account (which includes online created and stored documents), Garmin nuvi GPS device, Nikon Coolpix Digital Camera and storage media, the Gunbroker.com and Western Union accounts, IP addresses, and stored GPS locations.

## SUMMARY

Digital evidence can help answer many questions in an investigation ranging from the whereabouts of a victim at a given time, to the state of mind of the offender. Therefore, evidence on computers and networks should be included whenever feasible in crime reconstructions. At the same time, care must be taken when interpreting the abstracted behavioral evidence that is stored on computers. People use technology in creative ways that can complicate the forensic analysis process, particularly when attempts are made to conceal digital evidence. Computers also have many subsystems that interact in ways that can complicate the forensic analysis process. In all cases, given the malleability and multivalent nature of digital evidence, it is necessary to seek corroborating evidence from multiple independent sources. The risk of missing or misinterpreting important details highlights the importance of utilizing the scientific method to reach objective conclusions that are solidly based in the evidence.

# REFERENCES

Alles, E. J., Geradts, Z. J., & Veenman, C. J. (2009). Source camera identification for heavily JPEG compressed low resolution still images. *Journal of Forensic Sciences, 54*(3), 628–638.

Casey, E. (2002). Practical approaches to recovering encrypted digital evidence. *International Journal of Digital Evidence,* Fall 2002 *1*(3).

Casey, E. (2002). Error, uncertainty and loss in digital evidence. *International Journal of Digital Evidence, 1*(2).

Casey, E., & Stellatos, G. (2008). The impact of full disk encryption on digital forensics. *ACM SIGOPS Operating Systems Review, 42*(3).

Casey, E., Ferraro, M., & Nguyen, L. (2009). Investigation delayed is justice denied: proposals for expediting forensic examinations of digital evidence. *Journal of Forensic Science,* Fall 2009.

Cohen, M. (2007). Advance carving techniques. *Digital Investigation, 4*(3–4), 119–128.

Kurosawa, K., Kuroki, K., & Akiba, N. (2009). Individual camera identification using correlation of fixed patter noise in image sensors. *Journal of Forensic Sciences.*

McMenamin, J. (2007). Gaumer convicted of rape, murder: Prosecutors seeking death penalty for UMBC student, who met victim online. *Baltimore Sun.*

Murphey, J. (2007). Automated Windows event log forensics. *Digital Forensics Research Workshop.*

Pereira, M.T. (2008). Forensic analysis of the Firefox 3 Internet history and recovery of deleted SQLite records. *Digital Investigation.*

# CHAPTER 3

# Electronic Discovery

James O. Holley, Paul H. Luehr, Jessica Reust Smith,
and Joseph J. Schwerha IV

## INTRODUCTION TO ELECTRONIC DISCOVERY

Electronic discovery or "e-discovery" is the exchange of data between parties in civil or criminal litigation. The process is largely controlled by attorneys who determine what data should be produced based on relevance or withheld based on claims of privilege. Forensic examiners, however, play crucial roles as technical advisors, hands-on collectors, and analysts.

Some examiners view electronic discovery as a second-class endeavor, void of the investigative excitement of a trade secret case, an employment dispute, or a criminal "whodunit." These examiners, however, overlook the enormous opportunities and challenges presented by electronic discovery. In sheer economic terms, e-discovery dwarfs traditional digital forensics and will account for $10.67 billion in estimated revenues by 2010 (Socha & Gelbman, 2008a).

This financial projection reflects the high stakes in e-discovery, where the outcome can put a company out of business or a person in jail. Given the stakes, there is little room for error at any stage of the e-discovery process—from initial identification and preservation of evidence sources to the final production and presentation of results. Failing to preserve or produce relevant evidence can be deemed spoliation, leading to fines and other sanctions.

In technical terms, electronic discovery also poses a variety of daunting questions: Where are all the potentially relevant data stored? What should a company do to recover data from antiquated, legacy systems or to extract data from more modern systems like enterprise portals and cloud storage? Does old data need to be converted? If so, will the conversion process result in errors or changes to important metadata? Is deleted information relevant to the case? What types of false positives are being generated by keyword hits? Did the tools

## CONTENTS

Introduction
to Electronic
Discovery ........... 63

Legal Context .... 66

Case
Management ..... 74

Identification
of Electronic
Data .................... 78

Forensic
Preservation
of Data .............. 83

Data
Processing ....... 106

Production of
Electronic
Data ................. 130

Conclusion ....... 132

Cases ............... 132

References ....... 132

## CASE STUDY: *COLEMAN v. MORGAN STANLEY*

In *Coleman v. Morgan Stanley*, after submitting a certificate to the court stating that all relevant e-mail had been produced, Morgan Stanley found relevant e-mail on 1600 additional backup tapes. The judge decided not to admit the new e-mail messages, and based on the company's failure to comply with e-discovery requirements, the judge issued an "adverse inference" to the jury, namely that they could assume Morgan Stanley had engaged in fraud in the underlying investment case. As a result, Morgan Stanley was ordered to pay $1.5 billion in compensatory and punitive damages. An appeals court later overturned this award, but the e-discovery findings were left standing, and the company still suffered embarrassing press like the *The Wall Street Journal* article, "How Morgan Stanley botched a big case by fumbling e-mails" (Craig, 2005).

used to process relevant data cause any errors or omissions in the information produced to lawyers? What file server data can be attributed to specific custodians? How can an examiner authenticate database reports? What can an examiner do to fill in the gaps after e-mail has been erroneously deleted?

Confusion over terminology between lawyers, forensic examiners, and lay people add to the complexity of e-discovery. For instance, a forensic examiner may use the term "image" to describe a forensic duplicate of a hard drive, whereas an IT manager may call routine backups an "image" of the system, and a lawyer may refer to a graphical rendering of a document (e.g., in TIFF format) as an "image." These differing interpretations can lead to misunderstandings and major problems in the e-discovery process, adding frustration to an already pressured situation.

Fortunately, the industry is slowly maturing and establishing a common lexicon. Thanks to recent definitions within the 2006 amendments to the U.S. Federal Rules of Civil Procedure (F.R.C.P.), attorneys and examiners now typically refer to e-discovery data as ESI—short for Electronically Stored Information. This term is interpreted broadly and includes information stored on magnetic tapes, optical disks, or any other digital media, even if it is not technically stored in electronic form. In addition, George Socha and Thomas Gelbman have created a widely accepted framework for e-discovery consulting known as the Electronic Discovery Reference Model (EDRM). Shown in Figure 3.1, the EDRM breaks down the electronic discovery process into six different stages.

The first EDRM stage involves information management and the process of "getting your electronic house in order to mitigate risk & expenses should electronic discovery become an issue." (Socha & Gelbman, 2008a). The next identification stage marks the true beginning of a specific e-discovery case and describes the process of determining where ESI resides, its date range and format, and its potential relevance to a case. Preservation and collection cover the harvesting of data using forensic or nonforensic tools. The processing stage then covers the filtering of information by document type, data range, keywords, and so on, and the conversion of the resulting data into more user-friendly formats for review by attorneys. At this stage, forensic examiners may be asked to apply their analysis to documents of particular interest to counsel.

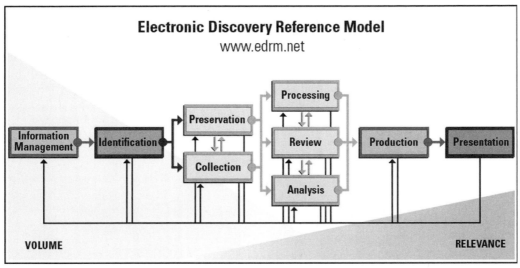

**FIGURE 3.1**

Diagram of the Electronic Discovery Reference Model showing stages from left to right (Socha & Gelbman, 2008a).

During production, data are turned over to an opposing party in the form of native documents, TIFF images, or specially tagged and encoded load files compatible with litigation support applications like Summation or Concordance. Finally, during the presentation stage, data are displayed for legal purposes in depositions or at trial. The data are often presented in their native or near-native format for evidentiary purposes, but specific content or properties may be highlighted for purposes of legal argument and persuasion.

---

The Electronic Discovery Reference Model outlines objectives of the processing stage, which include: "1) Capture and preserve the body of electronic documents; 2) Associate document collections with particular users (custodians); 3) Capture and preserve the metadata associated with the electronic files within the collections; 4) Establish the parent-child relationship between the various source data files; 5) Automate the identification and elimination of redundant, duplicate data within the given dataset; 6) Provide a means to programmatically suppress material that is not relevant to the review based on criteria such as keywords, date ranges or other available metadata; 7) Unprotect and reveal information within files; and 8) Accomplish all of these goals in a manner that is both defensible with respect to clients' legal obligations and appropriately cost-effective and expedient in the context of the matter."

---

This chapter explores the role of digital forensic examiners throughout these phases of e-discovery, particularly in large-scale cases involving disputes between organizations. It addresses the legal framework for e-discovery as well as unique forensic questions that arise around case management, identification and collection of ESI, and culling and production of data. Finally, this chapter describes common pitfalls in the complex, high-stakes field of e-discovery, with the goal of helping both new and experienced forensic examiners safely navigate this potential minefield.

## LEGAL CONTEXT

In the past few years, the complexity of ESI and electronic discovery has increased significantly. The set of governing regulations has become so intricate that even professionals confess that they do not understand all the rules. A 2008 survey of in-house counsel found that 79% of the 203 respondents in the United States and 84% of the 200 respondents in the United Kingdom were not up to date with ESI regulations (Kroll Ontrack, 2008). Although it is beyond the scope of this chapter to cover all aspects of the legal context of discovery of ESI, the points that are most relevant to digital investigators are presented in this section.

---

### PRACTITIONER'S TIP: INTERNATIONAL CONSIDERATIONS

This chapter focuses on the requirements of the United States, but digital examiners should be aware that even more stringent requirements may be present when evidence is in foreign countries. Most of Europe, for example, affords greater privacy protections to individuals in the workplace. Therefore, in countries such as France, it is often necessary to obtain the consent of an employee before conducting a search on his or her work computer. The very acts of imaging and reviewing a hard drive also may be subject to different country-specific regulations. Spanish rules, for instance, may require examiners to image a hard drive in the presence of a public notary, and analysis may be limited to information derived from specific keyword searches, not general roaming through an EnCase file. Thus, a civil examination in that country may look more like a computer search, which is subject to a criminal search warrant in the United States. For more information on conducting internal investigations in European Union countries, see Howell & Wertheimer (2008).

---

### Legal Basis for Electronic Discovery

In civil litigation throughout the United States, courts are governed by their respective rules of civil procedure. Each jurisdiction has its own set of rules, but the rules of different courts are very similar as a whole.[1] As part of any piece of civil litigation, the parties engage in a process called *discovery*. In general, discovery allows each party to request and acquire relevant, nonprivileged information in possession of the other parties to the litigation, as well as third parties (F.R.C.P. 26(b)). When that discoverable information is found in some sort of electronic or digital format (i.e., hard disk drive, compact disc, etc.), the process is called *electronic discovery* or *e-discovery* for short.

The right to discover ESI is now well established. On December 1, 2006, amended F.R.C.P. went into effect and directly addressed the discovery of ESI. Although states have not directly adopted the principles of these amendments *en masse*, many states have changed their rules to follow the 2006 F.R.C.P. amendments.

---

[1] For the purposes of this chapter, we are concentrating on the Federal Rules of Civil Procedure; however, each state has its own set of civil procedures.

## ESI Preservation: Obligations and Penalties

Recent amendments to various rules of civil procedure require attorneys—and therefore digital examiners—to work much earlier, harder, and faster to identify and preserve potential evidence in a lawsuit. Unlike paper documents that can sit undisturbed in a filing cabinet for several years before being collected for litigation, many types of ESI are more fleeting. Drafts of smoking-gun memos can be intentionally or unwittingly deleted or overwritten by individual users, server-based e-mail can disappear automatically following a system purge of data in a mailbox that has grown too large, and archived e-mail can disappear from backup tapes that are being overwritten pursuant to a scheduled monthly tape rotation.

Just how early attorneys and digital examiners need to act will vary from case to case, but generally they must take affirmative steps to preserve relevant information once litigation or the need for certain data is foreseeable. In some cases like employment actions, an organization may need to act months before a lawsuit is even filed. For example, in *Broccoli v. Echostar Communications*, the court determined that the defendant had a duty to act when the plaintiff communicated grievances to senior managers one year before the formal accusation. Failure to do so can result in severe fines and other penalties such as described next.

---

### CASE STUDY: *ZUBULAKE v. UBS WARBURG*

The seminal case of *Zubulake v. UBS Warburg* outlined many ESI preservation duties in its decision. Laura Zubulake was hired as a senior salesperson to UBS Warburg. She eventually brought a lawsuit against the company for gender discrimination, and she requested, "all documents concerning any communication by or between UBS employees concerning Plaintiff." UBS produced about 100 e-mails and claimed that its production was complete, but Ms. Zubulake's counsel learned that UBS had not searched its backup tapes. What began as a fairly mundane employment action turned into a grand e-discovery battle, generating seven different opinions from the bench and resulting in one of the largest jury awards to a single employee in history.

The court stated that "a party or anticipated party must retain all relevant documents (but not multiple identical copies) in existence at the time the duty to preserve attaches, and any relevant documents created thereafter," and outlined three groups of interested parties who should maintain ESI:

- **Primary players**: Those who are "likely to have discoverable information that the disclosing party may use to support its claims or defenses" (F.R.C.P. 26(a)(1)(A)).

- **Assistants to primary players**: Those who prepared documents for those individuals that can be readily identified.

- **Witnesses**: "The duty also extends to information that is relevant to the claims or defenses of any party, or which is 'relevant to the subject matter involved in the action'" (F.R.C.P. 26(b)(1)).

The Zubulake court realized the particular difficulties associated with retrieving data from backup tapes and noted that they generally do not need to be saved or searched, but the court noted:

> [I]t does make sense to create one exception to this general rule. If a company can identify where particular employee documents are stored on backup tapes, then the tapes storing the documents of "key players" to the existing or threatened litigation should be preserved if the information contained on those tapes is not otherwise available. This exception applies to all backup tapes.

In addition to clarifying the preservation obligations in e-discovery, the Zubulake case revealed some of the penalties that can befall those who fail to meet these obligations.

*(Continued)*

## CASE STUDY: *ZUBULAKE v. UBS WARBURG*—CONT'D

The court sanctioned UBS Warburg for failing to preserve and produce e-mail backup tapes and important messages, or for producing some evidence late. The court required the company to pay for additional depositions that explored how data had gone missing in the first place. The jury heard testimony about the missing evidence and returned a verdict for $29.3 million, including $20.2 million in punitive damages.

The Zubulake court held the attorneys partially responsible for the lost e-mail in the case and noted, "[I]t is not sufficient to notify all employees of a litigation hold and expect that the party will then retain and produce all relevant information. Counsel must take affirmative steps to monitor compliance so that all sources of discoverable information are identified and searched." (*Zubulake v. UBS Warburg*, 2004). Increasingly, attorneys have taken this charge to heart and frequently turn to their digital examiners to help assure that their discovery obligations are being met.

Rather than grappling with these challenges every time new litigation erupts, some organizations are taking a more strategic approach to prepare for e-discovery and engage in data-mapping before a case even begins. The two most fundamental aspects of being prepared for e-discovery are knowing the location of key data sources and ensuring that they meet regulatory requirements while containing the minimum data necessary to support business needs. The data-mapping process involves identifying pieces of data that are key to specific and recurring types of litigation (e.g., personnel files that are relevant to employment disputes). In turn, organizations attempt to map important pieces of data to functional categories that are assigned clear backup and retention policies. Organizations can then clean house and expunge unnecessary data, not to eliminate incriminating digital evidence, but to add greater efficiency to business operations and to reduce the amount of time and resources needed to extract and review the data for litigation.

In the best of all worlds, the data-mapping process cleanses a company of redundant data and rogue systems and trains employees to store their data in consistent forms at predictable locations. In a less perfect world, the data-mapping process still allows a company to think more carefully about its data and align an organization's long-term business interests with its recurring litigation concerns. For example, the data-mapping process may prompt an organization to create a forensic image of a departing employee's hard drive, especially when the employee is a high-ranking officer or is leaving under a cloud of suspicion.

## Determining Violations of the Electronic Discovery Paradi

As pointed out by the Zubulake decision, the consequences of failing to preserve data early in a case can be severe. Under F.R.C.P. Rule 37, a court has broad latitude to sanction a party in a variety of ways. Of course, courts are

## CASE STUDY: *QUALCOMM INC. v. BROADCOM CORP.*

In *Qualcomm Inc. v. Broadcom Corp.*, the underlying dispute centered on whether Qualcomm could claim a patent to video compression technology after it allegedly had participated in an industry standards-setting body known as the Joint Video Team (JVT). Qualcomm brought a lawsuit against Broadcom claiming patent infringement, but the jury ultimately returned a unanimous verdict in favor of Broadcom.

During all phases of the case, Qualcomm claimed that it had not participated in the JVT. Qualcomm responded to numerous interrogatories and demands for e-mails regarding its involvement in the JVT. When a Qualcomm witness eventually admitted that the company had participated in the JVT, over 200,000 e-mails and other ESI were produced linking Qualcomm to the JVT! The court determined that Qualcomm had intentionally and maliciously hidden this information from Broadcom and the court. As a result Qualcomm had to pay sanctions (including attorney fees) of over $8 million and several attorneys for Qualcomm were referred to the State Bar for possible disciplinary action.

most concerned about attorneys or litigation parties that intentionally misrepresent the evidence in their possession, as seen in the Qualcomm case.

The following 10 recommendations are provided for investigators and in-house counsel to avoid the same fate as Qualcomm (Roberts, 2008):

1. Use checklists and develop a standard discovery protocol;
2. Understand how and where your client maintains paper files and electronic information, as well as your client's business structures and practices;
3. Go to the location where information is actually maintained—do not rely entirely on the client to provide responsive materials to you;
4. Ensure you know what steps your client, colleagues, and staff have actually taken and confirm that their work has been done right;
5. Ask all witnesses about other potential witnesses and where and how evidence was maintained;
6. Use the right search terms to discover electronic information;
7. Bring your own IT staff to the client's location and have them work with the client's IT staff, employ e-discovery vendors, or both;
8. Consider entering into an agreement with opposing counsel to stipulate the locations to be searched, the individuals whose computers and hard copy records are at issue, and the search terms to be used;
9. Err on the side of production;
10. Document all steps taken to comply with your discovery protocol.

This is a useful and thorough set of guidelines for investigators to use for preservation of data issues, and can also serve as a quick factsheet in preparing for depositions or testimony.

## Initial Meeting, Disclosures, and Discovery Agreements

In an effort to make e-discovery more efficient, F.R.C.P. Rule 26(f) mandates that parties meet and discuss how they want to handle ESI early in a case.

### PRACTITIONER'S TIP: MEET AND CONFER

Lawyers often depend on digital examiners to help them prepare for and navigate a Rule 26(f) conference. The meeting usually requires both technical and strategic thinking because full discovery can run counter to cost concerns, confidentiality or privacy issues, and claims of privilege. For example, an organization that wants to avoid costly and unnecessary restoration of backup tapes should come to the table with an idea of what those tapes contain and how much it would cost to restore them. At the same time, if a party might be embarrassed by personal information within deleted files or a computer's old Internet history, counsel for that party might be wise to suggest limiting discovery to specific types of active, user documents (.DOC, .XLS, .PDF, etc.). Finally, privilege concerns can often be mitigated if the parties can agree on the list of attorneys that might show up in privileged documents, if they can schedule sufficient time to perform a privilege review, and if they allow each other to "claw back" privileged documents that are mistakenly produced to the other side.

The initial meetings between the parties generally address what ESI should be exchanged, in what format (e.g., native format versus tiffed images; electronic version versus a printout, on CD/DVD versus hard drive delivery media), what will constitute privileged information, and preservation considerations. Lawyers must make ESI disclosures to each other and certify that they are correct. This process is especially constructive when knowledgeable and friendly digital investigators can help lawyers understand their needs, capabilities, and costs associated with various ESI choices. The initial meeting may result in an agreement that helps all the parties understand their obligations. This same agreement can help guide the parties if a dispute should arise.

### CASE STUDY: *INTEGRATED SERVICE SOLUTIONS, INC. v. RODMAN*

Consider the case of *Integrated Service Solutions, Inc. v. Rodman*. Integrated Service Solutions (ISS) brought a claim against Rodman, which in turn required information from a nonparty, VWR. VWR was subpoenaed to produce ESI in connection with either ISS or Rodman. VWR expressed its willingness to provide data but voiced several objections, namely that the subpoena was too broad, compliance costs were too great, and that ISS might obtain unfettered access to its systems (all common concerns).

VWR and ISS were able to reach a compromise in which ISS identified particular keywords, PricewaterhouseCoopers (PwC) conducted a search for $10,000, and VWR reviewed the resulting materials presented by PwC. However, the relationship between VWR and ISS deteriorated, and when VWR stated that it did not possess information pertinent to the litigation, ISS responded that it was entitled to a copy of each file identified by the search as well as a report analyzing the information.

The case went before the court, which looked at the agreement between the parties and held that ISS should receive a report from PwC describing its methods, the extent of VWR's cooperation, and some general conclusions. The court also held that VWR should pay for any costs associated with generating the report.

This case underscores several key principals of e-discovery. First, even amicable relationships between parties involved in e-discovery can deteriorate and require judicial intervention. Second, digital investigators should be sensitive to the cost and disclosure concerns of their clients. Third, digital examiners may be called upon to play a neutral or objective role in the dispute, and last, the agreement or contract between the parties is crucial in establishing the rights of each party.

## Assessing What Data Is Reasonably Accessible

Electronic discovery involves more than the identification and collection of data because attorneys must also decide whether the data meets three criteria for production, namely whether the information is (1) relevant, (2) nonprivileged, and (3) reasonably accessible (F.R.C.P. 26(b)(2)(B)). The first two criteria make sense intuitively. Nonrelevant information is not allowed at trial because it simply bogs downs the proceedings, and withholding privileged information makes sense in order to protect communications within special relationships in our society, for example, between attorneys and clients, doctors and patients, and such. Whether information is "reasonably accessible" is harder to determine, yet this is an important threshold question in any case.

In the Zubulake case described earlier, the employee asked for "all documents concerning any communications by or between UBS employees concerning Plaintiff," which included "without limitation, electronic or computerized data compilations," to which UBS argued the request was overly broad. In that case Judge Shira A. Scheindlin, United States District Court, Southern District of New York, identified three categories of reasonably accessible data: (1) active, online data such as hard drive information, (2) near-line data to include robotic tape libraries, and (3) offline storage such CDs or DVDs. The judge also identified two categories of data generally *not* considered to be reasonably accessible: (1) backup tapes and (2) erased, fragmented, and damaged data. Although there remains some debate about the reasonable accessibility of backup tapes used for archival purposes versus disaster recovery, many of Judge Scheindlin's distinctions were repeated in a 2005 Congressional report from the Honorable Lee H. Rosenthal, Chair of the Advisory Committee on the Federal Rules of Civil Procedure (Rosenthal, 2005), and Zubulake's categories of information still remain important guideposts (Mazza, 2007).

The courts use two general factors—burden and cost—to determine the accessibility of different types of data. Using these general factors allows the courts to take into account challenges of new technologies and any disparity in resources among parties (Moore, 2005). If ESI is not readily accessible due to burden or cost, then the party possessing that ESI may not have to produce it (see F.R.C.P. 26(b)). Some parties, however, make the mistake of assessing the burden and cost on their own and unilaterally decide not to preserve or disclose data that is hard to reach or costly to produce. In fact, the rules require that a party provide "a description by category and locations, of all documents" with potentially relevant data, both reasonably and not reasonably accessible (F.R.C.P. 26(a)(1)(B)). This allows the opposing side a chance to make a good cause showing to the court why that information should be produced (F.R.C.P. 26(a)(2)(B)).

These rules mean that digital examiners may have to work with IT departments to change their data retention procedures and schedules, even if only temporarily, until the parties can negotiate an ESI agreement or a court can decide what must be produced. The rules also mean that digital examiners may eventually leave behind data that they would ordinarily collect in many forensic examinations, like e-mail backups, deleted files, and fragments of data in unallocated space. These types of data may be relatively easy to acquire in a small forensic examination but may be too difficult and too costly to gather for all custodians over time in a large e-discovery case.

## Utilizing Criminal Procedure to Accentuate E-Discovery

In some cases, such as lawsuits involving fraud allegations or theft of trade secrets, digital examiners may find that the normal e-discovery process has been altered by the existence of a parallel criminal investigation. In those cases, digital examiners may be required to work with the office of a local US Attorney, State Attorney General, or District Attorney, since only these types of public officials, and not private citizens, can bring criminal suits.

There are several advantages to working with a criminal agency. The first is that the agency might be able to obtain the evidence quicker than a private citizen could. For example, in *United States v. Fierros-Alaverez*, the police officer was permitted to search the contents of a cellular phone during a traffic stop. Second, the agency has greater authority to obtain information from third parties. Third, there are favorable cost considerations since a public agency will not charge you for their services. Finally, in several instances, information discovered in a criminal proceeding can be used in a subsequent civil suit.

Apart from basic surveillance and interviews, criminal agencies often use four legal tools to obtain evidence in digital investigations—a hold letter, a subpoena, a 'd' order, and a search warrant.[2]

A criminal agency can preserve data early in an investigation by issuing a letter under 18 U.S.C. 2703(f) to a person or an entity like an Internet Service Provider (ISP). Based on the statute granting this authority, the notices are often called "f letters" for short. The letter does not actually force someone to

---

[2] Beyond the scope of this chapter are pen register orders, trap and trace orders, or wire taps that criminal authorities can obtain to collect real-time information on digital connections and communications. These tools seldom come into play in a case that has overlapping e-discovery issues in civil court.

produce evidence but does require they preserve the information for 90 days (with the chance of an additional 90 day extension). This puts the party with potential evidence on notice and buys the agency some time to access that information or negotiate with the party to surrender it.

Many criminal agencies also use administrative or grand jury subpoenas to obtain digital information as detailed in Federal Rules of Criminal Procedure Rule 17. The subpoenas may be limited by privacy rights set forth in the Electronic Communication Privacy Act (18 U.S.C. § 2510). Nevertheless, criminal agencies can often receive data such as a customer's online account information and method of payment, a customer's record of assigned IP numbers and account logins or session times, and in some instances the contents of historic e-mails.

Another less popular method of obtaining evidence is through a court "d" order, under 18 U.S.C. §2703(d). This rule is not used as often because an official must be able to state with "specific and articulateable" facts that there is a reasonable belief that the targeted information is pertinent to the case. However, this method is still helpful to obtain more than just subscriber information—data such as Internet transactional information or a copy of a suspect's private homepage.

Search warrants are among the most powerful tools available to law enforcement agencies (see Federal Rules of Criminal Procedure Rule 41). Agents must receive court approval for search warrants and must show there is probable cause to believe that evidence of a specified crime can be found on a person or at a specific place and time. Search warrants are typically used to seize digital media such as computer hard drives, thumb drives, DVDs, and such, as well as the stored content of private communications from e-mail messages, voicemail messages, or chat logs.

Despite the advantages of working a case with criminal authorities, there are some potent disadvantages that need to be weighed. First, the cooperating private party loses substantial control over its case. This means that the investigation, legal decisions (i.e., venue, charges, remedies sought, etc.), and the trial itself will all be controlled by the government. Second, and on a corollary note, the private party surrenders all control over the evidence. When government agents conduct their criminal investigation, they receive the information and interpret the findings, not the private party. If private parties wish to proceed with a civil suit using the same evidence, they will typically have to wait until the criminal case has been resolved.

It is imperative for digital examiners to understand the legal concepts behind electronic discovery, as described earlier. You likely will never know more than a lawyer who is familiar with all the relevant statutes and important e-discovery court decisions; however, your understanding of the basics will help you apply your art and skills and determine where you can add the most value.

## CASE MANAGEMENT

The total volume of potentially relevant data often presents the greatest challenge to examiners in an e-discovery case. A pure forensic matter may focus on a few documents on a single 80 GB hard drive, but an e-discovery case often encompasses a terabyte or more of data across dozens of media sources. For this reason, e-discovery requires examiners to become effective case managers and places a premium on their efficiency and organizational skills. These traits are doubly important considering the tight deadlines that courts can impose in e-discovery cases and the high costs that clients can incur if delays or mistakes occur.

### PRACTITIONER'S TIP: TOOL TESTING AND QUALITY ASSURANCE

Effective case management requires that examiners establish a strategic plan at the outset of an e-discovery project, and implement effective and documented quality assurance measures throughout each step of the process. Problems can arise from both technical and human errors, and the quality assurance measures should be sufficiently comprehensive to identify both. Testing and verification of tools' strengths and weaknesses before using them in case work is critical, however it should not lull examiners into performing limited quality assurance of the results each time the tool is used (Lesemann & Reust, 2006).

Effective case management requires that examiners plan ahead. This means that examiners must quickly determine where potentially relevant data reside, both at the workstation and enterprise levels. As explained in more detail later in this chapter (see the section, "Identification of Electronic Data"), a sit-down meeting with a client's IT staff, in-house counsel, and outside counsel can help focus attention on the most important data sources and determine whether crucial information might be systematically discarded or overwritten by normal business processes. Joining the attorneys in the interviews of individual custodians can also help determine if data are on expected media like local hard drives and file servers or on far-flung media like individual thumb drives and home computers. This information gathering process is more straightforward and efficient when an organization has previously gone through a formal, proactive data-mapping process, and knows where specific data types reside in their network.

Whether examiners are dealing with a well-organized or disorganized client, they should consider drafting a protocol that describes how they intend to handle different types of data associated with their case. The protocol can address issues such as what media should be searched for specific file types (e.g., the Exchange server for current e-mail, or hard drives and home directories for archived PST, OST, MSG, and EML files), what tools can be used during collection, whether deleted data should be recovered by default, what keywords and date ranges should be used to filter the data, and what type of deduplication should be applied (e.g., eliminating duplicates within a specific custodian's data set, or eliminating duplicates across all custodians' data). Designing a protocol at the start of the e-discovery process increases an examiner's efficiency and also helps manage the expectations of the parties involved.

A protocol can also help attorneys and clients come to terms with the overall volume and potential costs of e-discovery. Often it will be the digital examiner's job to run the numbers and show how the addition of even a few more data custodians can quickly increase costs. Though attorneys may think of a new custodian as a single low-cost addition to a case, that custodian probably has numerous sources of data and redundant copies of documents across multiple platforms. The following scenario shows how this multiplicative effect can quickly inflate e-discovery costs.

---

### THE POTENTIAL COST OF ADDING ONE MORE CUSTODIAN

One Custodian's Data:

Individual hard drive = 6GB of user data
Server e-mail = 0.50GB
Server home directory data = 1GB
Removable media (thumb drives) = 0.50GB
Blackberries, PDAs = 0GB (if synchronized with e-mail)

Scanned paper documents = 1GB
Backup tapes – e-mail for 12 mo × 0.50GB = 6GB
Backup tapes – e-docs for 12 mo × 1.0GB = 12GB

Potential data for one additional custodian = 28GB
Est. processing cost (at $1,500/GB) = $42,000

---

Digital examiners may also be asked how costly and burdensome specific types of information will be to preserve, collect, and process. This assessment may be used to decide whether certain data are "reasonably accessible," and may help determine if and how preservation, collection, processing, review, and production costs should be shared between the parties. Under Zubulake, a court will consider seven factors to determine if cost-shifting is appropriate (*Zubulake v. UBS Warburg*):

1. The extent to which the request is specifically tailored to discover relevant information.
2. The availability of such information from other sources.
3. The total cost of production, compared to the amount in controversy.
4. The total cost of production, compared to the resources available to each party.
5. The relative ability of each party to control costs and its incentive to do so.
6. The importance of the issues at stake in the litigation.
7. The relative benefits to the parties of obtaining the information.

In an attempt to cut or limit e-discovery costs, a client will often volunteer to have individual employees or the company's own IT staff preserve and collect documents needed for litigation. This can be acceptable in many e-discovery cases. As described in more detail later, however, examiners should warn their clients and counsel of the need for more robust and verifiable preservation if the case hinges on embedded or file system metadata, important dates, sequencing of events, alleged deletions, contested user actions, or other forensic issues.

If an examiner is tasked with preserving and collecting the data in question, the examiner should verify that his or her proposed tools are adequate for the job. A dry run on test data is often advisable because there will always be bugs in some software programs, and these bugs will vary in complexity and importance. Thus it is important to verify, test, and document the strengths and weaknesses of a tool before using it, and apply approved patches or alternative approaches before collection begins.

Effective case management also requires that examiners document their actions, not only at the beginning, but also throughout the e-discovery process. Attorneys and the courts appreciate the attention to detail applied by most forensic examiners, and if an examiner maintains an audit trail of his or her activities, it often mitigates the impact of a problem, if one does arise.

## FROM THE CASE FILES: DOCUMENTATION TO THE RESCUE

In a recent antitrust case, numerous employees with data relevant to the suit had left the client company by the time a lawsuit was filed. E-mail for former employees was located on Exchange backups, but no home directories or hard drives were located for these individuals. Later in the litigation, when the opposing party protested the lack of data available on former employees, the client's IT department disclosed that data for old employees could be found under shared folders for different departments. The client expressed outrage that this information had not been produced, but digital examiners who had kept thorough records of their collections and deliveries were able to show that data for 32 of 34 former employees had indeed been produced, just under the headings of the shared drives not under individual custodian names. Thus, despite miscommunications about the location of data for former employees, careful record-keeping showed that there was little missing data, and former employee files had been produced properly in the form they were ordinarily maintained, under Federal Rules of Civil Procedure Rule 34.

Documenting one's actions also helps outside counsel and the client track the progress of e-discovery. In this vein, forensic examiners may be accustomed to tracking their evidence by media source (e.g., laptop hard drive, desktop hard drive, DVD), but in an e-discovery case, they will probably be asked to track data by custodian, as shown in Table 3.1. This allows attorneys to sequence and prepare for litigation events such as a document production or the deposition of key witnesses. A custodian tracking sheet also allows paralegals to determine where an evidentiary gap may exist and helps them predict how much data will arrive for review and when.

**Table 3.1** Sample Tracking Sheet Summarizing ESI Preserved for Each Custodian

| NAME | Image Date | LAPTOP | | DESKTOP | | | EXCHANGE | HOME DIR |
| | | E-mail (GB) | E-Docs (GB) | Image Date | E-mail (GB) | E-Docs (GB) | E-mail (GB) | E-Docs (GB) |
| --- | --- | --- | --- | --- | --- | --- | --- | --- |
| John Doe | 10/10/2008 | 1.5 | 1.2 | 10/10/2008 | 0 | 2.1 | 1.8 | 5.5 |
| Jane Smith | 10/10/2008 | 4.4 | 0.8 | 10/11/2008 | 1.2 | 1.7 | 4.3 | 7.7 |

Case management is most effective when it almost goes unnoticed, allowing attorneys and the client to focus their attention on the substance and merits of their case, not the harrowing logistical and technical hurdles posed by the e-discovery process in the background. As described earlier, this means that examiners should have a thorough understanding of the matter before identification and preservation has begun, as well as a documented quality assurance program for collecting, processing, and producing data once e-discovery has commenced.

## IDENTIFICATION OF ELECTRONIC DATA

Before the ESI can be collected and preserved, the sources of potentially relevant and discoverable ESI must be identified. Although the scope of the preservation duty is typically determined by counsel, the digital investigator should develop a sufficient understanding of the organization's computer network and how the specific custodians store their data to determine what data exists and in what locations. Oftentimes this requires a more diligent and iterative investigation than counsel expects, however it is a vital step in this initial phase of e-discovery.

A comprehensive and thorough investigation to identify the potentially relevant ESI is an essential component of a successful strategic plan for e-discovery projects. This investigation determines whether the data available for review is complete, and if questions and issues not apparent at the outset of the matter can be examined later down the road (Howell, 2005). A stockpile of media containing relevant data being belatedly uncovered could call into question any prior findings or conclusions reached, and possibly could lead to penalties and sanctions from the court.

There are five digital storage locations that are the typical focus of e-discovery projects (Friedberg & McGowan, 2006):

- Workstation environment, including old, current, and home desktops and laptops
- Personal Digital Assistants (PDAs), such as the BlackBerry® and Treo®
- Removable media, such as CDs, DVDs, removable USB hard drives, and USB "thumb" drives
- Server environment, including file, e-mail, instant messaging, database, application and VOIP servers
- Backup environment, including archival and disaster recovery backups

Although these storage locations are the typical focus of e-discovery projects, especially those where the data are being collected in a corporate environment, examiners should be aware of other types of storage locations that may be relevant such as digital media players and data stored by third parties (for example,

Google Docs, Xdrive, Microsoft SkyDrive, blogs, and social networking sites such as MySpace and Facebook).

Informational interviews and documentation requests are the core components of a comprehensive and thorough investigation to identify the potentially relevant ESI in these five locations, followed by review and analysis of the information obtained to identify inconsistencies and gaps in the data collected. In some instances a physical search of the company premises and off-site storage is also necessary.

## Informational Interviews

The first step in determining what data exist and in what location is to conduct informational interviews of both the company IT personnel and the custodians. It is helpful to have some understanding of the case particulars, including relevant data types, time period, and scope of preservation duty before conducting the interviews. In addition, although policy and procedure documentation can be requested in the IT personnel interviews, it may be helpful to request them beforehand so they can be reviewed and any questions incorporated into the interview. Documenting the information obtained in these interviews is critical for many reasons, not least of which is the possibility that the investigator may later be required to testify in a Rule 30(b)(6) deposition.

For assistance in structuring and documenting the interviews, readers might develop their own interview guide. Alternatively, readers might consult various published sources for assistance. For example, Kidwell et al. (2005) provide detailed guides both for developing Rule 26 document requests and for conducting Rule 30(b)(6) depositions of IT professionals. Another source for consideration is a more recent publication of the Sedona Conference (Sedona Conference, 2008).

### IT Personnel Interviews

The goal of the IT personnel interviews is to gain a familiarity and understanding with the company network infrastructure to determine how and where relevant ESI is stored.

When conducting informational interviews of company IT personnel, IT management such as the CIO or Director of IT will typically be unfamiliar with the necessary infrastructure details, but should be able to identify and assemble the staff that have responsibility for the relevant environments. Oftentimes it is the staff "on the ground" who are able to provide the most accurate information regarding both the theoretical policies and the practical reality. Another point to keep in mind is that in larger companies where custodians span the nation if not the world, there may be critical differences in the computer and network infrastructure between regions and companies, and this process is complicated further if a company has undergone recent mergers and acquisitions. Suggested questions to ask IT personnel are:

- Is there a **centralized asset inventory system**, and if so, obtain an asset inventory for the relevant custodians. If not, what information is available to determine the history of assets used by the relevant custodians?

- Regarding **workstations**, what is the operating system environment? Are both desktops and laptops issued? Is disk or file level encryption used? Are the workstations owned or leased? What is the refresh cycle and what steps are taken prior to the workstations being redeployed? Are users permitted to download software onto their workstations? Are software audits performed on the workstations to determine compliance?

- Regarding **PDAs and cell phones**, how are the devices configured and synchronized? Is it possible that data, such as messages sent from a PDA, exist only on the PDA and not on the e-mail server? Is the BlackBerry® server located and managed in-house?

- What are the policies regarding provision and use of **removable media**?

- Regarding general **network** questions, are users able to access their workstations/e-mail/file shares remotely and if so what logs are enabled? What are the Internet browsing and computer usage policies? What network shares are typically mapped to workstations? Are any enterprise storage and retention applications implemented such as Symantec Enterprise Vault®? Is an updated general network topology or data map available? Are outdated topologies or maps available for the duration of the relevant time period?

- Regarding **e-mail servers**, what are their numbers, types, versions, length of time deployed and locations? What mailbox size or date restrictions are in place? Is there an automatic deletion policy in place? What logging is enabled? Are employees able to replicate or archive e-mail locally to their workstations or to mapped network shares?

- Regarding **file servers**, what are the numbers, types, versions, locations, length of time deployed, data type stored, and departments served. Do users have home directories? Are they restricted by size? What servers provide for collaborative access, such as group shares or SharePoint®? To which shares and/or projects do the custodians have access?

- Regarding the **backup environment**, what are the backup systems used for the different server environments? What are the backup schedules and retention policies? What is the date of the oldest backup? Have there been any "irregular" backups created for migration purposes or "test" servers deployed? What steps are in place to verify the success of the backup jobs?

- Please provide information on any other **data repositories** such as database servers, application servers, digital voicemail storage, legacy systems, document management systems, and SANs.

- Have there been any **other prior or on-going investigations or litigation** where data was preserved or original media collected by internal staff or outside vendors? If so, where does this data reside now?

Obtaining explicit answers to these questions can be challenging and complicated due to staff turnover, changes in company structure, and lack of documentation. On the flip side when answers are provided (especially if just provided orally), care must be taken to corroborate the accuracy of the answers with technical data or other reliable information.

## Custodian Interviews

The goal of the custodian interviews is to determine how and where the custodians store their data. Interviews of executive assistants may be necessary if they have access to the executive's electronic data. Suggested questions to ask are:

- How many **laptops and desktops** do they currently use? For how long have they used them? Do they remember what happened to the computers they used before, if any? Do they use a home computer for company-related activities? Have they ever purchased a computer from the company?

- To what **network shares** do they have access? What network shares are typically mapped to a drive letter on their workstation(s)?

- Do they have any **removable media** containing company-related data?

- Do they have a **PDA and/or cell phone** provided by the company?

- Do they use **encryption**?

- Do they use any **instant messaging** programs? Have they installed any unapproved software programs on their workstation(s)?

- Do they **archive their mail** locally or maintain a copy on a company server or removable media?

- Do they **access their e-mail and/or files remotely**? Do they maintain an online storage account containing company data? Do they use a personal e-mail address for company related activities, including transfer of company files?

The information and documentation obtained through requests and the informational interviews can assist in creating a graphical representation of the company network for the relevant time period. Although likely to be modified as new information is learned, it will serve as an important reference throughout the e-discovery project. As mentioned earlier, some larger corporations may have proactively generated a data map that will serve as the starting point for the identification of ESI.

## Analysis and Next Steps

Review and analysis of the information obtained is essential in identifying inconsistencies and gaps in the data identification and collection. In addition, comparison of answers in informational interviews with each other and against the documentation provided can identify consistent, corroborative information between sources, which is just as important to document as inconsistencies. This review and analysis is not typically short and sweet, and is often an iterative process that must be undertaken as many times as new information is obtained, including after initial review of the data collected and from forensic analysis of the preserved data.

### FROM THE CASE FILES: FINDING THE MISSING LAPTOP

E-discovery consultants had been brought in by outside counsel to a national publicly-held company facing a regulatory investigation into its financial dealings, and were initially tasked with identifying the data sources for custodians in executive management. Counsel had determined that any company-issued computer used by the custodians in the relevant date range needed to be collected, thereby necessitating investigation into old and home computers. Without an updated, centralized asset tracking system, company IT staff had cobbled together an asset inventory from their own memory and from lists created by previous employees and interns. The inventory showed that two Macintosh laptops had been issued to the Chief Operations Officer (COO), however only one had been provided for preservation by the COO, and he maintained that he had not been issued any other Macintosh laptop. The e-discovery consultants searched through the COO's and his assistant's e-mail that had already been collected, identifying e-mail between the COO and the IT department regarding two different Macintosh laptops, and then found corresponding tickets in the company helpdesk system showing requests for technical assistance from the COO. When confronted with this evidence, the COO "found" the laptop in a box in his attic and provided it to the digital investigator. Subsequent analysis of the laptop showed extensive deletion activity the day before the COO had handed over the laptop.

There are many challenges involved in identifying and collecting ESI, including the sheer number and variety of digital storage devices that exist in many companies, lack of documentation and knowledge of assets and IT infrastructure, and deliberate obfuscation by company employees. Only through a comprehensive, diligent investigation and analysis you are likely to identify all relevant ESI in preparation for collection and preservation.

### FROM THE CASE FILES: HAND-ME-DOWN SYSTEMS

In a standard informational interview, investigators were told by the IT department in the Eastern European division of an international company that IT followed a strict process of wiping the "old" computer whenever a new computer was provided to an employee. The investigators attempted to independently verify this claim through careful comparison of serial numbers and identification of "old" computers that had been transferred to new users. This review and analysis showed intact user accounts for Custodian A on the computers being used by Custodian B. The investigators ultimately uncovered rampant "trading" and "sharing" of assets, together with "gifting" of assets by high level executives to subordinate employees, thereby prompting a much larger investigation and preservation effort.

# FORENSIC PRESERVATION OF DATA

Having conducted various informational interviews and having received and reviewed documents, lists and inventories from various sources to create an initial company data map, the next step for counsel is to select which of the available sources of ESI should be preserved and collected. The specific facts of the matter will guide counsel's decision regarding preservation. Federal Rules of Evidence Rule 26(b)(1) allows that parties "may obtain discovery regarding any non-privileged matter that is relevant to any party's claim or defense – including the existence, description, nature, custody, condition, and location of any documents or other tangible things and the identity and location of persons who know of any discoverable matter."

Once counsel selects which sources of ESI are likely to contain relevant data and should be preserved in the matter, the next two phases of the electronic discovery process as depicted in Figure 3.1 include preservation and collection. **Preservation** includes steps taken to "ensure that ESI is protected against inappropriate alteration or destruction" and **collection** is the process of "gathering ESI for future use in the electronic discovery process."

> Preservation for electronic discovery has become a complicated, multi-faceted, steadily-changing concept in recent years. Starting with the nebulous determination of when the duty to preserve arises, then continuing into the litigation hold process (often equated to the herding of cats) and the staggering volumes of material which may need to be preserved in multiple global locations, platforms and formats, the task of preservation is an enormous challenge for the modern litigator. Seeking a foundation in reasonableness, wrestling with the scope of preservation is often an exercise in finding an acceptable balance between offsetting the risks of spoliation and sanctions related to destruction of evidence, against allowing the business client to continue to operate its business in a somewhat normal fashion. (Socha & Gelbman, 2008b)

Although the EDRM defines "preservation" and "collection" as different stages in electronic discovery for civil litigation, it has been our experience that preservation and collection must be done at the same time when conducting investigations, whether the underlying investigation is related to a financial statement restatement, allegations of stock option backdating, alleged violations of the Foreign Corrupt Practices Act, or other fraud, bribery, or corruption investigation. Given the volatile nature of electronic evidence and the ability of a bad actor to quickly destroy that evidence, a digital investigator's perspective must be different.

Electronic evidence that is not yet in the hands of someone who recognizes its volatility (i.e., the evidence has not been collected) and who is also absolutely committed to its protection has not really been preserved, regardless of the content of any preservation notice corporate counsel may have sent to custodians.

## PRACTITIONER'S TIP: DESTRUCTION OF EVIDENCE

Besides the case cited, we have conducted numerous investigations where custodians, prior to turning over data sources under their control, have actively taken steps to destroy relevant evidence in contravention of counsels' notice to them to "preserve" data. These steps have included actions like:

- Using a data destruction tool on their desktop hard drive to destroy selected files
- Completely wiping their entire hard drive
- Reinstalling the operating system onto their laptop hard drive
- Removing the original hard drive from their laptop and replacing it with a new, blank drive
- Copying relevant files from their laptop to a network drive or USB drive and deleting the relevant files from their laptop
- Printing relevant files, deleting them from the computer, and attempting to wipe the hard drive using a data destruction tool

- Setting the system clock on their computer to an earlier date and attempting to fabricate electronic evidence dated and timed to corroborate a story
- Sending themselves e-mail to attempt to fabricate electronic evidence
- Physically destroying their laptop hard drive with a hammer and reporting that the drive "crashed"
- Taking boxes of relevant paper files from their office to the restroom and flushing documents down the toilet
- Hiding relevant backup tapes in their vehicle
- Surreptitiously removing labels from relevant backup tapes, inserting them into a tape robot, and scheduling an immediate out-of-cycle backup to overwrite the relevant tapes
- Purchasing their corporate owned computer from the company the day before a scheduled forensic collection and declaring it "personal" property not subject to production

## FROM THE CASE FILES: PRESERVED BACKUP TAPES PUT BACK INTO ROTATION

We were retained by outside counsel as part of the investigation team examining the facts and circumstances surrounding a financial statement restatement by an overseas bank with US offices. The principal accounting issue focused on the financial statement treatment of certain loans the bank made and then sold. It was alleged that certain bank executives routinely made undisclosed side agreements with the purchasers to buy back loans that eventually defaulted after the sale. Commitments to buy back defaulted loans would have an affect on the accounting treatment of the transactions. Faced with pending regulatory inquiries, in-house counsel sent litigation hold notices to custodians and directed

IT staff to preserve relevant backup tapes. The preservation process performed by IT staff simply included temporarily halting tape rotations. But no one actually took the relevant tapes from IT to lock them away. In the course of time, IT ran low on tape inventory for daily, weekly and monthly backups. Eventually, IT put the relevant tapes back into rotation. By the time IT disclosed to in-house counsel that they were rotating backup tapes again, more than 600 tapes potentially holding relevant data from the time period under review had been overwritten. The data, which had been temporarily preserved at the direction of counsel was never collected and was eventually lost.

Forensic examiners might use a wide variety of tools, technologies, and methodologies to preserve and collect the data selected by counsel, depending on the underlying data source.[3] Regardless of the specific tool, technology, or methodology, the forensic preservation process must meet certain standards, including technical standards for accuracy and completeness, and legal standards for authenticity and admissibility.

Historically, forensic examiners have relied heavily on creating forensic images of static media to preserve and collect electronic evidence.[4] But more and more often, relevant ESI resides on data sources that can not be shut down for traditional forensic preservation and collection, including running, revenue generating servers or multi-Terabyte Storage Area Networks attached to corporate servers.

Recognizing the evolving nature of digital evidence, the Association of Chief Police Officers has published its fourth edition of *The Good Practice Guide for Computer-Based Electronic Evidence* (ACPO, 2008). This guide was updated to take into account that the "traditional 'pull-the-plug' approach overlooks the vast amounts of volatile (memory-resident and ephemeral) data that will be lost. Today, digital investigators are routinely faced with the reality of sophisticated data encryption, as well as hacking tools and malicious software that may exist solely within memory. Capturing and working with volatile data may therefore provide the only route towards finding important evidence." Additionally, with the advent of full-disk encryption technologies, the traditional approach to forensic preservation is becoming less and less relevant. However, the strict requirement to preserve and collect data using a sound approach that is well documented, has been tested, and does not change the content of or metadata about electronic evidence if at all possible, has not changed.

## Preserving and Collecting E-mail from Live Servers

Laptop, desktop, and server computers once played a supporting role in the corporate environment: shutting them down for traditional forensic imaging tended to have only a minor impact on the company. However, in today's

---

[3] Research performed by James Holley identified 59 hardware and software tools commercially or publicly available for preserving forensic images of electronic media (Holley, 2008).

[4] "Static Media" refers to media that are not subject to routine changes in content. Historically, forensic duplication procedures included shutting down the computer, removing the internal hard drive, attaching the drive to a forensic write blocker, and preserving a forensic image of the media. This process necessarily ignores potentially important and relevant volatile data contained on the memory of a running computer. Once the computer is powered down, the volatile memory data are lost.

business environment, shutting down servers can have tremendously negative impacts on the company. In many instances, the company's servers are not just supporting the business—they are the business. The availability of software tools and methodologies capable of preserving data from live, running servers means that it is no longer absolutely necessary to shut down a production e-mail or file server to preserve data from it. Available tools and methodologies allow investigators to strike a balance between the requirements for a forensically sound preservation process and the business imperative of minimizing impact on normal operations during the preservation process (e.g., lost productivity as employees sit waiting for key servers to come back online or lost revenue as the company's customers wait for servers to come back online).

Perhaps the most requested and most produced source of ESI is e-mail communication. Counsel is most interested to begin reviewing e-mail as soon as practicable after forensic preservation. Because the content of e-mail communications might tend to show that a custodian knew or should have known certain facts; or took, should have taken, or failed to take certain action; proper forensic preservation of e-mail data sources is a central part of the electronic discovery process. In our experience over the last 10 years conducting investigations, the two most common e-mail infrastructures we've encountered are Microsoft Exchange Server (combined with the Microsoft Outlook e-mail client) and Lotus Domino server (combined with the Lotus Notes e-mail client). There are, of course, other e-mail servers/e-mail clients in use in the business environment today. But those tend to be less common. In the course of our investigations, we've seen a wide variety of e-mail infrastructures, including e-mail servers (Novell GroupWise, UNIX Sendmail, Eudora Internet Mail Server and Postfix) and e-mail clients (GroupWise, Outlook Express, Mozilla, and Eudora). In a few cases, the company completely outsourced their e-mail infrastructure by using web-based e-mail (such as Gmail or Hotmail) or AOL mail for their e-mail communications.

## Preserving and Collecting E-mail from Live Microsoft Exchange Servers

To preserve custodian e-mail from a live Microsoft Exchange Server, forensic examiners typically take one of several different approaches, depending on the specific facts of the matter. Those approaches might include:

- Exporting a copy of the custodian's mailbox from the server using a Microsoft Outlook e-mail client
- In older versions of Exchange, exporting a copy of the custodian's mailbox from the server using Microsoft's Mailbox Merge utility (Exmerge)

- In Exchange 2007, exporting a copy of the custodian's mailbox using the Exchange Management Shell
- Exporting a copy of the custodian's mailbox from the server using a specialized third-party tool (e.g., GFI PST-Exchange Email Export wizard)
- Obtaining a backup copy of the entire Exchange Server "Information Store" from a properly created full backup of the server
- Temporarily shutting down Exchange Server services and making a copy of the Exchange database files that comprise the Information Store
- Using a software utility such as F-Response™ or EnCase Enterprise to access a live Exchange Server over the network and copying either individual mailboxes or an entire Exchange database file

Each approach has its advantages and disadvantages. When exporting a custodian's mailbox using Microsoft Outlook, the person doing the exporting typically logs into the server as the custodian. This can, under some circumstances, be problematic. One advantage of this approach, though, is that the newer versions of the Outlook client can create very large (>1.7GB) Outlook e-mail archives. For custodians who have a large volume of mail in their accounts, this might be a viable approach if logging in as the custodian to collect the mail does not present an unacceptable risk. One potential downside to this approach is that the Outlook client might not collect deleted e-mail messages retained in the Microsoft Exchange special retention area called "the dumpster," which is a special location in the Exchange database file where deleted messages are retained by the server for a configurable period of time. Additionally, Outlook will not collect any part of any "double-deleted" message. Double-deleted is a term sometimes used to refer to messages that have been soft-deleted from an Outlook folder (e.g., the Inbox) into the local Deleted Items folder and then deleted from the Deleted Items folder. These messages reside essentially in the unallocated space of the Exchange database file, and are different from hard-deleted, which bypass the Deleted Items folder altogether during deletion. Using Outlook to export a custodian's mailbox would not copy out any recoverable double-deleted messages or fragments of partially overwritten messages.

One advantage of using the Exmerge utility to collect custodian e-mail from a live Exchange server is that Exmerge can be configured to collect deleted messages retained in the dumpster and create detailed logs of the collection process. However, there are at least two main disadvantages to using Exmerge. First, even the latest version of Exmerge cannot create Outlook e-mail containers larger than 1.7GB. For custodians who have a large volume of e-mail in their account,

Microsoft Exchange stores mailboxes in a database comprised of two files: priv1.edb and priv1.stm. The priv1.edb file contains all e-mail messages, headers, and text attachments. The priv1.stm file contains multimedia data that are MIME encoded. Similarly, public folders are stored in files pub1.edb and pub1.stm. An organization may maintain multiple Exchange Storage Groups, each with their own set of databases. Collectively, all databases associated with a given Exchange implementation are referred to as an Information Store, and for every .EDB file there will be an associated .STM file (Buike, 2005).

the e-mail must be segregated into multiple Outlook containers, each less than about 1.7GB. Exmerge provides a facility for this, but configuring and executing Exmerge multiple times for the task and in a manner that does not miss messages can be problematic. Second, Exmerge will not collect any part of a double-deleted message that is not still in the dumpster. So there could be recoverable deleted messages or fragments of partially overwritten messages that Exmerge will not copy out.

## TOOL FEATURE: USING EXMERGE TO PRESERVE E-MAIL

Exmerge can be run with the Exmerge GUI or in batch mode from the command line. The screenshots in Figures 3.2 through 3.4 show the steps to follow to extract a mailbox, including the items in the Dumpster, using the Exmerge GUI.

To enable the maximum logging level for Exmerge, it is necessary to edit the Exmerge.ini configuration file, setting LoggingLevel to the value 3.

**FIGURE 3.2**

Configuring Exmerge to extract a custodian's mailbox from a live Exchange Server 2003 into a PST.

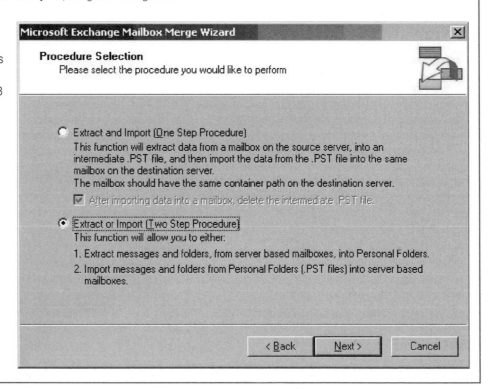

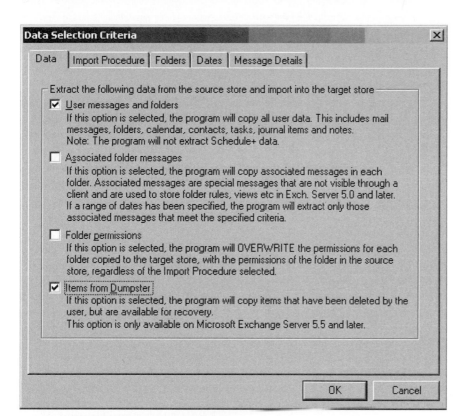

**FIGURE 3.3**
Configuring Exmerge to extract "Items from Dumpster."

**FIGURE 3.4**
If a custodian has multiple GB of e-mail on the server, this Exmerge screen allows the investigator to use date criteria to export the e-mail into date constrained PSTs, keeping the size of any one PST under 1.7GB.

With the release of Exchange Server 2007, Microsoft did not update the Exmerge utility. Instead, the latest version of Exchange Server includes new command-line functionality integrated into the Exchange Management Shell essentially to replace Exmerge.

> The Exchange Management Shell provides a command-line interface and associated command-line plug-ins for Exchange Server that enable automation of administrative tasks. With the Exchange Management Shell, administrators can manage every aspect of Microsoft Exchange 2007, including mailbox moves and exports. The Exchange Management Shell can perform every task that can be performed by Exchange Management Console in addition to tasks that cannot be performed in Exchange Management Console. (Microsoft, 2007a)

The Exchange Management Shell PowerShell (PS) Export-Mailbox command-let (cmdlet) can be used either to export out specific mailboxes or to cycle through the message store, allowing the investigator to select the mailboxes to be extracted. By default, the Export-Mailbox cmdlet copies out all folders, including empty folders and subfolders, and all message types, including messages from the Dumpster. For a comprehensive discussion of the Export-Mailbox cmdlet and the permissions required to run the cmdlet see Microsoft (2007b).

The following is the command to export a specific mailbox, "jsmith@company.com," to a PST file named `jsmith.pst`:

```
Export-Mailbox -Identity jsmith@company.com
    -PSTFolderpath c:\jsmith.pst
```

The following is the command to cycle through message store "MailStore01" on server named "EXMAIL01," allowing the investigator to select the mailboxes to be extracted:

```
Get-Mailbox -Database EXMAIL01\MailStore01 | Export-
    Mailbox -PSTFolderpath c:\pst"
```

---

### TOOL FEATURE: USING MICROSOFT EXCHANGE EXPORT-MAILBOX COMMAND-LET

The screenshots in Figures 3.5 through 3.7 show the steps to follow to cycle through message store "EMT" on the Exchange server named "MAIL2," allowing the investigator to select the mailboxes to be extracted.

(**Note**: The following screen captures were taken during a live investigation, however the names have been changed to protect custodian identities.)

```
Machine: 1094-old | Scope: mytestserver.com            _ □ ×
[PS] C:\>Get-Mailbox -Database mail2\EMT | Export-Mailbox -PSTFolderpath c:\pst
```

**FIGURE 3.5**

Using the Exchange Management Shell PowerShell (PS) Export-Mailbox command-let (cmdlet) to export a custodian's mailbox from an Exchange Server 2007 system.

```
Machine: 1094-old | Scope: mytestserver.com            _ □ ×
[PS] C:\>Get-Mailbox -Database mail2\EMT | Export-Mailbox -PSTFolderpath c:\pst

Confirm
Are you sure you want to perform this action?
Exporting mailbox content from the mailbox 'Jessica Smith' into .pst file
'c:\pst\jessica.smith.pst'. This operation may take a long time to complete.
[Y] Yes  [A] Yes to All  [N] No  [L] No to All  [S] Suspend  [?] Help
(default is "Y"):n

Confirm
Are you sure you want to perform this action?
Exporting mailbox content from the mailbox 'James Holley' into .pst file
'c:\pst\james.holley'. This operation may take a long time to complete.
[Y] Yes  [A] Yes to All  [N] No  [L] No to All  [S] Suspend  [?] Help
(default is "Y"):y

Confirm
Are you sure you want to perform this action?
Exporting mailbox content from the mailbox 'Eoghan Casey' into .pst file
'c:\pst\eoghan.casey.pst'. This operation may take a long time to complete.
[Y] Yes  [A] Yes to All  [N] No  [L] No to All  [S] Suspend  [?] Help
(default is "Y"):n
```

**FIGURE 3.6**

The cmdlet will cycle through each mailbox in the message store and allow the investigator to select which mailboxes will be extracted. In this example, James's mailbox is extracted but Jessica's and Eoghan's are not.

```
Machine: 1094-old | Scope: mytestserver.com            _ □ ×
[PS] C:\>Get-Mailbox -Database mail2\EMT | Export-Mailbox -PSTFolderpath c:\pst

 james.holley
    Moving messages. Deleted Items (360/600)
    [oooooooooooooooooo                                    ]
```

**FIGURE 3.7**

Confirmation that the extraction process is running and is extracting messages from the "Deleted Items" folder.

The most complete collection from a Microsoft Exchange Server is to collect a copy of the Information Store (i.e., the priv1.edb file and its associated .STM file for the private mailbox store as well as the pub1.edb and associated .STM file for the Public Folder store). The primary advantage of collecting the entire information store is that the process preserves and collects all e-mail in the store for all users with accounts on the server. If during the course of review it becomes apparent that new custodians should be added to the initial custodian list, then the e-mail for those new custodians has already been preserved and collected.

Traditionally, the collection of these files from the live server would necessitate shutting down e-mail server services for a period of time because files that are open for access by an application (i.e., the running Exchange Server services) cannot typically be copied from the server. E-mail server services must be shut down so the files themselves are closed by the exiting Exchange application and they are no longer open for access. This temporary shutdown can have a negative impact on the company and the productivity of its employees. However, the impact of shutting down e-mail server services is rarely as significant as shutting down a revenue-producing server for traditional forensic imaging. In some cases, perhaps a process like this can be scheduled to be done off hours or over a weekend to further minimize impact on the company.

More recently, software utilities such as F-Response™ can be used to access the live Exchange Server over the network and to preserve copies of the files comprising the Information Store. F-Response (to enable access to the live server) coupled with EnCase® Forensic or AccessData's FTK Imager® could be used to preserve the `.EDB` and `.STM` files that comprise the Information Store. Alternatively, F-Response coupled with Paraben's Network E-mail Examiner™ could be used to preserve individual mailboxes from the live server.

## TOOL FEATURE: F-RESPONSE—PRESERVATION OF AN EDB FROM A LIVE MICROSOFT EXCHANGE SERVER

F-Response (www.f-response.com/) is a software utility based on the iSCSI standard that allows read-only access to a computer or computers over an IP network. The examiner can then use his or her tool of choice to analyze or collect data from the computer. Different types of licenses are available, and the example shown in Figures 3.8 through 3.12 (provided by Thomas Harris-Warrick) is shown using the Consultant Edition, which allows for multiple computers to be accessed from one examiner machine.

The examiner's computer must have the iSCSI initiator, F-Response and the necessary forensic collection or analysis tools installed, and the F-Response USB dongle inserted in the machine. The "target" computer must be running the "F-Response Target code," which is an executable than can be run from a thumb drive.

### 1. Start F-Response NetUniKey Server

The first step is to initiate the connection from the examiner's computer to the target computer, by starting the F-Response NetUniKey server. The IP address and port listed are the IP and port listening for validation requests from the target computer(s).

### 2. Start F-Response Target Code on Target Computer

Upon execution of the F-Response Target code, a window will appear requesting the IP address and port of the examiner's machine that is listening for a validation request. After entering in this information, the window in Figure 3.9 will appear. The host IP address, TCP address, username and password must be identified.

### 3. Consultant Connector

The next step involves opening and configuring the iSCSI Initiator, which used to be completed manually. F-Response has released a beta version of Consultant Connector, however, which completes this process for you, resulting in read-only access to the hard drive of the target computer.

### 4. Preservation of EDB File

The Microsoft Exchange Server was live when accessed with F-Response, and it was not necessary to shut down the server during the collection of the EDB file using FTK Imager (see additional detail, further, on FTK Imager).

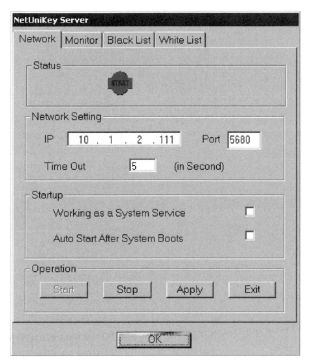

**FIGURE 3.8**

F-Response NetUniKey server.

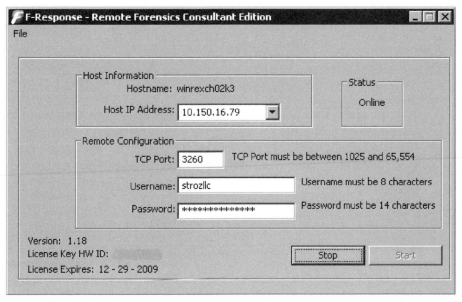

**FIGURE 3.9**

F-Response window on target computer.

**FIGURE 3.10**

F-Response Consultant Connector showing read-only access to hard drive of target computer.

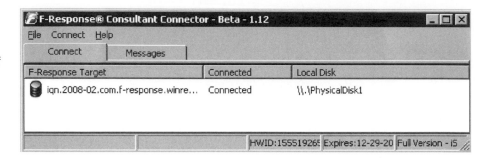

**FIGURE 3.11**

Live Microsoft Exchange Server on target computer.

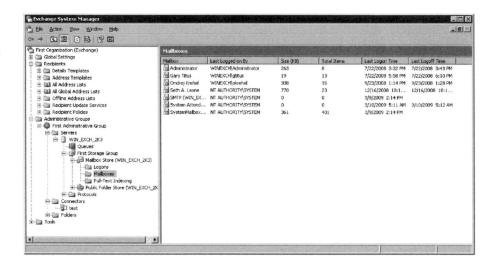

**FIGURE 3.12**

Successful collection of EDB file from live Microsoft Exchange Server using F-Response and FTK Imager.

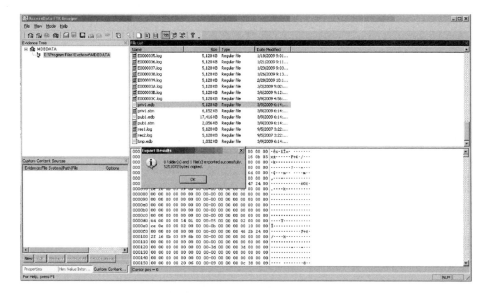

Another approach to collecting the `.EDB` and `.STM` files might be to collect a very recent full backup of the Exchange Server Information Store if the company uses a backup utility that includes an Exchange Agent. The Exchange Agent software will enable the backup software to make a full backup of the Information Store, including the `priv1.edb` file, the `pub1.edb` file, and their associated `.STM` files.

Once the Information Store itself or the collective `.EDB` and `.STM` files that comprise the Information Store are preserved and collected, there are a number of third-party utilities on the market today that can extract a custodian's mailbox from them. Additionally, if the circumstances warrant, an in-depth forensic analysis of the `.EDB` and `.STM` files can be conducted to attempt to identify fragments of partially overwritten e-mail that might remain in the unallocated space of the `.EDB` or `.STM` files.

## FROM THE CASE FILES: EVIDENCE IN UNALLOCATED SPACE OF MICROSOFT EXCHANGE DATABASE

This was the case in an arbitration. The central issue in the dispute was whether the seller had communicated certain important information to the buyer prior to the close of the transaction. The seller had received this information from a third party prior to close. The buyer claimed to have found out about the information after the close and also found out the seller possessed the information prior to close. The buyer claimed the seller intentionally withheld the information. An executive at the seller company had the information in an attachment to an e-mail in their inbox. Metadata in the Microsoft Outlook e-mail client indicated the e-mail had been forwarded. However, the Sent Items copy of the e-mail was no longer available. The employee claimed the addressee was an executive at the buyer company. The buyer claimed the recipients must have been internal to the seller company and that the buyer did not receive the forwarded e-mail.

The seller company hired us to conduct an exhaustive search for a copy of the forwarded e-mail throughout their own internal e-mail archives, including forensic images of all key executives' laptop and desktop computers as well as a forensic examination of the current e-mail server and e-mail server backup tapes. The purpose of the examination was to attempt to determine the addressees of the forwarded e-mail. The buyer company refused to examine their own archives and refused to allow a forensic examination of their computers. Both Exmerge and Paraben's Network E-mail Examiner found the e-mail in the Inbox of the seller employee—neither tool found a copy of the forwarded message. However, a forensic examination of the .EDB file uncovered fragments of the relevant e-mail in the unallocated space of the seller's .EDB file. These fragments allowed the seller company to substantiate their claim of forwarding the message to the buyer. Although this kind of in-depth forensic recovery of fragments of a deleted e-mail is not always necessary, if the central issue might be decided by a single e-mail, the effort might be worthwhile.

In addition, some companies have been deploying enterprise level e-mail storage and management applications that they anticipate using not only to store and manage the company's e-mail data, but also to respond to discovery requests. In some cases, the application houses much of the archived e-mail data for the custodians, and could also be configured to maintain a copy of every e-mail that enters or leaves the Exchange environment, regardless of whether a user later deleted the e-mail from their account on the Exchange server. A forensic examiner may need to preserve data from these applications and should determine the tool's functionality and configuration from the company IT department to assist in this process. The importance of verifying the application's ability to provide accurate and complete information is discussed in Howell (2009).

## Preserving and Collecting E-mail from Lotus Domino Server

Unlike Exchange Server, where e-mail is contained in a unified database storage file (i.e., the `priv1.edb` file) and must be extracted from the `.EDB` file into `.PST` files for processing into a review environment, on Lotus Domino server each custodian will have their own separate e-mail file (IBM, 2007). Each custodian will have a Lotus Notes data file on the server that holds the custodian's e-mail, as well as other Lotus Notes items (e.g., Calendar items, To-Do lists, etc.). A complete collection from the live Lotus Domino server can be as simple as making a copy of each `.NSF` file assigned to a custodian. However, consider collecting `.NSF` files for all e-mail users at the time. If during the course of reviewing a custodian's e-mail it becomes apparent that new custodians should be added to the initial custodian list, you'll be better able to respond to the needs of the matter if e-mail for those new custodians has already been preserved and collected.

## PRACTITIONER'S TIP: LOTUS DOMINO CONSIDERATIONS

At least three considerations come to mind when working with Lotus Domino.

1. A custodian's `.NSF` file might not have a name that clearly links it to the custodian. For instance, the `.NSF` file for custodian Joe Smith could be called 123456.nsf. To confirm that you preserve the correct mail files, consider asking for a custodian/e-mail file cross reference.

2. Unlike Exchange, where the `.EDB` and `.STM` files are always open for access by Exchange Server services, each `.NSF` file should be open for access only during a replication event. Copying the `.NSF` files off the server should generally not be hampered by open file access and shutting down e-mail server services should not be necessary. One exception to this is the case where a custodian does not have a replica of his or her e-mail on the local computer: the custodian could access his or her e-mail directly from the server copy. In that case,

the `.NSF` file on the server might be open for access by the custodian's copy of Lotus Notes on his or her laptop/desktop as long as the Lotus Notes application is active. The custodian might need to close Lotus Notes on the laptop or desktop to release the `.NSF` file on the server.

3. Lotus Notes `.NSF` files can be protected with local encryption such that the user's ID file and password are required to open the `.NSF` file and access the e-mail data. After the `.NSF` has been opened in Lotus Notes using the ID file and password, the protection can be removed by creating a copy of the database file without encryption. Individual messages may also be protected even if the entire database file is not, and in most instances the ID file and password used at the time the message was protected must be used to decrypt the message. Messages that are individually protected have a value of "1" in the Lotus Notes field "Encrypted," which can be used to identify the messages if necessary.

Most of the electronic discovery review tools on the market today can take as input a native Lotus Notes .NSF file for processing into their review environment, so the .NSF files typically do not require further processing.

The tools commonly used to complete this collection could be as simple and cost-effective as xxcopy™ (see the next section for more details) or as complex as an EnCase Enterprise e-discovery suite.

## Preserving and Collecting Home Drives and Departmental Shares[5]

Several tools are available to the forensic examiner for preserving and collecting data from live file servers. Two of the more robust tools are FTK Imager by AccessData, which is free, and xxcopy, which is free for noncommercial use, and licensed for commercial use.

FTK Imager, which has a "lite" version that can be run on a server from CD or USB without installing the software on the server, has several advantages over xxcopy. First, FTK Imager can preserve certain metadata about files and folders and it containerizes the data into evidence containers. This protects the data and the metadata from accidental modification. Additionally, since FTK Imager is a forensic tool, it provides an opportunity to identify and attempt to recover deleted files from the live server.

---

### TOOL FEATURE: PRESERVING LOGICAL FILES USING FTK IMAGER

Using FTK Imager to preserve logical data, such as a custodian's home directory, from a live server is a simple process. The screenshot in Figure 3.13 shows the opening screen of FTK Imager and adding the live server as a logical drive.

Once the drive has been added as an evidence item, the files, including deleted files, are available for review and export as a logical image (AD1) (Figure 3.14).

After identifying the destination directory and filename of the local image file to be exported, the user can choose to generate a directory listing of all the files in the image, which is recommended for documentation and quality assurance purposes (Figure 3.15).

After the preservation is completed, a results window will open informing the user if the process was successful or not (Figure 3.16). This information, including a hash value for the logical image itself, is included in a log file that is automatically generated and saved in the destination directory. The generation of a hash value is another advantage of FTK Imager over xxcopy.

The AD1 logical image file should always be opened in FTK Imager after completion to verify that the data was preserved accurately and completely.

---

[5] By "home drive" we mean that personal network space assigned to a custodian for individual or personal use. Other than a system administrator with privileged access to the file server housing the home drives, only the custodian should be able to read files from and write files to their home drive. Contrast this with a departmental share where all employees assigned to a department (e.g., Finance, HR, Accounting, IT, etc.) map the departmental share to their local computer and have permission to read from and write to the shared space.

**FIGURE 3.13**

Adding a logical drive as an evidence item in FTK Imager.

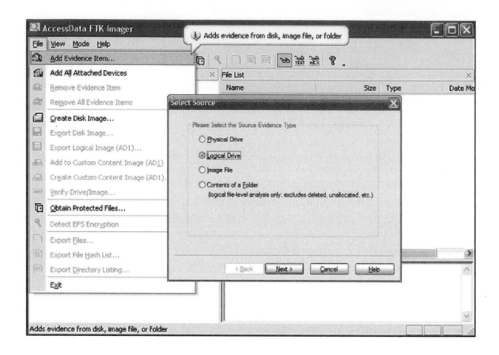

**FIGURE 3.14**

Review and export of files into a logical image file in FTK Imager.

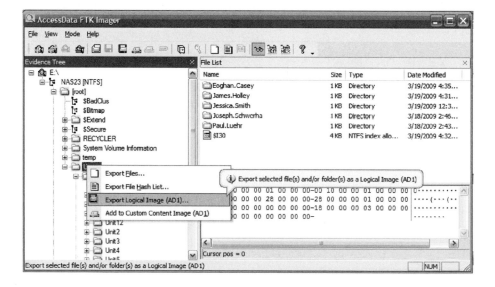

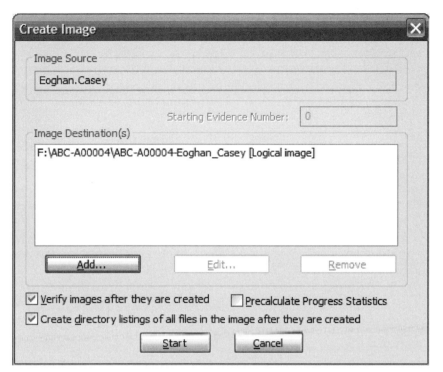

**FIGURE 3.15**
FTK Imager configured to capture a logical image of Eoghan Casey's home drive.

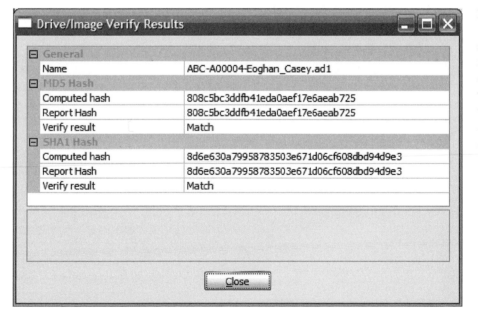

**FIGURE 3.16**
FTK Imager results window showing the MD5 and SHA1 hash values for the data to be acquired match the MD5 and SHA1 hash values of the data that was acquired – this is a verified acquisition.

The other useful tool for preserving logical files is xxcopy™ by Pixielab, Inc. (www.xxcopy.com/), which is based on the Microsoft xcopy command that can be used to preserve data from file servers. The xxcopy utility can be configured to generate a detailed log of the copying process, and can preserve the date and time metadata for the files and folders of both the original files being copied, and the copy of the files. In addition, xxcopy recently added Unicode support with version 2.97.3, the previous lack of which was a major disadvantage as xxcopy would not always log folders that were not copied due to Unicode characters in the folder name. However, xxcopy has several disadvantages compared with FTK Imager:

- xxcopy does not place the files it copies into a "container." The files remain loose files in a file system, subject to accidental change during future processing.

- xxcopy will not copy open files from the server. If a custodian has a file in his or her home drive open for editing—including a .PST or .NSF e-mail container—xxcopy will not copy the open file. However, if the optional logging facility is enabled during the copy process, xxcopy will add an entry in its log file for each live file it failed to copy.

- xxcopy does not calculate and preserve in its log a cryptographic hash of the files it copies. xxcopy relies on the MS Windows operating system to make complete and accurate copies of files. If MS Windows fails to make a complete and accurate copy of a file and also fails to report that the copy process failed, then xxcopy cannot determine that a copy of a file is incomplete.

- xxcopy cannot identify and recover any recently deleted files during the copy process (except files and folders that are still in the Recycle Bin).

An example xxcopy command line for preserving live server data from the folder S:\Jessica Smith Files\ to the folder D:\ES55\Jessica Smith Files\ is provided here:

```
xxcopy /H /K /E /PB /oAD:\ES55\Jsmith-log.log /TCA /
    TCC /TCW "S:\Jessica Smith Files" "D:\ES55\Jessica
    Smith Files"
```

An explanation of each switch used in this command follows. A full listing of the command line switches available can be found at www.xxcopy.com/xxcopy25.htm.

- /H includes hidden and system files
- /K maintains attributes
- /E includes subdirectories and empty directories
- /PB show progress bar
- /oA appends to error log in specified location

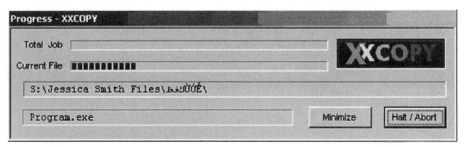

**FIGURE 3.17**
xxcopy progress bar.

- /TCA preserves last accessed dates
- /TCC preserves creation dates
- /TCW preserves last modified dates

The xxcopy progress bar provides some indication of the time required to complete the copying process (Figure 3.17).

The xxcopy log, specified using the /oA switch, provides information on whether the copy process is successful or not. In addition to review of this log, the examiner should always perform an independent comparison of number of files to be copied and number of files copied to ensure the copy process was accurate and complete (Figure 3.18).

There are other tools that are somewhat similar to xxcopy, including the Microsoft software utility Robocopy and Microsoft Backup; however each has its disadvantages for collections when compared to both FTK Imager and

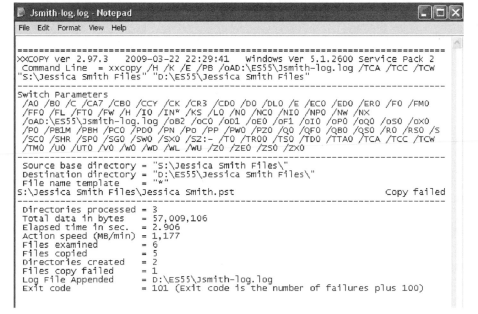

**FIGURE 3.18**
xxcopy log file showing that one file Jessica Smith.pst failed to copy. This was due to the file being in use when the copy process was run.

**FIGURE 3.19**

Demonstrating that
Robocopy maintains
metadata on files (but not
folders) it writes to the data
drive ABC-A00001 (see
folder named ABC-A00004)
but changes metadata on
both files and folders on
the original source server
(see folder named Eoghan.
Casey).

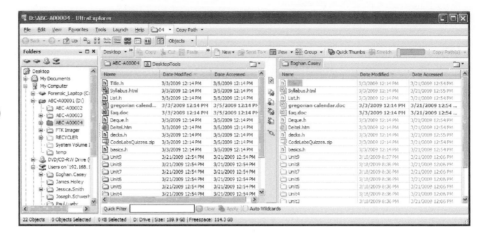

xxcopy. Robocopy is the most similar to xxcopy, and has the same disadvantages, namely that it does not containerize the files it copies, will not copy open files from the server, and does not calculate a cryptographic hash of the files it copies. Robocopy, however, has an additional disadvantage—although it preserves date-time metadata on the copies of the files it makes, it updates the access date of the original files left behind (Figure 3.19). This certainly contravenes a fundamental forensic principle to not alter the original data if at all possible, and for this reason, given the other options available, we do not recommend using Robocopy to preserve data from a live server.

Another utility, called Microsoft Backup, differs from xxcopy and Robocopy in that it does "containerize" the files it backs up into a .BKF file. However, Microsoft Backup shares the same fundamental flaw as Robocopy, where it preserves date-time metadata on the copies of the files it makes, but updates the access date of the original files left behind. For this reason, given the other options available, we do not recommend using Microsoft Backup to preserve data from a live server.

Of course, do not forget about the backup tapes of the servers. A full backup made during the timeframe of interest and before anyone was aware of an investigation or litigation may be the only place to find some files that were deleted from the server either intentionally or in the normal course of business. Backup tapes are a crucial source of this historical data.

## Preserving and Collecting Data from Transactional Systems and Databases

Preserving and collecting data from complex transactional or database systems (e.g., SAP, Oracle Financials, JD Edwards, Equity Edge, etc.) offers the forensic examiner a challenge. Traditional forensic imaging and backup tapes may preserve the data, but will generally not make the data accessible and useable to a third party. Additionally, in most cases, the forensic examiner will not be qualified to run the application that houses and interacts with the data and the application itself will not likely have facilities for conducting the required data analytics supporting the investigation or litigation. Those factors together mean that generally, preserving and collecting the data in a useable fashion will mean extracting it from its proprietary environment and importing it into a nonproprietary environment.

The extraction process will generally be driven by the requirements of the litigation or investigation, including defining applicable date constraints, selecting specific accounting codes or company codes, and finalizing data sources (e.g., accounts payable, accounts receivable, journal entries, or data from CRM systems, ERP systems, or HR systems, etc.). In some cases, the database system may contain standard reporting modules that can be run to extract data from the system in a text file format. In other cases, the forensic examiner will work with a programmer or administrator of the database system to develop customized reports or queries. The output of the report or query process will be the data selected for collection and preservation transformed into a flat text-based format able to be uploaded into a nonproprietary database environment.

An important aspect of the extraction process will be an independent review of the extraction/report queries before they are run to verify they do not include unapproved constraints that might restrict the extracted data. Additional queries should also be run whose outputs constitute quality control checks of the output data to be compared to corresponding queries of the data after import into the new environment. This is typically accomplished with row or record counts as well as control totals of numeric fields. After importing the data into a nonproprietary database system, the count of imported rows or records can be compared to the count of exported rows or records and the sum of an imported numeric field can be compared to the control total calculated of that same field prior to extraction. This enables the forensic examiner to evaluate the import process and verify the imported data matches the output of the approved queries. Absent these kinds of quality control procedures, there could be import errors that go undetected. These errors could have an impact on the output of analytical procedures executed on the data.

As with e-mail server and file server data, backup tapes of the database or transactional data systems can be very important. For instance, some financial systems retain detailed records for only a few fiscal years and, at some scheduled process, drop the detailed records and maintain only summary data afterward. Available full backups of the system might be the only mechanism for recovering some detailed records that have been deleted by the system after their defined retention period.

## Preserving and Collecting Data from Other Data Sources

There are a variety of other data sources that will be sought in the course of formal discovery, including data from cell phones or personal digital assistants that might be synchronized with a custodian's laptop e-mail client as well as entertainment devices like iPods. Personal digital devices can store hundreds of gigabytes of data and are likely candidates for preservation and collection for review and production. As technology progresses and capabilities like WiFi, digital video/audio/photograph, and GPS are integrated into the devices, they will store more and more information relevant to what a person knew and when they knew it or the actions a person took or failed to take.

The targeted data on a new generation cell phone or PDA is likely to be e-mail, calendar items, call logs, GPS location information to correlate with other timing data; videos or photographs taken with the camera or stored on the phone; and other types of user data a custodian might store on their cell phone or PDA. Additionally, the phones will contain a type of data not usually found on a personal computer—the ubiquitous text message. In the normal configuration, text messages sent from phone to phone bypass the corporate e-mail server and are not recorded there. So the data will likely be found only on the cell phone itself.

Software tools allowing preservation and collection of cell phone and PDA data are becoming more readily available, even as the number of different models of phones and devices expands. Once the data are preserved and collected, the traditional user data will be processed for review and production just like any other user data. However, another type of analysis will likely be important for an investigation, including whether the user data on the cell phone or PDA is consistent with user data from other sources. Additionally, the call logs, text messages, and GPS information might be analyzed and correlated with other information to reconstruct a timeline of key events.

## Evidence Chain of Custody and Control

A key aspect of electronic data preservation and collection in formal discovery is initiating and maintaining chain of custody and control of the electronic data. A well-documented chain of custody process allows the data to be submitted as evidence in a court or other legal or administrative proceeding. The Federal Rules of Evidence Rule 1001 states, "If data are stored in a computer or similar device, any printout or other output readable by sight, shown to reflect the data accurately, is an 'original'." A well-documented chain of custody process will be required to demonstrate that the data preserved and collected has not changed since the preservation and collection and that any printouts of the data are accurate reflections of the original data. Absent good chain of custody procedures, an adverse party might raise a claim as to the accuracy of the data in an effort to have the data withheld from admission.

The legal requirement that the data preserved and collected accurately reflect the original has many implications in the technical application of electronic discovery. For instance, if original data on a file server are preserved using a simple copy–paste procedure, the content of the copy will likely be an accurate representation of the original, but the metadata about the original will be changed on the copy. If at some time in the future the matter requires an inspection of the Date Created of a key document, the copy preserved with a copy–paste procedure will not have the same Date Created as the original, even if the content of the copy is digitally identical to the original. This is not to suggest that preservation and collection via a copy–paste procedure automatically makes electronic evidence inadmissible. After all, the content of the copy will most likely be identical to the content of the original and a printout from the copy will likely accurately reflect the original. But the means used to preserve and collect the data, if not a more robust forensic procedure, can have an impact on your future use of the data and metadata when electronic discovery questions are necessarily formatted into forensic analysis questions.

## Preserving and Collecting Backup Tapes

Many of the systems covered in earlier paragraphs of this section are routinely backed up by a company for disaster recovery purposes. It will be important for the forensic examiner to understand the universe of available backup tapes for each of the systems, when tapes are rotated, which tapes are kept long term, and when tapes are destroyed. At the initial stages of the matter, the company should provide (or in some cases be compelled to create new) a complete backup tape inventory for both current systems and during the relevant time period (if different) detailing at least the following information:

- Tape identifier/label
- Tape format (e.g., DDS, LTO, DLT, etc.)
- Backup date/time
- Names(s) of server(s)/system(s) targeted for backup
- Type of backup on the tape (e.g., a full backup, incremental or differential)
- Current location of the tape (e.g., in the backup device, in the server room, in off-site storage, etc.)
- Scheduled rotation

It is not unusual for a company to make full backups of their systems on a weekly basis during the weekend hours and to make incremental or differential backups during the work week. Full backups of large data sets can take time and resources away from the servers, and incremental or differential backups only back up the subset of data that changed since the last full backup. Most companies will keep weekly or monthly full backups for some period of time and might keep an annual full backup for a number of years. In the highly regulated financial and pharmaceutical industries, we typically find that month-end and year-end backup tapes are kept much longer than in the nonregulated industries.

## FROM THE CASE FILES: COSTLY TAPE PROCESSING

Backup tapes can be a contentious issue. In one matter we worked on, a company in a highly regulated industry had more than 30,000 backup tapes in off-site storage. Compounding the matter, the company did not have a reliable inventory of the tapes that described in any detail the contents of the tapes such that some tapes could be eliminated from the pool of tapes to be reviewed. Because any of the tapes might have held relevant nonprivileged data, all tapes were initially cataloged to provide a suitable inventory from which to make selections for data restoration and processing. Had the company kept a reliable log of tapes in off-site storage, including some indication of what was on a tape or even what backup tape media types (e.g., DDS, DLT, DLT IV) were used to back up servers containing relevant data, the company could have saved a considerable amount of money on tape processing.

Do not underestimate the value of backup tapes. Though processing them can take time, they contain a snapshot of the server at a period of time before the litigation or investigation began, before anyone knew data on the systems might be produced to another party, and before someone or some process might have deleted potentially relevant and nonprivileged data.

## DATA PROCESSING

Having preserved and collected perhaps a mountain of data for counsel to review, the next phase of the electronic discovery process is—naturally—data processing. Although data processing will be focused on accomplishing many objectives discussed in the introductory section of this chapter, the overarching goals for data processing are data transformation and data reduction. The data must be transformed into a readable format so that counsel can review the data for relevancy and privilege and the volume of data must be reduced, typically through filtering for file types, duplicates, date, and keywords, in a manner that does not compromise the completeness of any future production.

## FROM THE CASE FILES: LARGE QUANTITIES OF DATA

The Enron case highlights the steady growth in both volume and importance of electronic data in corporate environments. Andrew Rosen, President of ASR Data Acquisition and Analysis, a computer forensics firm hired by Arthur Andersen to preserve electronic records and to attempt to recover deleted computer records related to the matter, estimated his firm preserved approximately "268 terabytes—roughly 10 times the amount of data stored by the Library of Congress" in the form of hundreds of hard drives. All that data had to be reviewed. If all the digital content were printable ASCII text printed singled sided, reviewers would have to look at 76.9 billion pages of paper—a stack more than 4,857 miles tall (Holley, 2008).

The forensic examiner's role in this phase of the e-discovery process ultimately depends on the processing strategy for review purposes decided by counsel. An examiner is typically involved with extracting the user files from the preserved data, including the forensic images and the data preserved from servers, using a tool such as EnCase Forensic. Filtering the data for duplicates, date, and keywords, and transforming the data to a reviewable format can be performed either by examiners using forensic software or other processing tools, or with an electronic discovery database. These electronic discovery databases are robust, comprehensive database platforms. Most are able to perform filtering for file type, duplicates, date, and keywords. Other advanced systems also provide advanced analytics such as concept searching, concept categorization, e-mail thread analysis, "near" duplicate identification, and/or social networking analysis. These database platforms facilitate counsel review and ultimate production by either hosting the data online or by outputting responsive data to load files for review with in-house review tools such as Concordance or Summation.

There are many different processing strategies for review purposes employed by counsel. Counsel considers many factors when deciding on a strategy, and though discussion of all of these factors are outside the scope of this chapter, we have found that data volume, costs, and upcoming production deadlines are the most frequent factors considered. Three of the more common approaches are:

- Upload all the user files extracted from the preserved data into an electronic discovery database and perform the data filtering in the database.
- Use forensic software or other processing tools such as dtSearch to filter the data and transform it into reviewable format.
- Use a hybrid approach where the extracted data is first reduced through filtering with forensic software or other processing tools and then is uploaded into an electronic discovery database for review and/or further filtering.

Forensic examiners should understand how data are uploaded, stored, and searched in the electronic discovery databases both because they are often responsible for providing the data to be uploaded, and also for instances where they are required to either assist with formulating the keywords or perform quality assurance on the results, as further described in the production section of this chapter. It is even more imperative for forensic examiners to understand the tools they use to extract user files from preserved data, filter for duplicates, date, and keyword, and transform for review. The focus of this section is on performing these tasks and completing the necessary quality assurance to ensure accurate and complete results.

## Exctracting and Processing Data from Forensic Images

For almost every matter, counsel will have a list of custodians and will direct forensic images of custodian laptop and desktop computers to be preserved. Processing data from those forensic images into a review environment can be a technically complex procedure with many decision points. Counsel must determine which file types are most likely to be relevant; whether processing will include attempts to identify and recover deleted files; how to handle compressed or encrypted files; what level of forensic review, if any, will be accomplished for high priority and/or lower priority custodians; whether attempts will be made to identify and recover fragments of deleted files from unallocated space; whether personal data will be excluded from upload into the review environment; and more.

### PRACTITIONER'S TIP: UNDERSTAND THE CASE AND CONTEXT

Certain types of data may be identified as relevant only after a diligent forensic examiner reviews the forensic image(s) in a case. Therefore, forensic examiners must have an understanding of the case background and what kind of ESI is being sought in order to identify relevant items when they come across them. Furthermore, forensic examiners should not become overly reliant on rote checklists and automated methods for extracting predetermined file types, or they risk missing entire classes of relevant items. Such an oversight could lead to incomplete productions, and provide grounds for sanctions as discussed in the legal section earlier in this chapter.

### *Relevant File Types*

One of the first decisions counsel must make that has an impact on data reduction is to determine which file types are potentially relevant to the matter. In almost every matter, e-mail and office documents will be processed into the review environment. But there are other matters where unique file types play a part. If a custodian works in an engineering department, for example, the engineering drawings themselves (which can be quite large when created in a computer-aided design (CAD) application) might be relevant and they would be extracted for review. However, they might be excluded from extraction if the dispute does not center on the CAD drawings themselves.

### FROM THE CASE FILES: DATA REDUCTION

In one matter we worked on, digital camera pictures in JPEG file format were relevant to the dispute. Counsel asked us to design a processing methodology for extracting the digital camera JPEG files from the forensic image while ignoring typical web page JPEG graphic files. Since the files have the same extension, a simple search for all .JPG files would extract too many files for counsel to review. Complicating this was the fact that some of the relevant digital camera images were also in the web cache folders. But counsel had no interest in reviewing all the typical JPEG images that continue to proliferate in the web cache folders. Our approach to the process involved analyzing samples of the relevant digital camera pictures, developing signatures from them that identified them distinctly from web page image files, and analyzing file system activity patterns when web page images are created on the hard drive. Using those data elements, we were able to isolate the web page images from all other JPEG files, significantly reducing the number of JPEG files counsel had to review in the matter.

Extracting files from forensic images is typically done using a variety of techniques, but the most complete technique checks a file's signature instead of a file's extension. A file *signature* refers to a unique sequence of data bytes at the beginning of a file that identifies the file as a specific file type. For instance, a file whose first four bytes are "%PDF" can be identified as a likely Adobe Acrobat Portable Document Format file, even if its extension is not .PDF. The file signature will be a better indicator of the file's contents than is its extension. This is especially important where a company maps a custodian's local My Documents folder to their network home drive and has implemented Client Side Caching. In this situation, all documents in the My Documents folder actually reside on a file server housing the custodian's home drive. Local copies of the files are available to the custodian to be opened and edited when the custodian is offline, but the local copies of the file are not actually contained in the My Documents folder, they do not have their real document names, and they have no extensions. The Microsoft Windows operating system maintains a local database that maps the actual files to the names the custodian expects to see. In actuality, the files are contained in the C:\Windows\CSC folder and they have names like 80001E6C or 80001E60 without extensions. An extraction procedure that relies exclusively on extensions will not identify the relevant files in the Client Side Cache folder. Additionally, if a custodian has renamed file extensions in an effort to hide files (e.g., renaming myfile.doc to myfile.tmp) then the renamed files will not be extracted if the extraction procedure looks exclusively for file extensions.

### Identifying and Recovering Deleted Files and Folders

Forensic tools commonly available today have robust capabilities to identify and recover deleted files in the normal course of processing. As discussed in the legal section of this chapter, Rule 26(a)(2)(B) exempts from discovery information that is "not reasonably accessible" and the Advisory Committee identified deleted data that requires computer forensics to restore it as one data source that might not be reasonably accessible. Whether or not to include recoverable deleted files in a discovery effort is a decision that ultimately needs to be made by counsel.

### Compressed or Encrypted Files

Compressed file archives (e.g., zip, rar, tar, cab, 7z, etc.) will be extracted and examined to determine if they contain relevant file types. The processing must be able to recursively extract files from the archive because a compressed archive can be included in another compressed archive. Encrypted or password-protected files need to be identified and a log generated. Once notified, counsel will decide whether additional actions such as attempts to "crack" the password or approaching the respective custodian are necessary.

### Nontext-based Files

Counsel will decide whether nontext-based files such as TIFF images of scanned documents or PDF files will be extracted and processed into review. Typically, a well-constructed keyword search through the nontext data will not find hits because the files are not encoded in a text format. Therefore, searching the nontext-based files will require either running an Optical Character Recognition (OCR) program against the images to render the text of the pages or manual/visual review.

### Forensic Review of High Priority Custodian Computers

If allegations or suspicions of potential evidence tampering exist, there are a number of forensic questions that could be answered for each of the custodians at issue.

- Is this actually the custodian's computer? Do they have a user profile on the system? When was the user profile first created and used? When was the user profile last used? If the system has an asset tag, does the asset tag agree with information contained in the company's asset tracking database?

- Does it appear that someone may have used a data destruction tool on the hard drive to destroy files?

- When was the operating system installed? Does that correlate with IT records about this computer asset?

- Is there evidence suggesting the custodian copied files to a network drive or external drive and deleted the files?

- Is there evidence to suggest someone may have tampered with the system clock?

- Is there evidence to suggest any massive deletion of files from the system prior to imaging?

Although it might not be practical to conduct this forensic analysis by default on all hard drives for all custodians, it could provide valuable information if conducted on the hard drives of the most critical custodians. Indeed, the ability to answer these types of questions is one reason why creating a forensic image of computers is the preferred method of data preservation compared to preserving only active files or custodian-selected files.

### Recovering Fragments of Deleted Files from Unallocated Space

Any frequently used computer is likely to have hundreds of thousands, if not millions, of file fragments in the computer's unallocated space. In civil discovery matters though, these file fragments are rarely seen as "reasonably accessible" and therefore not necessary to be recovered and processed into a review environment. That can be seen as an extraordinary effort and can be an expensive proposition. However, for investigations, it might be appropriate for the most important custodians. Fragments of files recovered from unallocated space will not have file system metadata associated with them—therefore you will not necessarily be able to determine with any certainty when a file was created, modified, accessed, or deleted. In fact, you might not even be able to determine that the fragment was part of a document that the user deleted. File fragments can be created in many ways that do not relate to a custodian deleting files, including:

- The custodian accessing or opening a file whose content is subsequently temporarily cached to the local hard drive
- The custodian or the Microsoft operating system optimizing the hard drive, moving files from one location on disk to another and leaving fragments of the files in their old location
- A virus program quarantining and then deleting a file that is subsequently partially overwritten
- Microsoft Office or an e-mail application creating and then deleting temporary files that are subsequently partially overwritten, resulting in a fragment
- The WinZIP compression and archiving program creating and deleting temporary copies of files that have been extracted for viewing, which are subsequently partially overwritten

If the file is of a type that contains embedded metadata, for example Microsoft Office files and Adobe Acrobat files, this embedded information may be able to be recovered. This embedded metadata can include dates of creation, modification, last saved, and last printed, as well as the author. These dates would not necessarily correspond to the file system metadata. Because file fragments often provide almost no information that can help determine when they were created, by whom or by what process they were created, and how they came to be file fragments, great care must be used when examining them and making judgments about them.

### Isolating Personal Data

Some custodians use their company-owned computer as if it were their own personal computer. We've worked on matters where custodians have stored their personal income tax records, private family pictures, social security records, and immigration and naturalization records on the company's computer. In some cases, counsel has requested that this data not be extracted from the forensic image nor processed into the review environment. This might be problematic if the custodian's personal data are comingled with company data, and is often best achieved through the creation of a detailed protocol signed off on by the custodian and the company's counsel. Similar issues often arise when the custodian list includes a company's Board of Directors and the board member has not been diligent in keeping board-related data separate from the data generated from his or her day-to-day job at his or her respective employer. In some cases, a detailed protocol that specifies the identification of relevant board-related data, through performing the collection, preservation, and processing on site at the respective board member's home or employer may be necessary.

### Exploring Web Usage

Counsel may be particularly interested in whether the primary custodians might have used web-based e-mail services in an effort to circumvent the company e-mail system. Additionally, Instant Messaging services and proxy services will be important to review for the most important custodians. Counsel may also ask that recoverable web mail message and Instant Message chat logs be extracted from the images and processed into the review environment.

---

## FROM THE CASE FILES: WEB-BASED E-MAIL

We worked on one Foreign Corrupt Practices Act investigation looking into the practices of an overseas office of a US company. The overseas executives of the company used their corporate e-mail accounts for their normal day-to-day activities, but used free web-based e-mail accounts to conduct their illegal activities. We recovered web mail from one executive that specifically identified topics to be discussed only via the web mail service and indicating the executive knew the US offices had the ability to monitor all corporate e-mail servers and traffic globally.

---

## PRACTITIONER'S TIP: PROCESSING PROTOCOL USING ENCASE

Over time we've developed the following high-level work flow for processing forensic images supporting electronic discovery matters. This work flow is designed to be used with the EnCase forensic software. You might adapt the work flow to your local needs and tools:

1. Update chain of custody documents as necessary.
2. Update evidence database as necessary.
3. Review forensic preservation memo as necessary.
4. Prepare backup copy of forensic image as necessary.
5. Create new EnCase case and add/import image.
6. Adjust case time zone settings as necessary.
7. Validate sector count and verify image hash.
8. Validate logical data structures.
9. Run recover folders tool.
10. Hash all files and validate file signatures.
11. Export EnCase all files list.
12. Filter active user files.
13. Export EnCase active user files list.
14. Copy folders—filtered active user files.
15. Filter active e-mail files.
16. Export EnCase active e-mail files list.
17. Copy folders—filtered active e-mail files.
18. Filter deleted user files.
19. Export EnCase deleted user files list.
20. Copy folders—filtered deleted user files.
21. Filter deleted e-mail.
22. Export EnCase deleted e-mail files list.
23. Copy folders—filtered deleted e-mail.
24. Identify web mail files.
25. Export EnCase web mail list.
26. Export web mail.
27. Verify file counts—user files, e-mail archives, recovered deleted data, web mail.
28. Verify total size on disk.
29. MD5 sum all exported files—save hash log.
30. Import EnCase all files list into SQL.
31. Import EnCase filtered files list(s) into SQL.

*(Continued)*

---

**PRACTITIONER'S TIP: PROCESSING PROTOCOL USING ENCASE—CONT'D**

32. Import hash log into SQL.
33. Quality check hash log against EnCase filtered file list(s).
34. Convert e-mail as necessary.
35. Save conversion logs.
36. Quality check e-mail conversion process.
37. Recover deleted e-mail from active and deleted e-mail containers.
38. Count all extracted files by type.
39. Count all mail files and mail items inside the files.
40. Quality check all forensic processing.
41. Send to e-discovery team for processing into review:

- Extracted active user files
- Extracted active e-mail containers/archives
- Extracted active web mail
- Recovered deleted user files
- Recovered deleted e-mail containers/archives
- Recovered deleted e-mail from e-mail containers
- Processing logs and counts
- Converted e-mail
- Forensic processing documentation

42. Update chain of custody documents as necessary.
43. Update evidence database as necessary.
44. Prepare forensic processing memo for binder.

---

## Processing Data from Live E-mail, File Servers, and Backup Tapes

Data preserved and collected from live e-mail and file servers present very few processing challenges to the forensic examiner. E-mail extracted from the live Exchange and Domino e-mail servers will likely proceed directly into the filtering stage without further preprocessing. If the e-mail comes from some other system (e.g., GroupWise, UNIX Sendmail, etc.) and the review tool does not support the native e-mail in that format, then the forensic examiner might convert the e-mail into PST format prior to processing. This conversion should be done only when absolutely necessary as the conversion process is a prime opportunity to introduce data loss and/or corruption. Many tools exist to do this conversion, but it is important to choose carefully and test the tool's e-mail conversion and logging capabilities. The conversion process must not lose e-mail or attachments, must maintain e-mail-attachment relationships, must not change important metadata elements, and must fully document the conversion process. After the conversion has taken place, there should be significant quality assurance steps taken to ensure that the conversion was accurate and complete.

Files preserved and collected from live file servers will likely be processed using the same procedures as for forensic images. The files will be subjected to the same selection and filtering criteria so that there is a consistent approach to user files. The process is typically simpler, however, as there is much less comingling of user files with system files than on forensic images.

When processing backup tapes, it is not uncommon for counsel to ask a vendor to first catalog select tapes to test the accuracy of the company's tape inventory. Particularly if some sampling will be done of the tapes, counsel must be confident that the sampling methodology is relying on a sound inventory as its basic starting point. Cataloging a selection of tapes and comparing the actual results to expected results will provide a measure of confidence that the tape inventory is accurate or will suggest that the tape inventory is not reliable. Once the data from specific e-mail and file server backup tapes are restored, then the data will be processed using the same tools and methods as for the live server e-mail and live file server data.

## Data Reduction through Deduplication

Deduplication can reduce the load on counsel, who typically will review documents for relevance and privilege prior to production. Deduplication essentially identifies, using some algorithm, that a file presented to the processing tool is a copy of a file already in the data set for review. Once a file is identified as a duplicate of another file already in review, the new file can be suppressed (although the tool should not "forget" that it found the duplicate).

There are essentially two major deduplication methodologies: per-custodian deduplication and global deduplication. In the per-custodian model, all data for custodian Mike is deduped only against other data also preserved and collected from Mike's data sources. If a file exists on Mike's hard drive and a copy of the file is recovered from Mike's home drive on the live file server and several copies of the file are restored from multiple backup tapes of the file server, then counsel should expect to see and review only one copy of the file for Mike. Other custodians might also have a copy of the file, but Mike's copy will not be deduped against Jane's copy. Likewise, an e-mail contained in Mike's Sent Items folder will be deduped only against other e-mail sources for Mike. If several instances of the e-mail server are restored from backup tape, and a copy of the e-mail exists in Mike's account on each restored tape, then counsel should expect to see the e-mail only once in their review of Mike's data. Recipients of the e-mail who are custodians and who have not deleted the e-mail may also have a copy of the e-mail in their holdings.

The other major deduplication methodology is global deduplication. In this methodology, once the first copy of a unique file is identified using a specific deduplication algorithm, all other copies of that same file will be considered duplicates regardless of custodian. If both Mike and Jane have a copy of a file on their hard drive, the first one to be processed will be added to the review environment and the second one will be suppressed (although the tool should not "forget" that it found the duplicate).

Careful attention should be paid to the technical implementation of the deduplication algorithm. For e-documents, the most common algorithm used to identify duplicates is the MD5 hash. Identifying e-mail duplicates is slightly more complicated as tools typically identify duplicates by hashing the values of a number of different e-mail fields (e.g., sender, recipient, cc, bcc, subject, body text, attachment titles) in a predetermined order. Therefore, depending on the fields used by the tool, there may be different determinations between tools of what is and is not a duplicate e-mail. Not only that, but in some tools the fields used to deduplicate are optional, so different fields can be chosen for different projects.

## FROM THE CASE FILES: THE IMPORTANCE OF TOOL VALIDATION

A commercially available tool had a number of different optional fields available to deduplicate Lotus Notes e-mail, including author, recipients, date and time, number of attachments, and e-mail body. It was only through use of the tool and review of the results that it became obvious not all fields were being used as deduplication criteria, regardless of whether or not they were chosen by the user. Consultation with the developer revealed that there was a "bug" in the tool whereby with Lotus Notes e-mail the e-mail body was not being used to compare potential duplicates, even if the e-mail body was selected by the user as one of the criteria. This bug was specific to deduplication of Lotus Notes e-mail and not Microsoft Outlook. This bug obviously had the capacity to erroneously eliminate unique messages through the deduplication process, an unacceptable situation. Fortunately this bug was identified before the processing was finalized and we were able to ensure that the complete data set was provided to counsel.

The testing and validation of tools with a robust test set that is representative of different e-mail types and real-world scenarios is very important. However, it is not realistic to require testing of every possible scenario before using a tool, nor is it possible to test every type of human error that could take place. This is another reason why it is imperative to perform the necessary quality assurance steps at every step of the electronic discovery process.

Some of the deduplication tools keep detailed records of their automated deduplication decisions, making it relatively easy to show that multiple custodians had a copy of a specific document. However other tools make a deduplication decision and then do not log the fact that the duplicate file existed, or the process of saving the log is not automatic and must be performed manually after each data set has been processed. If Jane has a copy of a file processed into the review environment and later another copy of the same file is processed for Mike, a record should be created and saved that documents Mike had a copy of the file.

Custodian level deduplication is generally preferred by counsel because it allows a wide variety of review strategies to be developed. First, counsel might assign an associate to perform a first-level review of all documents in Mike's holdings to develop a detailed understanding of Mike's communication patterns, including topics on which Mike routinely provides comments and insights, as well as topics of conversation where he is typically only an observer. A reviewer focused on understanding Mike's role in and actions on behalf of a company will need to have access to all of Mike's documents. In a global deduplication methodology, if a document was first processed for Jane and later processed for Mike and Mike's copy was suppressed as a duplicate, the associate might not know Mike had a copy of the document, even if the application did record the fact. Custodian level deduplication also allows for custodian-specific searches to be performed.

Other review strategies certainly exist. Counsel might assign an associate to do a first level review of all documents related to a specific transaction, regardless of custodian or all documents related to a specific period of time to get a sense for official corporate actions in a specific fiscal quarter. Counsel may also determine that the time and cost savings generated by using a global deduplication methodology, resulting in less documents to review, is more important than immediately being able to determine which custodian had which document in their data set. This is often the strategy chosen if counsel is confident that the information on what custodian had which document can be provided at a later date if necessary. Typically, for global deduplication to meet counsel's long-term needs, the application must track and facilitate some level of access to the original document for every custodian that held the document.

## Data Reduction through Keyword Searching

Keyword searching provides perhaps the greatest potential to drastically reduce the data volume to a manageable, reviewable level. However it is also a process that if not performed correctly has the potential to significantly impact the completeness and accuracy of the data provided to counsel for review and included in the ultimate production.

Almost every major electronic discovery database platform provides some facility both for preculling, where the data is searched and only responsive data made available for review by counsel, and searching in the review environment, which can be performed by or for counsel.

As mentioned earlier, forensic examiners should understand how data are uploaded, stored, and searched in the electronic discovery databases both because they are often responsible for providing the data to be uploaded (especially if their company owns a proprietary electronic discovery database), and also for instances where they are required to either assist with formulating the keywords or perform quality assurance on the results.

When the forensic examiner is performing the keyword searching, understanding the searching process of the tool used is even more crucial. This understanding is important from a technical perspective to ensure that the keyword search results are accurate and complete, and also to identify crux areas of the process that would benefit from vigorous quality assurance. In addition, understanding the searching process is also important from the perspective of assisting counsel with developing an effective keyword search strategy. There are three core components of the searching process that must be understood:

- How the tool indexes the document content, and how documents that cannot be indexed are handled
- The data sources being searched
- How to formulate a smart, targeted keyword list with the tool's specific keyword syntax and advanced searching capabilities

Additional details on these three core components follow. A comprehensive test example using the tool dtSearch Desktop is also included, to provide additional demonstrative information and highlight the importance of understanding the three core components and performing quality assurance at each step of the searching process.

---

## TOOL FEATURE: dtSEARCH DESKTOP—INDEXING AND KEYWORD SEARCHING MICROSOFT OUTLOOK PST DATA

The dtSearch suite includes a range of indexing and searching products including dtSearch Desktop, dtSearch Network, and dtSearch Web, all of which are based on dtSearch's text retrieval engine. In our experience, we have found that dtSearch is a robust, highly configurable indexing and searching tool for electronic documents and many types of e-mail, including Microsoft Outlook. dtSearch also makes the engine available to developers to allow users to create added functionality if necessary. dtSearch is able to identify certain documents it could not index because of corruption or specific types of encryption and password protection, but does not identify documents with unsearchable text, such as scanned PDF files. Additionally, dtSearch is not able to index Lotus Notes e-mail or perform deduplication. The configurable nature of dtSearch can become a liability if the user is not diligent about reviewing the settings before conducting the index and search.

Proper planning and consideration of indexing preferences in relation to the keywords being searched is essential before beginning the indexing, as is documentation of the preferences being used to ensure consistency among data sets and to answer questions that may arise in the future. The consequences of errors in the search process are often high, including providing an incomplete production to counsel when the mistake is overlooked and work having to be redone when the mistake is caught.

In the following example, dtSearch Desktop was used to index four Microsoft Outlook .PST files consisting of publicly available Enron data and test data generated by the authors.

### 1. Setting the Indexing Preferences

After the keyword list has been finalized and a searching strategy determined, the first step in using any searching tool that utilizes an indexing engine is to set the indexing preferences. Depending on the tool, the examiner may be able to choose how certain letters and characters are indexed. As shown in Figure 3.20, in dtSearch each letter and character can either be indexed as a letter, space, or hyphen, or be ignored.

### 2. Creating an Index

When creating the index through the dtSearch Index Manager, the user has the option to index the data with case and/or accent sensitivity. In most cases, you will not want to index the data with case or accent sensitivities to ensure that a complete set of responsive data is identified. However, when the client has requested small acronym keywords such as NBC or ABC, this may result in too many false positives. One solution would be to index the data twice, once with case sensitivity turned on and one without. The small acronym keywords could be searched in the case-sensitive index and all other keywords searched in the noncase-sensitive index.

*(Continued)*

## TOOL FEATURE: dtSEARCH DESKTOP—INDEXING AND KEYWORD SEARCHING MICROSOFT OUTLOOK PST DATA—CONT'D

**FIGURE 3.20**

Configuring Indexing Options in dtSearch.

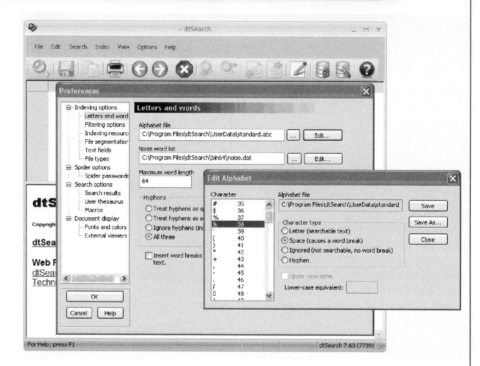

Choosing the Detailed index logging option will generate a log of all items indexed and all items not indexed, or only partially indexed (Figure 3.21).

### 3. Index Summary Log

When the index has finished, a log can be viewed that summarizes the number of files indexed and the number of files not indexed, or only partially indexed. A more detailed log that lists each file can also be accessed. Figure 3.22 depicts the summary log and then the more detailed log listing the two items only partially indexed.

When the original messages are located, it is determined that the attachment to the message with the subject "Ken Lay Employment Agreement" is corrupt, and the attachment to the message with the subject "RE: Target" is password protected. As they are listed under partially indexed, the e-mail itself and any other attachments to the e-mail would have been successfully indexed.

The items either not indexed or only partially indexed should be documented as exceptions to the search process, and either provided to the client for review or further work performed in an attempt to make them available for searching (such as cracking the password protection on the file).

### 4. Keyword Searching

After the data have been indexed and any exceptions noted, the data can be keyword searched. dtSearch can import a list of keywords, or keywords can be run one at a time in the Search window. Figure 3.23 shows a search for the keyword "apples & oranges" using the Search window, with no files retrieved as responsive.

However, remember that the ampersand symbol "&" is by default indexed as a space, and is also a special search symbol meaning "synonym." For example, the keyword "fast&" would also return as responsive the word "quickly." Therefore

*(Continued)*

## TOOL FEATURE: dtSEARCH DESKTOP—INDEXING AND KEYWORD SEARCHING MICROSOFT OUTLOOK PST DATA—CONT'D

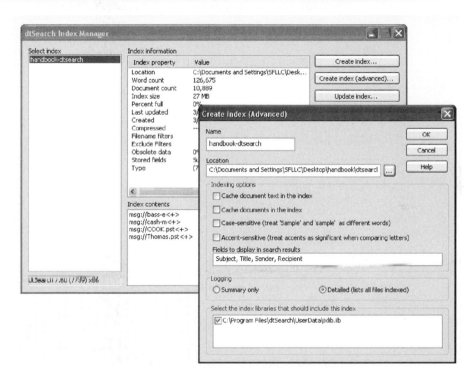

**FIGURE 3.21**

Enabling Detailed index logging in dtSearch.

the previous search is not searching literally for the term "apples & oranges" but is interpreting the search as an incorrect synonym search. If the keyword is changed to "apples oranges", responsive e-mail items are identified as shown in Figure 3.24. These types of errors are a common mistake when the user does not fully understand dtSearch's search syntax, and highlight the importance of performing a test with a known dataset, indexed with the preferences being used in the case, and searching for the case search terms.

Similarly, it is important to note that dtSearch cannot index the content of files with no searchable text (dtSearch does index the metadata for these files), and also does not identify them as being only partially indexed. As shown in Figure

3.25, the keyword "written agreement" identifies no hits when searching a scanned PDF containing the keyword.

We have implemented work-arounds to this issue by running a grep command through the dtSearch index files themselves to identify PDF files containing a small number of indexed words.

### 5. Copying Out Results

After the keyword search, responsive files can be copied out, preserving the folder structure as well as dates of creation, modification, and last access as shown in Figure 3.26. Always check the folder to which the data was copied to ensure that the number of files copied out is accurate.

**FIGURE 3.22A**

Summary log of items partially indexed by dtSearch.

### Index Update Report

| | |
|---|---|
| Index | C:\Documents and Settings\SFLLC\Desktop\handbook\dtsearch\handbook-dtsearch |
| Actions | Create Add |
| Result | OK |
| Start | 3/15/2009 10:19:53 AM |
| End | 3/15/2009 10:21:59 AM |

**Documents indexed**

| | |
|---|---|
| Total words in index | 126,675 |
| Total documents in index | 10,889 |
| Documents indexed | 10,889 |
| Bytes indexed | 195,839 kb |
| Documents removed | 0 |

**Documents not indexed**

| | |
|---|---|
| Documents not indexed | 0 |
| Encrypted files | 0 |
| Unreadable files | 0 |
| Skipped as "binary" | 0 |

**Documents partially indexed**

| | |
|---|---|
| Partially encrypted files | 1 |
| Partially unreadable files | 1 |

**FIGURE 3.22B**

Detailed log of items partially indexed by dtSearch.

**Index:** C:\Documents and Settings\SFLLC\Desktop\handbook\dtsearch\handbook-dtsearch
**Update started:** 3/15/2009 10:19:53 AM

Click here for the summary report.

**Ken Lay Employment Agreement - {44012000}.msg**
　　msg://Outlook/COOK.pst/Inbox/Ken Lay Employment Agreement - {44012000}.msg
　　*Partially corrupt*
　　Size: 36,352  Type: Outlook MSG  WordCount: 215  Result: Partially unreadable

**RE_ Target {c4062000}.msg**
　　msg://Outlook/COOK.pst/Inbox/RE_ Target {c4062000}.msg
　　*Partially encrypted*
　　Size: 69,632  Type: Outlook MSG  WordCount: 1,333  Result: Partially encrypted

## How Documents Are Indexed

There are a number of different indexing engines available on the market today. The indexing engine prepares the documents for searching generally by creating a full-text index of the contents of the documents. Some indexing tools also index metadata about the documents and make the metadata searchable as well (e.g., document names and document properties). The more advanced indexing tools understand compound document formats and provide a capability to search the contents of compound documents.

Given the wide variety of file types and ways they can be damaged or secured, tools used for keyword searching will not be able to index certain file types that are relevant to a case, due to corruption, lack of searchable text (e.g., scanned

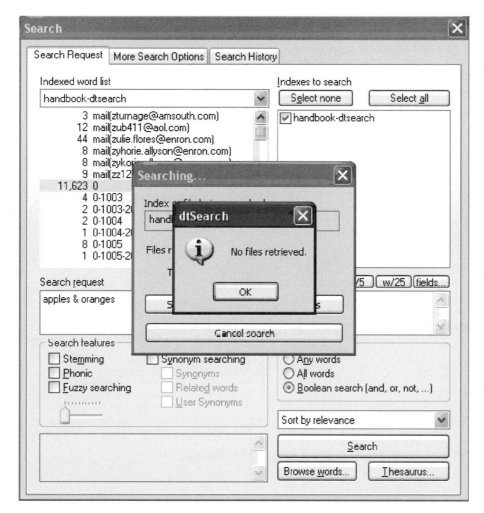

**FIGURE 3.23**
dtSearch keyword results
showing no items retrieved
for keyword "apples &
oranges".

PDF), encryption, or password protection. It is important to know what file types your tool cannot search and how the tool deals with files it cannot index. Detailed logging of the files the tool can and cannot index is an important feature to enable both a thorough evaluation of the tools' capabilities, as well as an adequate quality assurance review of the results.

Some tools have more fundamental limitations that forensic examiners must be cognizant of in order to avoid mistakes. For instance, some tools used to perform keyword searches in e-discovery support only ASCII keyword searching and cannot be used to search for keywords in Unicode format. As another example, some tools index data in such a way that a keywords can be case sensitive. Some keyword search tools used to index and search the data

**FIGURE 3.24**

dtSearch keyword results showing two items retrieved for keyword "apples oranges".

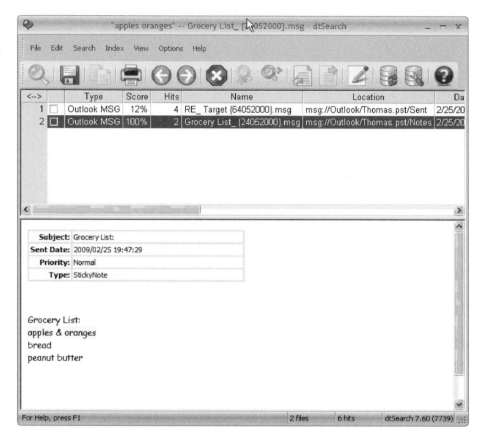

**FIGURE 3.25**

dtSearch keyword results showing no items retrieved for keyword "written agreement" visible in a scanned PDF.

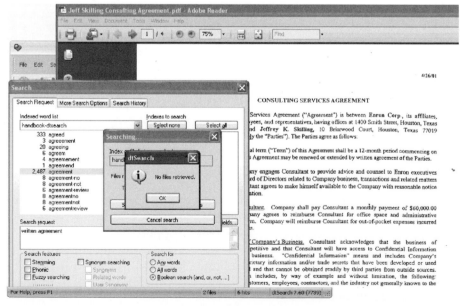

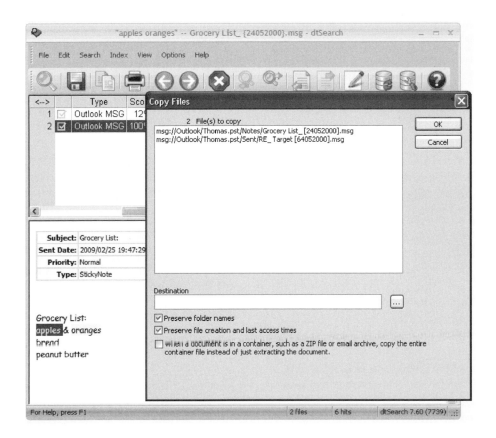

**FIGURE 3.26**
Extracting files of interest using dtSearch.

necessarily rely on many other software programs to process the data. For example, searching Microsoft Outlook data almost always requires the use of the Outlook API. Therefore, tool testing and validation should not be limited to any specific e-discovery tool, but should include the programs they incorporate. A good example of this is the Microsoft Outlook bug where the body of e-mails created with pre 2003 versions of Outlook are blank when opened with an unpatched version of Outlook 2003. The tool did not index contents of these e-mails, but the failure was not a flaw of limitation of the tool itself. Because the unpatched version of Microsoft Outlook provided no data to the index engine, the tool had no data to index. This was a failure of the Outlook API upon which the tool relied.

In addition to the basic functionality of keyword searching tools, the index settings are a key component of the indexing engine. Most have dictionaries of noise words that will not be indexed (e.g., "and", "if", "because") and also enable you to build a custom dictionary of noise words that can be project-

or matter-specific. Other configuration options might include how specific characters such as "&", ".", "-", and "," are indexed. For example, in dtSearch hyphenated words can be indexed in one of four ways. First, hyphens can be indexed as spaces, such that first-class would be indexed as "first" and "class" with each word separately searchable. Second, by treating the hyphens themselves as searchable, "first-class" would be indexed only as "first-class". A search for "first" or "class" would not find "first-class". Third, by ignoring hyphens, "first-class" would be indexed as "firstclass". And finally, "first-class" might be indexed all three ways to enable a more thorough search. Some index settings might enable you to index field names in XML files and index NTFS Summary Information Streams along with the document content.

Still other options might enable you to completely ignore certain languages or to include in the index several different languages. The tool's approach to indexing punctuation will be important to keyword construction. If the tool indexes the period, then you would be able to search for "Ph.D" or "gmail. com". But if the tool does not index periods, then search terms constructed to find e-mail addresses must not use the period. In addition, some tools use the ampersand as a special character (e.g., synonym), so using a keyword with an ampersand will not return that keyword.

### What the Data Sources Are

Developing a robust search strategy requires an understanding of the types of documents to be searched and their content. Search terms designed to comb through formal corporate documents will be different than search terms designed to parse through more informal e-mail communications where custodians might routinely use abbreviations or slang terminology. Effectively searching through even more informal communications mediums like instant messaging might require using search terms that are almost unrecognizable as words (e.g., "r u there", or "doin?", or "havin sup with my peeps").

### Developing Targeted Keywords

The initial keyword list is usually generated by counsel, however the forensic examiner can and should provide guidance and insight into the formulation of keywords and what keywords could generate an excessive number of false positives. A careful review of each keyword on the list and consideration of what it is designed to uncover and what it is designed to accomplish should be performed to ensure the most precise results possible. For example, in one case we worked on, counsel developed a list of key terms containing over 800 words. The list was not well focused, and returned hundreds of thousands of false positive results. Similarly, very short keywords (e.g. acronyms and other terms that are only two or three characters) can also be problematic. The same situation occurs when the contents of document metadata is not taken into account (for example searching Microsoft Word documents for "Microsoft"), or keywords that are included in standard nomenclature such as the disclaimer wording at the bottom of most company e-mails.

Certain keywords that may not generate excessive false positives in one data set will do so in another. To provide some insight into the number of responsive documents before the results are produced for review, it can be helpful to generate for counsel a keyword hit summary report detailing the number of hits and/or the number of documents per keyword. Oftentimes the keyword list is subject to negotiation between the two parties, and this keyword search summary report can be used to show cause for reconsideration or editing of certain keywords due to the number of hits they would generate.

When counsel must also review documents both for relevance and for privilege, it is typical for counsel to develop two or more distinct keyword lists. One list of terms will help counsel to identify potentially privileged materials for privilege review. This list typically contains names of the outside law firms that have been retained by the company for legal advice in the past, as well as the names and e-mail addresses of attorneys from the firms who have been involved in privileged communications with the company's executives and staff. Additionally, the list will likely contain the names and e-mail addresses of in-house counsel. Other words might help counsel find and review documents related to specific issues where the company sought legal advice in the past, including "legal advice", "privileged", "work product", "work-product", and perhaps other terms.

## PRACTITIONER'S TIP: CHECKING THE RESULTS

Before keywords are finalized it can be beneficial for the examiner to review the data before running the search. In instances where counsel provides a custodian's company e-mail address and asks for all e-mails to and from that e-mail address, it may be prudent to review the data to try and determine whether the custodian's e-mail address changed at any point due to changes in company e-mail address nomenclature (e.g., "j_smith@company.com" changed to "jsmith@company.com"), the custodian's change of department (e.g., "jsmith@company.com" or "jsmith@company-investments.com"), or a change of name. In addition, depending on a number of factors including the mail server configuration and method of collection, the custodian's e-mail address is not always preserved in the specific e-mail field. The field is populated with the custodian's name (e.g., "Smith, John") but the link between the name and the e-mail address has been lost. For Outlook mail, Figure 3.27 depicts the error generated when the e-mail is viewed and the custodian name clicked in an attempt to view the e-mail address.

A search for the e-mail address "jsmith@company.com" would not return an e-mail with only the custodian's name in the field as responsive if this link had been lost.

**FIGURE 3.27**
Error generated by Microsoft Outlook when the link between the name and the e-mail address has been lost.

Counsel will construct the other list of terms specifically to find documents potentially relevant to the matter under review. The keyword list should not be taken lightly—attorney review hours flow from the list. To the extent key terms can be precisely developed to focus on the matter under review, attorney review hours will be saved.

## FROM THE CASE FILES: BUILDING A BETTER KEYWORD LIST

We have conducted a number of investigations that can be similarly categorized (e.g., stock option back dating, revenue recognition, FCPA compliance, etc.). We've examined the keywords used in those matters to explore which keywords across the matters tended to uncover documents that an attorney subsequently marked as a HOT document and which data sources tended to contain the HOT documents. We've used this historical data to assist counsel in developing not only a prioritized custodian list, but also a prioritized data preservation and collection plan and a prioritized data processing and review plan.

### Advanced Keyword Searching Concepts

Keywords can lead counsel to relevant documents; however simple keywords like "revenue" or "recognition" can lead to a tremendous volume of irrelevant documents—expending significant attorney time in the review process. If the real issue is a company's standard revenue recognition policies and how they were implemented or circumvented in specific cases, then the matter may require more complex keyword searching capabilities. Typically, this is accomplished with keyword completion, Boolean expressions, keyword stemming, phonic searching, field searching, and keyword synonym capabilities.

### Keyword Completion

Keyword completion allows a search term to specify how a keyword must start but does not specify how the word must end. For example, "rev*" (where the * represents the unspecified part of the term) will find "revenue", "revolution", "revocation", and any other word that starts with "rev". The keyword "rec*" will find "recognize", "recognition", "recreation", and any other word that begins with "rec". When used alone, keyword completion tends to be overinclusive. But when combined with other advanced search capabilities, keyword completion allows some powerful search capabilities where the precise use of a single word might not be known.

### Boolean Expressions

With Boolean expressions, a complex keyword can be constructed to narrow the focus of the search. The Boolean expression may typically include AND, OR, NOT, and WITHIN. For example, **rev* w/5 rec*** will find all occurrences of the word "revenue" when it occurs within five words of "recognition", but it will not find single occurrences of either word.

### Keyword Stemming

Keyword stemming is a capability to extend a search to find variations of a word. For example, the keyword "implement" would find "implemented" and "implementing" if the stemming rules are properly constructed.

### Phonic Searching

Phonic searching extends a search to find phonetic variations of a word (i.e., other words that sound like the search term and start with the same letter. For example, a phonic search for "Smith" would return "Smyth", "Smythe", and "Smithe". Phonic searches can return false positives, but can also help find documents where spelling errors occurred.

### Keyword Synonym Searching

Synonym searching extends a search to return synonyms of the keywords. Typically, the process relies on a thesaurus created either by the search team or supplied by a vendor. Synonym searching can also return false positives, but might help the reviewers understand more about the language and phrases certain custodians use.

### Keyword Field Searching

Field searching allows for keywords to be searched against only certain parts, or fields, of a document. For example, an e-mail address could be searched against only the "From" field of an e-mail data set to identify all e-mails sent from that address. This search would not find the e-mail address keyword in the e-mail body or in any of the other fields such as "To," "CC," or "BCC."

As the keywords become more complex, the need for quality assurance at each step of the searching process becomes increasingly important. The keyword list should be reviewed by multiple people for typographical and syntax errors, complex terms should be tested to ensure they are formulated correctly, and the results reviewed for completeness and accuracy.

## Data Reduction through Advanced Analytics

As mentioned briefly before, on the market today are e-discovery database platforms with advanced analytical capabilities that go well beyond traditional keyword or Boolean searching. Concept searching, concept categorization or "clustering," e-mail thread analysis, near duplicate analysis, social networking analysis, and other types of advanced analytics enable counsel to further reduce the mountain of electronic files for review, quickly identifying and focusing on the more relevant files. The addition of these advanced analytical capabilities allow for automatic identification and grouping of documents based on their topic or concept rather than on specific keywords.

There are a number of approaches that various tools take to enable more advanced analytics. For example, Autonomy uses Information Theory and Bayesian Inference to put mathematical rigor into their analytics engine.[6] Bayesian inference techniques enable the development of advanced algorithms for recognizing patterns in digital data. Although Autonomy supports traditional keyword searching and Boolean searching with which counsel is very likely familiar, the software also employs mathematically complex algorithms to recognize patterns occurring in communications and to group documents based on those patterns. The software "learns" from the content it processes and groups documents based on statistical probability that they relate to the same concept. As more data is processed, the software continues to learn and the probabilities are refined. Using this approach, Autonomy allows counsel to begin reviewing the documents most likely to contain relevant material first and then to migrate their review to other material as new information emerges.

Cataphora takes a different approach to enabling advanced search and analytics by using standard and custom ontologies as well as a branch of mathematics called Lattice Theory (Stallings, 2003). Originally a term used by philosophers, ontology "refers to the science of describing the kinds of entities in the world and how they are related." (Smith, Welty, McGuinness, 2004). As defined by Tom Gruber, "In the context of computer and information sciences, an ontology defines a set of representational primitives with which to model a domain of knowledge or discourse. The representational primitives are typically classes (or sets), attributes (or properties), and relationships (or relations among class members)" (Liu & Ozsu, 2009). By precisely defining individuals, classes (or sets, collections, types or kinds of things), attributes, relations, functions, restrictions, rules, axioms (or assertions), and events that can occur in a domain, an ontology models a domain. That complex model can then be applied to a data set and the data can be visualized based on the model. For example, an ontology about baseball might describe "bat," "ball," "base," "park," "field," "score," and "diamond" and the interactions among those things whereas an ontology about jewelry might describe "cut," "color," "clarity," "carat," "ring," "diamond," "bride," "engagement," and "anniversary." Using this ontology, documents related to the baseball diamond would be grouped together, but grouped separately from documents related to a jewelry business. In a dispute with another jeweler, one party might quickly identify and mark as nonresponsive all the documents related to baseball, even though they contain the keyword "diamond."

Attenex takes yet another approach to grouping documents and also presents a visual depiction of their content to reviewers. During processing, Attenex identifies nouns and noun phrases and groups documents based on the frequency

---

[6] See www.autonomy.com/content/Technology/autonomys-technology-unique-combination-technologies/index. en.html.

with which words commonly appear together based on statistical analysis. In the visual depiction of the related documents, the word or phrase that causes the documents to group together is directly available to the reviewer. In this manner, documents that contain similar content—though not necessarily identical content—are visually grouped together to enable counsel to review them all at essentially the same time.

Stroz Friedberg's e-discovery database platform Stroz Discovery (www.strozlic.com) implements two approaches to categorize documents. The first approach uses pattern matching and rules-based analysis to encapsulate the logic contained within a reviewer's coding manual. In another approach, statistical algorithms are used to build a classification model from a sample learning-set that was coded by the client. The software learns how counsel coded the learning- set, develops a classification model based on what it sees, then applies the model to new, uncoded documents. These technologies can also be used in a hybrid of automatic and manual coding to suggest document codes or to pre-annotate documents prior to counsel reviewing the documents (see Figure 3.28, provided by Christopher Cook).

There are other applications used in e-discovery that provide advanced analytics. A summary discussion of these applications, including aspects that set them apart from one another, is beyond the scope of this chapter. Consult the 2008 Socha-Gelbmann Electronic Discovery Survey (www.sochaconsulting.com/2008survey/) for a review of software providers and service providers.

**FIGURE 3.28**

Stroz Discovery using advanced analysis to suggest document codes.

The Sedona Conference has also published an excellent summary of different technologies that hold promise for data reduction in e-discovery (Sedona Conference, 2007).

Forensic examiners should be aware that these technologies and applications exist, as they can be useful when performing analysis in other contexts such as determining document distribution and identifying different versions of documents in a theft of intellectual property case.

## Data Transformation and Review

After the data processing has been completed, the next phase is transformation of the data into a format for counsel review, and then the subsequent review of that data by counsel. Forensic examiners are typically not involved in the data transformation and review phases, especially in instances where data was processed with an e-discovery database platform that will also host the data for review by counsel. It is also our experience that forensic examiners are not often asked to "transform" the data for review, which is typically done by creating a load file so the responsive data can be uploaded into a review tool such as Concordance or Summation. In instances where this is requested, there are tools such as Discovery Assistant that can perform this process. As with any tool, the examiner should ensure that he or she has a thorough understanding of how the tool functions, and performs sufficient quality assurance to ensure a complete and accurate result.

## PRODUCTION OF ELECTRONIC DATA

Data identified by the attorneys to produce to the opposing party is often provided after having been converted to an image format such as Adobe PDF or TIFF, and is delivered with a corresponding load file containing associated fielded information about each file. A digital examiner or investigator may be asked to verify the accuracy and completeness of the information before it is produced to the opposing party. In these instances, the following quality assurance steps should be included:

- **Data Volume**: The examiner should verify that the number and types of files to be produced equals the number in the production set. For example, in most load files original single documents are broken up into document families, with each member of the document family having its own row or entry in the load file. In this way, an e-mail message would be recorded in one row of the load file, and the attachment to the e-mail would be recorded in a different row, with one of the fields for both entries documenting the e-mail and attachment relationship. Therefore if the examiner is attempting to confirm that 400 e-mails were included in the production, and there are 700 entries in the load file, the examiner would need to further segregate the e-mails and their attachments to ensure an accurate count and comparison.

- **Metadata**: The examiner should verify that the metadata recorded in the load file is consistent and accurate. This is often achieved through reviewing a suitable sample set, as the sheer number of files in the production datasets precludes the ability to review each metadata field for each file. This review should encompass both an overall general review of the fields and format, and a comparison of specific documents and their corresponding metadata in the load file to verify that the load file information accurately represents the metadata of the native file. The examiner should check that all required fields are present and populated with valid information in a consistent format. Special attention should be paid to the date fields to ensure that all dates are formatted consistently, especially in cases where data from multiple countries were processed.

- **Image Files**: If documents have been converted to file formats such as TIFF or PDF, the examiner should review a suitable sample set to verify that the image file accurately represents the native file.

- **Text Fields or Files**: In instances where documents have been converted to image files, the text of a document can be included for searching purposes either as a field in the load file or as a separate text file. If this is the case, the examiner should review a suitable sample set to confirm that the text provided is complete and accurate.

- **Exception Files**: The examiner should verify that any files not provided in the production dataset were listed as an exception file, and accurately identified as such. There are some files, such as database files, that, due to their format, are not able to be converted to an image file. The examiner should discuss with the attorneys how best to handle these files; one option is to provide the files in native format.

## FROM THE CASE FILES: THE IMPORTANCE OF QUALITY ASSURANCE

Digital examiners had been tasked with completing quality assurance of production load files of native e-documents and e-mail that had been created by an outside e-discovery vendor, and were to be delivered to the government regulatory agency. By performing the preceding quality assurance steps on the production load files, the digital examiners identified missing data and inaccurate fields, including missing nonmessage items such as calendar items and notes in the native Lotus Notes database files, that the vendor had not processed nor listed on the exception report, inconsistent date formats populated in the date fields, such that some entries were recorded as DD/MM/YYYY and some recorded as MM/DD/YYYY, and inconsistent field headers between different load files. The examiners reported these anomalies to the vendor who reproduced accurate and complete load files.

## CONCLUSION

The e-discovery field is complex, and the technical and logistical challenges routinely found in large e-discovery projects can test even the most experienced digital forensic examiner. The high stakes nature of most e-discovery projects leave little room for error at any stage of the process—from initial identification and preservation of evidence sources to the final production and presentation of results—and to be successful an examiner must understand and be familiar with their role at each stage. The size and scope of e-discovery projects require effective case management, and essential to effective case management is establishing a strategic plan at the outset, and diligently implementing constructive and documented quality assurance measures throughout each step of the process.

## CASES

*Broccoli v. Echostar Communications*, 229 F.R.D. 506 (D. MD 2005)

*Coleman (Parent) Holdings, Inc. v. Morgan Stanley & Co., Inc.*, 2005 WL 679071 (Fla. Cir. Ct. Mar. 1, 2005), rev'd on other grounds, *Morgan Stanley & Co. Inc. v. Coleman (Parent) Holdings, Inc.*, 955 So.2d 1124 (Fla. Dist. Ct. App. 2007)

*Integrated Service Solutions, Inc. v. Rodman*, Civil Action No. 07-3591 (E.D. Pa. November 03, 2008)

*United States v. Fierros-Alaverez*, 2008 WL 1826188 (D. Kan. April 23, 2008)

*Qualcomm Inc. v. Broadcom Corp.*, 548 F.3d 1004 (Cal. 2008)

*Zubulake v. UBS Warburg LLC*, 217 F.R.D. 309, 322 (S.D.N.Y. 2003)

*Zubulake v. UBS Warburg LLC*, No. 02 Civ. 1243 (SAS), 2004 U.S. Dist. LEXIS 13574, at *35 (S.D.N.Y. July 20, 2004)

## REFERENCES

ACPO. (2008). *The Good Practice Guide for Computer-based Electronic evidence*. (4th ed.). Available online at www.7safe.com/electronic_evidence/

Buike, R. (2005). *Understanding the exchange information store*. MSExchange.org. Available online at www.msexchange.org/articles/Understanding-Exchange-Information-Store.html

Craig, S. (2005). How Morgan Stanley botched a big case by fumbling emails. *The Wall Street Journal*, A1.

Federal rules of evidence. Available online at www.law.cornell.edu/rules/fre/rules.htm

Friedberg, E., & McGowan, M. (2003). Electronic discovery technology. In A. Cohen & D. Lender (Eds.), *Electronic discovery: Law and practice*, Aspen Publishers.

Holley, J. (2008). *A framework for controlled testing of software tools and methodologies developed for identifying, preserving, analyzing and reporting electronic evidence in a network environment*. Available online at www.infosec.jmu.edu/reports/jmu-infosec-tr-2008-005.php

Howell, B. (2005). Strategic planning at outset of e-discovery can save money in the end. *Digital Discovery & e-Evidence, 5*(2).

Howell, B., & Wertheimer, L. (2008). Data detours in internal investigations in EU countries. *International Law & Trade*.

Howell, B. (2009). Lawyers on the Hook: Counsel's professional responsibility to provide quality assurance in electronic discovery. *Journal of Securities Law, Regulation & Compliance, 2*(3).

IBM. (2007). *The History of Notes and Domino*. Available online at www.ibm.com/developerworks/lotus/library/ls-NDHistory/

Kidwell, B., Neumeier, M., & Hansen, B. (2005). *Electronic discovery*. Law Journal Press.

Kroll Ontrack. (2008). *ESI Trends Report*.

Lesemann, D., & Reust, J. (2006). No one likes surprises in e-discovery projects. And quality assurance and strategic planning can reduce their number. *Digital Discovery & e-Evidence, 6*(9).

Mazza, M., Quesada, E., & Sternberg, A. (2007). In pursuit of FRCP1: Creative approaches to cutting and shifting the costs of discovery of electronically stored information, 13 *Rich. J.L. & Tech., 11*, 101.

Microsoft. (2007a). *Using the Exchange Management Shell*. Microsoft TechNet. Available online at http://technet.microsoft.com/en-us/library/bb123778.aspx

Microsoft. (2007b). *How to Export Mailbox Data*. Microsoft TechNet. Available online at http://technet.microsoft.com/en-us/library/bb266964.aspx

Moore, J. W. (2000). *Moore's federal practice* (3rd ed.) LexisNexis.

National Institute of Standards and Technology. (2004). *Digital Data Acquisition Tool Specification, Version 4*. Available online at www.cftt.nist.gov/disk_imaging.htm

Roberts, K. (2008). *Qualcomm fined for "monumental" e-discovery violations—possible sanctions against counsel remain pending*. Litigation News Online, American Bar Association. Available online at www.abanet.org/litigation/litigationnews/2008/may/0508_article_qualcomm.html

Rosenthal, L. H. (2005). Memorandum from Honorable Lee H. Rosenthal Chair, Advisory Committee on the Federal Rules of Civil Procedure to Honorable David F. Levi, Chair, Standing Committee on Rules of Practices and Procedure (May 27, 2005). Available online at www.uscourts.gov/rules/supct1105/Excerpt_CV_Report.pdf

Sedona Conference. (2007). *The Sedona conference best practices commentary on search and retrieval methods*. Available online at www.thesedonaconference.org/dltForm?did=Best_Practices_Retrieval_Methods___revised_cover_and_preface.pdf

Sedona Conference. (2008). "Jumpstart Outline": Questions to ask your client and your adversary to prepare for preservation, rule 26 obligations, court conferences and requests for production, May 2008. Available online at www.thesedonaconference.org/dltForm?did=Questionnaire.pdf.

Smith, M. K., Welty, C., & McGuinness, D. L. (2004). *OWL web ontology language guide*. Available online at www.w3.org/TR/2004/REC-owl-guide-20040210/#StructureOfOntologies

Socha, G., & Gelbman, T. (2008a). 2008 Socha-Gelbman electronic discovery survey report.

Socha, G., & Gelbman, T. (2008b). *Preservation node*. Available online at www.edrm.net/wiki/index.php/Preservation_Node

Stallings, W. (2003). *Cryptography and network security: Principles and practice* (3rd ed.). Addison-Wesley.

Tamer, O. M., & Ling, L. (2009). *Encyclopedia of database systems*. Springer (in press). See http://tomgruber.org/writing/ontology-definition-2007.htm

# CHAPTER 4

# Intrusion Investigation

**Eoghan Casey, Christopher Daywalt, and Andy Johnston**

## INTRODUCTION

Intrusion investigation is a specialized subset of digital forensic investigation that is focused on determining the nature and full extent of unauthorized access and usage of one or more computer systems. We treat this subject with its own chapter due to the specialized nature of investigating this type of activity, and because of the high prevalence of computer network intrusions.

If you are reading this book, then you probably already know why you need to conduct an investigation into computer network intrusions. If not, it is important to understand that the frequency and severity of security breaches has increased steadily over the past several years, impacting individuals and organizations alike. Table 4.1 shows that the number of publicly known incidents has risen dramatically since 2002.

These security breaches include automated malware that collects usernames and passwords, organized theft of payment card information and personally identifiable information (PII), among others. Once intruders gain unauthorized access to a network, they can utilize system components such as Remote Desktop or customized tools to blend into normal activities on the network, making detection and investigation more difficult. Malware is using automated propagation techniques to gain access to additional systems without direct involvement of the intruder except for subsequent remote command and control. There is also a trend toward exploiting nontechnological components of an organization. Some of this exploitation takes the form of social engineering, often combined with more sophisticated attacks targeting security weaknesses in policy implementation and business processes. Even accidental security exposure can require an organization to perform a thorough digital investigation.

## CONTENTS

Introduction......135

Methodologies 139

Preparation......143

Case Management and Reporting . 157

Common Initial Observations...170

Scope Assessment.....174

Collection.........175

Analyzing Digital Evidence..........179

Combination/ Correlation ......191

Feeding Analysis Back into the Detection Phase ...............202

Conclusion.......206

References.......206

135

**Table 4.1** Number of Publicly Known Incidents Compiled from http://datalossdb.org (January 2009)

| Year | # of Incidents Known | Change |
|------|---------------------|--------|
| 2002 | 3 | NA |
| 2003 | 11 | +266% |
| 2004 | 22 | +100% |
| 2005 | 138 | +527% |
| 2006 | 432 | +213% |
| 2007 | 365 | −15.5% |
| 2008 | 493 | +35% |

## FROM THE CASE FILES: ACCIDENTAL EXPOSURE

A service company that utilized a wide variety of outside vendors maintained a database of vendors that had presented difficulties in the past. The database was intended for internal reference only, and only by a small group of people within the company. The database was accessible only from a web server with a simple front end used to submit queries. The web server, in turn, could be accessed only through a VPN to which only authorized employees had accounts. Exposure of the database contents could lead to legal complications for the company.

During a routine upgrade to the web server software, the access controls were replaced with the default (open) access settings. This was only discovered a week later when an employee, looking up a vendor in a search engine, found a link to data culled from the supposedly secure web server.

Since the web server had been left accessible to the Internet, it was open to crawlers from any search engine provider, as well as to anyone who directed a web browser to the server's URL. In order to determine the extent of the exposure, the server's access logs had to be examined to identify the specific queries to the database and distinguish among those from the authorized employees, those from web crawlers, and any that may have been directed queries from some other source.

Adverse impacts on organizations that experienced the most high impact incidents, such as TJX and Heartland, include millions of dollars to respond to the incident, loss of revenue due to business disruption, ongoing monitoring by government and credit card companies, damage to reputation, and lawsuits from customers and shareholders. The 2008 Ponemon Institute study of 43 organizations in the United States that experienced a data breach indicates that the average cost associated with an incident of this kind has grown to $6.6 million (Ponemon, 2009a). A similar survey of 30 organizations in the United Kingdom calculated the average cost of data breaches at £1.73 million (Ponemon, 2009b).

Furthermore, these statistics include only those incidents that are publicly known. Various news sources have reported on computer network intrusions into government-related organizations sourced from foreign entities (Grow, Epstein & Tschang, 2008). The purported purpose of these intrusions tends to be reported as espionage and/or sabotage, but due to the sensitivity of these types of incidents, the full extent of them has not been revealed. However, it is safe to say that computer network intrusions are becoming an integral component to both espionage and electronic warfare.

In addition to the losses directly associated with a security breach, victim organizations may face fines for failure to comply with regulations or industry security standards. These regulations include Health Insurance Portability and Accountability Act of 1996 (HIPAA), the Sarbanes-Oxley Act of 2002 (SOX), the Gramm-Leach-Bliley Act (GLBA), and the Payment Card Industry Data Security Standard (PCI DSS).

In the light of these potential consequences, it is important for the digital forensic investigators to develop the ability to investigate a computer network intrusion. Investigating a security breach may require a combination of file system forensics, collecting evidence from various network devices, scanning hosts on a network for signs of compromise, searching and correlating network logs, combing through packet captures, and analyzing malware. The investigation may even include nondigital evidence such as sign-in books and analog security images. The complexity of incident handling is both exciting and daunting, requiring digital investigators to have strong technical, case management, and organizational skills. These capabilities are doubly important when an intruder is still active on the victim systems, and the organization needs to return to normal operations as quickly as feasible. Balancing thoroughness with haste is a demanding challenge, requiring investigators who are conversant with the technology involved, and are equipped with powerful methodologies and techniques from forensic science.

This chapter introduces basic methodologies for conducting an intrusion investigation, and describes how an organization can better prepare to facilitate future investigations. This chapter is not intended to instruct you in technical analysis procedures. For technical forensic techniques, see the later chapters in this text that are dedicated to specific types of technology. This chapter also assumes that you are familiar with basic network intrusion techniques.

A theoretical intrusion investigation scenario is used throughout this chapter to demonstrate key points. The scenario background is as follows:

## INVESTIGATIVE SCENARIO
## Part 1: Evidence Sources

A company located in Baltimore named CorpX has learned that at least some of their corporate trade secrets have been leaked to their competitors. These secrets were stored in files on the corporate intranet server on a firewalled internal network. A former system administrator named Joe Wiley, who recently left under a cloud, is suspected of stealing the files and the theft is believed to have taken place on April 2, 2009, the day after Joe Wiley was terminated. Using the following logs, we will try to determine how the files were taken and identify any evidence indicating who may have taken them:

- Asavpn.log: Logs from the corporate VPN (192.168.1.1)
- SecEvent.evt: Authentication logs from the domain controller

- Netflow logs: Netflow data from the internal network router (10.10.10.1)
- Server logs from the SSH server on the DMZ (10.10.10.50)

Although the organization routinely captures network traffic on the internal network (10.10.10.0), the data from the time of interest is archived and is not immediately available for analysis. Once this packet capture data has been restored from backup, we can use it to augment our analysis of the immediately available logs.

In this intrusion investigation scenario, the organization had segmented high-value assets onto a secured network that was not accessible from the Internet and only accessible from certain systems within their network as shown in Figure 4.1.

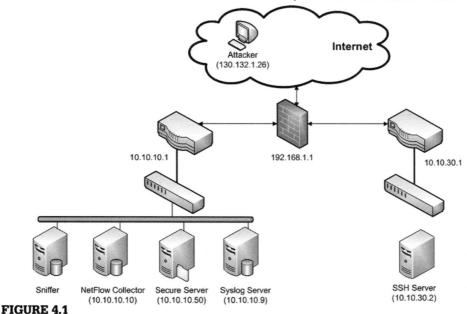

**FIGURE 4.1**

Network topology and monitoring for the intrusion investigation scenario used in this chapter.

Specifically, their network is divided into a DMZ (10.10.30.0/24) containing employee desktops, printers, and other devices on which sensitive information isn't (or at least shouldn't be) stored. In order to simplify remote access for the sales force, a server on DMZ can be accessed from the Internet using Secure Shell (SSH) via a VPN requiring authentication for individual user accounts. The internal network (10.10.10.0/24) is apparently accessible only remotely using Remote Desktop via an authenticated VPN

connection. The intranet server (10.10.10.50) provides both web (intranet) and limited drive share (SMB) services. In addition to isolating their secure systems, they monitored network activities on the secured network using both NetFlow and full packet capture as shown in Figure 4.1. However, they did not have all of their system clocks synchronized, which created added work when correlating logs as discussed in the section on combination/correlation later in this chapter.

# METHODOLOGIES

## The Incident Response Lifecycle

There are several different prevalent methodologies for responding to and remediating computer security incidents. One of the more common is the Incident Response Lifecycle, as defined in the NIST Special Publication 800-61, "Computer Security Incident Handling Guide." This document, along with other NIST computer security resources, can be found at http://csrc.nist.gov. The lifecycle provided by this document is shown in Figure 4.2.

01282

**FIGURE 4.2**

NIST Incident Response Lifecycle (Scarfone, Grance & Masone, 2008).

The purpose of each phase is briefly described here:

- **Preparation**: Preparing to handle incidents from an organizational, technical, and individual perspective.
- **Detection and Analysis**: This phase involves the initial discovery of the incident, analysis of related data, and the usage of that data to determine the full scope of the event.
- **Containment, Eradication and Recovery**: This phase involves the remediation of the incident, and the return of the affected organization to a more trusted state.
- **Post-Incident Activity**: After remediating an incident, the organization will take steps to identify and implement any lessons learned from the event, and to pursue or fulfill any legal action or requirements.

The NIST overview of incident handling is useful and deserves recognition for its comprehensiveness and clarity. However, this chapter is not intended to provide a method for the full handling and remediating of security incidents. The lifecycle in Figure 4.2 is provided here mainly because it is sometimes confused with an intrusion investigation. The purpose of an intrusion investigation is not to contain or otherwise remediate an incident, it is only to determine what happened. As such, intrusion investigation is actually a subcomponent of incident handling, and predominantly serves as the second phase (Detection and Analysis) in the NIST lifecycle described earlier. Aspects of intrusion investigation are also a component of the Post-incident Activity including presentation of findings to decision makers (e.g., writing a report, testifying in court). This chapter will primarily cover the process of investigating an intrusion and important aspects of reporting results, as well as some of the preparatory tasks that can make an investigation easier and more effective.

---

### PRACTITIONER'S TIP: KEEP YOUR FOCUS

Forensic investigators are generally called to deal with security breaches after the fact and must deal with the situation as it is, not as an IT security professional would have it. There is no time during an intrusion investigation to bemoan inadequate evidence sources and missed opportunities. There may be room in the final report for recommendations on improving security, but only if explicitly requested.

---

### Intrusion Investigation Processes: Applying the Scientific Method

So if the Incident Response Lifecycle is not an intrusion investigation methodology, what should you use? It is tempting to use a specialized, technical process for intrusion investigations. This is because doing something as complex as tracking an insider or unknown number of attackers through an enterprise computer network would seem to necessitate a complex methodology. However, you will be better served by using simpler methodologies that will guide you in the right direction, but allow you to maintain the flexibility to handle diverse situations, including insider attacks and sophisticated external intrusions.

In any investigation, including an intrusion case, you can use one or more derivatives of the scientific method when trying to identify a way to proceed. This simple, logical process summarized here can guide you through almost any investigative situation, whether it involves a single compromised host, a single network link, or an entire enterprise.

1. **Observation**: One or more events will occur that will initiate your investigation. These events will include several observations that will represent the initial facts of the incident. You will proceed from these facts to form your investigation. For example, a user might have observed that his or her web browser crashed when they surfed to a specific web site, and that an antivirus alert was triggered shortly afterward.

2. **Hypothesis**: Based upon the current facts of the incident, you will form a theory of what may have occurred. For example, in the initial observation described earlier, you may hypothesize that the web site that crashed the user's web browser used a browser exploit to load a malicious executable onto the system.

3. **Prediction**: Based upon your hypothesis, you will then predict where you believe the artifacts of that event will be located. Using the previous example hypothesis, you may predict that there will be evidence of an executable download in the history of the web browser.

4. **Experimentation/Testing**: You will then analyze the available evidence to test your hypothesis, looking for the presence of the predicted artifacts. In the previous example, you might create a forensic duplicate of the target system, and from that image extract the web browser history to check for executable downloads in the known timeframe. Part of the scientific method is to also test possible alternative explanations—if your original hypothesis is correct you will be able to eliminate alternative explanations based on available evidence (this process is called falsification).

5. **Conclusion**: You will then form a conclusion based upon the results of your findings. You may have found that the evidence supports your hypothesis, falsifies your hypothesis, or that there were not enough findings to generate a conclusion.

This basic investigative process can be repeated as many times as necessary to come to a conclusion about what may have happened during an incident. Its simplistic nature makes it useful as a grounding methodology for more complex operations, to prevent you from going down the rabbit hole of inefficient searches through the endless volumes of data that you will be presented with as a digital forensic examiner.

The two overarching tasks in an intrusion investigation to which the scientific method can be applied are *scope assessment* and *crime reconstruction*. The process of determining the scope of an intrusion is introduced here and revisited in the section, "Scope Assessment," later in this chapter. The analysis techniques associated with reconstructing the events relating to an intrusion, and potentially leading to the source of the attack, are covered in the section, "Analyzing Digital Evidence" at the end of this chapter.

**FIGURE 4.3**

Scope assessment process.

### Determining Scope

When you begin an intrusion investigation, you will not know how many host and network segments have been compromised. In order to determine this, you will need to implement the process depicted in Figure 4.3. This overall process feeds scope assessment, which specifies the number of actually and potentially compromised systems, network segments, and credentials at a given point in time during the investigation with the ultimate goal of determining the full extent of the damage.

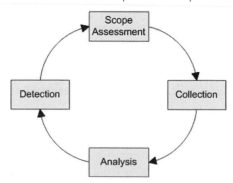

The phases in the process are described here:

1. **Scope Assessment**: Specify the number of actually and potentially compromised systems, network segments, and credentials at a given point in time during the investigation.

2. **Collection**: Obtain data from the affected systems, and surrounding network devices and transmission media.

3. **Analyze**: Consolidate information from disparate sources to enable searching, correlation, and event reconstruction. Analyze available data to find any observable artifacts of the security event. Correlate information from various sources to obtain a more complete view of the overall intrusion.

4. **Detection**: Use any of the artifacts uncovered during the analysis process to sweep the target network for any additional compromised systems (feeding back into the Scope Assessment phase).

The main purpose of the scope assessment cycle is to guide the investigator through the collection and analysis of data, and then push the results into the search for additional affected devices. You will repeat this cycle until no new compromised systems are discovered. Note that depending upon your role, you may be forced to halt the cycle when the target organization decides that it is time to begin containment and/or any other remediation tasks.

## FROM THE CASE FILES: FAILURE TO DETERMINE SCOPE

The initial investigation into a data breach of a major commercial company focused on its core credit card processing systems, and found evidence of extensive data theft. Digital investigators were dedicated to support the data breach of the credit card systems, and were not permitted to look for signs of intrusion in other areas of the company. One year later, it was discovered that the same attackers had gained unauthorized access to the primary servers in one of the company's largest divisions one year before they targeted the core credit card systems. The implications of this discovery were far-reaching. Not only did the intruders have access to sensitive data during the year prior to the discovery of the intrusion, they had continuous access during the year that digital investigators were focusing their efforts on the core credit card processing systems. If the earlier intrusion had been discovered during the initial investigation, there would have been a better chance of finding related digital evidence on the company's IT systems. However, two years after the initial intrusion, very limited information was available, making it difficult for digital investigators to determine where the intrusion originated and what other systems on the company's network were accessed. Until digital investigators learned about the earlier activities, they had no way to determine how the intruders originally gained unauthorized access to the company's network. As a result, remediation efforts were not addressing the root of the problem.

In certain cases, the evidence gathered from the victim network may lead to intermediate systems used by the attacker, thus expanding the scope of the investigation. Ultimately, the process depicted in Figure 4.3 can expand to help investigators track down the attacker.

---

## PRACTITIONER'S TIP: GET IT IN WRITING!

As with any digital investigation, make sure you are authorized to perform any actions deemed necessary in response to a security breach. We have dealt with several cases in which practitioners have been accused of exceeding their authorization. Even if someone commands you to perform a task in an investigation, ask for it in writing. If it isn't written down, it didn't happen. Ideally the written authorization should provide specifics like who or what will be investigated, whether covert imaging of computers is permitted, what types of monitoring should be performed (e.g., computer activities, eavesdropping on communications via network or telephones or bugs, surveillance cameras), and who is permitted to examine the data. Also be sure that the person giving you written authorization is authorized to do so! When in doubt, get additional authorization.

---

## PREPARATION

Sooner or later, almost every network will experience an information security breach. These breaches will range from simple spyware infections to a massive, intentional compromise from an unknown source. Given the increasing challenges of detecting and responding to security breaches, preparation is one of the keys to executing a timely and thorough response to any incident. Any experienced practitioner will tell you that it is more straightforward to investigate an incident when the problem is detected soon after the breach, when evidence sources are preserved properly, and when there are logs they can use to reconstruct events relating to the crime. The latest Ponemon Institute study indicates that the cost of data breaches were lower for organizations that were prepared for this type of incident (Ponemon, 2009a).

Therefore, it makes sense to design networks and equip personnel in such a way that the organization can detect and handle security events as quickly and efficiently as possible, to minimize the losses associated with downtime and data theft. Preparation for intrusion investigation involves developing policies and procedures, logging infrastructure, configuring computer systems as sources of evidence, a properly equipped and trained response team, and performing periodic incident response drills to ensure overall readiness.

## PRACTITIONER'S TIP: USE HOME FIELD ADVANTAGE

Digital investigators should use their knowledge and control of the information systems to facilitate intrusion investigation as much as feasible. It is important for digital investigators to know where the most valuable information assets (a.k.a., crown jewels) are located. Since this is the information of greatest concern, it deserves the greatest attention. Furthermore, even if the full scope of a networkwide security breach cannot be fully ascertained, at least the assurance that the crown jewels have not been stolen may be enough to avoid notification obligations.

Developing an understanding of legitimate access to the crown jewels in an organization can help digital investigators discern suspicious events. Methodically eliminating legitimate events from logs leaves a smaller dataset to examine for malicious activity. For instance, connections to a secure customer database may normally originate from the subnet used by the Accounting Department, so connections from any other subnet within the organization deserve closer attention. In short, do not just instrument the Internet borders of an organization with intrusion detection systems and other monitoring systems. Some internal monitoring is also needed, especially focused monitoring of systems that contain the most valuable and sensitive data.

Beyond being able to monitor activities on hosts and networks, it is useful to establish baselines for host configuration and network activities in order to detect deviations from the norm. Added advantage can be gained through strategic network segmentation prior to an incident, placing valuable assets in more secure segments, which can make containment easier. Under the worst circumstances, secure segments can be completely isolated from the rest of the network until remediation is complete.

One of the most crucial aspects of preparation for a security breach is identifying and documenting the information assets in an organization, including the location of sensitive or valuable data, and being able to detect and investigate access to these key resources. An organization that does not understand its information assets and the associated risks cannot determine which security breaches should take the highest priority. Effective intrusion investigation is, therefore, highly dependent on good Risk Management practices. *Without a Risk Management plan, and the accompanying assessment and asset inventory, incident handling can become exceedingly difficult and expensive.* An intelligent approach to forensic preparedness is to identify the path these information assets take within the business processes, as well as in the supporting information systems. Data about employees, for example, will likely be maintained in offices responsible for Personnel and Payroll. Customer information may be gathered by a sales force and eventually end up in an Accounting office for billing. Such information may be stored and transmitted digitally around the clock in a large business. Security measures need to be put in place to safeguard and track this information and to insure that only appropriate parties have access to it.

Being able to gauge the relative severity of an incident, and knowing when to launch an investigation is the first step in effective handling of security breaches. The inability to prioritize among different incidents can be more harmful to a business than the incidents themselves. Imagine a bank that implemented an emergency response plan (designed for bank robberies) each time an irate customer argued with a manager over unexplained bank charges. Under these conditions, most banks would be in constant turmoil and would lose most of their customers. In information security, incidents must undergo a triage process in order to prioritize the most significant problems and not waste resources on relatively minor issues.

This section of the text enumerates some of the more important steps that can be taken to ensure that future intrusion investigations can be conducted more effectively. Note that this section is not intended to be comprehensive with respect to security recommendations; only recommendations that will assist in an investigation are listed.

## PRACTITIONER'S TIP: DON'T JUST LOOK IN THE LAMPLIGHT FOR YOUR LOST KEYS

When preparing an organization from a forensic perspective, it is important to look beyond expected avenues of attack, since intrusion often involve anomalous and wily activities that bypass security. Therefore, effective forensic preparation must account for the possibility that security mechanisms may not be properly maintained or that they may be partially disabled through improper maintenance. Moreover, all mechanisms may work exactly as intended, yet still leave avenues of potential exploitation. A prime example of this arises in security breach investigations when firewall logs show only denied access attempts but will not record a successful authentication that may be an intrusion. In such cases, it is more important to have details about successful malicious connections than about unsuccessful connection attempts. Therefore, logs of seemingly legitimate activity, as well as exceptional events, should be maintained.

As another example, social engineering exploits often target legitimate users and manipulate them into installing malware or providing data that can be used for later attacks. Intrusion Prevention/Detection Systems will record suspicious or clearly hostile activity, but investigation of sophisticated attacks requires examination of normal system activity as well. Social engineering attacks do not exploit technological vulnerabilities and normally do not carry any signatures to suggest hostile activity. It is important to realize that, in social engineering attacks, all technological components are behaving exactly as they were designed to. It is the design of the technology, and often the design of the business process supported by the technology, that is being exploited. Since an exploit may not involve any unusual transactions within the information systems, the forensic investigator must be able to investigate normal activity, as well as exceptional activity, within an IT infrastructure. For this reason, preparing for an incident also supports the ongoing information assurance efforts of an organization, helping practitioners maintain the confidentiality, integrity and availability of information.

## Asset/Data Inventory

The rationale for this is straightforward. To protect an organization's assets, and investigate any security event that involves them, we must know where they are, and in what condition they are supposed to be. To benefit an intrusion analysis several key types of asset documentation should be kept, including:

- **Network topology**. Documents should be kept that detail how a network is constructed, and identify the logical and physical boundaries. A precisely detailed single topology document is not feasible for the enterprise, but important facets can be recorded, such as major points of ingress/egress, major internal segmentation points, and so on.

- **Physical location of all devices**. Forensic investigators will inevitably need to know this information. It is never a good situation when digital investigators trace attacker activity to a specific host name, and nobody at the victimized organization has any idea where the device actually is.

- **Operating system versions and patch status**. It is helpful to the intrusion investigator to understanding what operating systems are in use across the network, and to what level they are patched. This will help to determine the potential scope of any intrusion.

- **Location of key data**. This could be an organization's crown jewels, or any data protected by law or industry regulations. If an organization maintains data that is sufficiently important that it would be harmed by the theft of that data, then its location should be documented. This includes the storage location, as well as transit paths. For example, credit data may be sent from a POS system, through a WAN link to credit relay servers where it is temporarily stored, and then through a VPN connection to a bank to be verified. All of these locations and transit paths should be documented thoroughly for valuable or sensitive data.

Fortunately, this is a standard IT practice. It is easier to manage an enterprise environment when organizations know where all of their systems are, how the systems are connected, and their current patch status. So an organization may already be collecting this information regularly. All that a digital investigator would need to know is how to obtain the information.

## Policies and Procedures

Although they might not be entertaining to read and write, policies and procedures are necessary for spelling out exactly how an organization will deal with a security event when it occurs. An organization with procedures will experience more efficient escalations from initial discovery to the initiation of a response. An organization without procedures will inevitably get bogged down in conference calls and arguments about how to handle the situation, during which the incident could continue unabated and losses could continue to mount. Examples of useful policies and procedures include:

- **Key staff**: This will define all individuals who will take part in an intrusion investigation, and what their roles will be. (See the section, "Organizational Structure" of this chapter for a description of common roles.)

- **Incident definition and declaration thresholds**: These will define what types of activity can be considered a security incident and when an organization will declare that an incident has occurred and initiate a response (and by extension an investigation).

- **Escalation procedures**: These will define the conditions under which an organization will escalate security issues, and to whom.

- **Closure guidelines**: These will define the conditions under which an incident is considered closed.

- **Evidence handling procedures**: These will define how items of evidence will be handled, transferred, stored, and otherwise safeguarded. This will include chain of custody and evidence documentation requirements, and other associated items.

- **Containment and remediation guidelines**: This will define the conditions under which an organization will attempt to contain and remediate an incident. Even if this is not your job as an investigator, it is important to understand when this will be done so that you can properly schedule your investigation to complete in time for this event.

- **Disclosure guidelines**: These will specify who can and should be notified during an investigation, and who should not.

- **Communication procedures**: These will define how the investigative team will communicate without alerting the attacker to your activity.

- **Encryption/decryption procedures**: These will define what is encrypted across an organization's systems, and how data can be decrypted if necessary. Investigative staff will need access to the victim organization's decryption procedures and key escrow in order to complete their work if the enterprise makes heavy use of on-disk encryption.

In terms of forensic preparation, an organization must identify the mechanisms for transmission and storage of important data. Beyond the data flows, policies should be established to govern not just what data is stored, but how long it is stored and how it should be disposed of. These policies will not be determined in terms of forensic issues alone, but forensic value should be considered as a factor when valuing data for retention. As with many issues involving forensic investigation and information security in general, policies must balance trade-offs among different organizational needs.

## Host Preparation

Computer systems are not necessarily set up in such a way that their configuration will be friendly to forensic analysis. Take for example NTFS Standard Information Attribute Last Accessed Time date-time stamp on modern Windows systems. Vista is configured by default not to update this date-time stamp, whereas previous versions of Windows would. This configuration is not advantageous for forensic investigators, since date-time stamps are used heavily in generating event timelines and correlating events on a system.

It will benefit an organization to ensure that its systems are configured to facilitate the job of the forensic investigator. Setting up systems to leave a more thorough audit trail will enable the investigator to determine the nature and scope of an intrusion more quickly, thereby bringing the event to closure more rapidly. Some suggestions for preparing systems for forensic analysis include:

- Activate OS system and security logging. This should include auditing of:
  - Account logon events and account management events
  - Process events
  - File/directory access for sensitive areas (both key OS directories/files as well as directories containing data important to the organization)
  - Registry key access for sensitive areas, most especially those that involve drivers and any keys that can be used to automatically start an executable at boot (note that this is available only in newer versions of Windows, not in Windows XP)

---

### PRACTITIONER'S TIP: WINDOWS AUTORUN LOCATIONS

Aren't sure which locations to audit? Use the tool autoruns from Microsoft (http://technet.microsoft.com/en-us/sysinternals/bb963902.aspx) on a baseline system. It will give you a list of locations on the subject system that can be used to automatically run a program. Any location fed to you by autoruns should be set up for object access auditing. Logs of access to these locations can be extremely valuable, and setting them up would be a great start. This same program is useful when performing a forensic examination of a potentially compromised host. For instance, instructing this utility to list all unsigned executables configured to run automatically can narrow the focus on potential malware on the system.

---

- Turn on file system journals, and increase their default size. The larger they are, the longer they can retain data. For example, you can instruct the Windows operating system to record the NTFS journal to a file of a specific size. This journal will contain date-time stamps that can be used by a forensic analyst to investigate file system events even when the primary date-time stamps for file records have been manipulated.

- Activate all file system date-time stamps, such as the Last Accessed time previously mentioned in Vista systems. This can be done by setting the following Registry DWORD value to 0: `HKLM\SYSTEM\CurrentControlSet\Control\FileSystem\NtfsDisableLastAccessUpdate`

- Ensure that authorized applications are configured to keep a history file or log. This includes web browsers and authorized chat clients.

- Ensure that the operating system is not clearing the swap/page file when the system is shut down, so that it will still be available to the investigator who images after a graceful shutdown. In Windows this is done by disabling the Clear Virtual Memory Pagefile security policy setting.

- Ensure that the operating system has not been configured to encrypt the swap/page file. In newer versions of Windows, this setting can be found in the Registry at `HKLM\SYSTEM\CurrentControlSet\Control\FileSystem\NtfsEncryptPagingFile.`

- Ensure that the log file for the system's host-based firewall is turned on, and that the log file size has been increased from the default.

---

**PRACTITIONER'S TIP: HOST-BASED TRACES**

Right about now, you might be saying something along the lines of "But attackers can delete the log files" or "The bad guys can modify file system date-time stamps." Of course there are many ways to hide one's actions from a forensic analyst. However, being completely stealthy across an enterprise is not an easy task. Even if they tried to hide their traces, they may be successful in one area, but not in another. That is why maximizing the auditing increases your chances to catch an attacker. To gain more information at the host level, some organizations deploy host-based malware detection systems. For instance, one organization used McAfee ePolicy Orchestrator to gather logs about suspicious activities on their hosts, enabling investigators to quickly identify all systems that were targeted by a particular attacker based on the malware. Let us continue the list for some helpful hints in this area.

---

- Configure antivirus software to quarantine samples, not to delete them. That way if antivirus identifies any malicious code, digital investigators will have a sample to analyze rather than just a log entry to wonder about.

- Keep log entries for as long as possible given the hardware constraints of the system, or offload them to a remote log server.

- If possible, configure user rights assignments to prevent users from changing the settings identified earlier.

- If possible, employ user rights assignments to prevent users from activating native operating system encryption functions—unless they are purposefully utilized by the organization. If a user can encrypt data, they can hide it from you, and this includes user accounts used by an attacker.

---

**PAGEFILE PROS AND CONS**

Note that this will leave the pagefile on disk when the system is shut down, which some consider a security risk. Note that some settings represent a tradeoff between assisting the investigator and securing the system. For example, leaving the swap/page file on disk when the system is shut down is not recommended if the device is at risk for an attack involving physical access to the disk. The decision in this tradeoff will depend upon the sensitivity of the data on the device, and the risk of such an attack occurring. Such decisions will be easier if the organization in question has conducted a formal risk assessment of their enterprise.

## Logging Infrastructure

The most valuable resources for investigating a security breach in an enterprise are logs. Gathering logs with accurate timestamps in central locations, and reviewing them regularly for problems will provide a foundation for security monitoring and forensic incident response.

Most operating systems and many network devices are capable of logging their own activities to some extent. As discussed in Chapter 9, "Network Analysis," these logs include system logs (e.g., Windows Event logs, UNIX syslogs), application logs (e.g., web server access logs, host-based antivirus and intrusion detection logs), authentication logs (e.g., dial-up or VPN authentication logs), and network device logs (e.g., firewall logs, NetFlow logs).

### A LOG BY ANY OTHER NAME...

The National Institute of Standards and Technology publication SP800-92, "Guide to Computer Security Log Management" provides a good overview of the policy and implementation issues involved in managing security logs. The paper presents log management from a broad security viewpoint with attention to compliance with legally mandated standards. The publication defines a log as "a record of the events occurring within an organization's systems and networks." A forensic definition would be broader: "any record of the events relevant to the operation of an organization's systems and networks." In digital investigation, any record with a timestamp or other feature that allows correlation with other events is a log record. This includes file timestamps on storage media, physical sign-in logs, frames from security cameras, and even file transaction information in volatile memory.

Having each system keep detailed logs is a good start, but it isn't enough. Imagine that you have discovered that a particular rootkit is deleting the Security Event Logs on Windows systems that it infects, and that action leaves Event ID 517 in the log after the deletion. Now you know to look for that event, but how do you do that across 100,000 systems that each store their logs locally? Uh-oh. Now you've got a big problem. You know what to look for, but you don't have an efficient way to get to the data.

### PRACTITIONER'S TIP: MAKING DO WITHOUT CENTRALIZED LOGGING

When a centralized source of Windows Event logs is not available, we have been able to determine the scope of an incident to some degree by gathering the local log files from every host on the network. However, this approach is less effective than using a centralized log server because individual hosts may have little or no log retention, and the intruder may have deleted logs from certain compromised hosts. In situations in which the hosts do not have synchronized clocks, the correlation of such logs can become a very daunting task.

The preceding problem is foreseeable and can be solved by setting up a remote logging infrastructure. An organization's systems and network devices can and should be configured to send their logs to central storage systems, where they will be preserved and eventually archived. Although this may not be feasible for every system in the enterprise, it should be done for devices at ingress/egress points as well as servers that contain key data that is vital to the organization, or otherwise protected by law or regulations. Now imagine that you want to look for a specific log event, and all the logs for all critical servers in the organization are kept at a single location. As a digital investigator, you can quickly and easily grab those logs, and search them for your target event. Collecting disparate logs on a central server also provides a single, correlated picture of all the organization's activity on one place that can be used for report generation without impacting the performance of the originating systems. Maintaining centralized logs will reduce the time necessary to conduct your investigation, and by extension it will bring your organization to remediation in a more timely manner.

There are various types of solutions for this, ranging from using free log aggregation software (syslog) to commercial log applications such as Splunk, which provide enhanced indexing, searching, and reporting functions. There are also log aggregation and analysis platforms dedicated to security. These are sometimes called Security Event Managers, or SEMs, and a common example is Cisco MARS. Rolling out any of these solutions in an enterprise is not a trivial task, but will significantly ease the burden of both intrusion analysts as well as a variety of other roles from compliance management to general troubleshooting. Due to the broad appeal, an organization may be able to leverage multiple IT budgets to fund a log management project.

## PRACTITIONER'S TIP: NETWORK-LEVEL LOGGING

To gain better oversight of network-level activities, it is useful to gather three kinds of information. First, statistical information is useful for monitoring general trends. For instance, a protocol pie chart can show increases in unusual traffic whereas a graph of bytes/minute can show suspicious spikes in activity. Second, session data (e.g., NetFlow or Argus logs) provide an overview of network activities, including the timing of events, end-point addresses, and amount of data. Third, traffic content enables digital investigators to drill into packet payloads for deeper analysis.

Because central log repositories can contain key information about a security breach, they are very tempting targets for malicious individuals. Furthermore, by their nature, security systems often have access to sensitive information as well as being the means through which information access is monitored. Therefore, it is important to safeguard these valuable sources of evidence against misuse by implementing strong security, access controls, and auditing. Consider using network-based storage systems (network shares, NFS/AFS servers, NAS, etc.) with strong authentication protection to store and provide access to sensitive data. Minimizing the number of copies of sensitive data and allowing access only using logged authentication will facilitate the investigation of a security breach.

Having granular access controls and auditing on central log servers has the added benefit of providing a kind of automatically generated chain of custody, showing who accessed the logs at particular times. These protective measures can also help prevent accidental deletion of original logs while they are being examined during an investigation.

### PRACTITIONER'S TIP: OVERSIGHT

Technical controls can be undermined if a robust governance process is not in place to enforce them. An oversight process must be followed to grant individuals access to logging and monitoring systems. In addition, periodic audits are needed to ensure that the oversight process is not being undermined.

A common mistake that organizations make is to configure logging and only examine the logs after a breach occurs. To make the most use of log repositories, it is necessary to review them routinely for signs of malicious activity and logging failures. The more familiar digital investigators are with available logs, the more likely they are to notice deviations from normal activity and the better prepared they will be to make use of the logs in an investigation. Logs that are not monitored routinely often contain obvious signs of malicious activities that were missed. The delay in detection allows the intruder more time to misuse the network, and investigative opportunities are lost. Furthermore, logs that are not monitored on a routine basis often present problems for digital investigators, such as incomplete records, incorrect timestamps, or unfamiliar formats that require specialized tools and knowledge to interpret.

### PRACTITIONER'S TIP: INCOMPLETE LOGS

We have encountered a variety of circumstances that have resulted in incomplete logs. In several cases, storage quotas on the log file or partition had been exceeded and new logs could not be saved. This logging failure resulted in no logs being available for the relevant time period. In another case, a Packeteer device that rate-limited network protocols was discarding the majority of NetFlow records from a primary router, preventing them from reaching the central collector. As a result, the available flow information was misleading because it did not include large portions of the network activities during the time of interest. As detailed in Chapter 9 (Network Investigations), NetFlow logs provide a condensed summary of the traffic through routers. They are designed primarily for network management, but they can be invaluable in an investigation of network activity.

Incomplete or inaccurate logs can be more harmful than helpful, diverting the attention of digital investigators without holding any relevant information. Such diversions increase the duration and raise the cost of such investigations, which is why it is important to prepare a network as a source of evidence.

A simple and effective approach to routine monitoring of logs is to generate daily, weekly, or monthly reports from the logs that relate to security metrics in the organization. For instance, automatically generating summaries of authentication (failed *and* successful) access activity to secure systems on a daily basis can reveal misuse and other problems. In this way, these sources of information can be used to support other information assurance functions, including security auditing. It is also advisable to maintain and preserve digital records of physical access, such as swipe cards, electronic locks, and security cameras using the same procedures as those used for system and network logs.

## Log Retention

In digital investigative heaven, all events are logged, all logs are retained forever, and unlimited time and resources are available to examine all the logged information. Down on earth, however, it does not work that way. Despite the ever-decreasing cost of data storage and the existence of powerful log management systems, two cost factors are leading many organizations to review (or create) data retention policies that mandate disposal of information based on age and information type. The first factor is simply the cost of storing data indefinitely. Although data storage costs are dropping, the amount of digital information generated is increasing. Lower storage costs per unit of data do not stop the total costs from becoming a significant drain on an IT budget if all data is maintained in perpetuity (Gartner, 2008). The second factor is the cost of accessing that data once it has been stored. The task of sifting through vast amounts of stored data, such as e-mail, looking for relevant information can be overwhelming. Therefore, it is necessary to have a strategy for maintaining logs in an enterprise.

> Recording more data is not necessarily better; generally, organizations should only require logging and analyzing the data that is of greatest importance, and also have non-mandatory recommendations for which other types and sources of data should be logged and analyzed if time and resources permit. (NIST SP800-92)

This strategy involves establishing log retention policies that identify what logs will be archived, how long they will be kept, and how they will be disposed of. Although the requirements within certain sectors and organizations vary, we generally recommend having one month of logs immediately accessible and then two years on backup that can be restored within 48 hours. Centralized logs should be backed up regularly and backups stored securely (off-site, if feasible).

Clearly documented and understood retention policies provide two advantages. First, they provide digital investigators with information about the logs themselves. This information is very useful in planning, scheduling, and managing an effective investigation from the start. Second, if the organization is required by a court to produce log records, the policies define the existing business practice to support the type and amount of logs that can be produced.

It is important to make a distinction between routine log retention practices and forensic preservation of logs in response to a security breach. When investigating an intrusion, there is nothing more frustrating than getting to a source of evidence just days or hours after it has been overwritten by a routine process. This means that, at the outset of an investigation, you should take steps to prevent any existing data from being overwritten. Routine log rotation and tape recycling should be halted until the necessary data has been obtained, and any auto deletion of e-mail or other data should be stopped temporarily to give investigators an opportunity to assess the relevance and importance of the various sources of information in the enterprise. An effective strategy to balance the investigative need to maximize retention with the business need for periodic destruction is to snapshot/freeze all available log sources when an incident occurs. This log freeze is one of the most critical parts of an effective incident response plan, promptly preserving available digital evidence.

## Network Architecture

Note that the approach to network architecture issues may need to vary with the nature of the organization. In the case of a university or a hospital, for instance, there may be considerable resistance to decrypting HTTPS traffic at a proxy. As with all other aspects of preparedness, the final design must be a compromise that best serves *all* of the organization's goals.

The difficulty in scoping a network intrusion increases dramatically with the complexity of the network architecture. The more points of ingress/egress added to an enterprise network, the more difficult it becomes to monitor intruder activities and aggregate logs. In turn, this will make it more difficult to monitor traffic entering and leaving the network. If networks are built with reactive security in mind, they can be set up to facilitate an intrusion investigation.

- Reduce the number of Internet gateways, and egress/ingress points to business partners. This will reduce the number of points digital investigators may need to monitor.
- Ensure that every point of ingress/egress is instrumented with a monitoring device.
- Do not allow encrypted traffic in and out of the organization's network that is not sent through a proxy that decrypts the traffic. For example, all HTTPS traffic initiated by workstations should be decrypted at a web proxy before being sent to its destination. When organizations allow encrypted traffic out of their network, they cannot monitor the contents.
- Remote logging. Did we mention logging yet? All network devices in an organization need to be sending their log files to log server for storage and safe keeping.

## Domain/Directory Preparation

Directory services, typically Microsoft's Active Directory, play a key role in how users and programs are authenticated into a network, and authorized to perform specific tasks. Therefore Active Directory will be not only a key source of information for the intrusion investigator, but will also often be directly targeted by advanced attackers. Therefore it must be prepared in such a way that intrusion investigators will be able to obtain the information they need. Methods for this include:

- Remote logging. Yes, we have mentioned this before, but keeping logs is important. This is especially true for servers that are hosting part of a directory service, such as Active Directory Domain Controllers. These devices not only need to be keeping records of directory-related events, but logging them to a remote system for centralized access, backup, and general safekeeping.

- Domain and enterprise administrative accounts should be specific to individual staff. In other words, each staff member that is responsible for some type of administrative work should have a unique account, rather than multiple staff members using the same administrative account. This will make it easier for digital investigators to trace unauthorized behavior associated with an administrative account to the responsible individual or to his or her computer.

- Rename administrator accounts across all systems in the domain. Then create a dummy account named "administrator" that does not actually have administrative level privilege. This account will then become a honey token, where any attempt to access the account is not legitimate. Auditing access attempts to such dummy accounts will help digital investigators in tracing unauthorized activity across a domain or forest.

- Ensure that it is known which servers contain the Global Catalog, and which servers fill the FSMO (Flexible Single Master Operation) roles. The compromise of these systems will have an effect on the scope of the potential damage.

- Ensure that all trust relationships between all domains and external entities are fully documented. This will have an impact on the scope of the intrusion.

- Use domain controllers to push policies down that will enforce the recommendations listed under "Host Preparation" later in this chapter.

## Time Synchronization

Date and time stamps are critical pieces of information for the intrusion investigator. Because an intrusion investigation may involve hundreds or thousands of devices, the time settings for these devices should be synchronized. Incorrect timestamps can create confusion, false accusations, and make it more difficult to correlate events using multiple log types. Event correlation and reconstruction can proceed much more efficiently if the investigators can be sure that multiple sources of event reports are all using the same clock. This is *very* difficult to establish if the event records are not recorded using synchronized clocks. If one device is five minutes behind its configured time zone, and another device is 20 minutes ahead, it will be difficult for an investigator to construct an event timeline from these two systems. This problem is magnified when dealing with much larger numbers of systems. Therefore, it is important to ensure that the time on all systems in an organization is synchronized with a single source.

**TIME SYNCHRONIZATION**

- Windows: How Windows Time Service Works (http://technet.microsoft.com/en-us/library/cc773013.aspx)
- UNIX/Linux: *Unix Unleashed 4th edition*, Chapter 6
- Cisco: Network Time Protocol www.cisco.com/en/US/tech/tk648/tk362/tk461/tsd_technology_support_sub-protocol_home.html

## Operational Preparedness, Training and Drills

Following the proverb, "For want of a nail the shoe was lost," a well-developed response plan and well-designed logging infrastructure can be weakened without some basic logistical preparation. Like any complex procedure, staff will be more effective at conducting an intrusion investigation if they have been properly trained and equipped to preserve and make use of the available evidence, and have recent experience performing an investigation.

## PRACTITIONER'S TIP: STOCK YOUR TOOLCHEST

Responding to an incident without adequate equipment, tools, and training generally reduces the effectiveness of the response while increasing the overall cost. For instance, rushing out to buy additional hard drives at a local store is costly and wastes time. This situation can be avoided by having a modest stock of hard drives set aside for storing evidence. Other items that are useful to have in advance include a camera, screwdrivers, needle-nose pliers, flashlight, hardware write blockers, external USB hard drive cases, indelible ink pens, wax pencils, plastic bags of various sizes, packing tape, network switch, network cables, network tap, and a fire-resistant safe. Consider having some redundant hardware set aside (e.g., workstations, laptops, network hardware, disk drives) in order to simplify securing equipment and media as evidence without unduly impacting the routine work. If a hard drive needs to be secured, for instance, it can be replaced with a spare drive so that work isn't interrupted. Some organizations also employ tools to perform remote forensics and monitoring of desktop activities when investigating a security breach, enabling digital investigators to gather evidence from remote systems in a consistent manner without having to travel to a distant location or rely on untrained system administrators to acquire evidence (Casey, 2006).

Every effort should be made to send full-time investigators and other security staff to specialized training every year, and there is a wide variety of incident handling training available. However, it will be more difficult to train nonsecurity technical staff in the organization to assist during an incident. If the organization is a large enterprise, it may not be cost- and time-effective to constantly fly their incident handlers around the country or around the world to collect data during incidents. Instead the organization may require the help of system and network administrators at various sites to perform operations to serve the collection phase of an intrusion investigation (e.g., running a volatile data script, collecting logs, or even imaging a system). In this situation it will also not be cost-effective to send every nonsecurity administrator to specialized incident handling training, at the cost of thousands of dollars per staff member. A more effective solution is to build an internal training program, either with recorded briefings by incident handling staff or even computer-based training (CBT) modules if the organization has the capability to produce or purchase these. Coupled with explicit data gathering procedures, an organization can give nonsecurity technical staff the resources they need to help in the event of an intrusion.

In addition to training, it is advisable to host regular response drills in your organization. This is especially the case if the organization does not experience security incidents frequently, and the security staff also performs other duties that do not include intrusion investigation. As with any complex skill, one can get out of practice.

## CASE MANAGEMENT AND REPORTING

Effective case management is critical when investigating an intrusion, and is essentially an exercise in managing fear and frustration. Managing an intrusion investigation can be a difficult task, requiring you to manage large, dispersed teams and to maintain large amounts of data. Case management involves planning and coordinating the investigation, assessing risks, maintaining communication between those involved, and documenting each piece of media, the resulting evidence, and the overall investigative process. Continuous communication is critical to keep everyone updated on developments such as new intruder activities or recent security actions (e.g., router reconfiguration). Ideally, an incident response team should function as a unit, thinking as one. Daily debriefings and an encrypted mailing list can help with the necessary exchange of information among team members. Valuable time can be wasted when one uninformed person believes that an intruder is responsible for a planned reconfiguration of a computer or network device, and reacts incorrectly. Documenting all actions and findings related to an incident in a centralized location or on an e-mail list not only helps keep everyone on the same page, but also helps avoid confusion and misunderstanding that can waste invaluable time.

The various facets of case management with respect to computer network intrusions are described in the following sections.

## Organizational Structure

There are specific roles that are typically involved in an intrusion investigation or incident response. Figure 4.4 is an example organizational chart of such individuals, followed by a description of their roles.

Who are these people?

- **Investigative Lead**: This is the individual who "owns" the investigation. This individual determines what investigative steps need to be taken, delegates them to staff as needed, and reports all results to management. The "buck" stops with this person.

- **Designated Approval Authority**: This is the nontechnical manager or executive responsible for the incident response and/or investigation. Depending on the size of the organization, it could be the CSO, or perhaps the CIO or CTO. It is also the person who you have to ask when you want to do something like take down a production server, monitor communications, or leave compromised systems online while you continue your investigation. This is the person who is going to tell you "No" the most often.

- **Legal Counsel**: This is the person who tells the DAA what he or she must or should do to comply with the law and industry regulation. This is one of the people who will tell the DAA to tell you "No" when you want to leave compromised devices online so that you can continue to investigate. This person may also dictate what types of data need to be retained, and for how long.

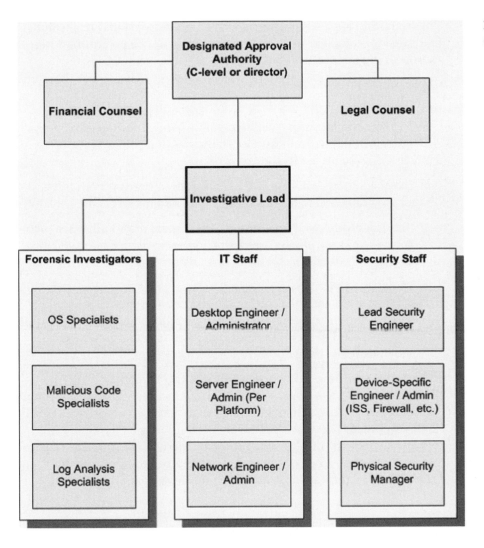

**FIGURE 4.4**
Organizational chart.

- **Financial Counsel**: This is the person who tells the DAA how much money the organization is losing. This is one of the people you'll have to convince that trying to contain an incident before you have finished your investigation could potentially cost the organization more money in the long run.

- **Forensic Investigators**: These are the digital forensics specialists. As the Investigative Lead, these are the people you will task with collection and analysis work. If the team is small, each person may be responsible for all digital forensic analysis tasks. If the organization or team is large, these individuals are sometimes split between operating system, malware, and log analysis specialists. These last two skills are absolutely required for intrusion investigations, but may not be present in other forms of digital investigation.

- **IT Staff**: These are the contacts who you will require to facilitate your investigation through an organization.

  - The Desktop Engineers will help you to locate specific desktop systems both physically and logically, and to facilitate scans of desktop systems across the network.

  - Server Engineers will help you to locate specific servers both physically and logically, and to facilitate scans of all systems across the network.

  - Network Engineers will help you to understand the construction of the network, and any physical or logical borders in place that could either interfere with attacker operation, or could serve as sources of log data.

  - Directory Service (Usually Active Directory) Administrators will help you to understand the access and authorization infrastructure that overlays the enterprise. They may help you to deploy scanning tools using AD, and to access log files that cover user logins and other activities across large numbers of systems.

- **Security Staff**: These individuals will assist you in gathering log files from security devices across the network, and in deploying new logging rules so that you can gather additional data that was not previously being recorded. These are also the people who may be trying to lock down the network and "fix" the problem. You will need to keep track of their activities, whether or not you are authorized to directly manage them, because their actions will affect your investigation.

## PRACTITIONERS TIP: MINIMIZE EVIDENCE DYNAMICS

It is not uncommon for some technical staff to take initiative during an incident, and to try and "help" by doing things like port scanning the IP address associated with an attack, running additional antivirus and spyware scans against in-scope systems, or even taking potentially compromised boxes offline and deleting accounts created by the intruders. Unfortunately, despite the best intentions behind these actions, they can damage your investigation by alerting the intruder to your activities. You will need to ensure that all technical staff understands that they are to take no actions during an incident without the explicit permission of the lead investigator or incident manager.

Any organization concerned about public image or publicly available information should also designate an Outside Liaison, such as a Public Relations Officer, to communicate with media. This function should report directly to the Designated Approval Authority or higher and probably should not have much direct contact with the investigators.

## Task Tracking

It can be very tempting just to plunge in and start collecting and analyzing data. After all, that is the fun part. But intrusion investigations can quickly grow large and out of hand. Imagine the following scenario. You have completed analysis on a single system. You have found a backdoor program and two separate rootkits, and determined that the backdoor was beaconing to a specific DNS host name. After checking the DNS logs for the network, you find that five other hosts are beaconing to the same host name. Now all of a sudden you have five new systems from which you will need to collect and analyze data. Your workload has just increased significantly. What do you do first, and in what order do you perform those tasks?

To handle a situation like this, you will need to plan your investigation, set priorities, establish a task list, and schedule those tasks. If you are running a group of analysts, you will need to split those tasks among your staff in an efficient delegation of workload. Perhaps you will assign one person the task of collecting volatile data/memory dumps from the affected systems to begin triage analysis, while another person follows the first individual and images the hard drives from those same devices. You could then assign a third person to collect all available DNS and web proxy logs for each affected system, and analyze those logs to identify a timeline of activity between those hosts and known attacker systems. Table 4.2 provides an example of a simple task tracking chart.

**Table 4.2** Example Chart for Tracking Tasks for Case Management Purposes

| | | Investigative Plan | | |
|---|---|---|---|---|
| Step | Task | Relevant Procedures | Assigned To | Status |
| 1 | Volatile data acquisition for devices server-03 and server-04 | Proc-006 | Bob Analyst & Jane Analyst | Complete 04/14/09 |
| 2 | Disk acquisition for devices server-03 and server-04 | Proc-003 | Bob Analyst & Jane Analyst | In Progress |
| 3 | Netflow and firewall log acquisition for site XYZ | Proc-010 | Tim Analyst | In Progress |
| 4 | Sniffer deployment to Reston site at network border | Proc-019 | Tim Analyst | Not begun |

Task tracking is also important in the analysis phase of an intrusion investigation. Keeping track of which systems have been examined for specific items will help reduce missed evidence and duplicate effort. For instance, as new intrusion artifacts emerge during investigations like IP addresses and malware, performing ad hoc searches will inevitably miss items and waste time. It is important to search all media for all artifacts; this can be tracked using a chart of relevant media to record the date each piece of media was searched for each artifact list as shown in Table 4.3. In this way, no source of evidence will be overlooked.

**Table 4.3** Example Chart for Tracking Artifact Searches Performed on All Systems within Scope for Case Management Purposes

| Host | Artifact List 1 (Active) | Artifact List 1 (Unalloc) | Artifact List 2 | Artifact List 3 |
|------|--------------------------|---------------------------|-----------------|-----------------|
| Workstation-32 | 2/12/2009 | 2/13/2009 | 2/15/2009 | 2/18/2009 |
| Fileserver-1 | 2/12/2009 | 2/13/2009 | 2/15/2009 | 2/17/2009 |
| E-mailserver-2 | 2/12/2009 | 2/13/2009 | 2/15/2009 | 2/19/2009 |

## PRACTITIONER'S TIP: CASE MANAGEMENT vs. PROJECT MANAGEMENT

If case management sounds like project management, that's because it is. Common project management processes and tools may benefit your team. But that doesn't mean that you can use just any project manager for running an investigation, or run out immediately to buy MS Project to track your investigative milestones. A network intrusion is too complicated to be managed by someone who does not have detailed technical knowledge of computer security. It would be more effective to take an experienced investigator, who understands the technical necessities of the trade, and further train that individual in project management. If you take this approach, your integration of project management tools and techniques into incident management will go more smoothly, and your organization may see drastic improvements in efficiency, and reductions in cost.

## Communication Channels

By definition, you will be working with an untrusted, compromised network during an intrusion investigation. Sending e-mails through the e-mail server on this network is not a good idea. Documenting your investigative priorities and schedules on this network is also not a good idea. You should establish out-of-band communication and off-network storage for the purposes of your investigation. Recommendations include the following:

- Cell network or WiMAX adapters for your investigative laptops. This way you can access the Internet for research or communication without passing your traffic or connecting to the compromised network.

- Do not send broadcast e-mail announcements to all staff at an organization about security issues that have arisen from a specific incident until after the incident is believed to have been resolved.
- Communicate using cell phones rather than desk phones, most especially if those desk phones are attached to the computing environment that could be monitored easily by intruders (i.e., IP phones).

---

## PRACTITIONER'S TIP: BE PARANOID

When investigating a security breach, we always assume that the network we are on is untrustworthy. Therefore, to reduce the risk that intruders can monitor our response activities, we always establish a secure method for exchanging data and sharing updated information with those who are involved in the investigation. This can be in the form of encrypted e-mail or a secure server where data.

---

## Containment/Remediation versus Investigative Success

There is a critical decision that needs to be made during any security event, and that decision involves choosing when to take defensive action. Defensive action in this sense could be anything from attempting to contain an incident with traffic filtering around an affected segment to removing malware from infected systems, or rebuilding them from trusted media. The affected organization will want to take these actions immediately, where "immediately" means "yesterday." You may hear the phrase, "Stop the bleeding," because no one in charge of a computer network wants to allow an attacker to retain access to their network. This is an understandable and intuitive response. Continued unauthorized access means continued exposure, increased risk and liability, and an increase in total damages. Unfortunately, this response can severely damage your investigation.

When an intrusion is first discovered, you will have no idea of the full extent of the unauthorized activity. It could be a single system, 100 systems, or the entire network with the Active Directory Enterprise Administrator accounts compromised. Your ability to discover the scope of the intrusion will often depend upon your ability to proceed without alerting the attacker(s) that there is an active investigation. If they discover what you are doing, and what you have discovered so far about their activity, they can take specific evasive action. Imagine that an attacker has installed two different backdoors into a network. You discover one of them, and immediately shut it down. The attacker realizes that one of the backdoors has been shut off, and decides to go quiet for a while, and not take any actions on or against the compromised network. Your ability to then observe the attacker in action, and possibly locate the second backdoor, now has been severely reduced.

## Attribute Tracking

In a single case, you may collect thousands of attributes or artifacts of the intrusion. So where do you put them, and how do you check that list when you need information? If you are just starting out as a digital investigator, the easier way to track attributes is in a spreadsheet. You can keep several worksheets in a spreadsheet that are each dedicated to a type of artifact. Table 4.4 provides an example attribute tracking chart used to keep a list of files associated with an incident.

You could also keep an even more detailed spreadsheet, by adding rows that include more granular detail. For example, you could add data such as file system date-time stamps, hash value, and important file metadata to Table 4.4 to provide a more complete picture of the files of interest in the table. However, as you gradually add more data, your tables will become unwieldy and difficult to view in a spreadsheet. You will also find that you will be recording duplicate information in different tables, and this can easily become a time sink. A more elegant solution would be a relational database that maintains the same data in a series of tables that you can query using SQL statements from a web front-end rather than scrolling and sorting in Excel. However, developing such a database will require that you be familiar with the types of data that you would like to keep recorded, and how you typically choose to view and report on it.

There are third-party solutions for case management. Vendors such as i2 provide case management software that allows you to input notes and lists of data that can be viewed through their applications. The i2 Analysts Notebook application can also aid in the analysis phase of intrusion investigation by automating link and timeline analysis across multiple data sets, helping digital investigators discern relationships that may not have been immediately obvious, and to visualize those relationships for more human-friendly viewing. This type of tool can be valuable, but it is important to obtain an evaluation copy first to ensure that it will record all the data that you would like

**Table 4.4** Example Chart for Tracking Attributes for Case Management Purposes

| Name | Path | Host | Description |
|------|------|------|-------------|
| abc.exe | C:\windows | Workstation-10 | Backdoor program that beacons over HTTPS to host badguy.dyndnsprovider.net. See Report X for full details. |
| def.sys | C:\windows\ system32 | Workstation-10 | Rootkit driver that hides abc.exe file and associated process. See Report X for full details. |

to track. A third-party solution will be far easier to maintain, but not as flexible as a custom database. Custom databases can be configured to more easily track attributes such as file metadata values than could a third-party solution. You may find that a combination of third-party tools and custom databases suits your needs most completely.

## Attribute Types

An intrusion investigation can potentially take months to complete. During this time, you may be collecting very large amounts of data that are associated with the incident. Examples of common items pertinent to an intrusion investigation are described in this section, but there are a wide variety of attributes that can be recorded. As a general rule, you should record an artifact if it meets any of the following criteria:

- It can be used to prove that an event of interest actually occurred.
- It can be used to search other computers.
- It will help to explain to other people how an event transpired.

Specific examples of attributes include the following.

### Host Identity

You will need to identify specific hosts that are either compromised or that are sources of unauthorized activity. These are often identified by:

- **Internal host name**: For example, a compromised server might be known as "app-server-42.widgets.com." These names are also helpful to remember as internal technical staff will often refer to their systems by these names.

- **IP address**: IP addresses can be used to identify internal and external systems. However, be aware that internal systems may use DHCP, and therefore their IP may change. Record the host name as well.

- **External host name**: It is common for modern malware to beacon to a domain name rather than an IP address. This allows the attacker to maneuver these beacons around IP blocks by using dynamic DNS to quickly change the IP associated with the DNS host name.

---

**PRACTITIONERS TIP: KEEPING TRACK OF DYNAMIC DNS**

Some intruders will frequently change the IP addresses associated with DNS host name beacon targets. In some cases, we have tracked the changes with a quick script that performs name resolution queries (e.g., using nslookup) on these domains at regular intervals, and dumps the results into a CSV file that you can either open as a spreadsheet or import into a database.

### Files of Interest

You will also need to track files of interest. In an intrusion, this could be files such as malicious executables, keystroke logs, e-mail attachments, configuration files for subverted programs, and so on. The things you will need to track about them include, at a minimum:

- File names
- Full storage path
- Hash value
- File system date-time stamps
- Key strings
- Key metadata values

### Operating System and Application Configuration Settings

Attackers will often use their own code with specific configuration settings or modify the configuration settings of legitimate programs and the operating system. These configuration settings should be examined for distinctive details pertaining to the intrusion.

#### FROM THE CASE FILES: REMOTE DROP LOCATION

An attacker was using the software OpenVPN to set up a tunnel from a credit relay server to an external system. This tunnel was used to steal PCI data from that system, and from others. The IP address to which the tunnel was initiated was recorded in the configuration file for the OpenVPN program.

### Indicators of Execution

Another valuable type of data to track is indicators of execution. For example, as detailed in Chapter 5, "Windows Forensic Analysis," when attackers run their own code, or use programs from the compromised system, Windows systems may record this activity in items such as:

- **Prefetch files**: Execution time is based on both file system and embedded date-time stamps.
- **Link files**: Execution time is based on file system date-time stamps.
- **Registry "Userassist" keys**: Execution is based on a date-time stamp kept inside the key.
- **Active processes**: Execution time is based on the uptime of the process subtracted from the current time of the system. This is also the potential timeframe of execution for any DLLs loaded into a given process.
- **Log entries**: There are a wide variety of log entry types that track program execution. Common examples are Windows System Log entries that show service starts and stops, and Windows Security Log entries that show general process starts and stops (as long as auditing is turned on for such an event).

### Account Events

User account events may also be linked to intrusion-related activity. You will need to be able to record activity such as:

- Unauthorized user accounts
- Compromised user accounts
- Logon/logoff times for accounts of interest
- New user account creations
- Changes in user account permissions

---

**PRACTITIONER'S TIP: USER ACCOUNT IDENTIFIERS**

When recording a user account on a Windows system, you should also record its SID. This is because in some places, user activity is recorded only with the SID, not with the username itself.

---

### Network Transmissions and Sessions

During your investigation you may identify and need to record occurrences of network transmissions, or extended network communication sessions between two hosts. From these events, you will need to record the following data if available:

- Date-time stamp
- Source and destination IP address
- Source and destination host name
- Source and destination port numbers (if TCP or UDP is in use)
- Transmission content (if visible)
- Transmission size (number of bytes transmitted in each direction)
- Network location where the event was observed

### General Event Tracking

For case management and analysis purposes, it is necessary to maintain an event timeline. This timeline will typically consist of a collection of occurrences that somehow are established by collections of other artifacts. Maintaining a time-line document helps identify gaps in understanding that need to be addressed, and supports the analysis process of understanding how an intrusion developed. Table 4.5 shows a brief example of a short, related chain of events, and how each event has multiple sources of evidence corroborating that the event occurred.

## Reporting

Intrusion investigations can be very complicated engagements, involving many distributed systems and spanning long periods of time. These investigations bring with them their own set of reporting challenges, including those described in this section.

**Table 4.5** Example Chart for Tracking Events for Case Management and Crime Reconstruction Purposes

| Date | Time | Event | Evidence Source |
|---|---|---|---|
| 3-16-09 | 1532 | Execution of c:\windows\system32\123.exe on workstation-48.widgets.com. | Item 002d: Security Event Log for workstation-48<br>Item 002c: NTFS Create time for 123.exe on workstation-48 |
| 3-16-09 | 1532 | DNS query for abc123.badguy.com from host workstation-48.widgets.com. Resolution successful to IP 555.555.555.555. | Item 003: Sniffer log – packet 166<br>Item 010: DNS log |
| 3-16-09 | 1533 | Port 443 TCP session initiated from workstation-48.widgets.com to 555.555.555.555. Session length 5 minutes. Session conformed to SSL. | Item 003: Sniffer log – packet 376<br>Item 007: HTTP Proxy Log |

### Fact versus Speculation

You will sometimes arrive to investigate an intrusion months or even years after it has been in progress. This, combined with the fact that most modern enterprises do not rigorously collect and preserve security event data, means that many of the details of the intrusion will be lost permanently. The primary role of a forensic investigator is to report facts. However, an intrusion investigator may be required to speculate, depending upon his or her employer. For example, the results of an intrusion investigation may be used in an attempt to better secure a network, or to determine whether the organization has a notification obligation. Although the results may not have yielded a definitive answer to the point of entry or exfiltration of data, the investigator may be required to make a best guess so that the organization can take some action.

If you find yourself in the position where you are being asked to speculate, make sure that your report clearly differentiates between what is fact and what is speculation. This is common for corporate investigations. In this situation speculate only where specifically asked to do so by your customer, and make sure that you clearly indicate what evidence there is for your guess, and where there is no concrete evidence. However, if you are asked to speculate in a forensic report in a criminal investigation, you should refuse.

## PRACTITIONER'S TIP: PROBABILITY IN DIGITAL INVESTIGATIONS

There is a distinction between baseless speculation and probability based on available evidence. When available evidence does not lead to a definitive answer, digital forensic practitioners may be asked to render an opinion on the likelihood of a particular aspect of the investigation. For instance, if there is no solid evidence showing that sensitive information was stolen by intruders, an organization may want some measure of the risk to help them reach a decision on the best course of action. After carefully analyzing the evidence, digital investigators can indicate the probability of exposure using the terms "possible" and "probable," or "unlikely," "likely," and "most likely" depending on the level of certainty. A general approach for coming up with this type of probability is covered in (Casey, 2002, 2004).

### *Reporting Audiences*

Digital investigators will generally have several different audiences for their reports in an intrusion investigation. Nontechnical managers will want to know only the bottom line. That is, when you will know exactly what happened, and when they can start fixing it. If you are not close to fulfilling either one of these requests, you need to have a clear explanation as to why you are not.

Technical staff needs to be supplied with the information they require to do their job. If they are supposed to be monitoring specific IPs, they will need updated lists of those addresses. If they are supposed to retain certain types of data, they will need to know precisely which data, and for how long.

Managers who are still or formerly were technical will not want the same information as technical managers, but will often want to hear the basic event timeline in shallow technical detail. They won't be concerned with granular attributes of the attack, but will want to know some technical details of the initial attack, and how the attacker is moving throughout the network.

Law enforcement needs concrete evidence of the crime and its apparent source to obtain subpoenas and search warrants. For instance, providing the IP addresses used by attackers and the associated time periods can enable law enforcement to obtain information from Internet service providers (ISPs) that enable them to apprehend the attacker. In some cases you may also be asked to provide details about artifacts found on compromised systems that might be stored on the intruder's computer, enabling law enforcement to show linkage between the attacker and victim systems. It is critical that the information you provide law enforcement is complete and accurate, since the actions they take can have broad consequences, potentially mobilizing search and seizure teams and detaining suspected individuals. If you mistype an IP address or do not account for time-zone differences, it will be your fault when the wrong person is subjected to the attention of law enforcement.

### *Interim Reports*

Shortly after you are asked to begin a digital investigation, it is not uncommon to be asked when you will be finished. Although intrusion investigations can easily span months, digital investigators must provide information as soon as is feasible to support important decisions, including whether to involve law enforcement, whether they should notify customers, and when it is advisable to initiate remediation measures. During this time, you will be expected to deliver regular reports, both written and oral. These reports may include anywhere from daily briefings to weekly updates. The key will be in determining how to deliver these interim reports, and what information to include.

As time goes on, your explanations will need to stay firm, as the pressure will mount on you to complete your investigation. Interim reports can easily turn into arguments as the managers of a compromised organization will want to move immediately to remediation. The longer your investigation takes, the more frustrated they will become. If you have some improvement to show, this will make your job easier.

During your interim reports, make sure that technical managers receive an ever-expanding storyline. "We now know that the attacker has done X, Y, or Z." These individuals will also need updates on the effectiveness of your search. "We were able to scan X number of devices since our last report, and the result was Y new infections." Nontechnical managers will simply need an estimated time to completion.

## COMMON INITIAL OBSERVATIONS

Security incidents can start in a variety of ways. How you initially discover an incident will determine how you proceed in the beginning of the investigation. Some of the more common initial observations are described next.

### Antivirus Alerts

It is not uncommon for an intrusion to begin with one or more alerts from antivirus programs. It is tempting to treat the malicious code that is detected by antivirus software as low-threat, mindless malware infection, like some random virus that happened to be accidentally copied to one of your computers. It is also tempting to assume that if antivirus found it, then your defenses did their job, and you're good to go, no further action necessary. This assumption can be a critical mistake.

Upon an antivirus alert, remember that you still do not know the following:

- How long the malicious files were actually on the system (unless the antivirus alert was specific to a file just copied through some medium)

- Whether or not they were placed there intentionally as part of a compromise or by accidental infection through unsafe web browsing or similar activity
- Whether or not there is additional, undetected malicious files on the system
- Whether or not the malicious code (if it includes backdoor functionality) has been used to remotely access the system, and possibly to use it to target other internal devices

The only way to discover the answer to these questions is to conduct analysis on the systems that received the alerts, and to determine the full extent of malicious code presence, and any other unauthorized activity that may have occurred on that system, or against other systems.

---

## FROM THE CASE FILES: OPENING A CAN OF WORMS

A large company discovers antivirus alerts on five systems, each for the exact same backdoor program. At this point, all the company knew was that they had five systems running the same backdoor program. They did *not* know how long those backdoor programs had been there, or what was done with them.

This company could have treated this event as a simple virus infection, but instead they chose to treat it as a security incident, and a possible intentional compromise. Some time later, forensic analysis of those systems, and subsequent searches through the enterprise revealed at least 80 systems that had different variations of the same backdoor as well as other rootkit and backdoor software that had not been detected by the company's antivirus software. This included the compromise of over 30 servers. Antivirus alerts were the initial window into this intrusion.

---

## IDS Alerts

An alert from an intrusion detection system is a direct warning of attempted unauthorized activity. This is the main purpose of an IDS. However, before using IDS alerts to spur a forensic exam, ensure that your organization has properly tuned its sensors and rule set. Otherwise you will spend too much time chasing down false positives. Also, you should specify in your policy exactly what types of IDS alerts you will use to trigger further data gathering from the target device. For example, conducting a full acquisition and analysis of an Internet accessible web server because it was port scanned might easily be a waste of resources. Hosts on the Internet are randomly scanned on a frequent basis. However, if your IDS detected a reverse shell spawned from the same server, you would want to treat that alert more seriously.

## E-mail with Suspicious Contents

E-mail is a common delivery vector for malicious payloads, and as an initial vector of entry into large corporations and government organizations. If someone reports that they have received an e-mail from an unknown source and that they have followed a link contained within, or opened an attachment that was delivered with the e-mail, this may constitute a security event that will require an investigation. Once a user executes a phishing or spear phishing attack payload, they may have installed malicious code onto their system. There may still be an issue even if the e-mail comes from a known source, but the attachment was unexpected, as source addresses can be spoofed. In some cases, spear phish attacks will originate from an organization that has been compromised to another organization that is a business partner. By routing the e-mail attack through a compromised organization, it will appear to be more legitimate, and will therefore be more likely to be opened.

## System and Application Crashes

Malicious code, from exploits to rootkits, is typically not created through a robust software development lifecycle, with a significant testing and evaluation phase that is intended to work out bugs. Because of this, attackers may cause a target application or operating system to crash. This can be a first warning to a user or administrator that there may be a security problem. Obviously you cannot treat every OS or application error as an attack, but there are certain circumstances where such an event is more likely to be a security problem, including:

- The crash results from the opening of an e-mail attachment.
- A web browser crashes upon viewing a specific web page.
- An operating system continues to crash, and IT staff cannot successfully identify the problem.
- An otherwise stable server crashes, particularly a Domain Controller or other critical system.

### FROM THE CASE FILES

A corporate user receives an e-mail message from an individual claiming to act for a government agency, soliciting a response for a Request For Proposals (RFP) that is attached to the e-mail as a Microsoft Word document. Because the user is a member of the sales staff, he opens the e-mail. After all, responding to RFPs is how he earns a living. However, when he opens the document, Microsoft Word crashes. He tries again, with the same result. He then forwards the document to a work associate, who tries to open the RFP. Word crashes on his system as well. The user then notifies the help desk. A member of the help desk staff tries to open the document,

and when Word crashes on his system, he recognizes this as a security issue, and notifies security staff.

Analysis revealed that (1) the Word document contained malicious code that would download additional malware from an overseas location when the Office document was opened, and (2) The "From" line of the e-mail included an e-mail address for a nonexistent individual. Three systems were infected at this point, but this spear phish attack was detected early because a help desk worker was knowledgeable enough to understand that under certain circumstances, an application crash can be a symptom of attack.

Crashes as a result of an attack will continue to become less prevalent over time, as more malicious code is developed professionally for organized crime and state-related entities. However it can still be a common indicator of an intrusion.

## Blacklist Violations

Over time, an organization may develop blacklists that contain signs of unauthorized or malicious activity in network traffic. These lists are often in the form of specific, known-bad IP addresses or DNS host names, but could also be other descriptors such as port numbers associated with specific backdoors or unauthorized chat programs. When an internal host is detected attempting to reach one of these external systems or using a disallowed port, this is a sign that a compromise may have occurred and an investigation may be required. You should set investigative thresholds that depend upon the nature of the blacklisted item. For example, some blacklisted items may require a more immediate response. An IP address associated with a previous intrusion may be treated differently from a DNS host name associated with a publicly known worm. Likewise you may observe some traffic that is more likely a sign of misuse than compromise, such as AOL Instant Messenger traffic from a user that did not realize that it was against your company policy. Some government organizations also maintain blacklists that may be available to digital investigators in certain cases.

## Abnormal Patterns of Network Traffic

Although there are not necessarily any set rules for this, there are general behavior patterns that may indicate a compromise when seen in network traffic. Some common examples include:

- Workstations sending significantly more data outbound than they receive
- Devices that generate a high volume of traffic in either direction that are not intended for massive traffic volume
- Devices that are communicating using abnormal ports/protocols, or an unusually high variety of ports/protocols

## External Notifications

The worst way to find out about a security incident is when somebody from outside your organization tells you about it. Unfortunately, this sometimes happens. These situations will vary widely depending upon the exact evidence presented to you by the outside party, and so your investigation will be crafted to match.

> **FROM THE CASE FILES**
>
> In 2007, a retail chain corporate office received a phone call from a major credit card vendor. It turns out that this vendor had traced the theft of thousands of credit card numbers to that retail chain. As a CISO, this is not how you want to start your day. As you may guess, a security incident was rightfully declared.

# SCOPE ASSESSMENT

Identifying the full scope of an intrusion is one of the primary goals of the investigation. Keeping in mind that a security breach could have occurred before it was detected, it is a good practice to extend analysis to a time before the initial detection. Furthermore, it is important to look beyond a single compromised computer when considering the method of intrusion and the scope of a security breach. It is generally necessary to assume that other computers or devices on the network were involved in or impacted by the breach.

The scope of an intrusion consists of the following:

- **Actual scope**: Devices and network segments on which intruder activity is verified to have taken place.
- **Potential scope**: All devices for which the attacker has (1) network access and (2) valid credentials. For example, if the attacker can communicate with server-01 through DCE/RPC and SMB/CIFS, and the attacker has credentials for that system, then it is potentially within scope.

The answer to the question of scope will include several key pieces of data:

- What devices were directly compromised and where are those devices located?
- What host/network/domain credentials were compromised?
- For which hosts/networks/domains are those credentials valid, and where are those assets?
- What hosts/networks/domains have trust relationships with compromised assets?

To better understand the intent of these questions, consider the following example.

Suppose you discover a single potentially compromised workstation. You collect data from it, and conduct analysis on that system. Your analysis reveals that the attacker used the pwdump utility to extract the local password hashes. These hashes included the local administrator account. The same password is used for all local administrator accounts for all desktops on the entire domain. This was probably done to ease the burden of help desk staff and desktop engineers by preventing them from having to remember too many passwords. However, the fact that this credential has been stolen means that every device that utilizes the same local admin password is now in the potential scope of incident. They are not necessarily in the actual scope, as you have not verified whether or not any direct unauthorized action was taken against those devices, but they must be considered at significant risk nonetheless. This is most especially true if the system you first discovered has been compromised for any length of time. Once proper credentials have been stolen, an attacker can move between Windows systems in a matter of minutes.

In the beginning of an incident, you will have only your initial observations to guide your scope assessment, and so your scope will be mostly potential. As you collect data, analyze it, and then use your discoveries to find additional compromised systems, both your actual and potential scopes may continue to expand, and will hopefully become more concrete. *All* devices in the potential scope of the incident will need to be searched for known artifacts. This process is covered later in this chapter.

# COLLECTION

For the most part, the collection of evidence for network intrusions is similar to collections for any other digital investigation, as detailed in Casey (2004). In general, the data you choose to collect will be driven by the needs of the investigation. However, we would like to reinforce a few specific points here.

When dealing with a network that has not been prepared adequately from a forensic standpoint, it is generally necessary to have a meeting with select IT personnel to identify potential log sources. Explain from the outset that the goal is to identify any sources of information with timestamps that could have recorded events related to the incident, including security related devices (e.g., firewalls, IDS, intrusion prevention or antivirus agents) as well as system management systems (e.g., NetFlow logs, bandwidth monitoring, web proxy logs). Through such discussion, and review of associated documentation, it is often possible to generate a list of the most promising sources of information on the victim network. This information gathering meeting is also an opportunity to develop a coordinated preservation plan, instructing specific individuals to preserve backup tapes or provide access to systems that contain log data.

## PRACTITIONER'S TIP: RUFFLED FEATHERS

Your job as a forensic investigator involves reconstruction of events from available data. It does not involve apportioning blame for an incident. Unfortunately, many of the technical support staff upon whom you will depend for information will suspect that your findings may be used to apportion blame, anyway. Given the dynamics of most organizations, they may be right. This can place the digital investigator in a delicate situation in which some investigative activities could be taken as implied criticism. The next Practitioner's Tip: Trust but Verify, is a case in point. If the network administrator tells you that a firewall is blocking packets to TCP port 139 and you then generate such traffic to test that statement, it may seem that you don't "believe" what you have been told. Your best defense in these cases is your own professionalism. It really doesn't matter whether or not you believe anything you are told. It is your job to verify everything you can. It might help if you emphasize that you need to "illustrate" the information rather than "verify" it, however. Your final product will be a report, and the results of any tests you run will be included to illustrate the characteristics of the network and the systems under examination. This is not just a verbal trick, but a valid and useful way to approach your professional responsibilities.

In some instances it may be necessary to rely on someone who is more familiar with a given system to help collect certain data, particularly when you do not have the necessary password or expertise. Whenever feasible, guide the individual through the collection process, document the steps taken as completely and accurately as possible (e.g., taking screenshots or saving queries), and ask questions about the resulting data to ensure that all of the required information is preserved. When dealing with complex systems such as databases or security event management systems, it may be necessary to perform trial queries or samplings to determine whether the output contains the required data. During this process, digital investigators generally refine what is needed from the system and learn more about the logs and associated systems, which can be invaluable from an analysis standpoint.

## PRACTITIONER'S TIP: TRUST BUT VERIFY

When you have to rely on a system administrator's description of the network, and of how and what events are logged to interpret your evidence, do not assume that everything you are told is correct. In so far as possible, verify what you are told empirically. If for instance, you are told that certain packets are blocked on the network, try to generate them and make sure they are blocked. If you are told that certain events will generate a given pattern of log records, try to duplicate those events and examine the log records for verification. This is part of identifying and reducing the number of assumptions you are making. Similarly, if you are told that specific activities are not logged, consider asking multiple system administrators. In one case, one system administrator asserted that the domain controllers did not retain DHCP logs, making it difficult to determine which users were assigned specific IP addresses during the time of interest. However, another system administrator was posed the same question and directed investigators to a logon script he had written to record useful information each time a user logged into a Windows system in the domain, including the username, computer name, MAC address, and IP address. This recorded information was sufficient for digital investigators to complete their work.

## Live Collection

In the field of digital forensics it is traditional to shut down systems, and then create a forensic duplicate of the hard drives. Once that has been done in an intrusion case, the targeted organization will typically want to clean the system and then place it back online. As mentioned previously in this chapter, early remediation of compromised systems can tip the attacker off about the investigation. On one hand, it is common for Windows workstations to go offline for long periods. People shut their computers down at night, or take their laptops home. So if you took a workstation or two down to image, the attacker might not notice, as long as the device is not re-imaged or cleaned afterward, thereby removing their persistent malware. However it is not common for high availability systems to go offline. If you took down all three domain controllers for a single domain overnight to image, this will look more suspicious to the attacker, and you will be exposing the investigation to discovery.

So it is more beneficial to leave compromised systems online until the investigation has completed. If you choose to pursue this course of action, this means that sooner or later, you will do some live forensic preservation. Live forensic preservation has been considered detrimental, largely because the data is constantly changing and you are not supposed to change evidence that will be used in court. There are several counterpoints to this:

- You may not be a criminal investigator. If this is the case, your first responsibility may be to protect the target organization, not to prosecute a criminal, and so it is more important for you to not tip off the attacker.

- Even if you are a criminal investigator, your ability to apprehend the perpetrator may still be irrevocably damaged by tipping him or her off to the investigation. You will have to decide whether or not the fact that the system is changing while you copy it is that large of a problem.

- The systems in question may be critical to the business operations of the organization, and taking it out of service could cause greater damage to the organization than the intrusion you are investigating.

The reality is that much digital evidence cannot be collected except while it is changing. The most obvious example of this is the contents of computer memory. When investigating an intrusion, it is usually necessary to collect volatile data including information about running processes, open files, and active network connections. Although executing any command on a live system will alter its state and overwrite portions of memory, this does not make the acquired data any less useful in an investigation. If you are to collect data from a live system, you must simply be able to indicate that the act of gathering the data did not have an impact on the actual facts that you report as evidence of the intrusion. Having said this, when extensive examination and searching of a compromised system is required, it is advisable to acquire a full forensic duplicate of data for offline examination.

One of the risks when acquiring evidence from a live system when investigating an intrusion is that the subject system could be compromised to such a degree that the operation of even trusted incident response tools is skewed. For instance, system files or the kernel may have been modified to destroy data or return incomplete information. Therefore, it is generally recommended to acquire the full contents of memory prior to executing other utilities on the live system.

## Forensic Acquisition of Memory

Although we would argue that the contents of memory should be collected in almost every case, it is especially vital in an intrusion investigation for several reasons:

- Memory can contain artifacts of an intrusion, just as a disk can. In fact, some types of artifacts can often be found only in memory (as opposed to on disk), such as currently running processes, or currently active network connections.

- Moreover, these artifacts may be remotely searchable. If you have visibility into physical memory across your enterprise, then you can search for known artifacts in memory to identify additional compromised systems during your scope assessment.

- Some malicious code is memory-resident *only*. This means that there is no file on disk corresponding to the process that is active in memory on the computer. Once the contents of memory are lost, so is the malicious code. If you do not collect memory, you will miss these types of malicious programs.

- Some malicious code contains key data, such as passwords, or even segments of code, in an encrypted form that only decrypts in memory. Although is it usually possible in theory to decrypt the executable as stored on the disk, it is often much more convenient to examine the decrypted code in memory.

- Volatile data can be collected more quickly than full disk images. If you are in a triage situation, where you are just trying to determine whether a system has or has not been compromised, you can quickly gather volatile data and select pieces of data from disk to make this assessment.

- Volatile data takes up less storage space than full disk images. If you are trying to collect enough data remotely to make an assessment as to whether or not a system has been compromised, volatile data and select pieces of data from disk can easily be transmitted across networkwide area network links. This makes it easier for you to utilize a remote agent (person or program) to collect this data and transmit it to you at your location.

For these reasons, a full memory dump should be collected wherever possible from compromised systems. Forensic preservation and examination of memory specifically, and volatile data in general, is covered in *Malware Forensics* (Malin, Casey & Aquilina, 2008).

## Network Packet Capture

Computer intrusions typically involve computer networks, and there is always going to be the potential for valuable evidence on the network transmission medium. Capturing network traffic can give investigators one of the most vivid forms of evidence, a live recording of a crime in progress (Casey, 2004). This compelling form of digital evidence can be correlated with other evidence to build an airtight case, demonstrating a clear and direct link between the intruder and compromised hosts. The problem is that this medium is volatile.

If you are not capturing traffic on a network link when a transmission of interest is sent, then it is lost. You will never have access to that data. It is advisable that you begin capturing traffic in the beginning of an incident, at least for the devices that are exhibiting the initial symptoms of a security event.

Later during the incident, you will be able to readjust your monitoring locations based upon more detailed results of your analysis. In an ideal world, you would be able to capture all network traffic entering and leaving any network segment that is in the potential scope of the incident, as well as data to and from your network management and data "crown jewels." But your organization most likely does not have the capacity for network traffic collection on this scale, so you will need to prioritize your captures. Your priority should be to collect network traffic to and from known compromised systems, so that you can collect enough information to be able to identify specific artifacts that can be used later to detect attacker activity across other network devices already in place, such as firewalls, proxy servers, and IDS sensors.

## PRACTITIONER'S TIP: MAKE A COPY OF THE ENTIRE LOG

Whenever you encounter a source of logs on a network, preserve the entire original log for later analysis, not just portions that seem relevant at the time. The reason for this admonition is that new information is often uncovered during an investigation and the original logs need to be searched again for this information. If you do not preserve the original log, there is a risk that it will be overwritten by the time you return to search it for the new findings. When exporting logs from any system, make sure that DNS resolution is not occurring because this will slow the process and may provide incorrect information (when DNS entries have changed since the time of the log entry).

## ANALYZING DIGITAL EVIDENCE

The ultimate goal of an intrusion investigation can vary depending on the situation, and can be influenced by business concerns, cost-benefit analysis, due diligence considerations, admissibility in court, and so on. In some cases the goal may be to locate and remediate all systems that the intruder accessed. In other cases the goal may be to determine whether the attacker stole sensitive data. In still other cases the goal may be to determine whether the victim network was used as a platform for illegal activities. When an intrusion results in significant damage or loss, the goal may be to apprehend and prosecute the attackers (Casey, 2006). The fact that the goal can vary underscores the importance of defining and documenting that goal from the start.

Regardless of the ultimate goal, digital investigators need to ascertain the method through which the intruders gained access, the time (or times) that this access occurred, where the attacks came from, and what systems and data were exposed. Answering these questions requires some degree of forensic reconstruction, including a combination of temporal, functional, and relational analysis of available data.

Date and time correlation is by far one of the most effective intrusion analysis techniques. There is such an abundance of temporal information on computers and networks that the different approaches to analyzing this information are limited only by our imagination and current tools. Temporal analysis can be summed up by the following statement: Look for other events that have occurred around the same date and time as one or more events already identified as related to the intrusion. Here are some examples:

- Look for other malicious or unknown executables with date-time stamp values close to a known piece of malware. Many intrusions involve more than one malware file. If you can find one, there is a good chance that there are more files created, written or modified around the same time as that file.

- Look for log entries that show processes being started, stopped, or experiencing errors during your known timeframe. For example, some malware adds itself as a service, and Event Log entries can be generated in Windows when a service is started. Poorly coded malware and exploits also will often crash legitimate systems, leaving traces in OS logs and crash dumps.

- Look for authentication log entries during your known timeframe. Attackers will often move through networks using stolen credentials because this is less obvious than using exploits or fake accounts. If you can correlate the logon of legitimate accounts to known-bad events, then you may be able to discover which accounts are being used by an attacker, or even that you have an insider problem.

## PRACTITIONER'S TIP: DATE-TIME STAMP TAMPERING

For the past several years, it has been common for malicious code to modify its own file system date-time stamps. For example, some programs will change their NTFS Standard Information Attribute date-time stamps to match those of legitimate Windows system DLLs. However it is not as common for malware to modify every date-time stamp. So in your searches for date-related information, remember to check all file system date-time stamps, as well as those in file metadata and other embedded values.

The key with items listed earlier is date and time. You will not have the time to manually inspect every crash dump file on your enterprise, but you should check the crash dumps on in-scope systems that occur at the same time as other known bad activity.

The goal of functional analysis is to understand what actions were possible within the environment of the offense, and how the intruder's toolkit works. Functional analysis includes reviewing network device configuration to determine what the intruder could access. For instance, if a firewall was configured to block connections from the Internet to the targeted systems, then investigators must figure out how the intruder bypassed the firewall restrictions (e.g., by connecting through an intermediate system within the network, or having insider assistance).

Relational analysis involves studying how the various systems involved in a compromise relate to each other and how they interact. For instance, trust relationships between systems need to be explored in order to determine whether the intruder used them to gain access to additional systems.

## INVESTIGATIVE SCENARIO
## Part 2a: Forensic Analysis

We will begin our digital investigation by examining NetFlow activity for web and SMB protocols over the internal network. NetFlow is a routing management tool developed by Cisco, as detailed in Chapter 9, "Network Analysis." Many routers can be configured to dump a stream of network activity information to designated servers. The data does not record individual packet information, but a higher-level of communication called flows. These can be seen as records of closely associated traffic for particular packet exchange sessions. As detailed in Chapter 9, analysis of NetFlow logs in this scenario reveals a significant amount of traffic from the intranet server at 10.10.10.50 to the VPN at 192.186.1.1 on April 2, 2009 around 22:40. This information enables us to start an event timeline, shown in Table 4.6.

**Table 4.6** Initial Timeline of Events in the Intrusion Investigation Scenario Used in this Chapter

| Time | Description | Source of Data | Comments |
|---|---|---|---|
| 2009apr02 22:40 | HTTP access to intranet server 10.10.10.50 | Netflow | Data consistent with file transfers in the 100000K range. |

Now, with the timeline as a guide, we look in the web server access logs on the intranet server (10.10.10.50). Note that Microsoft Internet Information Server (IIS) logs' timestamps are in UTC by default. In this scenario, the other logs use the local Eastern Daylight Savings time zone (UTC-0400). The necessary adjustment for time zone should be noted in the timeline's comments field.

```
200  9-04-03 02:38:10 W3SVC1 10.10.10.50 GET /iisstart.htm - 80 - 192.168.1.1
Mozilla/4.0+(compatible;+MSIE+6.0;+Windows+NT+5.1) 200 0 0
2009-04-03 02:38:10 W3SVC1 10.10.10.50 GET /images/snakeoil1.jpg - 80 - 192.168.1.1
Mozilla/4.0+(compatible;+MSIE+6.0;+Windows+NT+5.1) 200 0 0
2009-04-03 02:38:10 W3SVC1 10.10.10.50 GET /images/snakeoil2.jpg - 80 - 192.168.1.1
Mozilla/4.0+(compatible;+MSIE+6.0;+Windows+NT+5.1) 200 0 0
```

(Continued)

## INVESTIGATIVE SCENARIO—CONT'D

```
2009-04-03 02:38:10 W3SVC1 10.10.10.50 GET /images/snakeoil3.jpg - 80 - 192.168.1.1
  Mozilla/4.0+(compatible;+MSIE+6.0;+Windows+NT+5.1) 200 0 0
2009-04-03 02:38:10 W3SVC1 10.10.10.50 GET /images/snakeoil4.gif - 80 - 192.168.1.1
  Mozilla/4.0+(compatible;+MSIE+6.0;+Windows+NT+5.1) 200 0 0
2009-04-03 02:38:10 W3SVC1 10.10.10.50 GET /images/snakeoil5.jpg - 80 - 192.168.1.1
  Mozilla/4.0+(compatible;+MSIE+6.0;+Windows+NT+5.1) 200 0 0
2009-04-03 02:38:10 W3SVC1 10.10.10.50 GET /images/snakeoil7.jpg - 80 - 192.168.1.1
  Mozilla/4.0+(compatible;+MSIE+6.0;+Windows+NT+5.1) 200 0 0
2009-04-03 02:38:10 W3SVC1 10.10.10.50 GET /images/snakeoil8.jpg - 80 - 192.168.1.1
  Mozilla/4.0+(compatible;+MSIE+6.0;+Windows+NT+5.1) 200 0 0
2009-04-03 02:38:10 W3SVC1 10.10.10.50 GET /images/snakeoil6.jpg - 80 - 192.168.1.1
  Mozilla/4.0+(compatible;+MSIE+6.0;+Windows+NT+5.1) 200 0 0
2009-04-03 02:38:10 W3SVC1 10.10.10.50 GET /images/snakeoil9.jpg - 80 - 192.168.1.1
  Mozilla/4.0+(compatible;+MSIE+6.0;+Windows+NT+5.1) 200 0 0
2009-04-03 02:38:10 W3SVC1 10.10.10.50 GET /images/snakeoil10.jpg - 80 - 192.168.1.1
  Mozilla/4.0+(compatible;+MSIE+6.0;+Windows+NT+5.1) 200 0 0
2009-04-03 02:38:10 W3SVC1 10.10.10.50 GET /images/snakeoil11.jpg - 80 - 192.168.1.1
  Mozilla/4.0+(compatible;+MSIE+6.0;+Windows+NT+5.1) 404 0 2
2009-04-03 02:38:10 W3SVC1 10.10.10.50 GET /images/snakeoil12.jpg - 80 - 192.168.1.1
  Mozilla/4.0+(compatible;+MSIE+6.0;+Windows+NT+5.1) 200 0 0
2009-04-03 02:38:10 W3SVC1 10.10.10.50 GET /images/snakeoil13.jpg - 80 - 192.168.1.1
  Mozilla/4.0+(compatible;+MSIE+6.0;+Windows+NT+5.1) 200 0 0
```

These web server access logs show access to a series of JPEG files in the "snakeoil" series from the VPN (192.168.1.1). The timestamps, adjusted to UTC-0400, do not quite match those on the NetFlow logs. This may be due to a small discrepancy between the clock setting on the intranet server and the clock on the router that generated the NetFlow records. Such discrepancies appear often in the infrastructure of many organizations and need to be noted and eventually accounted for as detailed in the correlation section later in this chapter.

Fortunately for the organization, its security design did not permit remote VPN access to the most secure files on the intranet server. A functional analysis of the network configuration confirms that the company secrets could not have been accessed directly via the VPN. At this point in the investigation it would seem that CorpX's most sensitive data was protected from unauthorized access (to be continued…).

The principle of Occam's Razor is frequently misconstrued to mean that the simplest answer must be the correct one. Thus, the principle could be used to justify laziness in scientific inquiry. In fact, the principle states that an explanation of any phenomenon should be based on as few assumptions as possible. In the context of intrusion investigation, we can apply this principle by employing the scientific method, conducting experiments, and relying on available evidence.

## INVESTIGATIVE SCENARIO
## Part 2b: Employing the Scientific Method
## a.k.a. Practitioner's Tip: Challenge Your Assumptions

When conducting any investigation, it is important to consider alternative possibilities and to try to disprove your own conclusions. For instance, when investigating a security breach, do not rule out the possibility that someone gained physical access to the computer rather than compromised it via the network, or vice versa. For instance, in the intrusion investigation scenario used in this chapter, the company secrets stored on the intranet server could not be accessed directly via the VPN. However, by performing a relational analysis (looking at how various systems on the network can interact) and a functional analysis (checking to see whether certain systems could access the intranet server), we found that systems on the DMZ could access corporate secrets on the intranet server.

Further analysis of NetFlow logs reveals an unusually large quantity of data being transferred from the intranet server (10.10.10.50) to a host on the DMZ (10.10.30.2) at around the time of concern as summarized in Table 4.7.

**Table 4.7** Summary of NetFlow Traffic from Intranet Server on Secure Network (10.10.10.50) to SSH Server on DMZ Network (10.10.30.2)

| Start | End | Src Port | Src Port | Dst IP | Dst Port | Bytes |
|---|---|---|---|---|---|---|
| 0402.23:12:51.699 | 0402.23:12:51.711 | 10.10.10.50 | 139 | 10.10.30.2 | 54825 | 173 |
| 0402.23:12:51.711 | 0402.23:12:51.723 | 10.10.10.50 | 139 | 10.10.30.2 | 54826 | 173 |
| 0402.23:12:47.432 | 0402.23:12:52.184 | 10.10.10.50 | 445 | 10.10.30.2 | 54824 | 2421 |
| 0402.23:12:51.723 | 0402.23:12:52.292 | 10.10.10.50 | 139 | 10.10.30.2 | 54827 | 1700 |
| 0402.23:13:09.035 | 0402.23:28:03.157 | 10.10.10.50 | 445 | 10.10.30.2 | 54828 | 31304 |

The network diagram identifies 10.10.30.2 as an SSH server, which are usually UNIX-based systems. An individual with knowledge of the CorpX network could establish a VPN connection, log onto the SSH server in the DMZ, and from there access the files containing company secrets on the intranet server. Examining these NetFlow records confirms that, starting at around 23:13 and ending at 23:28, connections were established between the SSH server and ports 139 and 445 on the intranet server. The ports 139 and 445 are generally associated with the SMB protocol, indicating that a network file share on the intranet server was accessed at this time. In the correlation section later in this chapter, we will look for correlating events in other logs to develop a more complete picture of what occurred.

Still, at this stage of the investigation, it is not safe to rule out alternate possibilities. The IP address (10.10.30.2) used to gain unauthorized access to the company secrets is assigned to a system in the DMZ. Based on what we have been told, all DMZ systems are on the premises. At this point we have a computer on the premises in use at 11 PM, and it is possible that someone on the premises was responsible for these activities. Therefore, any physical security data, such as logs or security camera records, should be checked to see if any on-premises activity has been recorded. In this scenario, the physical security systems indicated that nobody was on the premises at the time in question, making this possibility very unlikely. Nonetheless, when you can prove that an alternate hypothesis is invalid rather than assume it, the effort is not wasted (recall the role of falsification in the scientific method).

To get a clearer sense of whether files of concern were stolen, digital investigators can check whether the files on the intranet server were accessed at the time of the suspicious activity (provided last accessed times are enabled as discussed earlier in this chapter). However, when dealing with a server that is critical to the operation of CorpX, it is preferable not to shut the system down and create a full forensic duplicate. In such situations, digital investigators can use a remote forensics tool to examine the file system while the server is still running. In this way, the needed digital evidence can be obtained in a forensically sound manner while maintaining business continuity. Figure 4.5 shows ProDiscover IR being used to examine the intranet server from the intrusion investigation scenario used in this chapter. Note that the remote forensic tool must be set to the

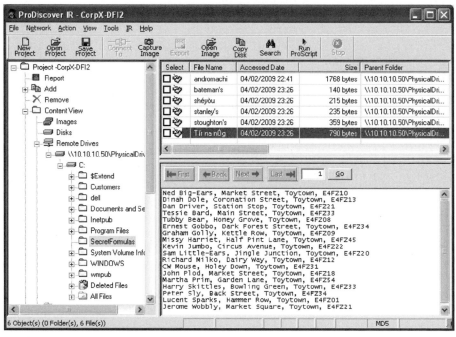

**FIGURE 4.5**

A remote forensic preview of intranet server using ProDiscover IR.

same time zone as the system being examined in order to display timestamps accurately. This remote forensic preview reveals that secret formula files were indeed last accessed during the time of concern. Specifically, five of the six secret files on the server were last accessed on April 2, 2009 at 23:26, which is during the time someone logged into the SSH server on the DMZ and accessed a network file share on the intranet server. In short, it looks very likely that someone took CorpX's trade secrets! Now the big question on everyone's mind is who stole their data (to be continued…).

Once digital investigators confirm a serious problem such as theft of valuable information, it is generally necessary to delve more deeply into available sources of evidence and combine findings to form a comprehensive reconstruction of the crime. Techniques and tools for performing forensic analysis of NetFlow and other common types of network data are covered in Chapter 9. The remainder of this chapter covers techniques and tools for pulling all available data in an investigation together to reconstruct a more complete understanding of events surrounding a security breach.

## Host-based Analysis Techniques

Many analysis techniques used in network intrusion investigations are similar to those used in other types of digital investigations. Here are some of the techniques that are particularly useful when attempting to track down an intrusion.

### Hash Correlation

A common method of analyzing data is to identify specific files via hash value. There are two general ways to proceed. You can identify known-good files via hash so as then to be able to focus on files that are unknown. Conversely, you can identify known-bad files by hash value that you have previously discovered. This second technique is especially useful in identifying malware used on multiple systems in an intrusion, and in network traffic. Once you discover one system on which a program has been used, you can hash that executable and search for files with that hash value on other systems.

### Fuzzy Hashing and Segmentation Hashing

Classic file hashing and correlation via hash value is done by hashing entire files, and comparing those values to the hash values of other full files to identify identical files. Skilled attackers understand this, and will make small modifications to their malicious executables so that the backdoor they drop on one system will not have the same hash value as a backdoor dropped onto another system. Fortunately, there are hashing techniques that allow you to compare parts of a file to parts of other files, rather than the file as a whole. These techniques are called *fuzzy hashing* and *segmentation hashing*. Segmentation hashing is the process of collecting hash values for chunks of a file that are a specific size. For example, you could hash a file in 50 byte chunks, collecting a hash value for bytes 1–50, 51–100, and so on. Fuzzy hashing is often a more effective method. Fuzzy hashing algorithms choose sections of a file to hash based upon probable similarities. You can then compare the fuzzy hash values from a known-bad file to a set of unknown executables, to determine if they share a percentage of their instructions in common. This is especially effective in determining if two files that are not identical are nonetheless related. An example of a tool that performs this is `ssdeep` (http://ssdeep.sourceforge.net/).

### Process Structure Correlation

Identification of a malicious process will lead you to other artifacts. In a memory dump, the name of a process and its PID (Process Identifier) number will map to other things such as:

- **Loaded DLLs**: This may include libraries supplied by the attacker that you did not previously locate, and their storage location.

- **File handles**: This may include other files supplied by the attacker.

- **Registry handles**: This will tell you what Registry keys are being accessed by the process, possibly including the Registry keys used to automatically start the executable at boot.

- **Network sockets and connections**: The PID will be linked to any related listening sockets or active connections. This can tell you one or more ports that the process uses, and possibly with what other hosts it is communicating.

- **Execution path**: The full path to the original file used to execute the program. Even if the file has been deleted since, this can lead you to a directory used by the attacker for other activities. This may also include command line options used to start the program, which can be useful when conducting malicious code analysis.

- **Parent process**: You can determine the parent process of the malicious process. This can tell you how it was started, and other related data. For example, if a malicious process was started by Internet Explorer, then it may be that it was created as the result of an Internet Explorer exploit.

- **Structure comparison**: If the process is not shown in the basic process list, but is present in another structure such as the linked list of EPROCESS blocks, then it may be that there is a rootkit attempting to hide the process.

### Directory Correlation

It is common for an attacker to store multiple malicious files in the same directory. If you discover one file related to the intrusion, you can take a look at the other files in the same directory to see if any of them look suspicious. This may be unrealistic if the directory in question is something like `C:\windows\system32`, which is clogged with legitimate files, but for less populated directories this is worth a try.

### Keyword/Regex Search

A keyword or regular expression search is the process of searching an item of evidence for specific characters or character patterns that are either considered suspicious or are direct signs of unauthorized activities. For example, an attacker may have packed his or her code with a specific packing tool that has a unique or unusual name for the packed sections of the executable. If you find one such program, you may be able to find other programs packed with this same program by searching for that executable section name.

Over time you will aggregate a generic set of keywords that you find are useful in more than one intrusion investigation. Even if you know nothing about a new case, you could use these terms for an initial keyword search for suspicious items. For example, intruders that are not skilled enough to write their own code will often use public tools such as `pskill` from Microsoft. This program, and some of the other pstools contain the string "Sysinternals," referencing the former company of the author. A keyword search for this string, though it may yield false positives, may also lead you to tools used by the intruder stored alongside these common programs.

## Unknown Code Assessment

In an increasing number of cases it is necessary to analyze malicious programs found on a compromised system. The results of such analysis can give digital investigators additional leads such as files placed on the system or IP addresses of remote systems. In addition, malware analysis can enable digital investigators to decode file contents or network traffic that was otherwise inaccessible. The complete process of analyzing malware in a forensic manner is beyond the scope of this chapter and is covered in detail in *Malware Forensics* (Malin, Casey & Aquilina, 2008). However, given the importance of this aspect of intrusion investigation, it deserves some attention here.

When you do discover unknown executable code that may be related to unauthorized activity, you will need to assess that code to determine its functionality and the artifacts of its execution. This will include attempting to determine information such as:

- Unique metadata signature of executable files
- Unique text strings found in the files
- Any additional files created, deleted, or modified by the malware
- Additional files required for the malware to operate
- The names of any processes that the malware attempts to hide, terminate, inject itself into, etc.
- Any Registry keys that are manipulated, or any other modifications of system configuration
- Listening ports opened by the code
- Target of any network communication initiated by the malware, and the protocols used
- Methods for interacting with the code, and signatures that can be used to identify it on the network

There are several different types of activities that can be used to determine this type of information, and they are described in the following subsections.

### Automated Scanning

You can use automated tools to identify and deconstruct the code to determine its function. Tools usable for this range from typical antivirus programs to those that attempt to automatically unpack an executable, and even run it in a sandbox to determine how it functions.

### Static File Inspection

You can inspect a static file with some simple techniques to determine some basic pieces of information. This includes using programs to extract readable strings from the file, examine executable file metadata, and check library dependencies.

### Dynamic Analysis

Execute the code to observe its actions. This will also typically require you to interact with the code to some extent to elicit its full functionality. In some cases you will need to create programs with which the code can interact across network links in a test environment. This type of analysis may involve simple tools that log the behavior of programs on the system, or it may require that you use a debugger to run the code in a more controlled environment.

### Disassembly and Decompilation

This is the process of taking a binary executable and reverting it back to either assembly code or to the higher-level language in which it was constructed. This is not an exact process, as compiler optimizations will have changed the code sufficiently that you will not be able to determine the exact original instructions, but you will be able to determine overall functionality.

## Initial Processing

Most of your analysis tasks and techniques will be selected based upon the facts of the investigation. However, there are some tasks that can and should be performed regardless of the conditions. Most of these are processes you can simply kick off when you receive the evidence, and let run over night. When they are complete, the evidence will be in a better position to analyze and you will have more information to go on. The steps are as follows.

### PRACTITIONER'S TIP: PARALLEL PROCESSING

There will be times when you are in an extreme rush, and do not have the time to tie up your primary analysis system performing these processes. In this case, you will obviously have to proceed manually in an attempt to find what you need. But even if you must start manual analysis immediately, it would benefit you to have another system conducting these operations in the event that you will need their results at a later date.

### *Initial Processing: Host Analysis*

These steps are specific to the processing of host-based data.

1. **Hash verification**. Verify the hash value of evidence transferred into your possession to verify its integrity.

2. **Create a working copy**. If you only have one copy of the image, create a working copy and store the original. Verify the hash value of your working copies.

3. **Verify time settings**. Check and note the time settings of the device, and check responder notes to see if the device time was accurate. You will not be able to properly correlate events from multiple sources unless you know how their time settings are configured, and whether or not the time of the device was accurate.

4. **Recover deleted files**. Have your forensic tool undelete/recover any deleted files that it sees, if it does not do so automatically. This is so they can be directly included in any future searches or analysis steps.

5. **File signature analysis**. Use your tool to automatically tag any files that either do not have a valid file signature or where the signature does not match the file extension (assuming you are analyzing an operating system where this matters).

6. **Carve files**. Attackers will commonly delete some malicious programs once they are finished with them. You should always carve any executable files and libraries that can be recovered from slack and unallocated space.

7. **Calculate file hashes and compare to known files**. This can be used to immediately identify known-bad files, and will also provide you with additional information regarding other files as you conduct your manual searches later.

---

### PRACTITIONER'S TIP: LEST WE FORGET

When filtering files out of view because they have hashed out to be a known-good file (or for any other reason), do not forget to put them back into view when you have completed the specific search you are doing. Even activities relating to legitimate files can be valuable to an investigation, and inadvertently excluding files from analysis can result in incomplete understanding of events.

---

8. **Antivirus scan**. The attacker may be using malicious code that is already known to some antivirus vendors, or is obvious enough to trigger a generic alert. You should scan every possibly compromised system with multiple antivirus packages. This will require that you mount the evidence files as a logical drive so that an antivirus scanner can see the files.

9. **Packer detection scan**. It is common for intruders to pack, or obfuscate their code. Sometimes these obfuscations contain known patterns that can be identified using tools specialized for such a search. This can be a quick way to find malware that is not known to antivirus software, but does contain a known-packer signature.

10. **Index files**. Index the system images using a tool like PTK (www.dflabs.com) or FTK (www.accessdata.com). This will link individual files to the strings that they contain. This is a time-consuming process, but it will make your subsequent keyword searches occur much more quickly.

11. **Generic keyword search**. You should always kick off a search for your generic intrusion keywords in the beginning of a new analysis operation.

12. **Case-specific keyword search**. For the very first system you analyze in a given case, you may not yet have identified any case-specific keywords. But for every subsequent system, you will have such a list that will include attributes such as known-bad IP addresses and host names, and unique malware strings. So a keyword search for any known case keywords should be conducted for every new system found.

### Initial Processing: Log Analysis

These steps are specific to the processing of log files.

1. **Hash verification**. Verify the hash value of evidence transferred into your possession to verify its integrity.

2. **Create a working copy**. If you have only one copy of the log file, create a working copy and store the original. Verify the hash value of your working copies.

3. **Check the file to verify the format of the log entries**. Many log analysis applications can process only certain log formats. If you attempt to import an incompatible format into a log analysis program that does not understand it properly, you may miss data and never even know.

4. **Line count**. Determine how many lines the log file has so that you will know if it will be possible to review it manually or if it will need to be filtered.

5. **Determine time span**. Always check the date-time stamps for the first and last log entries to determine if the log file even covers the timeframe of interest, and check responder notes to see if the device time was accurate. You don't want to spend an hour analyzing log files from today when you are trying to correlate events that occurred a week ago. Note that an intruder may have tampered with the system clock settings and make sure that the timestamps from a compromised system are consistent.

### Initial Processing: Malicious Code

1. **Hash verification**. If you were given the malware rather than extracting it from a host, verify the hash value of evidence transferred into your possession to verify its integrity.
2. **Create a working copy**. If you have only one copy of the file, create a working copy and store the original. Verify the hash value of your working copies.
3. **Antivirus scan**. Scan the malware with as many antivirus packages as you can to see if the malware is already known.
4. **Fuzzy hash**. Create fuzzy hash values for the file and compare it to the other malware in your library to see if there is a link.
5. **Automated sandbox scan**. If you have access to an automated sandbox, you should have the sandbox process the malicious code to determine if it automatically reveals any artifacts.
6. **Packer detection scan**. As mentioned in the host-based list earlier, a packer detection scan can help you to determine if the code is obfuscated in a known way. Some such programs will also attempt to automatically unpack the executable for you.

The complete process of examining Windows and Linux systems for evidence of intrusion and traces of malware is covered in more detail in *Malware Forensics* (Malin, Casey & Aquilina, 2008) with examples of associated tools.

## COMBINATION/CORRELATION

Ideally, in an intrusion investigation, we should be able to determine the scope of an intrusion and establish the continuity of offense, connecting the virtual dots from the target systems back to the intruder. We have a better chance of obtaining a complete and accurate picture of events when we combine information from multiple independent sources to increase the completeness and accuracy of our understanding of an intrusion.

The most common approach to correlating logs is to look at particular time periods of interest in an effort to find related events recorded in multiple logs.

---

### INVESTIGATIVE SCENARIO
### Part 3a: Log Correlation and Crime Reconstruction

Back to the big question of who stole CorpX's data. The timeline, based primarily on NetFlow logs, puts the start of the suspicious SMB network file share activities at 23:12:47 from IP address 10.10.30.2. Examining the Security Event logs on the intranet server around this time period, and searching for the string 10.10.30.2, yields a successful logon record timestamped 23:11:30, as shown in Figure 4.6. The user name is "ow3n3d," which is not a user account that

*(Continued)*

## INVESTIGATIVE SCENARIO—CONT'D

**FIGURE 4.6**

Logon entry on intranet server corresponding to unauthorized file share access.

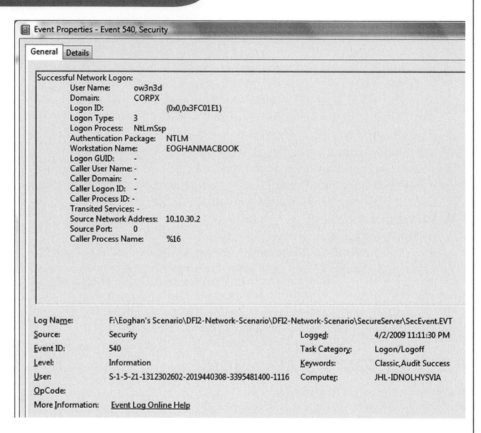

system administrators at CorpX recognize, suggesting that it is not a legitimate account.

Searching the Security Event logs around this time period for other occurrences of the "ow3n3d" account, we find that it was originally created and was granted Administrative access rights just a few minutes earlier at 10:56:06 by someone using the administrator account (Table 4.8).

Further examination of the Security Event logs during this period reveal that the individual who used the administrator account to create the "ow3n3d" account connected to the intranet server via the VPN (192.168.1.1) using Remote Desktop. Pertinent details about the logon and logoff events associated with this suspicious use of the administrator account are provided in Table 4.9. As a point of interest, observe that the event log entries in Table 4.9 captured the name of the attacker's

machine (EVILADMIN) even though it was a remote system on the Internet that was connected into the target CorpX network via VPN. When an intruder uses a Windows system to establish a VPN connection into the target network and access Windows servers within the network, some distinctive information like the attacker's machine name can be transferred into the Security Event logs of the target systems.

So, to learn more about the intruder, it is necessary to examine logs generated by the VPN. Unfortunately, the clock on the VPN device was incorrect, making it more difficult to correlate its logs with logs from other systems. Therefore, we must take a detour in our analysis to figure out the clock offset of the VPN device. But first, we need to update the timeline with results from our latest analysis as shown in Table 4.10.

**Table 4.8** Security Event Log Entries on Intranet Server Showing the Administrator Account Being Used to Create the Suspicious "ow3n3d" Account

| Date-time | Event ID | Event Details |
|---|---|---|
| 4/2/2009 22:43 | 624 | Account Management "ow3n3d\|CORPX\|%{S-1-5-21-1312302602-2019440308-3395481400-1116}\|Administrator\|CORPX\|(0x0,0x3F9D99F)\|-\|ow3n3d\|ow3n3d\|ow3n3d@CorpX.local\|-\|-\|-\|-\|-\|%%1794\|%%1794\|513\|-\|0x0\|0x15\|" |
| 4/2/2009 22:43 | 628 | Account Management "ow3n3d\|CORPX\|%{S-1-5-21-1312302602-2019440308-3395481400-1116}\|Administrator\|CORPX\|(0x0,0x3F9D99F)\|-" S-1-5-21-1312302602-2019440308-3395481400-500 "User Account password set: Target Account Name: ow3n3d Target Domain: CORPX Target Account ID: %{S-1-5-21-1312302602-2019440308-3395481400-1116} Caller User Name: Administrator Caller Domain: CORPX Caller Logon ID: (0x0,0x3F9D99F)" |
| 4/2/2009 22:56 | 636 | Account Management "CN=ow3n3d,DC=CorpX,DC=local\|%{S-1-5-21-1312302602-2019440308-3395481400-1116}\|Administrators\|Builtin\|%{S-1-5-32-544}\|Administrator\|CORPX\|(0x0,0x3F9D99F)\|-" S-1-5-21-1312302602-2019440308-3395481400-500 "Security Enabled Local Group Member Added: Member Name: CN=ow3n3d,DC=CorpX,DC=local Member ID: %{S-1-5-21-1312302602-2019440308-3395481400-1116} Target Account Name: Administrators Target Domain: Builtin Target Account ID: %{S-1-5-32-544} Caller User Name: Administrator Caller Domain: CORPX Caller Logon ID: (0x0,0x3F9D99F) Privileges: -" |

**Table 4.9** Windows Security Event Logs Showing the Intruder Logging into the Intranet Server Using the Administrator Account The connection is using Remote Desktop (RDP) and is coming through the VPN (192.168.1.1).

| Date-time | Event ID | Event Details |
|---|---|---|
| 4/2/2009 22:40 | 528 | "Administrator\|CORPX\|(0x0,0x3F9D99F)\|10\|User32 \|Negotiate\|JHL-IDNOLHYSVIA\|{792d8992-c006-e32b-73c6-af350297e798}\|JHL-IDNOLHYSVIA $\|CORPX\|(0x0,0x3E7)\|5240\|-\|192.168.1.1\|1041" S-1-5-21-1312302602-2019440308-3395481400-500 "Successful Logon: User Name: Administrator Domain: CORPX Logon ID: (0x0,0x3F9D99F) Logon Type: 10 Logon Process: User32 Authentication Package: Negotiate Workstation Name: JHL-IDNOLHYSVIA Logon GUID: {792d8992-c006-e32b-73c6-af350297e798}" |
| 4/2/2009 22:46 | 683 | Session disconnected from winstation: User Name: Administrator Domain: CORPX Logon ID: (0x0,0x3F9D99F) Session Name: RDP-Tcp#9 Client Name: EVILADMIN Client Address: 192.168.1.1 |
| 4/2/2009 22:55 | 682 | Session reconnected to winstation: User Name: Administrator Domain: CORPX Logon ID: (0x0,0x3F9D99F) Session Name: RDP-Tcp#11 Client Name: EVILADMIN Client Address: 192.168.1.1 |
| 4/2/2009 22:56 | 683 | Session disconnected from winstation: User Name: Administrator Domain: CORPX Logon ID: (0x0,0x3F9D99F) Session Name: RDP-Tcp#11 Client Name: EVILADMIN Client Address: 192.168.1.1 |

**Table 4.10** Updated Timeline of Events in Intrusion Investigation Scenario

| Time (Apr 2, 2009) | Description | Source of Data | Comments |
|---|---|---|---|
| 22:40 | HTTP access to web server 10.10.10.50 | Netflow | Data consistent with file transfers in the 100000K range. Follow-up with web server logs. |
| 22:40 | HTTP access to corporate data | IIS logs | Files in snakeoil series, identified as sensitive by X Corporation. IIS logs in GMT+0000. |

*(Continued)*

**Table 4.10** Updated Timeline of Events in Intrusion Investigation Scenario—Cont'd

| Time (April 2, 2009) | Description | Source of Data | Comments |
| --- | --- | --- | --- |
| 22:40–22:46 | Administrator account logged into intranet server via the VPN | Server Event Logs | |
| 22:43 | User name: ow3n3d created using administrator account | Server Event Logs | |
| 22:55–22:56 | Administrator granted access to share server from client EVILADMIN coming through VPN using Remote Desktop | Server Event Logs | |
| 22:56 | User name: ow3n3d granted access rights on share server from client EVILADMIN | Server Event Logs | |
| 23:11 | Login to share server from SSH Server, User name: ow3n3d | Server Event Logs | |
| 23:13–23:28 | SMB communication with share server 10.10.10.50 | NetFlow | Communication to SSH server, 10.10.30.2, in DMZ, possibly SAMBA. Follow-up with share server logs. |

## Resolving Unsynchronized Date-time Stamps

Failure to maintain consistent, accurate time in log servers is one of the greatest stumbling blocks to log correlation. Clocks on Cisco devices are particularly prone to drift and must be maintained using NTP. If the logs are recent and the investigator has access to the logging systems, it may be possible to establish the relative time offset with some confidence. Unfortunately, the existence of the offset casts doubt on the consistency of the offset. If the clocks are 10 minutes out of synchronization now, it reduces our confidence that they were no more or less than 10 minutes out of synchronization one month ago.

The best approach to correlating two unsynchronized logs is to identify an event, or a pattern of events, that generates a record in both logs simultaneously. The timestamps for the event can be compared and the time offset computed. In the chapter scenario, for example, the timestamps in logs associated with the VPN device do not match those on other systems on the network. Since we do not yet know which, if either, system was properly calibrated, we will use the intranet server logs as our working time baseline.

Fortunately, the Cisco VPN device in use at CorpX was configured to record access attempts to resources on the intranet web server. Comparing the web access log entry for the snakeoil1.jpg file with the corresponding entry in the VPN log, we see that the date-time stamps generated by the VPN are 58 minutes and 25 seconds behind.

### Web access log entry on intranet server (UTC):

```
2009-04-03 02:38:10 W3SVC1 10.10.10.50 GET /images/
   snakeoil1.jpg - 80 - 192.168.1.1 Mozilla/4.0+(compatib
   le;+MSIE+6.0;+Windows+NT+5.1) 200 0 0
```

### Corresponding VPN log entry:

```
Apr 02 2009 21: 39:45: %ASA-6-716003: Group <DfltGrpPolicy>
   User <jwiley> IP <130.132.1.26> WebVPN access GRANTED:
   http://10.10.10.50//images/snakeoil1.jpg
```

Even this approach to determining clock offsets can result in errors and confusion. Digital investigators may inadvertently select a log source that has an inaccurate timestamp as the basis for correcting time offsets, thus throwing off all the times in their analysis. This situation can be avoided by looking for more than one reference point across the various logs. In the preceding example, incorporating NetFlow logs in the calculation of clock offset reveals that the router clock was 77 seconds ahead of the intranet server. Even such a small offset can create confusion when developing an intrusion timeline. In short, the more independent sources of evidence that can be correlated and the more events that can be correlated across the logs, the more likely we are to get an accurate picture of events.

## INVESTIGATIVE SCENARIO
## Part 3b: Putting Together Pieces of the Puzzle

Having determined that date-time stamps in the VPN logs need to be adjusted by adding one hour, we are ready to continue our analysis into who stole CorpX's trade secrets. Examining the VPN logs for the times of interest reveals that the data thief authenticated with the VPN using the jwiley user account at 22:37:49 and accessed the intranet web server. The intruder subsequently connected to the intranet server using Remote Desktop at the time the ow3n3d account was created as shown in the following VPN log entry (having added 58 minutes, 25 seconds):

```
Apr 02 2009 22: 55:21: %ASA-6-716003:
    Group <DfltGrpPolicy> User <jwi-
    ley> IP <130.132.1.26> WebVPN access
    GRANTED: rdp://10.10.10.50/
```

VPN logs also show that the ow3n3d account was later used to authenticate to the VPN at 23:08:42, and established an SSH connection with the SSH server in the DMZ (10.10.30.2). Examination of authentication logs on the SSH server for this time period show that the intruder logged in using the jwiley account between 23:12 and 23:30. This was the only account logged into the SSH server during the period when trade secrets on the intranet server were accessed.

Furthermore, the following entries in /var/secure.log on the SSH server show that the jwiley account was used at 23:30:15 to establish an sftp session, potentially to transfer the stolen trade secrets off of the system onto the intruder's computer.

```
Apr 2 23:30:15 Shell.CorpX.com com.apple.
    SecurityServer[22]: checkpw() succeeded,
    creating credential for user jwiley
Apr 2 23:30:15 Shell.CorpX.com com.apple.
    SecurityServer[22]: checkpw() succeeded,
    creating shared credential for user jwiley
Apr 2 23:30:15 Shell.CorpX.com com.apple.
    SecurityServer[22]: Succeeded authorizing right
    system.login.tty by client /usr/sbin/sshd for
    authorization created by /usr/sbin/sshd
Apr 2 23:30:15 Shell.CorpX.com sshd[4025]:
    Accepted keyboard-interactive/pam for
    jwiley from 10.10.20.1 port 1025 ssh2
Apr 2 23:30:15 Shell.CorpX.com
    sshd[4037]: subsystem request for sftp
```

In all the pertinent VPN log entries, including those relating to the jwiley and ow3n3d accounts, the thief's originating IP address was recorded 130.132.1.26. With the proper legal authorization, the Internet Service Provider (ISP) responsible for that IP address may be able to provide information about the subscriber who was using that IP address at the time. This information could lead to a search warrant of the intruder's home and seizure of his computers, which we would search for traces of the stolen data, check to see if the machine name was EVILADMIN, and look for other linkage with the intrusion and data theft.

Although digital investigators follow the trail left by an intruder, it is important to document the key findings into a logical progression of events, as discussed in the section, "Case Management," earlier in this chapter (see Table 4.5). To demonstrate this in the context of the investigative scenario for this chapter, we have developed the timeline of events shown in Table 4.11.

Recall that this documentation process serves several purposes, and is an effective tool to reaching a clearer understanding of events relating to an intrusion. In addition to helping us keep track of our findings, this type of chronological event tracking chart provides everyone involved in an ongoing investigation with an overview of what is known about the intrusion, and where there are still gaps in knowledge. In the longer term, this documentation can be included in a final report and can be an invaluable memory aid for testimony, summarizing the most important events.

**Table 4.11** Timeline of Events in Intrusion Investigation Scenario with Times Corrected for Clock Offsets

| Time (April 2, 2009) | Description | Source of Data | Comments |
|---|---|---|---|
| 22:37 | jwiley account authenticated to VPN | VPN Logs | VPN timestamps assumed offset 58 mins, 25 secs from intranet server. |
| 22:39 | HTTP access to web server 10.10.10.50 | VPN Logs | Files in snakeoil series, identified as sensitive by X Corporation. |
| 22:39 | HTTP access to web server 10.10.10.50 | Netflow | Data consistent with file transfers in the 100000K range. Follow-up with web server logs. NetFlow time-stamps assumed offset by 77 seconds from intranet server. |
| 22:39 | HTTP access to corporate data | IIS logs | Files in snakeoil series, identified as sensitive by X Corporation. IIS logs in GMT+0000. |
| 22:46 | Administrator granted access to share server from client EVILADMIN coming through VPN using Remote Desktop | Server Event Logs | |
| 22:56 | User name: ow3n3d granted access rights on share server from client EVILADMIN | Server Event Logs | |
| 23:08 | ow3n3d account authenticated to VPN | VPN Logs | |

*(Continued)*

**Table 4.11** Timeline of Events in Intrusion Investigation Scenario with Times Corrected for Clock Offsets—Cont'd

| Time (April 2, 2009) | Description | Source of Data | Comments |
|---|---|---|---|
| 23:12–23:30 | User jwiley accesses 10.10.30.2 via SSH through VPN | Logs on 10.10.30.2 | |
| 23:11 | Login to share server from SSH Server, User name: ow3n3d | Server Event Logs | |
| 23:13–23:28 | SMB communication with share server 10.10.10.50 | Netflow | Communication to SSH server, 10.10.30.2, in DMZ, possibly SAMBA. Follow-up with share server logs. |
| 23:30 | User jwiley accesses 10.10.30.2 via sftp through VPN | Logs on 10.10.30.2 | |

*Intranet timestamps are being used as baseline pending further information.*

Although most tools organize and correlate logs by time, there are other systems for organizing evidence. In some cases it may make more sense to organize by file ownership, for instance, or IP of origin. Any characteristics or traces of the intrusion that you can extract from logs or compromised hosts may be useful to search various data sources.

---

**PRACTITIONER'S TIP: WHAT CARE I FOR TIME?**

Quite often one correlation method, such as a timeline, will point to other types of correlation. In the case scenario, we saw an access by a machine named EVILADMIN. We should check the logs for other systems accessed by EVILADMIN in the past (remember the point about looking back *before* the time of detection). Mind you, we ultimately strive to incorporate our findings into a bigger and better timeline, but there would be nontemporal correlations within the master sequence. We like time. Events and time go together so nicely.

---

During an intrusion investigation, available data sources are searched repeatedly as the investigation progresses and investigators find new information, such as IP addresses, nonstandard ports, or communication methods used by the intruders. Therefore, it is important for digital investigators to be conversant with tools and techniques for correlating and searching various sources of data.

## TOOL FEATURE: LOG CORRELATION TOOLS

Splunk (www.splunk.com) is one of the most flexible log correlation tools available. Although Splunk does recognize some specific log formats, it uses a flexible approach to extract features from any log data, and indexes log data to enable quicker searches. The data input screen of Splunk is shown in Figure 4.7 with the specific `cisco_syslog` format specified.

**FIGURE 4.7**

Adding a Cisco syslog file to Splunk.

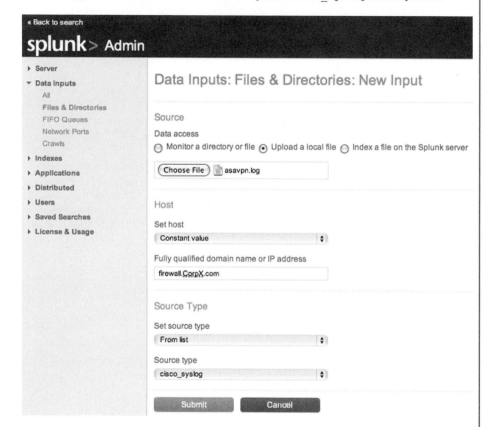

Unlike many other log correlation tools that require logs to be in a well-defined format, Splunk does not depend on specific log formats, and recognizes timestamps of most kinds. In practical terms, digital investigators can load every available log (defined loosely to include any record with a timestamp) into Splunk, including file system information, server logs, and network traffic, and examine these disparate sources together. This is the definition of correlation! The main caveat is that logs must generally be in plain text for Splunk to understand them. Fortunately, most binary data sources can be converted to text. The following commands were used to convert logs from the intrusion investigation scenario using this chapter into text format for input into Splunk:

- **Windows Security Event logs**: LogParser "SELECT * FROM SecEvent.Evt WHERE (TimeGenerated > '2009-04-02 09:00:00') and (EventID IN (528;529;540; 624;628;636;682;683))" –q -i:EVT –o:CSV
- **NetFlow**: flow-print -f 5
- **Network traffic**: tcpdump -r 20090323-gooddryrun. pcap -tttt -vv -n

Note that conversion can introduce errors, particularly in date-time stamps. For instance, make sure that the system used to convert Windows Event logs has its clock and time zone set to the same values as the original logs.

*(Continued)*

## TOOL FEATURE: LOG CORRELATION TOOLS—CONT'D

Once all available logs have been loaded and indexed in Splunk, they can be viewed and queried with the ease of a search engine. Splunk has the ability to correlate on any feature in log files, including IP address, host name, username, and message text. Clicking on any value in a given log entry will cause Splunk to search its index for all items containing that value. In addition to searching for specific items in the logs, the timeline feature can be used to perform temporal analysis. Splunk provides a histogram of events per unit time that digital investigators can use to observe high concentrations of activity, and drill down into potentially significant time periods. In addition, results can be restricted by date range. Combining the filtering and histogram features of Splunk enables digital investigators to locate periods of suspicious activities. All these features are shown in Figure 4.8, where the digital investigator is viewing logs between the times 22:50 and 23:00 on April 2, 2009 that

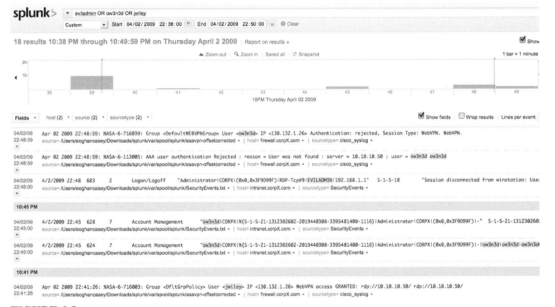

**FIGURE 4.8**

Splunk being used to correlate logs from multiple sources, filtering by time and keywords.

contain the keywords ow3n3d or eviladmin (Splunk treats an asterisk as a wildcard). Observe in Figure 4.8 that Splunk normalizes the differently formatted date-time stamps in the logs, thus enabling the correlation.

Because Splunk indexes log data, it shows how available strings relate to information being entered in the query field as shown in Figure 4.9.

An added benefit from a forensic perspective is that Splunk retains the original logs and provides a "Show source" option,

**FIGURE 4.9**

Splunk showing how many items are in the logs relating to the search string ow3n3d.

*(Continued)*

## TOOL FEATURE: LOG CORRELATION TOOLS—CONT'D

enabling digital investigators to view important events in their original context.

Among Splunk's shortcomings is the lack of a feature to adjust for time zone differences or clock offset. Digital investigators must make necessary adjustments prior to loading data into Splunk. Difficulties can arise when input data has multiple date-time stamps in each record (e.g., file system information), making it necessary to create a custom template for the specific format. In addition, the ability to recognize most timestamp formats comes with a price. Splunk can mistak-

enly identify nontimestamps as timestamps. Before performing analysis, digital investigators should test each type of data they are loading into Splunk to verify that it is interpreting each log source as expected.

Other tools that can be useful for log correlation but rely on specific log formats include xpolog (www.xplg. com) and Sawmill (www.sawmill.net). There are also more expensive commercial log correlation tools like CS-MARS from Cisco, nFX from NetForensics, and NetDetect or from Niksun.

When dealing with the more skilled adversary, investigators should always look at the logs for signs of subterfuge such as hardware clock tampering, missing entries, or time gaps. It is important to perform this type of examination on raw logs prior to import into a database or other tool because entries that have timestamps out of sequence with their surrounding entries can be critical from a forensic perspective. Since most analysis tools simply order entries by their timestamps, it will not be evident from these tools that there are entries out of sequence.

## FEEDING ANALYSIS BACK INTO THE DETECTION PHASE

Once you have identified specific artifacts related to an intrusion, you will then be able to search the enterprise for those artifacts, thereby identifying additional compromised systems and network segments. This involves searching several types of structures, primarily systems, network communication links, and directories.

### Host-based Detection

Host-based detection sweeps involve auditing all hosts within the potential scope of the incident to determine if they possess any of the known artifacts of the incident. These artifacts exist either in memory, or in the primary nonvolatile data storage used by the operating system. The primary types of artifacts for which you will need to be able to sweep include:

- Filenames and file naming conventions
- File metadata values or specific string contents
- Registry keys or configuration file contents

- Log messages
- Process names and execution paths
- Process library load outs and file handle lists
- Loaded driver modules
- Specific discrepancies between kernel structures, or between a kernel structure and results of kernel API queries

Searching for these artifacts is not an easy task. There are several constraints that will affect your ability to sweep for these artifacts.

## Enterprisewide Visibility

Your first problem will be obtaining access to all systems in the potential scope of the incident. For example, if the attacker has compromised domain-level credentials, then all systems in the domain are in the potential scope of the incident. This means you will need to search each and every system in that domain for known artifacts to determine if they had malicious code installed upon them, even if this includes thousands of systems. If you do not conduct this search, you will risk there being undetected, compromised hosts. This assumes that the devices in the domain are of an operating system capable of running the malware. For example, a Vista system may not execute malware specifically written for XP SP2, let alone Mac OS X.

From a simple enterprise management perspective, this means that you will need the ability to deploy agents to all such systems and/or remotely poll the operating system or a preexisting agent for the specific information that you require. This brings us back to the Preparation phase of the Incident Response Lifecycle. Many organizations are not set up for this, and that can be a barrier to an effective investigation.

Furthermore, in an enterprise there will invariably be staff members on travel, or people who simply have their systems turned off. You can't search a system that is at a customer site in another country, or that isn't even powered on. Your best option is to trigger searches when systems authenticate to the network, so that the next time a remote worker returns to the office, or connects via a VPN an agent is loaded or a remote search is initiated.

Finally, you will have systems that are not part of your network authentication and authorization structure, such as experimental systems that haven't been added to one of your domains, student-owned systems at a university, or wireless systems on an airport's public wireless network. These systems will not respond to searches or agents pushed out through the directory. Searches of these devices will have to be conducted separately at a greater administrative overhead, if you even know they exist and where they are. This is another reason that a proper asset inventory is essential to an intrusion investigation. You cannot search devices of which you are completely unaware.

## Hardware Load

You will also have to deal with the fact that you will be taxing the remote system you are trying to search. Conducting operations such as searching the entire directory structure, and parsing every executable file to identify specific metadata is not a trivial task. At organizations that have three to five year turnover rates for their workstations, you will significantly slow down the older systems during these searches. If possible, conduct your searches during off hours. Otherwise, prepare your help desk to field complaint calls about systems "acting slow."

## Circumventing Rootkit Interference to Conduct Artifact Sweeps

Remember that if the system you are searching is compromised, malicious code already running on the system may actively attempt to hide itself from standard OS queries for file system and process data. Because of this, you will not be able to trust that a simple API query for an artifact type returned a proper result. For example, you may attempt to obtain a list of DLLs in `C:\windows\system32` to determine if a specific Trojan DLL is present, but just because the result is negative does not mean that the file is not there.

There are several ways to deal with this. First, you can attempt to query for artifacts directly at the structures for which you are searching. In other words, imagine again that you are searching system32 for a specific DLL. Rather than your tool (whatever it may be) issuing a query to kernel32.dll as part of the public Windows API, you could open a handle directly to the MFT (Master File Table) of an NTFS volume and search it directly, thereby circumventing basic rootkit API hooks. This is a common technique used by remote forensic tools. Similar techniques are available for searching for other types of artifacts. However, if the target system is already running a rootkit, you cannot be absolutely sure that a way has not been found to circumvent this type of technique.

Another method is to compare structures and assess for discrepancies. Not only could you query the MFT directly, but you can also compare the contents of the MFT with the results of a directory listing via API call. This is how some rootkit detection programs work, and you should have this capability as well.

## Tool Options

There are different options for software tools that will actually enable you to conduct such a search:

- **Custom Scripts**: You can utilize custom scripts to query for different artifacts. For example, WMI scripting is a robust method for querying the Windows operating system directly for artifacts.

- **Specialized Forensic Tools**: There are several forensic tools that are designed for remote forensic searches. EnCase Enterprise and

ProDiscover IR are two examples. Note that there are significant differences in their feature sets and methods. Both tools offer custom scripting so that you can automate searches for artifact types, but there is also significant cost for such tools.

- **Forensic Access Facilitators**: A new remote forensic tool type has emerged that grants remote access directly to remote system memory and disks completely separate from the analysis platform being used to assess those structures. One tool that accomplishes this at this time is called F-Response. You can deploy F-Response agents, and then simply search the remote systems with lower cost forensic tools that do not inherently include remote search capabilities. Note however, that F-Response offers only agent-based access to remote systems.

## Network-based Detection

Network-based Intrusion Detection, or NIDS, is a more commonly developed practice, and is essentially already covered by common intrusion detection methodologies. Devices that exist at network choke points, such as IDS sensors, firewalls, and application proxies can be used to search ingress/egress network traffic for specific artifacts that you have discovered during your analysis tasks. These artifacts will typically be one of the following:

- IP addresses of known victims or external hosts involved in the intrusion
- DNS host names involved in the intrusion
- TCP/UDP port numbers used in attack-related traffic
- Specific ASCII or hex values found in packets associated with incident-related traffic
- Abnormal protocol header values directly associated with incident-related traffic
- Volumes of traffic, either abnormal for a particular host in a compromised network segment, or abnormal for direction in a specific direction (i.e., a workstation exhibiting excessively heavy egress traffic)

For example, if during your analysis of a malicious code sample, you discover that it communicates to several specific hosts via port 80 and embeds instructions inside valid HTML, all of these things can be searched using the network devices just mentioned. You can configure your firewall to log access to the IP addresses in question, and though you may not be able to simply monitor for port 80 access, you can configure web proxies to search for specific HTML signatures that correlate to the unauthorized traffic. Searching for artifacts such as these at network borders will assist you in identifying additional hosts.

As mentioned previously in this chapter, you will probably not be able to deploy a sufficient number of sniffers to cover all points of ingress/egress on your network to monitor for unauthorized activity. However you can use the devices already in play.

## CONCLUSION

Intrusion investigation is an exciting and dynamic process that requires strong technical skills and effective case management, often requiring a team of digital investigators and forensic examiners. In practice it sometimes seems like controlled chaos, particularly when an intruder is still active on the victim systems. Digital investigators have a better chance of navigating the challenges and complexities of intrusion investigations if they follow the scientific method and scope assessment cycle. In addition, the success of this type of investigation depends heavily on having a mechanism to keep track of the investigative and forensic subtasks.

## REFERENCES

Casey, E., & Stanley, A. (2004). Tool review: Remote forensic preservation and examination tools. *Digital Investigation, 1*(4).

Casey, E. (2002). Error, uncertainty and loss in digital evidence. *International Journal of Digital Evidence, 1*(2).

Casey, E. (2004). *Digital evidence & computer crime* (2nd ed.). Academic Press, San Diego, CA.

Casey, E. (2004). Network traffic as a source of evidence: Tool strengths, weaknesses, and future needs. *Journal of Digital Investigation 1*(1).

Casey, E. (2006). Investigating sophisticated security breaches. *Communications of ACM, 49*(2).

Gartner Press Release. (2008). *Gartner Says Companies Should Implement Information Access Technologies, Rather Than Buying More Storage, to Manage Old Corporate Data.* STAMFORD, Conn.

Grow, B., Epstein, K., & Tschang, C. C. (2008). The new e-spionage threat. *Business Week.* Available online at www.businessweek.com/magazine/toc/08_16/B4080magazine.htm

Malin, C., Casey, E., & Aquilina, J. (2008). *Malware Forensics.* Syngress.

Ponemon Institute. (2009a). *2008 Annual study: US Cost of a Data Breach.*

Ponemon Institute. (2009b). *2008 Annual study: UK Cost of a Data Breach.*

Scarfone, K., Grance, T., & Masone, K. (2008). *Computer security incident handling guide, special publication 800-61, revision 1.* National Institute of Standards and Testing. Available online at http://csrc.nist.gov/publications/nistpubs/800-61-rev1/SP800-61rev1.pdf

**PART**

# Technology

# CHAPTER 5

# Windows Forensic Analysis

**Ryan D. Pittman and Dave Shaver**

## INTRODUCTION

Despite the proliferation and growing popularity of other user interfaces, such as Macintosh OS X and Ubuntu (a flavor of Linux), Microsoft's Windows operating systems remain the most popular in the world. In fact, sources have reported that over 90% of the computers in use today are running some version of the Windows operating system.[1] This is not surprising given the almost endless variation that can be found in Windows products, their relative ease of use for the average computer owner, and the virtual stranglehold on marketing Microsoft has enjoyed for so many years (particularly before recent inroads by a resurgent Apple, Inc.). Microsoft operating systems have even found an audience in nontraditional quarters, as scores of Macintosh users have learned to use products like Apple's Boot Camp or Parallels virtualization software to run Windows on their Intel-based Macintosh hardware. Private users, Fortune 500 companies, and government agencies alike all overwhelmingly have chosen Windows systems as their primary technology infrastructures.

In light of this, it should not be surprising that the majority of systems that digital investigators will be called upon to examine will be running a Windows operating system. The ease of use of Windows appeals to criminals and "evil-doers" the same as it does to the grandmother down the street. And both the longevity and popularity of Windows have made it a favorite target of virus authors, hackers, and industrial saboteurs. So, whether investigating child pornography, intellectual property theft, or Internet Relay Chat (IRC) bot

**CONTENTS**

Introduction.....209

Windows, Windows Everywhere......210

NTFS Overview..........215

Forensic Analysis of the NTFS Master File Table (MFT)...............223

Metadata..........230

Artifacts of User Activities..........235

Deletion and Destruction of Data..................273

Windows Internet and Communications Activities..........279

Windows Process Memory............285

BitLocker and Encrypting File System (EFS)....287

[1]http://marketshare.hitslink.com/report.aspx?qprid=8

**209**

RAIDs and
Dynamic
Disks...............292

Cases...............299

References.......299

infection, it is a safe bet that knowledge of Windows operating systems, and its associated artifacts, will aid investigators in their task.

This chapter provides technical methods and techniques to help practitioners extract and interpret data of investigative value from computers running Windows operating systems. An important aspect of conducting advanced forensic analysis is understanding the mechanisms underlying fundamental operations on Windows systems like the boot process, file creation and deletion, and use of removable storage media. In addition, by understanding how to aggregate and correlate data on Windows systems, digital investigators are better able to get the "big picture" (such as an overall theory of user action and a timeline), as well as overcoming specific technical obstacles. For example, in a case where a file's primary creation time on the system is questioned, due to information related to the file's transfer as shown in packet capture data or firewall logs, lesser known file system date-time stamps, embedded application metadata, and link files could all help ascertain the provenance of the file.

## WINDOWS, WINDOWS EVERYWHERE...

Although there are numerous different versions of Microsoft Windows, older versions (such as Windows 9x, NT, ME, and even 2000) are somewhat outdated and are no longer widely used. It is, of course, not out of the question that the investigator could come across systems running one these older versions, but it is far more likely that they will encounter one of the newer versions currently in widespread use for home, corporate, and government environments: Windows XP, Windows Vista, and (for server environments) Windows Server 2003 or 2008. Microsoft also offers additional variations for handheld devices, such as Windows CE, but handheld devices will not be the focus of this chapter. At the time of this writing, an even newer version of Windows (Windows 7; previously codenamed "Blackcomb" and "Vienna") is on the horizon and already in Beta release.[2] Although these different versions of Windows share common characteristics, there are differences that present quirks and features that can prove useful (and sometimes frustrating) to the forensic examiner.

It is important for forensic examiners to understand the Windows startup process for a number of reasons beyond simply interrupting the boot process to view and document the CMOS configuration. First, when less experienced digital investigators inadvertently boot an evidentiary system, a knowledgeable forensic examiner may need to explain which files were altered in the startup

---

[2]All references to Windows 7 throughout this chapter are a product of *preliminary* testing by the author with a Beta release (Build 7000) of Windows 7 Ultimate, and are for informational purposes only. Investigators and examiners are reminded of the importance of performing their own testing and research prior to offering opinions.

process, and demonstrate that no user-created files or other data of evidentiary significance were modified. Second, forensic examiners often need to determine which version of the operating system was running and when it was installed. Third, when investigating malware or other possible system subversion, it is generally necessary to examine each aspect of the startup process for signs of tampering.

A very helpful file in Windows NT/2000/XP/2k3 is the `boot.ini` file, which can provide the examiner with information pertaining to the version of the operating system installed on a particular system partition as shown in Figure 5.1. This file may show multiple boot options that are available to the user, including multiple operating systems on different partitions. Windows setup logs (e.g., `c:\windows\setuplog.txt` and `c:\windows\debug\netsetup.log`) can also provide good information about how Windows was installed and configured.

Further, querying the `SOFTWARE\Microsoft\Windows NT\Current Version` registry subkey (using a standard registry editor, such as `regedit`, or another forensic viewer) in any of the modern Windows distributions (including Windows 7) can provide a wealth of operating system information, including the installed product and current version, install date, registered owner and organization, and even service pack number.

## Windows XP

Windows XP has been a standard Microsoft OS for workstations for years. Since it hit the scene in 2001, millions of Windows users have grown comfortable with its user-friendly interface, comparatively efficient operation, and improvements over previous versions such as Windows 2000 and Windows ME. Windows XP comes in three primary editions (i.e., Home, Media Center, and Professional), which were targeted at different parts of Microsoft's workstation computing customers. From a file system standpoint, XP continues to run on top of the File Allocation Table (FAT) and New Technology File System (NTFS) structures with which examiners have grown familiar.[3] The boot sequence for XP shown in Figure 5.2 is likewise fairly straightforward, and mirrors that of several previous versions as well as Windows Server 2003.

**FIGURE 5.1**

`Boot.ini` file from a system running Windows XP Professional.

---

[3]Support for additional file systems can be added to Windows using third-party drivers like the EXT2 Installable File System (www.fs-driver.org/).

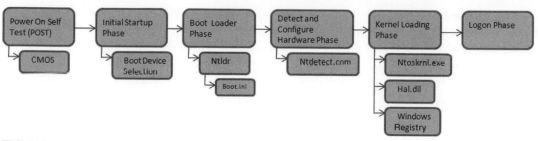

**FIGURE 5.2**

Windows XP boot sequence.

## FROM THE CASE FILES: COMPUTERS DON'T LIE

A recent examination of a Windows server and analysis of its IIS 6.0 web logs confirmed that the system had indeed been compromised, and even revealed the source of the attack. The logs provided a suspicious IP address, the operating system used in the compromise (Windows XP), and the suspect's web browser (Avant). The IP address led investigators to an ISP, and eventually to a suspect in the intrusion. However, the suspect denied all involvement in the compromise and stated that his computer was running Windows 98 (as had always been the case). This was of course discouraging news for investigators, who were sure they had their man. Despite the suspect's protestations, investigators seized his computer anyway (per their search warrant) and shortly began the forensic examination. A search of the hard drive revealed a deleted `boot.ini` file that appeared to have been deleted mere days after the compromise of the web server, clearly showing that Windows XP Professional had been installed on the system, thereby punching a hole in the suspect's story.

There are many features in Windows XP that can be very useful for forensic examiners. Evidence of user actions is often recorded in areas (such as Internet history, Event logs, Prefetch files, `thumbs.db` files, and link files) that are easy to view for the trained digital investigator with the right tool. However, other challenges (such as analyzing restore points, analysis of data in the Windows registry, collection and analysis of memory, dealing with RAIDs and dynamic disks, overcoming Windows encryption, and documenting data destruction) can present a much greater challenge, even for more experienced digital investigators. Regardless of its utility, Microsoft stopped selling XP in 2008, but plans to continue support for this beloved Windows version until 2014, which means it will most likely be a big part of examiners' lives for many years to come.

Throughout this chapter, unless otherwise stated, discussions of Windows XP operation and artifacts also generally apply to Windows Server 2003 systems.

### Windows Vista (and related systems)

Windows Vista, which many still remember under its development code name of "Longhorn," was officially released in 2007 and, like XP before it, was intended by Microsoft to become the de facto OS for workstations. Vista, like XP (and the upcoming Windows 7), is available in multiple editions (i.e., Starter, Home Basic and Basic N, Home Premium, Business and Business N,[4] Enterprise, and Ultimate), each with its own capabilities and features; for example, Vista Home allows users to back up documents, and Vista Enterprise allows the creation of true-clone copies of the entire hard disk/partitions for later recovery or creation of identical systems.

Also similar to XP, Vista, 2k8, and 7 take advantage of the NTFS file system and add the concept of Transactional NTFS (TxF). Implemented together with the Kernel Transaction Manager (KTM), TxF was designed to make NTFS more robust by treating file operations as transactions that can be rolled back or reapplied as necessary in the case of catastrophic system failure. Most of Microsoft's official literature suggests that Vista cannot be installed and run on FAT32. However, although this may be true from a simplistic or tech support standpoint, there are several tips and tweaks that will allow Vista to be installed on a FAT32 partition, so it is possible the digital investigator could encounter such a scenario. Before Vista was released, it was thought it would be based on a new file system (WinFS) under development by Microsoft. However, shortly before Vista's release, problems in development caused Microsoft to shelve the new file system temporarily, leaving Vista to utilize NTFS as its primary base.[5]

Although Vista, 2k8, and 7 are not yet as familiar to users as XP, the same is also true for most IT professionals and digital investigators. Vista presents a unique challenge in that, particularly for many younger forensic examiners, it represents the first *significantly* new and different version of Windows to be released in their careers. Vista, 2k8, and 7 share many features and capabilities with XP that examiners have grown to know and love, but they are fundamentally different from their older cousin in many aspects. Vista, Server 2008, and 7 depart from XP's tried-and-true path, even at such a basic level as the boot sequence, introducing things like the Windows Boot Loader and Boot Configuration Data (BCD), depicted in Figure 5.3.

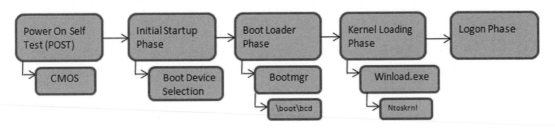

**FIGURE 5.3**
Windows Vista boot sequence.

---

Some of the things that make Vista and its cohorts unique are also things that could aid examiners in their investigations, as detailed later in this chapter. For example, the Shadow Copy feature (which has its roots in the system restore and other snapshot-type capabilities under Windows XP) is enabled by default in Vista Business, Enterprise, and Ultimate editions and makes incremental backup copies of files and folders to aid in document recovery. The Windows Search (also called Instant Search) feature in Vista indexes most of the user files and folders (including e-mail) to aid users in searching for particular files. In addition, Vista makes greater use of metatags (essentially metadata) and encourages users to add their own information to important files. Unfortunately though, for every potential advantage that Vista presents, it shares most of the complexities of XP and then some. Examples of potential obstacles when examining a Vista system include (but are certainly not limited to):

- Pathing differences between Vista and XP (e.g., `\Users\<user name>\AppData\Local` in Vista versus `\Documents and Settings\<username>\Local Settings` in XP)
- Differences in Recycle Bin data structures
- BitLocker encryption
- The fact that Vista does not (by default) track the Last Accessed times for files and folders
- ReadyBoost (in which flash or removable media is utilized as a disk cache)

The bottom line is that the advent of Windows Vista, Server 2008, and Windows 7 does not mean that examiners need to panic. Vista, Server 2008, and 7 are similar enough (particularly in the file systems they utilize) to their XP and 2k3 predecessors that a digital investigator proficient in examining one should feel fairly comfortable in the others. With that said, this chapter will attempt to highlight (where applicable) differences between the artifacts and examinations of the newer Windows operating systems, as they depart from previous versions.

Throughout this chapter, unless otherwise stated, discussions of Windows Vista operation and artifacts also generally apply to Windows Server 2008 and Windows 7.[6]

## WinFS

It is, perhaps, easiest to cover WinFS first, as it is not *currently* something that forensic examiners encounter in the field. Microsoft started developing WinFS

---

[6]Windows Vista, Windows Server 2008, and Windows 7 Beta are all very similar; however, 2k8 is separated from the other two primarily by the fact that many services, processes, and features enabled by default in Vista and 7 Beta are disabled by default in 2k8, and must be discreetly and explicitly enabled by the user.

for Vista but postponed its release and planned to include it in the Windows 7 operating system. However, at the time of this writing, Beta releases of Windows 7 still appear to be based on an NTFS file system, and contain most of the same system files found on XP and Vista computers running on top of NTFS. The WinFS file system is relational (similar to a true database) and organizes data by content and attributes. This type of structure is touted by Microsoft and others eagerly awaiting its release as a great boost to efficiency, and that any file system built on such a framework will provide an unparalleled level of data organization. Although this remains to be seen, Microsoft continues to work on the file system under the code name Project Orange, and beta versions have been made available to willing testers. Although it is unclear when or if WinFS will eventually become a file system standard, it definitely appears that the project is not dead and Microsoft seems committed to its further research and development.

# NTFS OVERVIEW

While the world waits for WinFS, most modern Windows workstations and servers are using the much more familiar NTFS. NTFS is an alternative to FAT file systems (e.g., FAT12, FAT16, FAT32) and can be utilized by Windows NT/2k/XP/2k3/Vista/2k8 operating systems. The current version is NTFS 3.1, which has been used in Windows XP and later OS releases. Among improvements in NTFS file systems are increased file size potential (roughly 16TB versus 4GB for FAT32), increased volume size potential (roughly 256TB versus 2TB for FAT32), and the recording of Last Accessed times (in Windows NT/2k/XP/2k3, and in Vista/2k8/7 if enabled). In addition, NTFS uses a data structure called the Master File Table (MFT) and entries called index attributes instead of a file allocation table (FAT) and folder entries in order to make the access and organization of data more efficient. These and other key features of NTFS of interest to forensic examiners are covered in this section.

## NTFS Internal Files

The primary internal files that NTFS uses to track data, sometimes referred to as metadata files, are summarized in Table 5.1. If nothing else, the presence of these internal files on a system being examined (or traces of these files in unallocated space) should indicate to an examiner that the system was formatted as NTFS.

It general, the dates and times associated with these files are set when the files are first created on the volume and do not change over time with use of the system. As such, the dates and times of these internal files (particularly the Created Date) can be used as an indication of when the volume was last formatted as NTFS. All of these files have their function, and can be analyzed to the $n^{th}$ degree, but a few of them can be very useful to the investigator.

**Table 5.1** Descriptions of Internal NTFS Files

| Filename | $MFT Record | General Function |
| --- | --- | --- |
| $MFT | 0 | Functions like a table of contents for data on the Volume |
| $MFTMirr | 1 | Used for system recoverability |
| $LogFile | 2 | Used for system recoverability |
| $Volume | 3 | Contains information about the formatted volume |
| $AttrDef | 4 | Lists attributes supported by the formatted volume |
| $Bitmap | 6 | Tracks cluster usage on the volume |
| $Boot | 7 | Points to the volume boot sector on the disk |
| $BadClus | 8 | Tracks the location of bad clusters on the disk |
| $Secure | 9 | In Windows 2000 and later, stores security descriptors |

## CASE STUDY: *JOHNSON v. WELLS FARGO*

In May 2008, a U.S. District Court in Nevada heard a motion on behalf of a defendant alleging that the plaintiff in the case reformatted two hard disk drives possibly containing evidence that the plaintiff falsified documentation to support his claims. The defendant informed the plaintiff of the intent to compel production of the hard disk drives in September 2007; however, the defendant's "forensic computer expert" (the label applied to the defendant's digital investigator in court filings) concluded, upon examination of the system files on the reformatted hard disk drives, that one of the drives was reformatted a mere five days after the plaintiff was notified that he would be compelled to produce it, and the second drive was reformatted only 10 days later. As a result, the Court found that the plaintiff destroyed potential evidence and a jury instruction adverse to the plaintiff was ordered in the case as a result of his actions.

## $MFT

Forensic examiners require an in-depth understanding of the MFT to interpret and verify what forensic tools are displaying and to retrieve additional information about deleted files beyond what is available using automated software.

Fundamentally, the MFT is organized in a series of records, each with its own number (called a record number or file identifier). Each record is 1024 bytes in length, making it easy to view them in any tool that allows the examiner to customize text style or view size. This standard record length also makes it easy to locate a particular file's entry in the MFT by multiplying the file's record number (reported by most forensic software) by 1024 and then proceeding to that File Offset (FO) within the $MFT file; this FO represents the first byte of the file's MFT record. MFT records in Windows NT and 2000 begin with the distinctive byte sequence FILE*, and MFT records in other versions of Windows (including Vista, 2k8, and 7) begin with FILE0. Individual MFT records generally refer to a single file, although exceptions exist when you consider special cases, such as files in alternate data streams.

The MFT and its component records are discussed in greater depth in the section, "Forensic Analysis of the NTFS Master File Table" later in this chapter.

## $LogFile

The $LogFile is used by the file system as a type of transaction log, utilized for stability and recoverability in case of a catastrophic event. Transaction logging assists Windows by allowing for the system to be restored to a consistent state in the event of a catastrophic failure. In essence, transactions are recorded as complete or incomplete, signifying to the file system that they should be redone (completed) or undone (uncompleted) after a failure to ensure the stability of the system.

Even though the exact structure and decoding of the $LogFile is not widely known, it would not take an examiner long to notice recognizable data structures within the file. For example, the $LogFile contains references (although, sometimes fragmentary) to MFT records and index buffers (essentially folder entries, in NTFS). MFT records (which will generally show the record header, Standard Information Attribute, Filename Attribute, and sometimes even the resident data of a file) can be located within the $LogFile by searching for the record header strings FILE0 or FILE* (case sensitive). Index buffers, likewise, can be located by searching for their own unique header string, INDX (case sensitive), as shown in Figure 5.4.

Similarly, the header string for link files (the utility of which are detailed in the section, "Artifacts of User Activity" later in this chapter) can be found within the $LogFile as shown in Figure 5.5 by searching for the hexadecimal sequence \x4c\x00\x00\x00\x01\x14\x02.

These artifacts can obviously be found elsewhere on the system, but the value in the $LogFile is the persistency of its data. Although a file may be permanently deleted from the computer, its link file likewise eliminated and its MFT record overwritten, transaction data pertaining to this file (in the form of MFT records, index buffers, or link files) do not change. So, it is possible to find a reference in the code of the $LogFile to a file or folder that no longer exists on the system, along with many important data about that file, such as the

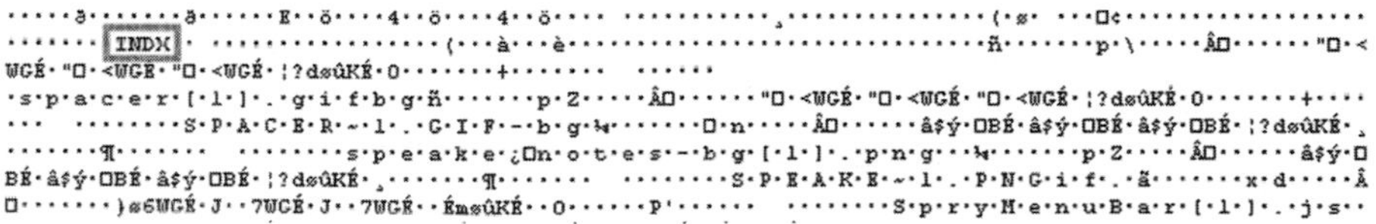

**FIGURE 5.4**

Index buffer found in $LogFile by searching for INDX.

**FIGURE 5.5**

Fragment of a link file found in the `$LogFile`.

```
··□·······/······/······L·········Å·····FO·····ÚUQN&6É··qý^¶LÉ··□OH&6É·□à···············□····PàOÐ ê·ì·<Ø··
+00│<·······K·i·d·s··········t·Y^□8ÓHDg·3½i ('G··Yr?$D□ÅU□þkO±θ·2·□à··Y9Š··yoda.jpg·(·····ïMY9Š-v9·58E··y·o·d·a·.·j·
p·g············c···············b···········¼á4·····C:\Documents and Settings\Kids\My Documents\yoda.jpg· ·.··.·\·.·
·\·K·i·d·s·\·M·y··D·o·c·u·m·e·n·t·s·\·y·o·d·a·.·j·p·g·+·C:·\·D·o·c·u·m·e·n·t·s··a·n·d··S·e·t·t·i·n·g·s·\·K·i·d·s·\·M
·y··D·o·c·u·m·e·n·t·s········X······desktop·········□¡ÀÑÑ│+Fx²│<j·[OJšÅÎà¡Ý·¿□··MÒŠ)□¡ÀÑÑ│+Fx²│<j·[OJšÅÎà¡Ý·¿□··MÒŠ)
```

file's name, file and parent MFT record numbers, and times and dates associated with the file or folder.

Some forensic suites (such as EnCase) have the ability to parse `$LogFile` entries as part of their base package as shown in Figure 5.6.

Although there are only a few readily available automated tools that can parse the `$LogFile`, the data structures within the file are fairly well documented (as described earlier), and an examiner could write a custom script in Perl, Python, or other useful language to parse the data.

## $Volume

The `$Volume` file is another internal NTFS file that can be useful to the examiner. The `$Volume` data object itself will be displayed by most forensic tools but the `$Volume` file is resident within the MFT and contains only attributes (none of which are a Data Attribute). Therefore, this file will appear as an empty file in most forensic software, as seen in Figure 5.7 with the blank lower right pane.

To view the useful information within the `$Volume`, which primarily consists of the volume's name (label), the examiner must go directly to MFT record

**FIGURE 5.6**

EnCase forensic $LogFile Parser module (under the Case Processor EnScript).

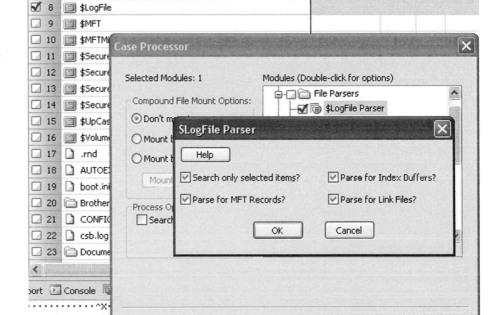

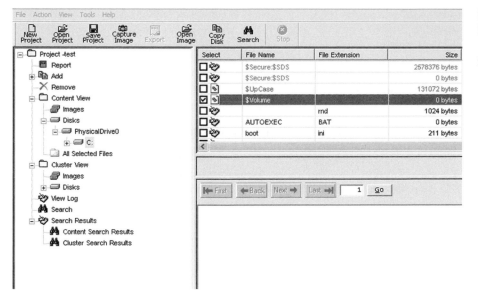

**FIGURE 5.7**
ProDiscover Basic showing
$Volume as an empty
file, with no size.

3 (the fourth record, starting at record 0) and view the resident information (Figure 5.8).

## Data Access Control

One of the key features of NTFS is its increased security over FAT file systems. This security manifests itself in many ways, but perhaps the most noticeable is an access control list (ACL) that governs read-write-execute access to Windows files and folders. Security descriptors stored in the $Secure file, an internal NTFS file that is actually three data streams, details ownership and access information for files and folders on the file system. This ownership and access information is often quite important to an examiner attempting to determine who had access

**FIGURE 5.8**
Volume label data within the
MFT record for $Volume.

to (or who is responsible for) a particular data object. For example, an examiner seeking a clue as to which user account was used to download a particular pornographic picture usually need only look at the picture's owner in NTFS.

Although these ownership and access values in the $Secure file can be interpreted manually, it is fairly complex and requires data from several different internal NTFS files, so it is far easier for examiners to use a third-party tool.

## TOOL FEATURE: INTERPRETING OWNERSHIP INFORMATION

Forensic tools such as EnCase and FTK Imager (which is free) make getting file ownership and permission information a snap by allowing the examiner to simply highlight a file or folder and look at the object's details as shown in Figure 5.9(a) and (b).

Other solutions such as cacls.exe (a native Windows utility), AccessEnum (http://technet.microsoft.com/en-us/sysinternals/bb897332.aspx), and filestat.exe by Foundstone (a division of McAfee, Inc.) can also provide information on file ownership and access permissions on a live running machine.

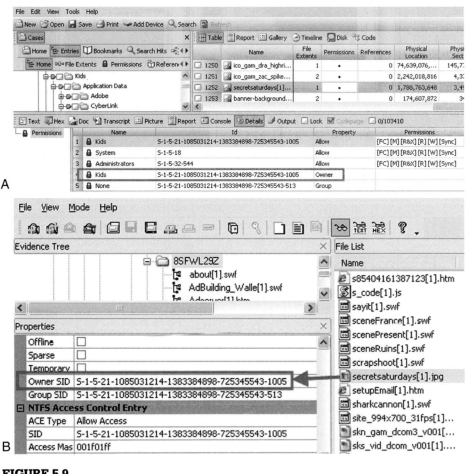

A

B

### FIGURE 5.9

(a) File permissions viewed in EnCase. (b) File permissions viewed in FTK Imager.

## File Streams

Another aspect of NTFS is its use of file streams, also called alternate data streams (ADSs), to store information. This feature was originally designed to increase compatibility with Macintosh systems, but has grown to be used by "bad guys" and developers alike. As previously mentioned (when talking about the $Secure file), Windows makes use of file streams for some of its record keeping, but ADSs can also be used to hide data. A file held in the ADS of another file has no icon of its own and is not displayed to the user by Windows; however, a user can nonetheless still access a file placed in an ADS and even run it directly from the ADS without having to extract it from its hidden location. Following are the very simple command-line strings used to place a file (an executable, in this case) into the ADS of another file and run the secreted file from that location. The result of this operation is the execution of rootkit.exe, even if the original rootkit.exe file has been deleted in Windows Explorer.

```
type rootkit.exe > c:\windows\notepad.exe:rootkit.exe
start c:\windows\notepad.exe:rootkit.exe
```

For that reason, contraband or malicious files (such as this rootkit secreted in an ADS by a hacker) are obviously of interest to an examiner.

---

### TOOL FEATURE: ALTERNATE DATA STREAMS

Although most third-party forensic suites will detect these streams as a normal part of the file system (for example, EnCase describes them as "File, stream"), there are other tools that can provide additional assistance. For example, Streams by Mark Russinovich (http://technet.microsoft.com/ en-us/sysinternals/bb897440.aspx) or LADS by Frank Heyne Software (www.heysoft.de/en/software/lads.php?lang=EN) can be quite helpful in locating data in ADSs on a booted system as shown in Figure 5.10.

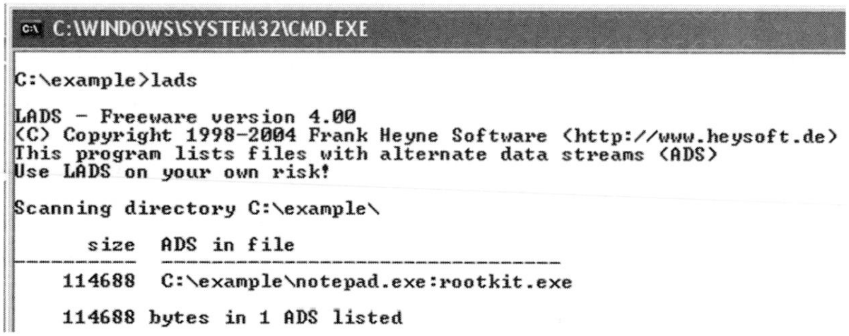

```
C:\WINDOWS\SYSTEM32\CMD.EXE

C:\example>lads

LADS - Freeware version 4.00
(C) Copyright 1998-2004 Frank Heyne Software (http://www.heysoft.de)
This program lists files with alternate data streams (ADS)
Use LADS on your own risk!

Scanning directory C:\example\

     size   ADS in file
----------  -----------------------------------------
   114688   C:\example\notepad.exe:rootkit.exe

   114688 bytes in 1 ADS listed
```

**FIGURE 5.10**
Example of LADS output.

## Data Compression

The NTFS file system provides Windows users with the ability to compress data on the disk, thereby saving space. When files, folders, or even whole NTFS volumes are compressed, Windows applies an industry standard algorithm to replace redundant data with a placeholder that takes up less room. Decompression is then handled on-the-fly by the OS when a particular piece of data is accessed by the user. Data objects that are compressed carry an attribute of "C" (and are often seen as blue) when viewed in Windows Explorer.

NTFS can also take advantage of something Macintosh users have enjoyed for years to save space—sparse files. Sparse files are files whose useful data area is given allocated space on the disk, whereas the portion of the file's data that is not required by the application to which the file belongs in essence is discarded by being placed in unallocated space. When the file is read, the specified portions of the file's code are read by an application, and the nonspecified portions are simply replaced with zeros in memory. This process allows for much larger files to be allocated much less space on disk, thereby conserving storage resources. Sparse files will be identified as such by most forensic tools, when tracking file cluster usage as shown in Figure 5.11.

## Reparse Points

Another advantage of NTFS over FAT file systems is its ability to take advantage of reparse points. Reparse points are files or folders that essentially function as links, but contain additional information about the objects or locations to which they point. This additional information allows file system filters to treat the data in different ways. Reparse points can function as hard links (a file with more than one name), symbolic links (file to file), junction points (folder to folder), or mount points (folder to volume). Reparse points are used to a far greater extent in Windows Vista, Server 2k8, and Windows 7 than in previous versions of the operating system. For example, the C:\Documents and Settings folder with which most examiners are familiar in Windows XP still exists in Windows Vista; however, the folder has very little content and is nothing more than a reparse point that leads to the C:\Users folder as shown in Figure 5.12.

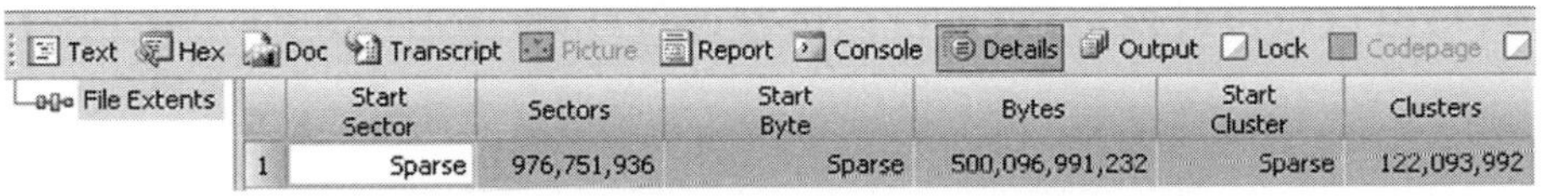

**FIGURE 5.11**

A sparse file viewed in EnCase.

| | Start Sector | Sectors | Start Byte | Bytes | Start Cluster | Clusters |
|---|---|---|---|---|---|---|
| 1 | Sparse | 976,751,936 | Sparse | 500,096,991,232 | Sparse | 122,093,992 |

Text · Hex · Doc · Transcript · Picture · Report · Console · Details · Output · Lock · Codepage

File Extents

**FIGURE 5.12**
The Documents and Settings folder is only a reparse point in Windows Vista.

# FORENSIC ANALYSIS OF THE NTFS MASTER FILE TABLE (MFT)

## $MFT Record Basics

Each MFT record has its own data structure, to include slack that occurs between the end of the last attribute in the record and the beginning of the subsequent MFT record. Decoding the data in the records can sometimes be tricky, and is normally handled by a forensic tool, but it can be done by hand in the absence of one of these tools or for validation purposes. For example, examining the two bytes located at record offset 22 within a file's MFT entry indicates the status of the file (Table 5.2).

In addition to data such as the file status flag described earlier, which resides in each record header (normally the first 56 bytes of the record in XP and later), MFT records are composed of attributes that each have a specific function and structure. Each individual attribute has its own header, which (among other things) identifies the attribute and gives the size of the attribute. It is also useful to understand that these attributes can be resident (meaning, they exist within a given MFT record) or nonresident (meaning, they exist outside a given MFT record, elsewhere on the disk, and are simply referenced within the record). Among these attributes, the Standard Information Attribute (SIA), Filename Attribute (FNA), and Data Attribute can be most helpful from a forensic perspective.

## Standard Information Attribute (SIA)

The SIA is a resident attribute identified via the hexadecimal sequence \x10\x00\x00\x00. This attribute is the source of the date-time stamps interpreted

**Table 5.2** Significance of Flags Found at Record Offset 22 in an MFT Record

| Flag | Significance |
| --- | --- |
| 00 00 | Deleted file |
| 01 00 | Allocated file |
| 02 00 | Deleted directory |
| 03 00 | Allocated directory |

and displayed by Windows and most forensic tools in reference to a particular file or folder. Beginning at offset 24 within the attribute stream (i.e., 23 bytes after the \x10 in the attribute identifier), the next 32 bytes make up the File Created, Last Modified, [MFT] Entry Modified, and Last Accessed date-time stamps in FILETIME format.

## PRACTITIONER'S TIP: DATE-TIME STAMP DIFFERENCES BETWEEN NTFS AND FAT

NTFS date-time stamps differ from those recorded on FAT systems in several key ways. First, it is important to note that NTFS and FAT date-time stamps do not reside in the same locations; whereas NTFS uses the $MFT as a primary repository for date and time metadata, FAT systems record dates and times within folder entries. Another major difference is that NTFS date-time stamps are recorded in UTC, regardless of the time zone set for the system, whereas FAT date-time stamps are recorded in local time; this distinction is important, particularly when interpreting the date-time stamps manually. In addition, NTFS represents date-time stamps using the FILETIME format, which represent the number of 100 nanosecond intervals since January 1, 1601 and can be interpreted by most forensic tools, including free tools such as DCode by Digital Detective (see Figure 5.13).

The FILETIME format is different from the DOSDATETIME that is primarily used in FAT, which is 4 bytes and starts in January 1, 1980. To confuse matters, on FAT systems the resolution of create time on FAT is 10 milliseconds (additional bytes are used to record hundredths of a second), whereas write time has a resolution of 2 seconds, and access time has a resolution of 1 day, allowing the examiner to be less specific about when a file or folder was last accessed on the file system (Microsoft, 2009a). Even within NTFS, the use of Last Accessed date-stamps can vary. For example, NTFS delays updates to the last access date-time stamps by up to 1 hour after the last access (Microsoft, 2009a). Furthermore, by changing (or adding) the registry value HKEY_LOCAL_MACHINE\System\CurrentControlSet\Control\FileSystem\NtfsDisablelastAccessUpdate in Windows XP to "1" (DWORD), XP will no longer update the Last Accessed times/dates of file and folders. It should also be noted that this setting (i.e., no update) is the default setting for Windows Vista.

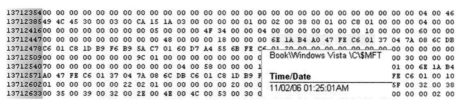

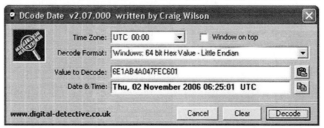

**FIGURE 5.13**

Interpretation of Windows 64-bit date by EnCase above, set to EST, and DCode (www.digital-detective. co.uk/freetools/decode.asp) below, set to UTC.

## Filename Attribute (FNA)

The FNA is a resident attribute identified via the hexadecimal sequence \x30\ x00\x00\x00. Among the data contained in the FNA for a particular file are a reference to its parent folder (by MFT record number), the file's physical and logical size, its Unicode file name, and (like the SIA) a set of four 64-bit dates and times. Beginning at offset 32 *within the attribute stream* (i.e., 31 bytes after the \x30 in the attribute identifier), the next 32 bytes make up the File Created (8 bytes), Last Modified (8 bytes), [MFT] Entry Modified (8 bytes), and Last Accessed date-time stamps (8 bytes). However, whereas the dates and times held in the SIA are updated as a user accesses and modifies a file, the dates and times in the FNA are set when the referenced file is first created on the volume and are *generally* not updated through normal system usage.

---

### PRACTITIONER'S TIP: DETECTING DATE-TIME STAMP TAMPERING

The fact that the FNA is not typically updated when the SIA is altered can be significant for an examiner that suspects a file's dates and times have been artificially manipulated. For example, if the file signed_contract.doc were to have dates in its SIA that predate those in its FNA, this could be evidence (particularly in conjunction with other indicators) that the file's dates were manipulated using a tool such as Timestomp. Timestomp is a part of The Metasploit Project's MAFIA (Metasploit Anti-Forensic Investigation Arsenal; www.metasploit.com/research/projects/antiforensics/) and is capable not only of *changing* SIA date-time stamps but of blanking them out entirely. The GUI tool called Attribute Changer (www.petges.lu/) can also be used to change SIA date-time stamps. Although these tools are easy to use and make manipulating SIA date-time stamps a snap, they are currently unable to manipulate the FNA date-time stamps, thereby providing examiners another basis upon which to deduce their use.

There are undocumented circumstances where date-time stamps in the FNA are changed under normal circumstances, such as when a file is renamed (Mueller, 2009). However, these changes are independent of the SIA information. Although there are exceptions when both SIA and FNA date-time stamps are updated, the vast majority of them apply to Windows system files that are not of temporal concern to investigators.

---

## Data Attribute

An MFT record's Data Attribute can be very important to examiners, chiefly because it contains either the actual data itself (resident) or a pointer to where the data resides on the disk (nonresident). A resident Data Attribute contains the actual data of the file referenced by the MFT record; this occurs when the data the file contains is relatively small in size (usually less than 600 bytes), so small text files (such as boot.ini or Internet cookies) are often held as resident files. For larger files, the MFT contains a list of the clusters allocated to that file, called *data runs*. As shown in Figure 5.14, a resident file can be easily distinguished from a nonresident file by the fact that the first byte of the resident file does not occur at the beginning of a sector and it has no file slack, both of which are normal aspects of a nonresident file stored elsewhere on the disk.

**FIGURE 5.14**

Comparison of resident and nonresident Data Attributes.

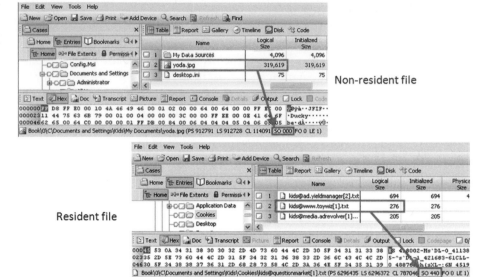

Non-resident file

Resident file

## Finding the Data

Whether resident or nonresident, a Data Attribute is marked in the MFT record by the hexadecimal sequence \x80\x00\x00\x00. Figure 5.15 shows the division of attributes within a single MFT record containing a resident Data Attribute.

In this instance (Figure 5.15), the contents of the file are very easy to find, because they reside within their own MFT record. However, when the Data Attribute is nonresident, information in the MFT record must be decoded to

**FIGURE 5.15**

Single MFT record with resident Data Attribute.

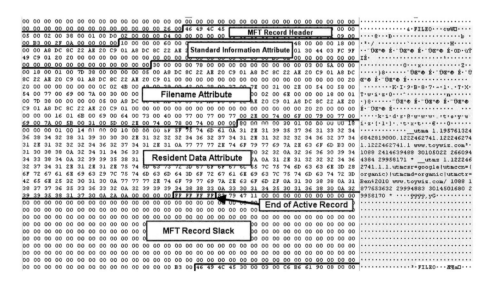

```
20 00 00 00 00 00 00 00 0D 01 69 00 6D 00 61 00 67 00 65 00 30 00 30 00 30 00 35 00 2E 00 6A
00 70 00 67 00 00 00 00 00 80 00 00 00 50 00 00 00 01 00 00 00 00 00 03 00 00 00 00 00 00 00 00
00 00 11 00 00 00 00 00 00 00 40 00 00 00 00 00 00 00 20 01 00 00 00 00 00 00 15 1A 01 00 00
00 00 00 15 1A 01 00 00 00 00 00 41 0C 34 4A 12 01 31 06 71 24 01 00 00 00 D0 81 E1 FF FF FF FF
82 79 47 11 00 00 00 00 00 00 00 00 00 00 00 00 00 00 00 00 00 00 00 00 00 00 00 00 00 00 00 00
```

**FIGURE 5.16**
Nonresident Data Attribute for file with two fragments.

locate the data on the disk. Examine the nonresident Data Attribute for the file image05.jpg in Figure 5.16.

The first boxed byte in Figure 5.16 (\x01) is found at offset 8 within the attribute and acts as a flag showing that the attribute is nonresident. The second boxed set of bytes (\x40\x00), when interpreted little-endian, gives the offset from the beginning of the attribute to the first data run (0x0040 = 64 bytes). The third set of boxed bytes (\x15\x1A\x01\x00\x00\x00\x00\x00), when interpreted little-endian, provides the logical size of the referenced file (0x011A15 = 72213 bytes in size). The last two sets of boxed bytes (\x41\x0C\x34\x4A\x12\x01 and \x31\x06\x71\x24\x01) are the two data runs for the referenced file, indicating that the file occupies two noncontiguous clusters (i.e., two fragments) on the disk.

Examining the first of the data runs, the examiner must break down the bytes as shown in Figure 5.17. The first byte in the run (\x41) is the header and must be viewed as two nibbles. The first number (4) indicates the number of bytes used to calculate the data's starting cluster on the disk, and the second number (1) denotes the number of bytes that (when converted little-endian) give the total number of contiguous clusters in this data stream (fragment). Finally, adding the two nibbles together (4+1) gives the length of this data run (5), not including the header byte. This is how the bytes breakdown:

Interpreting the length little-endian tells the examiner that there are 12 contiguous clusters in this first data run; interpreting the Starting Cluster tells the examiner that the file begins in cluster 17975860 (0x01124A34). So, the first part of this file begins at cluster number 17975860 and fills the subsequent 11 clusters; if the forensic examiner wanted to carve this first fragment, he or she would start at the first byte of cluster 17975860 and stop at the last byte of cluster 17975871.

Interpreting the second data run is a little bit different. The bytes in all data runs after the first are grouped similarly, but instead of a starting cluster, the bytes

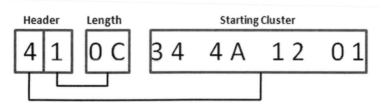

**FIGURE 5.17**
Breakdown of data run for a nonresident Data Attribute.

identified by the first nibble in the data run header represent the *offset* from the starting cluster of the *previous data run* (i.e., the starting cluster for the second data run is relative to the starting cluster of first data run, the starting cluster of third data run is relative to the starting cluster of second data run, and so on). In Figure 5.16, the second data run (\x31\x06\x71\x24\x01) denotes a fragment that is six contiguous clusters in length, which begins 74865 clusters (\x012471) after the starting cluster of the previous data fragment (17975860 + 74865 = 18050725). So, if the examiner wanted to carve this second fragment, he or she would start at the first byte of cluster 18050725 and stop at the last byte of cluster 18050730. But, if the examiner wanted only to carve the logical file (not the entire physical file, which includes file slack), she would need to carve only as many bytes from cluster 18050730 as required to match the file's 72213 byte logical size. Once the data from the second (and, in this case, last) file fragment has been carved, they can be merged back together by the examiner to form the original file, image05.jpg.

## PRACTITIONER'S TIP: DATA RUNS WITH NEGATIVE OFFSETS

It is not uncommon for files on NTFS to have fragments that reside farther toward the beginning of the drive than their previous data fragments, creating a situation where the relative offset from the starting cluster of the previous data run is actually a negative number. The process of interpreting these data runs to locate data fragments on the disk is a bit more complicated when an offset is negative, rather than positive. A data run whose high bit is 1, rather than 0 as depicted in Figure 5.18, should be padded, if needed, and interpreted as a signed value.

For example, consider the data run \x31\x06\x83\x18\xFF. When the relative offset data is read little-endian, the value to

be interpreted is read as \xFF\x18\x83. Because the high bit is 1, the offset data should be padded with \xFF and interpreted as a signed long value in order to provide an accurate offset. The expression is padded to create an even number of bytes. Data runs containing three bytes in their relative offset are padded to four bytes (with \x00 for unsigned and \xFF for signed runs) and interpreted as *long* values. Data runs containing two bytes in their relative offset do not need to be padded, and are interpreted simply as unsigned or signed *short* values.

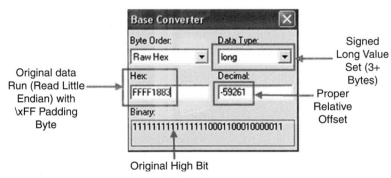

**FIGURE 5.18**
Using a base converter utility to pad and convert a negative data run.

Why might it be important to understand the procedure of interpreting MFT entries to locate where data are stored? Imagine for a moment that `image05.jpg` was actually a contraband photograph upon which the fate of the forensic examiner's case relied. Suppose that contraband image was copied to an NTFS-formatted thumb drive and then wiped from the source disk, so the only place it then resided was on the portable media. Last, assume that when investigators turned up the heat, the suspect reformatted the thumb drive with another file system (FAT32, for example). If a forensic examiner located the MFT record for `image05.jpg` in unallocated space on the thumb drive, the examiner could use the Data Attribute to locate and carve the fragments of the file (provided they have not been overwritten), going a long way to proving both the suspect's possession of the image and his attempt to destroy the evidence. Because MFT data runs provide the location for all file fragments, it may be possible to recover an entire deleted file even when it is fragmented. Recovering fragmented files on FAT is more difficult because folder entries store only the starting cluster of a file.

## NTFS File Deletion

In the same vein, it is quickly worth mentioning what happens in NTFS when a file is deleted (as opposed to simply being sent to the Recycle Bin). When a file is deleted in NTFS, many different things happen "under the hood," but among the observable behaviors important to examiners are:

- The deleted file's entry is removed from its parent index, and the file system metadata (i.e., Last Written, Last Accessed, Entry Modified) for the file's parent *folder* are updated. It is also possible that the metadata for the deleted file itself may be updated because of how the user interacted with the file in order to delete it (e.g., right-clicking on the file). However, examiners should exercise caution before drawing any conclusions from the metadata of a deleted file without other supporting or related evidence found elsewhere on the file system.

- The two bytes located at record offset 22 within the file's MFT record are changed from `\x01\x00` (allocated file) to `\x00\x00` (unallocated file).

- The appropriate locations in `$Bitmap` are modified to show that both the space occupied by the MFT record and the space previously occupied by the file itself are now unallocated and ready for reuse.

Deleting a file in NTFS can also cause changes to the `$LogFile`, `\$Extend\$UsrJrnl`, and `\$Extend\$Quota` internal files. The minutiae of deleting a file from an NTFS file system are covered in Carrier (2005). A more practical interpretation of file deletion (e.g., who deleted a file or when) is discussed in greater depth in the section, "Deletion and Destruction of Data" later in this chapter.

# METADATA

Metadata has been a focus of the forensic community for some time now. Ever since examiners figured out that there might be more to a file than meets the eye, they have been interested in what other data exist (other than what is visible to the casual user) that might provide an extra nugget of evidence in an investigation. Metadata is simply (to cite the most overused computer forensic definition of all time) data about data; it is information that describes or places data in context, without being part of the data that is the primary focus of the user (e.g., the graphic part of a JPEG photograph). Generally speaking, there are two types of metadata: file system metadata and application (or file) metadata.

## File System Metadata

The majority of file system metadata in NTFS resides within the internal files (e.g., $MFT, $Secure), which leads to them, not surprisingly, also being called NTFS metadata files. Although file system metadata like file permissions, file status (active versus deleted), and information about whether a file is resident or nonresident can be useful in the right context, the aspect of file system metadata that often draws the most attention is the date-time stamp information. Windows and most forensic tools display only the date-time stamp information held in the Standard Information Attribute (SIA) of the MFT record, largely because these are the date-time stamps that get updated when a file or folder is copied, moved, written to, or otherwise worked with on the system (this is in contrast to the date-time stamps held in FNA, which are set when the file is first created on the volume and generally do not change thereafter).

Despite the eagerness of the layperson to take this file system metadata as gospel in an investigation, forensic examiners must help place these times in context, which is not always an easy task. The behavior of Windows date-time stamps can vary wildly depending on the exact action taken with a file or folder. For instance, moving a file from one volume to another using drag-and-drop or command line will update the file's create date, whereas right-clicking and choosing Cut and then Paste will retain the original file's create data. Forensic examiners must also be aware of special circumstances affecting date-time stamps; for example, files extracted from an archive (such as a .ZIP or .RAR file) can often carry date-time stamps with them from the system upon which they were first archived. A more obscure phenomenon called *file tunneling* causes a new file to inherit the file system metadata of another file that existed previously in a directory (Microsoft, 2007a). The best principle is to test and validate before rendering any opinion as to the significance of a particular date-time stamp at issue, especially if that opinion is going to be used as an important part of a legal decision. If possible, attempt to recreate the circumstances at issue in the investigation and observe and evaluate the results carefully.

## FROM THE CASE FILES: BACKDATING

A recent investigation focused on a government server, which was found to be beaconing out to another country. The start date of the beaconing traffic gave investigators an approximate date for the compromise of the victim machine, as they began developing their timeline. However, during the forensic examination of the compromised system, the source of the beaconing was found to be a piece of malware (keylogger) whose File Created date-time stamp (as displayed by several different forensic tools) predated the beginning of the beaconing by almost two years. Investigators began to wonder if the system had actually been compromised much earlier than they originally thought. But, upon more detailed examination of the file's MFT record, and manual translation of the dates and times held in the FNA for the malware and associated files, investigators confirmed that the malware had most likely been created on the system at a date and time that very neatly matched the start of the beaconing traffic, confirming their original timeline. This discovery led to suspicion of SIA date-time stamp alteration on the part of the intruder and the location of a date-time stamp modification utility.

With these exceptions in mind, and assuming no file-tunneling behavior, the date-time stamps in the SIA generally have the following significance:

- **File Created**: This date-time stamp usually shows when a file or folder was created on a volume and can be one of the most valuable date-time stamps for investigators. For instance, when an existing file is *copied*, the File Created date-time stamp of the new copy is set to the current time (the new copy retains the Last Written and Entry Modified date-time stamps of the original file). Similarly, if a file is *moved* onto a different volume using the Windows command line or drag-and-drop feature, the File Created date-time stamp of the new copy is set to the current time (moving a file within the same volume does not alter the File Created date-time stamp). However, if a file is *moved* onto a different volume using the Cut and Paste menu options, the File Created date-time stamp remains unchanged (the Last Accessed and Entry Modified date-time stamps would most likely change).

- **Modified** (Last Written): This date-time stamp represents the last time the $DATA attribute of a file was altered. For example, if a user opened a .BAT file, edited the content, and resaved the file, the file's Last Written time will most likely be updated as well. In contrast, if the user opened the same file, read the contents, and then closed the file without making any change, the Last Written time would not be updated.

- **Last Accessed**: This date-time stamp represents the most recent time a file or folder was accessed by the file system. This date-stamp does not necessarily indicate that a file was opened; simply placing the mouse over the filename in Windows Explorer can update the last accessed date. Furthermore, although an update of this date-time stamp *can* be a result of an action taken by the user (e.g., opening and reading the file), it could also be the result of automatic or innocuous system actions (e.g., antivirus scan or file backup). As such, the true value of the Last Accessed timestamp should be carefully evaluated by the examiner in context with other file system evidence. Also keep in mind that NTFS delays updates to the Last Accessed date-time stamps by up to one hour after the file was accessed. Despite its fickle nature, however, it can generally be assumed that the Last Accessed time/date of a file or folder on a system can be updated by the file system only when the system is running, and can be used as a guide to help determine general system usage.

- **SIA Modified** (Entry Modified): This date-time stamp represents the last time any attribute in the MFT record for the file or folder was modified. Reasons for an update to this date-time stamp can include changing a file's location on the disk, another data stream being added to the file, or a change in the file's name.

## Application Metadata

Unlike file system metadata, application metadata is found within the files to which it refers (such as Microsoft Office files, `.PDF` files, and digital photographs). This information, generally placed or recorded by the application used to create or work with the file, can provide valuable information for the investigator.

Although numerous types of files contain application metadata, Microsoft Office documents are most notorious for recording ancillary information, a circumstance that has become even more pronounced with the use of embedded tags in Microsoft Office 2007 and Windows Vista. Office documents regularly carry Created, Modified (Last Written), and Accessed date-time stamps, which may appear to be similar to the date-time stamps used by NTFS, but they are much less susceptible to casual modification and can sometimes tell the investigator more about the file itself. For example, the file shown in Figure 5.19 was copied to a removable storage device (formatted NTFS) on November 29, 2008, which caused its file system metadata to be updated. However, a closer examination of the file reveals application metadata that suggest the file was actually created on August 11, 2008. Which date-time stamp is correct? Both are accurate in their own way: the file system Created date indicates the date and time the file was created on the volume being examined, whereas the application metadata Created date indicates when the document actually came into being. Although different, both these date-time stamps can be useful to the investigator.

According to Microsoft, data such as the author's name, initials, company or organization, and computer name, as well as a document's storage location,

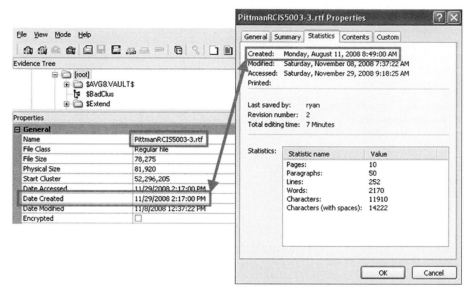

**FIGURE 5.19**
File system Created date
versus application metadata
Created date.

revision and version number, template information, comments, and previous authors can all be stored within the metadata of an Office document (Microsoft, 2007b). The question for investigators is how to get to that data with a minimum of trouble. The data can, of course, be found and interpreted manually by the examiner, but with so much recent focus on the value of metadata in Office documents many tools have been developed to assist in its analysis.

## TOOL FEATURE: MICROSOFT OFFICE METADATA EXTRACTION

There are add-ons or scripts that have been authored to work with well-known forensic suites that parse some application metadata. For example, the Office Metadata.enpack shown in Figure 5.20 works to parse Office metadata for display in the EnCase Version 6 interface and can process hundreds or thousands of file simultaneously.

Other third-party applications can also parse and display Office metadata in a user-friendly GUI format like Pinpoint Laboratories' Metaviewer (www.pinpointlabs.com/new/utilities.html) shown in Figure 5.21 and Metadata Miner Catalogue (http://peccatte.karefil.com/Software/Catalogue/MetadataMiner.htm).

These tools can provide the investigator with a good summary of an Office document's application metadata. However, it should be noted that some application metadata may not be displayed. For example, Object Linking and Embedding (OLE) streams within a Word document (created prior to Office 2003 or containing unaccepted or rejected Track Changes) can also contain information about the last 10 authors and save locations of the document (metadata that is not often cleaned via conventional privacy programs). Obtaining this information can be a bit trickier, but tools such as the `wmd.pl` script can help the investigator locate and interpret these important data (Carvey, 2009).

**FIGURE 5.20**

Output from Lance Mueller's Office Metadata. enpack (www.forensickb. com/).

Book\1\C\160GB USB drive\▮▮▮▮▮▮▮▮▮▮▮▮▮▮\Humor\Greatest Hacker in the WORLD.doc

Title: Greatest Hacker in the WORLD
Subject:
Author: Gateway_User
Keywords: Comments:
Last Saved By: Gateway_User
Template: Normal.dot
Version: Microsoft Word 10.0
Revision: 1
Create Date: 04/29/05 10:01:00AM
Last Revision Date: 04/29/05 10:01:00AM
Number of Pages: 1
Number of Words: 1171
Number of Characters: 6681
Number of Paragraphs: 15
Number of Words: 1171

**FIGURE 5.21**

Output from Pinpoint Laboratories' Metaviewer.

**Pinpoint Metaviewer**

**Metaviewer**

**PINPOINT** LABORATORIES

**OLE Metadata**

| | | | | |
|---|---|---|---|---|
| File Name: | Greatest Hacker in the W | Keywords: | | |
| Title: | Greatest Hacker in the W | Manager: | | |
| Author: | Gateway_User | Last Saved By: | Gateway_User | |
| Comments: | | Word Count: | 1171 | |
| App Name: | Microsoft Word 10.0 | Page Count: | 1 | |
| Version: | 10.6735 | Paragraph Count: | 15 | |
| Date Created: | 4/29/2005 10:01:00 AM | Line Count: | 55 | |
| Date Last Printed: | | Character Count: | 6681 | |
| Date Last Saved: | 4/29/2005 10:01:00 AM | Chars (incl. spaces): | 7837 | |
| Total Edit Time: | 0 | Byte Count: | 0 | |
| Template: | Normal.dot | Presentation Format: | | |
| Shared: | False | Slide Count: | 0 | |
| Subject: | | Note Count: | 0 | |
| Category: | | Hidden Slides: | 0 | |
| Company: | Gateway | Multimedia Clips: | 0 | |

**File System Metadata**

| | | | | |
|---|---|---|---|---|
| File Path: | F:\160GB USB drive\GSI | File Size: | 30208 | |
| Created Date: | 6/4/2007 11:14:23 AM | MD5 Hash: | 390BA2F7974AE59F2655 | |
| Last Modified: | 4/29/2005 11:01:30 AM | SHA-1 Hash: | A3BA8A4FC4174C07A0A | |
| Last Accessed: | 11/29/2008 10:15:47 AM | SHA-256 Hash: | 3EBB5D662C8E0F6E585 | |

Exit    Browse ...    Copy All    Copy Selected

An investigator should also examine files of interest in a raw form to determine whether they contain additional useful metadata. Tools have been known to miss common metadata such as the last 10 authors' information often found in Microsoft Word documents, and there may be additional metadata that is not recovered using available automated tools. One example, presented by Eoghan Casey at the 2009 meeting of the American Academy of Forensic Sciences, demonstrated the existence and forensic usefulness of less widely known embedded metadata, including date-time stamps in the root entry of Microsoft Office documents. Another example detailed the concealment of entire data files (such as a `.JPG,` an `.MP3,` and a `.ZIP` file) in the "unknown parts" and "unknown relationships" portions of Microsoft Office 2007 metadata (Park et al., 2008).

Forensic examiners should be aware that metadata associated with Microsoft Office documents can be altered using freely available tools.

---

### FROM THE CASE FILES: METADATA TAMPERING

It should also be remembered that both types of date-time stamps (file system and application) can be modified manually and may require a bit of extra work on the part of the investigator. Consider the scenario of a Word document (`Company Safety Plan.doc`) found on the laptop computer of a tech-savvy CEO 14 days after a devastating fire gutted his company headquarters and cost a maintenance employee his life. The CEO, being sued for wrongful death and negligence in connection with his failure to create and publish such a document, claimed it was proof that the Company implemented a safety plan the week prior to the employee's death. An examination of the file's SIA metadata in FTK and application metadata in Metaviewer ostensibly showed that the Word document was created and last modified eight days before the fire; however, also found on the CEO's computer were MiTeC's Structured Storage Viewer (www.mitec.cz/Downloads/SSView.zip) and Attribute Changer (www.petges.lu/). Becoming suspicious, the forensic examiner checked the document's FNA, which revealed date-time stamps recorded three days after the fire. When confronted with the evidence, the CEO admitted to creating the document after the fire and changing its application metadata with Structured Storage Viewer, then readjusting its SIA with Attribute Changer to further obfuscate evidence of his tampering.

---

# ARTIFACTS OF USER ACTIVITIES

When an individual accesses a computer system and puts it through its paces, many artifacts are generated that forensic examiners can use to reconstruct the individual's activities. Systems running Windows are a wealth of such usage data and can be the key to many forensic puzzles, provided the forensic examiner can find and properly interpret these artifacts.

## Logging onto (and off of) a System

Information pertaining to when and how a user logs onto a Windows system can be valuable to an investigator. In cases involving unauthorized access, theft of intellectual property, or even child pornography, data surrounding user accounts and logon procedures can go a long way toward proving the overall incident and creating a timeline.

From the very first Windows screen, users are subjected to settings that govern how they interact with the system, which can be examined by the forensic examiner. For example, looking in the Windows registry can provide information pertaining to whether the logon screen displays the name of the last user to logon, whether or not a user is able to shut down the computer from the logon screen without first authenticating to the system, what username (with its associated domain, if present) was last used to logon to the system, and whether the system uses the Windows Welcome screen or the classic logon prompt for user logon.

---

## REGISTRY KEYS RELATING TO LOGON

SOFTWARE\Microsoft\Windows\CurrentVersion\policies\
    system\dontdisplaylastusername (DWORD=1 means
    the name of the last logged on user is not displayed)
SOFTWARE\Microsoft\Windows\CurrentVersion\poli-
    cies\system\shutdownwithoutlogon (DWORD=1
    means a user is able to shut down the computer with-
    out first logging on)

SOFTWARE\Microsoft\WindowsNT\CurrentVersion\
    Winlogon\DefaultUserName (DefaultDomainName)
    (String values showing the last username and domain/
    workgroup/computer logged in plain text)
SOFTWARE\Microsoft\WindowsNT\CurrentVersion\
    Winlogon\LogonType (DWORD=1 means the Windows
    Welcome screen is used)

---

Another setting that can be helpful to investigators trying to make the case for monitoring an employee's activity or justifying a search of their computer is whether the system presented any type of warning banner to the user. As shown in Figure 5.22, string values found at SOFTWARE\Microsoft\Windows\

**FIGURE 5.22**

Registry values entered to present legal warning messages at system startup.

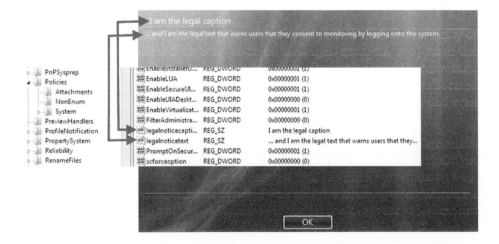

`CurrentVersion\policies\system\` control the warning banner window caption and the text of the warning displayed to users before the logon screen is reached; blank values mean that no warning banner is shown.

There are a number of artifacts that forensic examiners can use to glean information about user account activities on a system. For example, a quick glance at the File Created date-time stamp for a user's `Documents and Settings` folder and the associated `NTUSER.DAT` file (often considered to be the fifth important registry hive, after SAM, SECURITY, SOFTWARE, and SYSTEM) can reveal when the user account was first created on the system as shown in Figure 5.23.

Looking at the Last Written date-time stamp of a user's `NTUSER.DAT` file can also be used as an indication of the last date and time a user logged off of the system. As such, comparing `NTUSER.DAT` Last Written date-time stamps with the date and time the system was last shut down (as evidenced by data interpreted from the `SYSTEM\<current control set>\Control\Windows\ShutdownTime` subkey) could provide an indication of which user last shut down the system.

Focusing more specifically on the user accounts themselves can also be quite revealing. The names of user accounts used to logon to a system can be found by examining the `SAM\SAM\Domains\Account\Users\Names` subkey in the SAM registry hive. This location contains subkeys named with the friendly names of Windows user accounts for both local and domain accounts that have been used on the system.

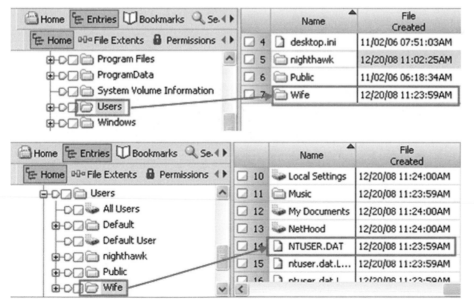

**FIGURE 5.23**

Account creation time can often be assumed by viewing the user folder and `NTUSER.DAT` File Created date-time stamps for the user.

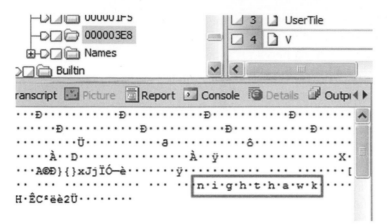

**FIGURE 5.24**

Content of the V value showing the username nighthawk associated with Relative Identifier 000003E8 (decimal 1000).

The SAM\SAM\Domains\Account\ Users subkey has several other subkeys representing user accounts. These subkeys' names, when interpreted via a base converter, each correspond with the Relative Identifier (RID) of a single user account. For example, the subkey 0001F4, when converted from a hexadecimal to a decimal value, translates to 500, which is the RID of the built-in administrator account. Within each of these subkeys with hexadecimal names are two important values: F and V. The V value can provide the examiner with the means of linking the RID to a user account, because it normally contains a user account name in human-readable format (Unicode). For instance, Figure 5.24 shows the nighthawk user account under the subkey value 003E8, which translates into a RID of 1000, associated with a normal user on the system.

The F value contains important information about the behavior of the user account as shown in Figure 5.25. For example, interpreting bytes 8 through 15 as a Windows FILETIME value provides the last date the account was logged in. In addition, data in the F value contains the date of the last password change (bytes 24–31), the date of account expiration (bytes 32–39), and the date of the last failed login attempt (bytes 40–47).[7] These date-time stamps can be

**FIGURE 5.25**

Date-time stamps contained within the F value for the user account.

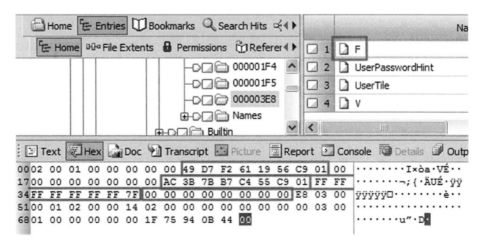

---

[7] If the password has never been set or changed, the date of last password change will match the account creation date.

particularly useful in an intrusion investigation, where a pattern of failed log-ins followed by the logon of a specific account could be very telling regarding the methodology of the attacker and the means of compromise.

Another way to link a user account with a specific SID is to look at the `SOFTWARE\Microsoft\WindowsNT\CurrentVersion\ProfileList` subkey shown in Figure 5.26. This location contains additional subkeys named with the full SID and RID of each user account used to logon via the system. An advantage of the `ProfileList` subkey is that it may also contain information for users that have been deleted from the system, whereas the SAM registry hive may not. Because profile folders are generally named after the user account to which they are tied, examining the `ProfileImagePath` value can likewise link a user account to a specific SID.

It should be noted that it can sometimes be difficult to tell if a user account is tied to the local machine or a domain. For example, a forensic examiner may see two or more SIDs ending in an RID of 500 (the RID associated with the administrator account); on the surface this seems impossible, as the SID/RID is meant to uniquely identify each user account on the system. However, it is the SID portion of the number, and not the RID, which makes each account unique, as one is the local administrator and the others are domain adminis-trator accounts.

In order to identify which accounts are local accounts, the investigator can examine the `SECURITY\Policy\PolAcDmS` subkey. When the last 16 bytes of the (`Default`) value are interpreted as unsigned 32-bit integers, they trans-late into the SID belonging to the *local machine* (Figure 5.27).

So, using the example of the `nighthawk` user account, a comparison of Figures 5.26 and 5.27 reveals that the `nighthawk` user account is a *local* user account. If the translated hexadecimal value in `PolAcDmS` *differed* from that of the SID associated with the nighthawk account in the `ProfileImagePath` value, it can be assumed that the nighthawk account was a domain account. Further, examining and translating the (`Default`) value for `PolPrDmS` subkey would reveal the SID of the primary domain to which the system is connected, and the value could be compared with the SIDs of the suspected domain accounts on the computer.

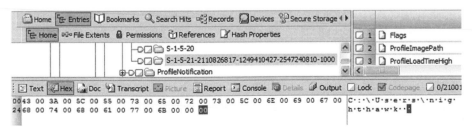

**FIGURE 5.26**

Content of the `ProfileImagePath` value for the `nighthawk` user account.

**FIGURE 5.27**

Translation of the last 16 bytes of the (Default) value as unsigned 32-bit integers.

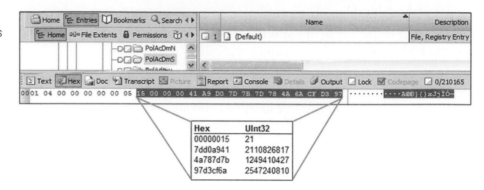

## Windows Event Logging

One of the primary sources of information regarding user and system activities are the Windows event logs. By default Windows 2k/XP/2k3 store event logs in c:\windows\system32\config (the same folder that the primary Windows registry hives reside). There are three core log files available in this location: AppEvent.evt, SecEvent.evt, and SysEvent.evt. However, the advent of newer Microsoft applications, such as Microsoft Office 2007 and Internet Explorer 7, has created additional log files, such as Osession.evt and Internet.evt.[8] Domain controllers and DNS servers can have additional event logs, including File Replication, Directory Service, and DNS event logs. Windows XP provides a good example of the pre-Vista event logs, and is the focus of this section.

In Windows XP, the Event Log service is started automatically when the system is booted and records log events in the files described earlier. The contents of the event logs can be viewed by a Windows user via the Event Viewer snap-in for the Microsoft Management Console (MMC), or using c:\windows\system32\eventvwr.exe. In the most general terms, the Application event log records information related to installed software (such as failures or configuration issues), the Security event log records information related to security and access to resources (such as user logons and logoffs), and the System event log records information related to the Windows operating system.

By default, the Security event log is not enabled for Windows workstations, but is enabled by default for most Server installations, and can be configured to log most actions on the system. An investigator can determine whether or not security logging was enabled for a particular system by examining the (Default)

---

[8] This filename seems to vary with the version of the operating system installed, as users researching this topic using a German version of Windows XP (http://computer.forensikblog.de/en/2007/05/weird_ie7_event_log.html) found a file called Windows.evt (with a space in between the "s" and the ".") rather than Internet.evt.

value (in hex) for the registry subkey `SECURITY\Policy\PolAdtEv`. It is the first byte in the hex string for this value that reflects the status of security logging for the system:

> \x00 = Auditing is disabled (meaning the security log will most likely be empty)
>
> \x01 = Auditing is enabled (meaning the security log is set to record at least some audit events)

The further decoding of the hexadecimal string can reveal exactly what security events the system is set to log, and at what level (i.e., success, failure, or both), and is fairly well documented (Microsoft, 2006).

Each log entry can include the date and time of the event being recorded, the user account and computer responsible for the event, an event ID, and a description of the event. The event description is generally constructed from detailed messages in the registry and several related `.DLL` files. Therefore, care must be taken when examining event logs on a different system since variations in versions of the operating system and installed applications may result in incorrect or incomplete error messages. The EventID.net web site provides the investigator with a tremendous resource for analyzing event IDs found in individual event properties as demonstrated in Figure 5.28.

Event descriptions can also be very useful to the investigator, as they can contain additional data about the cause of the event and provide critical information such as usernames, computer names, IP addresses, and applications related to the event, such as a system logon or service failure.

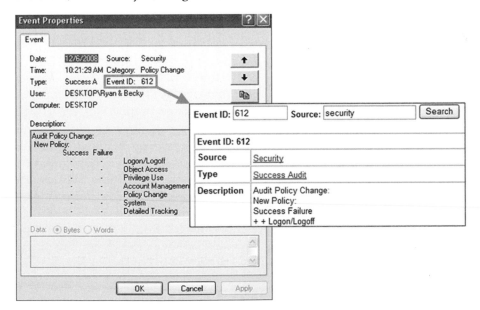

**FIGURE 5.28**

Security event viewed via the Event Viewer and the corresponding event ID looked up via www.eventid.net.

## FROM THE CASE FILES: EVENT LOG CLUES

Event logs can be very revealing. In a recent network intrusion investigation, malware was placed on the compromised Windows system in the early morning hours, when no users should have been accessing the system. The vulnerability and method used to transfer the malware were unknown. However, examination of the system event files revealed the system's antivirus software began attempting to quarantine the malware from a specific user's profile the week before, thereby providing investigators with help on their timeline and a starting point for their investigation

In another recent case, a suspect used VNC-style remote desktop software (already installed on the system and configured with a weak password) to repeatedly gain unauthorized access to a victim Windows server. However, unbeknownst to the attacker, every time he used the remote desktop application to log on, an entry capturing his IP address and username was added to the Windows event logs, eventually leading investigators to his workstation elsewhere in the same company.

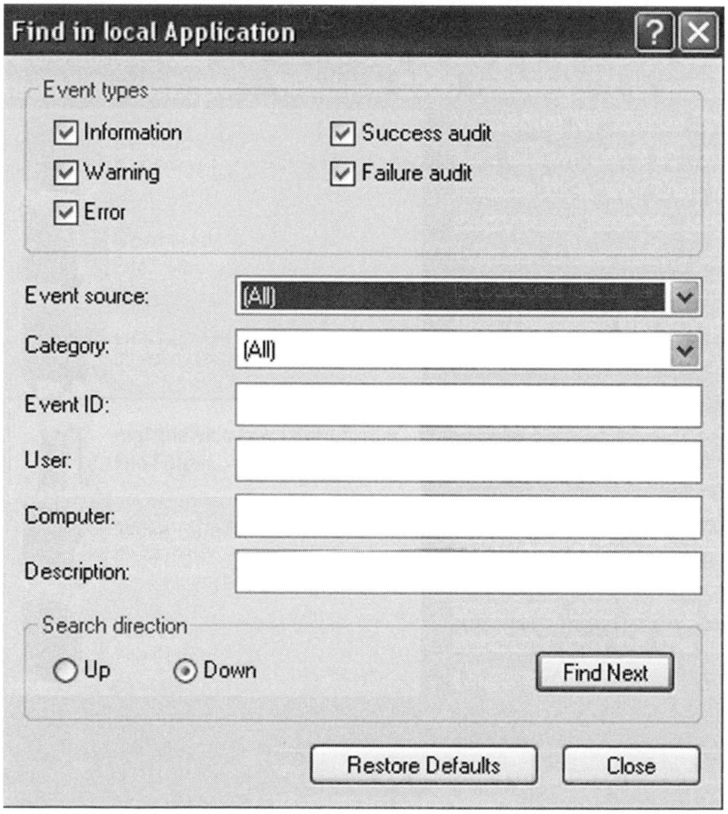

**FIGURE 5.29**

Find... functionality for Windows Event Viewer.

For the forensic examiner, viewing, searching, and analyzing event logs can sometimes be a challenge. Copying the event log files out of an image using a forensic tool and opening the logs via the Event Viewer on an examination box (particularly one that is running the same version of the examined operating system) can have the advantages of displaying events in a user-friendly format, providing more complete event descriptions (as the Event Viewer draws on native Windows DLLs), and providing the examiner a limited search functionality with which to locate specific types of events or descriptions (see Figure 5.29).

However, Windows Event Viewer may not be the best choice for examining large numbers of event logs. Log files can also require alterations to headers within the logs themselves using a hex editor if the files are corrupt before they can be read. A primary cause of event log corruption is the fact that they were copied or imaged from a live, running system. Under these conditions, there are a number of specialized tools for processing event logs that will likely serve the examiner better.

## TOOL FEATURE: WINDOWS EVENT LOGS

Microsoft's Log Parser utility can provide a powerful means of querying and searching event logs. This tool can require a background in structured query language (SQL) to avoid a steep learning curve (Giuseppini et al., 2005). As an alternative to one of these solutions, examiners could also use the Python-based tool GrokEVT (http://projects.sentinelchicken.org/grokevt/). Forensic suites like EnCase can parse Windows event logs in an automated fashion, although the text or comma separated values (.CSV) output can be a bit difficult to work with.

Deleted event logs can also be located in unallocated space by searching for their distinctive LfLe (\x4c\x66\x4c\x65) file header. The format of 2k/XP/2k3 is fairly straightforward and the data is user-readable (Unicode ASCII) so raw records can be interpreted with relative ease. For a detailed analysis of the binary format of .EVT files and useful utilities for parsing them directly see Carvey (2009).

The Windows logging process has been entirely revamped in Vista, debuting over 30 new log files, changing the file structure of the logs (using a well-documented XLM format), changing their file extension to .EVTX, and giving them a new location (c:\windows\system32\winevt\logs). Also changed are the Event IDs in Vista. Although it does not appear to be completely consistent, many of the new event IDs are derived from adding 4096 to the old event ID codes. As an example, Vista event ID 4624 replaced the 2k/XP/2k3 event ID 528 (and 540) for successful logons. Failed logon attempts are recorded in Vista under event ID 4625. Like in 2k/XP/2k3, it is possible for an examiner to locate and recover deleted Vista event files (the file signature is ElfFile), but reading the recovered data is a bit more complicated owing to the linked XML structure of .EVTX files. For a detailed examination of the Vista .EVTX file format from a forensic perspective, see Schuster (2007).

## Link Files

Link files (.LNK extension) are simply shortcuts, which point to another file or folder. Users sometimes create these shortcuts intentionally for convenient access to particular items, but more often Windows creates link files automatically in an attempt to assist the user and speed up operations. Windows places link files in various locations, including a user's Desktop, Start Menu, and Recent folders, as well as in application data areas and restore points.

The mere presence of a link file can be significant because it may indicate that the user opened a particular file or folder. For example, finding a link file in a user's Desktop folder called my_lolitas.lnk, which points to a folder containing hundreds of pictures of minors in lewd or lascivious poses, would make it far more difficult for the user to claim he had no knowledge of the folder's existence. By the same token, finding a link file in a user's `Recent` folder called `hot_credit_cards.xls.lnk`, which points to the spreadsheet on a piece of removable media, would make the user's arguments against his access of the spreadsheet much less plausible. Further, each link file, as an object on the file system, has its own set of date-time stamps, which can provide the examiner with data indicating when the link file was created or last used, based on the Last Written date-time stamp.

Information stored inside the link file can also be very valuable from a forensic perspective, because it provides details about the link's target file. Link files can contain data showing the full path to the target file (even on removable media or network shares that are no longer connected), the volume label, and volume serial number of the volume upon which the target file resides as shown in Figure 5.30.[9] The four-byte volume serial number can be located immediately preceding the byte sequence `\x10\x00\x00\x00` prior to the start of the full path (or the volume label, if a label is present). The bytes of the volume serial number are little-endian, and must be read from right to left.

The drive letter assigned to the volume upon which the target resides and the dates and times of the target file (as opposed to the dates and times of the link file itself) can also be found in the link file. The date-time stamps found within the link file that refer to the link's target are standard Windows 64-bit dates and times (8-bytes in length) and can be found at the following offsets from the beginning of the link file:

- Bytes 28–36: Created date-time stamp for the target file
- Bytes 36–44: Last Accessed date-time stamp for the target file
- Bytes 44–52: Last Written date-time stamp for the target file

**FIGURE 5.30**

Analysis of a link file showing the full path to the target file (highlighted), as well as the volume serial number (`\x34\xE1\x25\x17`) and volume label `super_ cool` for the volume on which the target resides.

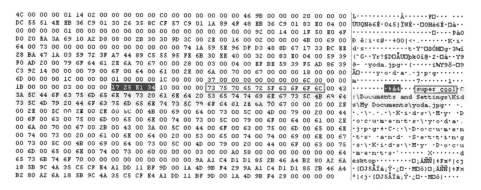

---

[9] A volume label (if present) is generally assigned to a volume by a user and can be changed at any time, whereas the volume serial number is a unique value applied to a Windows volume when it is formatted and is difficult for average users to alter without reformatting the volume.

Note that the sequence of these date-time stamps (created, accessed, written) is different from the more common sequence in NTFS and FAT file systems (created, written, accessed).

---

## TOOL FEATURE: LINK FILE ANALYSIS

Although this link file data can easily be interpreted manually, most forensic suites have the ability to assist the examiner in doing so. One tool that is very handy for link file analysis is MiTeC's free Windows File Analyzer utility (www.mitec. cz/wfa.html). When pointed to a folder of shortcut files, which could be copied out of a disk image using a forensic tool, the Windows File Viewer parses the link files and provides the underlying data in a concise, printable report format (Figure 5.31).

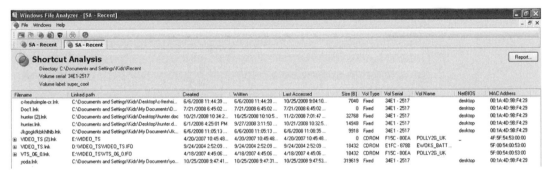

### FIGURE 5.31
Sample output from MiTeC's Windows File Analyzer shortcut analysis.

---

It should be noted that the data within a link file only reflects the state of the target file when the link file was last updated (usually, when the target file was opened on the volume). For example, if a link file's target was deleted from the volume on which it resides, the link file would then most likely contain outdated path, volume, and time/date information, provided the link file itself was not also deleted. However, this behavior can also be helpful to the investigator, as link files can be found to provide information about target files and folders to which the investigator can no longer find reference on the active file system.

## Prefetch Files

Prefetch files (.PF extension) are a specialized file type, similar to link files, used by Windows XP/2k3/Vista/7 operating systems to speed up the running of executable files.[10] Windows XP and Vista, in particular, prefetch application data to run those applications more efficiently on subsequent executions.

---

[10] Prefetching is turned off in Windows Server 2008.

These files, located by default in the `c:\windows\prefetch` folder, can provide a great deal of data about files executed on a system.

When a program (such as `calc.exe`) is executed on a system (locally or remotely), information relating to the execution of that program is saved in a prefetch file that is named as follows: the executable name, a dash, and a hexadecimal value used to represent the path from which the file was executed (e.g., `c:\windows\prefetch\calc.exe-DCD22666.pf`). Information contained within each prefetch file can include the date and time the executable was last run from its current location (8 bytes beginning at file offset 120; 64-bit Windows FILETIME value in UTC), as well as the number of times the executable has been run from its current location (4 bytes beginning at file offset 144; interpreted little-endian) as shown in Figure 5.32.

In addition, the path and name of the `.DLL` files the executable requires to run and the path to the executable itself (which can be found by searching for the name of the executable within the code of the prefetch file) can also be found. Further, by examining the date-time stamps of the prefetch file itself, an examiner may be able to draw conclusions about when the executable was first run (i.e., created date of the prefetch file) from its current location.

Although prefetching is enabled by default (at least boot prefetching in Windows Server 2k3 and 2k8), it can be disabled by a user modifying the `SYSTEM\<current control set>\Control\Session Manager\Memory Management\PrefetchParameters\EnablePrefetcher` value (DWORD "0"=Disabled; "1"=Application prefetching only; "2"=Boot prefetching only; "3"=Application and boot prefetching). Further, it should be noted that the prefetch folder can hold up to 128 prefetch files; however, when this upper limit is reached the prefetch files for the 96 *least used programs* are automatically deleted to make more room, leaving the 34 prefetch files with the highest run count.

**FIGURE 5.32**
Last run time/date (8 bytes) and the run count (4 bytes) data within the prefetch file.

```
0000 | 11 00 00 00 53 43 43 41-0f 00 00 00 8e 33 00 00 | ····SCCA·····3··
0010 | 43 00 41 00 4c 00 43 00-2e 00 45 00 58 00 45 00 | C·A·L·C·.·E·X·E·
0020 | 00 00 57 e1 43 6d 6e 80-20 50 65 89 03 00 00 00 | ··WáCmn· Pe·····
0030 | 00 00 90 7c 00 00 00 00-00 f0 0a 00 00 00 00 00 | ···|·····ð······
0040 | 1c cc fd b5 20 70 be 88-40 cd fd b5 3a 57 cd 02 | ·Ìýµ p¾·@Íýµ:WÍ·
0050 | 00 00 00 00 98 00 00 00-23 00 00 00 54 03 00 00 | ········#···T···
0060 | 72 02 00 00 ac 20 00 00-bc 0e 00 00 68 2f 00 00 | r···¬ ··¼···h/··
0070 | 01 00 00 00 26 04 00 00-d8 11 2f d6 de 57 c9 01 | ····&···Ø·/ÖÞWÉ·
0080 | 00 00 00 00 00 00 00 00-00 00 00 00 00 00 00 00 | ················
0090 | 02 00 00 00 01 00 00 00-00 00 00 00 38 00 00 00 | ············8···
00a0 | 00 00 00 00 32 00 00 00-02 00 00 00 38 00 00 00 | ····2·······8···
00b0 | 37 00 00 00 66 00 00 00-35 00 00 00 02 00 00 00 | 7···f···5·······
00c0 | 6f 00 00 00 05 00 00 00-d2 00 00 00 34 00 00 00 | o·······Ò···4···
00d0 | 04 00 00 00 74 00 00 00-02 00 00 00 3c 01 00 00 | ····t·······<···
```

Prefetch files can easily be analyzed by hand in small numbers. However, larger numbers of prefetch files (such as a system's entire `Prefetch` folder) may require the use of scripts or plug-ins available with an examiner's favorite forensic suite, or a third-party tool like MiTeC's Windows File Analyzer covered in the previous section.

## Installed Programs

The programs installed on an examined system can often have a bearing on an investigation as well. Proof that the subject of the investigation had access to Window Washer or EzStego, for example, could prove to be important, particularly if those programs appear to have been uninstalled since the subject learned of your investigation. In addition to prefetch and link (e.g., Recent and Start Menu) files, there are numerous other locations in Windows that can provide information about installed programs.

The first and most obvious location is the `c:\program files` folder. This folder holds files and folders created when an application is installed, and is often used as the location from which a program executes (for example, `c:\program files\microsoft office\office12\winword.exe`). Finding a program folder in this location, and examining the date-time stamps on the folder and related files, can give an examiner an indication of when the program was installed (i.e., File Created dates) and when the program was last used (i.e., Last Accessed or Last Written dates; remember prefetch!). In Windows Vista and Windows 7, a folder called `ProgramData` is also located on the root of `c:` and contains application-specific data for Windows programs such as Media Player and Windows Defender. Keep in mind that some programs (such as printer software) create folders directly on the root of the partition.

Another installed program goldmine is application data folders under each user's profile in the following locations:

> `c:\Documents and Settings\<user folder>\Application Data` (Windows XP)
> `c:\Documents and Settings\<user folder>\Local Settings\Application Data` (Windows XP)
> `c:\Users\<user folder>\AppData` (Windows Vista and 7)
> `c:\ProgramData` (Windows Vista and 7)

These folders contain application-specific data for third-party programs installed by the user. For instance, the folders and registry entries depicted in Figure 5.33 show remnants of a data destruction program named Window Washer. Folders in these locations also have a far greater chance of not being deleted or removed when a program is uninstalled by the user and can provide proof of a program's installation and removal long after it is taken off the system.

**FIGURE 5.33**

Examination of installed software locations in the folder structure and Windows registry.

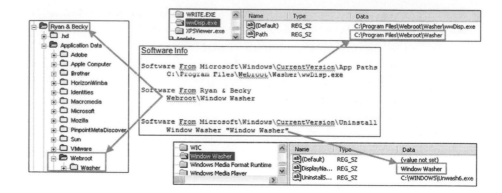

Examiners should use caution before jumping to conclusions about what user account installed the programs in these application data locations. The mere fact that these program folders exist under a particular user's folder does not necessarily mean they were actually installed by that user. Even the file and folder permissions can be misleading. In Figure 5.34, the VMware folder is reported as having an owner of "Kids," despite the fact that this user account was unprivileged and did not have the power to install programs. In other words, VMware was installed by another user account, despite the

**FIGURE 5.34**

Folder ownership data for the VMware application folder under the "Kids" user account.

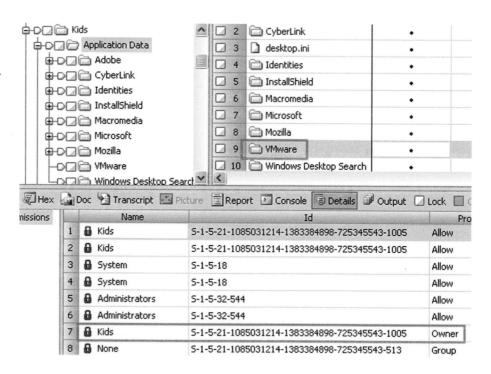

ownership information associated with this folder. This situation can arise when a privileged account is used to install a program that can be used by all user accounts on the system.

Not surprisingly, the Windows registry is also a vast repository of information pertaining to installed programs. Under `Software` each user's NTUSER.DAT file contains application-specific data that pertains to their user account and can be used not only as an indication that a program was installed, but also that the user account interacted with it in some way (keep in mind that this could include unknowing interaction by the user). In addition, the Windows `SOFTWARE` registry hive contains similar subkeys for installed programs, which could be associated with any users of the system. The Windows `SOFTWARE` registry hive also contains a list of file extensions in the `SOFTWARE\Classes` subkey shown in Figure 5.35. These file extensions represent file types that can be managed by some program on the system and could contain legacy data about installed programs.

Data pertaining to programs that are (or were at one time) installed on a system can also be found in the following registry locations:

```
SOFTWARE\Microsoft\Windows\CurrentVersion\AppPaths
SOFTWARE\Microsoft\Windows\CurrentVersion\Uninstall
```

The installed program data in the registry (in both NTUSER.DAT and SOFTWARE) tends to be even more persistent than the application data folders, and examination of the subkey Last Written date could indicate when a program was installed.

## Thumbnail Cache Files

`Thumbs.db` files are compound files that contain smaller (thumbnail) images of folders and files viewed in Windows Explorer, as well as the last modified date-time stamps of the viewed files. On Windows systems prior to Vista, when a user chooses to view the contents of a folder in `Thumbnails` view, a `thumbs.db` file is automatically created in that folder containing the thumbnail images of the folder's contents. When additional files are added to the folder viewed in `Thumbnails` view, the `thumbs.db` file is updated to include thumbnail images of those files, and the Last Accessed, Last Written, and Entry Modified date-time stamps of the `thumbs.db` are updated.

**FIGURE 5.35**

SOFTWARE\Classes registry data showing evidence of EnCase installed on the system.

**FIGURE 5.36**

Analysis of a `thumbs.db` file.

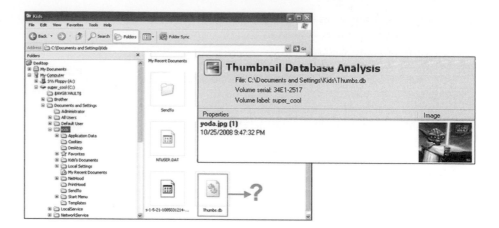

A bonus for forensic examiners is that thumbnail images can remain in the `thumbs.db` file even after the actual object to which the thumbnail image pertains has been deleted. For example, Figure 5.36 shows that the file `yoda.jpg` is no longer present in the `c:\Documents and Settings\Kids` folder; however, when the `thumbs.db` file in that folder is analyzed, evidence of the file's presence in that location (and its content) can still be seen. The date-time stamp for the `yoda.jpg` thumbnail denotes the date and time the thumbnail was first added as an entry in the `thumbs.db` file. The metadata of the `thumbs.db` file itself does not change when other file objects within its folder are deleted, because the `thumbs.db` itself is not updated.

On Vista and 7, these thumbnail cache files are held in a different location than in previous versions of Windows. Rather than residing in the individual folders to which they pertain, thumbnail cache files are centralized for each user, in the users' `AppData\Local\Microsoft\Windows\Explorer` folders. Thumbnail images are stored in four different sizes by the OS, requiring four different files to hold the contents: `thumbcache_32.db`, `thumbcache_96.db`, `thumbcache_256.db`, and `thumbcache_1024.db`.

## TOOL FEATURE: EXTRACTING DETAILS FROM THUMBS.DB

The best way to analyze thumbnail files is with an automated tool. Plenty of third-party tools, such as MiTeC's Windows File Analyzer, are also available to view the contents of `thumbs.db` files. However, Windows File Analyzer does not currently recognize `thumbcache_32.db`, `thumbcache_96.db`, `thumbcache_256.db`, and `thumbcache_1024.db` files as thumbnail caches. Tools suites like EnCase and FTK make short work of thumbnail cache files and provide an examiner quick access to the underlying images by analyzing the files' compound structure.

Another thumbcache file, located in the same folder as these size-related thumbnail caches, is the `thumbcache_idx.db` file. This file acts as an encoded index containing information regarding the path to the various locations where the actual picture files (represented by the thumbnails in the thumb-cache files) reside on the disk. Forensic suites such as EnCase use the data within this index file to automatically resolve image paths for the examiner. However, if the actual image to which a thumbnail refers has been deleted, it will no longer have a valid reference in the `thumbcache_idx.db`, and even forensic tools will be unable to resolve the path to which a thumbnail refers. It should also be noted that the Disk Cleanup utility in Vista/2k8/7 clears the users' thumbnail caches by default.

## Printer Files

Information on Windows systems can also be found in connection with a computer's configured printer and printing activity. A system running Windows can generally be set to send data to a printer in Raw or Enhanced Metafile (EMF) formats (although there are variations of these two). Both formats result in the creation of two file types (a shadow file and a spool file) in the `c:\windows\system32\spool\printers` folder when a system is set to spool print jobs. The files are named as complimentary pairs; for example, one job sent to the printer results in the creation of one `FP00001.SHD` file and one `FP00001.SPL` file for the same job (regardless of the number of pages in the printed job), while the next print job results in the creation of `FP00002.SHD` and `FP00002.SPL`. Both shadow and spool files can contain information useful to an investigator.

The shadow file (file extension .SHD) created when a job is sent to the printer can contain information about the job itself, such as the printer name, computer name, files accessed to enable printing, user account that created the print job, the selected print processor and format, the application used to print the file, and the name of the printed file (which can be a Uniform Resource Locator (URL) if the file is a web page printed via a browser). This data can all be seen in Unicode using a hex editor or forensic software.

Although the shadow file contains mostly administrative and configuration data about the print job, the spool file (file extension `.SPL`) contains the actual data to be printed. Among the information that can be seen in the code of an EMF-format spool file using a hex editor or like tool are the name of the printed file and the print format, but the true value is the printed pages themselves. A spool file will contain one EMF for each page in the job sent to the printer, with each page marked (conveniently) by the uppercase letters EMF (`\x45\x4D\x46`).

First the good news… Viewing the printed pages held in the spool files can be fairly simple. For example, EnCase automatically converts the 41 bytes

**FIGURE 5.37**
Conversion of EMF data using EnCase.

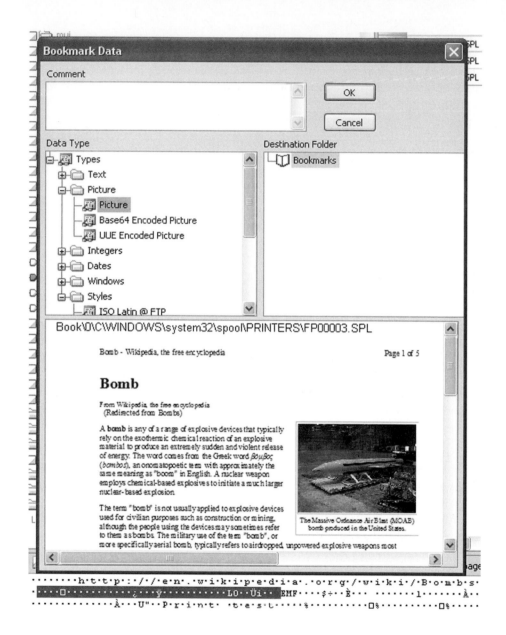

**FIGURE 5.37**
Conversion of EMF data using EnCase.

immediately prior to each EMF in the spool file to a user-viewable format by bookmarking the data as a picture (Figure 5.37).

Another tool, the free EMF Spool Viewer (www.codeproject.com/KB/printing/EMFSpoolViewer.aspx), can likewise allow the investigator to view spooled pages in a simple and user-friendly interface.

Now the bad news… Print spool and shadow files are extremely perishable and by default are kept only until a job is successfully printed, after which they are automatically deleted from the system. Persistent `.SPL` and `.SHD` files are generally found in only one of two circumstances:

1. There was some problem with the print job that prevented it from completing successfully (e.g., the printer being out of paper, a communication problem between the sending system and the printer, or the chosen printer not being powered on).

2. The sending system is configured to keep printed documents as shown in Figure 5.38, thereby retaining backup or tracking copies of jobs sent to the printer.

The examiner should also remember that many organizations, particularly large private-sector companies, retain copies of printed documents on central servers in order to comply better with modern legal and regulatory requirements. And, even if all spool files have been deleted prior to examination, they could still be located in unallocated space on an examined system by searching for the EMF marker.

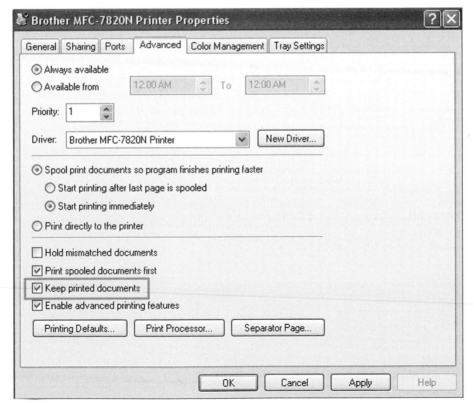

**FIGURE 5.38**

System configured to retain .SPL and .SHD files after printing.

## Recycle Bin

The Recycle Bin (sometimes called `Recycler, Recycled, or $Recycle. Bin` depending on the version of Windows) is nothing more than another folder in Windows. Users will commonly respond that they deleted a file, when what they really mean is that they sent the file to the Recycle Bin. When a file is moved to the Recycle Bin, it is not deleted, but rather the pointer to the file (most significantly, the file's name and the information pertaining to the file's parent folder) is updated to reflect the file's new logical location.

By default, when users press the Delete key (or choose the right-click `Delete...` option), they are asked if they would like to send the file/folder to the Recycle Bin. This process can be circumvented by holding the Shift key while pressing the Delete button or using the `del` command from the console. Additionally, the user could configure the system to bypass the Recycle Bin altogether by editing the Recycle Bin properties via a right-click menu option, which changes the DWORD value for `NukeOnDelete` from 0 to 1 in the `SOFTWARE\Microsoft\Windows\CurrentVersion\Explorer\BitBucket` subkey. Also located in the `BitBucket` subkey are the values for determining the maximum percentage of the drive the Recycle Bin can consume and whether or not the system is set to apply Recycle Bin settings globally or independently to all volumes (Figure 5.39).

A separate Recycle Bin folder is maintained for each user on a Windows system. Each user's Recycle Bin is named with the user's full SID, which includes the identifiers for the local machine or the domain and the user's RID on the local machine or domain. On versions of Windows prior to Vista, the SID-named folder was not created for a user until he or she accessed the Recycle Bin (usually by causing something to be sent there).

Pre-Vista Windows Recycle Bins contain a file called `INFO2`, which acts as an index and repository of information about files sent to the Recycle Bin. When a file is moved to the Recycle Bin, the file is renamed to begin with a "D" (presumably for "deleted"), followed by the drive letter where the file previously resided, an incremented number, and the file's original file extension (e.g., Dc3.doc). Although the file's name is changed, the data's physical location

**FIGURE 5.39**

Recycle Bin settings in the Windows registry.

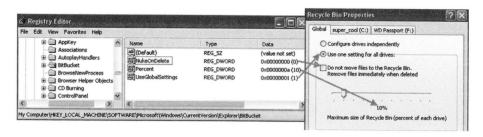

on the disk, its size, and code are unchanged, and the file can still be opened or viewed with little trouble. Each file moved to the Recycle Bin gets its own record in the INFO2 file, with each record being 800 bytes in length (280 bytes in 95, 98, and ME). These INFO2 file records contain important information that examiners can interpret and use in their investigations.

As shown in Figure 5.40, among the important data in each INFO2 record are the full path for the file's *original* location (record offset 0; variable length), the date and time the file was moved to the Recycle Bin (record offset 268; 8 bytes), and the file's physical size (record offset 280; 2 bytes).

In addition, the record index numbers (record offset 264; 4 bytes) can be used to determine in what order files were moved to the Recycle Bin and how many other files may have existed in that location at the time they were moved. The INFO2 begins numbering records at 1 (0 in Windows 95/98) and continues to increment records as items are added to the Recycle Bin. The INFO2 record count is reset only when the Recycle Bin is empty and the user logs off the system; otherwise the record continues to increment from the last used index number. If there are no deleted files in the Recycle Bin, the INFO2 file still exists but will contain only a 20 byte header. The Last Written date-time stamp for the INFO2 file in an empty Recycle Bin reflects the date and time the Bin was last emptied by the user.

One tool for interpreting INFO2 records is Foundstone's Rifiuti command-line utility (www.foundstone.com/us/resources/proddesc/rifiuti.htm). This program provides record index numbers, date and time of deletion, full original path, and physical size of the files in the Recycle Bin, all output in a tab-delimited format suitable for opening in Microsoft Excel. The Windows File Analyzer also parses and displays INFO2 records in a report-ready format. However, even if the examiner uses one of these automated tools to parse the INFO2's active data, it should be noted that it is very common to see old INFO2 record data in the file slack of allocated INFO2 files. Therefore, it is important to also examine INFO2 records using a forensic tool to ensure that no information is overlooked.

**FIGURE 5.40**

Content of user's Recycle Bin folder and INFO2 file (full original path and deletion date-time stamp highlighted) viewed in EnCase.

**FIGURE 5.41**

EnCase view of files in
`$Recycle.Bin` on
a Windows Vista system;
the `$T` file (codc shown
at bottom) contains the
file's deletion date-time
stamp and original path
(in Unicode).

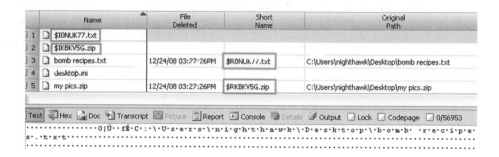

The Vista Recycle Bin operates differently from that of its earlier cousins. In Vista (and 7), the Recycle Bin folder has been renamed `$Recycle.Bin`, and (in contrast to Windows 2k/XP/2k3) a Recycle Bin subfolder (named with a user's full SID/RID) is created for a user the first time he or she logs on, *regardless of whether or not anything has been deleted*. In another departure, the index-like INFO2 file has been replaced by a process of using two files to correspond with every one file sent to the Recycle Bin.

When a file is sent to the Vista Recycle Bin, it is renamed with a pseudorandom filename beginning with $R and ending in the file's original extension; this $R file contains the file's original content. Along with the $R file, another file (beginning with $I and named to be complimentary with the $R file) is created and contains the file's date and time of deletion (file offset 16; 8 bytes) and the file's path at the time of deletion (file offset 24; variable length; in Unicode) as shown in Figure 5.41.

## Connection of External Devices

Increasingly, digital investigators are encountering cases that involve the use of removable media, USB devices, specifically. Whether the investigation deals with theft of intellectual property, the possession of child pornography, embezzlement, or even computer intrusion, USB devices could potentially be related to the crime. As such, examiners often need to get some idea of when, how many, and what types of USB devices have been connected to the computer(s) they are examining.

The Windows registry houses a wealth of information pertaining to USB devices that have been connected to a system. Data found in the `SYSTEM\<ControlSet###>\Enum\USBSTOR` subkey shown in Figure 5.42 can be particularly helpful.

The first-level subkeys under `USBSTOR`, such as `Disk&Ven_SanDisk&Prod_Cruzer_Mini&Rev_0.2` in Figure 5.42, are device class identifiers taken from device descriptors and used to identify a specific kind of USB device. The second-level subkeys (e.g., `SNDK5CCDD5014E009703&0` in Figure 5.42) are unique instance identifiers used to identify specific devices within each class.

The unique instance identifier of a device is either the device's serial number or (if the device does not have a serial number reported in its device descriptor) a pseudorandom value derived by Windows to uniquely identify the device.[11] Each unique instance identifier generally represents one USB device; so, seeing two different unique instance identifiers under one device class identifier could indicate that two different devices of similar type and manufacture were plugged into the system (such as two different 4GB SanDisk Cruzer thumb drives). The unique class identifier can also be used to obtain other information important to the investigator. For example, being that the unique instance identifier generally stays the same for a specific device on each Windows system to which it is connected, seeing the same unique instance identifier on multiple systems can be an indicator of the same device's use with each of those computers. Further, by write-protecting a seized USB device and plugging it into a virgin forensic computer, an examiner could record the unique instance identifier (and other device information) populated in the forensic computer's registry and compare it to the registry of a suspect system to determine if that seized device had been similarly connected.

**FIGURE 5.42**

Entries in the SYSTEM\ <ControlSet###>\ Enum\USBSTOR subkey.

---

## PRACTITIONER'S TIP: FORENSIC EXAMINATION OF USB ARTIFACTS

Tests performed with several hardware USB write-blockers have shown that Windows often populates a unique instance identifier for the write-blocking device rather than the suspect USB device, so a software write-blocking method may be preferred. Whether a hardware or software USB write-blocking method is selected, the examiner should perform tests in advance with nonevidence media and observe and record the results.

---

A device's unique identifier can also be found by viewing the Device Instance Id under the device's properties in the Windows Device Manager on a running system to which the device is connected as shown in Figure 5.43.

Additionally, by searching for a device's unique instance identifier in the c:\ windows\setupapi.log file, an examiner can determine the first time a USB device was connected to a system.

---

[11] If the second character of the unique instance identifier is an ampersand ("&"), the value is Windows-generated and not the result of a serial number reported by the device itself.

**FIGURE 5.43**

Viewing a device's properties in the Windows Device Manager reveals the device's unique identifier, which can be matched to a corresponding registry subkey in the USBSTOR.

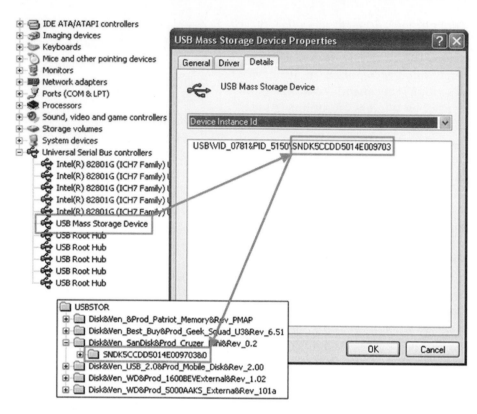

```
[2008/12/20 16:54:28 1084.7 Driver Install]
#-019 Searching for hardware ID(s): usbstor\
    disksandisk_cruzer_mini_____0.2_,usbstor\
    disksandisk_cruzer_mini_____,usbstor\
    disksandisk_,usbstor\sandisk_cruzer_
    mini_____0,sandisk_cruzer_mini_____0,usbstor\
    gendisk,gendisk
#-018 Searching for compatible ID(s): usbstor\disk,usbstor\
    raw
#-198 Command line processed: C:\WINDOWS\system32\services.
    exe
#I022 Found "GenDisk" in C:\WINDOWS\inf\disk.inf;
    Device: "Disk drive"; Driver: "Disk drive"; Provider:
    "Microsoft"; Mfg: "(Standard disk drives)"; Section
    name: "disk_install".
#I023 Actual install section: [disk_install.NT]. Rank:
    0x00000006. Effective driver date: 07/01/2001.
```

```
#-166 Device install function: DIF_SELECTBESTCOMPATDRV.
#I063 Selected driver installs from section [disk_install]
    in "c:\windows\inf\disk.inf".
#I320 Class GUID of device remains: {4D36E967-E325-11CE-
    BFC1-08002BE10318}.
#I060 Set selected driver.
#I058 Selected best compatible driver.
#-166 Device install function: DIF_INSTALLDEVICEFILES.
#I124 Doing copy-only install of "USBSTOR\
    DISK&VEN_SANDISK&PROD_CRUZER_MINI&REV_0.2\
    SNDK5CCDD5014E009703&0".
#-166 Device install function: DIF_REGISTER_COINSTALLERS.
```

Further, the examiner can locate the following registry subkeys:

```
SYSTEM\<ControlSet###>\Control\DeviceClasses\{53f56307-
    b6bf-11d0-94f2-00a0c91efb8b}
SYSTEM\<ControlSet###>\Control\DeviceClasses\{53f5630d-
    b6bf-11d0-94f2-00a0c91efb8b}
```

Subkeys in these locations can be seen to correspond with specific devices by unique instance identifier, with the Last Written date-time stamp on the device subkey indicating the last time the device was connected to the system (Figure 5.44).

The &0 at the end of the unique instance identifiers (whether serial number or Windows-derived) can be incremented to denote a related device. For example, when a U3-enabled device is plugged into a system, it actually results in the creation of two virtual USB devices, a CD-Rom device and a Disk device; if the unique instance identifier for the virtual CD-Rom device is 6&38b32a79&0, it is likely that the complimentary virtual Disk device will be 6&38b32a79&1.

**FIGURE 5.44**

The Last Written date-time stamp of the corresponding device subkey in `DeviceClasses` indicates that the device was connected to the system on 05/04/07.

**FIGURE 5.45**

Drive letters listed in the registry subkey SYSTEM\ MountedDevices.

\DosDevices\A:
\DosDevices\C:
\DosDevices\D:
\DosDevices\E:
\DosDevices\F:

Values located under each unique instance identifier subkey can include the ParentIdPrefix (not always populated) and FriendlyName for each device. The FriendlyName is nothing more than a more detailed and less complex description of the device, which can contain manufacturer and model information (such as "Patriot Memory USB Device").

It should be noted that numerous devices can report the same FriendlyName value, so this should not be used as a reliable means of unique device identification. The ParentIdPrefix is a Windows-derived value that (if present) can be used to link each device with additional information. For example, the SYSTEM\ MountedDevices subkey often contains values similar to those in Figure 5.45.

The underlying data associated with each of these device values contains a description of the device that was last mounted on that drive letter, including the device's ParentIdPrefix as detailed in Figure 5.46.

## TOOL FEATURE: EXAMINING USB ARTIFACTS

Forensic examiners seeking to analyze USB activity on a system they are examining can, of course, conduct their analysis manually. However, tools do exist to make the analysis easier, or at least a bit faster. Many of the forensic tool suites (e.g., EnCase, FTK, etc.) have scripts or add-on functionality that allow an examiner to dig the USBSTOR information from the registry and display it in a report-style format. UVCView is a Microsoft development tool (http://msdn.microsoft.com/en-us/library/aa906848.aspx) that allows examiners to view USB device descriptors (the source of much of what is populated in the registry); it can be difficult to find, but at the time of this writing it is available at ftp://ftp.efo.ru/pub/ftdichip/Utilities/UVCView. x86.exe. Another popular tool is USBDeview by NirSoft, which reads the SYSTEM hive to which it is pointed and attempts to do much of the association between USBSTOR, DeviceClasses, and MountedDevices data for the user. Whatever tool is chosen, the examiner should always validate the results before placing them in a report or taking them to court.

**FIGURE 5.46**

Matching a USB device to its last mounted drive letter via its ParentIdPrefix.

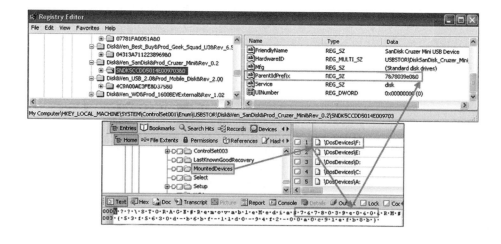

Recent research by Rob Lee (Mandiant) and Harlan Carvey has also shed light on the `HKLM\Software\Microsoft\Windows Portable Devices\ Devices` subkey, which contains data similar to that in the `USBSTOR`, including a history (partial, at least) of USB devices plugged into Windows Vista and Windows 7 systems. An added benefit of this subkey is that it can show that multiple different devices were mounted under a particular drive letter on the system (e.g., `E:\`), thereby providing a longer historical record for an examiner; this is in contrast to the `MountedDevices` subkey discussed earlier, which shows only the last device mounted under a particular drive letter. The `port_dev.pl` plugin for RegRipper (www.regripper.net/) parses data from the `Windows Portable Devices\Devices` subkey and provides easy-to-read output, including each listed device's `FriendlyName`, serial number (or unique identifier), and drive letter under which the device was mounted (providing these data are available in the subkey).

## PRACTITIONER'S TIP: USB TRACES IN LINK FILES

Forensic examiners should also keep in mind that link files can be an excellent source of data about the connection of external devices. Recall that link files contain the full path to their target file, including the drive letter and serial number of the volume on which the target file resides. Matching the volume serial number in a link for a target file opened from removable media with the volume serial number of a seized USB thumb drive, and then matching that USB thumb drive to a specific computer via the registry is a pretty good way to get an investigation rolling.

## Pagefile.sys and Hiberfil.sys

Like their UNIX/Linux counterparts, Windows systems often have a need to swap data out of volatile memory to a location on the disk. However, whereas most *nix systems have a whole partition (small as it may sometimes be) dedicated to this swap space, Windows systems tend to use one single file, `pagefile.sys`. `Pagefile.sys` (or simply, the page file) is created when Windows is installed and is generally 1 to 1.5 times the size of the installed system RAM on XP systems. The settings for the size of the page file, as well as whether the file is cleared at shutdown or disabled entirely can be found in the `SYSTEM\<ControlSet###>\Control\Session Manager\Memory Management` registry subkey.

The page file has intrigued examiners for years because theoretically it could contain any data that was held in memory for long after a system was powered down; these data could include unpacked executables, unencrypted passwords, encryption and communications keys, live chat messages, and more. However, the challenge has always been how to extract usable data from the mass of digital detritus often found within the `pagefile.sys`. One strategy is to use a tool like `strings.exe` (http://technet.microsoft.com/en-us/sysinternals/

Sign in

Windows Live ID: this_is_my_email_address@hotmail.com
(example555@hotmail.com)

Password: ••••••••••••••••

Forgot your password?

☑ Remember me on this computer (?)
☐ Remember my password (?)

[ Sign in ]

Use enhanced security

**FIGURE 5.47**

Windows live e-mail login prompt.

bb897439.aspx) or BinText (www.foundstone.com/us/resources/proddesc/bintext.htm) to attempt to pull out user-readable text from the page file. This can be effective, but even the elimination of all the "machine code" characters can leave the investigator looking through line after line of "48dfhs9bn" and "%__<>" strings, unable to discern the meaning of the seemingly random data. Another strategy is to look for recognizable data structures. As just a few examples, looking for executable headers (\x4d\x5A\x90), searching for URL prefixes (e.g., http:// or www.), or locating the text PRIVMSG (which precedes each message sent in many IRC chat clients) could pay dividends, depending on the type of investigation. Further, understanding the geographic relationship between data can be helpful. Consider the e-mail login prompt in Figure 5.47.

To the user the password appears masked by dots; however, the computer sees the underlying data and the password to be used is held in RAM. If a search of the pagefile.sys revealed the user's e-mail address, it is not out of the realm of possibility that the user's password could be in close proximity and easily identified, particularly if it is a user-friendly word or phrase.

The hiberfil.sys is similar to the page file, but rather than being used as active swap space, the hiberfil.sys is a repository for the contents of RAM (in a compressed format) when a system is told to hibernate (such as when the lid of a laptop is closed).

Vista handles hibernation a bit differently than previous Windows versions in that it has three related modes: sleep, hibernation, and hybrid sleep-hibernation. In sleep mode, the system continues to supply minimal power to RAM maintaining the contents and not requiring the system to use the hiberfil.sys. Hibernation, on the other hand, causes the contents of RAM to be saved to the hiberfil.sys for restoration when the system "wakes up." The hybrid sleep-hibernation mode takes advantage of both techniques, continuing to supply low-level power to RAM *and* saving the contents to the hiberfil.sys for redundancy. The SandMan Project is specifically aimed at assisting investigators in performing forensic analysis of Windows hibernation files (http://sandman.msuiche.net/).

Many examiners have also begun to encounter ReadyBoost used in conjunction with Vista systems. ReadyBoost uses up to 4GB of flash memory (usually in the form of a USB device or flash card) as a memory cache (virtual memory); specifically, Vista uses the flash memory to store data important for the function of the memory manager. An advanced version of ReadyBoost is also listed as a feature for Windows 7, removing the 4GB size restriction for utilized flash memory. Although the user can enjoy the speed gains from ReadyBoost, its use has little impact for the forensic examiner. A file called `Readyboost.sfcache` is created on the flash media used for ReadyBoost, but the file is (unfortunately for the examiner) 128-bit AES encrypted and represents nothing other than that the device was used for that purpose.

## Restore Points and Shadow Copies

System restore functionality (or simply, restore points) have been used in Windows since the introduction of Windows ME and have been a part of every nonserver Windows OS since then.[12] In an effort to increase recoverability, the creation of restore points (RPs) is turned on by default (although it can be manually disabled, of course), causing an RP to be created when a major change occurs to the system (such as the installation of a major piece of software), on a regular schedule (such as daily), or when the user manually creates an RP. It should also be noted that system restore functionality is disabled automatically unless at least 200MB of space (300MB in Vista) are available on the system for its use.

In Windows XP, when an RP is created, backup versions of the Windows registry (i.e., SAM, SECURITY, SOFTWARE, SYSTEM, and users' NTUSER.DAT files), along with other files listed in the Monitored File Extensions list (including .EXE, .INI, and .LNK files), are created and stored in the System Volume Information folder (Microsoft, 2008a). This folder is normally protected and inaccessible to users without system-level authority, even to members of the administrators group (although system authority is not hard to come by on most Windows systems). Data in the System Volume Information area are stored in subfolders named with a capital "RP" followed by the number of the restore point (in sequence) from RP0 as shown in Figure 5.48. An examination of the File Created date-time stamp for each RP folder can provide an indication of when the backup was initiated.

```
C:\System Volume Information\_restore{08601ED4-F51B-4629-9991-33F368C96C73}>DIR
 Volume in drive C is super_cool
 Volume Serial Number is 34E1-2517

 Directory of C:\System Volume Information\_restore{08601ED4-F51B-4629-9991-33F3
68C96C73}

12/27/2008  12:23 AM                 154 drivetable.txt
12/26/2008  05:11 PM               6,566 fifo.log
09/29/2008  05:16 PM      <DIR>          RP143
09/30/2008  11:38 AM      <DIR>          RP144
10/01/2008  12:16 PM      <DIR>          RP145
12/19/2008  05:07 PM      <DIR>          RP146
10/02/2008  08:14 PM      <DIR>          RP147
10/03/2008  08:17 PM      <DIR>          RP148
10/04/2008  09:17 PM      <DIR>          RP149
10/07/2008  04:02 PM      <DIR>          RP150
```

**FIGURE 5.48**

Restore points seen via the console with system-level privileges.

---

[12] System Restore can be installed in Windows 2003 (www.msfn.org/win2k3/sysrestore.htm), but it is a tweak not supported by Microsoft. It should also be noted that in Vista, system restore cannot be used for disks smaller than 1GB or that are formatted FAT32.

Information about how and what data are kept (or not kept, in the case of the first subkey) is primarily held in two registry locations:

```
SYSTEM\<ControlSet###>\Control\BackupRestore
SOFTWARE\Microsoft\Windows NT\CurrentVersion\
    SystemRestore
```

Information in the `SystemRestore` key can be particularly instructive, as it can include data pertaining to several characteristics, including:

- Whether the system restore function is disabled (`DisableSR`; DWORD=0x00000001 means disabled).

- How often RPs are scheduled to be created (`RPGlobalInterval`; DWORD value representing seconds, default is 0x00015180=86400 seconds=24 hours in Windows XP and Vista).

- The percentage of storage on the disk that can be used for RPs (`DiskPercent`; DWORD value representing percentage, maxed out at 0x0000000c=12% in Windows XP). Be aware that in Windows Vista, there is no practical limit on the total size that can be given to system restore data, although by default it is set at 15% of the drive. The built-in utility `vssadmin.exe` can be used to set storage limits; if no size is specified, there theoretically is no limit to the amount of space that can be used for system restore data.

- The number of days to retain restore points (`RPLifeInterval`; DWORD value representing seconds, default is 0x0076a700=7776000 seconds=90 days in Windows XP). Windows Vista has a default `RPLifeInterval` value of DWORD=0xffffffff, which means there is virtually no time limitation on how long old RPs are retained.

Examining data in restore points can provide a picture of the examined system at some point in the past. Consider a laptop computer that is examined with the goal of determining whether it had ever been connected to a particular corporate network or domain; by examining the data contained within registry hives backed up in past restore points it may be possible to prove the laptop's connection to the network in question, and even provide an approximate timeframe for its connection. Further, consider a case involving the execution of malicious code from a piece of removable media; if no traces of the removable media or code can be found on the active system, an examination of the system's RPs could lead to the discovery of link files and USBSTOR data for the device and file carrying the code.

Viewing registry data in ME/XP system restore points is not unlike viewing the data in its nonbacked-up state. For example, backed up registry hives found in the `c:\system volume information\_restore{…}\RP###\`

snapshot location can be parsed and viewed the same as any registry hive found in the `c:\windows\system32\config` folder. Forensic tools such as EnCase and FTK make viewing these backup hives a breeze, but almost any tool or technique designed to examine registry hives (e.g., USBDview) could be made to work similarly on the backups thereof. The backups can even be copied out of an image and loaded directly into the Windows Registry Editor on a forensic workstation for examination (see Figure 5.49).

**FIGURE 5.49**

SYSTEM hive from an RP viewed in the Windows Registry Editor via the Load Hive… option.

Viewing the other (nonregistry) files backed up in RPs can likewise be as simple as the examiner using their favorite viewer. It is important to note that nonregistry files in ME/XP RPs are renamed with an "A" followed by a seven-digit number and the file's original file extension; however, the file's code is not affected by the name change. For example, an examiner could copy all the `.LNK` files out of a restore point in a forensic image and parse them with Windows File Analyzer, the same as they could have done with files from a user's `c:\Documents and Settings\<username>\Recent` folder.

In addition to the backed up registry hives and nonregistry files, several other files can normally be found in XP RP folders that can provide examiners with information. For example, the `fifo.log` file shown in Figure 5.50 contains a list of restore points that have aged out or been purged (on a first in/first out basis, hence "fifo") and the dates of their deletion. Another log file, `rp.log`, can contain data pertaining to what event (e.g., Avg8 Update or System Checkpoint) caused the restore point to be created.

It should also be noted that restore points can be found on removable media, such as external hard drives. These restore points can provide examiners with

```
C:\System Volume Information\_restore{08601ED4-F51B-4629-9991-33F368C96C73}>type
 fifo.log
09/16/08-19:21:54 : Fifoed RP1 on drive C:\
09/16/08-19:21:54 : Fifoed RP2 on drive C:\
09/16/08-19:21:54 : Fifoed RP3 on drive C:\
09/16/08-19:21:54 : Fifoed RP4 on drive C:\
09/16/08-19:21:54 : Fifoed RP5 on drive C:\
09/16/08-19:21:56 : Fifoed RP6 on drive C:\
09/16/08-19:21:56 : Fifoed RP7 on drive C:\
09/16/08-19:21:56 : Fifoed RP8 on drive C:\
09/16/08-19:21:56 : Fifoed RP9 on drive C:\
09/16/08-19:21:56 : Fifoed RP10 on drive C:\
09/16/08-19:21:56 : Fifoed RP11 on drive C:\
```

**FIGURE 5.50**

Contents of the `fifo.log` file showing deletion of restore point data.

valuable information about data that resided on the removable drive at a previous point in time, as well as provide a means of potentially tying a particular device to a particular system.

Like with many other Windows artifacts, Vista, 2k8, and 7 are completely different animals entirely when it comes to dealing with restore point data. Restore points in Vista are tied into the volume shadow service (also called the shadow copy or previous versions feature in Vista), are created every 24 hours (by default) or when a major change occurs (such as software installation or user-initiated restore point creation), and can consume up to 15% of total drive space (by default). Although this also holds true for Window 7, the Shadow Copy Service is off by default on Windows Server 2008.

The Previous Versions feature is nearly transparent for the user, as files and folders are scanned once a day (by default) and a copy is saved if their content differs from that of the last scan or RP creation. A user need only right-click on a file or folder object in Vista (Business, Enterprise, or Ultimate) and choose Restore Previous Versions to search for and select previous versions that can be quickly recovered.

Although the system restore data, including the shadow copy data, are still located in the `c:\system volume information` folder, gone are the convenient `RP`-named files, which have been replaced by files with large GUID-style names (Figure 5.51).

The forensic community at large is just starting to understand and document the file structure of these new system restore data files (Hargreaves, 2008; Lee, 2008). However, data in these files are *not encrypted or compressed* by default and can be searched in several ways. The first way is in the same manner as many other large data files, such as the `pagefile.sys` or the unallocated clusters data object shown in many forensic tools. But, like data in the `pagefile.sys` or unallocated clusters, files may be fragmented and difficult to recover intact. Using his or her favorite forensic tool, an examiner can run keyword searches (to include creating indexes) over these files, carve for known data types like images or Office documents as discussed in Chapter 2, "Forensic Analysis," and even recover specific data objects (such as MFT records) with minimal effort.

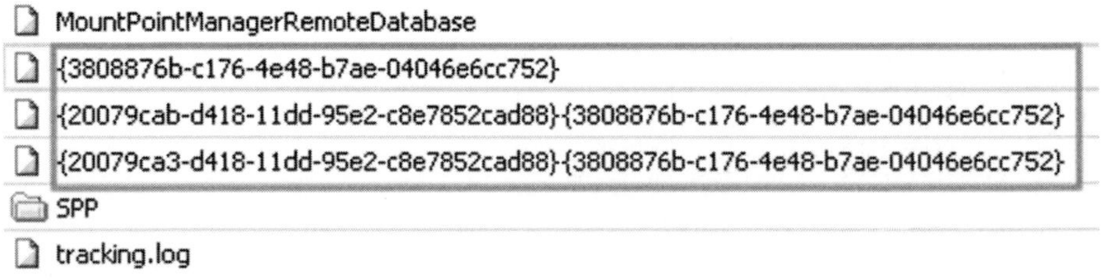

**FIGURE 5.51**

Restore point/shadow copy data in Vista.

MountPointManagerRemoteDatabase

{3808876b-c176-4e48-b7ae-04046e6cc752}

{20079cab-d418-11dd-95e2-c8e7852cad88}{3808876b-c176-4e48-b7ae-04046e6cc752}

{20079ca3-d418-11dd-95e2-c8e7852cad88}{3808876b-c176-4e48-b7ae-04046e6cc752}

SPP

tracking.log

Another method for searching the system restore data is a bit more complex, but can prove more beneficial. The first step is to extract the System Volume Information folder out of the Vista/2k8/7 forensic image onto the root of another drive. The drive can then be connected to a forensic system (or virtual machine) running Windows Vista; running the command `vssadmin list shadows` in the console (run as administrator) will list all shadow copy volumes on the local and any connected disks as shown in Figure 5.52.

Once the shadow copies are located (and the examiner has obtained their names), they can then create a link to the shadow copy data, thereby mounting each shadow copy volume on the forensic system. The examiner can use a command line such as:

```
mklink /d c:\ryan-shadowcopy-5 \\?\GLOBALROOT\Device\
    HarddiskVolumeShadowCopy5\
```

Note that the trailing (last) backslash in the preceding command line is required for the command to execute properly. If this command is successful, the system should report the successful creation of a symbolic link to the data within the shadow copy volume and the examiner can simply double-click the link to gain access to the underlying data (from a previous time period in the history of the system) in the familiar Windows Explorer interface. Furthermore, with the shadow copy volume mounted, the examiner could then add the folder into a forensic tool like FTK Imager in Figure 5.53, and create a forensic image of the logical data (files and folders) contained therein.

Yet another option is to boot the forensic image in a virtual machine (or restore to a physical disk and boot in another machine) and simply examine the snapshot data in its native Windows environment, as it could have been viewed by the user, by reverting to previous restore points or manually examining

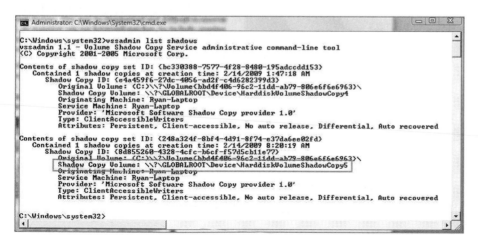

**FIGURE 5.52**

Example `vssadmin` output.

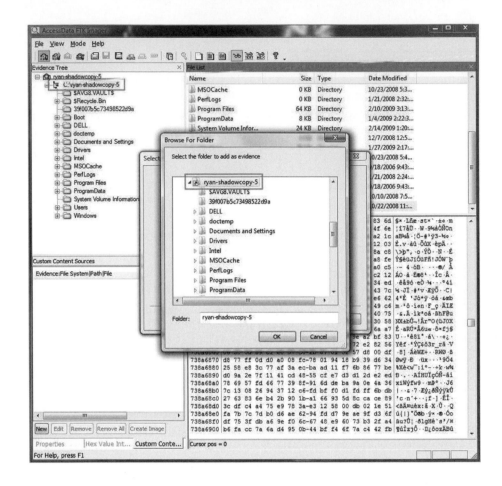

previous versions of individual files or folders. ShadowExplorer (www. shadowexplorer.com) can also assist the examiner by providing a user-friendly interface in which to explore previous version data on all Vista releases. For example, although the shadow copy service is present in Vista Home Basic, users are not provided the Restore Previous Versions right-click option as they are in Enterprise and Ultimate, making tools like ShadowExplorer particularly helpful.

## Other Vista Artifacts

This chapter has already highlighted quite a few differences between Vista/ Server 2k8 (and, in many cases, 7) and previous version of Windows, but there are still many more features and quirks that can have applicability to forensic examiners. For example, seeing a folder called `Program Files (x86)` alongside the regular `Program Files` folder means that the installed OS is a 64-bit version; the x86 folder remains for compatibility reasons (e.g., 32-bit program installation). Although that may be just an interesting piece of trivia to some investigators, other features are much more substantial.

For example, a new security measure, called file system virtualization, is implemented in Vista/2k8/7 and prevents unprivileged users and applications from placing data in protected system areas (such as `Program Files` and `System32` folders, or the Windows registry). As part of a larger User Access Control (UAC) system, which is based on the security concept of least-privilege and ensures users and processes run with normal permission unless administrator privileges are specifically requested/authorized, these restrictions could make it difficult for some applications (such as Internet Explorer) to function properly. As such, each user is assigned locations to which applications can write data, without that data actually residing in a protected location on the system, where it could pose a greater security threat. When virtualization is enabled for a particular application (as it is for Internet Explorer by default, but not for applications like `cmd.exe`), data that needs to be written to a protected location is actually redirected to a location belonging to the user responsible for the data, such as `c:\Users\<user>\AppData\Local\VirtualStore` folder. Even though the application is still able to read and interact with the data, it remains safely out of the protected system location.

As another example, Vista has some advanced indexing and search capabilities that, although present in earlier versions of Windows, are more readily available and accessible to Vista users. For the locations that are indexed by default (usually each user's `Start Menu` and e-mail, as well as `c:\Users` and its subfolders excluding the `Default` user folder) and the locations added by the user, Vista maintains its indexes in `c:\ProgramData\Microsoft\Search\data\Applications\Windows\Projects\SystemIndex\Indexer\CiFiles` folder. An examiner can determine what locations are included in the indexes by examining the subkeys located at `SOFTWARE\Microsoft\Windows Search\CrawlScopeManager\Windows\SystemIndex\WorkingSetRules`. Locations *potentially indexed* by Vista will be listed in numbered subkeys, each of which contains (among other things) the information summarized in Table 5.3.

The indexes created from the included locations can be searched by the examiner using keywords, which can be particularly fruitful if Windows indexed encrypted, encoded, or obfuscated files while they were open, decoded, and being worked with, thereby providing the examiner with access to information that is no longer readily available elsewhere on the system.

**Table 5.3** Information in the Registry Relating to Each Location That Is Indexed by Vista

| Value Name | Data Type | Data Value | Significance |
|---|---|---|---|
| Include | DWORD | 0x00000000 | The location is *not* included in the indexes |
| Include | DWORD | 0x00000001 | The location *is* included in the indexes |
| IncludeSubdirs | DWORD | 0x00000000 | *None* of the location's children are included in the indexes |
| IncludeSubdirs | DWORD | 0x00000001 | *At least one* of the location's children is included in the indexes |
| URL | SZ | Variable | Path to location that could be indexed |

Vista and 7 users can likewise search indexed locations using Windows' built-in search functionality, and can save searches (with the specified search criteria and data tags) in order to speed up future searches for the same material. A user's c:\Users\<username>\Searches folder can contain records of these searches saved by the user in the form of XML files with .SEARCH-MS extensions (Figure 5.54).

File system virtualization, indexing, and searching are just three substantial examples of additional Vista/2k8-specific features that many investigators may not have dealt with before. Other features, such as SuperFetch (the preloading of commonly used programs into memory to reduce load times) and the ability of certain versions (such as Enterprise and Ultimate) to perform full automatic, scheduled backups, can also have implications for the examiner, depending on the nature of the investigation.

## PRACTITIONER'S TIP: FINDING ROUTINE BACKUPS

The availability of convenient backup mechanisms on modern operating systems increases the likelihood that average users will maintain routine backups of their data. These backups can provide forensic examiners with valuable information, particularly when incriminating data has been deleted by the user but is saved in a routine backup. In addition to looking for removable mass storage devices and artifacts of USB connections, digital investigators may find artifacts of routine backups in the registry. Information related to recent backups on Vista (such as LastResultTarget, LastResultTime, LastResultSuccess, TotalSize, DeviceProduct, DeviceSerial, DeviceVendor, and DeviceVersion) can be found in the SOFTWARE\Microsoft\Windows\CurrentVersion\WindowsBackup\SystemImageBackup subkey.

Examiners are encouraged to install Vista, Server 2k8, and/or 7 on test machines (virtual environments are convenient) in order to further document the forensic artifacts left behind by their use that may not have been covered in this chapter and better understand how those unique artifacts can apply to a particular case they may be investigating.

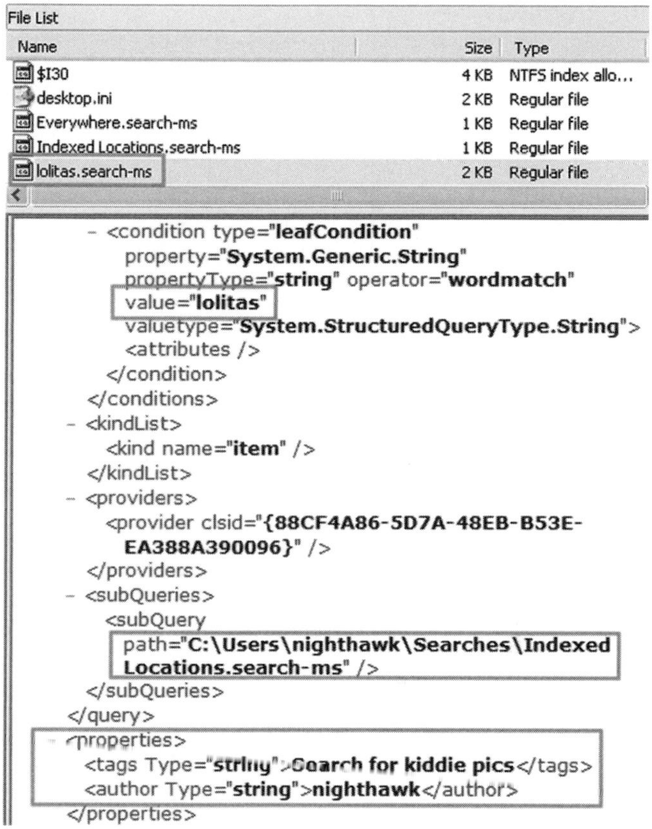

## Registry Potpourri

It is easy to see that the worth of the Windows registry in computer forensic investigation cannot be overstated. Almost any aspect of a well-planned examination has the potential to uncover pertinent evidence in the registry. Which begs the question, what more is there to find that has not been covered already? The answer is *plenty*!

For example, some of the most often examined areas of the registry are generally called *user assist keys* or most recently used (MRU) keys; the subkeys and values in these areas hold information that Windows has deemed important to helping the user perform small tasks on the system, such as opening often used files or speeding up access to certain resources. Consider the following subkey in Windows XP:

```
- <condition type="leafCondition"
    property="System.Generic.String"
    propertyType="string" operator="wordmatch"
    value="lolitas"
    valuetype="System.StructuredQueryType.String">
    <attributes />
  </condition>
  </conditions>
- <kindList>
    <kind name="item" />
  </kindList>
- <providers>
    <provider clsid="{88CF4A86-5D7A-48EB-B53E-
        EA388A390096}" />
  </providers>
- <subQueries>
    <subQuery
      path="C:\Users\nighthawk\Searches\Indexed
        Locations.search-ms" />
  </subQueries>
  </query>
- <properties>
    <tags Type="string">Search for kiddie pics</tags>
    <author Type="string">nighthawk</author>
  </properties>
```

**FIGURE 5.54**

Portion of a Windows Vista saved search file.

```
NTUSER.DAT\Software\Microsoft\Search Assistant\ACMru
```

Figure 5.55 demonstrates that the values and data under this subkey (and its children) provide information about user searches via the Windows Search Companion (most often accessed by right-clicking a folder and choosing Search… or from the Start button). The values are incremented beginning at zero, with the lowest numbers representing the most recently searched for items.

Another helpful location is `NTUSER.DAT\Software\Microsoft\ Internet Explorer\TypedURLs`, which contains a list of the last 25 URLs typed into the Internet Explorer address bar (i.e., pages visited by means other than simply clicking on a link). Like with the values under `Search Assistant`, the lowest numbered values represent the most recent additions to the list, but the values in `TypedURLs` begin numbering at one instead of zero (URL1). When the limit of 25 is reached, the values are disposed of in a first in/first out (FIFO) operation.

**FIGURE 5.55**

Examination of the currently logged on user's search activity.

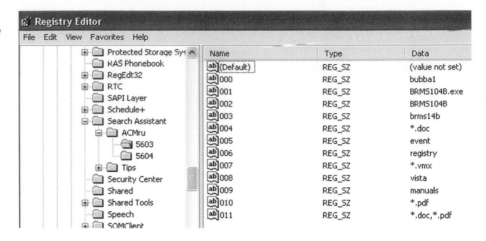

**FIGURE 5.55**

Examination of the currently logged on user's search activity.

Programs or locations opened by a user from the Start→Run... location can be found in NTUSER.DAT\Software\Microsoft\Windows\CurrentVersion\Explorer\RunMRU. The values in this location are displayed as a series of letters, beginning at "a," the key to which lies with the MRUList value (Figure 5.56).

The data contained in the MRUList value shows an ordering of the other values based *roughly* on the last time the value was accessed (although, it actually has more to do with the order in which values are displayed in the drop-down menu under Start→Run...). So, in the example seen in Figure 5.56, the data in value h was the most recently accessed (in this case, opening Windows Explorer to view the System32 folder), with the programs listed in values g, c, f, a, e, b, and d having been last accessed via Start→Run... in that order

**FIGURE 5.56**

RunMRU subkey containing last items run from Start→Run....

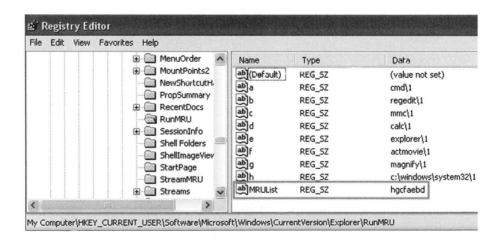

(descending). However, it must be noted that the MRUList value is updated (and the value list reordered) only when a *new* program or location that is not already on the list is added (meaning, if the user were to rerun cmd via Start→Run…, the data seen in Figure 5.56 would not change).

These examples are just scratching the surface of the wealth of data contained in the Windows registry that could help examiners. Everything from autostart locations (that are of prime importance in intrusion/malware investigations), to recently opened Office documents, to instant messaging (IM) and peer-to-peer (P2P) data, to shared folders and mapped drives, to default printer information and much more can all be found in the wizard's bag that is the Windows registry; the trick is knowing where to look and how to translate or interpret what resides there.

## TOOL FEATURE: REGISTRY ANALYSIS

Many forensic suites, such as EnCase, FTK, and ProDiscover, have specialized functionality or scripts designed to access these (and many more) useful locations in the registry. Other third-party tools like RegRipper, Windows Registry Recovery, and Registry File Viewer (www.snapfiles.com/get/rfv.html) can aid the examiner in a quick rip-and-strip of subkeys of interest in specific registry hives. For a more in-depth look at registry data from a forensic perspective, including a spreadsheet listing useful locations and registry analysis tools on the DVD that accompanies the book, see Carvey (2009).

It should also be noted that, as registry hives have their own internal structures, it is possible to identify and recover deleted registry data using forensic tools like EnCase. The RegLookup tool also includes a recovery algorithm for deleted Registry keys (Morgan, 2008). Another option for recovering deleted registry data is regslack.pl, written by Jolanta Thomasson (www.regripper.net/RegRipper/RegRipper/regslack.zip).

## DELETION AND DESTRUCTION OF DATA

Specific actions of users are often at the heart of a digital investigation. "When were they logged on? What Internet sites did they visit? Did they send any e-mail?" But one question that is asked over and over again, it seems, is "did the user knowingly delete or destroy any data, particularly if that destruction was done to prevent investigators from obtaining benefit from it?" In many civil and criminal cases, users (and indeed, whole organizations) are placed under legal directives to make every effort to retain and protect from destruction the data deemed relevant to a current or future inquiry; when these types of directives are violated, it is called "spoliation" and can mean the difference between winning or losing a contested legal action. As such, digital investigators are often called upon to attempt to answer this important question, but (unfortunately) it is not always as easy a question to answer as it sounds.

## FROM THE CASE FILES: SPOLIATION

In September 2006, an appeal was filed with the Ninth Circuit Court of Appeals to review the decision of a lower court pertaining to allegations by a plaintiff of accounting irregularities on the part of his former employer (named as the defendant in the case) [*Leon v. IDX Systems Corp.*, 2006 U.S. App. LEXIS 23820 (9th Cir. Sept. 20, 2006)]. A digital investigator for the defendant found that, shortly after the plaintiff's suit was filed, over 2200 files and folders had been deleted or rendered unrecoverable on the plaintiff's employer issued laptop computer. Faced with the evidence, the plaintiff admitted he deleted numerous files and used a wiping program in an attempt to remove traces of those files from the unused space on his computer. As a result of the plaintiff's actions, the Court dismissed his case against his former employer, and even went so far as to levy a $65,000 spoliation sanction against him for acting in bad faith. The Court of Appeals upheld the dismissal of the case and spoliation sanction against the plaintiff.

## Data Destruction

In the case of actual destruction of data (e.g., wiping), there are several techniques that can be used in attempts to verify that data was actually destroyed and (if so) who did the destroying. For example, data destruction tools sometimes leave behind distinguishable patterns; specific files and folders that have been wiped can have their names changed to something nonsensical and may show something a bit more obvious, such as aaaaaaaaaaaa.aaa or DELETED_DELETED_DELETED_DELETED. By locating nondeleted files of the same logical size, the digital investigator may even be able to find an unaltered copy of the wiped data. The same types of data patterns can be seen in large chunks in unallocated space as a result of some disk cleaning tools (although it can sometimes be difficult to distinguish massive \x00 patterns as wiping as opposed to pure unused disk space). Other tools, such as the Windows-native utility cipher.exe, wipe free space (by default) with seemingly random data as shown in Figure 5.57.

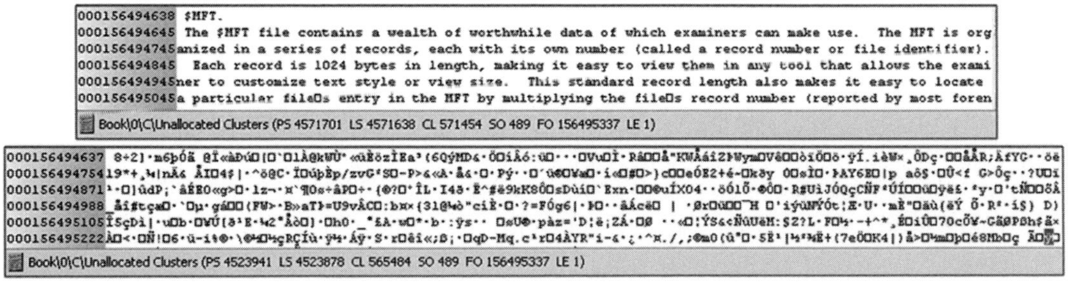

**FIGURE 5.57**

Data at file offset 156494638 within the Unallocated Clusters, compared with the data at the same location after the execution of cipher /W:c:\.

The good news is that all is not lost if a wiping tool was used to destroy data. Many times, the fact that a wiping tool was run at all is itself evidence and can have a bearing on the outcome of a case. An investigator, first attempting to establish the presence of a data destruction utility, can perform keyword and hash searches against the evidence looking for hits on terms or files associated with known data destruction utilities, but this method can be a bit hit-or-miss. An investigator should also thoroughly examine installed program locations as discussed in the section on installed programs earlier in this chapter. Registry entries for installed utilities and autostart locations can likewise be quite revealing. Other artifacts of installation, such as a link file for an installed program in a user's Start Menu can indicate the presence of an installed data destruction tool. Even if the tool has already been removed from the system, it is often still possible to locate artifacts indicating such a program was installed. Many automated uninstall programs miss vital areas where evidence was created at installation, such as prefetch files for the execution of program installer packages or executables used to start the program as a running service. Further, data in Windows "helper" registry areas (such as `SOFTWARE\Microsoft\Windows\CurrentVersion\ShellExtensions\Approved`) often persist.

Once evidence of a data destruction tool is located, proving who may have used it and when can be a little trickier. Windows artifacts like link files, prefetch files, system event logs, and wiping application log files can provide good affirmative evidence of a utility's use. As detailed earlier in this chapter, link files contain date-time stamps and path data pertaining to their target file and can provide an indication that a particular program was accessed, even if the program itself is no longer visible on the examined evidence. Prefetch files are even more helpful, as demonstrated in Figure 5.58, providing evidence that the program was executed on the system, how many times it was run, the location from where it was run, and the last date and time it was executed on the system. MRU registry entries and locations such as `NTUSER.DAT\Software\Microsoft\Windows\ShellNoRoam\MUICache`, which contains entries created by Windows Explorer when an application window is run, can also be examined for proof that a particular data destruction tool was executed.

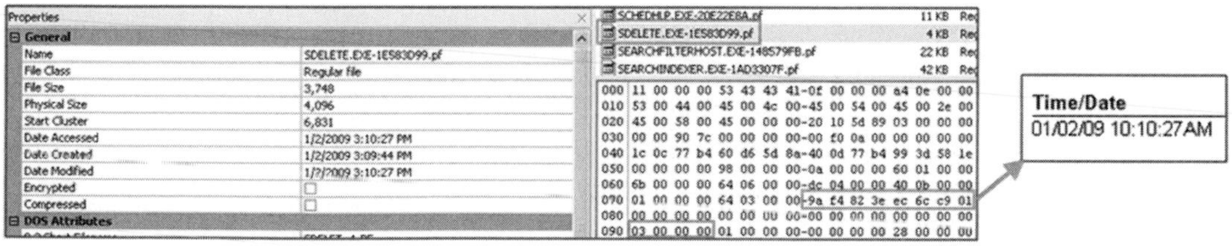

**FIGURE 5.58**

Showing prefetch file analysis, highlighting run count and last run time.

An examination of link files and registry hives in system restore points can also be helpful for the investigator searching for evidence of data destruction. Data in these locations can all be correlated to help "paint the complete picture."

An investigator should remember that no *selective* data destruction software is perfect, and unless examining an entire volume or disk that has been wiped, chances are that the investigator will be able to find some evidence of the wiping tool's use (Geiger, 2005; Brill 2006a, 2006b).

## Defragmentation

Another method of data destruction that can be encountered by investigators is that resulting from the execution of Windows (or third-party) cluster defragmentation tools. Defragmentation takes data structures that are spread across the disk (such as the $MFT or a 1.3GB .AVI file with numerous file extents) and places them into contiguous clusters (if possible), thereby speeding up system operation and improving the experience for the user (Kessler, 2007). As the defragmentation process takes data from one location on the disk and writes it to another, the rewritten data often overwrites data in unallocated space that could have been identified by the digital investigator, thereby making it more difficult to recover deleted files and folders.

Determining whether or not an examined system has recently been defragmented can be a challenge. A clue can be provided by the location of any third-party defragmentation utilities that may have been installed by the user. For example, locating artifacts such as those in Figure 5.59 are a strong indicator that the user may not be utilizing Windows' built-in defragmentation capabilities.

**FIGURE 5.59**

Installed third-party defragmentation utility.

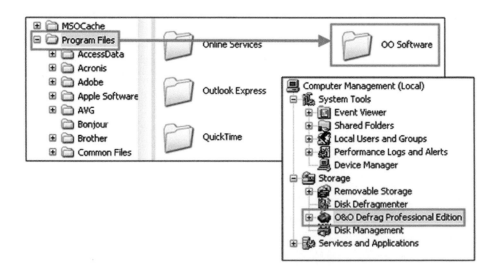

When examining a disk in a forensic suite, showing all files and sorting by the number of file extents or fragments in each file could provide the investigator with an overall impression of the level of fragmentation on the disk. Further, restoring an image to an external drive (or booting it in a virtual environment) and using Windows to analyze the level of file fragmentation can help give the investigator a sense of how recently defragmentation occurred. For example, if the Information Technology (IT) department does not regularly defragment hard drives, and the examined system reportedly has been in constant use for three months by a member of the Sales department, it would seem unusual if the level of file fragmentation on the disk was only 1%.

Defragmentation on a Windows system generally occurs in one of three ways:

- Manual defragmentation by the user
- User-scheduled defragmentation
- Windows automatic (limited) defragmentation

Manual defragmentation by a user (in Windows, not with a third-party utility) generally is accomplished via the Microsoft Management Console (`mmc.exe`). `Mmc.exe` can be run via the `Start→Run...` menu and is accessed by running the Windows Disk Defragmenter utility from the `Start→Programs→Accessories→System Tools` shortcut. As such, if a manual defragmentation was run by the user, it could be indicated by an update to the Last Accessed date-time stamps for `mmc.exe`, or the Defragmenter snap-in for the console (`dfrg.msc`). However, at best the Last Accessed date-time stamp for `mmc.exe` would indicate only the last possible time a manual defragmentation *could have* been run in this manner, considering the fickle nature of Windows' Last Accessed times. A more reliable date/time group would be the last run date and time found in the prefetch file for `mmc.exe`, as this would indicate the last time it actually was executed.

User-scheduled and Windows automatic (limited) defragmentation operations do not generally utilize the Microsoft Management Console, and updates to `mmc.exe` artifacts (e.g., link files, Run... data, MRU subkeys, prefetch files, etc.) are much less likely. If defragmentation was scheduled by the user, evidence of the scheduled task may be found in the Windows Scheduled Tasks Explorer (XP) or Task Scheduler (Vista and 7). Windows stores scheduled tasks in `.JOB` files under the `c:\windows\tasks` folder.

Despite not being scheduled by the user, the Windows automatic (limited) defragmentation is scheduled to run about every three days by default (on Windows XP and newer systems) in order to maintain peak efficiency for key system files (Russinovich & Solomon, 2001). The defragmentation does not apply to the disk or volume as a whole, but is focused on a specific subset of files listed in the `layout.ini` file in the `c:\windows\prefetch` folder. User-created files and folders are not generally included in this type of defragmentation, but the automatic defragmentation does have the potential to overwrite data in unallocated space. When the automatic defragmentation is run, files such as `defrag.exe` and `dfrgntfs.exe` (and their associated artifacts) are utilized and may be updated, but `mmc.exe` is not utilized. Further, observing a very low level of fragmentation in the files listed in `layout.ini`, and a much higher level of fragmentation in user-created or nonsystem files, could indicate that automatic defragmentation (as opposed to full manual or user-scheduled defragmentation) had taken place.

## File Deletion

Evidence of file deletion (as opposed to destruction/wiping) by a particular user presents its own set of challenges, particularly since no specific program or utility is required to delete a file in Windows. Simply sending a file to the Recycle Bin (as covered in depth earlier in this chapter) is not (by the most common forensic definition) actual deletion of the file; however, a user sending a file to the Recycle Bin is often viewed as legally significant in a case where the user was supposed to be preserving or protecting data. Further, a file in the Recycle Bin is usually easy to identify and data provided by INFO2 records or $I files (Vista/7 Recycle Bin operation) can help the investigator pinpoint where the file was when it was deleted, as well as when the data was sent to the Bin and by which user account. Even if the Recycle Bin is empty, looking at the Last Written date-time stamp on the associated INFO2 record can provide the investigator with valuable data about the approximate time the Recycle Bin was cleared.

Forensic examiners can often recover data and associated metadata for deleted files, even when Recycle Bin information is not available. In particular, when dealing with NTFS, a recovered MFT entry can provide all the information a forensic examiner needs about deleted data (Fellows, 2009).

For digital investigators, knowing the mechanics is often a far cry from knowing who deleted the file and when. Most forensic suites have the ability to identify deleted and partially overwritten files, distinguishing them via different icons or information in the files' descriptions as shown in Figure 5.60.

**FIGURE 5.60**

Identification of a deleted file by three popular forensic software suites.

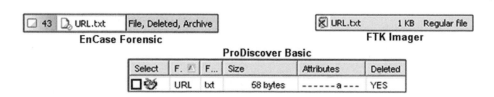

Determining exactly when a file was deleted can be problematic. The best rule of thumb is to recognize that a file's SIA dates and times are not generally updated again *after* the file is deleted from the system (as the file system no longer recognizes the file as active data). Therefore, it is possible to assume that a deleted file's most recent SIA date-time stamp represents the last time anything happened to the file *prior* to its deletion; meaning, the file was active on the file system at the date and time listed in the most recent date-time stamp and any deletion of the file would have had to occur after that time/date. This type of determination is far from precise, but can help at least narrow the window of time for a file's deletion. An examination of the other activities occurring on the system at the time of the deleted file's last date-time stamp could assist the investigator in making a more specific determination of when a particular file was most likely deleted. Further, any available data backups for the examined system can be invaluable in determining when files or folders actually were removed from the system.

## PRACTITIONER'S TIP: DETERMINING TIME OF DELETION

A common mistake that forensic examiners can make is to assume that the Last Accessed date-time stamps of deleted files show when the files were deleted. Although it may seem logical in theory that a file would be accessed at the time it was deleted, this is not always true. For instance, deleting an entire folder does not update the Last Accessed date-time stamp of the files it contains (try it!). As another example, when a user causes Internet Explorer to clear the Temporary Internet Files (e.g., `Tools→Delete Browsing History…→Delete Files…`, in Internet Explorer 7), it does not update the Last Accessed dates of the files. Without other supporting evidence, the only statement an examiner can safely make about a deleted file based solely on its Last Accessed date-time stamp is that it was not deleted *prior* to the date indicated by that piece of metadata.

Determining who deleted the file can be even more difficult and often has to be obliquely proven by attempting to correlate system usage data (such as logged on users, etc.) with the last date-time stamps on the deleted file. A determination regarding who deleted a file can also be circumstantially supported by file permissions data (file owner, who has deletion rights, etc.), clues from the location of the deleted file (e.g., `c:\Documents and Settings\<username>\My Documents`), and link files and MRU registry data that pointed to the data in its active state, but the investigator must correlate and weigh each piece of evidence carefully before opining on the source of a file's deletion.

## WINDOWS INTERNET AND COMMUNICATIONS ACTIVITIES

Very often in an investigation, another important aspect of user activity is the user's interactions with the Internet. In this modern age, the Internet has become a vital part of people's everyday lives, delivering everything from e-mail to stock quotes, from weather to groceries, and everything in between. It is not unusual that one suspect (or victim) may have Gmail, Hotmail, and Yahoo! e-mail accounts, an iTunes Store account, MySpace and Facebook profiles, data storage online at MobileMe, and use µTorrent and Limewire on a regular basis, and access all of these before they even leave the house for work in the morning!

Although it would be nearly impossible in this chapter to document every aspect of a Windows system's potential interaction with the Internet, there are a few applications and artifacts that investigators and examiners are likely to encounter on almost every Windows computer.

## Internet Explorer

Internet Explorer is the web browser that Microsoft has integrated with its products since the late 1990s, and remains one of the most popular web browsers in circulation today. Although it faces competition from other browsers (e.g., Firefox, Opera, and Google's Chrome), Internet Explorer can still be found on almost every Windows computer. At the time of this writing, the current version of Internet Explorer is version 8.0.

If a user utilizes Internet Explorer to interact with the Internet, an examiner should be able to find several artifacts to assist in their investigation. In addition to registry artifacts, such as `TypedURLs` (discussed earlier in this chapter), the Internet Explorer file artifacts generally fall into three categories:

- Cookies
- Internet history
- Web cache

The term *cookie* (in addition to being a delicious treat) refers to a small text file usually downloaded to user workstations from web servers when sites hosted by those web servers are visited. The purpose of cookies varies depending on the web server, but they can be used for authentication or session tracking, as well as communicating user preferences to the server. Although these text files can be difficult to decode, they often contain references to URLs, domain names, usernames, and dates and times that can be of use to the investigator (although, these data can be encoded). Although the presence of a URL in a cookie is not proof positive that the user visited that URL, it is strong circumstantial evidence.

Cookie files are located in the `C:\Documents and Settings\<username>\Cookies` (Windows 2k/XP/2k3) or `C:\Users\<username>\AppData\Roaming\Microsoft\Windows\Cookies` (Windows Vista/2k8/7) folder and are organized through the use of an `index.dat` file. The `index.dat` files in these user folders track the cookies, and contain 256-byte records detailing important information such as the last time the cookie was modified and accessed (FILETIME format), the number of times the site that owns the cookie was visited, the username that caused the cookie to be deposited, and the URL to which the cookie pertains.

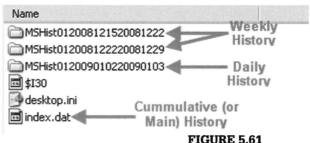

**FIGURE 5.61**

Contents of a User's `History.IE5` folder.

A user's Internet history is located in the `C:\Documents and Settings\<username>\Local Settings\History\History.IE5` (Windows 2k/XP/2k3) or `C:\Users\<username>\AppData\Local\Microsoft\Windows\History\History.IE5` (Windows Vista/2k8/7) folder, and (like cookies) is organized via `index.dat` files. However, in contrast to the single `index.dat` file used for cookies, Windows uses multiple folders and `index.dat` files for different types of Internet Explorer history as detailed in Figure 5.61.

A user's history `index.dat` files contain 128-byte records that track Internet sites visited by a user, as well as files opened via Internet Explorer or Windows Explorer. These records can be parsed to provide information such as the name and URL of the site (or file) visited and the number of times it was visited. The records also contain multiple timestamps, the significance of which vary slightly between the cumulative (main), daily, and weekly history files:

- **Cumulative (Main) History**: In the Main History `index.dat` file, the two primary timestamps both represent the last time a URL was visited and are recorded in consecutive 8-byte (FILETIME format) runs; both date-time stamps are recorded in GMT.

- **Daily History**: In the Daily History `index.dat` file, the two primary time stamps pertaining to the last time a URL was visited are similarly recorded in consecutive runs, but the first date-time stamp is recorded in local time, and the second is recorded in GMT.

- **Weekly History**: In the Weekly History `index.dat` file, the two timestamps are again present, but their significance is different; whereas the first date-time stamp still represents the last time a URL was visited and is recorded in local time, the second date-time stamp represents the date (in GMT) when the Daily History `index.dat` file (of which the record was previously a part) was archived into the Weekly History `index.dat` file.

Whereas the history files are simply record after record of tracking data, the actual files downloaded from the Internet as a part of normal web browsing with

Internet Explorer are added to the user's web cache. The web cache is located in the `C:\Documents and Settings\<username>\Local Settings\Temporary Internet Files\Content.IE5` (Windows 2k/XP/2k3) or `C:\Users\<username>\AppData\Local\Microsoft\Windows\Temporary Internet Files\Content.IE5` (Windows Vista/2k8/7) folder, further divided into a series of subfolders with seemingly random 8-byte (8-character) names. As with the other folders related to Internet Explorer, the cache is organized via its own `index.dat` file, located in the `Content.IE5` folder.

The `index.dat` file for the web cache includes a listing of the cache sub-folder names, as well as 128-byte records containing information such as the URL from which the file was downloaded, the number of times that URL was visited, the name and size of the cached file, and multiple date-time stamps. Some of the more useful dates and times found in the `index.dat` file for each cached object include:

- The last time the file was modified on the web server (FILETIME format; GMT)
- The file's "last checked" time, which corresponds with the last time the file was accessed to determine if a newer version should be downloaded from the pertinent web server (FILETIME format; GMT); this normally occurs each time the URL that "owns" the file is visited
- The file's last accessed time (DOSDATETIME format; GMT)
- The file's created time (DOSDATETIME format; GMT)

All the previously mentioned `index.dat` files can be parsed manually. However, examination of cookie, history, and web cache files is made much easier using a forensic tool or third-party viewer.

---

### TOOL FEATURE: EXAMINING INDEX.DAT FILES

Many forensic suites, such as EnCase, automate the search for Internet artifacts and parse the data in the `index.dat` files for easy viewing. In addition, tools such as MiTeC's Windows File Analyzer, Systenance Software's Index. dat Analyzer (www.systenance.com/indexdat.php), or NirSoft's IECookiesView (www.nirsoft.net/utils/iecookies. html), IECacheView (www.nirsoft.net/utils/ie_cache_viewer. html), and IEHistoryView (www.nirsoft.net/utils/iehv.html) can provide an examiner a quick and useful view of a user's Internet Explorer usage data.

---

## Windows Chat

Since the dawn of IRC, the ever-expanding Internet and ceaselessly advancing technology has made people crave personal contact over their computers. Microsoft sought to answer that craving with Windows Messenger, a chat client that first hit the scene in 2001, integrated with Windows XP. Windows

Messenger has since been fazed out (or at least, is no longer under active development) in favor of Windows Live Messenger and related products.

It is not unusual in the investigation of a Windows computer to find artifacts from Windows Messenger or its newer cousins (which includes MSN Messenger). Because there have been so many different iterations of the various Windows chat clients over the years, it is not practical to discuss each and every one in fine detail. However, there are some tools and other resources that could be useful for the examiner confronted with potential Windows chat client evidence.

Paraben Corporation's Chat Examiner can recover contact lists and saved messages from several different iterations of MSN Messenger (as well as ICQ, Yahoo Messenger, Trillian, Skype, Hello, and Miranda) and is a solid tool from a well-known forensic tool vendor. Belkasoft's Forensic IM Analyzer shown in Figure 5.62 also makes short work of saved IM data for MSN and Windows Live Messengers (as well as ICQ, Skype, Yahoo Messenger, MySpaceIM, &RQ, Miranda, SIM-IM, QIP, QIP Infium, Hello, Trillian, QQ, and AIM).

Because of the great variety of messenger programs (which seems to be growing by the month) and their increased use as a communication medium, the research on Windows chat clients is ongoing; fortunately, the people conducting this research often choose to release their findings to provide forensic examiners with additional details and support in conducting their Windows chat client examinations (Dickson, 2006; Parsonage, 2008 ; van Dongen, 2007).

## Windows E-mail Clients

E-mail clients, such as Microsoft Outlook and Outlook Express, enable users to send and receive e-mail (via SMTP, POP, and IMAP), manage newsgroups, and organize helpful information, such as contacts and calendars. The forensic artifacts related to these mail clients are numerous, but here is a quick overview of each program.

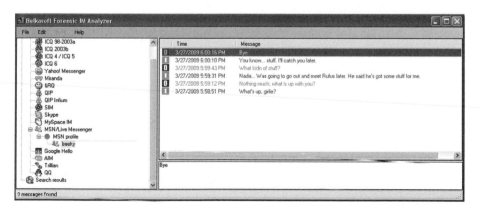

**FIGURE 5.62**

Search results in Belkasoft's Forensic IM Analyzer tool (http://belkasoft.com/bfia/en/Forensic_Instant_Messenger_Analyzer.asp).

Microsoft Outlook is an e-mail client that is part of the Microsoft Office suite of utilities. It provides a popular platform (particularly in larger organizations) for e-mail management. The primary data file types associated with Outlook are personal storage (.PST) and offline storage (.OST) files. These .PST and .OST files contain a user's e-mail, calendar, contacts, and other data that allow Outlook to function effectively for the user. The default location for these files is the `C:\Documents and Settings\<username>\Local Settings\Application Data\Microsoft\Outlook` folder in XP, and each user maintains their own Outlook data files.

There is a wide variety of different ways for an examiner to get at the data within a .PST or .OST file. Perhaps the easiest (if not most forensically sound) is to add a .PST file into Outlook on a forensic workstation via the File→Open→Outlook Data File… option. Once the .PST file is opened in Outlook, the examiner can access and view the user's mail and other Outlook objects as if they were the user themselves. If the .PST is password protected, this is obviously more of challenge, but there are a host of programs available for cracking .PST passwords. Other than Outlook itself, virtually any forensic suite worth its salt will process Outlook data files for viewing and searching by the examiner.

## TOOL FEATURE: OUTLOOK CONVERSION

It may be necessary to convert an .OST file into a .PST file before opening it with Microsoft Outlook, as .OST files cannot generally be read unless the user is connected to its home network. Tools such as Stellar Information Systems Limited's Stellar Phoenix Mailbox Exchange Desktop (www.stellarinfo.com/exchange-ost-recovery.htm), Recoveronix Limited's Recovery for Exchange OST (www.officerecovery.com/recovery-for-exchange-ost/index.htm *very* expensive), and Chily Softech Private Limited's OST to PST (www.ost2pst.net/; does not work with Outlook 2003) can do it.

Further, the advantage of using a forensic suite to parse e-mail is that many of them can recover deleted objects (such as messages, contacts, etc.) from the unallocated space within .PST and .OST files. Outlook data files have their own structures, similar to their own file systems, complete with unallocated space in which examiners can find snippets of deleted conversations and even entire messages, with the right forensic tool.

Microsoft Outlook Express is similar to Outlook, but it has been historically bundled with Windows OSs and Internet Explorer, rather than Microsoft Office. In Windows Vista and later, Outlook Express was replaced by Windows Mail and Windows Live Mail, but the concept was still the same: give consumers a slim, easy-to-use mail and news reader without all the overhead of Microsoft Outlook. In contrast to Outlook, Outlook Express utilizes .DBX files as its primary data file type. However, the good news is that .DBX files serve roughly the same purpose as Outlook .PST and .OST files, and almost every forensic tool that can handle Outlook data files can parse and search Outlook Express .DBX files in a similar manner. The default location for .DBX files in XP/2k3 and earlier is C:\Documents and Settings\<username>\ Local Settings\Application Data\Identities\<{long GUID-style value}>\Microsoft\Outlook Express.

Windows Mail in Vista and later operating systems is significantly different than Outlook or Outlook Express. Instead of .PST, .OST, or .DBX data files, Windows Mail maintains message data in plain-text .EML files, located under a user's profile at C:\Users\<username>\AppData\Local\ Microsoft\Windows Mail\Local Folders. It should also be noted that users can encrypt Windows Mail fairly easily as part of Windows' normal operation, so Windows Mail message content may not always be easily readable for the examiner.

## WINDOWS PROCESS MEMORY

The collection and analysis of memory on Windows machines is an enormous, complex, and often confusing subject, about which entire volumes have been written. So, rather than trying to reinvent the wheel or cram 75 pages of material into a few paragraphs, this section's purpose is to give digital investigators some quick forensic hits (such as ways to collect memory from a Windows system) and direct them to other sources of information on the subject that cover it very well, in great instructional depth.

The collection and analysis of Windows memory (RAM) has been getting a lot of attention from the forensic community of late owing to the large amount of data that can potentially have a bearing on an investigation. Everything from the version of Windows, to the unpacked code of running executables, to unencrypted passwords, to remote connections can be found in RAM; however, the problem has always been how to get the memory out and analyze it to maximum effect.

Due to a flurry of recent research and innovation, much of it spurred by the Digital Forensic Research Workshops (DFRWS) memory challenges, the art of capturing memory has presented investigators with a host of different choices. Hardware approaches like the Tribble (Grand & Carrier, 2004), dumping memory via FireWire (Martin, 2007), and even freezing memory chips to maintain data after power has been removed (Halderman et al., 2008) all have been researched and written about, but the average investigator in the field may not find them very practical. If the examined system is running in a VMware virtual environment (or the forensic image has been booted in a virtual environment by the investigator), suspending the virtual machine will cause the contents of memory to be saved down to a .VMEM file, which the investigator can then mine for data. Creating a crash dump that contains the contents of memory is also a possibility for systems with 2GB of RAM or less (Microsoft, 2006b; 2009b), but investigators may hesitate to have such a large impact on the examined system. Beyond using these types of techniques, many investigators find it easier (and forensically safer) to use a software-based approach, implemented in such a way as to be repeatable and accomplish the primary goal of having minimal impact on the examined system (NIST, 2008).

Popular (and effective) software tools for capturing the contents of RAM are the different varieties of the *nix dd.exe utility (DD), which is also very popular for creating images of entire volumes or hard drives. DD allows the investigator to identify the contents of RAM as a single data object and direct its acquisition to a piece of external media, or even across the network.

## TOOL FEATURE: FORENSIC ACQUISITION OF MEMORY

The Defense Computer Forensic Laboratory's dcfldd. exe is a powerful forensic acquisition tool (http://dcfldd. sourceforge.net/). A very basic command-line for running dcfldd.exe to capture RAM follows, but it should be noted that different tools (even different versions of the same tool) may take different arguments, which should be tested thoroughly by the investigator before use in the field:

dcfldd.exe if=\\.\PhysicalMemory of=f:\memory\ram-dump. dd conv=noerror hashlog=f:\memory\ram-dump.dd.md5

It should also be noted that access to the Physical-Memory object in user mode is restricted in Windows 2k3/Vista/2k8/7 and currently prevents this type of operation using dcfldd.exe. Other tools are available that can circumvent this prohibition. For instance, HBGary's FastDump Pro is a commercial tool that supports all 32- and 64-bit Windows operating systems from Windows 2k to Server 2k8, and can acquire data from systems with more than 4GB of RAM (www.hbgary.com/products-services/fastdump-pro/). In addition, Mandiant's Memoryze (www.mandiant.com/software/memoryze.htm), ManTech Memory DD (www.mantech.com/msma/MDD.asp), Matthieu Suiche's win32dd (www.msuiche.net/2008/06/14/capture-memory-under-win2k3-or-vista-with-win32dd/), and HBGary's FastDump Community Edition (www.hbgary.com/products-services/fastdump-pro/) are all effective, free options for forensically acquiring RAM from Windows system.

Many forensic suites now also have the ability to dump the contents of RAM. Technology Pathway's ProDiscoverIR (www.techpathways.com/ProDiscoverIR.htm) and EnCase (winen.exe) have the capability to acquire physical memory in a forensically sound manner, but it must be noted that they also cost money.

Another option for investigators that do not want to capture the entire contents of RAM, but want to focus on specific processes, is to use a tool that can target specific process memory space. Command-line tools, such as Microsoft's Userdump.exe (http://support.microsoft.com/kb/241215), Tobias Klein's pd.exe (www.trapkit.de/research/forensic/pd/index.html), and Arne Vidstrom's pmdump.exe (www.ntsecurity.nu/toolbox/pmdump/) can all be used to target specific running processes (such as a process that has crashed or is known to be malicious) without having to dump the entire contents of memory. One of HBGary's other free tools is Flypaper (www.hbgary.com/products-services/flypaper/), which traps the contents of running processes in memory, making it very handy in malware and malicious logic investigations. Other GUI tools, such as Mark Russinovich's Process Explorer (Figure 5.63; technet.microsoft.com/en-us/sysinternals/bb896653.aspx), allow investigators to target running processes and obtain debug dumps and strings analyses for processes of interest.

So, once an investigator has the contents of memory, what should he or she do with it? Traditionally, `strings.exe` (or similar tool such as BinText) has been used to glean information from full or process specific memory dumps created with one of the methods or tools already discussed. However, there are at least as many memory *analysis* tools and techniques as there are ways of acquiring memory. The shortest way to discuss memory analysis (and specifically memory analysis tools) is to say that almost every company mentioned earlier with a tool for acquisition of physical memory also has another tool or means to analyze that memory. As an example, HBGary's Responder products (commercial) have turned memory analysis into child's play, leveraging advanced malware analysis plug-ins and full Unicode searching to dynamically debug and create analysis reports on the fly. In addition, Mandiant's Memoryze and Tobias

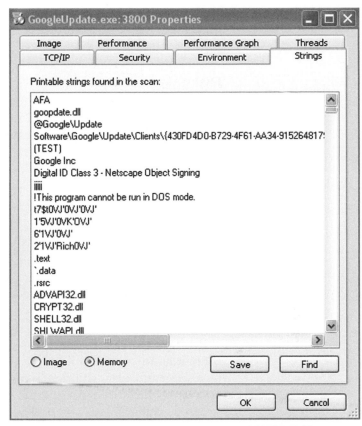

**FIGURE 5.63**

Process Explorer strings output for specific process memory.

Klein's Memory Parser are examples of free tools that have endeavored to make memory analysis easier and more fruitful for the investigator, and these are just the beginning. Another free memory dump analysis tool is Volatile System's Volatility Framework (www.volatilesystems.com/default/volatility).

For more information on the why and (most importantly) how of Windows memory collection and analysis see Malin, et al. (2008) and Carvey (2009).

## BITLOCKER AND ENCRYPTING FILE SYSTEM (EFS)

Microsoft has two primary built-in implementations of user-level Windows encryption, BitLocker and the Encrypting File System (EFS). The major difference between the two is that EFS encrypts only a user's folders and files (e.g., Office documents, etc.), whereas BitLocker is used to encrypt entire volumes. BitLocker and EFS both have advantages and disadvantages, and users (particularly, more sophisticated users) have begun to make liberal use of both. Although both types of encryption are relatively easy to implement, unforeseen problems (e.g., computer crash and OS corruption) could leave users facing the same difficulties encountered by forensic examiners in dealing with encrypted data: How do I get the unencrypted data back?

## BitLocker

BitLocker, which hit the scene with the advent of Windows Vista, is (at the time of this writing) available in Vista Enterprise and Ultimate, as well as Server 2k8 (and is listed as a planned feature in Windows 7). According to Microsoft, its stated purpose is to protect "against data theft or exposure on computers that are lost or stolen, and offers more secure data deletion when computers are decommissioned" (Microsoft, 2008b). It does this by providing users with a built-in "whole-disk" encryption solution.

BitLocker is designed to function together with a hardware chip called a Trusted Platform Module (TPM) (usually built into the system/motherboard), which stores the encryption/decryption keys (called a Full Volume Encryption Key, or FVEK) and releases them only after verifying the integrity of early boot components and boot configuration data. In short, the practical effect is that the TPM will allow a BitLocker-encrypted drive to be booted (and decrypted) only if the drive is located in its original computer. BitLocker and its TPM can also work in conjunction with a PIN and/or a USB device containing the required keys.[13] To properly function, BitLocker requires at least two partitions, with one being reserved as a system partition of at least 1.5GB on which boot files and the Windows Pre-execution environment are stored, and the identification of such a partitioning scheme could indicate BitLocker's use.

Regardless of the specific implementation, failing to recognize the use of BitLocker in advance of acquiring a traditional forensic image can leave the examiner unable to access the data in the image. A quick look at each volume's primary volume boot sector (sector offset 3) can reveal whether the volume is BitLocker-encrypted. In place of the normal OEM vendor name (usually NTFS in Vista), the examiner will see -FVE-FS- (\x2d\x46\x56\x45\x2d\x46\x53\x2d), indicating that the volume is covered by Full Volume Encryption (BitLocker). Alternately, when digital investigators are dealing with a live system, on a computer running a BitLocker-capable version of Vista (or Server 2k8), executing the `manage-bde.wsf` script will display the BitLocker status of volumes for which it has been implemented. If the script is run and no results are returned, it is usually safe to assume that BitLocker is not being used on the system.

---

[13] Certain BitLocker configurations can work solely with a USB device, eliminating the requirement for a built-in TPM.

---

**PRACTITIONER'S TIP: BRING YOUR OWN TOOLS**

As with most commands/binaries used in incident response, examiners should roll with their own tools, and (if at all possible) not rely on those already present on the system to be examined. Examiners should also note that they may be required to run this script in conjunction with the Windows script host, `cscript.exe`. Both `manage-bde.exe` and `cscript.exe` are located in `c:\windows\system32` and can be added to a response toolkit.

---

Ideally, forensic examiners want to have the keys to decrypt an encrypted drive. BitLocker keys (64-bytes in length) are held in memory while the system is up and running, and researchers are making an effort to develop practical methods for locating and then utilizing such information (Kornblum, 2009). However, these techniques are in their early development and may not be feasible in certain investigations. The simplest approach is to recover the key when the system is still running and digital investigators can use the `manage-bde.wsf` script to obtain the BitLocker recovery password (Mueller, 2008). Running the following command in the console will provide an examiner with the recovery key and numerical recovery password for the specific BitLocker-encrypted volume (`D:\`, in this example):

```
cscript manage-bde.wsf –protectors –get d:
```

Once the examiner has the recovery password, a copy of the BitLocker-encrypted drive can be connected to a forensic system running Vista (or a BitLocker-aware forensic suite, such as EnCase Forensic with its Decryption Suite module) and the data can be recovered by simply supplying the recovery password when prompted.

Once running, it is possible to temporarily disable BitLocker (e.g., `cscript manage-bde.wsf –protectors –disable d:`). It is also possible to permanently decrypt the data via the BitLocker Drive Encryption interface, if permitted to do so by the data/drive owner; however, permanently decrypting the data would mean a tremendous impact on the *in situ* state of data on the drive, which is a situation normally eschewed in forensic and legal circles. With that said, the best way to image a computer running BitLocker may be to image it live (e.g., obtain a logical image of the BitLocker-encrypted volume). Although this is not the preferred method of forensic imaging according to traditional forensic dogma, obtaining a logical image from a running system does currently represent an examiner's best chance to obtain valid, usable data for the furtherance of their investigation, while (if done with proper forensic tools and methodology) having a far more minimal impact on the affected system.

So, what are an examiner's options? The investigator can always hold out hope that the owner of the system they wish to examine will consent to the examination and the booting of their computer, and willingly provide any items needed to boot the system (e.g., PIN, FVKE on USB, etc.).[14] Within corporate or government environments running BitLocker-encrypted systems, a network administrator will often have a master key to unlock the computers. However, once a protected computer is booted in such a manner, the data is still technically encrypted, meaning if the system were to lose power the data would again become unreadable.

It should also be noted that Windows 7 contains another BitLocker feature that will be of interest to investigators: the ability to BitLocker-encrypt removable media (such as a thumb drive) via a user-friendly right-click option. Once encrypted, a BitLockered-thumb drive, for example, will be protected from unauthorized access when not plugged into the Windows 7 machine that encrypted it. Such a drive will be transparently accessible to the user when plugged into its home machine, and accessible via password when plugged into any other computer running a Windows OS.

**FIGURE 5.64**

An EFS-encrypted folder viewed in Windows Explorer.

Desktop
File Folder

Downloads
File Folder

Links
File Folder

nighthawk's encrypted folder
File Folder

Saved Games
File Folder

Videos
File Folder

## EFS

The ability to use EFS to encrypt data has been around since the release of Windows 2000 (although it is notably absent from distributions such as Windows XP Home Edition and Windows Vista Home Basic), and allows users to easily apply encryption to select files and folders in a way that is more or less transparent. During the encryption process, keys are generated that are tied to a user's Windows username/password combination. The decryption of protected data is seamlessly accomplished for the logged on user (because the correct credentials were supplied when they logged onto Windows); however, anyone outside of that user's authenticated session will be unable to view the underlying data of an EFS-encrypted file.

Like with BitLocker, failing to recognize that files or folders are EFS-encrypted prior to imaging evidence can have significant repercussions. The names of files and folders encrypted with EFS are most often displayed as green in the Windows Explorer interface, and seeing such "green names" on a live, running machine can be the first clue that EFS-encrypted data exists (Figure 5.64).

---

[14] If practical, law enforcement officers should always include items such as passwords and PINs in their affidavits for subpoenas and search warrants.

**FIGURE 5.65**

Identification of EFS-encrypted files using `efsinfo.exe`.

Examiners can also choose to use tools such as `efsinfo.exe` (a part of the Windows XP Service Pack 2 Support Tools) to identify EFS-encrypted data along with the user account that is able to decrypt them as shown in Figure 5.65.

Most forensic tools will also identify EFS-encrypted data as demonstrated in Figure 5.66, although special steps will still have to be taken to view the data in its unencrypted form.

If EFS-encrypted data objects are located prior to imaging, obtaining unencrypted logical copies of the objects is always an option to insure against later inability to access the data on the forensic image. However, if EFS-encrypted data is encountered within a forensic image, the examiner does have other options.

Many forensic tools offer the ability to decrypt EFS files automatically, provided the proper user password is known (or guessed, or cracked) and entered as appropriate. As such, obtaining the proper password is the key (if you'll pardon the pun). The easiest way to obtain a user's Windows password is to ask the user; you never know, the user (or his or her system administrator) could surprise you by providing it willingly. Failing that, numerous options exist for the exporting of SAM and SYSTEM registry hives from a forensic image and

**FIGURE 5.66**

An EFS-encrypted folder viewed in EnCase.

the subsequent cracking or unmasking of passwords using the examiner's tool of choice (e.g., PRTK, Cain & Abel, 0phcrack, SAMInside, Linux, etc.). Before undertaking a true cracking action, though, the examiner may want to complete the following in the interest of avoiding unneeded frustration:

- Attempt to guess the password based on things you know about the user or information supplied from other sources.

- Dump the Windows protected storage area (which can include saved passwords and autocomplete data) from the registry using a tool such as Protected Storage Explorer by Forensic Ideas (www.forensicideas.com/tools.html).

- Attempt to brute-force the password using a dictionary file filled with common passwords or passphrases, or a dictionary created by indexing the user's favorite web sites.

- Understand the difference between cracking an LM password and trying to crack an NTLM password.

## TOOL FEATURE: DECRYPTING EFS

Once the proper username/password combination is obtained, decrypting EFS files becomes child's play. Figure 5.67 shows ElcomSoft's Advanced EFS Data Recovery Tool (www.elcomsoft.com/aefsdr.html), which can scan a drive for EFS-encrypted files and available EFS encryption keys, and enables the examiner to decrypt located keys using a Windows user password, and can even perform dictionary attacks on encrypted keys. If the correct password is sup-

plied, the examiner is given the option to save all files that can be decrypted with that password in their decrypted (reviewable) state.

The EnCase Decryption Suite (EDS) and its built-in Analyze EFS… option can also be used to automatically locate EFS key files and then allow examiners to enter user passwords that will automatically be used to decrypt EFS data.

**FIGURE 5.67**

AEFSDR used to locate and decrypt EFS-encrypted files.

## RAIDs AND DYNAMIC DISKS

A Redundant Array of Inexpensive Disks, or RAID, is nothing more than a group of hard drives that function as one for the purpose of increased storage and data recoverability. RAIDs are identified primarily by how data are stored on them. Although there are numerous variations, there are three common levels very often encountered by examiners:

- **RAID 0**: Two or more drives across which the data are spanned (striped). Data access in this configuration is very efficient; however, if one drive fails, all data are lost.

- **RAID 1**: Two or more drives across which the data are mirrored. This provides the ultimate in redundancy and recoverability; however, data access (particularly write operations) can be slowed by the need to create two or more copies and space/cost concerns can become prohibitive.

- **RAID 5**: Three or more drives across which the data are spanned (striped) with data parity built-in for recoverability. This configuration is one of the most popular, as it provides a good mix of speed, storage, and data recoverability; if one drive fails, data can be rebuilt based on the parity stripes on the remaining drives.

RAIDs can be created with software (using dynamic disks) or hardware and can be internal or external. Software RAIDs can easily be created using built-in Windows functionality (Figure 5.68).

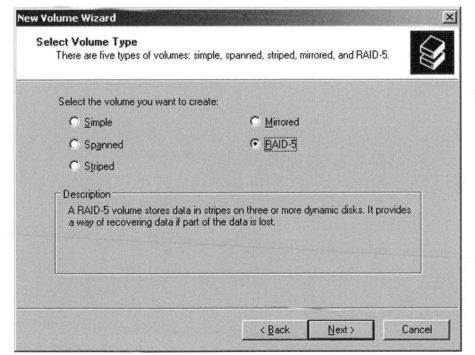

**FIGURE 5.68**

Windows interface for creation of a software RAID.

For a software RAID or dynamic disk, the operating system is booted, and then puts the drives together logically prior to the completion of the boot up sequence. Once the drives are configured properly, Windows sees them as a single drive and is ready to take advantage of the increased storage space and (depending on the type of RAID) data redundancy. Software RAIDs are an attractive option for users not wanting to invest in more expensive hardware options; however, software RAIDs take resources away from Windows and, as such, are less common than hardware RAIDs in enterprise and government infrastructures. The Registry key SYSTEM\<current control set>\Services\dmio\Boot Info\Primary Disk Group can provide additional information about the last dynamic disk mounted by the Windows system.[15]

An easy method to determine if a computer is using dynamic disks (particularly when all the examiner has access to are forensic images of the system) is to look at the last 1MB of the suspect hard drive. Flags similar to those seen in Figure 5.69 (e.g., PRIVHEAD) indicate the examined drive was configured as a dynamic disk (as opposed to a basic disk). It should also be remembered that systems cannot boot from dynamic disks; for this reason, most laptops disable dynamic disk functionality.

Dynamic disks are managed by the Logical Disk Manager (LDM), which maintains a database of partition information for the dynamic disks within a system.

**FIGURE 5.69**

PRIVHEAD flag seen in last 1MB of a dynamic disk.

```
4FFFFFE00   50 52 49 56 48 45 41 44   00 00 33 51 00 02 00 0B   PRIVHEAD..3Q....
4FFFFFE10   01 C9 9A 01 82 0B B0 7E   00 00 00 00 00 00 00 0A   .É..*~.......
4FFFFFE20   00 00 00 00 00 00 07 FF   00 00 00 00 00 00 07 40   ......ÿ.......@
4FFFFFE30   31 37 30 61 37 36 63 63   2D 33 35 39 30 2D 34 37   170a76cc-3590-47
4FFFFFE40   65 36 2D 39 66 65 34 2D   64 34 34 65 36 34 38 64   e6-9fe4-d44e648d
4FFFFFE50   61 36 61 38 00 00 00 00   00 00 00 00 00 00 00 00   a6a8............
4FFFFFE60   00 00 00 00 00 00 00 00   00 00 00 00 00 00 00 00   ................
4FFFFFE70   31 62 37 37 64 61 32 30   2D 63 37 31 37 2D 31 31   1b77da20-c717-11
4FFFFFE80   64 30 2D 61 35 62 65 2D   30 30 61 30 63 39 31 64   d0-a5be-00a0c91d
4FFFFFE90   62 37 33 63 00 00 00 00   00 00 00 00 00 00 00 00   b73c............
4FFFFFEA0   00 00 00 00 00 00 00 00   00 00 00 00 00 00 00 00   ................
4FFFFFEB0   37 36 61 39 35 31 66 64   2D 35 64 66 39 2D 34 64   76a951fd-5df9-4d
4FFFFFEC0   65 65 2D 61 31 35 39 2D   35 37 64 64 38 35 65 61   ee-a159-57dd85ea
4FFFFFED0   63 63 61 65 00 00 00 00   00 00 00 00 00 00 00 00   ccae............
4FFFFFEE0   00 00 00 00 00 00 00 00   00 00 00 00 00 00 00 00   ................
4FFFFFEF0   44 61 76 65 2D 75 7A 76   70 36 7A 62 31 37 6C 44   Dave-uzvp6zb17lD
4FFFFFF00   67 30 00 00 00 00 00 00   00 00 00 00 00 00 00 00   g0..............
4FFFFFF10   00 02 00 00 00 00 00 00   00 00 00 00 00 00 00 00   ................
4FFFFFF20   00 00 3F 00 00 00 00 02   7F CB 73 00 00 00 00 02   ..?.....Ës.....
4FFFFFF30   7F F8 00 00 00 00 00 00   00 08 00 00 00 00 00 00   ø.............
4FFFFFF40   00 00 02 00 00 00 00 00   00 07 FD 00 00 00 01 00   ........ý....
4FFFFFF50   00 00 01 00 00 00 00 00   00 05 C9 00 00 00 00 00   .........É....
```

---

[15] The current control set for a system can be determined by looking at the SYSTEM\Select\Current value. The DWORD value corresponds with the current control set number (e.g. 0x00000001 (1) = ControlSet001).

## TOOL FEATURE: READING LOGICAL DISK MANAGER

A free tool from Windows Sysinternals (LDMDump) is available to assist examiners in reading the LDM on a running system (http://technet.microsoft.com/en-us/sysinternals/bb897413. aspx). The system examined in Figure 5.70 has four physical drives; one basic disk (d0) contains the operating system, and the other drives support a three-dynamic disk RAID (d1).

When examiners just have access to forensic images (as opposed to the suspect machine in its running state), the image could be mounted as a physical disk on a forensic system (via a tool such as Guidance Software's Physical Disk Emulator module for EnCase or GetData's Mount Image Pro) and LDMDump used to further examine its configuration.

```
C:\Documents and Settings\Administrator\Desktop\LdmDump>ldmdump.exe /d0

Logical Disk Manager Configuration Dump v1.03
Copyright (C) 2000-2002 Mark Russinovich

Disk does not have LDM database.

C:\Documents and Settings\Administrator\Desktop\LdmDump>ldmdump.exe /d1

Logical Disk Manager Configuration Dump v1.03
Copyright (C) 2000-2002 Mark Russinovich

PRIVATE HEAD:
Signature           : PRIVHEAD
Version             : 2.11
Disk Id             : 4b676395-7217-41f8-8587-17627b7132e7
Host Id             : 1b77da20-c717-11d0-a5be-00a0c91db73c
Disk Group Id       : 76a951fd-5df9-4dee-a159-57dd85eaccae
Disk Group Name     : Dave-uzvp6zb171Dg0
Logical disk start  : 3F
Logical disk size   : 27FCB73 (20473 MB)
Configuration start : 27FF800
Configuration size  : 800 (1 MB)
Number of TOCs      : 1
TOC size            : 7FE (1023 KB)
Number of Configs   : 1
Config size         : 5C9 (740 KB)
Number of Logs      : 1
Log size            : E0 (112 KB)
```

**FIGURE 5.70**

Output of LDMDump for an examined system using dynamic disks.

In the case of a hardware RAID, a hardware controller on the motherboard or in the form of an add-in card (e.g., 3ware or Promise Technology) presents the individual drives as a single disk prior to the operating system booting. Once the OS is booted, a user can interact with the RAID as if it were a single drive. The hardware controller is the key to the RAID's configuration and accessing data on the RAID can be very difficult if the drives are removed.

## RAID Acquisition

The proper forensic acquisition of RAIDs can be a difficult skill for investigators to master. The data on a RAID must be preserved in a way that maximizes its integrity and accessibility, while minimizing impact on the examined system. When it is time to image a RAID, there are two primary considerations that need to be addressed:

1. Can the system maintaining the RAID be powered off? Many organizations cannot afford critical server downtime, so shutting down the system may not be a practical option.

2. Should the component RAID drives be imaged together or individually? Imaging the drives individually may be necessary because of driver or storage issues but can lead to complications when it comes time to process and examine the images.

In light of many organizations' unwillingness to allow a RAID server to be shut down for imaging, live acquisitions in Windows are very common (and usually fairly straightforward). If you have administrator credentials (or can be given admin credentials by a system administrator), the fastest and simplest live imaging method is to run your favorite imaging tool (e.g., AccessData's FTK Imager or a forensic version of DD, such as DCFLDD) from a thumb drive.

The image can either be saved to a formatted storage drive (NTFS is a good choice) connected directly to the RAID system, or sent across a network. If connecting the destination drive directly to the RAID, the examiner should choose the fastest bus available in order to minimize acquisition and verification times:

eSATA 3Gbits: up to 3Gbits/second
FireWire 800: up to 800Mbits/second
USB 2.0: up to 480Mbits/second
FireWire 400: up to 400Mbits/second
USB 1.1: up to 12Mbits/second

Once the drive is connected, a command line like the following can be used with DCFLDD to capture an image of the running RAID:[16]

```
dcfldd.exe if=<disk to be imaged> of=/
   mnt/<destination>/image.img conv=synch,noerror
   hashlog=/mnt/<destination>/image.md5 bs=1024
```

If sending the image across the network, transfer speed is also an issue. Ensuring both the RAID server and the computer receiving the image have Gigabit (10/100/1000) Ethernet cards will increase image acquisition and verification speeds greatly:

Fast Ethernet (10/100): up to 100Mbits/second
Gigabit Ethernet (10/100/1000): up to 1Gbit/second

When imaging across the network, a storage device is connected to a remote system (such as the examiner's laptop computer) and then shared out as a network resource; the storage device can then be mounted as a network share

---

[16] This is simply an example and may not fit every situation or the particular version of the tool chosen by the examiner. Each examiner should fully test and validate the tools they use prior to using them for forensic work in the field.

on the RAID system and used as the destination for the forensic image. If you have enterprise class forensic tools, such as Guidance Software's EnCase Enterprise or AccessData's FTK Enterprise, they also make excellent choices for imaging live, running RAID systems across the network.

If the RAID system can be shutdown, the easiest method for imaging a hardware RAID is often for the examiner to boot the system using their favorite boot CD and save the image to an external hard drive connected via the fastest bus available. In this scenario, the hardware RAID controller provides the RAID configuration data, without which the RAID cannot be properly "seen" and accessed by an operating system. As such, the primary consideration when using a boot disk is choosing a disk with the correct drivers for the hardware RAID controller. Newer forensic boot disks (such as the latest version of Helix from www.e-fense.com) have drivers for most RAID controllers the examiner will encounter. However, if the proper driver is not included on the boot disk, it can often be downloaded from the controller manufacturer's web site and loaded (in the boot disk environment) via a USB thumb drive.

Although it should be the last resort, sometimes the examiner will be forced to image the drives of a RAID individually and logically reassemble them prior to the start of the forensic examination. However, before undertaking this course of action, an examiner (or first responder/evidence collector) should make every effort to record information pertaining to the RAID's configuration before shutting down the system. For example, data such as the RAID type (e.g., RAID0, RAID1, RAID5), the order of drives, and stripe size and direction will be invaluable when it comes to reconstructing the RAID for examination.

## TOOL FEATURE: RAID RECONSTRUCTION

Although many forensic tools are capable of reconstructing RAID drives imaged individually, one of the best is Runtime Software's RAID Reconstructor (www.runtime.org/raid.htm). Runtime's GetDataBack for NTFS or FAT can also be used to locate the partitions within the reconstructed RAID and pull the restored RAID into the examiner's favorite forensic tool for examination.

Guidance Software's EnCase Forensic suite is also adept at rebuilding both software and hardware RAIDs. For a software RAID, the process is as simple as adding all the component disks to the EnCase interface, right-clicking the OS/boot disk (which is where the software RAID configuration data is stored), and choosing Scan Disk Configuration…; the result will be that EnCase reconstructs the software RAID for the examiner and displays its contents as a virtual disk object for examination.

Piecing together a hardware RAID from forensic images of individual disks is a bit trickier. The primary problem the examiner faces is knowing how to properly order the drives/images and what stripe size to choose, which can be a challenge if the examiner was not the person who created the images. Similar to reconstructing a software RAID, once the stripe size and drive order is known, reconstructing a hardware RAID is fairly straightforward using EnCase (Guidance Software, 2009):

*(Continued)*

## TOOL FEATURE: RAID RECONSTRUCTION—CONT'D

1. Select all component disks in the Devices tab and choose Edit Disk Configuration....
2. Choose the RAID type (e.g., RAID0, RAID1, RAID5, etc.) and enter stripe size.
3. Right-click in the Component Devices area and add the component disks in the correct order.

If the information entered for the RAID is correct, EnCase will reconstruct the hardware RAID for the examiner and display its contents as a virtual disk object for examination. EnCase even allows examiners to use NULL devices in circumstances where a drive for a RAID utilizing parity (such as RAID5) is missing or damaged.

## FROM THE CASE FILES: REBUILDING RAID

During a recent intrusion investigation, a server that was suspected to be compromised was shipped to investigators. The server hardware arrived severely damaged, but (luckily) its five hard drives remained viable. The server's owner stated he believed the server was a RAID, but he was unsure of what type. Investigators sought the help of one of their crack forensic examiners. After imaging each drive, the examiner added the images into EnCase only to find that all the disks showed up as Unused Disk Space with no readily visible file system (characteristic of a RAID). The examiner

converted the EnCase evidence files to DD images via FTK Imager, added the images to RAID Reconstructor, and rebuilt the disks into a single RAID image. He then added the image to GetDataBack for NTFS and identified three partitions, noting the locations of the three volume boot sectors. The examiner added the rebuilt RAID image back into EnCase as a raw image file and rebuilt the three partitions (a simple right-click operation in EnCase). With the partitions rebuilt, a full examination of the RAID could be conducted to aid the investigation.

### NASs and SANs

Network-attached storage (NAS) or a storage area network (SAN) can also present special challenges to an examiner. A NAS is typically a smaller device, which, as its name implies, provides storage space to network users. Because there are numerous NAS vendors, with numerous unique and proprietary configurations, there is no set procedure to image them. However, two of the techniques described earlier for imaging a RAID (i.e., taking the NAS apart and imaging the drives separately or mounting the NAS as a logical share and obtaining a live, logical image of it) can be very effective.

SANs are more common in large corporate and government infrastructures and are normally very large. What makes a SAN an efficient method for large-scale storage is how it allocates space to users; space given to a user is called a Logical Unit Number, or LUN. Somewhere on the network there is a server dedicated to the allocation of the LUNs and the maintenance of the SAN; this server is connected to the SAN via a Host Bus Adapter (HBA).

There are two primary choices for acquiring a forensic image of a SAN:

- From a computer connected to the SAN, a system administrator can assign the examiner read-only privileges to the LUNs in question, which can then be imaged live (similar to a standard RAID). If possible, the examiner should ask the system administrator to temporarily remove all access to the LUNs by other users until the image and verification are finished.

- The connected computer can be shut down and booted using a forensic boot disk. Once booted, specific LUNs can be imaged as described earlier. If using this technique, the examiner must ensure the boot disk has the correct HBA drivers or the examiner will not be able to properly access the LUNs.

## CASES

*Johnson v. Wells Fargo Home Mortgage, Inc.*, 2008 WL 2142219 (D. Nev. May 16, 2008)
*Leon v. IDX Systems Corp.*, 2006 U.S. App. LEXIS 23820 (9th Cir. Sept. 20, 2006)

## REFERENCES

AccessData. (2009). *Registry Quick Find Chart.* Available online at www.accessdata.com/media/en_us/print/papers/wp.Registry_Quick_Find_Chart.en_us.pdf

Brill, A. (2006a) The Brill files: An investigative report on data wiping utilities—Part one. *Kroll Ontrack Newsletter,* 4(5). Available online at www.krollontrack.com/newsletters/cccfn_0506.html.

Brill, A. (2006b). The Brill files: An investigative report on data wiping utilities—Part two. *Kroll Ontrack Newsletter,* 4(6). Available online at www.krollontrack.com/newsletters/cccfn_0606.html

Carrier, B. (2005). *File system forensic analysis.* Addison-Wesley.

Carvey, H. (2009). *Windows forensic analysis* (2nd ed.). Syngress Media.

Dickson M. (2006). An examination into MSN Messenger 7.5 contact identification. *Journal of Digital Investigation,* 3(2), 79–83.

Fellows, G. (2009). The joys of complexity and the deleted file. *Journal of Digital Investigation,* 2(2), 89–93.

Geiger, M. (2005). Evaluating commercial counter-forensic software. In *Proceedings of DFRWS 2005.* Available online at www.dfrws.org/2005/proceedings/geiger_counterforensics_slides.pdf

Giuseppini, G., Burnett, M., Faircloth, J., & Kleiman, D. (2005). *Microsoft log parser toolkit.* Syngress Media.

Grand, J., & Carrier, B. (2004). A hardware-based memory acquisition procedure for digital investigations. *Journal of Digital Investigation,* 1(1), 1742–2876. Available online at www.digitalevidence.org/papers/tribble-preprint.pdf

Guidance Software. (2009). *How to Acquire RAIDs.* Available online at www.guidancesoftware.com/support/articles/acquireraids.asp.

Halderman, J. A., Schoen, S. D., Heninger, N., Clarkson, W., William Paul, W., Calandrino, J. A., et al. (2008). Lest we remember: Cold boot attacks on encryption keys. In: *Proceedings 17th USENIX security symposium* (Sec '08). San Jose. Available online at http://citp.princeton.edu/memory/

Hargreaves, C., Chivers, H., & Titheridge, D. (2008). Windows Vista and digital investigations. *Digital Investigation Journal, 5*(1–?), 34 48.

Kessler, M. (2007). *Maintaining Windows 2000 peak performance through defragmentation.* Microsoft Technet. Available online at http://technet.microsoft.com/en-us/library/bb742585.aspx

Lee, R. (2008). *VISTA shadow volume forensics.* SANS Computer Forensics and E-Discovery Blog. Available online at http://sansforensics.wordpress.com/2008/10/10/shadow-forensics/

Malin, C., Casey, E., & Aquilina, J. (2008). *Malware forensics.* Syngress Media.

Martin, A. (2007). FireWire memory dump of a Windows XP computer: A forensic approach. Available online at www.friendsglobal.com/papers/FireWire%20Memory%20Dump%20of%20Windows%20XP.pdf

Microsoft. (2006a). *How to determine audit policies from the registry.* Available online at http://support.microsoft.com/kb/246120;EN-US;q246120

Microsoft. (2006b). *How to configure system failure and recovery options in Windows.* (Q307973; http://support.microsoft.com/kb/307973)

Microsoft. (2007a). *Windows NT contains file system tunneling capabilities.* Available online at http://support.microsoft.com/kb/172190

Microsoft. (2007b). *How to minimize metadata in Office documents.* Available online at http://support.microsoft.com/kb/223396;en-us;223396

Microsoft. (2008a). *Monitored file name extensions.* http://msdn.microsoft.com/en-us/library/aa378870.aspx.

Microsoft. (2008b). BitLocker drive encryption. Microsoft Technet. Available online at http://technet.microsoft.com/en-us/windows/aa905065.aspx

Microsoft. (2009a). *File Times.* Microsoft Developer Network. Available online at http://msdn.microsoft.com/en-us/library/ms724290(VS.85).aspx

Microsoft. (2009b). *Windows feature lets you generate a memory dump file by using the keyboard.* (Q244139 http://support.microsoft.com/kb/244139)

Mueller, L. (2008). *Incident response—Recovering a BitLocker recovery password before system shutdown.* Professional Blog. Available online at www.forensickb.com/2008/01/incident-response-recovering-bitlocker.html

Mueller, L. (2009). *Detecting timestamp changing utilities. Professional Blog.* Available online at http://www.forensickb.com/2009/02/detecting-timestamp-changing-utlities.html

NIST. (2008). *Computer Security Incident Handling.* NIST Special Publication 800-61 Rev 1. Available online at http://csrc.nist.gov/publications/nistpubs/800-61/sp800-61.pdf

Park, B., Park, J., & Lee, S. (2008). Data concealment and detection in Microsoft Office 2007 files. *Journal of Digital Investigation, 5*(3–4), 104–114.

Parsonage, H. (2008). *The forensic recovery of instant messages from MSN Messenger and Windows Live Messenger.* Available online at http://computerforensics.parsonage.co.uk/downloads/MSNandLiveMessengerArtefactsOfConversations.pdf

Russinovich, M., & Solomon, D. (2001). Windows XP: Kernel improvements create a more robust, powerful, and scalable OS. *MSDN Magazine.* Available online at http://msdn.microsoft.com/en-us/magazine/cc302206.aspx

Schuster, A. (2007). *Introducing the Microsoft Vista event log file format.* Available online at www.dfrws.org/2007/proceedings/p65-schuster.pdf

van Dongen W.S. (2007). Forensic artefacts left by Windows Live Messenger 8.0. *Journal of Digital Investigation, 4*(2), 73–87.

# CHAPTER 6

# UNIX Forensic Analysis

Cory Altheide and Eoghan Casey

## INTRODUCTION TO UNIX

UNIX originated in the depths of Bell Labs in the late 1960s. During the 1970s it became widely used in academia, and in the 1980s AT&T released UNIX System V, which saw widespread commercial use. Meanwhile, researchers at UC Berkeley were developing a plethora of useful code additions to the UNIX core, including core networking code that is still in use in modern operating systems. Over time, the licensing costs of these later releases of AT&T's UNIX led the maintainers of the Berkeley Software Distribution to release a UNIX derivative completely free from any AT&T code—the first such release was 4.4BSD-Lite, the precursor of all modern BSD operating systems.

Around the same time, an enterprising Finn named Linus Torvalds released a free Unix clone that would run on the cheap, ubiquitous Intel 386 platform. Together with the GNU userland utilities it became the system known as Linux (or GNU/Linux).

Today, UNIX and Unix-like systems are used for many purposes, from low-end embedded systems to the most powerful supercomputing clusters in the world. In addition to the two main "open" Unix-like systems, several commercial UNIX systems derived from System V are still in use today. Before we discuss them, let us clarify some terminology.

### Unix vs. UNIX vs. Unix-like

Today the UNIX trademark and specification are controlled by the Open Group (www.unix.org/what_is_unix.html). There is a certification program to determine if an operating system (or portion thereof) meets the specification. As there is a cost associated with this process, the free Unix variants are not

## CONTENTS

Introduction to UNIX ............... 301

Boot Process .... 304

Forensic Duplication Consideration .. 306

File Systems .... 306

User Accounts .......... 326

System Configuration .. 328

Artifacts of User Activities ......... 329

Internet Communications ............. 339

Firefox 3 ........... 339

Cache .............. 344

Saved
Session.............344

E-Mail
Analysis...........345

Chat Analysis... 350

Memory and
Swap Space .....351

References.......351

UNIX certified, and thus are not "UNIX." To avoid confusion, we will refer to all systems that share common Unix characteristics as *Unix-like*.

## Linux

*Linux* is used to describe any number of operating systems based upon the Linux kernel. These systems generally use code from the GNU project for the core of their userland utilities, and thus you may hear the term *GNU/Linux* used as well. It can be argued that the more cumbersome GNU/Linux is a more correct description of the total system, however Linux is the more common usage. Linux systems are packaged in *distributions*. A distribution generically refers to a collection of applications and a Linux kernel. These are usually wrapped together on installation media, and will often come with specific branding, distribution-specific modifications, and a package management system to enable the addition of new or updated software. Popular general purpose distributions include RedHat/Fedora, Ubuntu, Slackware, and SuSE.

Many purpose-specific distributions exist. These are generally stripped down compared to their general-use counterparts, and include distributions designed to operate as web application platforms, wireless routers, firewalls and intrusion detection systems, digital video recorders, and many more. Linux also powers large clusters of low-end computers that operate as a single super-computer. Examples of this setup include the most powerful ranked supercomputing cluster in the world at Los Alamos National Laboratory (www.top500.org/system/9707) and the infrastructure behind Google (http://highscalability.com/google-architecture). At the other end of the scale, Linux powers the current generation of ultraportable netbooks, including the ASUS Eee PC and the One Laptop per Child project.

Given the steady increase in use, it is increasingly probable that at some point in your career you will need to investigate a Linux-based system. Fortunately, familiarity with Linux will transfer over to the other Unix-like systems to varying degrees. At the very least you will be better off knowing Linux than not knowing any Unix-like systems at all.

### The BSDs

"The BSDs" refers to the line of Unix-like systems that can trace their origins (directly or indirectly) to the 4.4BSD lineage. Today, this includes FreeBSD, NetBSD, and OpenBSD, FreeBSD being the most widely used of the three. To make very broad generalizations, FreeBSD is used in applications where network throughput and stability is the highest priority, OpenBSD is used in applications where security is the paramount concern, and NetBSD is used when hardware portability is desired. This is not to say that OpenBSD or NetBSD are any less reliable than FreeBSD—after all, NetBSD originated as a fork of the FreeBSD code, and OpenBSD originated as a fork of NetBSD. However, OpenBSD is designed with security as its priority, and NetBSD is designed to be as portable as possible, with ports existing for the Sega Dreamcast and the DEC VAX.

BSD-based desktops and laptops are few and far between, but they do exist (www.pcbsd.org). You are most likely to encounter a BSD-based machine if your investigation involves a web server; particularly of a hosting provider or other enterprise-level web service.

## Commercial Unix Operating Systems

There are a number of Unix-like systems developed by computer companies for their specific hardware, including Sun, IBM, Hewlett Packard (HP), and Silicon Graphics, Inc. (SGI).

Solaris is Sun Microsystem's commercial Unix offering that originated in 1992 and is still used extensively in corporate data centers. Originally developed for Sun's own SPARC processor, modern Solaris runs capably on both 32- and 64-bit Intel x86 processors. Additionally, Sun moved to an open source model in 2005 with the release of *OpenSolaris*. Strengths of Solaris include the ZFS file system, which is capable of holding a 16 exabyte file (should this ever become physically possible), and robust clustering and virtualization support. Solaris systems are not commonly used by individuals, but can be found in business use. If your investigation brings you to one Solaris system, there is a good chance you will end up investigating many more.

AIX is IBM's commercial Unix, which runs on IBM systems using POWER processors. AIX systems are often deployed to run a specific application or applications that leverage the DB2 database and robust availability. AIX is closely tied to the IBM hardware it runs on, and has a reputation for incredible reliability. Due to the cost of the required hardware, AIX systems are almost never seen outside of corporate use. As with Solaris systems, if you need to investigate one system, be prepared to encounter many more.

HP-UX is HP's commercial Unix, which is tied closely to the HP hardware on which it runs. It has similar positives (reliability, clustering) and negatives (cost) compared to the other commercial Unixes. It is also not usually found outside of corporate data centers, and is also generally found in large deployments.

IRIX is a commercial Unix developed by SGI for their hardware that was widely used to support computer animation and graphical rendering.

In this chapter we will focus primarily on Linux but will make an effort to point out differences and caveats when dealing with other systems where applicable. For the most part, userland utilities are either identical or have interoperable analogs on all the Unix-like systems—dealing with kernel-level information and hardware access is where things diverge quickly.

> **FROM THE CASE FILES: IRIX CONTRABAND DROP BOX**
>
> An organization found that intruders had gained unauthorized access to one of their SGI IRIX systems and were using it to store credit card data stolen from various e-commerce sites. Although the computer contained useful evidence relating to the group that was stealing data, no law enforcement agency was equipped to examine an IRIX system. After several weeks of confusion, information security personally in the organization were asked to mount the file system read only from another Unix system and extract the stolen data for law enforcement and credit card companies. To this day, there is very limited support for IRIX in most forensic tools, making recovery of deleted files a challenge.

## BOOT PROCESS

It is important for forensic examiners to understand the Unix system startup process. Knowledge of startup files can help forensic examiners determine which version of the operating system was running and when it was installed. In addition, when an evidentiary Unix system is inadvertently booted, it may be necessary to explain which files were involved in the startup process and assert that no user-created files or other data of evidentiary significance were modified. Furthermore, because of its open design, almost any aspect of the boot process can be altered, so you need to know where to look for malicious modification.

On system boot, after BIOS checks are performed, bootloader code in the Master Boot Record (MBR) is run. The bootloader loads and executes the kernel, which subsequently spawns the first process identifier (PID 1), called *init*. From this point the boot process differs between Linux and BSD. There are two major styles of system initialization in the Unix world, and these are unsurprisingly tied to Unix's bifurcated lineage. The two styles are System V and BSD. At the time of this writing BSD systems only ever use BSD style initialization; however, Linux systems may use either style depending upon the distribution.

The first step in the Linux boot process is loading the kernel. The kernel is generally found in the /boot directory and will be referenced by the boot loader. Next, the initial ramdisk (initrd) is loaded to device drivers, file system modules, logical volume modules, and other items that are required for boot but that aren't built directly into the kernel.

Once the boot loader loads the kernel, the kernel proceeds to initialize the system hardware before starting /sbin/init (PID 1). The init process starts all other processes on the system. Once init starts, there are two distinct ways in which it will proceed to bring up a Unix-like system—System V[1] style and BSD[2] style. Linux distributions generally follow System V examples for most things, including init's tasks and processing runlevels.

## FROM THE CASE FILES: SUBTLE SOLARIS SNIFFER

When investigating a Solaris system that was being used to break into other computers on the victim network, we found more subtle remnants of an earlier intrusion. Taking advantage of the fact that system administrators infrequently inspect or alter the kernel on their system, an intruder placed a sniffer startup file in the kernel directory on a Solaris system. The startup file contained the following lines, ensuring that the sniffer, named update and update. hme for redundancy, would be executed each time the system was rebooted.

```
# more /kernel/pssys
1 "./update -s -o output"
1 "./update.hme -s -o output.hme"
```

Forensic examination of the system revealed that various executables placed on the system by the intruder had been compiled with a non-Solaris compiler. In addition, we found the sniffer files and associated output files in /usr/ share/man/tmp, another location that system administrators rarely visit.

```
# ls -altc
total 156
-rw-r--r--    1    root    root    23787    Jun 12 07:52 output.hme
drwxr-xr-x    2    root    root    512      Jun  6 17:20 .
drwxr-xr-x   40    bin     bin     1024     Jun  6 17:20 ..
-rw-r--r--    1    root    root    50       Jun  6 17:20 output
-rwxr-xr-x    1    root    root    25548    Jun  6 17:20 update
-rwx------    1    root    root    25996    Jun  6 17:20 update.hme
```

The sniffer files contained usernames and passwords, and also captured the intruder logging into the compromised server remotely. These logs showed the intruder taking the sniffer logs and other sensitive files from the system.

## System V

In addition to being the most common init style across Linux distributions, System V `init` is also used by Solaris and HP-UX. System V `init` reads the /etc/inittab file to determine the default *runlevel*. A runlevel is a numeric descriptor for the set of scripts a machine will execute for a given state. On most Linux distributions, runlevel 3 is synonymous with a full multi-user console (i.e., command line) environment, whereas runlevel 5 is a graphical environment.

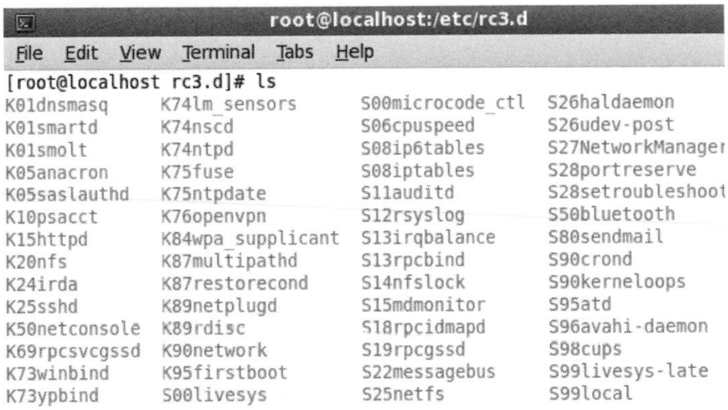

Note that each entry in a runlevel directory is actually a symbolic link to a script in /etc/init.d/ that will be started or stopped depending on the name of the symlink. Each script contains myriad variables and actions that will be taken to start or stop the service gracefully.

As you can see in Figure 6.1, there are numerous places an intruder can set up

**FIGURE 6.1**

Contents of an RC3.d directory showing a variety of scripts used to start and stop services on a Linux system.

```
root@localhost:/etc/rc3.d
File  Edit  View  Terminal  Tabs  Help
[root@localhost rc3.d]# ls
K01dnsmasq        K74lm_sensors      S00microcode_ctl   S26haldaemon
K01smartd         K74nscd            S06cpuspeed        S26udev-post
K01smolt          K74ntpd            S08ip6tables       S27NetworkManager
K05anacron        K75fuse            S08iptables        S28portreserve
K05saslauthd      K75ntpdate         S11auditd          S28setroubleshoot
K10psacct         K76openvpn         S12rsyslog         S50bluetooth
K15httpd          K84wpa_supplicant  S13irqbalance      S80sendmail
K20nfs            K87multipathd      S13rpcbind         S90crond
K24irda           K87restorecond     S14nfslock         S90kerneloops
K25sshd           K89netplugd        S15mdmonitor       S95atd
K50netconsole     K89rdisc           S18rpcidmapd       S96avahi-daemon
K69rpcsvcgssd     K90network         S19rpcgssd         S98cups
K73winbind        K95firstboot       S22messagebus      S99livesys-late
K73ypbind         S00livesys         S25netfs           S99local
```

a script to help them maintain persistent access to a compromised system. Careful review of all of the scripts involved in the boot process is mandatory in such a scenario.

## BSD

The BSD init process is a bit less complex. BSD init reads the script at /etc/rc to determine what system services are to be run, configuration information is read from /etc/rc.conf, and additional services to run from /etc/rc.local. This is the extent of init configuration for OpenBSD, whereas current FreeBSD and NetBSD also read additional startup scripts from the /etc/rc.d/ directory.

---

### FROM THE CASE FILES: t0rnKit BACKDOOR

Forensic examination of a compromised Linux server revealed that it had the t0rnkit rootkit installed. To ensure that a component of the rootkit was restarted whenever the system was rebooted, the following lines were added to the "/etc/rc.d/rc.sysinit" file.

```
# Xntps (NTPv3 daemon) startup..
/usr/sbin/xntps -q
# Xntps (NTPv3 deamon) check..
/usr/sbin/xntpsc 1>/dev/null 2>/dev/null
```

Closer inspection of the xntps executable revealed that it was part of the rootkit and not a legitimate part of the system.

---

## FORENSIC DUPLICATION CONSIDERATION

The dd command has existed on Unix systems long before digital forensics was a twinkle in the eye. Now this utility has become a de facto standard for creating forensic duplicates of storage media and volatile memory, and has been ported to other operating systems. This simple concept has evolved into specialized tools like dcfldd, which maintains audit and integrity log for forensic documentation purposes, and ddrescue, which has more flexibility in dealing with damaged media.

Acquiring a forensic image of a hard drive using these utilities provides a raw copy of the data that can be viewed using forensic tools like TSK, X-Ways, EnCase, and FTK. However, Unix systems that use Logical Volume Management (LVM) to enable resizing of partitions present a challenge for forensic practitioners. A forensic duplicate of a hard drive in such a system cannot be parsed by most forensic tools currently because the tools do not understand LVM. Therefore, it is necessary to activate the LVM and create a forensic duplicate of each partition individually.

## FILE SYSTEMS

Although volatile data collection and analysis has recently received more mainstream attention than in the past, analysis of the contents of the file system remains as important as ever. To properly understand the "magic" taking place behind the curtains of many forensics tools, the examiner must first understand how a given file system functions. Additionally, understanding where these functions diverge

## PRACTITIONER'S TIP: FORENSIC DUPLICATION OF LVM

The presence of an LVM configured disk will become immediately apparent when you look at the partition type (8e), which is displayed as Linux_LVM as shown here using `fdisk`.

```
# fdisk -l
Disk /dev/sda: 8589 MB, 8589934592 bytes
255 heads, 63 sectors/track, 1044 cylinders
Units = cylinders of 16065 * 512 = 8225280 bytes
Disk identifier: 0x0006159f

   Device Boot      Start        End      Blocks    Id  System
/dev/sda1  *             1         25      200781    83  Linux
/dev/sda2              26       1044    8185117+    8e  Linux LVM
```

The next step is to scan all disks and display the name associated with the LVM as shown next for a volume group named "VolGroup00."

```
# pvscan
PV /dev/sda2    VG VolGroup00    lvm2 [7.78 GB / 32.00 MB free]
Total: 1 [7.78 GB] / in use: 1 [7.78 GB] / in no VG: 0 [0 ]
```

In order to access the individual volumes it is necessary to activate the Volume Group as shown here:

```
# vgchange -a y VolGroup00
2 logical volume(s) in volume group VolGroup00 now active.

# lvs
LV VG Attr Lsize Origin Snap% Move Log Copy%
LogVol00 VolGroup00 -wi-a- 7.25G
LogVol01 VolGroup00 -wi-a- 512.00M
```

Image each logical partition as usual:

```
# dd if=/dev/VolGroup00/LogVol00 bs=4k of=/mnt/images/LogVol00.dd
# dd if=/dev/VolGroup00/LogVol01 bs=4k of=/mnt/images/LogVol01.dd
```

from what the user expects enables exploitation of these gaps to the advantage of the examiner—this is the basis for recovery of "deleted" data.

Most current Linux systems use the Ext3 file system. Ext3 is the successor of Ext2, which added journaling but retained Ext2's underlying structure otherwise. In fact, an Ext3 volume will happily mount as Ext2 if the user issues the mount command appropriately. Many other file systems are available via the Linux kernel, including ReiserFS, XFS, and JFS. For the purposes of brevity, we will discuss Ext3 (and indirectly Ext2). For a detailed examination of various file systems we recommend *File System Forensic Analysis* (Carrier, 2006). We will be using the same abstraction model presented in Carrier 2006, as it presents a clear and accurate view of the file system without resorting to inaccurate analogy.

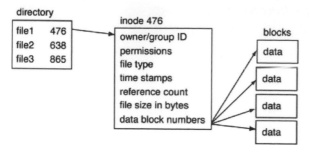

**FIGURE 6.2**

Depiction of the relationship between a directory, inode, and data blocks.

The logical progression of file system layers (as described by Carrier) from lowest to highest is as follows (Figure 6.2).

A *disk* refers to a physical storage device—a SCSI or SATA hard drive, for example. A *volume* is created using all or part of one or more disks. A single disk may contain several volumes, or a volume may span several disks, depending on configuration. The term "partition" is often used interchangeably for a volume—Carrier makes a distinction wherein a partition is limited to a single physical disk, and a volume is a collection of one or more partitions. Put simply, a volume describes a number of sectors on a disk or disks in a given system. A *file system* is laid down on a volume, and describes the layout of files and their associated metadata.

So, on a simple single-disk Linux system, the *partition table* describes the division of the disk into two *partitions/volumes*—one for swap and one for the actual *file system*. This file system is divided into *blocks* that contain the *content* of the files. These *blocks* in turn are described by *inodes*, and these *inodes* are described by *directories* containing *filenames*.

The lowest level data contained within a file system is *content*. Content is what is in the file—the data. *Metadata* is data *about* data—date and time information, ownership, and other data dependent upon the specific file system in question. The filename layer is the layer at which human users are most comfortable operating—this includes directories and filenames.

### Unix Date-time Stamps

The Unix date-time format is a 32-bit value representing the number of seconds since 00:00:00 on 1st January 1970.

---

**PRACTITIONER'S TIP: INTERPRETING UNIX DATE-TIME STAMPS**

In addition to seeing Unix date-time stamps represented in hexadecimal format, forensic examiners will encounter Unix date-time stamps in a numeric format, which is a string of 10 digits. For instance, the Unix date-time stamp 0x45C08766 is equivalent to the digital value 1170245478, which is easily converted using Perl as shown here:

```
$ perl -e "print scalar(gmtime(1170245478))"
Wed Jan 31 12:11:18 2007
```

Some applications running on Windows systems use the Unix date-time format. For instance, Firefox maintains records of web browsing activity in a file named history.dat with dates in Unix format.

A utility developed for Windows systems called DCode can interpret Unix date-time stamps (www.digital-detective. co.uk/freetools/decode.asp).

---

On Unix systems, file system date-time stamps are set in UTC, making it necessary to adjust file system dates to the correct time zone. The time zone settings on most Unix systems are stored in a file that is referenced by the /etc/localtime symbolic link. For instance, the following Perl command converts a Unix date-time stamp to local time (e.g., US Eastern time zone).

## Date-time Stamp Analysis

Unix systems maintain up to four date-time stamps. Each of the four time-stamps stored in an Ext inode are updated by different actions. We'll address them in their most commonly referenced order: (M) A C (and D).

The M-time (modification) is updated when the *content* of a file or directory is *modified*. For a file, this is triggered by any alteration of the content. The content of a directory's blocks is filenames, so the deletion or creation of a file in a directory will cause its M-time to update.

The A-time (access) is the most frequently updated—this will change whenever the *content* of a file or directory is read. Actions that cause the content of a file to be read include copying, moving from one volume to another, or simply opening the file. As mentioned previously, directories are simply files that have file-names as their content, so listing the contents of a directory is sufficient to cause that directory's A-time to be updated. Additionally, reading the content of any file will cause the A-time of that file as well as the directory containing that file to be updated.

The C-time (change time) is updated when the *inode* is altered. This happens when any of the metadata for a file or directory is changed, including either of the previously mentioned timestamps, a file or directory being copied or moved, or the permissions of a file or directory being modified. The C-time is not to be mistaken with the creation date of a file.

Finally, the D-time is updated when a file was deleted. This timestamp will only be set in deleted inodes.

Macintosh systems running Unix operating systems have additional date-time stamps as detailed in Chapter 7, "Macintosh Forensic Analysis."

On Unix systems, altering the modification or access time of any file is trivially done using the touch command. However, altering either of these timestamps in this manner updates the C-time. Additionally, preventing the updating of access times at all can be achieved using the noatime option to the mount command. When examining a machine possibly controlled by a savvy adversary, keep a healthy skepticism if you encounter strange (or strangely convenient) timestamps.

The C-time is of particular interest, as this timestamp cannot be easily altered to a specific value. In an investigation where the timing of events is key this may be your truest source of temporal information.

All file system activity can be conveniently displayed as a timeline using the mac-time utility from TSK. This program is used to create a log-style listing sorted by each timestamp entry in a supplied "*body*" file. A "body" file is a listing of files in a particular format, often referred to as "*mactime*" format. An appropriate body file can be generated using the `fls` program, also a part of TSK, as demonstrated here:

```
#fls -r -m / {image_file} > bodyfile
```

Alternatively, the output from `fls` can be piped directly to `mactime` to avoid the creation of an intermediary file as demonstrated here:

```
#fls -r -m / {image_file} | mactime -b -
```

The `mactime` utility can be instructed to present timestamps only for a certain time period as shown here:

```
#mactime -b bodyfile 04/01/2009-04/12/2009
```

We can combine these to generate a timeline that only shows the activity on the "/home" volume occurring on May 30, 2009. Note that in this example we are running `fls` against the volume (/dev/sda9) directly as opposed to creating a raw image file first.

```
fcculive:~# fls -r -m /home /dev/sda9 | mactime -b -
    05/30/2009 > timeline.txt
```

The resultant file has 200 lines—all this activity was generated during a very simple graphical logon session. Timeline investigations of intrusions occurring over a period of months or years on heavily used systems can grow into the millions of entries!

```
Sat May 30 2009 18:54:22    4096 m.c d/drwx------ 1000        1000    3694600  /home/user/.gnome2
Sat May 30 2009 18:54:23    4096 m.c d/drwxr-xr-x 1000        1000    3694637  /home/user/.nautilus
                             919 mac -/-rw------- 1000        1000    3695648  /home/user/.gnome2/update-notifier-C1885d
(deleted-realloc)
                             919 mac -/-rw------- 1000        1000    3695648  /home/user/.nautilus/saved-session-3BVPUU
Sat May 30 2009 18:54:27     818 m.c -/-rw------- 1000        1000    3695590  /home/user/.bash_history
Sat May 30 2009 18:56:15    4096 .a. d/drwx------ 1000        1000    3694597  /home/user/.gconf
                            4096 .a. d/drwx------ 1000        1000    3694599  /home/user/.gconf/apps
                            4096 .a. -/drwx------ 1000        1000    3694599
/home/user/.gnome2/panel2.d/default/launchers/gnome-terminal.desktop (deleted-realloc)
Sat May 30 2009 18:56:16    4096 .a. d/drwx------ 1000        1000    3694601  /home/user/.gnome2/keyrings
                           15267 .a. -/-rw-r--r-- 1000        1000    3694603  /home/user/.xsession-errors
                             105 .a. -/-rw------- 1000        1000    3694604
/home/user/.gnome2/keyrings/.keyringT8QNQU (deleted-realloc)
                             105 .a. -/-rw------- 1000        1000    3694604  /home/user/.gnome2/keyrings/login.keyring
                             217 m.c -/-rw------- 1000        1000    3695646  /home/user/.Xauthority
Sat May 30 2009 18:56:17     675 .a. -/-rw-r--r-- 1000        1000    3694594  /home/user/.profile
                            3116 .a. -/-rw-r--r-- 1000        1000    3694595  /home/user/.bashrc
                              28 m.c -/-rw------- 1000        1000    3694712  /home/user/.dmrc
Sat May 30 2009 18:56:18     463 m.c -/-rw-r--r-- 1000        1000    3694608
/home/user/.dbus/session-bus/4aa19355324ed7c15b5f3dfc49b05af9-0
```

```
                       4096 .a. d/drwx------ 1000      1000     3694625   /home/user/.gconf/desktop
                       4096 .a. d/drwx------ 1000      1000     3694627   /home/user/.gconf/desktop/gnome
Sat May 30 2009 18:56:19    4096 m.c d/drwxr-xr-x 1000  1000     3694593   /home/user
                        159 m.c -/-rw------- 1000      1000     3694614   /home/user/.ICEauthority
                       4096 .a. d/drwx------ 1000      1000     3694682   /home/user/.gconf/desktop/gnome/screen
                       4096 .a. d/drwx------ 1000      1000     3694735
/home/user/.gconf/desktop/gnome/screen/default
                        259 .a. -/-rw------- 1000      1000     3695645
/home/user/.gconf/desktop/gnome/screen/default/0/%gconf.xml
                        259 .a. -/-rw------- 1000      1000     3695645
/home/user/.gconf/desktop/gnome/screen/default/0/%gconf.xml.new (deleted-realloc)
Sat May 30 2009 18:56:20    4096 .a. d/drwxr-xr-x 1000  1000     3694593   /home/user
                       4096 .a. d/drwxr-xr-x 1000      1000     3694615   /home/user/.gnome2/share/fonts
                       4096 .a. d/drwxr-xr-x 1000      1000     3694616   /home/user/.gnome2/share/cursor-fonts
                          2 mac -/-rw-r--r-- 1000      1000     3694617   /home/user/.gnome2/share/cursor-
fonts/fonts.dir
                          2 mac -/-rw-r--r-- 1000      1000     3694618   /home/user/.gnome2/share/fonts/fonts.dir
                          0 .a. -/-rw------- 1000      1000     3694628
/home/user/.gconf/desktop/gnome/%gconf.xml
                       4096 .a. d/drwx------ 1000      1000     3761585
/home/user/.gconf/desktop/gnome/peripherals
                       4096 .a. d/drwx------ 1000      1000     3761647
/home/user/.gconf/desktop/gnome/peripherals/keyboard
                          0 .a. -/-rw------- 1000      1000     3761648
/home/user/.gconf/desktop/gnome/peripherals/keyboard/%gconf.xml
                       4096 .a. d/drwx------ 1000      1000     3761650
/home/user/.gconf/desktop/gnome/peripherals/keyboard/host-quincy
Sat May 30 2009 18:56:21    4096 .a. d/drwx------ 1000  1000     3694629
/home/user/.gconf/desktop/gnome/accessibility
                       2087 .a. -/-rw------- 1000      1000     3694632
/home/user/.gconf/desktop/gnome/accessibility/keyboard/%gconf.xml
                       2087 .a. -/-rw------- 1000      1000     3694632
/home/user/.gconf/desktop/gnome/accessibility/keyboard/%gconf.xml.new (deleted-realloc)
Sat May 30 2009 18:56:22    4096 m.c d/drwx------ 1000  1000     3694611   /home/user/.gnupg
                         28 .a. -/-rw------- 1000      1000     3694612   /home/user/.gnupg/gpg.conf
                       4096 .a. d/drwx------ 1000      1000     3694619   /home/user/.ssh
                         40 .a. -/-rw------- 1000      1000     3694620   /home/user/.gnupg/trustdb.gpg
                          0 .a. -/-rw------- 1000      1000     3694621   /home/user/.gnupg/pubring.gpg
                          0 .a. -/-rw------- 1000      1000     3694623   /home/user/.gnupg/secring.gpg
                        594 .a. -/-rw------- 1000      1000     3762203
/home/user/.gconf/desktop/gnome/remote_access/%gconf.xml
                        594 .a. -/-rw------- 1000      1000     3762203
/home/user/.gconf/desktop/gnome/remote_access/%gconf.xml.new (deleted-realloc)
                        594 .a. l/-rw------- 1000      1000     3762203
/home/user/afflib-3.3.4/conf26974 (deleted-realloc)
Sat May 30 2009 18:56:23    4096 m.c d/drwx------ 1000  1000     3694597   /home/user/.gconf
                        181 mac -/-rw------- 1000      1000     3694606   /home/user/.gconf/.testing.writeability
(deleted-realloc)
                        181 mac -/-rw------- 1000      1000     3694606
/home/user/.gconf/desktop/gnome/applications/window_manager/%gconf.xml
                        181 mac -/-rw------- 1000      1000     3694606
/home/user/.gconf/desktop/gnome/applications/window_manager/%gconf.xml.new (deleted-realloc)
                        181 mac -/-rw------- 1000      1000     3694606
```

```
/home/user/.gnupg/.#lk0x8287c60.quincy.3495 (deleted-realloc)
                         4096 .a. d/drwx------ 1000      1000      3694633
/home/user/.gconf/desktop/gnome/applications
                         4096 m.c d/drwx------ 1000      1000      3694635
/home/user/.gconf/desktop/gnome/applications/window_manager
                         4096 .a. d/drwx------ 1000      1000      3694657   /home/user/.gconf/apps/panel
                         2010 .a. -/-rw------- 1000      1000      3694688
/home/user/.gconf/apps/panel/objects/object_1/%gconf.xml
                         2010 .a. -/-rw------- 1000      1000      3694688
/home/user/.gconf/apps/panel/objects/object_1/%gconf.xml.new (deleted-realloc)
                         4096 .a. d/drwx------ 1000      1000      3694689
/home/user/.gconf/apps/panel/objects/object_0 (deleted-realloc)
                         4096 .a. d/drwx------ 1000      1000      3694689   /home/user/.gconf/apps/panel/toplevels
                         4096 .a. d/drwx------ 1000      1000      3694697
/home/user/.gconf/apps/panel/objects/object_0/bottom_panel_screen0
                         1961 .a. -/-rw------- 1000      1000      3694698
/home/user/.gconf/apps/panel/objects/object_0/bottom_panel_screen0/%gconf.xml
                          778 .a. -/-rw------- 1000      1000      3694700
/home/user/.gconf/apps/panel/objects/object_0/bottom_panel_screen0/background/%gconf.xml
                          778 .a. -/-rw------- 1000      1000      3694700
/home/user/.gconf/apps/panel/objects/object_0/bottom_panel_screen0/background/%gconf.xml.new (deleted-realloc)
                         4096 m.c d/drwx------ 1000      1000      3761652
/home/user/.gconf/desktop/gnome/peripherals/keyboard/host-quincy/0
                          134 mac -/-rw------- 1000      1000      3761742
/home/user/.gconf/desktop/gnome/peripherals/keyboard/host-quincy/0/%gconf.xml
                          134 mac -/-rw------- 1000      1000      3761742
/home/user/.gconf/desktop/gnome/peripherals/keyboard/host-quincy/0/%gconf.xml.new (deleted-realloc)
Sat May 30 2009 18:56:24    4096 .a. d/drwx------ 1000      1000      3833980
/home/user/.gconf/desktop/gnome/connected_servers
                            0 .a. -/-rw------- 1000      1000      3833981
/home/user/.gconf/desktop/gnome/connected_servers/%gconf.xml
                         4096 .a. d/drwx------ 1000      1000      3833982
/home/user/.gconf/desktop/gnome/connected_servers/1
                          455 .a. -/-rw------- 1000      1000      3833983
/home/user/.gconf/desktop/gnome/connected_servers/1/%gconf.xml
                          455 .a. -/-rw------- 1000      1000      3833983
/home/user/.gconf/desktop/gnome/connected_servers/1/%gconf.xml.new (deleted-realloc)
Sat May 30 2009 18:56:25      82 mac -/-rw-r--r-- 1000      1000      3694636
/home/user/.metacity/sessions/117f0001010001243709783000000034170001.ms
                         4096 m.c d/drwx------ 1000      1000      3694641/home/user/.metacity/sessions
                         1917 .a. -/-rw------- 1000      1000      3694656
/home/user/.gconf/apps/panel/applets/clock_screen0/%gconf.xml
                         1917 .a. -/-rw------- 1000      1000      3694656
/home/user/.gconf/apps/panel/applets/clock_screen0/%gconf.xml.new (deleted-realloc)
                         4096 .a. d/drwx------ 1000      1000      3694659/home/user/.gconf/apps/panel/applets
                         1929 .a. -/-rw------- 1000      1000      3694662
/home/user/.gconf/apps/panel/applets/workspace_switcher_screen0/%gconf.xml
                         1923 .a. -/-rw------- 1000      1000      3694666
/home/user/.gconf/apps/panel/applets/window_list_screen0/%gconf.xml
                         1924 .a. -/-rw------- 1000      1000      3694670
```

```
/home/user/.gconf/apps/panel/applets/show_desktop_button_screen0/%gconf.xml
                        1924 .a. -/-rw------- 1000     1000     3694670
/home/user/.gconf/apps/panel/applets/show_desktop_button_screen0/%gconf.xml.new (deleted-realloc)
                        1917 .a. -/-rw------- 1000     1000     3694672
/home/user/.gconf/apps/panel/applets/mixer_screen0/%gconf.xml
                        1917 .a. -/-rw------- 1000     1000     3694672
/home/user/.gconf/apps/panel/applets/mixer_screen0/%gconf.xml.new (deleted-realloc)
                        1922 .a. -/-rw------- 1000     1000     3694674
/home/user/.gconf/apps/panel/applets/window_menu_screen0/%gconf.xml
                        1922 .a. -/-rw------- 1000     1000     3694674
/home/user/.gconf/apps/panel/applets/window_menu_screen0/%gconf.xml.new (deleted-realloc)
                        4096 .a. d/drwx------ 1000     1000     3694683 /home/user/.gconf/apps/panel/objects
                        1878 .a. -/-rw------- 1000     1000     3694686
/home/user/.gconf/apps/panel/objects/object_2/%gconf.xml
                        1878 .a. -/-rw------- 1000     1000     3694686
/home/user/.gconf/apps/panel/objects/object_2/%gconf.xml.new (deleted-realloc)
                        1910 .a. -/-rw------- 1000     1000     3694692
/home/user/.gconf/apps/panel/objects/email_launcher_screen0/%gconf.xml
                        1910 .a. -/-rw------- 1000     1000     3694692
/home/user/.gconf/apps/panel/objects/email_launcher_screen0/%gconf.xml.new (deleted-realloc)
                        1909 .a. -/-rw------- 1000     1000     3694694
/home/user/.gconf/apps/panel/objects/browser_launcher_screen0/%gconf.xml
                        1909 .a. -/-rw------- 1000     1000     3694694
/home/user/.gconf/apps/panel/objects/browser_launcher_screen0/%gconf.xml.new (deleted-realloc)
                        1812 .a. -/-rw------- 1000     1000     3694696
/home/user/.gconf/apps/panel/objects/menu_bar_screen0/%gconf.xml
                        1812 .a. -/-rw------- 1000     1000     3694696
/home/user/.gconf/apps/panel/objects/menu_bar_screen0/%gconf.xml.new (deleted-realloc)
                        4096 .a. d/drwx------ 1000     1000     3694701
/home/user/.gconf/apps/panel/objects/object_0/top_panel_screen0
                        2193 .a. -/-rw------- 1000     1000     3694702
/home/user/.gconf/apps/panel/objects/object_0/top_panel_screen0/%gconf.xml
                         778 .a. -/-rw------- 1000     1000     3694704
/home/user/.gconf/apps/panel/objects/object_0/top_panel_screen0/background/%gconf.xml
                         778 .a. -/-rw------- 1000     1000     3694704
/home/user/.gconf/apps/panel/objects/object_0/top_panel_screen0/background/%gconf.xml.new (deleted-realloc)
                        1925 .a. -/-rw------- 1000     1000     3694763
/home/user/.gconf/apps/panel/applets/notification_area_screen0/%gconf.xml
                        1925 .a. -/-rw------- 1000     1000     3694763
/home/user/.gconf/apps/panel/applets/notification_area_screen0/%gconf.xml.new (deleted-realloc)
Sat May 30 2009 18:56:26    4096 .a. d/drwx------ 1000     1000     3694661
/home/user/.gconf/apps/panel/applets/workspace_switcher_screen0
                        4096 .a. d/drwx------ 1000     1000     3694663
/home/user/.gconf/apps/panel/applets/workspace_switcher_screen0/prefs
                        4096 .a. d/drwx------ 1000     1000     3694665
/home/user/.gconf/apps/panel/applets/window_list_screen0
                        4096 .a. d/drwx------ 1000     1000     3694667
/home/user/.gconf/apps/panel/applets/window_list_screen0/prefs
                        4096 .a. d/drwx------ 1000     1000     3694669
/home/user/.gconf/apps/panel/applets/show_desktop_button_screen0
Sat May 30 2009 18:56:28    5515 .a. -/-rw-r--r-- 1000     1000     3694653
```

```
/home/user/.gnome2/panel2.d/default/launchers/gnome-terminal-1.desktop
Sat May 30 2009 18:56:35      4096 .a. d/drwx------ 1000     1000     3694673
/home/user/.gconf/apps/panel/applets/clock_screen0
                              4096 .a. d/drwx------ 1000     1000     3694675
/home/user/.gconf/apps/panel/applets/clock_screen0/prefs
                              4096 .a. d/drwx------ 1000     1000     3694677
/home/user/.gconf/apps/panel/applets/clock_screen0/prefs/timezones
Sat May 30 2009 18:56:36      4096 .a. d/drwx------ 1000     1000     3694679
/home/user/.gconf/apps/panel/applets/mixer_screen0
                              4096 .a. d/drwx------ 1000     1000     3694681
/home/user/.gconf/apps/panel/applets/window_menu_screen0
Sat May 30 2009 18:56:37 318749 .a. -/-rw------- 1000              1000     3694624
/home/user/.gnupg/secring.gpg.lock/registry.i486.bin
                            318749 .a. -/-rw------- 1000     1000     3694624
/home/user/.gnupg/secring.gpg.lock/registry.i486.bin.tmp017CQU (deleted-realloc)
                              4096 .a. d/drwx------ 1000     1000     3694671
/home/user/.gconf/apps/panel/applets/notification_area_screen0
Sat May 30 2009 18:57:26      4096 m.c d/drwx------ 1000     1000     3694663
/home/user/.gconf/apps/panel/applets/workspace_switcher_screen0/prefs
                              4096 m.c d/drwx------ 1000     1000     3694667
/home/user/.gconf/apps/panel/applets/window_list_screen0/prefs
                               445 mac -/-rw------- 1000     1000     3694668
/home/user/.gconf/apps/panel/applets/workspace_switcher_screen0/prefs/%gconf.xml
                               445 mac -/-rw------- 1000     1000     3694668
/home/user/.gconf/apps/panel/applets/workspace_switcher_screen0/prefs/%gconf.xml.new (deleted-realloc)
                              4096 m.c d/drwx------ 1000     1000     3694675
/home/user/.gconf/apps/panel/applets/clock_screen0/prefs
                               156 mac -/-rw------- 1000     1000     3694676
/home/user/.gconf/apps/panel/applets/clock_screen0/prefs/timezones/%gconf.xml
                               156 mac -/-rw------- 1000     1000     3694676
/home/user/.gconf/apps/panel/applets/clock_screen0/prefs/timezones/%gconf.xml.new (deleted-realloc)
                              4096 m.c d/drwx------ 1000     1000     3694677
/home/user/.gconf/apps/panel/applets/clock_screen0/prefs/timezones
                               670 mac -/-rw------- 1000     1000     3694678
/home/user/.gconf/apps/panel/applets/window_list_screen0/prefs/%gconf.xml
                               670 mac -/-rw------- 1000     1000     3694678
/home/user/.gconf/apps/panel/applets/window_list_screen0/prefs/%gconf.xml.new (deleted-realloc)
                              1823 mac -/-rw------- 1000     1000     3695651
/home/user/.gconf/apps/panel/applets/clock_screen0/prefs/%gconf.xml
                              1823 mac -/-rw------- 1000     1000     3695651
/home/user/.gconf/apps/panel/applets/clock_screen0/prefs/%gconf.xml.new (deleted-realloc)
Sat May 30 2009 18:57:45      4096 m.c d/drwx------ 1000     1000     3694598 /home/user/.gconfd
Sat May 30 2009 19:00:24     15267 m.c -/-rw-r--r-- 1000     1000     3694603 /home/user/.xsession-errors
Sat May 30 2009 19:00:59        58 mac -/-rw-r--r-- 1000     1000     3694648 /home/user/.gnome/gnome-
vfs/.trash_entry_cache
                              4096 .a. d/drwxr-xr-- 1000     1000     3694650 /home/user/.gnome2/nautilus-scripts
                                28 .a. -/-rw------- 1000     1000     3694712 /home/user/.dmrc
                               268 .a. -/-rw------- 1000     1000     3694778
/home/user/.nautilus/metafiles/file:///home/user/Desktop.xml
                               818 .a. -/-rw------- 1000     1000     3695590 /home/user/.bash_history
                                35 .a. -/-rw------- 1000     1000     3695643 /home/user/.lesshst
```

```
                                 4096 .a. d/drwx------ 1000      1000     3761663  /home/user/.thumbnails/normal
Sat May 30 2009 19:01:00   8328283136 .a. -/-rwxr-xr-x 1000     1000     3695636  /home/user/Ubuntu-desktop.raw.img
                               563784 .a. -/-rw-r--r-- 0         0        3695641  /home/user/.fonts.cache-1
Sat May 30 2009 19:01:09         4096 .a. d/drwxr-xr-x 1000      1000     3694638  /home/user/Desktop
                                 4096 .a. d/drwxr-x--- 1000      1000     3694754  /home/user/Desktop/Downloads
                                  555 mac -/-rw------- 1000      1000     3695652  /home/user/.nautilus/metafiles/x-
nautilus-desktop:///.xml
                                 4096 .a. d/drwxrwxrwx 501       501      3760134  /home/user/bloom-1.0.1
                                 4096 .a. d/drwxr-xr-x 0         0        3768760  /home/user/vmware-tools-distrib
Sat May 30 2009 19:01:10         4096 .a. d/drwxrwxrwx 501       501      3694743  /home/user/sleuthkit-3.0.1
                                15042 .a. -/-rwxr-xr-x 1000      1000     3694766  /home/user/mount_ewf-20080513.py
                                 5269 .a. -/-rw-r--r-- 1000      1000     3695609  /home/user/patches.txt
                              2613248 .a. -/-rw-r--r-- 1000      1000     3695647  /home/user/fls
                             26721262 .a. -/-rw-r--r-- 1000      1000     3695649  /home/user/err
                                 4096 .a. d/drwxrwxrwx 501       501      3760159  /home/user/aimage-3.2.0
                                 4096 .a. d/drwxrwxrwx 501       501      3760189  /home/user/ataraw-0.2.0
                                 4096 .a. d/drwxrwxrwx 501       501      3760217  /home/user/bulk_extractor-0.0.10
                                 4096 .a. d/drwxrwxrwx 501       501      3760246  /home/user/fiwalk-0.4.3
                                 4096 .a. d/drwxrwxrwx 21252     21252    3760292  /home/user/afflib-3.3.4
                                 4096 .a. d/drwxr-xr-x 0         0        3760298  /home/user/ptk
                                 4096 .a. d/drwxrwxrwx 1000      1000     3760699  /home/user/pyflag-0.87-pre1
                                 4096 .a. -/drwxrwxrwx 1001      1001     3761589  /home/user/fiwalk-0.4.3/confdefs.h
(deleted-realloc)
                                 4096 .a. d/drwxrwxrwx 1001      1001     3761589  /home/user/fiwalk-0.5.1
                                 4096 .a. -/drwxr-xr-x 1000      1000     3762204  /home/user/afflib-3.3.4/conftest.undefs
(deleted-realloc)
                                 4096 .a. d/drwxr-xr-x 1000      1000     3762204  /home/user/forensics
Sat May 30 2009 19:01:20          112 mac -/-rw------- 1000      1000     3695584  /home/user/.nautilus/metafiles/file:///
                                                                                   home.xml
Sat May 30 2009 19:01:28            0 ma. -/-rw-r--r-- 1000      1000     3695653  /home/user/new file~
Sat May 30 2009 19:01:40         4096 ..c d/drwx------ 1000      1000     3694609  /home/user/.gnome2_private
                                  159 .a. -/-rw------- 1000      1000     3694614  /home/user/.ICEauthority
                                  217 .a. -/-rw------- 1000      1000     3695646  /home/user/.Xauthority
                                 4096 .a. d/drwx------ 1000      1000     3760283  /home/user/.gconf/apps/gedit-2
                                 4096 .a. d/drwx------ 1000      1000     3761656  /home/user/.gconf/apps/gedit-
2/preferences
                                    0 .a. -/-rw------- 1000      1000     3761657  /home/user/.gconf/apps/gedit-
2/preferences/%gconf.xml
                                 4096 .a. d/drwx------ 1000      1000     3761658  /home/user/.gconf/apps/gedit-
2/preferences/ui
                                    0 .a. -/-rw------- 1000      1000     3761659  /home/user/.gconf/apps/gedit-
2/preferences/ui/%gconf.xml
                                 4096 .a. d/drwx------ 1000      1000     3761660  /home/user/.gconf/apps/gedit-
2/preferences/ui/statusbar
Sat May 30 2009 19:01:41         7450 .a. -/-rw-r--r-- 1000      1000     3694774  /home/user/.gnome2/accelsgedit
Sat May 30 2009 19:01:45          553 .a. -/-rw-r--r-- 1000      1000     3695023  /home/user/.gnome2/gedit-metadata.xml
                                67895 mac -/-rwx------ 1000      1000     3695650  /home/user/.gconfd/saved_state
                                67895 mac -/-rwx------ 1000      1000     3695650  /home/user/.gconfd/saved_state.tmp
(deleted-realloc)
Sat May 30 2009 19:01:48         4096 m.c d/drwx------ 1000      1000     3694655  /home/user/.gconf/apps/gnome-screensaver
                                  143 mac -/-rw------- 1000      1000     3694772  /home/user/.gconf/apps/gnome-
screensaver/%gconf.xml
                                  143 mac -/-rw------- 1000      1000     3694772  /home/user/.gconf/apps/gnome-
screensaver/%gconf.xml.new (deleted-realloc)
```

```
                            141 mac -/-rw------- 1000        1000      3761653  /home/user/.gconf/apps/gedit-
2/preferences/ui/statusbar/%gconf.xml
                            141 mac -/-rw------- 1000        1000      3761653  /home/user/.gconf/apps/gedit-
2/preferences/ui/statusbar/%gconf.xml.new (deleted-realloc)
                           4096 m.c d/drwx------ 1000        1000      3761660  /home/user/ .gconf/apps/gedit-
2/preferences/ui/statusbar
                           4096 mac d/drwx------ 1000        1000      3981318  /home/user/.gconf/apps/nautilus
                           4096 mac l/drwx------ 1000        1000      3981318
/home/user/.mozilla/firefox/8u20d7t5.default/lock (deleted-realloc)
                            137 mac -/-rw------- 1000        1000      3981364
/home/user/.gconf/apps/nautilus/%gconf.xml
                            137 mac -/-rw------- 1000        1000      3981364
/home/user/.gconf/apps/nautilus/%gconf.xml.new (deleted-realloc)
                            137 mac -/-rw------- 1000        1000      3981364
/home/user/.mozilla/firefox/8u20d7t5.default/places.sqlite-journal (deleted-realloc)
Sat May 30 2009 19:02:17     58 m.c -/-rw-r--r-- 1000        1000      3694664
/home/user/.gedit-save-PDO8UU (deleted-realloc)
                             58 m.c -/-rw-r--r-- 1000        1000      3694664  /home/user/new file
                              0 ..c -/-rw-r--r-- 1000        1000      3695653  /home/user/new file~
Sat May 30 2009 19:02:18   4096 m.c d/drwx------ 1000        1000      3694649  /home/user/.nautilus/metafiles
                            215 mac -/-rw------- 1000        1000      3695031  /home/user/.gconfd/saved_state.orig
(deleted-realloc)
                            215 mac -/-rw------- 1000        1000      3695031
/home/user/.nautilus/metafiles/file:///home/user.xml
                            215 mac -/-rw------- 1000        1000      3695031
/home/user/.nautilus/metafiles/file:///home/user.xmlDHPsbV (deleted-realloc)
Sat May 30 2009 19:02:21   7450 m.c -/-rw-r--r-- 1000        1000      3694774  /home/user/.gnome2/accelsgedit
                            553 m.c -/-rw-r--r-- 1000        1000      3695023  /home/user/.gnome2/gedit-metadata.xml
                          18516 m.c -/-rw-r--r-- 1000        1000      3695654  /home/user/.recently-used.xbel
                          18516 m.c -/-rw-r--r-- 1000        1000      3695654  /home/user/.recently-used.xbel.33P1UU
(deleted-realloc)
                             75 mac -/-rw-r--r-- 1000        1000      3695655  /home/user/.gnome2/gedit-2
                             75 mac -/-rw-r--r-- 1000        1000      3695655  /home/user/.gnome2/gedit-2.HET1UU
(deleted-realloc)
Sat May 30 2009 19:02:25  18516 .a. -/-rw-r--r-- 1000        1000      3695654  /home/user/.recently-used.xbel
                          18516 .a. -/-rw-r--r-- 1000        1000      3695654 /home/user/.recently-used.xbel.33P1UU
(deleted-realloc)
Sat May 30 2009 19:02:29     58 .a. -/-rw-r--r-- 1000        1000      3694664/home/user/.gedit-save-PDO8UU (deleted-
realloc)
                             58 .a. -/-rw-r--r-- 1000        1000      3694664/home/user/new file
```

(Carrier, B. (2005). *File system forensic analysis*. Addison-Wesley Professional.)

## Root Directory

The primary data structures that make up ext2/ext3 are simply data streams with a defined format. The following example of an ext2 formatted floppy disk is provided to demonstrate the simplicity of these structures and their relationships. A forensic duplicate of this floppy disk is available at www.disclosedigital .com/DiscloseDigital/Digital_Evidence_files/ext2-floppy-02132004.zip.

The root directory's inode is always inode 2 and is shown here in WinHex:

```
Offset          0  1  2  3  4  5  6  7     8  9  A  B  C  D  E  F

00007000       02 00 00 00 0C 00 01 02    2E 00 00 00 02 00 00 00       ................
00007010       0C 00 02 02 2E 2E 00 00    0B 00 00 00 14 00 0A 02       ................
00007020       6C 6F 73 74 2B 66 6F 75    6E 64 00 00 0C 00 00 00       lost+found.....
00007030       14 00 0A 02 64 69 72 65    63 74 6F 72 79 31 00 00       ...directory1..
00007040       0E 00 00 00 14 00 09 01    69 6E 64 65 78 2E 64 61       .......index.da
00007050       74 00 00 00 15 00 00 00    20 00 05 01 66 69 6C 65       t.........file
00007060       33 70 00 00 00 00 00 00    10 00 05 01 66 69 6C 65       3p.........file
00007070       32 32 2E 73 11 00 00 00    24 00 05 01 66 69 6C 65       22.s....s...file
00007080       34 34 2E 73 00 00 00 00    14 00 0A 01 68 61 6E 64       44.s.......hand
00007090       6C 65 2E 70 64 66 00 00    13 00 00 00 68 03 0C 01       le.pdf......h...
000070A0       44 43 50 5F 31 37 32 32    2E 4A 50 47 00 00 00 00       DCP_1722.JPG....
000070B0       54 03 0A 01 2E 66 69 6C    65 33 2E 73 77 70 00 00       T....file3.swp..
000070C0       00 00 00 00 40 03 0B 01    2E 66 69 6C 65 33 2E 73       ...@...file3.s
000070D0       77 70 78 00 00 00 00 00    00 00 00 00 00 00 00 00       wpx................
```

Using the following format, we can translate these directory entries.

| bytes | Directory Entry |
|-------|-----------------|
| **4** | **Inode number** |
| 2 | This directory entry's length |
| 1 | File name length in bytes |
| 1 | File type (1=regular file 2=directory) |
| **x** | **File name** |

The root directory translated into the following, where unknown metadata associated with deleted files are indicated with a question mark.

| Inode | Entry length | Name length | TypE | Name |
|-------|--------------|-------------|------|------|
| 11 | 20 bytes | 10 bytes | dir | lost+found |
| 12 | 20 bytes | 10 bytes | dir | directory1 |
| 14 | 20 bytes | 9 bytes | file | index.dat |
| 21 | 32 bytes | 5 bytes | file | file3 |
| ? | ? | 5 bytes | file | file2 |
| 17 | 36 bytes | 5 bytes | file | file4 |
| ? | ? | 10 bytes | file | handle.pdf |
| 19 | 872 bytes | 12 bytes | file | DCP_1722.JPG |
| ? | ? | 10 bytes | file | .file3.swp |
| ? | ? | 11 bytes | file | .file3.swpx |

This information, and the contents of subdirectories, can be extracted from a forensic duplicate with TSK using "fls -f linux-ext2 -r -p -u ext2-floppy-021304.dd" (the –r option recurses through folders and –p provides full path names). Although knowing just the filename may be useful in some investigations, having just filenames without their associated metadata is generally of limited value.

## Locating File Metadata and Content

To determine important details about the file, including where the content of a file is stored, first we must get information about the overall structure of the disk from the superblock. This structure is located after the boot block, 1024 bytes from the beginning of the disk (offset 1024 = 400 hex).

The superblock is a dense structure with many fields and looks like this in raw form:

```
Offset          0  1  2  3  4  5  6  7    8  9  A  B  C  D  E  F
00000400        B8 00 00 00 A0 05 00 00   48 00 00 00 F5 01 00 00    ... ...  H...õ...
00000410        A5 00 00 00 01 00 00 00   00 00 00 00 00 00 00 00    ¥................
00000420        00 20 00 00 00 20 00 00   B8 00 00 00 B6 5E 2C 40    . ... ...¶^,@
00000430        B6 5F 2C 40 05 00 1A 00   53 EF 01 00 01 00 00 00    ¶_,@....Sï... ...
00000440        47 CE 26 40 00 4E ED 00   00 00 00 00 01 00 00 00    GÎ&@.Ní.........
00000450        00 00 00 00 0B 00 00 00   80 00 00 00 00 00 00 00    .........€.........
00000460        02 00 00 00 01 00 00 00   65 7E FD E6 C4 DF 41 2F    ......e~ýæÄßA/
00000470        AE 5D A8 88 70 E0 0F DF   00 00 00 00 00 00 00 00    ®]¨^pà.ß.........
```

The values in this data can be interpreted using the defined format of the superblock.

The format of the ext2 superblock is as follows:

| Bytes | Meaning | Value |
|---|---|---|
| 4 | Total number of inodes | 000000B8 = 184 |
| 4 | Filesystem size in blocks | 000005A0 = 1440 |
| 4 | Number of reserved blocks | 00000048 = 72 |
| 4 | Free blocks counter | 000001F5 = 501 |
| 4 | Free inodes counter | 000000A5 = 165 |
| 4 | Number of first useful block (always 1) | |
| 4 | Block size (as a power of 2, using 1024 bytes as the unit) | |
| 4 | Fragment size | |
| 4 | Number of blocks per group | 2000 = 8192 |
| 4 | Number of fragments per group | 2000 = 8192 |
| 4 | Number of inodes per group | 000000B8 = 184 |
| 4 | Time of last mount operation | B65E2C40=Feb 13 2004 05:20:54 GMT |
| 4 | Time of last write operation | B65F2C40=Feb 13 2004 05:25:10 GMT |
| 2 | Mount operations counter | 05=5 |
| 2 | # mount operations before check | 1A |
| 2 | Magic signature | 53EF |
| 2 | Status flag | 01 |

| Bytes | Meaning | Value |
|---|---|---|
| 2 | Behavior when detecting errors | 01 |
| 2 | Minor revision level | 00 |
| 4 | Time of last check | 47CE2640=Feb 9 2004 00:03:19 GMT |
| 4 | Time between checks | ED4E00=15552000 |
| 4 | OS where filesystem was created | 00 |
| 4 | Revision level | 01 |
| 2 | Default user ID for reserved blocks | 00 |
| 2 | Default group ID for reserved blocks | 00 |
| 4 | Number of first nonreserved inode | 0B=11 |
| 2 | Size of on-disk inode structure | 80=128 bytes |
| 2 | Block group number of this superblock | |
| 4 | Compatible features bitmap | |
| 4 | Incompatible features bitmap | |
| 4 | Read-only-compatible features bitmap | |
| 16 | 128-bit filesystem identifier | |
| 16 | Volume name | |
| 64 | Path of last mount point | |
| 4 | Used for compression | |
| 1 | Number of blocks to preallocate | |
| 1 | Number of blocks to preallocate for directories | |
| 818 | Nulls to pad out 1024 bytes | |

To facilitate the interpretation process, X-Ways has an ext2 superblock template that can be applied to the preceding data as shown in Figure 6.3.

Immediately following the superblock is the first Group Descriptor structure that contains the location of the inode table (there is only one group on a floppy disk).

```
Offset            0 1 2 3 4 5 6 7    8 9 A B C D E F
00000800          03 00 00 00 04 00 00 00    05 00 00 00 F5 01 A5 00      ........õ.¥.
00000810          03 00 00 00 00 00 00 00    00 00 00 00 00 00 00 00      ...........
```

The format of the group descriptor is as follows, and can also be viewed using the ext2 Group Descriptor template in X-Ways.

| Bytes | Meaning | Value |
|---|---|---|
| 4 | Block number of block bitmap | 000003 |
| 4 | Block number of inode bitmap | 000004 |
| 4 | Block number of first inode table block | 000005 |
| 2 | Number of free blocks in the group | 01F5=501 |
| 2 | Number of free inodes in the group | 00A5=165 |
| 2 | Number of directories in the group | 0003 |
| 2 | Alignment to word | 0000 |
| 4 | Nulls to pad out 24 bytes | 00000000 |

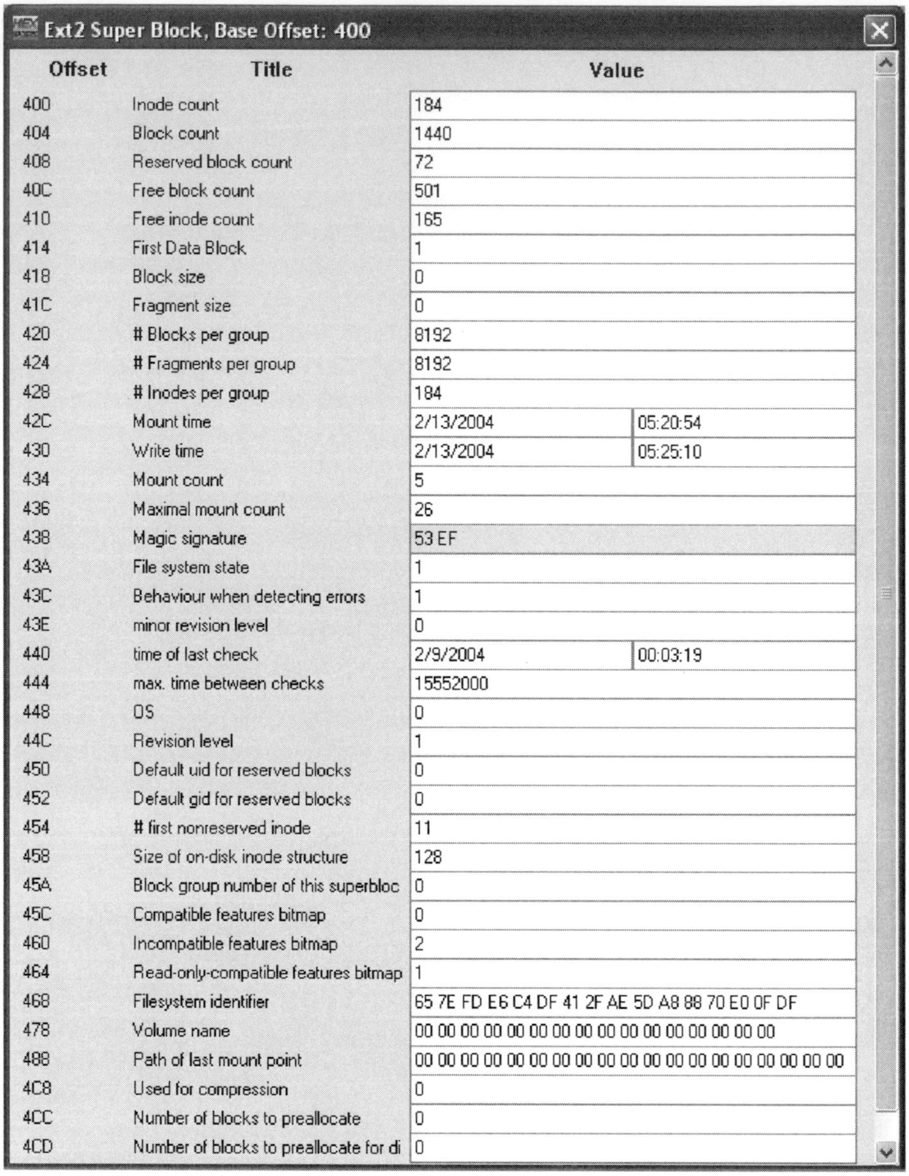

**FIGURE 6.3**

Superblock viewed through
X-Ways template.

**FIGURE 6.3**

Superblock viewed through X-Ways template.

| Offset | Title | Value | |
|--------|-------|-------|---|
| 400 | Inode count | 184 | |
| 404 | Block count | 1440 | |
| 408 | Reserved block count | 72 | |
| 40C | Free block count | 501 | |
| 410 | Free inode count | 165 | |
| 414 | First Data Block | 1 | |
| 418 | Block size | 0 | |
| 41C | Fragment size | 0 | |
| 420 | # Blocks per group | 8192 | |
| 424 | # Fragments per group | 8192 | |
| 428 | # Inodes per group | 184 | |
| 42C | Mount time | 2/13/2004 | 05:20:54 |
| 430 | Write time | 2/13/2004 | 05:25:10 |
| 434 | Mount count | 5 | |
| 436 | Maximal mount count | 26 | |
| 438 | Magic signature | 53 EF | |
| 43A | File system state | 1 | |
| 43C | Behaviour when detecting errors | 1 | |
| 43E | minor revision level | 0 | |
| 440 | time of last check | 2/9/2004 | 00:03:19 |
| 444 | max. time between checks | 15552000 | |
| 448 | OS | 0 | |
| 44C | Revision level | 1 | |
| 450 | Default uid for reserved blocks | 0 | |
| 452 | Default gid for reserved blocks | 0 | |
| 454 | # first nonreserved inode | 11 | |
| 458 | Size of on-disk inode structure | 128 | |
| 45A | Block group number of this superbloc | 0 | |
| 45C | Compatible features bitmap | 0 | |
| 460 | Incompatible features bitmap | 2 | |
| 464 | Read-only-compatible features bitmap | 1 | |
| 468 | Filesystem identifier | 65 7E FD E6 C4 DF 41 2F AE 5D A8 88 70 E0 0F DF | |
| 478 | Volume name | 00 00 00 00 00 00 00 00 00 00 00 00 00 00 00 00 | |
| 488 | Path of last mount point | 00 00 00 00 00 00 00 00 00 00 00 00 00 00 00 00 00 00 00 00 | |
| 4C8 | Used for compression | 0 | |
| 4CC | Number of blocks to preallocate | 0 | |
| 4CD | Number of blocks to preallocate for di | 0 | |

Some of this information can be obtained with TSK using `fsstat -f ext2-floppy-021304.dd`.

This tells us that the inode table is located in block 5, and we know from the superblock that each block is 1024 bytes (offset 5120 = 1400 hex). In raw form, the beginning of the inode table looks like this:

```
Offset          0  1  2  3  4  5  6      7  8  9  A  B  C  D  E  F
00001400       00 00 00 00 00 00 00     00 49 CE 26 40 49 CE 26 40    .....IÎ&@IÎ&@
00001410       49 CE 26 40 00 00 00     00 00 00 00 00 00 00 00 00    IÎ&@..........
00001420       00 00 00 00 00 00 00     00 00 00 00 00 00 00 00 00    ..............
00001430       00 00 00 00 00 00 00     00 00 00 00 00 00 00 00 00    ..............
00001440       00 00 00 00 00 00 00     00 00 00 00 00 00 00 00 00    ..............
00001450       00 00 00 00 00 00 00     00 00 00 00 00 00 00 00 00    ..............
00001460       00 00 00 00 00 00 00     00 00 00 00 00 00 00 00 00    ..............
00001470       00 00 00 00 00 00 00     00 00 00 00 00 00 00 00 00    ..............
00001480       ED 41 00 00 00 04 00     00 77 5F 2C 40 AA 5F 2C 40    íA...w_,@ª_,@
00001490       AA 5F 2C 40 00 00 00     00 00 00 04 00 02 00 00 00    ª_,@..........
```

The format of inodes is as follows:

| bytes | value |
|---|---|
| 2 | File type and access rights |
| 2 | Owner identification |
| 4 | File size in bytes |
| 4 | file last accessed time |
| 4 | inode last changed time |
| 4 | file last modified |
| 4 | file deletion time |
| 2 | Group identifier |
| 2 | Hard links counter |
| 4 | Number of data blocks of the file |
| 4 | File flags |
| 4 | Operating system specific |
| 4 | Pointer to first data block |
| 56 | 14 more pointers to data blocks |
| 4 | File version (for NFS) |
| 4 | File access control list |
| 4 | Directory access control list |
| 4 | Fragment address |
| 8 | Operating system specific |

Applying the X-Ways ext2 inode template enables us to view this information in a more readable form as shown for inode 11 in Figure 6.4.

The metadata associated with individual files on a forensic duplicate can be displayed with TSK using the istat command (e.g., istat -f linux-ext2 ext2-floppy-021304.dd 11).

Using this information, such as filenames and block numbers, you can locate and extract the active files on this disk. For example, the entry in the root

**FIGURE 6.4**

Inode viewed through X-Ways template.

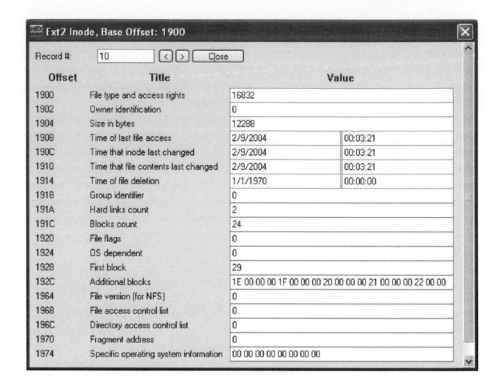

directory tells us that the text file named file3 is associated with inode 21, which in turn tells us that it starts at block 1034 and is 61 bytes in length. Going to offset 102800 (1034 blocks x 1024 bytes/block = 1058816 = 102800 hex) brings us to the start of the file as shown here:

```
Offset     0  1  2  3  4  5  6  7   8  9  A  B  C  D  E  F

00102800   54 68 69 73 20 66 69 6C  65 20 77 61 73 20 63 72   This file was cr
00102810   65 61 74 65 64 20 61 74  20 61 72 6F 75 6E 64 20   eated at around
00102820   30 30 3A 32 33 20 6F 6E  20 46 72 69 64 61 79 2C   00:23 on Friday,
00102830   20
```

## Useful Features of UNIX File Systems

When performing a forensic analysis of Unix file systems, there are features that should be inspected beyond just the file date-time stamps. As shown in Figure 6.3, the last time a Unix file system was mounted is recorded, which should be consistent with other activities on the system.

File permissions can also be revealing in a case, enabling digital investigators to determine which user account was used to create a particular file, or which group of users had access to data of concern.

Because Unix systems break portions into the disk into block groups, data of similar types are often stored in the same area of the disk, facilitating more efficient and focused searching for deleted data. For instance, efforts to recover deleted logs can focus on the /var/logs partition.

Unix systems in an Enterprise are often configured with some remote storage locations, which can be seen in /etc/fstab as shown here:

```
/dev/hda1           /                   ext2        defaults            1 1
/dev/hda7           /tmp                ext2        defaults            1 2
/dev/hda5           /usr                ext2        defaults            1 2
/dev/hda6           /var                ext2        defaults            1 2
/dev/hda8           swap                swap        defaults            0 0
/dev/fd0            /mnt/floppy         ext2        user,noauto         0 0
/dev/hdc            /mnt/cdrom          iso9660     user,noauto,ro      0 0
none                /dev/pts            devpts      gid=5,mode=620      0 0
none                /proc               proc        defaults            0 0
remote-server:/home/accts              /home/accts             nfs
bg,hard,intr,rsize=8192,wsize=8192
remote-server:/var/spool/mail          /var/spool/mail nfs
bg,hard,intr,noac,rsize=8192,wsize=8192
```

In this instance, all files in user home directories are stored on a remote server named remote-server along with spooled e-mail. Therefore, preserving just the hard drive of the single system would not preserve all potentially relevant files associated with the use of that system. It would also be necessary to preserve files stored on the remote server.

## Deleting and Recovering Data

When a file is deleted, its inode link count is set to zero, the directory entry is removed (and may be added as slack to a previous entry). In addition, the inode table is updated to show that the inode is no longer in use, and the block bitmap is updated to release blocks. In some versions of Linux file systems, the inode reference is set to zero and an additional deleted date stamp is updated. This process allows forensic examiners to recover deleted filenames and deleted inodes (and the associated data on disk) but makes it difficult to associate deleted filenames with deleted inodes.

The most effective strategy to recover deleted data is to examine deleted inodes, which are listed in the inode tables. Although the deleted inode does not contain a filename, it does provide useful metadata including dates, attributes, and location of data on disk. For smaller files, the inode contains a list of the actual blocks that contains data from the deleted file. The inode for larger files reference indirect blocks, which are simply lists of the actually allocated blocks.

Deleted files can be listed with TSK using fls with the -d option (deleted) as shown here for the same floppy disk used in previous examples:

```
% fls -f linux-ext2 -r -p -d ext2-floppy-021304.dd
r/- * 0:     file2
r/- * 0:     handle.pdf
r/- * 0:     .file3.swp
r/- * 0.     .file3.swpx
```

There is no date-time information associated with these files because we do not know with which inode they were associated. Older versions of the ext2 file system did not zero out the inode numbers making it easier to associate a deleted filename with its associated inode. Because the inode is not available in newer versions of ext2, the `fls` output does not give us much information, so let us look at the associated inodes in more detail using `ils`.

```
% ils -f linux-ext2 ext2-floppy-021304.dd
class|host|device|start_time
ils|raven|ext2-floppy-130204.dd|1077912300
st_ino|st_alloc|st_uid|st_gid|st_mtime|st_atime|st_ctime|st_dtime|
   st_mode|st_nlink|st_size|st_block0|st_block1
1|a|0|0|1076285001|1076285001|1076285001|0|0|0|0|0|0
15|f|0|0|1076285446|1076285446|1076649861|1076649861|100644|0|47|58|0
18|f|500|500|1076648869|1076648869|1076649898|1076649898|100664|0|80117|
   626|627
```

How do we associate the filenames with the appropriate inodes? We compare the metadata in each inode with metadata associated with each file to determine links. The preceding results show us that inode 15 referred to a 47-byte file and inode 18 referred to a 80117-byte file (in bold). By extracting the contents of inodes 15 and 18 using `icat` and determining what type of data they contain, we can make an educated guess about at least one of the files.

```
% icat -f linux-ext2 ext2-floppy-021304.dd 15 > unknown-file-inode15
% file unknown-file-inode15
unknown-file-inode15: ASCII text
% cat unknown-file-inode15
This file was created on Feb 8 at around 19:10
```

Note that cat is a standard UNIX command that is used to concatenate and print files, whereas `icat` is part of TSK and is used to print inodes.

```
% icat -f linux-ext2 ext2-floppy-021304.dd 18 > unknown-file-inode18
% md5sum unknown-file-inode18
MD5(unknown-file-inode18)= 490ab7557538a4c4b5d6f75ce51384ff
% file unknown-file-inode18
unknown-file-inode18: PDF document, version 1.2
% ls -l
-rw-r--r-- 1 user wheel        47 Feb 27 15:19 unknown-file-inode15
-rw-r--r-- 1 user wheel     80117 Feb 27 15:17 unknown-file-inode18
```

Ordering the date-time stamps of unallocated inodes using the `mactime` utility combined with the `ils -m` option, we can see when the inodes were last modified, last accessed, and deleted.

```
% ils -f linux-ext2 -m ext2-floppy-021304.dd | mactime
Feb 08 2004 19:03       0 mac ----------    0      0    1     <alive-1>
Feb 08 2004 19:10      47 ma. -rw-r--r--    0      0   15     <dead-15>
Feb 08 2004 00:07   80117 ma. -rw-rw-r--  500    500   18     <dead-18>
Feb 08 2004 00:24      47 ..c -rw-r--r--    0      0   15     <dead-15>
Feb 08 2004 00:24   80117 ..c -rw-rw-r--  500    500   18     <dead-18>
```

The only item with activity around 19:10 on Feb 8 is inode 15, indicating that it was named file2.

Another useful phenomenon on Unix file systems from a forensic perspective is the persistence of deleted inodes. When a file is deleted, the corresponding inode will retain some metadata associated with the file until the inode is reused. Therefore, deleting a file effectively freezes its metadata until that inode is overwritten by a new file, which may not occur for months or longer (Farmer & Venema, 2005). When large numbers of files are created and deleted, such as when an intruder installed malicious code on a compromised system, these traces can remain in the inode table for a long time.

## PRACTITIONER'S TIP: LOST FILES

When a file system is damaged on a Unix-like system, an automated process may place recovered files in a directory named `lost+found` at the root of the damaged volume. The contents of files within these `lost+found` directories may be of interest in a forensic examination, but it may be difficult to determine where they were originally located on the system. Confusingly, EnCase places a list of recoverable deleted files in an area called `Lost Files` within the user interface of the forensic tool (see Figure 6.6b later in this chapter). There is no relation between the `lost+found` directory on a Unix system and the `Lost Files` area in EnCase.

## Out-of-Place Inodes

In findings first described in *Forensic Discovery* by Farmer and Venema (2005), the authors made the discovery that inodes are typically allocated in fairly linear fashion, and that wildly outlying inodes may be used to find replaced binaries, and trace them back to their original creation location. You can list the inode number of a file using the –i flag to `ls` as demonstrated here:

```
[root@localhost /bin]# ls -fli
...
1278043 -rwxr-xr-x 1 root root     61 2007-08-28 20:43 gunzip
1278002 -rwxr-xr-x 1 root root   7316 2007-10-04 22:45 dbus-uuidgen
1277976 -rwxr-xr-x 1 root root  18476 2007-10-30 12:52 env
1278058 -rwxr-xr-x 1 root root  53036 2007-10-30 12:52 chown
```

```
164019   -rwxr-xr-x 1 root root 99564 2007-10-30 12:52 ls
1277988  -rwxr-xr-x 1 root root 19200 2007-10-30 12:52 basename
1278034  -rwxr-xr-x 1 root root 19804 2007-10-29 03:41 alsaunmute
1278027  -rwxr-xr-x 1 root root 52044 2007-10-05 11:15 sed
1278030  -rwxr-xr-x 1 root root 84780 2007-10-17 06:30 loadkeys
```

Note that the `ls` binary's inode number is not in the same range as the other items in the "`/bin`" directory. Where did it come from? Searching for other files with similar inodes reveals the answer as shown:

```
find / -xdev -print | xargs ls -id | sort -n
164017 /tmp/toolkit.tgz
164018 /tmp/.toolkit/eraser.tar
164019 /bin/ls
164020 /tmp/toolkit/.chroot
...
```

We can be pretty certain at this point that ls wasn't modified as part of a standard system update.

## USER ACCOUNTS

The "`/etc/passwd`" file contains a list of users and the full path of the associated home directories. The passwords for user accounts are generally stored in "`/etc/shadow`" (provided a centralized authentication mechanism is not in use).

A typical entry in the "`/etc/passwd`" file is shown here with a description of each field:

```
user:x:500:500::/home/user:/bin/bash
```

1. username
2. Hashed password field (deprecated in favor of "`/etc/shadow`")
3. User ID (UID)
4. *primary* group ID (GID)—note that a user can belong to any number of groups. This information is stored in "`/etc/group`."
5. GECOS comment field, generally used for a full username or a more descriptive name for a daemon account
6. User's home directory
7. Shell/program to run upon initial login

The "`/etc/passwd`" file will usually be fairly lengthy even on a single user system. An old trick that is still occasionally seen in the wild is to add an additional UID 0* user somewhere in the middle of these default accounts—an attempt to fade into the noise. (Note that any user with UID 0 is the functional equivalent of root.)

The "/etc/group" file has a somewhat similar format, with fewer fields. A typical selection of entries will look like the following:

```
root:x:0:root
bin:x:1:root,bin,daemon
daemon:x:2:root,bin,daemon
wheel:x:10:root
```

The first field is the group name, second is the hash of the group password (password protected groups are not typically used), the third is the GID, and the fourth is a comma-separated list of the members of the group. Additional unauthorized users in the root or wheel groups are suspicious and warrant further investigation.

The /etc/shadow file is the final piece of the authentication puzzle. It stores encrypted user passwords and related information.

```
root:id="10330"$gsGAI2/j$jWMnLcOzHFtlBDveRqw3i/:13977:0:99999:
  7:::
bin:*:13826:0:99999:7:::
...
gdm:!!:13826:0:99999:7:::
user:id="10330"$xSS1eCUL$jrGLlZPGmD7ia61kIdrTV.:13978:0:99999:7:::
```

Again, the fields are as follows:

1. Username
2. Encrypted password
3. Number of days since the epoch (1 Jan 1970) that the password was last changed
4. Minimum days between password changes
5. Maximum time password is valid
6. Number of days prior to expiration to warn users
7. Absolute expiration date
8. Reserved for future use

One item to note is that the daemon accounts bin and gdm don't have an encrypted password. Since these are not user accounts they have a null or invalid password field to prevent them from being used for an interactive login. Any non-user accounts that *do* have encrypted password fields should be investigated.

The root user is all-powerful on a standard Linux system. As such, gaining access to this user's privileges is usually of paramount importance to an intruder. For this and other reasons, access to root is usually strictly controlled. Unfortunately, some users may require root privileges to run certain programs or perform specific tasks beyond the capabilities of a normal user. The two interactive methods are via the su and sudo commands.

The su command requires that the user knows the root password—the user is literally logging in as root from within their current session. Nothing is to stop the user from logging in directly as root in the future. In a shared-root password environment, you have no accountability in the event that the root user does something disastrous, malicious or not. This problem is solved by sudo, which allows for fairly fine-grained distribution of root powers to non-root users. This is controlled by the "/etc/sudoers" file. You should examine this file for spurious or otherwise unauthorized entries or modifications if the particulars of your investigation indicate that an existing user was operating beyond their authority.

Even when a user account is deleted from a Unix system, the home directory can be left behind. Therefore, it can be fruitful to look in the "/home" directory for user data.

## SYSTEM CONFIGURATION

Unix does not have the equivalent of a Registry in Microsoft Windows. Instead, Unix systems use configuration files that are generally text-based. Although this transparency has the potential of making forensic examinations more straightforward, reducing the need to interpret data stored in proprietary formats, it is necessary to understand what information these configuration files contain.

### Scheduled Tasks

There are two methods of scheduling a command to be executed automatically at a preset time: at and cron. The cron process is the main method for scheduling a task to run at some point (or points!) in the future on a Linux system. Intruders may create a cron job on a compromised system to periodically launch a backdoor or beacon to enable them to regain entry.

There are two primary locations where cron will look for jobs to process: "/var/spool/cron," which will contain the user IDs of any users who have entered cron jobs using the crontab command, and "/etc/crontab", which will list additional locations for systemwide cron jobs. Generally these are found in the directories "/etc/cron.hourly," "/etc/cron.daily," "/etc/cron.weekly," and "/etc/cron.monthly."

These locations (and any others referenced in /etc/crontab) should be examined for unauthorized jobs. This is an old but still extremely popular and effective way to maintain access on a compromised Unix system.

The at command provides similar functionality to cron and creates job files in "/var/spool/cron."

# ARTIFACTS OF USER ACTIVITIES

When conducting a forensic examination of a computer system, it is often necessary to determine how a specific user accessed the system and what that user did. Unlike Microsoft Windows with its wide array of artifacts of system usage, Unix systems record relatively little information beyond some common log files.

Unix systems can keep extensive logs of the activities of individuals within the system. The degree of detail in these logs varies depending on the configuration of the machine, but all Unix systems have some basic logs described here.

## Logging onto (and off of) a System

When a user logs into a Unix system, they may be presented with information about the previous logon to that account, which is stored in the `lastlog` file. At that point, the `lastlog` and `utmp` files are updated with information about current logon session, including the time and host name. The `utmp` file contains information about active login sessions that can be displayed using the `who` or `w` command. The same information that is entered in the `utmp` file is appended to the `wtmp` log file, which is a simple user logon/logoff database common on most forms of Unix, including Mac OS X. The difference between these two files is that `utmp` entries are cleared when the user logs off, whereas the entries in `wtmp` are retained indefinitely.

On Unix systems, the default locations are "`/var/run/utmp`" and "`/var/log/wtmp`". Each entry in the `wtmp` database includes the user login name, device name, and host name, if remote. In addition, the `wtmp` database will generally have the time of logon and logoff, which can be helpful when trying to determine which user accounts were connected to the system at the time of interest.

The `last` command is used to query the `wtmp` database to determine who logged into a system and when they logged out. However, as can be seen in the first line of Table 6.1, the last command on most systems truncates the host

**Table 6.1** Unix `wtmp` Logs Viewed Using the Last Command

| oisin% last | | | |
|---|---|---|---|
| usera | pts/1 | s-pc1.bigscom.co | Sat Nov 11 11:08 - 11:08 (00:00) |
| usera | pts/1 | 192.168.1.100 | Sat Nov 11 11:03 - 11:04 (00:00) |
| usera | console | | Sat Nov 11 10:55 - 11:14 (00:18) |
| reboot | system boot | | Sat Nov 11 10:54 |
| usera | pts/5 | 192.168.1.110 | Fri Sep 8 19:24 - 00:07 (04:43) |
| usera | ftp | 192.168.1.110 | Fri Sep 8 19:13 - 19:13 (00:00) |
| usera | pts/4 | 192.168.1.110 | Fri Sep 8 19:12 - 00:07 (04:55) |
| usera | console | | Fri Sep 8 19:03 - 19:35 (00:32) |

**FIGURE 6.5**

Entries in a Unix wtmp database viewed using EnCase.

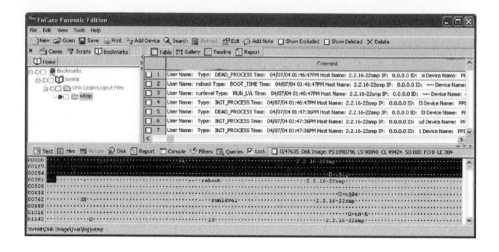

name, making it necessary to use a customized version of last to process the wtmp file or obtain the host name from somewhere else.

The wtmp database can also be parsed using an EnScript as shown in Figure 6.5.

There are a number of potential problems to be aware of when it comes to these logon records. Not all programs make an entry in wtmp in all cases. For instance, sshd does not make an entry in wtmp when someone connects using scp or using the port forwarding feature of SSH. Also, because different systems have slightly different wtmp formats (as defined in the system's "/usr/include/utmp.h" include file), programmers sometimes create programs that create improperly formatted entries in the wtmp database. For instance, some versions of MIT's Kerberized Telnet daemon create logout entries with the same time as the corresponding logon entry, causing sessions to be displayed as 0 minutes long. Additionally, the wtmp database can be corrupted by an incomplete write, making it necessary to analyze each log entry carefully using customized programs (Blank-Edelman, 2000).

## Syslog

Unix also maintains system logs (a.k.a. syslog) that can either be stored locally or sent to a remote system. These logs show incoming connections to servers and outgoing connections to WiFi. The following log entries show a Linux computer connecting to a WiFi Access Point named AWPERUCES.

```
Oct 29 23:02:41 twinklingstar NetworkManager: <info> Will activate
  connection 'eth1/AWPERUCES'.
<cut for brevity>
```

```
Oct 29 23:02:41 twinklingstar NetworkManager: <info> Activation (eth1)
  New wireless user key for network 'AWPERUCES' received.
Oct 29 23:02:41 twinklingstar NetworkManager: <info> Activation (eth1)
  Stage 1 of 5 (Device Prepare) scheduled...
Oct 29 23:02:41 twinklingstar NetworkManager: <info> Activation (eth1)
  Stage 1 of 5 (Device Prepare) started...
Oct 29 23:02:41 twinklingstar NetworkManager: <info> Activation (eth1)
  Stage 2 of 5 (Device Configure) scheduled...
Oct 29 23:02:41 twinklingstar NetworkManager: <info> Activation (eth1)
  Stage 1 of 5 (Device Prepare) complete.
Oct 29 23:02:41 twinklingstar NetworkManager: <info> Activation (eth1)
  Stage 2 of 5 (Device Configure) starting...
Oct 29 23:02:41 twinklingstar NetworkManager: <info> Activation (eth1/
  wireless): access point 'AWPERUCES' is encrypted, and a key exists.
  No new key needed.
```

Unix systems can be configured to send syslog entries to a remote system by adding the following line to /etc/syslog.conf configuration file:

```
*.*     @remote-server
```

## FROM THE CASE FILES: RECOVERING DELETED SYSLOGS

Figure 6.6 shows the buffer overflow attack against a Linux server using two forensic analysis tools. The Sleuth Kit (TSK) has strong support for examining Unix file systems and was able to recover the name of the deleted log file as shown in Figure 6.6(a). Although EnCase recovered the deleted log file as shown in Figure 6.6(b), it was not able to recover the file name.

**FIGURE 6.6A**

Entries in a deleted log file on a compromised Unix system showing a buffer overflow attack viewed using TSK.

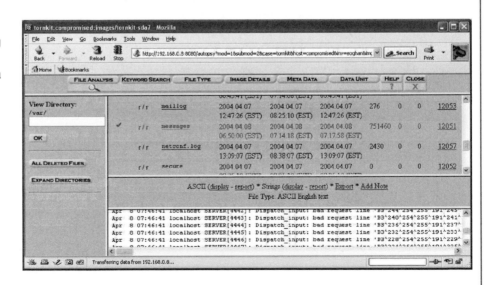

*(Continued)*

## FROM THE CASE FILES: RECOVERING DELETED SYSLOGS—CONT'D

**FIGURE 6.6B**

Entries in a deleted log file on a compromised Unix system showing a buffer overflow attack viewed using EnCase.

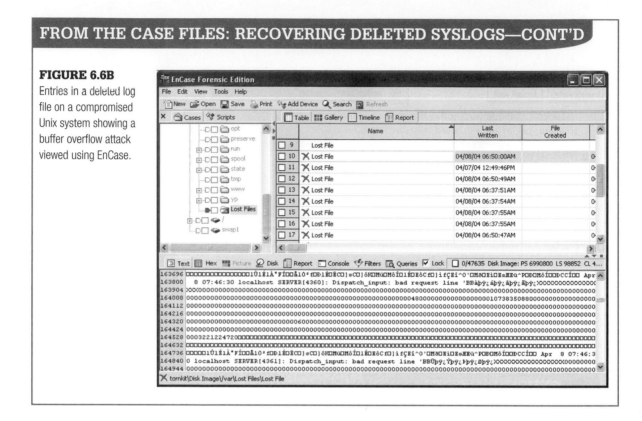

Notably, syslog uses an unreliable mechanism to send information to a central logging host, since it relies on the connectionless UDP protocol. In other words, a computer sends its log entries over the network to the syslog server on a remote computer but has no way of determining if the log entries reach their destination. If the syslog server is fortunate enough to receive the log entry, syslog timestamps the log entry with the date and time of the syslog server, not the sending host. Therefore, even if the clock on the sending host is accurate, the syslog server can introduce a time discrepancy. Also, the syslog server has no way of confirming the origin of a given log entry. So, it is possible to forge a log entry and send it to the syslog server, giving the false impression that a certain event occurred on a certain computer.

### Command History

A command history file is maintained for each user account on a Unix system, and contains recent commands executed under that account. The name of the command history files depends on the shell being used. It is most common to find .bash_history files in user home directories on a Linux system, and .history or .sh_history files on other Unix systems.

Command history files can be very useful for determining what a user or intruder did on a Unix system. The sample command history in Figure 6.7 shows the use of a secure deletion program (srm) to destroy the contents of a file named trade-secrets.tar.gz and a related folder.

Observe in Figure 6.7 that the command history does not show the date that each command executed. However, by examining the last accessed dates of files referenced in a command history file, it may be possible to determine when some of the activities occurred.

```
File  Edit  View  Terminal  Tabs  Help
twinkle@twinklingstar:~$ tail .bash_history
sudo apt-get install secure-delete
ls
srm trade-secrets.tar.gz
ls
srm -rf trade-secrets/
cd
ls
ls Documents/
ls Desktop/
exit
twinkle@twinklingstar:~$ █
```

**FIGURE 6.7**
Command history showing data destruction activities.

---

**FROM THE CASE FILES: INTRUDER ACTIVITIES**

A system administrator found a suspicious file on a Linux server within her organization and reported the problem to us. The file she had found contained the following, which turned out to be a rootkit.

```
% tar tvf aniv.tar
```

| | | | | | | |
|---|---|---|---|---|---|---|
| drwxr-xr-x | 2 | 512 | Mar | 8 | 17:02 | rkb |
| -rw-r--r-- | 1 | 358400 | Mar | 8 | 17:02 | BeroFTPD-1.3.3.tar.gz |
| -rw-r--r-- | 1 | 326 | Mar | 8 | 17:02 | readmeformountd |
| -rw-r--r-- | 1 | 757760 | Mar | 8 | 17:02 | root.tar.gz |
| -rwxr-xr-x | 1 | 8524 | Mar | 8 | 17:02 | slice2 |
| -rw-r--r-- | 1 | 6141 | Mar | 8 | 17:02 | mountd.tgz |
| -rw-r--r-- | 1 | 849920 | Mar | 8 | 17:02 | rkb.tar.gzb |

*(Continued)*

## FROM THE CASE FILES: INTRUDER ACTIVITIES—CONT'D

By the time we reached the location to examine the compromised system, the system administrator had restored the system from backup. As a result, there was limited information available about the intrusion. Fortunately, forensic examination of the system revealed the following command shell history, showing commands executed by the intruder:

```
% more .bash_history
w
pico /etc/passwd
mkdir /lib/.loginrc
cd /lib/.loginrc
/usr/sbin/named
ls
w
ls
/usr/sbin/named
ls
cd ~
```

```
ls
mv aniv.tar.gz /lib/.loginrc
cd /lib/.loginrc
tar zxf aniv.tar.gz
ls
cd aniv
ls
tar zxf rkb.tar.gz
ls
cd rkb
./install
```

Using this information, we were able to find aspects of the compromise that had not been obliterated when the system was restored from backup, including a user account that had been added by the intruder and would have allowed continued unauthorized access. In addition, we were able to look for similar signs of intrusion on other systems within the organization.

## Application Traces/Recently Opened Files

In addition to the earlier records of activities maintained by Unix systems, individual applications generate artifacts of user activities that can be useful in an investigation. Examples of traces that applications leave behind on Unix systems relating to user activities are provided here.

Gnome is the default desktop environment on some versions of Linux (e.g., Ubuntu), and is available for other versions of Linux. Gnome maintains lists of recently opened files in a number of locations, providing digital investigators with information about user account activities. For instance, Gnome maintains a list of recently opened files in a file named .recently-used.xbel in the home directory of each user account. In addition to the full path of the opened files, the entries in .recently-used.xbel contain the date-time stamp the file was opened and the application used to open the file. A sample of entries from this file are provided here.

```
grep "bookmark href" .recently-used.xbel
<bookmark href="file:///home/eoghan/Desktop/PTK_readme.pdf"
  added="2008-04-01T13:43:01Z" modified="2008-04-01T13:43:01Z"
  visited="2008-04-01T14:11:07Z">
<bookmark href="file:///media/MAXTOR160MB/Morgue/tornkit-image/torn
  bin.bmp" added="2008-04-01T14:52:04Z" modified="2008-04-01T14:52:04Z"
  visited="2008-04-01T14:52:11Z">
```

```
<bookmark href="file:///media/disk/Chapter10%20Mobile%20Network%20
  Investigations-20090408.pdf" added="2009-05-22T17:52:01Z"
  modified="2009-05-22T17:52:02Z" visited="2009-05-22T17:52:01Z">
<bookmark href="file:///media/disk/Chapter4-
  IntrusionInvestigation_05122009.doc" added="2009-05-22T18:38:16Z"
  modified="2009-05-22T18:38:16Z" visited="2009-05-22T18:43:25Z">
<bookmark
```

As this example demonstrates, this information can reveal the use of removable media.

Additional information about files that were opened using a particular user account can be found in files under the .gnome2 directory. For instance, the gnome2/gedit-metadata.xml and gnome2/evince/ev-metadata.xml files may contain names of files opened under a specific user account.

Some application like Open Office maintain their own list of recently used files. Figure 6.8 shows entries in a .recently-used file under a specific user account, providing the full path of files that were opened and the associated dates.

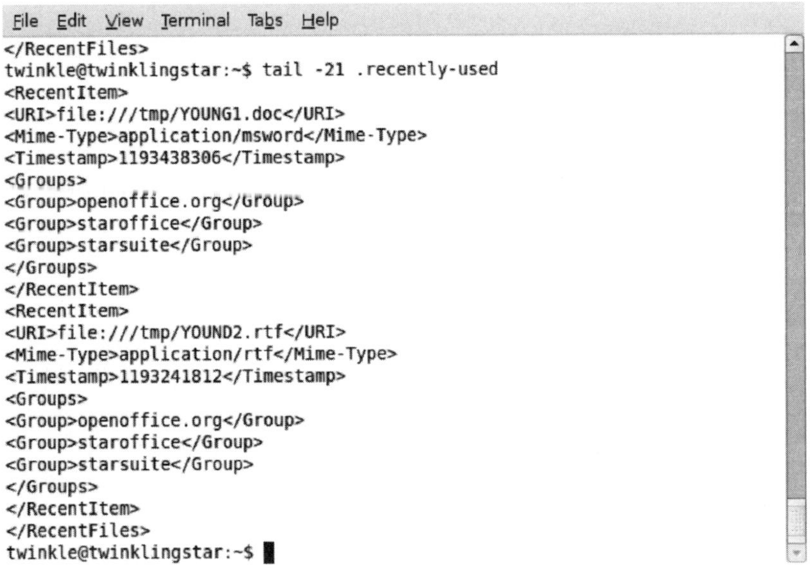

**FIGURE 6.8**
References to files that were opened recently using Open Office.

Similarly, the GIMP graphics viewing and editing program maintains a list of recently opened files in .gimp/documents under each user account as shown in Figure 6.9.

The Wireshark program for capturing network traffic as detailed in Chapter 9, "Network Analysis" maintains a list of recently used files and filters in the .wireshark/recent file under each user directory as shown in Figure 6.10.

Forensic examiners should experiment with the specific programs found on a subject computer to determine whether the application maintains historical

**FIGURE 6.9**

References to files that were opened recently using GIMP.

```
File  Edit  View  Terminal  Tabs  Help
twinkle@twinklingstar:~/.gimp-2.4$ cat documents
# GIMP documents
#
# This file will be entirely rewritten each time you exit.

(document "file:///media/disk/DCP_0551.JPG")
(document "file:///media/disk/DCP_0423.JPG")
(document "file:///media/disk/DCP_0418.JPG")
(document "file:///media/disk/DCP_0400.JPG")
(document "file:///media/disk/DCP_0367.JPG")
(document "file:///media/disk/DCP_0320.JPG")
(document "file:///media/disk/DCP_0314.JPG")
(document "file:///media/disk/DCP_0275.JPG")
(document "file:///media/disk/DSCN1433.JPG")

# end of documents
twinkle@twinklingstar:~/.gimp-2.4$ ls -alt documents
-rw------- 1 twinkle twinkle 505 2007-10-31 23:00 documents
twinkle@twinklingstar:~/.gimp-2.4$ █
```

**FIGURE 6.10**

References to files that were opened recently using Wireshark.

```
File  Edit  View  Terminal  Tabs  Help
twinkle@twinklingstar:~$ head -17 .wireshark/recent
# Recent settings file for Wireshark 0.99.6.
#
# This file is regenerated each time Wireshark is quit.
# So be careful, if you want to make manual changes here.

######## Recent capture files (latest last), cannot be altered through command l
ine ########

recent.capture_file: /media/disk/password-capture.dmp
recent.capture_file: /media/disk/pop-transfer.dmp

######## Recent capture filters (latest last), cannot be altered through command
 line ########

######## Recent display filters (latest last), cannot be altered through command
 line ########

recent.display_filter: (ip.addr eq 192.168.0.5 and ip.addr eq 131.243.1.10) and
(tcp.port eq 32788 and tcp.port eq 21)
recent.display_filter: (ip.addr eq 192.168.0.5 and ip.addr eq 130.132.50.23) and
 (tcp.port eq 32872 and tcp.port eq 110)
twinkle@twinklingstar:~$ █
```

details of usage. The possibilities are limited only by the number of applications that are available. For instance, the Nautilus file manager application can retain some information about files that were in use under a specific user account in the .nautilus directory, and a program called Midnight commander has similar information (see the DFRWS2008 Forensics Challenge at www.dfrws.org).

# Printing

Printing on Unix systems often is handled by the Common Unix Printing Solution (CUPS), which creates printer spool files in `"/var/spool/cups"` by default.

It is also possible to direct print spool files to a remote location by modifying the `"/etc/printcap"` configuration file.

When a file is printed, CUPS creates two files, a control file containing metadata and a data file containing the contents of the printed file in PostScript format. Figure 6.11 shows the contents of the `"/var/spool/cups"` folder on a Linux system, with control files starting with a "c" and data files starting with a "d" (deleted in this case).

The lower panel Figure 6.11 shows a CUPS control file with the username and other attributes associated with the print job. Control files are deleted only periodically (e.g., after 500 print jobs), but data files are deleted immediately after a document is printed.

| | | | | | | | | |
|---|---|---|---|---|---|---|---|---|
| r/r | c00001 | 2009.05.22 12:07:07 (EDT) | 2009.05.22 14:14:44 (EDT) | 2009.05.22 12:07:07 (EDT) | 1174 | 0 | 7 | 801322 |
| r/r | c00002 | 2009.05.22 13:52:26 (EDT) | 2009.05.22 14:14:44 (EDT) | 2009.05.22 13:52:26 (EDT) | 967 | 0 | 7 | 801324 |
| r/r | c00003 | 2009.05.22 14:14:50 (EDT) | 2009.05.22 14:14:43 (EDT) | 2009.05.22 14:14:50 (EDT) | 778 | 0 | 7 | 801325 |
| ✓  r/r | d00003-001 | 2009.05.22 14:14:50 (EDT) | 2009.05.22 14:14:43 (EDT) | 2009.05.22 14:14:50 (EDT) | 0 | 0 | 7 | 801321 |
| d/d | tmp/ | 2007.10.15 | 2009.05.22 | 2008.02.15 | 4096 | 0 | 7 | 801291 |

ASCII (display - report) * Hex (display - report) * ASCII Strings (display - report) * Export * Add Note
File Type: PDP-11 UNIX/RT ldp

ASCII String Contents Of File: /1/var/spool/cups/c00003

```
attributes-charset
utf-8H
attributes-natural-language
en-us
printer-uri
&ipp://localhost/printers/LaserJet_4000B
job-originating-user-name
eoghanB
job-name
        ffastfindI
document-format
application/postscriptB
```

**FIGURE 6.11**

The contents of `"/var/spools/cups"` on a Linux system showing file system metadata of control files and a deleted data file.

## FROM THE CASE FILES: PRINTING IP THEFT

An ex-employee of a company was suspected of stealing trade secrets. Although he admitted viewing documents of concern, he claimed that this was part of his job and that he had not taken them when he left the company. However, forensic examiners were able recover printer spool files from his Unix workstation, revealing that he had printed the documents of concern the day before he left the company. Faced with this evidence, the ex-employee admitted to taking printouts of the proprietary data.

Although the spool file containing the PostScript version of the document is generally deleted after printing is complete, it may be possible to recover these deleted spool files by carving in unallocated space of the `"/var"` partition for PDF documents. The beginning of a spool file ("/var/spool/cups/d00006-001") associated with the printed document "Chapter4-IntrusionInvestigation_05122009" is show here with the username eoghan, document name, and date of printing:

```
%!PS-Adobe-3.0
%%BoundingBox: (atend)
%%Creator: (OpenOffice.org 2.3)
%%For: (eoghan)
%%CreationDate: (Fri May 22 14:38:34 2009)
%%Title: (Chapter4-IntrusionInvestigation_05122009)
```

The items in this header provide useful signatures for file carving, as well as keyword searching of unallocated space for specific documents or all items printed by a specific user account.

For accounting purposes, the "/var/log/cups/page_log" records the number of pages (and sometimes the associated filenames) that each user printed at specific times. Although this log does not provide the contents of printed documents, it shows that a user account was in use at a particular time.

## Removable Media

Attaching a USB storage device of any kind will create a handful of entries in the syslog.log file. These entries will occur each time the device is connected to the system.

```
Oct 29 23:16:12 securesrv kernel: Initializing USB Mass Storage driver…
Oct 29 23:16:12 securesrv kernel: scsi2 : SCSI emulation for USB Mass
  Storage devices
Oct 29 23:16:12 securesrv kernel: usbcore: registered new interface
  driver usb-storage
Oct 29 23:16:12 securesrv kernel: USB Mass Storage support registered.
Oct 29 23:16:17 securesrv kernel: scsi 2:0:0:0: Direct-Access Sony
  Storage Media 0100 PQ: 0 ANSI: 0 CCS
Oct 29 23:17:52 twinklingstar gnome-keyring-daemon[5463]: adding
  removable location: volume_uuid_5B72_E2E9 at /media/disk
Oct 29 18:43:14 twinklingstar sudo: twinkle : TTY=pts/2 ; PWD=/tmp ;
  USER=root ; COMMAND=/bin/umount /media/disk
```

In addition, there may be references to files stored on removable media that were opened using applications on a Linux system.

## Deleting and Destroying Data

There are many userland utilities for obliterating data on Unix-like systems. Although these tools are generally effective at destroying data, forensic practitioners may be able to detect traces of their use as noted in the section on command history earlier in this chapter (see Figure 6.7).

Realizing the value of log files in a digital investigation, some offenders simply delete them. Some intruders will also clear entries from the `wtmp` database using specialized utilities to make it more difficult for digital investigators to reconstruct events relating to an intrusion. Fortunately, forensic practitioners may be able to recover deleted files or references to files that have been obliterated. Recall the example in Figure 6.6 earlier in this chapter, showing a recoverable deleted syslog file.

In addition, similar to the Recycle Bin concept in Microsoft Windows, when a user deletes a file within a graphical environment, the file is simply moved to a directory. For instance, the Gnome environment places files deleted by a user in the `.Trash` directory under the home directory. This feature enables users to restore files that were deleted accidentally, but also provides forensic examiners with useful information relating to user deletion activities.

# INTERNET COMMUNICATIONS

Unix systems provide a wide range of methods for accessing resources on the Internet. In addition to having web browsers and e-mail clients, Unix systems come with logon programs like SSH that are run from the command line to connect to other systems. This section details the remnants that such programs leave behind that can help digital investigators determine which remote systems were accessed.

## Secure Shell

Every time a user connects to a remote host using Secure Shell (SSH), that host's IP/host name and key are added to the `known_hosts` file, which can be helpful if an intruder used SSH to connect to another host, either on the local LAN or on the Internet as shown here:

```
$ cat .ssh/known_hosts
192.168.1.103 ssh-rsa
AAAAB3NzaC1yc2EAAAABIwAAAQEA4RjYT7I+f49a70MY6S/1YT63tCUDOz5Yt4N1RpeOtiV
Q9BBG23YO3/N+byoLs7dLPxuR+YR/Gg57YmNiF5 xu2EHM0ewoKL2Y3adjFTUoDhJTYaKg7u
3fqb1TxSERIEeHP2K1i0LaDxl6uDLOvNqy4H/f2Xt RuwXMDViysmjWPR0dCaTbj+D3jbO1U
cg5MIqRIctcM/AH3kF50xiBfamgINtsiJ/jDz9IEDUCXaN9/D+LBT/sw3PS8kWghYlylyHN
LruWQtp3heFekw2P/1eKqtaZHZuzf5QzUUyvLQhdQ60fOQmr3JN0jWIrulgRTSDORACHkVy
8YQUBbw2WbaC/Hw==
```

# FIREFOX 3

Firefox 3 stores the bulk of its internal data in SQLite 3 format database files. This is particularly useful for the forensic examiner because querying SQLite databases for information is easily performed with freely available tools (Tito, 2008). On Linux systems, Firefox profile information is stored under the user's home directory in the `.mozilla/firefox` directory.

In this directory you will find one or more folders and a file named profiles.ini. The content of this file will be similar to the following:

```
[General]
StartWithLastProfile=1

[Profile0]
Name=default
IsRelative=1
Path=u2wmsy3p.default
```

On launch, Firefox will read and process this file. In a multiple profile environment, StartWithLastProfile=1 tells Firefox to begin with the last used profile by default. The following stanza describes the first (and on this system, only) Firefox profile. In most normal uses a single profile named default will be present. The Path variable points to the directory under ~/.mozilla/firefox where this profile's data is stored.

Inside of each profile directory you will find numerous files and subdirectories. The most important files here will be the .sqlite files, which are the aforementioned SQLite 3 databases. We will be examining four of these databases in detail.

- **Cookies.sqlite**: stores data about cookies
- **Downloads.sqlite**: stores data about downloaded files
- **Formhistory.sqlite**: stores data about form submission inputs—search boxes, username fields, etc.
- **Places.sqlite**: stores the bulk of what would generally be considered "Internet history" data

Since these files are simply SQLite 3 databases, an investigator has many options when dealing with them. For our purposes we will use the SQLite Manager tool, available as a Firefox plug-in or a standalone XULRunner application (http://code.google.com/p/sqlite-manager/).

After exporting the user's Firefox profile, choose Connect Database from the Database menu, and browse to the exported profile directory as shown in Figure 6.12.

Next, select the database you'd like to examine and click Open. From here, you can browse the database structure, execute SQL queries, and export findings. You can also write data to the database, so you should use this tool only on working copies of data. A full discussion of the intricacies of SQL queries is outside of the scope of this book. However, most of these databases have simple schemas with one table of interest. For example, to view the data held in the cookies.sqlite database, you would execute the following command:

```
SELECT * FROM moz_cookies;
```

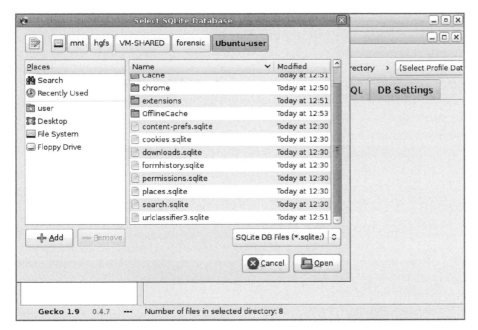

**FIGURE 6.12**
SQLite Manager.

An example of the results from this query are shown in Figure 6.13.

Entries in the cookies database may yield information as to the last time the user visited a site that requested a specific cookie, whether or not the user was registered or signed in at a particular site, and other state information.

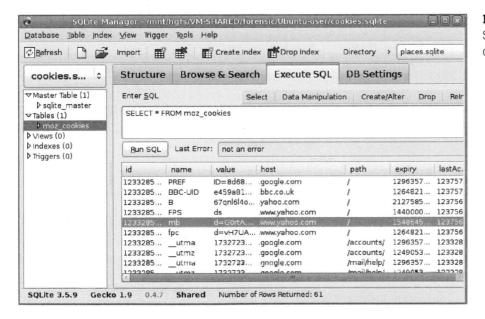

**FIGURE 6.13**
SQLite Manager:
cookies.sqlite.

The next Firefox database of interest is the `downloads.sqlite` database shown in Figure 6.14. As the name suggests, this file contains records of the files downloaded by the user. Based on the author's experimentation, the files that show up in this database are those that are handled by the Firefox Download Manager. Multimedia files handled by browser plug-ins and other items that end up in the browser cache will not show up in this database. The most important aspect of this particular database is that it allows the investigator to tie items found on the file system to specific URLs of origin—this could be the make or break point in a "Trojan defense" case.

**FIGURE 6.14**

SQLite Manager: downloads.sqlite.

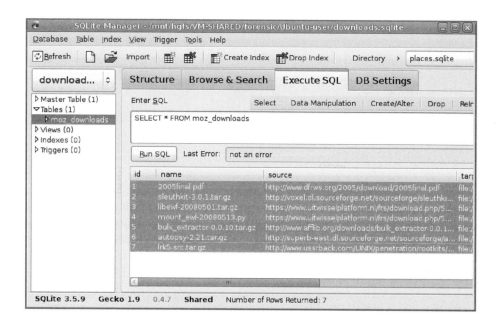

The formhistory.sqlite database contains entries typed into Form submission fields by the user. Key items of interest here may include addresses and subject lines of web mails, and search terms submitted to search engines.

The database that contains the items most regularly thought of as Internet history is places.sqlite. Unlike the previously discussed single-table databases, places.sqlite has a fairly involved schema, which has been detailed in its entirety by Chris Cohen at www.firefoxforensics.com/research/firefox_places_schema.shtml. For now, knowing that the id field in the moz_places table corresponds to the places_id in the moz_historyvisits table enables us to build a query that will produce relevant browsing history output.

The information of immediate concern in most web-related investigations is the URL visited and the time of that visit. These two items are found in the url field in the moz_plazes table and the visit_date in the moz_historyvisits table, respectively. The visit_date is stored in a modified Unix epoch time with an additional six digits of precision, so the data needs a bit of massaging before it appears to be anything remotely human-readable. The following sqlite statement will retrieve these two values from their respective tables and convert the visit_date to a more readable format:

```
SELECT
datetime(moz_historyvisits.visit_date/1000000,'unixepoch'),
  moz_places.url
FROM moz_places, moz_historyvisits
WHERE moz_places.id = moz_historyvisits.place_id
```
An example of the output from the above query is provided in Figure 6.15.

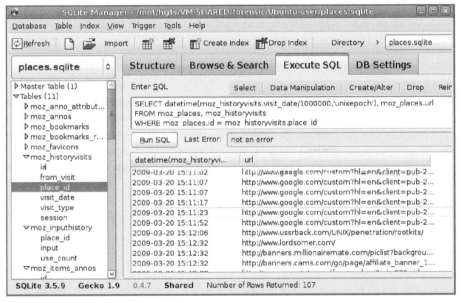

**FIGURE 6.15**
SQLite Manager: complex query of places.sqlite.

Various tools are available to assist in performing examinations of Firefox artifacts. The Firefox 3 Extractor is a command line tool that automates the process of extracting relevant data from the previously mentioned sqlite databases (www.firefoxforensics.com/f3e.shtml). In addition, as shown in Figure 6.16, FoxAnalysis is a GUI tool that simplifies and abstracts much of the database querying we've performed and supports date restrictions, keyword filtering, and various reporting options (http://forensic-software.co.uk/foxanalysis. aspx). Both tools are available free of charge.

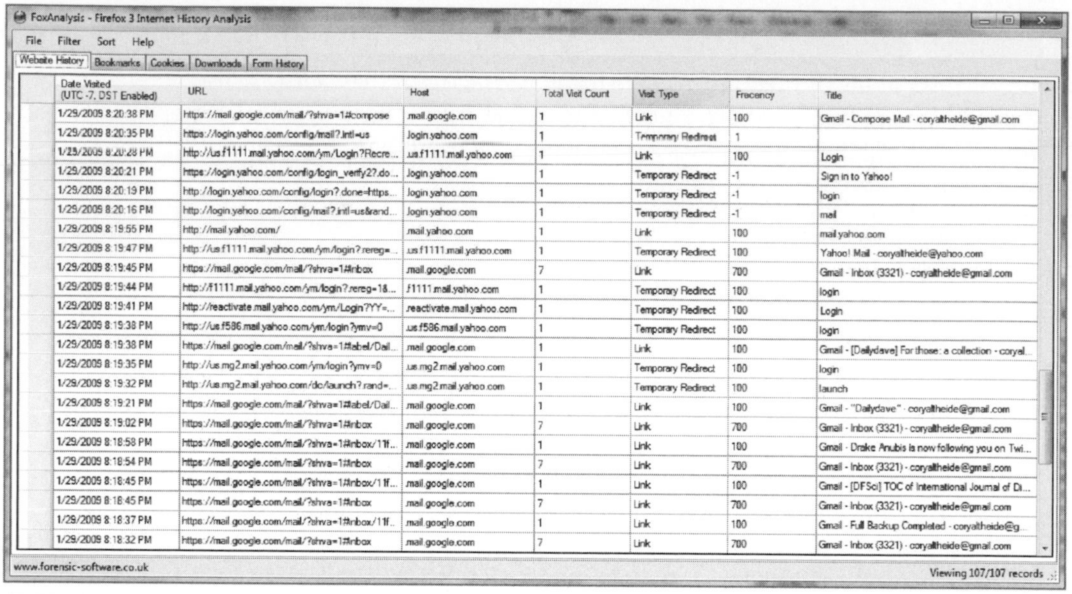

**FIGURE 6.16**
FoxAnalysis.

## CACHE

In addition to browser history files, a user's browser cache may be of investigative importance. The cache files are stored under the user's profile in a directory called Cache. Opening this directory for viewing will usually yield a stream of numbered unidentifiable files along with one cache map file (_CACHE_ MAP_) and three cache block files (_CACHE_00x_). These are binary files that contain information regarding the URLs and filenames associated with the cached data, as well as timestamp data. This information can be readily parsed and displayed by Cache View (www.progsoc.uts.edu.au/~timj/cv/) as shown in Figure 6.17, or MozillaCacheView (www.nirsoft.net/utils/mozilla_cache_ viewer.html).

## SAVED SESSION

In some cases, a file named `sessionstore.js` will be present in the user's profile directory. The function of this file is to recover the user's environment in the case of a crash or other unexpected shutdown. By replaying this file, Firefox is able to reopen the browser windows and tabs the user last had open. An excerpt from a sample `sessionstore.js` follows.

{state:{entries:[{url:"http://www.engadget.com/2009/02/06/intel-ships
-atom-n280-for-720p-netbooks-nvidias-ion-points/", title:"Intel ships
Atom N280 for 720p netbooks -- NVIDIA's Ion points, laughs", ID:1001, scroll:"0,1258"}], index:1},
title:"Intel ships Atom N280 for 720p netbooks -- NVIDIA's Ion points, laughs",
image:"http://www.blogsmithmedia.com/www.engadget.com/media/favicon-v2.ico", pos:10}], _
hosts:{'google.com':true, com:true,
'www.google.com':true, 'fedex.com':true, 'www.fedex.com':true,
'ups.com':true, 'wwwapps.ups.com':true, 'archlinux.org':true, org:true,
'wiki.archlinux.org':true, 'eeebuntu.org':true,
'www.eeebuntu.org':true, 'colinux.org':true, 'www.colinux.org':true,
'168.0.1':true, '0.1':true, 1:true, '192.168.0.1':true, '168.1.11':true, '1.11':true, 11:true,
'192.168.1.11':true}, width:1396, height:1027, screenX:0, screenY:19, sizemode:"normal",
cookies:[{host:".google.com", value:"105027", path:"/", name:"GMAIL_RTT"},

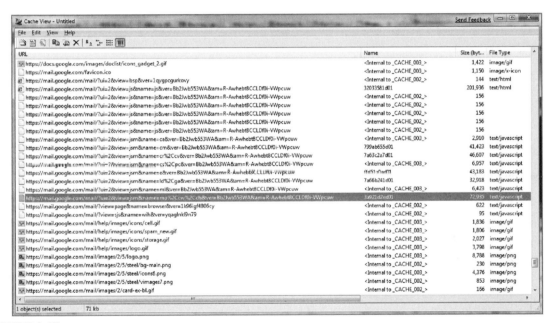

**FIGURE 6.17**
Cache View.

# E-MAIL ANALYSIS

Analysis of e-mail from Unix systems is, in general, fairly easy. Nearly all Unix e-mail clients and servers store mail on-disk in one of two plain-text formats—`mbox` or `Maildir`. The older `mbox` format consists of a single flat file, containing numerous e-mail entries, whereas the `Maildir` format stores each e-mail as a discreet file in a directory.

Both formats are plain text, so quickly searching for specific content can be performed without the need for any particular e-mail forensics utility. The key pieces are identifying the location of the mail files, identifying the format, and choosing your examination method. I will present two means of examining collected e-mail data.

User mail files are generally stored under the user's home directory; Mozilla Thunderbird stores its mail files in `.mozilla/thunderbird` directory in each user's home directory. In this directory you will find one or more profile directories, very similar to those discussed in the Firefox analysis section. In this profile directory there will be a folder named `Mail` that will have one or more subfolders—Thunderbird creates a separate folder for each mail account configured under a profile. Drilling down into one of these folders you should find a handful of files—those *without* extensions are the mbox format mail files which contain mail content. For example, the `Inbox` from the author's test machine begins with the following:

```
From - Thu Jan 29 20:54:02 2009
X-Account-Key: account2
X-UIDL: GmailIdfeefa85b3eb8620
X-Mozilla-Status: 0001
X-Mozilla-Status2: 00000000
X-Mozilla-Keys:
  X-Gmail-Received: 5e94fca9d660f8b9699e9a72fa54265243126ada
  Delivered-To: coryaltheide@gmail.com
  Received: by 10.65.153.7 with SMTP id f7cs8807qbo;
       Wed, 30 Nov 2005 12:22:58 -0800 (PST)
  Received: by 10.64.150.8 with SMTP id x8mr440592qbd;
       Wed, 30 Nov 2005 12:22:57 -0800 (PST)
  Received-SPF: fail
  Return-path: <authorsupport@elsevier.com>
```

The mail continues on with additional headers, then the mail body. This is followed by another "From " line. (**Note**: The capitalization as well as the trailing space is important.) The "From " line is the defined message delineator for the mbox format. Any line beginning with "From " is counted as a new mail.

Many of the commercial mail forensics tools utilized during examinations of Windows mail formats will be able to easily process any mbox or Maildir files. However, due to their simple and open natures, many free tools exist that will allow the examiner to quickly hone in on the specific data they are after. We examine two of these next—grepmail (http://grepmail.sourceforge.net) and Mairix (www.rpcurnow.force9.co.uk/mairix/).

## Grepmail

As its name implies, grepmail is a utility for searching for e-mail items that meet specific criteria, much in the same way the grep utility searches for lines or files that match certain patterns. The grepmail program has built-in knowledge of mail formats and thus gives the examiner more precision when defining search parameters. Although grepmail works only on mbox format mailboxes, it can parse compressed mailboxes, and can search through a number of mailboxes at once. The grepmail options of particular interest to examiners are noted as follows:

```
-b Search must match body
-d Specify a required date range
-h Search must match header
-H Print headers but not bodies of matching emails
-j Search must match status (A=answered, R=read, D=deleted,
O=old, F=flagged)
-Y Specify a header to search (implies -h)
```

One particularly interesting feature of grepmail is its date searching capabilities. Dates can be entered in a number of nonstandard formats. "02/21/09," "4:00am October fourth," and "today" are all valid date entries. Additionally, date searches can be constrained by keywords like "before," "since," or "between." This level of granularity may prove to be invaluable if your investigation revolves around specific times or dates.

For example:

```
grepmail -H -d "before 12:30am" 2009-February.mbox
```

This command will print the headers of all mail found in "2009-February. mbox" sent before 12:30 AM each day (the default date field to match is the "sent" date).

```
grepmail -j -a -d "after Feb 19" 2009-February.mbox
```

This will display the full content of all mail with a "deleted" status that was received after February 19.

Although certainly flexible and powerful, grepmail tends to slow down when dealing with very large mbox files (I have attempted to use grepmail on ~30GB mbox files). The grepmail program is well suited for queries against relatively small mailboxes and queries where a specific set of keywords, dates, and other search criteria are fixed before the search begins. Many legal discovery cases would fit this description. For investigations that don't have a fixed keyword list from the beginning, and those that may deal with very large mailbox, Mairix is a better choice.

## Mairix

The Mairix tool is quite a bit more complex than `grepmail`, but it is also quite a bit more powerful. We recommend a thorough read through the main page for a full understanding of the tool's capabilities, but hopefully this section will provide you with enough information to get started.

The key difference between Mairix and `grepmail` is that Mairix first builds an index, which is subsequently queried as the examiner performs searches. Additionally, Mairix is able to search both mbox and Maildir mail files. Unlike `grepmail`, you won't be able to simply jump into a shell and begin making queries. Searching with Mairix requires several steps. First, you need to create an `rcfile` that defines some variables Mairix needs to operate. Next, you build the index from your mailbox. Last, you query the index.

Our very minimal Mairix `rcfile` follows:

```
base=/forensics/mairix
mbox=2009-February.mbox
database=/forensics/mairix/.database
mfolder=mairix-out
```

`Base` defines the base path that Mairix will treat as its `root`; `mbox` points to the mbox file we'll be processing. This can be a colon-delimited set of mbox files. `Database` tells Mairix where to build its index. Finally, `mfolder` defines where Mairix will store the output from any subsequent queries. Search results are stored in Maildir format by default but this can be configured as necessary.

Next, we tell Mairix to build the index. This is achieved with a simple `mairix -f rcfile`, but adding a `-v` flag will increase verbosity and give you some progress information to watch while you wait. Indexing time will obviously increase with larger amounts of data.

```
root@ubuntu:/forensics/mairix# mairix -f rcfile -v
mairix 0.21, Copyright (C) 2002-2007 Richard P. Curnow
mairix comes with ABSOLUTELY NO WARRANTY.
This is free software, and you are welcome to redistribute it
    under certain conditions; see the GNU General Public License for
    details.
Finding all currently existing messages…
Starting new database
Scanning mbox /forensics/mairix/2009-February.mbox : 100% done
0 newly dead messages, 0 messages now dead in total
Scanning /forensics/mairix/2009-February.mbox[0] at [54,34758137]
Checking message path integrity
Checking to
Checking cc
Checking from
```

```
Checking subject
Checking body
Checking attachment_name
Wrote 1 messages (20 bytes tables, 0 bytes text)
Wrote 1 mbox headers (16 bytes tables, 37 bytes paths)
Wrote 16 bytes of mbox message checksums
To: Wrote 0 tokens (0 bytes tables, 0 bytes of text, 0 bytes of hit
   encoding)
Cc: Wrote 0 tokens (0 bytes tables, 0 bytes of text, 0 bytes of hit
   encoding)
From: Wrote 6 tokens (48 bytes tables, 39 bytes of text, 12 bytes of
   hit encoding)
Subject: Wrote 7 tokens (56 bytes tables, 42 bytes of text, 14 bytes
   of hit encoding)
Body: Wrote 112781 tokens (902248 bytes tables, 1056554 bytes of text,
   225562 bytes of hit encoding)
Attachment Name: Wrote 0 tokens (0 bytes tables, 0 bytes of text,
   0 bytes of hit encoding)
(Threading): Wrote 1 tokens (8 bytes tables, 45 bytes of text, 4 bytes
   of hit encoding)
```

Now we can query the index. Mairix supports a broad range of search operators. Chaining these together allows the investigator to quickly hone in on a small number of interesting e-mails that can be reviewed manually.

```
expr_i :           search expression (all expr's AND'ed together):
word    :          match word in message body and major headers
t:word  :          match word in To: header
c:word  :        : match word in Cc: header
f:word  :        : match word in From: header
a:word  :        : match word in To:, Cc: or From: headers (address)
s:word  :        : match word in Subject: header
b:word  :        : match word in message body
m:word  :        : match word in Message-ID: header
n:word  :        : match name of attachment within message
F:flags :        : match on message flags (s=seen,r=replied,f=flagged,
                     -=negate)
p:substring :    : match substring of path
d:start-end :    : match date range
z:low-high  :    : match messages in size range
bs:word :        : match word in Subject: header or body (or any other
                     group of prefixes)
s:word1,word2 :  : match both words in Subject:
s:word1/word2 :  : match either word or both words in Subject:
s:~word :        : match messages not containing word in Subject:
s:substring= :   : match substring in any word in Subject:
s:^substring= :  : match left-anchored substring in any word in Subject:
```

```
s:substring=2 :  match substring with <=2 errors in any word in
                     Subject:
```

We'll issue a query for a known-bad domain. Any mail arriving from this domain is suspicious at best.

```
root@ubuntu:/forensics/mairix# mairix -f rcfile f:hackerdomainz
Created directory /forensics/mairix/mairix-out
Created directory /forensics/mairix/mairix-out/cur
Created directory /forensics/mairix/mairix-out/new
Created directory /forensics/mairix/mairix-out/tmp
Matched 11 messages
```

The resulting mail files can be found in the "new" subdirectory.

## CHAT ANALYSIS

Unix-like systems generally come with simple chat utilities like talk and wall that enable users on a multiuser system to exchange messages. Because these chat programs will not generally work between computers that are separated by a firewall, they are not commonly used. Furthermore, these programs do not have an option to save log files. Therefore, forensic examiners will rarely encounter remnants of such chat activities.

A more common program used on Unix systems for chatting with others is Internet Relay Chat (IRC). There are a multitude of clients for accessing IRC, including BitchX and XChat. There are also bot programs like Eggdrop that provide access to IRC. Most IRC clients and bots can be configured to maintain logs that can be useful to forensic examiners. For instance, the XChat program will maintain logs of chat sessions in the `.xchat/xchatlogs` directory under a user's home directory.

One of the most commonly used Instant Messaging clients on Unix systems is Pidgin. This program enables users to communicate on most of the major IM systems on the Internet, including Yahoo, AOL, and MSN. All configuration files associated with Pidgin are stored in the `.purple` directory in each user's home directory. For example, Figure 6.18 shows an `accounts.xml` file that contains the IM accounts that the Pidgin program is configured to use.

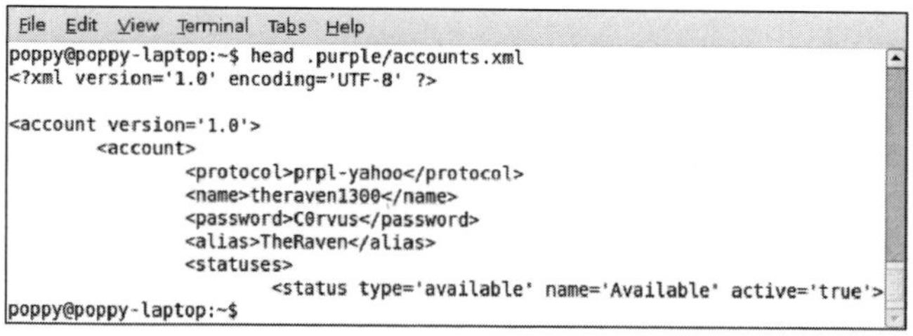

**FIGURE 6.18**

Yahoo username and password stored in the Pidgin configuration file named .purple/accounts.xml.

```
File  Edit  View  Terminal  Tabs  Help
poppy@poppy-laptop:~$ head .purple/accounts.xml
<?xml version='1.0' encoding='UTF-8' ?>

<account version='1.0'>
        <account>
                <protocol>prpl-yahoo</protocol>
                <name>theraven1300</name>
                <password>C0rvus</password>
                <alias>TheRaven</alias>
                <statuses>
                        <status type='available' name='Available' active='true'>
poppy@poppy-laptop:~$
```

In addition to logs that are intentionally saved by chat programs, forensic examiners may find traces of chat sessions in swap space on a Unix system as noted in the next section.

## MEMORY AND SWAP SPACE

Unix systems reserve a specific storage area for virtual memory, called *swap space*. Because this area is used to store data from memory temporarily, it can contain passwords, references to files that have been deleted from the system or were stored on removable media, and remnants of user activities such as chat logs and command history.

---

### FROM THE CASE FILES: RECOVERED COMMAND HISTORY IN SWAP SPACE

In one intrusion investigation, remnants of an old `.bash_history` file were recovered from swap simply using the strings command. This included items that were never written to the actual on-disk `.bash_history` file as shown here:

```
ls -lath .config/aweseome/rc.lua
vim .config/aweseome/rc.lua
xmodmap ~/.Xmodmap
ls -lath
less .config/aweseome/rc.lua
vim .config/aweseome/rc.lua
ls -lath
mkdir .config/awesome
```

```
mv .config/aweseome/rc.lua .config/awesome/
xmodmap ~/.Xmodmap
vim .xinitrc
kazehakase
mount /dev/sdb1
mkdir /mnt/thumb
sudo mkdir /mnt/
cd hachoir-core-1.2.1
python setup.py
./setup.py
python setup.py install
cd ../hachoir-regex-1.0.3
cd hachoir-parser-1.2.1
```

---

In some cases, it may be fruitful to search for remnants of web pages fetched (on clients) or rendered and served up (on servers).

Additional information can also be obtained from memory of Unix systems as detailed in Malin, Casey, and Aquilina (2008).

## REFERENCES

Blank-Edelman, D. N. (2000). *Perl for system administration: Managing multi-platform environments with Perl.* O'Reilly Media.

Carrier, B. (2005). *File system forensic analysis.* Addison-Wesley Professional.

Farmer, D. & Venema, W. (2005). *Forensic discovery.* Addison-Wesley Professional.

Malin, C. H., Casey, E. & Aquilina, J. M. (2008). *Malware forensics.* Syngress Media.

Tito, M. (2008). *Journal of Digital Investigation,* 5(1–2).

# CHAPTER 7

# Macintosh Forensic Analysis

Anthony Kokocinski

## INTRODUCTION

Apple Macintosh computers running Mac OS X are in widespread use, and can pose a challenge for many digital forensic examiners. Lack of regular exposure to Macintosh systems as a source of evidence make it harder for digital forensic examiners to become adept at locating and interpreting useful information on these systems. Even forensic examiners with some familiarity with these systems may not be sufficiently conversant to perform a forensic examination using Macintosh-based automated tool suites. It is generally most effective to conduct a forensic examination of Macintosh systems in a native Macintosh environment. However, this chapter makes an effort to address repeated requests over the years for guidance on how to conduct Macintosh forensics using Microsoft Windows-based forensic tool suites.

This chapter covers basic information on hardships encountered when processing Mac OS X 10.2–10.5 systems, provides tips on where to find configuration and user data, and breaks down a few application-specific data structures. A few new tools will be introduced and common forensic tool suites for Windows will be reviewed as appropriate to the data storage.

## IMAGING AND FILE SYSTEMS

Most Macintosh file systems are going to occur on easily identifiable media. Hard drives, optical discs, and thumb drives can all be formatted with Macintosh partitioning structure and file systems. These media can be imaged with traditional means and safety procedures. By now imaging computer systems, no matter what they are, should be ingrained into the brain of

## CONTENTS

Introduction.....353

Imaging and
File Systems....353

Macintosh
File Systems....355

Property
Lists.................359

User
Accounts..........359

Applications....364

System.............365

User Folders....370

User Folders:
Media Files......371

User Folders:
Applications....372

Wrap Up...........382

References.......382

**353**

any digital forensic examiner and will not be repeated here. However, there are several common misconceptions that forensic practitioners have when imaging Macintosh systems.

Although Windows-based operating systems do not always understand Macintosh on disk structures, this does not absolve forensic practitioners from employing write protection when acquiring a forensic duplicate. In some cases, Windows may alter areas of Macintosh formatted media and can cause irreparable damage by trying to recover the disk to a format it understands.

It is possible to image many Macintosh systems equipped with at least one FireWire port by setting the machine into target disk mode. This can be done in a number of ways; the most notable is by holding down the T key as it boots up. This is a set of hard-coded instructions in both the Open Firmware of PowerPCs and EFI of Intel-based Macintoshes. This process was created as a convenience for Macintosh users who wanted an easy way to transfer data between machines and had gotten used to the previous way of moving data through SCSI. Target disk mode basically turns a Macintosh computer into a very expensive external hard drive, and like hard drive enclosed circuitry, simply putting the computer into this mode does not alter any data. Because some Macintosh laptops have hard drives that are very difficult to remove, some practitioners took the risk of putting the evidentiary system in target disk mode and connecting it directly to a Windows examination machine without write protection, just to avoid taking apart an iBook. In addition, when the G5 towers first came out, SATA was a less familiar hard drive interface and there were no hardware write-blockers for SATA, so practitioners used target disk mode in favor of buying additional hardware.

There are risks associated with using target disk mode to acquire a forensic image of a hard drive. In addition to the aforementioned risks of not using a write-blocker, the target disk mode function is not available by default if there is a firmware password, and key depresses are ignored upon boot up, until the set OS is engaged.

An increasing number of forensic tools are incorporating features for examining Macintosh file systems, but they may not provide access to all on-disk structures. This has been a constant arms race between forensic suites, but it is often something that falls behind. In some instances, even some partition structures are not identified or are displayed correctly. If a single tool is relied upon without validation either manually or using another tool, then some information may be missing.

# MACINTOSH FILE SYSTEMS

File systems are often a bit overwhelming, particularly when there are several data structures involved. Some digital forensic examiners maintain that background knowledge for understanding the logical structures of laying down data on a hard drive to be important but hard to keep in your head at all times during an analysis. For the vast majority of situations, however, it is sufficient to understand that Macintosh file systems maintain most of their information in the Catalog and Extent files.

There are numerous resources containing a wide variety and depth concerning Macintosh file systems that will not be reiterated here (Casey, 2004; http://developer.apple.com/technotes/tn/tn1150.html). A number of important considerations to remember when looking at files on a Macintosh file system such as HFS, HFS+ HFSX are covered here.

## File System Date-time Stamps

The HFS+ and HFSX file systems support the following five date-time stamps:

- **Create Date**: When the file was created. Copying a file from one HFS volume to another generally preserves the create date.
- **Modified Date**: When the contents of the file was last changed.
- **Attribute Modified Date**: When attributes associated with the file were last altered, similar to the inode change time in UNIX. This can be updated without altering any of the data of the file. This is most commonly modified if the file is moved or renamed.
- **Accessed Date**: When the file was last accessed.
- **Backup Date**: A deprecated field that is not typically used.

These date-time stamps may not always be displayed or interpreted correctly by analysis tools. Figure 7.1 shows two forensic tools being used to view the same files on an HFS+ volume.

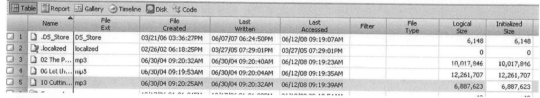

**FIGURE 7.1A**

An EnCase Table view of a folder of an HFS+ volume.

**FIGURE 7.1B**

An FTK file list of the same folder. FTK displays additional HFS data if configured by clicking the small columns button on the bottom file list pane.

## File Attributes

Macintosh operating systems can support file identification by both extension and type and creator codes. Forensic tools may not always display the type and creator codes, but they can be found in the Catalog tree alongside the other details about a file system object of interest. Other details contained in the Catalog tree that are often omitted by forensic tools include the Catalog Node Identifier (CNID) number, user and group numbers, and Unix-style file/folder permissions as shown in Figure 7.1(b).

## Data versus Resource Forks

Macintosh file systems natively contain multiple "forks" for a file. By default a data and resource fork are maintained. Since this is somewhat of a foreign concept to other file systems, the two forks are often displayed as two files by forensic examination tools. The forensic tools often provide some form of notation along with a resource fork to differentiate it as shown in Figure 7.2, and this fork often contains information that is much more difficult to understand on non-Macintosh systems.

## File Deletion

Because of the nature of HFS, HFS+, and HFSX volumes, recovery of deleted file system details is particularly difficult. Unlike many Windows and Unix systems, recovery of deleted file system information on Macintosh systems is nearly impossible because nodes in the Catalog file are so frequently overwritten. This is largely due to the B-tree balancing process in the Catalog file, which

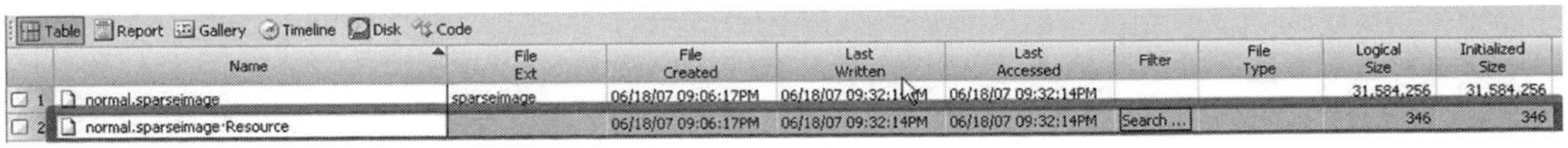

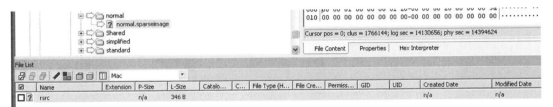

**FIGURE 7.2A**

EnCase shows resource forks in the same folder and with many of the same file attributes as the data fork. This is an example of a user's file vault sparseimage.

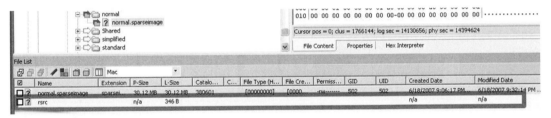

**FIGURE 7.2B**

FTK shows the RSRC as an additional stream contained within the original file. Notice no attribute data is shown. Same folder as before.

**FIGURE 7.2C**

By highlighting the folder in FTK, you can better see the two files side by side and the differences between the data fork of the file and the resource fork of the file.

obliterates previous file system details. Standard data carving techniques can be used to recover some file contents from Macintosh volumes, but only the data fork. This fork will retain what is a "typical" structure of media, document, application files with well-defined file formats, and header signatures that tools like Foremost rely on for carving as discussed in Chapter 2, "Forensic Analysis." The real difficulty comes in further correlation; pairing the carved data for each fork would be very difficult, especially since a lot of the data in resource forks is undocumented. Additionally, tying specific files to a user can be very difficult when file system details are no longer available in a Catalog file record. Therefore, attributing a file to a particular user is often possible only through forensic examination of data contents.

## Inodes

Lastly, although HFS, HFS+, and HFSX do not organize file data with inodes like many Linux or Unix file systems, files could be seen on the file system that have their names start with iNode and then contain a number (Figure 7.3).

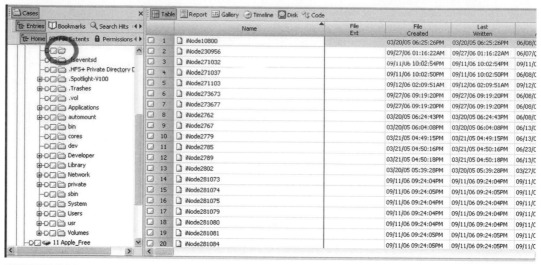

**FIGURE 7.3A**

EnCase displays the iNode files in a nameless folder. The name of this folder has unprintable characters. Previous versions of EnCase have had different interpretations of this folder; one previous name was Cases.

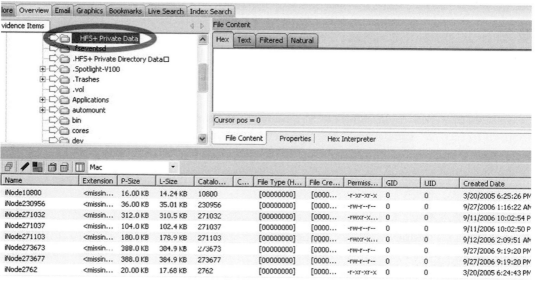

**FIGURE 7.3B**

FTK showing the same folder. FTK displays the folder name differently, either choosing not to display the unprintable characters or to use spaces as placeholders for them.

These are not inodes, nor are they typically seen during normal user usage. These files are the central location for data that is shared between hard links on a volume. This is the procedure that HFS+ uses to hard link files that share the same data with multiple names.

Although there can always be more said about imaging, partitioning structure, and file systems, for brevity this is as far as we will visit this topic in this chapter with some very notable exceptions in upcoming sections.

## PROPERTY LISTS

Before delving further into forensic analysis of Macintosh systems, it is important to have a solid understanding of property lists. Property lists, also referred to as `plist` files, are the greatest source of information for settings and configurations on Mac OS X. Property lists are often simple text files formatted in XML to be read on the system. Often they will contain text strings, Boolean values, and occasionally encoded binary data. Although these files can be examined using a text editor, it is most effective to view the hierarchical information in these files using an XML reader.

The only caveat to this is that in Mac OS X 10.4, the binary `plist` format became popular for a number of property lists. Although these binary files still contain XML data, they are not easily readable with the built-in viewers of some forensic tools. A free XML viewer that can be used to examine these files is plist Editor for Windows (www.ipodrobot.com), shown in Figure 7.4. This utility can be used to examine text `plist` files as well as binary ones, but may not display all the information in binary `plist` files in a usable format. Therefore, it is advisable to examine property list files using multiple tools to extract the most information.

## USER ACCOUNTS

During the course of any forensic analysis of a computer it is important to enumerate the user accounts on the system, and associate information with that user. Although it may be difficult to tie a person to an action without admission, it is much easier to tie an account to an action. For this attribution process, account enumeration is critical in any forensic analysis, and Macintosh OS X systems are no different. For account enumeration there are three critical pieces, user account information stored in the user database, the user's password(s), and user information on the volume.

**FIGURE 7.4**

plist Editor for Windows showing an exported `info.plist` file from Safari, and showing the version number for Safari on a Mac OS X 10.4 system.

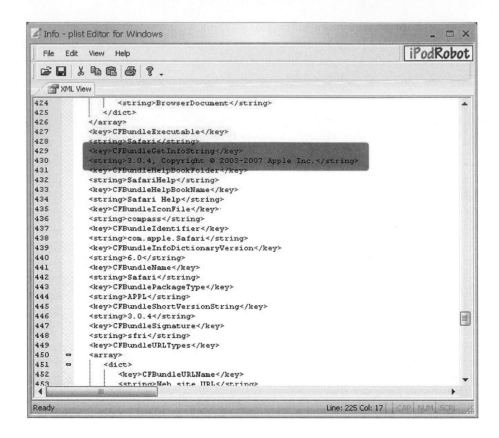

Depending on the version of Mac OS X that is being used on the system, user account information will be stored in different locations and formats. It is important to realize what kind of system you are looking at before trying to identify users. The most current version of Mac OS X, 10.5, stores this information in flat files located off the root of the drive at `/private/var/db/dslocal/`. Mac OS X 10.2–10.4 stores this information in a different location and format. Individual Store files store account information in a proprietary database format as shown in Figure 7.5, and are located in the `/private/var/db/netinfo/local.nidb/` folder.

Although these formats may look different as files, they carry the same types of information:

- Name, the name of the shell account.
- Realname, the name of the GUI account typically seen at login.
- User ID number (uid); user created accounts typically start from 501. This value can be useful for determining the owner of a specific file since the attributes of the file will generally contain the UID.

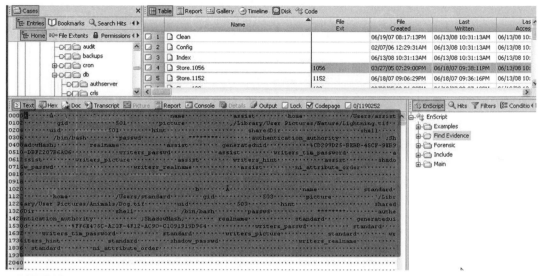

**FIGURE 7.5**

A display of EnCase showing one of the data stores in a Mac OS X 10.4 system. Highlighted is the user account information held in the NetInfo database.

- Group ID number (gid), is typically similar to the uid in later versions of Mac OS X.
- Picture, which corresponds to a picture on the drive that can be used for user identification from the GUI logon process.
- Authentication_authority, defines the type of security used for the password. Basic indicates the password is held in the database, Shadowhash indicates the password is held in a separate file.
- Home, the main folder on the system associated with the user account. This folder contains the user's desktop folder, and is the default location for user created and downloaded files. In addition, user specific configuration information is stored under this folder.
- Shareddir, which folder is by default shared when file sharing is turned on.
- Hint, if any text was supplied to the hint field during account creation.

As the databases progressed, new fields were added:

- Generateduid, a UUID field that was specific to each user. This would distinguish individual users generated between machines.
- Home_loc, a field to specify the file to be used as the Home folder, established for FileVault.

- Mcx_settings, an array set up to define parental control privileges. This regulates what a person can and cannot do on an account; able to be set only for nonadministrative users.
- Jpegphoto, a base64 encoded version of the logon picture, may supercede the picture field.

---

### PRACTITIONER'S TIP: EXAMINING USER ACCOUNT DETAILS

The information stored in the Directory Service structure of Mac OS X 10.5 is much easier to read using Windows-based forensic tools than the NetInfo structure of Mac OS X 10.2–10.4.

To pull the same information on a Mac OS X 10.5 system simply read the individual files in the `/private/var/db/dslocal/nodes/Default/users/`. Each of the user accounts will have a file in this folder. Some documents will have an underscore to begin the filename; typically these are system default accounts used for normal operation of the system. User generated accounts will typically not have this to start their name but this is not an absolute rule. Each of these files is a standard XML formatted `plist` file that can be examined with a text editor and interpreted using a `plist` viewer.

To pull the information out of the NetInfo database on Mac OS X 10.2–10.4 systems, simply copy the text from the `Store.#` files located in the `/private/var/db/NetInfo/local.nidb/` folder. With some forensic tools you can copy the ASCII text only out of the file; then that text can be read in a simple text editor. Alternately, export the entire file and run a strings tool against it to extract the ASCII text.

One exception when examining NetInfo formatted account details is that accounts with parental controls enabled will generally have to be examined in a different manner. In this situation, the `mcx_settings` file contains an XML data array that shows specifically what the account may or may not be allowed to do.

---

In additional to the information contained in the user account database, useful information is contained within the groups. The most notable is whether or not a user is a member of the administrator group. The accounts with administrative privilege in Mac OS X 10.2 through 10.4 are listed in the `Store.#` file containing the admin group definitions. For a Mac OS X 10.5 this information is stored in the `admin.plist` file under the `/private/var/db/dslocal/nodes/Default/groups/` folder.

After retrieving the account information from the subject system, there are a few critical pieces of information to note. For each account note the password hash (Mac OS X 10.2), the UUID (Mac OS X 10.3–10.5), and the Home folder (or file). These details are useful for identifying and accessing files on the system that are associated with a particular user account.

### User Account Passwords

In some cases, it may be desirable to know the password for a specific user account on a Macintosh system. For instance, if user areas are encrypted using FileVault, obtaining the user's password may provide access to the data of interest.

Login passwords for Mac OS X have had some evolution along with the rest of the operating system. In Mac OS X 10.2 the passwords were standard Unix-style eight-character passwords. Users could choose longer passwords, and there was an advantage to doing so, but the password required for login was truncated to the first eight. The hash for these passwords was saved in the traditional DES 128 format and a standard compilation of John the Ripper (www.openwall. com/john/) can crack these passwords with no alteration.

The password format and location changed in Mac OS X 10.3. Recall that this is the first version of Mac OS X that contains the UUID field for a user in the database. This UUID is needed to identify the password.

Starting with Mac OS X 10.3 the passwords were removed from the NetInfo database and stored instead in the `/private/var/db/shadow/hash/` folder of the system drive. The files within this folder are exactly the same as the UUID numbers pulled from the system files. These files contain a 104-character value that appears to be an NTLM hash crammed onto the front of a raw SHA1 password. This format of password hash can be attacked in two ways. The first 64 characters can be split off and formatted for John the Ripper to crack like a traditional NTLM password. However, this approach will only give you the first 14 characters of the password used on the system. If the password is longer than 14 characters you may have to crack the last 40 characters using a patched version of John the Ripper that supports raw SHA1 password hashes. Before installing a patched version of John the Ripper that does raw SHA1 passwords, be aware that later versions of Mac OS X use salted SHA1 passwords, which requires an additional modification to Jack the Ripper.

With Mac OS X 10.4 and 10.5 the shadowed passwords are still in the same location and linked to users with UUID numbers, but the internal format of the files has changed. Instead of 104 characters, the file contains 1240 characters. Also the NTLM hash is no longer stored by default. The NTLM hash will be stored only if the user account is enabled to accept Windows-style SMB clients as a form of file sharing. If this was not enabled, then the NTLM password will be all zeros.

The exact breakdown of the new shadowed file is unknown, but the first 64 characters represent an NTLM password if available, and characters 169 through 216 represent the new stored SHA1 hash. Observe that this value is 49 characters, which is longer than the 40 characters in Mac OS X 1.3. This is because the password is now salted, which makes brute force attacks more difficult because now cracking one password will make no difference for any of the others, unlike unsalted passwords. If the logon password is necessary, then having a fully patched version of John the Ripper, or another password cracker may be helpful.

Jaguar_user:<value>:::
NTLM_user:<value>:<value>:::
Panther_user:<value>:::
TigerLeopard_user:<value>:::

Once the passwords are on their way to being cracked, the last part of account enumeration can be conducted. Listed in the user account record will be where the home location is on the drive. With this information, document analysis can begin for that folder, with the assumption that all the documents and saved information can be attributed to the user. Unfortunately, without a software tool that can both identify ownership of the files and folders, as well as the permissions associated with them, it is difficult to establish ownership definitively, but general practice indicates that a user will store their documents in the Home folder.

## APPLICATIONS

Normally, during the course of an analysis it is important to note the applications installed on the system. The flexibility of Mac OS X may make this seem much harder than in earlier Macintosh systems. There are two types of executables for Mac OS X, command line binaries, and GUI applications. Most of the command line binaries will be installed in the default `/bin`, `/sbin`, `/usr/bin`, `/usr/sbin`, and many others consistent with Unix default folders. It is possible for users to install their own binaries, but this is for a higher skill level and will be discussed shortly. Most of the GUI applications can be found in `/Applications` and `/System/Library/Coreservices`. Most of the applications the system uses that are without direct user initiated control are in `/System/Library/Coreservices`. Most of the applications that the user uses are stored centrally in `/Applications`.

The `/Applications` folder on the root of the drive is the default location to install applications for most installers, and the typical place that users will install applications as well. Because of the structure of applications for Mac OS X, those locations are limitless. The `/Applications` folder contains subfolders for each application instead of executables. This is the way Mac OS hides the data from the casual user and makes installation and removal very easy. This folder structure is one example of how Mac OS X makes use of application bundles. A bundle is a way to group all the necessary libraries and executable code in one place. Each bundle contains pictures, language resources, plug-ins, and possibly multiple types of executable code. This allows the user to always see the same icon and applications, and for the system to load the pieces that it needs to support the structure. To make a parallel, it is as if all the `.DLL` files for a Windows application were stored in the same location as the application but generally hidden from view.

For most applications this makes installation as easy as drag and drop, and uninstallation as easy as throwing a folder into the trash. Because the code is always kept in the folder with the executable, and the user typically sees only the main icon, these applications can be put anywhere. Besides the /Applications folder, it is also common to find applications folders in the Home folder of a user. This is one of the spaces where Mac OS X will look for an application when you try to open a document.

Application bundles will typically start with a folder that has the extension .APP and contains a folder inside called "Contents". The Contents folder contains a number of resources, including a file called info.plist that contains some of the most important information that a forensic examiner can obtain regarding the application. This file will contain version information as shown in Figure 7.4, in addition to often listing the types of file extensions associated with it for use.

Binary executables may also be installed from additional sources. One way is to download the source code, then compile and install the program. This requires the installation of the developer's tools found typically in the /Developer folder on a drive. This usually advances the user level of the person on the system; a stop-gap for this can be to use one of the automatic application building frameworks available (e.g., fink or darwinports). Once installed on the system, these frameworks assist the user in building these binaries from source code. Many of these projects or binaries will create /opt or /usr/local folders, neither of which are standard on a Mac OS X system.

## SYSTEM

Outside of the user area are often some configuration files of how the system operates independent of each user. For instance, in Mac OS X 10.3 or higher versions, a master encryption password can be set for the computer by one of the administrative accounts and this master keychain is located in the /Library/Keychains/ folder. A number of other useful configuration files are summarized in this section.

The network setting is kept in various places for all versions of Mac OS X. It is always an XML property list but it can be very convoluted text. In Mac OS X 10.2 this is located at /private/var/db/SystemConfiguration/ preferences.xml. In Mac OS X 10.3–10.5 it is located at /Library/ Preferences/SystemConfiguration/preferences.plist. This file will contain all the networking settings for all the available interfaces, as well as different settings based on different locations. This file will also contain the name of the computer as Mac OS X sees itself, as shown here along with two Wi-Fi network connections used by this system sometime in the past.

```
<key>System</key>
<dict>
      <key>ComputerName</key>
      <string>Eoghan Casey's MacBook Pro</string>
      <key>ComputerNameEncoding</key>
      <integer>0</integer>
</dict>

<key>SSID_STR</key>
      <string>Port Networks Public Wi-Fi</string>
      <key>SecurityType</key>
      <string>Open</string>
      <key>Unique Network ID</key>
      <string>286EFFBD-0341-4AE5-9004-D288DE898175</string>
</dict>

<dict>
<key>SSID_STR</key>
      <string>belkin54g</string>
      <key>SecurityType</key>
      <string>Open</string>
      <key>Unique Network ID</key>
      <string>21B63E36-97DD-4843-A358-62FA6E84EF21</string>
```

If a user has changed the default workgroup for SMB sharing, that information will be stored in `/private/etc/smb.conf` for Mac OS X 10.2–10.4, and in `/private/var/db/smb.conf` for Mac OS X 10.5. Please note the location difference for Mac OS X 10.5 because there are multiple `smb.conf` files on the system; the one mentioned previously will have the workgroup if set, and the NetBIOS name if set by the system.

The built-in firewall settings are stored in the `com.apple.sharing.firewall.plist` file for Mac OS X 10.2 through 10.4, which is stored in `/Library/Preferences/` in plain text for Mac OS X 10.2 and 10.3. For Mac OS X 10.4 this becomes a binary property list file. For Mac OS X 10.5 this becomes a bit trickier; the firewall settings are located in part at `/Library/Preferences/com.apple.alf.plist` but this will list only specific application exceptions in addition to some preconfigured exceptions. If any of the services are set to run in sharing they will get an automatic pass. The most important field relating to the firewall operation is the globalstate, which can be set to 0 for off, 1 for essential only, and 2 for specific settings.

To figure out which services referenced in the firewall configuration file are actually running, it is necessary to look in the `/System/Library/LaunchDaemons/` folder and read through the configuration files. These configuration files control which services are set to run at startup and which are not. Specifically, services that are not configured to run will contain a Disabled field in their configuration `.plist` file. On older versions of Mac OS X, some `.plist` files for running services may be located in the `/Library/Preferences/` folder.

Printing on Mac OS X is handled through the CUPS service and will leave behind trace files that indicate printing, similar to some versions of Linux as detailed in Chapter 6, "UNIX Forensic Analysis." On Mac OS X, print spool files are located in `/private/var/spool/cups` and these files are named with a "c" and then five numbers starting sequentially with 00001. The file system dates of these files indicate when the associated file was printed. These files store useful information about each print job in a binary format, including the owner of the print job, the name of the print job, and details about the printer. Occasionally there may be files in this folder starting with a 'd' that contain a PostScript representation of what is being printed. These print spool files can be found on both the originating Mac OS X system and if there is one acting as the print server.

## Logs

There is one more part of the system settings that deserves some mention. Many of the running processes and daemons will store log files. The most common locations for the system are `/private/var/log/` and `/Library/Logs/`. Most log files are easy to attribute to their respective daemons, and are searchable for relevant information from your forensic tool suite. Unfortunately, many of these logs files are stored for a limited period of time, and some are stored for a limited amount of space on the drive. If these limitations are imposed upon log files, then they will typically be broken up into sequential versions and then rotated in order. They may be broken up by space or date—either way there are often multiple versions of a log file. Most of these log files are compressed with gzip or bzip2, requiring additional extraction before most forensic tool suites can search them for keywords. The compressed version of these logs may need to be extracted and expanded before being re-added to the forensic tool for text searches. Fortunately, once uncompressed, most of these log files are straight ASCII text and are easily searched.

### Connection of External Devices

To understand the value and challenges of these logs from a forensic perspective, consider the mounting of external devices in Mac OS X. Every version of Mac OS X, 10.2 through 10.5, seems to log this information differently. The most commonly used log is the `/private/var/log/system.log`. In version 10.2 a log entry containing the line "autodiskmount" is recorded every time an external disk is mounted. The information logged includes the disk/ slice, file system type, read/write status, volume name, and mount point for that volume. This behavior continues in 10.3, with a few exceptions. The process name has changed to "diskarbitrationd" so each log entry will have that name instead of "autodiskmount," and log entries will contain UUID values as identifiers for external devices. The UUID values are unique to the volume if it is a Macintosh native file system, and a FAT volume will register as all zeros.

---

**PRACTITIONER'S TIP: iPOD SHARING**

When external devices are attached to a Mac OS X system, a mount point is created in /Volumes that contains the volume name. Although such mount points are deleted after the device is removed, forensic examination may reveal their existence if they have not been overwritten. In one case, the subject of an investigation denied accessing a particular computer, but forensic examination showed that her iPod had been connected to the computer on a recent date.

---

There are fewer logs associated with external media in more recent versions of Mac OS X. In Mac OS X 10.4 the behavior is exactly the same as 10.3, but only for externally connected FireWire drives. Logs are no longer generated for USB connected drives. In Mac OS X 10.5 registering mount points for drives is dropped altogether. There is a workaround if Spotlight is running, since this application will occasionally try to update the file system identifier on a removable volume. This process is automatic and, if data on that volume was updated since last in a Mac OS X 10.5 machine, or the volume uncleanly unmounted, Spotlight will update the fseventsd information. This method has some issues though; it will not work if you have used that volume only in Mac OS X 10.5 machines or if no changes have be made to that volume since the last time it was put in that machine.

Additional logs that may provide information about connected external media are the `fsck_hfs.log` and the `DiskUtility.log`. Both can be found in the user's `Library/Logs` folder and a copy of the `fsck_hfs.log` can be found in the `/private/var/log` folder. The `fsck_hfs.log` will show anytime an HFS, HFS+, or HFSX volume was mounted. Unfortunately this log does not include the volume name, and does not distinguish between physical devices and disk images. Therefore, it is advisable to correlate information in `fsck_hfs.log` with either the `system.log` or the `DiskUtility.log`. The `DiskUtility.log` will show disk manipulations by the user through the Disk Utility or the helper application. This includes formatting disks, creating or mounting disk images, or burning optical discs.

### Logon/Logoff Activities

Mac OS X systems have many of the same logs associated with logon/logoff activities on Unix systems as detailed in Chapter 6, "UNIX Forensic Analysis." The `secure.log` found in `/private/var/log` can give an idea of not only user login and logoff activity, but also connection activity and security escalations through authenticated means. This log is always found in the same place, although in Mac OS X 10.2 it seems to not be used although a placeholder may exist.

Entries in `secure.log` can be referenced against the utmp, wtmp, or utmpx files on the Mac OS X systems. You can find the `utmp` and the successor `utmpx` in `/private/var/run/` and the `wtmp` file in the `/private/var/log/` folder. In Mac OS X 10.5 the `wtmp` log is replaced by the `asl.db` file and log in the `asl` folder both found in the `/private/var/log/` folder. All of these log files are different kinds of binary files; these files have no native viewer on a Windows machine.

It is important to note that all log files tend to rotate and may even be deleted as part of normal operation. Otherwise treat all entries as sequential; this may be an issue if the machine has been turned on and off intermittently over a period of years.

## Disk Images (and other Frameworks)

Disk image files on Mac OS X systems typically have a `.DMG` file extension, and they generally encapsulate a file system. There are a few common types of disk image files (uncompressed, compressed, and encrypted), and it can be challenge to deal with them inside of Windows-based forensic tools. Uncompressed disk image files can be extracted and then used as logical drives to be reinserted into your forensic tool suite. These can typically be added as if they were raw image files. Compressed disk images and encrypted disk images cannot be directly loaded into a forensic tool suite. A Mac OS X computer is needed to open these files. This issue applies to the implementation of FileVault on Mac OS X 10.3 through 10.5. In Mac OS X 10.3 and 10.4, FileVault disk images are represented as a `.sparseimage` file in the user's Home folder. In Mac OS X 10.5 this format was changed into a `.sparsebundle`, which helps integrate with their backup utility Time Machine.

## PRACTITIONER'S TIP: ACCESSING DATA WITHIN FILEVAULT

It is possible to mount an encrypted sparseimage file using a Mac OS X examination system, provided you can obtain the password for the user account. However, this is not possible on a Windows system. An alternate approach to opening an encrypted disk image that contains a user's FileVault protected data is to boot a clone of the system and log in as the user. In this way, you can log onto the system as the user, thus decrypting the FileVault protected data.

The reason that these disk images could be found anywhere on the system is because they are supported by no one specific program on the system, but a series of libraries running in the background as a framework to support this document type throughout the system. Another example of frameworks on the system is the support for QuickTime. The QuickTime framework supports a lot of the media usage on the Mac OS X system, from the iLife applications to the screensaver. These frameworks can be seen on the system in the /System/Library/Frameworks/ folder. Typically frameworks are used as support for multiple applications and functions on the system so that applications can share them.

## USER FOLDERS

User folders are areas where information may be stored by default or choice by a specific user while they operate Mac OS X. Although some targeted browsing of files may be used during the course of the investigation, much of the data in user folders will be encountered as a result of automated processes such as string searches or media reviews.

Before we start examining results of automated processes, there are a few important aspects of user folders to highlight. In Mac OS X 10.2 through 10.5 there are a few default folders that are created when a new account is created, some with default data. Some of these are not required for Mac OS X operation.

- **Desktop**: Folder where items on the desktop are placed, empty by default, required by all active accounts
- **Documents**: Empty, in version 10.5 has About Stacks.pdf in new accounts
- **Downloads**: Version 10.5 only has About Downloads.pdf in new accounts
- **Library**: Default data for Finder operation, required by all active accounts
- **Movies**: Empty
- **Music**: Empty
- **Pictures**: Empty
- **Public**: Contains a Drop Box folder with set permissions for sharing
- **Sites**: Default data for personal web sharing option

Only two folders are really necessary for using Mac OS X through the Finder; the others help with some of the additional functionality. Many of the empty folders are just suggested placeholders for those types of data, and are also the defaults for some of the Apple applications. Of course, users can create other folders, or remove these folders or store data anywhere on the drive. Even some default application behavior can be altered to save data in different locations. The notable exception is the `Library` folder. Many applications store their specific user data in the `Library` folder and cannot be set to a different location. This is where a great deal of information will be found as discussed in application-specific sections later in this chapter.

Similar to other user's folders, the Trash is in the user's Home folder. This is typically a hidden folder that is named `.Trash` and can be accessed by the user. This will contain documents the user has thrown out and, unlike the Windows Recycle Bin, the original location of the file is not preserved. This is the behavior for the boot volume. On external volumes the behavior is different. Since there is no user folder on an external volume, the Trash is organized at the root in a folder name `.Trashes`. Inside this folder are numbered folders that respond to the UID of the user that moved an item to the Trash and has not emptied it yet. That UID corresponds to the user that was logged in at the time and on that system. Because the Trash subfolders do not map to the UUID, only the UID, it may not be safe to conclude that a particular file was deleted by a certain user account simply based on its location in the Trash of a removable disk. Although there may be two documents in the `.Trashes/501` folder, they may have been thrown out by different users on different systems.

## USER FOLDERS: MEDIA FILES

The popular iLife suite of applications stores the majority of the media files in default locations within a user's Home folder. The files from iDvd are stored in `Documents`, the files from iPhoto are stored in `Pictures`, the files from iMovie are stored in `Movies`, and the files from iTunes are stored in `Music`.

By default iTunes stores its database in one folder, but it can be set to store data elsewhere. iTunes has one large database made up of many small files in a hierarchical structure. This structure is very complex and changes within the different versions of iLife but the media files should be very easy to view. Some caveats to this are the purchased media files from iTunes; some may be protected media and therefore unplayable. The media contained within those files however should be easy enough to determine from iTunes. Within each file purchased from iTunes whether protected or not, it will list the purchaser information. This may not be true for MP3 songs purchased elsewhere.

Similar to iTunes, iPhoto will organize the photos with a hierarchical structure with reference to date of import. iPhoto has a few major differences in organization. It will make use of link files for categorization as well as keeping multiple copies of the files that the user edited, so that an original to which a user can revert is always available. It may seem to someone who is browsing the folder that there are multiple versions of the file, although the user may see only one version of the file.

Unlike iTunes and iPhoto, iMovie and iDvd create separate project folders to contain different data. These are stored in `Movies` and `Documents`, respectively. Each of these folders may contain support media files for use in the project. Each project file uses the raw media similarly to iPhoto preserving the original data while just referencing any changes until a final movie is exported. This is why some movie files contained within may not play—they are just placeholders with references. Look for similar action within the DVD project folders as well.

iMovie underwent a significant change at some point for 2008 and, instead of project-specific folders, there are two folders in the `Movies` folder, `iMovie Events` and `iMovie Projects`. The first stores the raw DVD footage imported into iMovie and the second stores the project files, caches, and output from individual events. This gives the user the ability to pull from all media imported to make any movie. This centralizing of files makes it similar to iTunes and iPhoto.

It is possible to move some of these libraries as well as generate media content in other places—these are just the most common areas. Applications in the iLife suite change frequently so these are just guidelines rather than specific instructions of how to deal with this media. Fortunately, the content of the media is generally more important in an investigation than other factors.

## USER FOLDERS: APPLICATIONS

The configuration of a particular application and the usage artifacts it leaves behind can be very important in a forensic investigation. Many applications on Mac OS X property lists store configuration details and usage information, both as self-contained files as well as embedded in other files. The `Library/Preferences` folder under a user folder contains property lists for many applications, including records of recent activities. For instance, the following entries were extracted from the `com.apple.mail.search.plist` file, showing when the user searched e-mail for particular keywords.

```
<key>nist</key>
<dict>
      <key>IsForToDos</key>
      <false/>
      <key>ModDate</key>
      <date>2009-06-17T00:38:09Z</date>
      <key>RetypeAttempts</key>
      <integer>1</integer>
      <key>SearchField</key>
      <string>Subject</string>
      <key>UseCount</key>
      <integer>3</integer>
</dict>
<key>owen</key>
<dict>
      <key>IsForToDos</key>
      <false/>
      <key>ModDate</key>
      <date>2009-06-09T14:23:53Z</date>
      <key>RetypeAttempts</key>
      <integer>2</integer>
      <key>SearchField</key>
      <string>From</string>
      <key>UseCount</key>
      <integer>4</integer>
</dict>
```

Knowing what an individual was searching for in e-mail at a particular time may be of interest, and forensic examiners may also want to examine the contents of e-mail. This is just one example of the types of information that applications store in property list files on Mac OS X systems.

### FROM THE CASE FILES: PROPERTY LISTS

In one intellectual property theft case the suspect denied having accessed the files of concern, which were stored on a file server within the organization. An examination of property lists on his computer revealed several references to recently opened filenames, including those of concern. The property list showed the full path of each file stored on the server.

More recent versions of Mac OS X store configuration and usage details in SQLite3 database format. Use of these small databases began in Mac OS X 10.4 and became very prevalent in 10.5. A large number of these small databases are used to store and sort data for a variety of applications. This marks a drastic departure from previous convention for many of these applications as well as making sifting data out of it difficult for those not familiar with SQL commands.

Fortunately, inexpensive, user-friendly Windows-based programs like SQLite Database Browser (http://sqlitebrowser.sourceforge.net/) are available to examine these files as shown in Figure 7.6.

Once a file is loaded in SQLite Database Browser, the first tab of Database Structure shows how the data are organized, but it is the second Browse Data tab that is of the most use for forensic examination. This interface can be used

**FIGURE 7.6**

An example of the Safari `Cache.db` file in SQLite Database Browser.

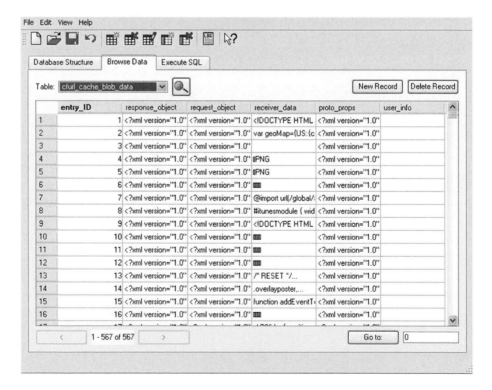

to select individual tables and examine the data they contain. Unfortunately, there is no easy way to dump the data all neatly cross-correlated so some work will have to be done either by hand or with the crafting of some SQL commands. This type of tool is necessary for reviewing many of the SQLite databases found on Mac OS X because these files are not currently interpreted by any forensic suite packages.

## Safari

The most commonly used application on computers is probably the web browser. Safari is the default browser included with Mac OS X systems, starting with Mac OS X 10.3 (it was available as a separate download for 10.2). Different versions of this browser store data in different locations and formats, and this browser is also affected by which version of Mac OS X upon which it is installed. It seems that the same version of Safari will store the cache data in different locations between Mac OS X 10.4 and 10.5. Some of the configuration information remains the same and some of it is a natural evolution of storage.

Each version maintains a list of configuration preferences in the `com.apple.Safari.plist` file in the user's `Library/Preferences` folder. In addition, usage artifacts found on different versions of Mac OS X are listed in Table 7.1.

**Table 7.1** Property Lists in a User's `Library/Safari` Folder Containing Safari Usage Information for Different Versions of Mac OS X

| Data | 10.2 | 10.3 | 10.4 | 10.5 |
|---|---|---|---|---|
| Bookmarks | Bookmarks.plist | Bookmarks.plist | Bookmarks.plist | Bookmarks.plist |
| Last session that was open, including multiple tabs | N/A | N/A | LastSession.plist | LastSession.plist |
| Browsing history | History.plist | History.plist | History.plist | History.plist |
| Downloaded items | Downloads.plist | Downloads.plist | Downloads.plist | Downloads.plist |
| Title bar icons | Icons folder | Icons folder | WebpageIcons.db | WebpageIcons.db |

An example of data contained in a Safari `History.plist` file is provided in Figure 7.7.

In Mac OS X 10.2 through 10.4, each user folder has 15 subfolders under `Library/Caches/Safari` that each have 15 subfolders, all of which contain cached data from recent web pages accessed using Safari as shown in Figure 7.8.

In Mac OS X 10.5 the storage of web browser cache data changes in more than one variation. Some systems will still have cache files and folders in

**FIGURE 7.7**

An exported Safari `History.plist` file from a Mac OS X 10.4 system.

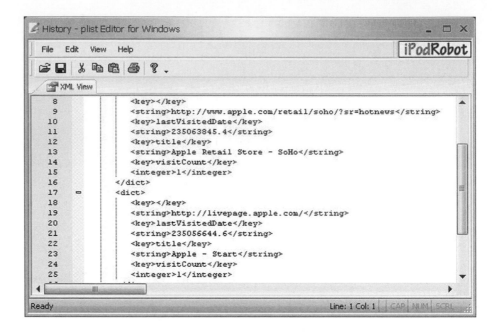

**FIGURE 7.8**

An example of the multiple nested folder structure for Safari web browsing cache on a Mac OS X 10.4 system displayed using FTK.

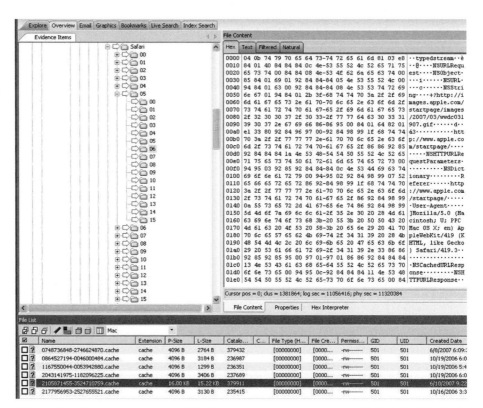

the previous location, but these are from an older version of Safari—either an older version in use on the system or the last time a previous version was used, leaving behind residual cache files. The first change the system made was to move the cache into a database originally located in the user's `Library/Caches/com.apple.Safari` folder. This was the `Cache.db` file, and it may still be present on systems. At some further point this file was moved to a centralized location in `/private/var/folders`. Here there will be a two-character folder owned by root that contains a subfolder named with a 28-character string. Inside those are different temporary folders. This appears to be the new temporary space for data as opposed to using `/var/tmp` on previous versions of Mac OS X. Inside the `-Caches-` folder are a number of subfolders containing cached data associated with various applications. Data associated with Safari is stored in a subfolder named `com.apple.Safari`, which includes the `Cache.db` file. Unfortunately the only way we can tie files cached by Safari back to a particular user account outside of content is through identification of permissions and ownership. This would be an issue for users who rely upon EnCase solely, since it does not display permissions associated with files on Mac OS X systems.

---

**FROM THE CASE FILES: CAUGHT IN THE CACHE**

Two individuals in an organization were suspected of having an affair, which was against company policy. They were both careful not to contact each other directly using e-mail or other common communication applications on their computers. However, they did share a web-based calendar to coordinate illicit meetings. Unbeknownst to them, the full calendar was cached by Safari on their computers.

---

Also with the switch to Mac OS X 10.4 a new folder appeared in the user's `Library/Caches/Metadata/Safari`. The first is the `Bookmarks` folder, which contains cache files that represent the bookmarks listed in the `Bookmarks.plist`. This folder persists in Mac OS X 10.5 and an additional `History` folder is added. This also contains cache files of all the places that have been viewed by the user. This will take the place of the cache folders found in earlier versions in the user's `Library/Safari` folder.

Because of the extra data in cache files for Safari along with cache data not being held in SQLite databases, deleted web page cache may prove very hard to reconstruct or to associate with a user.

## Mail

The next most popular application outside of the web browser is generally the e-mail client. On the Mac OS X this client is named Mail and also stores user-specific information in the user's `Library` folder. Configuration details for Mac

Mail, including the e-mail accounts and location of associated mailboxes on the system are stored in the `Library/Preferences/com.apple.mail` file.

In all versions of Mac OS X 10.2 through 10.5 most of the mail data is stored in the user's `Library/Mail` folder with slight variations by Mail version. Unlike Safari, Mail updates with the OS so you will not find the same version of Mail on different versions of Mac OS X, unless someone went to the trouble of replacing the application.

Mail in Mac OS X 10.2 and 10.3 essentially operates the same way. The main folder contains a folder for each account and one named `Mailboxes`. Each account folder name starts either with Mac or the connection type in capital letters, followed by a username@server structure. Each folder that starts with POP contains a file of current downloaded messages listed by id and another folder, `INBOX.mbox`. The `INBOX.mbox` folder contains configuration files for presentation in the Mail application and at least one file of ASCII mail text, essentially one large block of text that contains all the e-mails concurrently. Each account folder that starts with IMAP or Mac (which is an IMAP account) has a slightly different structure. There are `.imapbox` folders that contain a `CachedMessages` folder, which lists all the messages as sequential numbers with subversions indicating multipart messages as shown in Figure 7.9. The `Mailboxes` folder that

**FIGURE 7.9**

A representation of the `CachedMessages` folder for an IMAP account on a Mac OS X 10.3 system viewed using FTK.

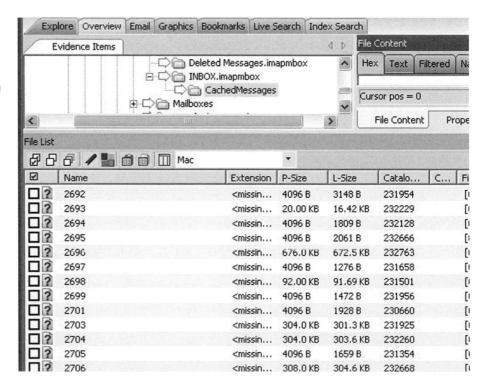

was mentioned earlier stores account independent messages, such as drafts or outgoing messages before they are associated with an account.

In Mac OS X 10.4 the format associated with Mail data changes slightly. The `POP` folders now follow a similar format to the IMAP listed earlier. The main folder contains an `INBOX.mbox/Messages/` folder. The e-mail messages are contained within as sequentially numbered EMLX files. These are the same type as before, just now with an extension. These files are still ASCII text.

Mac OS X 10.4 also introduces two new files for functionality. The first is `SmartMailboxes.plist`, which will sort the messages based upon filtering criteria without actually creating real mailboxes. The other is the `Envelope Index`, an SQLite database that contains calendar, message subject, e-mail addresses, and other information for easy searching of the data in the Mail application.

In Mac OS X 10.5 this evolution continues with further integration being supported by more SQLite databases. The individual e-mail files still have the same structure as Mac OS X 10.4. One of the new databases replaces the individual files that track downloaded messages by collating it into one file. An available feeds database file is updated from Safari as possible RSS feeds that can be subscribed to from within the Mail application.

## Address Book

The Address Book is another application that has embraced the SQLite and plist format for much of the data manipulation. For Mac OS X 10.2 through 10.4 the Address Book data was stored in the user's `Library/Application Support/Addressbook/` folder in a file named `Addressbook.data`. This was a proprietary file format that could be easily read only with the Address Book application itself. This changed in Mac OS X 10.5, and the `Addressbook.data` file may still exist, but it is leftover data no longer updated.

In Mac OS X 10.5 two structures seem to replicate that data. The `AddressBook-v22.abcddb` is an SQLite database that contains all the data in the Address Book. Interestingly, the same data is replicated in the `Library/Application Support/Addressbook/Metadata` folder, storing the same data in individual files as shown in Figure 7.10. There is an `.ABCDP` file for each contact as well as each group in the Address Book. These files build (or rebuild) the SQLite database upon launch of the application. The SQLite database is then used for the quick searching and the integration into the Mail and iChat application for address searching. Each `.ABCDP` file is just a property list and can be opened easily with Plist Editor.

## iCal

The default calendar application for Mac OS X is iCal. This application stores all the data in the user's `Library/Calendars` folder, except in version 10.4.

**FIGURE 7.10A**

An example of a limited Address Book database with one entry for Joe User viewed using SQLite database browser.

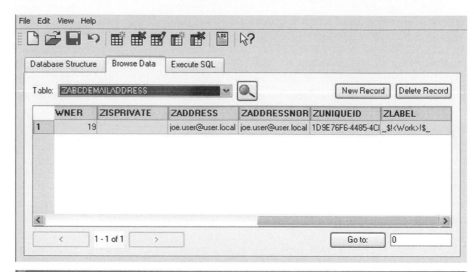

**FIGURE 7.10B**

The .ABCDP file that represents Joe User from the Address Book. The data is the same as in the Address Book database.

In Mac OS X 10.2 and 10.3 each calendar was represented by a .ICS file with the name of the calendar in the user's Library/Calendars folder. These files can be read either as text or with a calendar application.

In Mac OS X 10.4 this schema changed. Now the information is stored in the user's Library/Application Support/iCal folder. This folder contains several .calendar folders that represent each separate calendar. The information about which calendar is which is specified in the info.plist file contained in each folder. The data is stored in the corestorage.ics file also located in that folder.

Additionally, each event is also stored in the user's `Library/Caches/Metadata/iCal` folder. These are also broken down into folders for each calendar as well, although they do not seem to correlate the UUID values that each folder has for a name. In the cache, subfolders are individual `.icalevent` files, which are binary `plist` files that can be viewed with Plist Editor with no issue.

Mac OS X 10.5 changes the data storage location back to the user's `Library/Calendars` folder. A new file Calendar Cache is an SQLite database file that shows all the calendars integrated into one file as shown in Figure 7.11. Each calendar still has an individual folder with an `info.plist` file to identify the calendar.

For each calendar there is an `Events` folder named with a UUID value that contains each event in the calendar broken down into individual `.ICS` files as shown in Figure 7.12.

It is possible to see older versions of the calendar information stored in Mac OS X 10.5, so do not be surprised if there is data in the user's `Library/Caches/Metadata/iCal` or `Library/Application Support/iCal`. However, keep in mind that this is often older data, and most likely not with what the user is currently interacting. Although this may seem confusing and add work, it does provide a glimpse to previous activity.

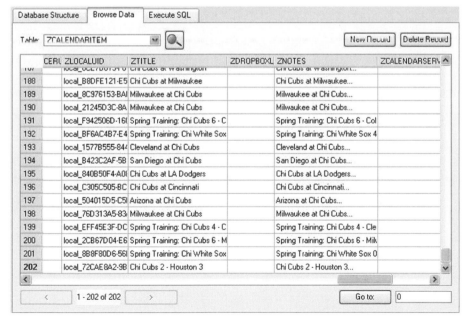

**FIGURE 7.11**
An example of the iCal database showing information in the calendar.

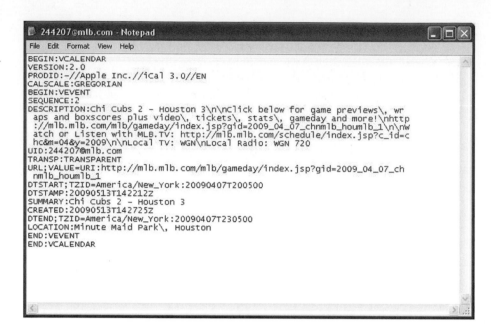

## WRAP UP

Hopefully this overview will assist in clarifying some of the issues of analyzing Mac OS X artifact data on a Windows system. Some of the forensic suites have different strengths, but there is no counterpart to every Mac OS X data structure. Largely notable exceptions are any of the encrypted files that are built-in such as FileVault or Keychains. The good information is that many of the most common data storage file types, plist and SQLite3 databases, are easily viewable on Windows with the addition of some free tools. This should suffice for all but the most complex of investigations involving Mac OS X artifacts.

## REFERENCES

Casey. (2004). http://developer.apple.com/technotes/tn/tn1150.html

# CHAPTER 8

# Embedded Systems Analysis

**Ronald van der Knijff**

## INTRODUCTION

When Joe checks his bank balance with a web browser on his mobile phone he immediately notices something is wrong. His balance is reduced to almost zero as a result of repeated daily cash withdrawals. Bewildered, he calls his bank to block his account. The bank investigates Joe's story and by correlating events from other customers, they find a suspicious point of sale terminal. The police officer involved seizes the point of sale terminal and sends it to the forensic laboratory for examination. At the forensic lab, fingerprint and DNA analysis is performed, assisted by a digital forensic expert to prevent any damage to the electronics and digital traces. Further analysis of the point of sale terminal reveals that it was maliciously manipulated with additional electronics to store and forward magnetic stripe data and entered PIN codes. The additional electronics uses a protected microcontroller to encrypt the customer data and a mobile phone with Wi-Fi for data transfer.

At the forensic laboratory some reference microcontrollers of the same type are used to develop a method to circumvent the read protection security. This method is then used to extract data from the program memory of the microcontroller found in the point of sale terminal. From the acquired memory data the cryptographic algorithm and the encryption key are reverse engineered. With this knowledge the encrypted data is decrypted resulting in a list of account numbers and PIN codes of compromised bank accounts. The flash memory from the seized mobile phone is also acquired. Although no SIM card is present in the mobile phone, some historical references to used SIM cards are found in the extracted data. With these references the telecom provider delivers subscription information leading to a suspect. The police find out that this suspect hired a car recently and when the navigation system of this

## CONTENTS

Introduction.....383

Definition and Operation.........384

Preserving Traces..............391

Data Collection.........397

Information Recovery..........413

Analysis and Interpretation of Results.........424

The Future.......430

Abbreviations...431

References.......433

car is examined a lot of waypoints close to other compromised point of sales terminals are found. The suspect is observed further and finally he and some other suspects are arrested. DNA material of one of the suspects matches with DNA found inside of the manipulated terminal. This evidence is presented in court by the prosecutor as strong evidence of attribution and is accepted by the judges.

This scenario is an example of cybercrime in which information technology is used both as the tool and target of a crime. Currently, the majority of digital forensics investigations involving embedded systems deal with more traditional criminal activities where information technology is used as an instrument without being an explicit target. For instance, homicide, drug dealing, terrorism, and child exploitation cases can have related digital evidence stored on mobile phones. However, as these systems become more sophisticated, there is a greater risk that they will be the target of attacks such as malicious code and data theft.

Embedded systems are probably the fastest growing source of forensic digital investigations. This is caused partly by technological developments where everything gets smaller, more portable, and wirelessly connected. The autonomous way in which embedded systems operate and leave digital traces, together with limited ways for users to access these traces also contributes to their forensic relevance.

This chapter starts with general information about how embedded systems work, followed by a description of methods and techniques for preserving, collecting, analyzing and interpreting the information they contain. It is important to note that some of the data acquisition methods described in this chapter can cause irreparable damage to the device. Even when experienced forensic examiners successfully acquire data, it may not be possible to return the device to its original working state. Given the number of abbreviations, the meaning of common terms is provided at the end of the chapter rather than expanding each one in the main text.

## DEFINITION AND OPERATION

An embedded system is a special-purpose computer system designed to perform one or a few dedicated functions, often with real time computing constraints. It is usually embedded as part of a complete device including hardware and mechanical parts (Wikipedia, 2008).

An embedded system can be defined as a computer system that is built in or "embedded" in a device of which it wholly or partially controls the functionality. The computer system and the device are indissolubly linked and one has no significance without the other (Parker, 1994).

These definitions are merely attempts to define the concept of embedded systems. An exact definition is impossible given the many manifestations of embedded systems and the rapid technological developments in this area. For the purposes of forensic examination, it is more practical to make a distinction between computer forensics for which dedicated hardware knowledge is required and computer forensics without the need for such specific knowledge. File system analysis for example, can be done without in-depth hardware knowledge, but to recover any additional information, the hardware characteristics of the storage medium need to be understood and they are mostly part of an embedded system (e.g., hard disk drive, tape unit, solid state disk).

## Overview of Devices

The following overview, which was compiled in connection with the year 2000 problem, illustrates the diversity of embedded systems (de Backer, 1999).

**Office systems**
- Telephones (fixed and mobile)
- Computers (notebook, palmtop, electronic organizers, PDA, smart card, etc.)
- Fax machines
- Answering machines
- Copiers

**Communication systems**
- Data links (hubs, routers, bridges, etc.)
- Switch systems (X25, Frame Relay, etc.)
- Telephone exchanges
- Calling systems
- Satellite links
- Radio and TV links

**Transport systems**
- Global positioning systems (GPS)
- Embedded systems in cars, buses, trams, trains, aircraft, ships (airbags, navigation, cruise control, electronic locks, etc.)
- Energy supply (petrol, gas, electricity, etc.) (pipelines)
- Monitoring systems
- Systems controlling (air) traffic
- Parking meters
- Ticket machines (parking tickets, etc.)
- Systems controlling times of public transport (trains, trams, buses, etc.)
- Radar systems
- Systems for luggage handling
- Check-in systems
- Speed detectors

**Household equipment**
- Audio, video, and communication equipment
- Clocks
- Ovens, microwaves
- Heating systems
- Thermostats
- Central heating installations
- Alarm installations

**Building management systems**
- Systems for energy saving
- Emergency systems (UPS, no-break installations, diesel generators, etc.)
- Heating systems
- Cooling systems
- Lifts, escalators
- Systems controlling access
- Systems for burglar alarms
- Systems for fire safety

*(Continued)*

- Registration systems
- CCTV cameras
- Safes
- Door locks

**Production systems**

- Computer-aided manufacturing (CAM) systems
- Computer-aided design (CAD) systems
- Systems for (controlling) energy (production) (electricity, gas, water, etc.)
- Systems for registering time
- Systems for marking date and/or time (expiry dates, etc.)
- Clock-driven pumps, valves, meters, etc.
- Test, monitoring, and control equipment (temperature, pressure, etc.)
- Simulation equipment
- Machines
- Robots
- Weighing equipment
- Implements, tools

**Banks**

- Cash dispensers
- Payment machines (e.g., with check cards, etc.)
- (Credit) card systems

**Medical systems**

- Infusion pumps
- Cardiac equipment
- Pacemaker
- Laboratory equipment
- Monitoring equipment
- Equipment for imaging and processing (radiography, tomography, magnetic resonance, ultrasound, etc.)
- Support equipment for organ functions
- Ventilation equipment
- Anaesthetic equipment
- Surgical equipment
- Nursing equipment
- Sterilizing and disinfecting equipment
- Medical filing systems

More recently, efforts have been made to categorize a subset of embedded systems called small-scale digital devices for forensic purposes (Harrill & Mislan, 2007).

**FIGURE 8.1**

Basic model of a computer system.

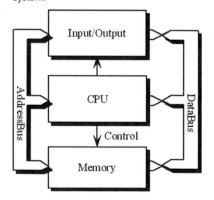

## Relevant Components and Their Basic Operation

Figure 8.1 shows the basic model of a computer system. Communication between the central processing unit (CPU), the memory and the input/output components (I/O), flows via the address bus, the data bus, and the control lines. The CPU reads instructions (the embedded software) from the memory, taking actions based on the type of instructions it receives. This action can, for example, consist of calculations carried out by the CPU or of transport of data to or from peripheral devices. For embedded systems, the integration of components is often higher than for open computer systems. For example, there are electronic organizers with a single chip that contains the CPU, the various memories, and the drivers for keyboard and display.

A wide variety of CPU architectures are used in embedded systems: from classic 8-bit types (Z80, 6800, 8051) to more recent processor families (ARM, MIPS, ×86). In addition to the obvious input and output peripherals such as the keyboard and the display there are many sensors and actuators for measuring input and controlling the output of processes. Think, for example, of infrared transmission (IrDA), radio communication (Bluetooth, Wi-Fi), as well as sensors for measuring position, temperature, pressure, or movement and actuators for controlling a valve, inflating an airbag, or locking a door. The input and output facilities intended for test and repair purposes are also important for forensic applications as summarized later in this section and discussed more comprehensively in the section on boundary-scan/JTAG later in this chapter.

## Memories

From a forensic examination perspective, memories are the most interesting embedded system components because they contain the most user related data. Memory refers to all semiconductor components of embedded systems that retain digital data. Besides memory, embedded systems can also contain other data storage media like hard drives or optical discs but these components can mostly be treated like open system components. For forensic examination of semiconductor memory it is important to know the main characteristics of different memory types.

### Read Only Memory (ROM)

ROM is nonvolatile[1] memory in which data are deposited during the production process and thereafter can only be read. ROM is used to store software and other static data. Embedded operating systems were often stored in ROM but this has changed since the introduction of flash memory.

### Programmable ROM (PROM)

PROM is nonvolatile memory in which data are deposited not during the production process but at a later programming stage and thereafter can only be read. Variations on the basic design have resulted in different programming concepts with the following distinguished names.

### Erasable PROM (EPROM)

EPROM is a PROM that can be erased as a whole with UV light and then reprogrammed (on the order of a hundred times).

### Electrically Erasable PROM (EEPROM)

EEPROM is a PROM in which each individual byte can be erased electrically (up to a million times for modern types). In embedded systems, EEPROM is mainly used for nonvolatile storage of dynamic data (configuration preferences, transactions, etc.).

### Flash

Flash is an EEPROM in which data can only be erased in blocks (up to a million times for modern types). Erasing results in a memory block that is

---

[1]Nonvolatile memory is a memory in which the data stored remains secure without power input. This in contrast to volatile memory in which the data is lost when the power supply is interrupted.

filled completely with 1s. Flash memory comes in two flavors: NOR flash and NAND flash, named after the basic logical structures of these chips. Contrary to NAND flash, NOR flash can be read byte by byte in constant time. This property allows more efficient execution of code and is the reason why NOR flash is often used when the primary goal of the flash memory is to store firmware.[2] Parts of NOR flash that are not occupied by firmware are then used for user data storage. In NAND flash, blocks are divided further into pages, for example 32 or 64 per block. A page is usually a multiple of 512 bytes in size, to emulate 512 byte sector size commonly found in file systems on magnetic media. Additionally, a page has a number of so-called spare area bytes, generally used for storing metadata such as error-correcting codes (ECC). Modern NAND flash uses multiple levels of electrical charge to store more than one bit in each cell. This mechanism and the limited amount of erase cycles cause bit errors during normal device operation. Modern NAND flash relies on error-correcting codes, stored in the spare area bytes, to detect and correct these errors. If errors cannot be recovered, a block is marked bad and another block is used instead.

Because of its high density of storage and fast access time, flash is emerging as a replacement for both ROM and EEPROM. NAND flash is the most used technology for the storage of multimedia data (music, photos, etc.) in embedded systems.

Such flash memory is often represented at the system level as an ATA disk with a FAT file system. The block structure has two important implications for forensic investigations. First, these systems are mostly built in such a way that deleted files are only marked in the FAT as deleted but can still be retrieved. After a disk formatting operation, the blocks might be physically erased, which makes recovery almost impossible. Second, different physical versions of one logical file can be present. This occurs when the size of the files is much smaller than the flash block size, which makes it more efficient to erase a block only if there is no more free space available in it. While there is free space, markings (available/unavailable) show which physical areas of memory are available. When there is no more free space in a block, only the active areas are copied to a free block and the old block is erased physically.

### Random Access Memory (RAM)

RAM is volatile memory that can be written to as well as read. RAM can be divided into Dynamic RAM (DRAM needs to be refreshed periodically) and

---

[2]Firmware is software that is embedded in a hardware device (like a mobile phone or a PDA). Because a processor needs byte-by-byte addressable memory for code execution, it is inefficient to store firmware in NAND flash. If program code is stored in NAND flash it needs to be completely transferred to RAM before a processor is able to execute the code.

Static RAM (SRAM does not need to be refreshed). In embedded systems, RAM is used as working memory and in combination with a battery for nonvolatile storage of dynamic data.

### Ferro Electric RAM (FeRAM)

FeRAM is a new, nonvolatile memory with the read and write characteristics of DRAM. For embedded systems, FeRAM has the potential in the future to replace all other types of memory as universal memory.

Table 8.1 summarizes the most important characteristics of the discussed memory types.

**Table 8.1** Main Characteristics of Different Memory Types

| Characteristics | ROM | PROM | EPROM | EEPROM | FLASH | DRAM | SRAM | FeRAM |
|---|---|---|---|---|---|---|---|---|
| Density | 6 | 1.5 | 4 | 1.5 | 6 | 4 | 1 | 5 |
| Retention time | ∞ | ∞ | 10 years | 10 years | 10 years | 0 | 0 | 10 years |
| Rewritable | n/a | 1 | 100 | $10^6$ | $10^6$ | ∞ | ∞ | $10^{16}$ |
| Writing speed | n/a | -- | - | - | + | ++ | ++ | ++ |
| Reading speed | + | ++ | + | + | + | + | ++ | + |

## Boot Loaders

A boot loader is the first program that runs on a system causing the system to become fully functional. For a personal computer the BIOS chip contains the boot loader code. When an embedded system is powered on or being reset, the CPU jumps to a particular point in memory (the so-called reset vector). This is where the primary boot loader is located. The primary boot loader might execute preparation tasks before it jumps to a memory location where the secondary boot loader resides, which finally starts the application code or the operating system. Typical preparation tasks include initializing processor registers, and copying the secondary boot loader and sometimes an operating system from flash to RAM. Primary boot loaders often contain flash reprogramming routines to receive, check, and install upgrades of the secondary boot loader code for debugging and in field upgrading tasks. How boot loaders can be used for forensic data acquisition will be explained later.

## Memory Management

Memory management refers to all methods used to store code and data in memory, keep track of their usage, and reclaim memory space when possible. At a low level this means a mapping between the physical chips and a logical address space via a memory map. At a higher level virtual address spaces with a memory management unit (MMU) might be used to give application programs the impression of contiguous working memory. In reality the memory may be physically fragmented into parts stored on different physical chips or other storage media. If a forensic examiner wants to know which physical memory locations of a device have been copied, in-depth knowledge of memory management is necessary as discussed in the section on data collection later in this chapter.

### Flash File Systems

An increasing number of embedded systems that use flash memory for file storage emulate a block device with standard 512-byte sectors, and use a standard file system (like FAT) on top of it. This block device emulation needs to support reclaiming of blocks that contain deleted data[3] (garbage collection). For reliable use of flash memory in a writable file system it is necessary to handle possible power loss between erase and subsequent write operations. Because erasing a block causes a block to deteriorate it is also desired to spread block erase operations as evenly as possible over the full range of physical blocks. The algorithms to do this are indicated as wear leveling and are often classified as sensitive intellectual property. Because blocks can become bad, block device emulation also needs to support bad block management. If the block device emulation and wear leveling techniques are not part of the file system they are part of a separate layer, called the flash translation layer. A more efficient use of flash memory is the use of a dedicated journaling flash file system (Jones, 2008). The implications of flash file systems on forensic data analysis are discussed in the section on file system recovery later in this chapter.

### Boundary-scan

Boundary-scan is a testing method to test or debug electronic components. Components can be chips but also printed circuit boards (PCBs). A lot of modern embedded systems on the market today are boundary-scan enabled. Boundary-scan has been standardized under industry standard IEEE1149.1 but is more widely known as JTAG, the acronym of the founders, the Joint Test Action Group (IEEE–Standards Association, 2001). Figure 8.2 shows the basic principles of a JTAG enabled printed circuit board.

JTAG enabled printed circuit boards use a dedicated interface, called the JTAG test access port (TAP), designed to be daisy-chained between different chips on a board. This interface can be used to shift data into so-called boundary-scan registers. These registers are built into chips especially for testing purposes and

---

[3]Deleted data is no longer used by the target system but can still be recovered; for example an SMS message deleted by the user but still present in flash memory because the flash block also contains active SMS messages.

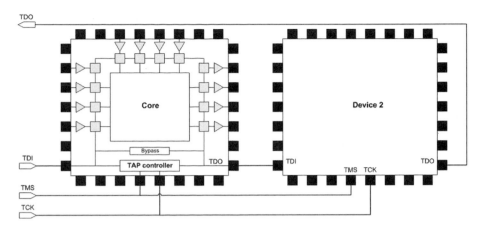

**FIGURE 8.2**
Two daisy-chained JTAG-enabled chips. The chip on the left shows the JTAG specific logic added to the chip's core structure.

are connected between chip I/O pins and their internal core logic. Depending on the state of the boundary-scan logic, the boundary-scan registers are invisible during normal operation of the device, connected to the I/O pins in external test mode, or connected to the internal core logic in internal test mode. With these operation modes it is possible to apply test vectors to a printed circuit board for testing connections between individual chips or control non-standardized test and debugging functionality of internal processor cores. The use of boundary-scan for forensic data acquisition is covered in the section on boundary-scan/JTAG later in this chapter.

## PRESERVING TRACES

Once an embedded system has been recognized as relevant to an investigation, preservation steps must be taken to guarantee the original state of all evidence including the digital evidence. This preservation process can be quite challenging when dealing with embedded systems. It is not always apparent whether an embedded system is switched on or off, and inadvertently switching off a system might also destroy important digital evidence. It is also not trivial to determine to which other components a particular system is connected and what influences those components can have on the target device.

With the enormous amount of existing embedded systems, their wide technological diversity, and the extremely rapid development of new products, it is not realistic to have off-the-shelf forensic solutions for every possible embedded system exhibit. With limited forensic resources it seems a better strategy to spend research and development time on components that occur in the majority of systems and also have a high likelihood of containing relevant digital clues that can be linked to individuals. Before usage in an actual forensic case, the developed semifinished examination methods need to be adapted and tested to work on a similar reference device. Adequate preservation measures are very important in this approach because it might take some time after the seizure of an exhibit until the actual data collection takes place.

## Nondigital Traces

In most actions related to preserving and collecting digital evidence, a form of physical contact will be established between the device and the examiners or their equipment. This contact might harm other forensic traces like fingerprints, DNA, or tool marks. Buttons, keyboards, and connectors for example are possible bearers for fingerprint traces and DNA. For high profile cases it is advisable to determine the optimal examination strategy with a team of forensic specialists from all relevant disciplines. Always try to record the initial state of the exhibits like the content of displays, the state of indicator lights, the position of switches, connections to other systems, or any visual damage.

---

### FROM THE CASE FILES

Skimming is the illegal copying of magnetic stripe data and accessory security codes from debit or credit cards. A popular skimming method adds recording electronics to existing automated teller machines (ATM) or point of sale terminals (POS). Forensic examination of skimming equipment is preferably done with a team consisting of fingerprint, DNA, and Information and Communication Technology (ICT) experts. ICT experts carry out the disassembling of the electronics and DNA experts sample relevant parts for DNA material.

Fingerprint experts know the most likely locations for fingerprint traces and prevent the other specialists from affecting these traces. DNA matches have been found based on material found on internal cable connectors. Skimming equipment often contains adhesive tape for connecting the rogue device to genuine parts of the ATM or POS terminal, which is a fruitful source for fingerprints. After DNA and fingerprint analysis, digitally stored data can be extracted and further analysis of the functionality can be done by ICT experts.

---

## Live versus Dead Dilemmas

An intuitive approach for collecting digital evidence from an embedded system is to first copy all data from volatile memory, then switch the system off and copy all data from nonvolatile memories. This approach has some practical difficulties. There is generally no easy method to access the data in the volatile memory (Feldman et al., 2008). Furthermore, switching off a device might also change data in nonvolatile memories. Some systems, for example, start a garbage collection procedure on flash memory as part of their shut down sequence. This garbage collection might overwrite blocks of deleted data possibly containing relevant information from the past. Other systems do this as part of their boot process so power cycling must be kept to an absolute minimum.

A more practical approach is to keep the system running and conserve the system in such a way that the risks of evidence alteration are minimized. Contacting the manufacturer regarding technical details is recommended. A dedicated examination procedure can then be developed on a similar reference system before the exhibit is further examined. Manufacturers may not be forthcoming; even with a court order they sometimes seem to delay a request until a prosecutor loses interest or the criminal trial takes place. Nondisclosure requirements from manufacturers don't have to prevent manufacturers from sharing information because a nondisclosure can also be signed by other people from whom the judge decides that they need to know specific details during a criminal trial.

## FROM THE CASE FILES

On 12 December 2007 part of the Netherlands suffered a power outage for almost 50 hours because an Apache helicopter from the Dutch air force hit a major power cable during a nighttime exercise. The aircraft's crew, who were using night vision goggles at the time of the accident, made an emergency landing without any injuries. A forensic quick response team immediately started investigating the case and embedded system specialists were asked to preserve and recover data from the Apache helicopter. With assistance from technical specialists from the Dutch air force the following sources of digital evidence were preserved:

- Data transfer cartridge (DTC), a memory module for storing flight related data like route, targets, and hazards that can be displayed onto a map during the flight

- Data downloaded from the Maintenance Data Recorder (MDR), a flight recorder with flight data, maintenance data, and audio with the last 30 minutes of cockpit communication

- Recordings from the Target Acquisition Designation System (TADS), a system primarily designed for usage in combination with weapon systems but also used for flight navigation

Data acquisition and analysis was done with both existing tools for this helicopter from manufacturer Boeing, and with specific forensic tools. Boeing generated a 170-page report from the MDC data with detailed technical information of the accident. TADS recording contained video images of the whole flight together with important flight data and audio recording of all internal and external communication. Because of Dutch law most of this information could be used only for the purpose of accident prevention and not for criminal or civil law (Onderzoeksraad Voor Veiligheid, 2009).

### Maintain Power

To prevent the loss of any data stored in volatile memory, try to ascertain whether the system has a power source and take precautions to ensure that this power supply does not fail. In addition to a regular power supply, many embedded devices have a backup battery. Study the technical manual in an effort to establish the capacity of the backup battery. When the capacity is not known, take the precaution of replacing the backup battery. Try this out on an identical reference device to make sure that no data are lost. Never remove the normal power source and the backup battery at the same time.

Mobile phones for example have at least one main battery and sometimes a backup battery for powering the real time clock when the phone is switched off. Mobile phones can be recharged via their original power adapter or via several universal charging solutions.

## FROM THE CASE FILES

It is not always immediately clear what role a battery plays in the working of an embedded system. During an investigation into an alarm mechanism used to detonate a bomb, the battery was removed, for the purpose of taking fingerprints, because there was no activity visible on the display. It later appeared that the complete alarm mechanism was supplied with power via this battery except the display, which was activated only after the display was connected to the main power circuit.

### Don't Cause Security Barriers

Volatile data can contain information relating to security barriers previously passed by the user. Think of password entry, biometric authentication, or encrypted partitions. As long as the device is switched on, the security system usually does not influence the extraction of data, but after it is switched off the access procedure must be reenacted.

For GSM and UMTS phones, for example, a PIN code or a PUK code might be needed to access the chip card inside the phone when the phone is switched on, as discussed in the procedural portion of the section on data collection later in this chapter.

### Isolate from Sensor Data and Network Connectivity

When initially preserving embedded systems, try to establish whether it has input or output components that can alter existing data. Global positioning devices for example are permanently reading positioning data from satellites. Navigation applications typically contain cyclical memory in which the last route taken is stored. When this information is relevant it is important not to move the system and to investigate whether it is possible to protect the cyclical memory against alteration. If it is not possible to prevent such alteration, then it will be necessary to examine the system on site.

Increasingly, embedded systems are being designed with networking capabilities. These network facilities might cause alteration of embedded system data from outside. A mobile phone that is switched on and connected to a network periodically exchanges data with that network. In addition to system data, individual personal data can change, for example, through incoming calls and incoming SMS messages. This may or may not be desirable depending on the situation. With a mobile phone, for example, it can be desirable to allow such data to be stored by the phone until all the transaction data related to the mobile phone has been acquired from the service provider.

Mobile phones, PDAs and other portable devices with valuable data might contain remote controllable self-destruct applications (DexMobile, 2008). These applications are meant to protect sensitive information after loss or theft but could also be used for antiforensic purposes. Unintended but exploitable self-destruct mechanisms exist that can be abused for antiforensics too (Leyden, 2001).

Forensic toolkits for mobile phone examination sometimes contain low-cost shielding solutions like special bags or shielded cabinets. It is important to realize that these solutions cause the battery to run down more quickly because the phone is using more power during network searching. When using such bags on a crime scene they need to be transferred to a protected area as quickly as possible. The most generic method for protecting live systems against wireless network originated data alteration is to store and examine them in a Faraday cage. A Faraday cage is an enclosure formed by conducting material that shields the interior from external electromagnetic radiation. All power and network connections in such a room are filtered to prevent external interference. Small Faraday cages exist with filtered power connections (LV Electronics, 2008). They can be used for preservation on crime scenes and powered during transport to bigger facilities for actual examination.

It is possible to think of situations in which it is inevitable that certain data in an embedded system will change. In such cases it is necessary to take such variations into account when assessing the integrity of the stored data. For instance, a mobile phone usually contains a real-time clock in which the data is changing continually. The value of this clock can be relevant (because most of the timestamps stored in the phone are taken from this clock) and certainly needs to be included in the report of forensic examination tools. The operative question is how to deal with this kind of dynamic data in the context of forensic integrity marks like MD5 values. Including such dynamic data in global device integrity calculations during acquisition is not desirable because it will cause the integrity mark to be different for each individual acquisition. This issue applies only to forensic acquisition of memory, since a global integrity mark is useful during subsequent analysis to check the overall integrity of digital evidence after using analysis tools on the data.

This is mainly an issue for logical extraction methods that use the regular operating system. The concern regarding dynamic data does not apply when acquiring physical memory via the JTAG interface because the normal operating system is not running and thus cannot change any data.

## Cleaning

Electronic devices that have been exposed to extreme conditions like fire or explosions need to be cleaned as soon as possible to preserve stored data and avoid further damage. The same holds for electronics that have been moisturized with water or blood, for example. Devices found in water or other fluids should be transported to a laboratory with the device submerged in the same fluid or in demineralized water and detached from batteries or other energy sources. Exposing these wet devices to air deteriorates the condition of the electronics much faster than when submerged. Blood in particular can be very damaging to printed circuit boards especially in combination with electrical power sources.

For cleaning printed circuit boards an ultrasonic cleaner and a mix of demineralized water with a nonionic surfactant like *Triton X-100* is very effective.

## Repair

Repair of an exhibit conflicts with the forensic principle of preserving the original state of the exhibit and is used only if no alternative methods exist or if there is no time or money for development of alternative examination methods.

During investigations of violent assaults, occasionally PDAs or mobile phones are encountered that have been damaged during the crime. Each digital clue can be relevant in such a case but there is not always enough time to wait for the development of dedicated low-level methods. In such cases attempts are made to repair an exhibit in order to use existing forensic tools that work only on fully functional devices.

Since it is widely known that forensic tools exist for reading (U)SIM cards from mobile phones, as discussed in the next section of this chapter, suspects sometimes try to make their (U)SIM card unusable (by biting it, stamping on it, etc.). Often the (U)SIM cards no longer work but it is possible to repair them. First, the plastic cover is removed with a scalpel on the opposite side of the card to the contact surfaces. Second, the epoxy material protecting the chip is removed using an etching solution in a fume cupboard. The damage to the chip can then be assessed under a microscope. If the silicon surface has been torn or pulverized, further (partial) data recovery attempts are very labor-intensive with a very small chance of success. If the only damage is in the wires connecting the silicon and the contact surfaces, tiny needles (microprobes) are placed on the chip at the points where the connecting wires were originally attached. These probes are connected electronically to a smart-card reader through which the (U)SIM card can then be accessed. Figure 8.3 shows a number of examples of (U)SIM card repairs.

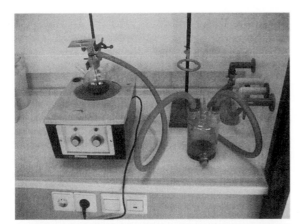

**FIGURE 8.3**
Examples of SIM repairs: removal of the epoxy layer (a); detail of broken connecting wire and the micro probes attached instead (b); SIM chip with irreparable damage (c).

# DATA COLLECTION

After an embedded system has been conserved and all potential evidence is preserved, an investigation needs to be carried out into what data it may contain and how this information can be accessed and read in a forensically sound manner. When it involves a commercial device, the preferred approach is to obtain the same type of device—an exemplar that can be compared with the exhibit. It can often be determined from the technical manual what kind of data can be present on a particular device and how this information can be protected, changed, and read out by the user. Additionally, technical documentation from the development phase or for maintenance and repair is valuable for retrieving information that is not of direct importance for the normal user. The data collection process can be divided into obtaining access and extracting data.

## Getting Access

In order to collect data from an embedded system, some kind of communication channel must be established to give commands to the device and receive response data. User level communication channels like key input and display output, cable connections, infrared transmission, Bluetooth and Wi-Fi are used whenever possible. Otherwise system-level access channels need to be found and made ready for use. Many embedded systems have special access channels for test and debug purposes. JTAG is a standardized example of such a test and debug channel. Finding, enabling, and using communication channels will be discussed further in the physical data acquisition sections later in this chapter.

More challenging access tasks are the ones penetrating the security that is protecting stored data. Security barriers like a PDA power-on password or a smart card PIN code need to be passed when the normal, user level, communication channels of a device are used for data collection. These logical security measures are circumvented when data are read directly from the memories. Alternately, it may be necessary to circumvent a physical protection, for example by removing an epoxy layer covering a smart card chip. For some devices, it may be possible to reactivate a test circuit that has been disabled by the manufacturer by removing or replacing a resistor. A number of methods and techniques for getting access are presented here.

### Procedural

In a number of cases gaining access is controlled via judicial procedures. This applies, for example, to get access to a (U)SIM smart card. (U)SIM ((Universal) Subscriber Identity Module) is a smart card with information about a UMTS or GSM subscriber stored electronically. Data in a (U)SIM can be protected with a PIN (Personal Identity Number). A PIN has four to eight digits, is requested after a phone is switched on, and is entered via the keypad of the phone. The number of attempts for entering a PIN is limited to three. If none of the attempts are successful the access to the protected data is blocked. This blockade can be lifted with a PUK (PIN Unblocking Key). A PUK has eight digits and is entered together with a newly chosen PIN. The number of attempts for entering a PUK is limited to 10. If none of these attempts are successful, most smart cards are configured to irreversibly block further PUK entry. In many countries PUKs can be obtained from the subscriber's network provider. For this the Integrated Circuit Card ID (ICCID) of the (U)SIM smart card is required plus, in most countries, judicial authorization. The ICCID is not protected with a PIN and can always be read out.

Procedures are also needed to access a mobile phone that is missing a (U)SIM card. Without a (U)SIM card, most mobile phones will not permit access to their normal input and output channels. This makes manual or logical data acquisitions problematic. Even if the phone permits access without a (U)SIM, it might contain data that is visible only after the particular (U)SIM card is inserted. Using another (U)SIM will likely not show the missing data and might even erase existing data in the phone memory. The phone evidently has a way to recognize the correct (U)SIM card, but a specially prepared (U)SIM can be used to let the phone "think" the missing (U)SIM is present. These programmable (U)SIMs are part of some forensic toolkits (Micro Systemation AB, 2006; Netherlands Forensic Institute, 2006). Most phones use the IMSI[4] and/or the ICCID to recognize a specific (U)SIM . This information can be found in call detail records of the network provider using the phone's IMEI[5] as a search key and the appropriate judicial authorization. The identifiers needed to clone a (U)SIM card can also be recovered from the phone memory by first acquiring physical memory and then locating and decoding the required information.

### Back-doors

Many systems for protecting access have a back-door built in deliberately with which the security can be circumvented. In some cases there is an extra password (a.k.a. master password) given in the technical documentation that always works. Some PDAs have a specific key combination that activates a system menu with an option to display portions of memory contents. The location of the password can be ascertained by studying these data on an exemplar device configured with a known password, after which the password of the exhibit itself can be retrieved. Mobile phones can contain a device password that must be entered as well as the (U)SIM PIN to use the phone. For some phones there are service sets generally used by repair centers that can be used to retrieve or circumvent these device passwords. Different approaches to finding back-doors are:

- Get in touch with the manufacturer.

- Search for documentation on the Internet. Searching on iPhone and passcode, for example, will quickly unveil a method to break the iPhone password protection (Zdziarski, 2008b).

---

[4]International Mobile Subscriber Identity, the subscriber identification number of the (U)SIM.

[5]International Mobile Equipment Identity, the identification number of the mobile phone.

- Trial and error on the basis of back-doors discovered previously. A combination of switching on a device and at the same time pressing certain keys often activates some service menu.

- Study communication interfaces. For many PDAs it is possible to make a complete backup on another exemplar of the same type. A complete backup means that all data, including the password, are transferred. The communication interface needed for the backup may be available to the user or may be for service purposes only. In the latter case a key combination is often needed to activate the port. Interface slots for extra hardware often offer possibilities for circumventing security.

- Reverse engineering by which the firmware is read and analyzed. A very useful tool for reverse engineering is the IDA Pro disassembler and debugger (Guilfanov, 2008). See the information recovery section later in this chapter for additional ways to use reverse engineering tools to examine data acquired from embedded systems.

**PRACTITIONER'S TIP**

Retrieving a back-door is time-consuming and often limited to one or just a few models. In addition there is the risk that a back-door will be removed in a product update as soon as this becomes generally known. For example, PDAs with older versions of Palm OS can be put in the debug mode via a *graffiti keystroke* after which an internal field in the Palm can be erased so that a password is no longer required. After this information became public Palm immediately announced that this fault in security would be rectified from Palm OS version 4.0 onward.

### *Measuring Memory*

A naïve password verification algorithm runs roughly as follows: the correct password is stored in nonvolatile memory and the password given by a user is stored temporarily. After the input is concluded (e.g., with the Enter key), the CPU compares the entered password with the stored password and stops the moment there is a difference. The protected data is released only if there is no difference between the entered and stored passwords. If the location of the password in the nonvolatile memory is not yet known, keying in a correct password on the exemplar and measuring the data and address buses can reveal this location. A logic analyzer is used for this kind of measurement.

The logic analyzer is physically attached to the pins of the memory chip representing the address and data bus of the embedded system (see Figure 8.4). The power supply must never be interrupted when measuring RAM. Extra precautions are often required to guarantee this, such as milling a casing without damaging the battery compartment.

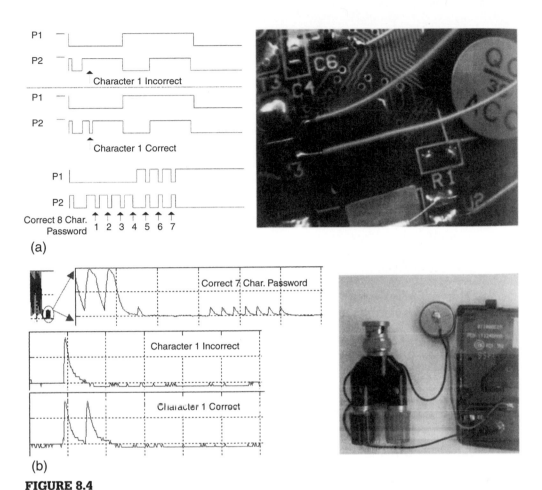

**FIGURE 8.4**

Relation between the correctness of a password character and a digital measuring point (a) and power consumption (b).

The address area of the password can be ascertained by studying these measurements after a number of experiments. Once the address area is known, the measurement can be adapted in such a way that only data related to these addresses is reproduced. With this arrangement the first character of an unknown password can be retrieved. By entering this first character during the subsequent measurement, the algorithm will run in the same way and report only after the comparison of the second character that the password entered is not correct. The second character is now known. The other characters of the password can be retrieved by repeating this procedure a number of times.

## Memory Injection

It is not always possible to retrieve the password using the method just described; for example when the password is not directly written in the memory but is hashed or encrypted, or when the number of consecutive false entered passwords is hard limited or causes an increasing input delay. The location of the password can often be established by making more measurements with different passwords. In these cases the password can be overwritten with the data of a known password.[6] The memory data belonging to that known password can be read from the exemplar device. If the location of the password has been established with the logic analyzer, a pattern generator can be connected to the memory chip programmed in such a way that the data is changed at the addresses where the password is located, thus replacing an unknown password with one that is known. The disadvantage of this method is that data is entered into the memory of the exhibit and the password information is thus altered. After the investigation has been concluded, the memory can be restored to its original state. Some logic analyzers contain their own pattern generators and these can be utilized. The Netherlands Forensic Institute has developed the Memory Toolkit for carrying out memory measurements and memory injections as discussed later in this section.

## Correlation Measurements

All the aforementioned methods of accessing memory on embedded systems work only if the address bus and data bus can be accessed by the measuring equipment. In compact systems in particular, all the memory components are integrated with the CPU in a chip and covered with a layer of epoxy (one-chip types). When dealing with such one-chip types, precise measurement of CPU related signals (rather than memory measurements) offers a solution. When dealing with the password verification algorithm described earlier, it is clear that a certain time elapses before the CPU reports that the password is incorrect. The more correct characters there are, the longer the process of checking will take. By measuring the time that is needed for the verification of a password entered it is possible to ascertain how many characters of the password entered are correct. The procedure for retrieving the complete password is then as follows:

1. Try all possible, one-character-long passwords (0...9, A...Z, a...z, etc.), and with each entry measure the time taken for verification.

---

[6]Instead of concentrating on the password, it may be possible to search for the password checking algorithm in the program memory and insert a variant that causes the password to always be assessed as correct. For this to work it must be possible to adapt the program memory (physical replacement with ROM or reprogramming with flash).

2. One of the measured time durations is significantly longer than the rest, the character that takes the longest time is the correct one (for example, Q).

3. Now repeat points 1 and 2, increasing the password to be tried by one character at a time, varying only the right-hand character and all the characters to the left of that are chosen as the characters found in step 2 (Q0...Q9, QA...QZ, Qa, ..., Qz, etc.).

The problem with this method is finding measuring points with password-dependent time variations. When measurements are made digitally with a logic analyzer on one-chip type devices, the most favorable approach is to measure as many accessible points as possible on the printed circuit board in the neighborhood of the chip. The measurement data can be transferred to a computer system and analyzed to locate measuring points that vary only for correct entered characters. When a (digital) oscilloscope is used for measurements, the power consumption can also give useful measurement data (Mangard et al., 2007). Figure 8.4 shows examples of both measurement methods.

### *Brute Force*

With the brute force method, a series of passwords (whether or not exhaustive) is entered into a system. When the order is chosen in such a way that the most likely passwords are tried first, this is known as password guessing.[7] In contrast to (U)SIMs and modern mobile operating systems, for example, a lot of devices have not limited the maximum number of consecutive incorrect attempts that can be made to enter a password. When dealing with embedded systems, users often select short, easy-to-guess passwords. The brute force method also has the great advantage that it is not usually destructive and can thus be tried first on an unknown system of which there is no other exemplar available. Some devices (e.g., BlackBerry, iPhone) will erase all data after a set number of incorrect password attempts. Depending on the type of system the password can be entered mechanically or electronically (see Figure 8.5 for a mechanic variant).

For a password hash read from embedded system memory, it is also possible to use *offline* password guessing or brute force. With this method hashes are calculated on a fast computer system and then compared with the extracted hash until a match is found. The found password is not necessarily the same as the original one because different passwords might have similar hashes.

**FIGURE 8.5**

A robot arm with camera for automatic password entry and response checking.

---

[7]The *correlation* method described here is also a form of brute force, not per password but per password character, which reduces the number of possibilities drastically.

## Manual Examination

A manual examination of embedded systems utilizes human computer interfaces like key input and display output, to extract as much data as possible. Reasons for choosing such a low-tech examination method include:

- In some cases, speed is more important than forensic soundness. If it is only important to know the value of the last trip counter of a car, it makes sense to switch on that car instead of spending a lot of time developing a forensically sound extraction procedure.

- With other methods it is not possible to extract certain evidence or to guarantee the integrity of certain data elements. Some mobile phones for example, have data cable connection points inside the battery compartment. Removing the battery to access these points may alter the date and time values of the phone. If these values are expected to be important they can be extracted via the user menu of the phone.

- The conversion of extracted data into information (decoding) is problematic. If no documentation is available on how specific data are formatted and all attempts to decode the data fail, the device itself might be a useful tool. In a mobile phone examination for example, data related to deleted voice dialing commands were found but it was not possible to play these voice tags with any available sound player. Through testing it was discovered how the phone coded the delete status of a voice tag and after flipping the deleted status data back to nondeleted, the voice tags could be played via the original phone.

The investigator needs to have the technical documentation for the system and needs to be experienced in manual examination of the target device. This will avoid data being unwittingly lost or affected.[8] All the operations need to be documented and it must be stated in the final report that the data have been extracted manually. Manual acquisition does not guarantee that all data are retrieved and also has the disadvantage of possible human (typographic) errors. For computer assisted manual examinations, forensic tools exist that use a camera and computer software for documenting screen contents during a manual examination (Fernico, 2007; Project-a-Phone, 2007).

---

[8]When mobile phones are being examined manually, it regularly happens that important data are overlooked due to inexperience of the investigator. For example, the investigator consults the last telephone numbers dialled but is not aware of a key combination specific to that model, which can also reveal the date and time.

## Logical Data Acquisition

Logical data acquisition refers to data extraction techniques without direct access to raw memory data. Logical data acquisition often uses common, high-level protocols to extract information elements that can be interpreted by a user without additional decoding. Most forensic phone software use as one of their methods, for example, the *Hayes command set*[9] to extract phone book entries, SMS messages, and call related data from mobile phones (Ayers et al., 2007). Some other popular protocols for logical data acquisition are SyncML, OBEX, IrMC, ActiveSync, Fbus, ISO7816-3. Another class of forensic logical data acquisition tools runs a kind of software agent on the exhibit, using the original operating system to transfer file system data to an examination host (Oxygen Software, 2008) or multimedia card (Me, 2008). Logical data acquisition methods do not generally capture deleted data.

Commercial, nonforensic, backup, and synchronization tools that can be used for logical data acquisition are available for many embedded systems, including marine and handheld GPS (Global Positioning System) units. In contrast to navigation systems in vehicles, handheld GPS units generally store position data rather than complete routes. Three types of position data can be distinguished:

- **Track-log**: A FIFO (first in/first out) buffer in which the current position of the GPS unit is continuously stored as soon as this differs from the original position.

---

[9]The Hayes command set, also referred to as AT commands, is a specific command-language used by most dialup modems. A lot of mobile phones and mobile data cards also use this command set.

- **Routes**: The series of points from the track-log where the alteration in course took place. This information is stored on the initiative of the user.
- **Waypoints**: Autonomous positions kept by the user that can often be provided with a brief text (Home, Pub, etc.).

A standardized interface exists for getting live position data from GPS equipment (NMEA). This interface is not very useful for forensic acquisition but data formatted according to NMEA specifications can sometimes be found in volatile or nonvolatile memories of GPS enabled devices. Various software is available for reading post-mortem position data and visualizing it on a map (GPS Utility Ltd, 2008; Forensic Navigation, 2008).

A vehicle electronic control unit (ECU) is another example of an embedded system that can be acquired logically. For vehicle systems that incorporate computer control, the assembly containing the microprocessor is called ECU. ECUs control vehicle functionality like antilock breaking, air bags, and seat-belt tensioners. ECUs get data from sensors measuring vehicle speed, wheel speed, deceleration, among others. They transmit control signals to actuators like valves, air bag igniters, and dashboard indicators. Within an ECU, nonvolatile data is saved in EEPROM or flash memory. This information usually includes diagnostic trouble codes (DTCs) and optional parametric crash data. Data obtained from one or more ECUs are often called *black box data*, and might be useful for forensic investigations. Connectors and connection protocols for vehicle diagnostics are highly standardized and a lot of commercial scanners exist. Most of these scanners can extract only the diagnostic error codes. Proprietary scanners are needed to extract manufacturer-specific data, which is often the most interesting from a forensic perspective (Ching-Yao Chan, 2000; Rosenbluth, 2001).

## FROM THE CASE FILES

Airbag data from the ECU of a crashed car was extracted and decoded with a method performed by the airbag manufacturer. The data showed deceleration values in a short interval around the airbag deployment. The differences between consecutive measurements on milliseconds interval times were so big that they could not be caused by the heavy weight of a car. Further examination of the ECU unit revealed a broken fastening bolt causing not the car movement to be registered but the ECU movement. This made the data useless for the initial question about the speed of the car just before the crash.

## Physical Data Acquisition

Physical data acquisition refers to data extraction techniques with direct access to real memory locations. This can be compared with bit-stream images of computer hard drives. Most built-in embedded system storage cannot be accessed with generic connection interfaces like ATA or SCSI for personal computers. The most generic connection interface for embedded system memories is the use of the physical connection points on the memory chips. Several chip package technologies exist (DIP, SIP, TSOP, PGA, LGA, BGA) and for each package technology a large number of variations are used in the number, the spacing, and the size of connection points. This diversity makes the use of physical connection points for forensic data acquisition expensive and impractical for generic use. Therefore, several less ideal methods of acquiring physical memory are commonly used.

### Software Agents

Software agents are pieces of software running on the exhibit device, assisting with, or responsible for, the physical data acquisition. These agents run on the normal operating system of the device and use Application Programming Interface (API) calls for low-level memory access, or they use a dedicated operating system for data acquisition. For this approach to work, the system needs to be accessible and must allow the execution of custom software. The Symbian OS, for example, has a low-level API function called *RRawDisk* that enables direct disk access (Breeuwsma et al., 2007). On Windows CE-based devices a similar approach can be used to read data from RAM and flash memory using ActiveSync and remote API calls (Hengeveld, 2003). For iPhone and iTouch devices a commonly used examination method puts commands on the system partition to remotely login to the device and copy the user partition via Wi-Fi to an examination machine (Zdziarski, 2008a; Hoog, 2009).

Because most software agents run on the normal operating system, precautions are needed for locked files or other processes changing the target data. Software methods can also be used to acquire RAM data but because the agent itself also uses RAM space it potentially overwrites interesting evidence in unallocated RAM areas (Schatz, 2007).

### Boot Loaders

As described earlier in this chapter boot loaders on embedded systems can contain functionality for direct access to memory locations. The interactive boot loader of a lot of HTC devices running Windows Mobile for example, can be activated by holding down the camera and power button and resetting the device. The boot loader's `d2s` command can be used on some devices to copy the contents of internal memory onto an inserted multimedia card or onto an examination system via the USB connector.

Instead of directly using the built-in boot loader functionality another approach uses the primary boot loader to transfer custom executable code to one of the writable device memories and to start executing that code. Embedded systems often have this flash loader functionality for in-field upgrading of firmware.

Additional boot loader functionality is widely used in the mobile phone world by both manufactures and hackers. Manufacturers use this method for debugging and repair and for in-field firmware upgrades. Apple, for example, distributes firmware upgrades for their iPhone and iPod devices via their iTunes software. iPhones can be switched into different upgrade modes; the most low-level one is used to update the boot loader itself and could also be used for forensic purposes. Hackers also use boot loader functionality to attack device security functions, installing custom firmware, or changing normal device behavior.[10] Flasher box is the common name for interface devices to connect mobile phones with computer systems for managing additional boot loader functionality. Flasher tools mostly contain a flasher box, control software, and a large number of cables to connect different phone models (GSM-Forum, 2008; Multi-com, 2008). Great care should be taken when using these tools for forensic examinations. Besides memory acquisition functionality, these tools sometimes have other options that are devastating in a forensic context like writing or erasing memory, changing serial numbers, or adding functionality. Before usage on an exhibit, a flasher tool needs to be tested on a similar device: once thoroughly to check the functionality, and preferably before each individual examination to train the examiner in using only the forensically sound options of such a tool (Al-Zarouni, 2007).

Forensic tools like XACT (Micro Systemation AB, 2008) and FTS Hex (FTS, 2008) use flash loader techniques for forensic acquisition of data from mobile phones and PDAs.

### Boundary-scan/JTAG

As discussed earlier in the chapter, boundary-scan technology is designed to apply test data to printed circuit boards and onboard device components. Boundary-scan can also be used to make physical data copies of memory chips (Breeuwsma, 2006). Usually memory chips do not have built-in JTAG functionality. Because they are connected to the address and data buses, boundary-scan can still be used to access the memory chips. Figure 8.6 shows how the JTAG external test mode can be used to access memory chips. Equipment needed to interact with JTAG can be found in the area of embedded system development (Signum Systems, 2009).

As a preface to discussing the forensic application of test circuits, the process of interacting with an embedded system memory via this interface is

---

[10]A very instructive open source project aimed at running Linux on iPhone hardware contains a custom developed boot loader that can be used to acquire flash data from iPhone memories via USB (Planetbeing, 2008).

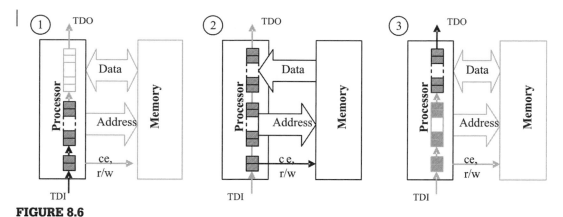

**FIGURE 8.6**
Using extest mode for accessing memory.

described here in general terms. The first test vector contains an address of a memory location and control signals (ce, r/w) with a read command. This test vector is clocked into the boundary-scan register using TDI (step 1 in Figure 8.6). After the test vector is shifted into the boundary-scan register it is activated with TMS, activating the address and command bus (step 2 in Figure 8.6). In response, the requested data from memory is placed on the data bus. In order to extract the requested data it is first necessary to execute a capture command with TMS to obtain a second test vector, containing the data from the data bus. This test vector with memory data is shifted out of the boundary-scan register and can be read from TDO (step 3 in Figure 8.6). Repeating this process with all possible memory addresses results in a complete memory image.

If an onboard processor supports JTAG to execute debug commands, it can also be used for data acquisition. Normally the execution of embedded software has to be stopped before debug commands can be executed. Examples of debug enabled chips are chips with an ARM7 or ARM9 core. These cores have some special registers to control the debug mode of the core. One register is used to put machine instructions in an instruction pipeline. For example, a value of a memory location can be read by placing an instruction to "store memory location to register R14" (for example, STR R[index], [R14]) in the pipeline and read the value of register R14 afterward. Because the core is still active in debug mode, memory locations might be based on virtual addresses because of an active memory manager.

Boundary-scan techniques can also be used to acquire data from RAM memory but precautions are needed to assure that the memories are regularly refreshed to keep the data valid.

### Physical Connectivity

The most generic way to acquire data from physical memory of an embedded system is to connect the acquisition device directly to the chip containing the target data. In this way the low-level access protocol as described by the chip's data sheet can be used to address each individual memory location. The most practical way for physical connectivity is to remove the chips from the printed circuit board and read the data with an external reader like a commercial device programmer. Because RAM memories will lose data without proper power and control signals, direct access needs to be done in circuit with special test clips applied over the existing chip pins. Special precautions are needed to avoid conflicts between the acquisition device and other components on the printed circuit board.

## FROM THE CASE FILES

On 9 May 2006 a 51-meter-long inland vessel loaded with 575 tons of copper sank after it was hit by an almost 200-meter-long tugboat. The 60-year-old boatman of the inland vessel was missing and found dead several days later. The GPS navigation device of the tugboat was known to store track-log coordinates in SRAM memory. A method was developed on a similar reference device to physically connect to the SRAM chips and acquire the data while the memory was still powered. From the acquired data all track-log points were recovered and plotted on a map. The boatman of the tugboat was found guilty of not changing his course on time while he could foresee a hit with his current course.

### Desoldering

For nonvolatile memory chips, physical removal is the most generic acquisition method. It can even be used if the system as a whole is not functioning anymore, after being burned, exposed to fluids, or deliberately damaged. Most nonvolatile memory chips nowadays are packed in a Thin Small-Outline Package (TSOP) or micro Ball Grid Array (BGA) casing. Dedicated desoldering equipment is preferred to prevent damaging the chips and thereby causing data loss. Figure 8.7 shows the preferred way to desolder TSOP chips. Hot air is blown on the edges of a TSOP chip. Therefore the temperature of the chip itself stays lower than the temperature of the solder connections. When the solder is melted a vacuum air gripper pulls the chip off.

Micro BGA chips don't have pins but instead use small balls on the bottom of the package for connecting the chip to the printed circuit board (Figure 8.8).

Micro BGA chips can be removed with hot air using a rework station. A rework station uses a temperature profile to heat up the printed circuit board and target chip in a controlled way, preventing

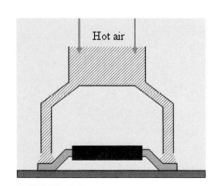

**FIGURE 8.7**

Removing TSOP chips with hot air.

chip damage and data loss caused by sudden temperature changes. The temperature profile is different for each chip and printed circuit board because the convection of heat is subject to many parameters like the thickness of the printed circuit board, the number of layers, the size of the nozzle and the chip size. Always practice on a reference model before removing a chip from an exhibit and use a temperature sensor mounted at the side of the memory chip for temperature logging.

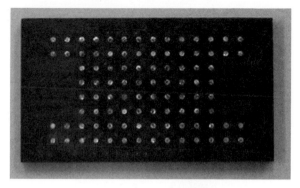

**FIGURE 8.8**

Example of a micro BGA chip.

### Preparation

Pins of a TSOP chip can be cleaned with solder wick and flux remover. If a micro BGA chip is removed from a printed circuit board the balls on the chip are damaged. Some solder is left behind on the chip and the rest is left behind on the printed circuit board, resulting in balls of different sizes. Since reading sockets are designed for virgin chips with balls of equal size, the differences in ball size on an unprepared, desoldered micro BGA chip result in bad connections. One solution to this problem is to repair the balls of the chip, a process called *reballing*. Although other methods are available the best method is to use a reballing machine (Retronix Ltd., 2008). This machine puts little balls of solder on the connection and locally melts it with a laser beam, but this machine is very expensive. An alternative solution to reballing is described in the next section.

### Connecting

After cleaning, the flash memory chip can be read with a commercial device programmer. These device programmers usually have several types of Zero Insertion Force (ZIF) sockets for connecting the chip to the programmer. Flash chips in TSOP casing usually use a package with 48 pins. Therefore most TSOP chips can be read with only one type of socket. Micro BGA chips, however, are found in many different sizes and differ greatly in number of balls and spacing between the balls (*pitch*). Usually these chips have casings between 40 and 167 balls, and will probably have even more in the future. Obtaining the correct socket to read a particular chip can be difficult because of the large number (over 40 and growing), high cost, and long delivery time. A solution for this problem is to use a socket that can be adapted for many types of chip casings; see Figure 8.9 (Logic Technology, 2008).

These sockets use spring contacts called *pogo pins* positioned into a matrix with one specific pitch. The chip is pressed onto the springs and the springs correct the difference in height of the balls. The memory chip is held into position by a locator. This locator is specific for each type of casing and can be made relatively easily with a milling machine.

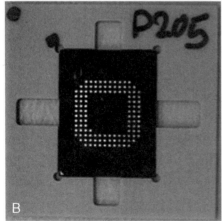

**FIGURE 8.9**

Universal socket (A) and locator with micro BGA chip (B).

### Reading

Memory chips can be read with commercially available device programmers (BPM Microsystems, 2008). A disadvantage is that a driver is needed for each type of memory chip. If a driver for a certain type of chip is not available, the manufacturer of the device programmer has to make this driver. This can take some time and is not always possible when a datasheet or reference chip is not available for evaluation and testing. An alternative approach is to use a custom-made universal memory chip reader. With such a reader, parameters like address bus size and data bus size are fully customizable. With NOR flash memory, a data structure can be read from the memory containing all necessary parameters for data extraction. This structure is part of the common flash interface standard (Jedec Solid State Technology Association, 2003). For NAND flash chips a limited number of different protocols exist. These protocols can be enumerated with software until the correct one is found. Due to the automatic configuration properties of a custom made universal flash chip reader, it is sometimes possible to read flash chips even without having a datasheet.

Not all flash can be addressed directly, especially NAND flash arrays that are part of multichip modules that are addressed via RAM buffers with configurable sizes. If different tools use different configurations or storage policies for the order of sector data and spare data, acquisition results will be ambiguous and hard to share between different information recovery tools. These problems can be avoided with the following conventions:

1. For direct addressable flash memory (possibly part of a multichip module): Store data exactly in the linear order, starting from address zero, as if the address bus of the memory array is directly controlled.

2. For flash memory that is not directly addressable, like NAND flash arrays (possibly part of a multichip module): Store data in page order, starting from address zero, using the internal memory map of the flash memory. For small page (e.g., 528 bytes) NAND flash this results in: <512 bytes main><16 bytes spare>…<512 bytes main><16 bytes spare>. For larger page NAND flash (e.g., 2112 bytes) this results in: <2048 bytes main><64 bytes spare>…<2048 bytes main><64 bytes spare>.

3. Store additional metadata describing the acquired chips and acquisition policies. For example:

- MemoryIdentifier: Unique string to identify different memories within one system;
- MemorySize: Size of the memory in bytes;
- MemoryEndians (only for word addressable chips): "Big" if the leftmost byte of a word is written to file first, "Little" otherwise.

When a modern NAND flash chip is acquired repeatedly and the acquisition results are compared, some bits might not be stable between different acquisitions. These erroneous bits are normally corrected by a connected controller that uses the error-correcting codes stored in the spare area of the flash and an error-correcting algorithm. The error-correcting algorithm needs to be known in order to perform the error correction without the controller after acquisition. Uncorrectable errors are most likely originating from blocks that are marked bad with some flag in the spare area or in another area reserved for metadata.

# INFORMATION RECOVERY

When all data have been acquired from a target device, recovery operations are needed to transform the low-level device data into human readable information. Information can originate from active data or deleted data.[11] Active data is guaranteed to be complete because it is used by the system in its current state.[12] Deleted data originates from past states of the system and is not necessarily complete. Information can be classified further into user-related information and system-related information. The term recovery is used for actions on both active and deleted data. Recovery techniques depend on the complexity of the embedded systems. Some systems don't have an operating system or file system, which sometimes results in data structures that are inspired more by the system programmers and not on standardized storage principles.

## Record Recovery

Data records are often used for information encoding in embedded system memories. The most basic variant just uses hard-coded memory locations and fixed data sizes possibly grouped into tables. More advanced variants use tag length value (TLV) encoding sometimes combined with relative pointers for linked list constructions. The generic method to reconstruct the information is reverse engineering of the firmware but mostly it is faster to use a reference device of the same brand and type and use trial-and-error methods with known data.

---

[11]Both active and deleted data can be essential or nonessential (Carrier, 2005). Take a timestamp from a call entry found in the memory copy of a mobile phone as an example. This timestamp is nonessential because it is related to the internal clock of the mobile phone. It can originate from active data or from data deleted by a user or a system process.

[12]In real-life systems even active data can be corrupt, caused by unhandled exceptions or implementation errors (e.g., a multimedia card from a photo camera that has been put in a card reader without write blocker on Windows XP).

---

### FROM THE CASE FILES

In 2004 a patient's death was probably caused by an overdose of medicine injected with an infusion pump. The cause of the overdose was unknown and the infusion pump was examined by a forensic laboratory. A primary goal of the forensic examination was to retrieve the last configured medicine dose. A reference device was obtained from the manufacturer and disassembled. The device contains an EEPROM memory for storage of nonvolatile data. The I/O lines of this EEPROM were analyzed during experiments with different medicine dose settings. The configured dose appeared to be written to a static EEPROM address when the device was switched off. With this knowledge the EEPROM of the questioned infuse pump was desoldered and read. The extracted dose value could not have caused an overdose but was also not consistent with the expected dose. During further technical analysis of the infusion pump no technical defects were found except for one user interface inconvenience that could lead to erroneous dose entries. Sometimes when a numerical key was pressed, a visual feedback signal was given but the key entry was not registered. Although this could be seen on the display it was reported as a probable cause for wrong dose entries.

---

The following software tools might be helpful in the process of record recovery.

### *Hex Editors*

Hex editors are the primary tool for analyzing unknown data from embedded system memories (BreakPoint Software, 2008; Casey, 2004). Besides common hex editor functionality like visual formatting, navigating, searching, and decoding of simple data types, the following features are very useful for record recovery:

- Color mapping applies a specific color to all bytes with a user-specified pattern. This is useful to recognize repeating patterns or to deemphasize uninteresting data.

- Bookmarks are useful to interactively find out how data are structured and to describe the individual fields of each record type. These bookmarks are linked to file addresses and can be saved and reloaded separate from the file containing the memory data. Figure 8.10 shows an example of WinHex bookmark functionality to dissect a deleted missed call record of a partial NOR flash copy from a Nokia 1600 phone.

- Structure definitions can be used to render binary data into structured data. Both WinHex and Hex Workshop support text files with application-specific syntax to specify different data structures. These data structures can be mapped to file addresses causing a more structured view of the data. This can be useful, for example, to find out how instances of a specific record type are grouped. Unfortunately these mappings cannot be saved for later reuse, only some basic decoding of built-in data types is supported, and there is no method for exporting the structured and partially decoded data.

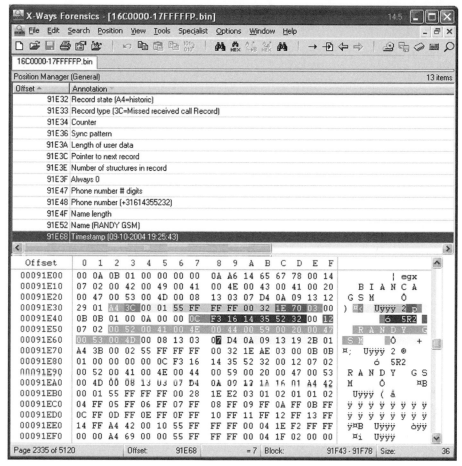

**FIGURE 8.10**

Using the bookmark functionality of WinHex to dissect a deleted missed call record of a partial NOR flash copy from a Nokia 1600 phone.

### IDA Pro Disassembler and Debugger

IDA Pro is a software tool built for disassembling and decompiling machine code (Eagle, 2008). This tool could be used to load data from embedded system memory that contains data encoding functions and to reverse engineer them to reconstruct relevant system and user information. Although possible, this would be very complex and time consuming. A more practical approach is to (ab)use IDA as an advanced hex editor with additional functionality for repeated decoding of memory data. This approach has two phases: A development phase that is performed once for each specific storage format, and a production phase where information from known storage formats can be extracted with a few mouse clicks. Figure 8.11 shows a screenshot of IDA during the development phase.

The development phase consists of the following steps:

1. The memory file is loaded into IDA as a binary file with the default metapc processor option and with all analysis options disabled because processor features are not needed. Different views, such as hexadecimal format or examining all strings that satisfy specific configurable criteria, can be useful for interpreting data structures. Similarly, reverse engineering functions, like applying different number and character formats and adding comments to different data parts, support the interactive process of finding out how data are structured. The goal of this step is to define structures for all record types of interest. Each structure may be specified up to the individual field details but this is not really necessary. For structure creation the IDA structure window can be used. Structure definitions can also be imported and exported in the format of the IDA built-in scripting language called IDC. This enables the use of external editing tools and structure reuse. The final result of this step is an IDC `StructureDefinition.idc` script with all relevant structure definitions for a specific storage format.

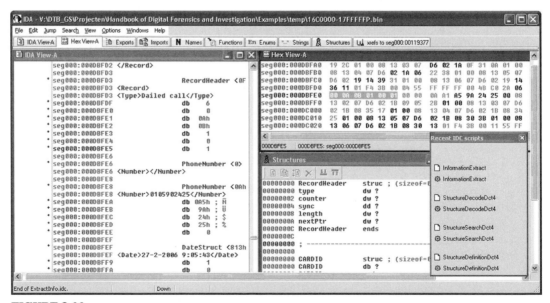

**FIGURE 8.11**

Using IDA Pro to recover data records from a Nokia DCT4 mobile phone memory.

2. After defining the structures, all addresses need to be found where these structures are used. In the early development phase this is done manually from the IDA view and with the Struct var... dialog. As soon as more knowledge is collected, IDC scripting can be used to automate this process. All identifiable structures are saved by IDA into cross-reference lists for later use. The ultimate goal of this step is to develop an IDC `StructureSearch.idc` script that finds all memory locations for each structure type.

3. The next step is to decode data from recovered structures into human readable information. This can be done interactively with IDA's commenting functionality. Decoded data are added as posterior comments to recovered data structures. A suitable markup language for this is XML. Again this process can be started manually, and as soon as specific encoding formats are understood well enough, the IDC scripting language can be used. This step results in a `StructureDecode.idc` script that decodes all data referenced by the structure cross-reference lists.

4. The last trivial step is an `InformationExtract.idc` script that exports all posterior comments to one XML file that can be viewed directly with a web browser or with additional formatting using a style sheet.

Scripts developed for a specific storage format can be used on data acquisition files originating from similar devices. The memory file just needs to be loaded into IDA and the four IDC scripts need to be loaded and executed one after each other.

## File System Recovery

File system recovery uses the acquired low-level data to rebuild the high level hierarchy of directories, subdirectories, and files. For data originating from flash file systems (as explained earlier in this chapter) this means finding out how the flash translation layer maps physical data to logical data and how the difference between active and delete data can be determined.[13] The result of this "flash translation layer analysis" is a method that splits the physical data into two parts: a part with all logical sectors in the right order belonging to the actual file system and another part with all other data not belonging to the (current) file system. The first part can be further analyzed by existing forensic tools for file system recovery (Carrier, 2005). Analysis of the second part is more complex and depends a lot on the setup and user behavior of the originating system.

---

[13]Technical documents about flash-based file storage often use the terms valid and invalid to distinguish memory locations belonging to active and deleted data.

## Data Carving

As discussed in Chapter 2, "Forensic Analysis," data carving is a technique that searches through acquired data for information that cannot be recovered via the original file system structures. Using common data carving tools directly on acquired data from flash memories might not give many useful results because the arrangement of blocks in flash can be very different from the way blocks are arranged on magnetic storage media. This difference is due to the behavior of the flash translation layer that is designed to maximize the life span of individual flash memory cells. Therefore, if generic data carving tools are used on data acquired from flash memories, it is preferred to preprocess the acquired data in such a way that the resulting sector order resembles the sector order commonly found on magnetic storage media.

Popular data carving targets for mobile phone examinations are photos and videos made with built-in cameras and deleted by users. Photos are mostly stored in JPEG format and videos in 3GP format with MPEG-4 or H.263 video streams and AAC or AMR for audio. After flash translation layer specific reordering of sector data, JPEG fragments can be carved with existing carving tools (Garfinkel, 2007). 3GP carving results are much better if carving is targeted toward individual video frames and when the carving tool also uses the metadata stored in 3GP formatted files (Luck & Stokes, 2008). After automatic carving tools are used, improved results can often be achieved with tool assisted manual examination. Most of the existing forensic tools are not publicly available (Bijhold et al., 2007). For 3GP analysis, *defraser* can be useful. Defraser is a forensic analysis application that can be used to detect full and partial multimedia files in datastreams (Netherlands Forensic Institute, 2007).

## Forensic Tools for Information Recovery

There are an increasing number of forensic tools especially designed to recover information from mobile phones, PDAs and navigation systems (Siedsma, 2008). These tools are useful for getting quick results but have major limitations from a forensic perspective. To a great extent these limitations are caused by small differences in firmware versions potentially causing big differences in resulting output. Current good practice is to use different tools, compare the differences, and additionally use hex editors and scripting tools for verification and additional searching.

Micro Systemation uses a promising approach to bridge the gap between physical and logical data acquisition with their XACT and .XRY products (Micro Systemation AB, 2008). XACT uses flash loader technology as one of the techniques for physical data acquisition. Data acquired from mobile phones and other sources can be added to an XACT project file and examined using the built-in hex editor. Reconstructed information can be added to nodes of different types. This can be done automatically with delivered data decoders or manually from within the XACT user interface. When a saved XACT project file is loaded into the .XRY reader, node data originating from so-called Catalog nodes are presented in a similar way to data originating from the .XRY logical acquisition tool. Node data can also be exported to files. Unfortunately the current version has no scripting functionality, which makes user-initiated decoding very impractical. Figure 8.12 shows data from a mobile phone, acquired and decoded with XACT and loaded into .XRY for further analysis and presentation. The header string ftyp3gp4 in Figure 8.12 is known to belong to video files.

## Information Recovery from a Samsung SGH-D500 Phone

A Samsung SGH-D500 phone contains a multichip package with RAM, NOR flash, and NAND flash. Physical data acquisition from the NOR and NAND flash memory results in two files: 32MB for the NOR flash and 132MB for the NAND flash. The NOR flash contains system data and user data stored in custom record formats. The NAND flash contains a FAT16 file system. Figure 8.13 depicts the NAND array structure as described in the datasheet (Samsung Electronics, 2004).

---

### FROM THE CASE FILES

After a fire, a man's burned body was discovered. The man turned out to be dead before the fire started. During the police investigation, the boyfriend of the victim's daughter was marked as suspect. A low quality picture and video file of the fire were found on his computer but not in the .XRY examination results of his mobile phone. JTAG was used to acquire the full NAND flash memory and Python scripts were used to reconstruct the logical sector order and FAT file system. No fragments of the questioned picture and video files were found in the reconstructed file system data.

The remaining acquired data allocated to the active FAT file system was reordered with a heuristic ordering method. In the ordered blocks 73% of data from the video file was found in consecutive logical blocks. The defraser tool (Netherlands Forensic Institute, 2007) was used to reconstruct the video content of this fragment and it turned out to contain similar content of a fire as visible in the video found on the suspect's PC. Five months after the fire, the daughter of the victim confessed to murdering her father with the assistance of her boyfriend.

---

Four 512-byte data sectors are grouped into one page together with four 16-byte parts of spare area data. The data sheet explains the assignment of the spare area bytes suggesting that logical sector numbers (LSN) should be stored in bytes 3 to 6 of each 16-byte spare area part (Figure 8.14).

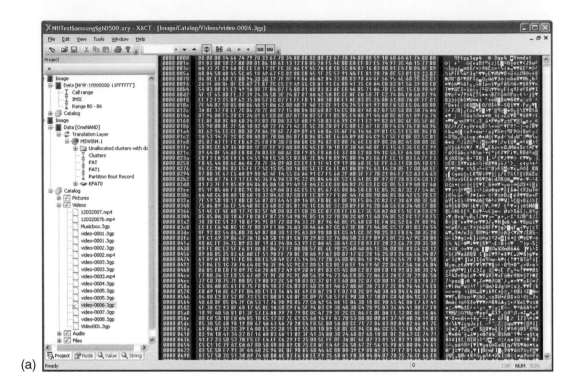

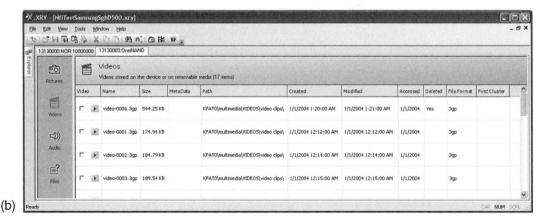

**FIGURE 8.12**

Mobile phone data acquired and decoded with XACT (a) and further analyzed with .XRY (b).

### Flash Translation Layer

Experiments with known data revealed that the LSN is stored in bytes 3 to 5 with the least significant byte first as demonstrated:

```
FFFF 5C35 00FE 00FF 0C03 CCFF
   FFFF FFFF
LogicalSectorNumber = 0x00355C =
   13660
FFFF 5D35 00FE 00FF F0FF 3CAA
   FEFF FFFF
LogicalSectorNumber = 0x00355D =
   13661
```

An acquired flash memory file gives different physical sectors with the same logical sector number. The first sector of each 128 Kbyte + 4 Kbyte block contains a four-byte block number starting on the twenty-first byte, and a four-byte block version starting on the seventeenth byte, as demonstrated:

```
5853 5231 6400 0000 0F00 0000 0100 0000 XSR1d . . .
0701 0000 0100 0000 FC00 0000 0000 0000 . . . . . .
BlockNumber = 00000001h = 1d
BlockVersion = 00000107h = 263d
```

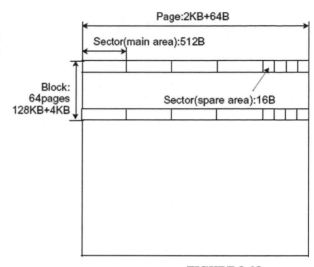

**FIGURE 8.13**

NAND array structure of the multichip package memory in a Samsung SGH-D500 phone.

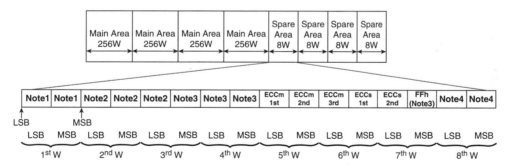

**NOTE:**
1) The 1st word of spare area in 1st and 2nd page of every invalid block is reserved for the invalid block information by manufacturer.
2) These words are managed by internal ECC logic. So it is recommended that the important data like LSN (Logical Sector Number) are written.
3) These words are reserved for the future purpose by manufacturer. These words will be dedicated to internal logic.
4) These words are for free usage.
5) The 5th, 6th and 7th words are dedicated to internal ECC logic. So these words are only readable. The other words are programmable by command.
6) ECCm 1st, ECCm 2nd, ECCm 3rd: ECC code for main area data.
7) ECCs 1st, ECCs 2nd: ECC code for 2nd and 3rd word of spare area.

**FIGURE 8.14**

Assignment of spare area bytes.

For physical sectors with identical logical sector numbers the physical sector with the highest physical address must be used within the block with the highest block version number. With this knowledge a sector list can be built containing items for each encountered logical sector number. Each list item is also a list containing all physical addresses of sectors with a specific logical sector number, sorted on block version and physical address within a block. An example fragment of such a list is shown here:

```
SectorList[23] = {0x01264f20, 0x01f77180}
SectorList[24] = {0x01265550, 0x01265340,
                  0x01265130, 0x01f77390}
SectorList[25] = {0x01265760, 0x01f775a0}
```

### Recovering the Actual File System

After building the sector list the actual file system can be recovered by appending 512 bytes (one data sector) from the flash memory, for each sector list item, starting from the first physical address in the sector list item (the addresses marked light gray above) to a file storing the complete file system. If a logical sector number is not present in the sector list, 512 dummy bytes are written to the output file. The resulting file can be further processed with file system forensic tools as described in Chapter 2, "Forensic Analysis."

### Recovering Other High Level File System Data

Not all acquired data from the flash memory data has been used to reconstruct the actual file system. The remaining data can contain remnants of older instances of the file system, such as when logical sectors belonging to a file that has been deleted and which logical sector numbers have been reused by the high level file system. This especially applies to small data objects with a high refresh frequency (e.g. FAT), so many remnants of older versions might exist in the flash memory file. In addition, portions of acquired memory can contain old file system information because those areas of memory were used by the embedded system's firmware for other purposes, such as workspace for the flash file system during flash memory clean-up operations.

The sector list introduced before contains information that can be used to reconstruct prior file system remnants. Assuming the first address of each sector list relates to the current file system, the subsequent addresses (marked dark gray earlier) can be used to generate an older instance of the file system. However, the older reconstructed file system will most likely not be complete or fully consistent since sectors that are not part of the current high level file system can be overwritten by the flash file system at any time.

For data carving purposes it is preferred to put all remaining data sectors in an order that maximizes the carving results. For this particular phone the following strategy proved to be useful:

1. For each item in the sector list, remove the first address because this address has already been used to generate the actual high level file system.

2. For each remaining item in the sector list with less address items than a certain threshold:

   (a) Initialize the current address item to the first address of the first sector list item.

   (b) Export this current address item and remove it from the sector list. Then look at all address items of the next sector list item and try to find the best match. The following heuristic is used for the matching:

      i. Is next sector: Because contiguous information is most likely put in adjacent physical sectors, if the absolute difference between the value of the current address item and the value of the next address item is equal to the sector size, this address is selected and no other addresses are matched.

      ii. Is next block: When a physical block is full, additional information is most likely saved at the start of a new allocated block. Therefore, if the value of the current address item is the last data sector of a block and the value of the next address item is the first data sector of a block, this address is selected and no further matching is done.

      iii. No match: Do not pick an address but repeat step (a), with the first address of the first item in the sector list in the hope that other physical sectors might exist that provide a better match.

   (c) If a match is found, go to (b) with the matched address as current item's address of the current sector list item.

3. Repeat step 2 until no sector list items exist with fewer address items than the threshold value.

4. All remaining items from the sector list are selected and their related data sectors are exported.

## ANALYSIS AND INTERPRETATION OF RESULTS

When all relevant low-level device data are converted into human readable information, the forensic value needs to be determined. The way to do this depends heavily on the modus operandi and the characteristics of the exhibits. In this section some aspects are covered that are specific for analysis and interpretation of evidence originating from embedded systems.

### Timestamps

Time aspects are important in most forensic investigations (Willassen, 2008). A timestamp is a recorded representation of a specific moment in time. Timestamps found in embedded systems originate from local clock chips or are derived from external systems with timestamp information like GPS, NTP, RDS, or SMS. Origin, transport, and storage format can cause different timestamps for the same time event. As a general rule, when acquiring data containing timestamp information, it is important to record an accurate time reference as close as possible to the moment when the timestamp is acquired. The time reference can be a radio controlled clock, a computer clock synchronized via the NTP protocol or any other accurate reference with known UTC offset.

---

### FROM THE CASE FILES

On 27 October 2005 a big fire in a prison complex at Amsterdam's Schiphol Airport killed 11 people and injured 15 others. During the forensic investigation a lot of digital traces were collected originating from SCADA[14] systems like surveillance, fire control, and personnel communication. Some of these systems were severely damaged by the fire. During data acquisition radio controlled clocks and NTP synchronized examination computers were used to annotate the differences between UTC time and the local time values on the different exhibits. The detected time differences varied between two minutes and 12 hours. From the recovered information a database with more then 500,000 time-synchronized events was reconstructed. From this database 14 events originating from three different sources were the most important for fact finding.

---

Timestamps are relative to the state of some local clock at a particular moment in time. Mobile phone timestamps, for example, can be relative to the built-in clock, the clock of the connected network or another external time reference. Some phones reset their clock value to a type-specific value after removal of the battery. Others phones have a backup energy source so depending on the capacity the clock keeps ticking. Still other phones

---

[14]SCADA generally refers to computer systems monitoring and controlling complex processes in buildings.

store their clock value in nonvolatile memory just before powering down and continue from this value after being switched on. Accuracy of built-in embedded system time references is not only depending on the clock chip but also on environmental conditions like temperature and the way a system uses the clock chip.

A wide variety of storage formats are used for storing timestamp data in embedded system memories. To illustrate, the timestamp "30 April 2008 14:30:59 UTC" is encoded as follows in some formats found in different mobile phone memories:

- 0x80400341039500 (ETSI SMS)
- 0xB19E0CA3 (Nokia)
- 0x07D8041E0E1E3B (Nokia)
- 0x26041E0E1E3B (Motorola)
- 0x00E129CB0E8B2EC0 (Symbian)
- 0x481882A3 (POSIX)

The evidentiary value of timestamps can be further analyzed by comparing timestamps originating from one event and generated by different systems. Most connection events for mobile phones, for example, generate local timestamps in the mobile phone memory but also in the call detail records of the service provider. SMS messages transmitted via a service provider toward a mobile phone, and stored in the phone memory with the original transmission format, have timestamps originating from the time reference of the service provider's message center. Timestamps from the service provider are in general more reliable than the local timestamps of the mobile phone.

A novel method for identifying the time when specific audio or video files are created uses the 50/60 Hz electrical network frequency (Grigoras, 2007). When digital equipment is used to record a conversation or event, it captures not only the intended speech but also the 50/60 Hz electrical network frequency (ENF). This might even occur if the recording device is battery-powered and in proximity to other mains-powered equipment or transmission cables. In a real electrical network the ENF is not fixed at precisely 50/60 Hz. Over time, frequency variations inevitably occur, principally because of differences between produced and consumed power. These variations can be used for forensic analysis using a reference frequency database recorded in a laboratory or obtained from the electrical network company. Forensic applications of ENF can not only be used to determine or verify when an audio or video file was recorded, but also to indicate the geographical area and to check the integrity of an embedded recording.

## Classification, Comparison, and Individualization

Classification, comparison, and individualization of mobile phones and associated data are illustrated next, with some examples.

### GSM and UMTS Phones

GSM or UMTS phones can be classified to a brand and type with their IMEI. IMEI is the abbreviation for International Mobile Equipment Identity, the unique number that each mobile phone (or other mobile device within GSM or UMTS) is obliged to have. The IMEI was introduced to uniquely identify all the mobile equipment present, independent of the subscribers who use this equipment. The IMEI of a device consists of 14 decimals supplemented with a check decimal, and can usually be found on a sticker under the battery and electronically in the nonvolatile memory. On most phones the IMEI can be extracted manually with the key combination *#06# and logically with the AT+CGSN AT-command. IMEIs ranges are registered by approved organizations and can often be queried to determine the brand and type from the IMEI number (International Numbering Plans, 2008). CDMA mobile phones have a similar identifier called the Mobile Equipment Identifier (MEID).

A phone can be used in the mobile network only with a valid IMSI (International Mobile Subscriber Identity). The IMSI is stored in the (U)SIM and is intended primarily for identifying the subscriber. IMSIs are structured with country and provider codes and administrated by the service providers and network providers.

---

### FROM THE CASE FILES

On 3 December 2002 IKEA received a blackmail letter stating that two explosive devices had been placed in IKEA shops in the Netherlands and a third device would be used unless a ransom was paid. The next day improvised explosive devices (IEDs) were found in two IKEA shops and were disarmed by a bomb squad. The IEDs consisted of an explosive charge, a detonator, and a mobile phone used as a remote controlled activator. The GSM phones had no SIM card but the detonators could still be activated with the built-in alarm clock or by pressing a keyboard button. A forensic examination of the nonvolatile memories of the phones revealed several IMSIs belonging to SIM cards that had been used in the phones before. These IMSIs were an important clue that led to several suspects, and after reading their phones and SIM cards, many cross links could be found (Figure 8.15). This information was accepted in court as important evidence to prove the link between the suspects and the IEDs.

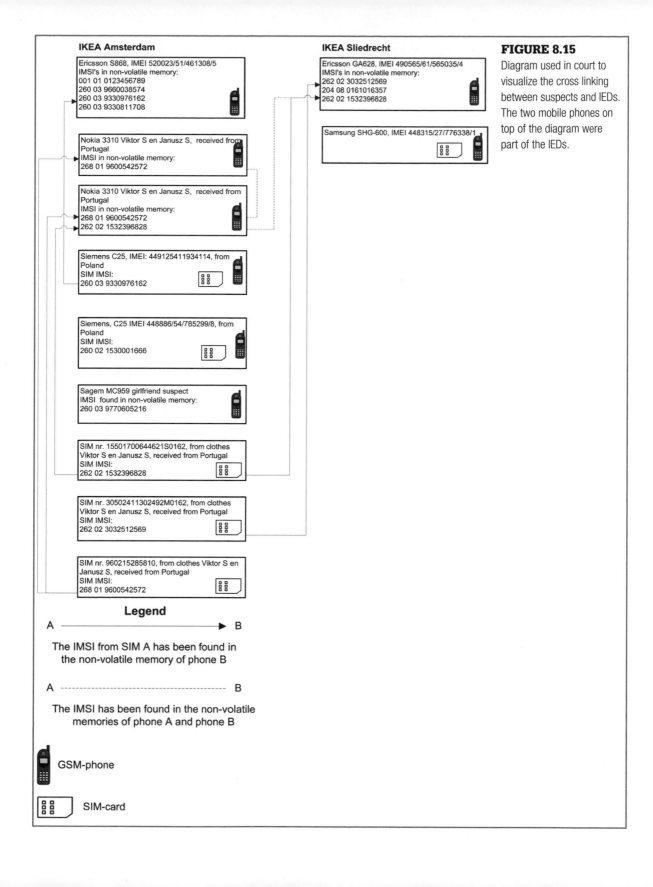

**IKEA Amsterdam**

Ericsson S868, IMEI 520023/51/461308/5
IMSI's in non-volatile memory:
001 01 0123456789
260 03 9660038574
260 03 9330976162
260 03 9330811708

Nokia 3310 Viktor S en Janusz S, received from Portugal
IMSI in non-volatile memory:
268 01 9600542572

Nokia 3310 Viktor S en Janusz S, received from Portugal
IMSI in non-volatile memory:
268 01 9600542572
262 02 1532396828

Siemens C25, IMEI: 449125411934114, from Poland
SIM IMSI:
260 03 9330976162

Siemens, C25 IMEI 448886/54/785299/8, from Poland
SIM IMSI:
260 02 1530001666

Sagem MC959 girlfriend suspect
IMSI found in non-volatile memory:
260 03 9770605216

SIM nr. 15501700644621S0162, from clothes Viktor S en Janusz S, received from Portugal
SIM IMSI:
262 02 1532396828

SIM nr. 30502411302492M0162, from clothes Viktor S en Janusz S, received from Portugal
SIM IMSI:
262 02 3032512569

SIM nr. 960215285810, from clothes Viktor S en Janusz S, received from Portugal
SIM IMSI:
268 01 9600542572

**IKEA Sliedrecht**

Ericsson GA628, IMEI 490565/61/565035/4
IMSI's in non-volatile memory:
262 02 3032512569
204 08 0161016357
262 02 1532396828

Samsung SHG-600, IMEI 448315/27/776338/1

**FIGURE 8.15**

Diagram used in court to visualize the cross linking between suspects and IEDs. The two mobile phones on top of the diagram were part of the IEDs.

### Legend

A ——————————→ B

The IMSI from SIM A has been found in the non-volatile memory of phone B

A - - - - - - - - - - - - - - - - B

The IMSI has been found in the non-volatile memories of phone A and phone B

GSM-phone

SIM-card

### Multimedia Data from a Specific Mobile Phone

After recovering (deleted) multimedia information like pictures, movies, or sounds, a legitimate forensic question is whether a specific item was made with the target phone. For this classification and individualization the following artifacts might be helpful in testing different hypotheses:

- File system information like file-naming schemes, file locations, and file timestamp information.

- Metadata from the multimedia formats like video codec, audio codec, audio bit rate, and timestamps. Table 8.2 shows some differences in file system information and metadata between different phone types.

- Photo Response Non-Uniformity (PRNU). PRNU is a relatively weak pattern of pixel-to-pixel sensitivity differences in digital image sensors. PRNU is primarily caused by varying sensitivity of individual pixels to light due to inhomogeneity and impurities in silicon wafers and

**Table 8.2** Comparison of File System Information and File Metadata for Video Files Made with Different Mobile Phones.

| Phone Brand/Type | File Name | Video Codec | Pixel Dimensions | | Display | Audio | |
| | | | Width | Height | Aspect Ratio | Codec | Bit Rate |
|---|---|---|---|---|---|---|---|
| Samsung SGH-E900 | SV_A0017.3gp | H.263 | 176 | 144 | "1.222" | AMR-NB | 8000 bps |
| Samsung SGH-E900 | SV_A0021.mp4 | MPEG-4 Visual | 320 | 240 | "4/3" | AMR-NB | 8000 bps |
| Samsung SGH-D500 | video-0001.3gp | MPEG-4 Visual | 176 | 144 | "4/3" | AMR-NB | 13 Kbps |
| Samsung SGH-D600 | video-0004.mp4 | MPEG-4 Visual | 352 | 288 | "1.222" | AAC LC | 64 Kbps |
| Samsung SGH-530e | SV_A0138.mp4 | MPEG-4 Visual | 320 | 240 | "4/3" | AMR-NB | 8000 bps |
| Samsung SGH-U600 | SV_A0004.3gp | H.263 | 176 | 144 | "1.222" | AMR-NB | 8000 bps |
| Nokia 6230 | Video015.3gp | H.263 | 128 | 96 | "4/3" | AMR-NB | 13 Kbps |
| Nokia 7610 | Video002.3gp | H.263 | 128 | 96 | "4/3" | AMR-NB | 13 Kbps |

imperfections introduced by the sensor manufacturing process. PRNU is believed to cause unique fingerprints of imaging sensors (Alles et al., 2008; Chen et al., 2007). Besides the questioned image material, PRNU for forensic identification also needs the camera in question for generation of reference data or existing reference data originating from that camera.

## (Past) Existence of Specific Files

Existing forensic tools for file system analysis try to recover data belonging to deleted information. These tools are not fully aware of the physical media from which the acquired data originates. This knowledge of the physical properties might improve the recovery process. Flash file systems, for example, often contain different versions of the same data objects because flash memory cannot be erased in small quantities. Especially for small objects (much smaller than the erase block size) with a high update frequency, a lot of old versions might exist outside of the normal high level file system. Data acquired from flash memories might contain additional data, belonging to past states of the file system, not accessible at the file system level.

File allocation tables and directory entries are an example of such artifacts. These items are updated frequently, and are relatively small compared to the erase block size of flash memory. This may result in a lot of physical instances of the same logical sector. To give an idea of the amount of different versions: in a case with a Samsung SGH-D500 mobile phone the acquired flash memory file contained 83 versions of some part of the FAT and 1464 versions of the `directory\multimedia\VIDEOS\video clips` where all user recorded video movies are stored by default. A common forensic tool will show the last version of the directory, possibly with some files marked as deleted but from the other versions of the directory data a significant amount of user behavior can be reconstructed. The same holds for other data objects although larger objects (like movie files) are likely to be (partly) overwritten earlier after deletion because they occupy complete flash blocks, which can be reused immediately after deletion.

## Determine Functionality

Another legitimate forensic question is to determine the functionality of a specific system. Some examples are fraud cases, where a specific electronic system is believed to copy magstripe data from financial cards and record entered PIN codes, or terrorist threat cases, where improvised explosive devices with remote-control electronics are used to trigger explosives. After acquisition and recovery of stored data the following techniques proved to be useful for determining functionality and behavior of embedded systems.

### Reconstruction of Electrical Diagrams From Electronic Equipment

The electrical diagram of basic printed circuit boards can be retrieved manually with a multimeter and established with the aid of CAD/CAM tools. For more complex systems additional inspection and analysis tools are needed. It might also be necessary to disassemble the equipment.

### Reconstruction of (Embedded) Software

Disassemblers and debuggers are the primary tools for determining the functionality of embedded software as discussed in the section on the IDA Pro Disassembler and Debugger earlier in this chapter. It is not always possible to extract embedded software from microcontroller memories, for example, because they are read-protected. Reverse engineering the microcontroller in order to bypass the protection mechanism is an expensive and time intensive solution. If source code is available from other sources (for example, from a seized computer), the following method can be used to find out whether the code in the program memory is based on the (source) code that has been discovered:

- The discovered source code is translated into machine code with the same development tools as found on the seized system.
- A microcontroller of the same type is programmed with this machine code.
- Two measurements are then made on the system under investigation. During the measurements all relevant input and output pins of the microcontroller are recorded, first with the target chip and then with the programmed reference chip.
- The measurement data consist of lists containing all points in time where pin data changed. Statements on the functionality of the target chip are depending on the similarity of both measurements.

This method can be used more generically to compare an evidentiary item with reference chips that have known functionality.

## THE FUTURE

Forensic investigation of embedded systems has grown out of its infancy and can now be classified as leading edge. Dedicated forensic tools are emerging, papers are being published, and an increasing number of people are getting involved in this area. There is still much work to be done. Low-level acquisition of embedded system memories can be performed by only a few highly specialized forensic laboratories, with the exception of a very limited set of devices that are currently supported by user-friendly tools. There are no standard procedures or test methods for low-level memory acquisition. The few tools for data analysis that currently exist are not good enough to rely on without case-by-case testing on reference devices. Most data analysis needs to be done with ad-hoc methods without much structural basis.

There is a high demand for cooperation with the industry because a lot of time is spent building knowledge about the working and behavior of systems that are designed and built by people who already have most of that knowledge but are not allowed to share it. Fast technological innovations and an increasing demand for more security to protect personal data stored in digital devices require an increase in the amount of resources for investigating these fascinating devices. Although research can improve forensic techniques for analyzing genetic materials like DNA, it is still possible to use existing methods on future traces because the fundamental makeup of the human race is not changing rapidly. Conversely, all current embedded systems will be replaced by different technology within a decade, and ongoing research is necessary to support forensic examination of current and future embedded systems.

## ABBREVIATIONS

| | |
|---|---|
| AAC | Advanced Audio Coding |
| AMR | Adaptive Multi-Rate |
| API | Application Programming Interface |
| ARM | Acorn RISC Machine |
| AT | Attention |
| BGA | Ball Grid Array |
| BIOS | Basic Input/Output System |
| CAD | Computer Aided Design |
| CAM | Computer Aided Manufacturing |
| CCTV | Closed Circuit Television |
| CDMA | Code Division Multiple Access |
| CPU | Central Processing Unit |
| DIP | Dual In-line Package |
| DNA | Deoxyribonucleic acid |
| DRAM | Dynamic Random Access Memory |
| DTC | Diagnostic Trouble Code |
| DUT | Device Under Test |
| ECC | Error-Correcting Code |
| ECU | Electronic Control Unit |
| (E)EPROM | (Electrically) Erasable PROM |
| ENF | Electrical Network Frequency |
| ETSI | European Telecommunications Standards Institute |
| FAT | File Allocation Table |

| | |
|---|---|
| FeRAM | Ferroelectric RAM |
| FIFO | First In/First Out |
| FPGA | Field Programmable Gate Array |
| GPS | Global Positioning System |
| GSM | Global System for Mobile Communications |
| I/O | Input/Output |
| ICCID | Integrated Circuit Card ID |
| ICT | Information and Communication Technology |
| IED | Improvised Explosive Device |
| IMEI | International Mobile Station Equipment Identity |
| IMSI | International Mobile Subscriber Identity |
| JTAG | Joint Test Action Group |
| LGA | Land Grid Array |
| LSN | Logical Sector Number |
| MIPS | Microprocessor without Interlocked Pipeline Stages |
| MMU | Memory Management Unit |
| NMEA | National Marine Electronics Association |
| NTP | Network Time Protocol |
| OBEX | Object Exchange |
| OS | Operating System |
| PCB | Printed Circuit Board |
| PDA | Personal Digital Assistant |
| PGA | Pin Grid Array |
| PIN | Personal Identity Number |
| POS | Point of Sale |
| POSIX | Portable Operating System Interface |
| PRNU | Photo Response Non-Uniformity |
| PROM | Programmable ROM |
| PUK | PIN Unblocking Key |
| RAM | Random Access Memory |
| RDS | Radio Data System |
| RISC | Reduced Instruction Set Computer |
| ROM | Read Only Memory |
| SAM | Secure Application Module |
| SCADA | Supervisory Control And Data Acquisition |
| SCSI | Small Computer System Interface |
| SIM | Subscriber Identity Module |
| SIP | System In Package |
| SMS | Short Message Service |
| SMT | Surface-Mount Technology |
| SRAM | Static Random Access Memory |
| TAC | Type Approval Code |

| TAP | Test Access Port |
|-----|-----|
| TCK | Test Clock |
| TDI | Test Data Input |
| TDO | Test Data Output |
| TLV | Tag Length Value |
| TMS | Test Mode Select |
| TRST | Test Reset |
| TSOP | Thin Small-Outline Package |
| UMTS | Universal Mobile Telecommunications System |
| UPS | Uninterruptible Power Supply |
| USB | Universal Serial Bus |
| USIM | Universal Subscriber Identity Module |
| UTC | Coordinated Universal Time |
| UV | Ultraviolet |
| XML | Extensible Markup Language |
| ZIF | Zero Insertion Force |

## REFERENCES

Al-Zarouni, M. (2007). Introduction to mobile phone flasher devices and considerations for their use in mobile phone forensics. In *Proceedings of 5th Australian Digital Forensics Conference*.

Alles, E. J., Geradts, Z., & Veenman, C. (2008). Source camera identification for low resolution heavily compressed images. In *International Conference on Computational Sciences and Its Applications*.

Ayers, R., Jansen, W., Delaitre, A., & Moenner, L. (2007). Cell phone forensic tools: An overview and analysis update. Available at http://csrc.nist.gov/publications/nistir/nistir-7387.pdf

Bijhold, J., Ruifrok, A., Jessen, M., Geradts, Z., Ehrhardt, S., & Alberink, I. (2007). Forensic audio and visual evidence 2004–2007: A review. In *15th INTERPOL Forensic Science Symposium*. Lyon, France. Available at www.forensic.to/webhome/enfsidiwg/Interpol-review-2007-audio-visual-evidence-paper.pdf

BPM Microsystems. (2008). Device programmers. Available at www.bpmmicro.com/

BreakPoint Software. (2008). Hex workshop hex editor. Available at www.hexworkshop.com/

Breeuwsma, M. (2006). Forensic imaging of embedded systems using JTAG (boundary-scan). *Digital Investigation, 3*, 32–42.

Breeuwsma, M., de Jong, M., Klaver, C., van der Knijff, R., & Roeloffs, M. (2007). Forensic data recovery from flash memory. *Small Scale Digital Device Forensic Journal, 1*.

Carrier, B. (2005). *File system forensic analysis*. Addison-Wesley Professional.

Casey, E. (2004). Tool review-WinHex. *Digital Investigation, 1*, 114–128.

Chen, M., Fridrich, J., Goljan, M., & Lukáš, J. (2007). Source digital camcorder identification using sensor photo response non-uniformity. *Proc. of SPIE Electronic Imaging*.

Ching-Yao, C. (2000). *Fundamentals of crash sensing in automotive air bag systems*. Warrendale, PA: Society of Automotive Engineers, Inc.

de Backer, C. (1999). Jaar-2000 checklist "Embedded systems". In *Millennium Forum 2000*. Brussels: Compendium.

DexMobile. (2008). *RobLock*. Available at www.dexmobile.com/roblock_wm.aspx

Eagle, C. (2008). *The IDA PRO book*. No Starch Press.

Feldman, A. J., Halderman, J. A., Clarkson, W., Paul, W., Calandrino, J. A., Appelbaum, J., et al. (2008). Lest we remember: Cold boot attacks on encryption keys. *Proc. 2008 USENIX Security Symposium*. Available at http://citp.princeton.edu/memory/

Fernico (2007). *ZRT*. Available at www.fernico.com/zrt.html

Forensic Navigation. (2008). *TomTology*. Available at www.forensicnavigation.com/

FTS. (2008). *Forensic Telecommunication Services Ltd*. Available at www.forensicts.co.uk/

Garfinkel, S. L. (2007). Carving contiguous and fragmented files with fast object validation. *Digital Investigation, 4*, 2–12.

GPS Utility Ltd. (2008). *GPS Utility*. Available at www.gpsu.co.uk/

Grigoras, C. (2007). Applications of ENF criterion in forensic audio, video, computer and telecommunication analysis. *Forensic Science International, 167*, 136–145.

GSM-Forum. (2008). *GSM-Forum*. Available at http://forum.gsmhosting.com/vbb/

Guilfanov, I. (2008). *IDA Pro disassembler and debugger*. Available at www.hex-rays.com/idapro/

Harrill, D. C., & Mislan, R. P. (2007). A small scale digital device forensics ontology. *Small Scale Digital Device Forensic Journal, 1*.

Hengeveld, W. J. (2003). *Set of win32 tools to investigate wince devices*. Available at www.xs4all.nl/~itsme/projects/xda/tools.html

Hoog, A., & Gaffaney, K.(2009). *iPhone forensics—annual report on iphone forensic industry*. Available at http://chicago-ediscovery.com/wpinstall/wp-content/uploads/2009/03/iPhone-Forensics-2009.pdf

IEEE Standards Association. (2001). IEEE Std 1149.1-2001 IEEE Standard Test Access Port and Boundary-Scan Architecture—Description.

International Numbering Plans. (2008). *International numbering plans*. Available at www.numberingplans.com

Jedec Solid State Technology Association. (2003). Common Flash Interface (CFI).

Jones, M. T. (2008). *Anatomy of Linux flash file systems*. Available at www.ibm.com/developerworks/linux/library/l-flash-filesystems/

Leyden, J. (2001). How to crash a phone by SMS. *The Register*. Available at www.theregister.co.uk/2001/11/28/how_to_crash_a_phone

Logic Technology. (2008). *Universal socket solution*. Available at www.logic.nl

Luck, J., & Stokes, M. (2008). An integrated approach to recovering deleted files from NAND flash data. *Small Scale Digital Device Forensic Journal, 2*.

LV Electronics. (2008). *RF Shielded test enclosures*. Available at www.lvelectronics.be/RF%20enclosures.htm

Mangard, S., Oswald, E., & Popp, T. (2007). *Power analysis attacks—revealing the secrets of smart cards*. Springer Science+Business Media, LLC

Mc, G. (2008). Internal forensic acquisition for mobile equipments. In *Proceedings of the International Parallel and Distributed Processing Symposium (IPDPS)*.

Micro Systemation AB. (2006). *SIM id-Cloner*. Available at www.msab.com/en/mobile-forensic-products/Sim-id-Cloner-mobile-forensic-tool/

Micro Systemation AB. (2008). *XACT*. Available at www.msab.com/en/mobile-forensic-products/XACT-mobile-forensic-application/

Multi-com. (2008). *gsm-technology.com*. Available at www.multi-com.eu/

Netherlands Forensic Institute. (2006). *TULP2G*. Available at tulp2g.sourceforge.net/

Netherlands Forensic Institute. (2007). *Defraser*. Available at sourceforge.net/projects/defraser/

Onderzoeksraad Voor Veiligheid. (2009). *Draadaanvaring Apachehelikopter Bommeler-waard. 12 December 2007* (Dutch). Available at www.onderzoeksraad.nl/docs/rapporten/Rapport_Apache_web.pdf

Oxygen Software. (2008). *Oxygen Forensic Suite*. Available at www.oxygen-forensic.com/

Parker, S. P. (1994). *McGraw-hill dictionary of scientific and technical terms*. (5th ed.). McGraw-Hill.

Planetbeing. (2008). *Linux on the iPhone*. Available at http://linuxoniphone.blogspot.com/

Project-a-Phone. (2007). *Project-a-phone*. Available at www.projectaphone.com/

Retronix Ltd. (2008). *Retronix PCB Repair Services*. Available at www.retronix.com/

Rosenbluth, W. (2001). *Investigation and interpretation of black box data in automobiles—A guide to the concepts and formats of computer data in vehicle safety and control systems*. ASTM.

Samsung Electronics. (2004). *Datasheet of the multi-chip package MEMORY, 256 Mbit (16 M ×16) synchronous burst, multi bank NOR flash memory / 512 Mbit(32 M×16) oneNAND, flash*2 / 128 Mbit(8M×16) synchronous burst uni-transistor random access memory*. Available at www.samsung.com

Schatz, B. (2007). BodySnatcher: Towards reliable volatile memory acquisition by software. In *Digital Forensics Research Conference 2007*. Available at www.dfrws.org/2007/proceedings/p126-schatz.pdf

Siedsma, C. (2008). *The electronic evidence information center—cellular/mobile phone forensics*. Available at www.e-evidence.info/cellarticles.html

Signum Systems. (2009). *JTAGjet*. Available at www.signum.com/Signum.htm?p=jtagjet.htm

Wikipedia contributors. (2008). Embedded system. In *Wikipedia, The Free Encyclopedia*. Available at http://en.wikipedia.org/w/index.php?title=Embedded_system&oldid=270845478

Willassen, S. Y. (2008). Methods for enhancement of timestamp evidence in digital investigations. Doctoral thesis. Norwegian University of Science and Technology. Available at www.diva-portal.org/smash/record.jsf?searchid=1&pid=diva2:124235

Zdziarski, J. (2008a). *iPhone forensics*. O'Reilly.

Zdziarski, J. (2008b). *iPhone passcode easily defeated*. Available at www.zdziarski.com/

# CHAPTER 9

# Network Investigations

Eoghan Casey, Christopher Daywalt, Andy Johnston,
and Terrance Maguire

## INTRODUCTION

Tracking down computer criminals generally requires digital investigators to follow the cybertrail between the crime scene and the offender's computer. The cybertrail can cross multiple networks and geographical boundaries, and can be comprised of many different kinds of digital evidence including proxy and firewall logs, intrusion detection systems, and captured network traffic. Dialup server logs at the suspect's Internet Service Provider (ISP) may show that a specific IP address was assigned to the suspect's user account at the time. The ISP may also have Automatic Number Identification (ANI) logs—effectively Caller-ID—connecting the suspect's home telephone number to the dialup activity. Routers on the ISP network that connect the suspect's computer to the Internet may have associated NetFlow logs containing additional information about the network activities under investigation. Each of these logs would represent steps on the trail.

Ideally, each step in the cybertrail can be reconstructed from one or more records from this evidence, enabling digital investigators to connect the dots between the crime scene and the offender's computer and establish the continuity of offense. If there is more than one type of evidence for a particular step, so much the better for correlation and corroboration purposes. Your reconstruction of events is like a scientific hypothesis. The more evidence you collect that is consistent with the hypothesis, the stronger the case for that hypothesis becomes.

Networks present investigators with a number of challenges. When the networks are involved in a crime, evidence is often distributed on many computers making collection of all hardware or even the entire contents of a network unfeasible.

## CONTENTS

Introduction.....437

Overview of Enterprise Networks.........439

Overview of Protocols..........442

Evidence Preservation on Networks....457

Collecting and Interpreting Network Device Configuration ...458

Forensic Examination of Network Traffic...............479

Network Log Correlation— A Technical Perspective......505

Conclusion.......516

References.......516

**437**

Also, evidence is often present on a network for only a split second—the windows of opportunity for collecting such volatile evidence are very small. Additionally, encryption software is becoming more commonplace, allowing criminals to scramble incriminating evidence using very secure encoding schemes. Furthermore, unlike crime in the physical world, a criminal can be several places on a network at any given time. A solid comprehension of computer networks and the application of forensic science principles to this technology is a prerequisite for anyone who is responsible for identifying, securing, and interpreting evidence on a network. To that end, this chapter provides an overview of network protocols, references to more in-depth materials, and discusses how forensic science is applied to networks. Furthermore, to help investigators interpret and utilize this information in a network-related investigation, this chapter focuses on the most common kinds of digital evidence found on networks, and provides information that can be generalized to other situations. This chapter assumes a basic understanding of network topology and associated technologies, as covered in Casey (2004).

## FROM THE CASE FILES: FOLLOWING THE CYBERTRAIL

It is not uncommon for intruders to maintain a trophy list of the systems they have compromised. In some cases, intruders inadvertently record their unauthorized actions with their own network capture programs. For instance, in one large-scale network intrusion the intruder placed a rootkit on over 40 servers, which included a sniffer that recorded network traffic.

Forensic examination of the compromised servers found sniffer logs created by the intruder's rootkit, showing the intruder gaining unauthorized access via a backdoor. These sniffer logs showed the IP address from which the intruder was connecting, enabling us to track the attacker back to the UUnet ISP. We promptly contacted the ISP and instructed them to preserve logs associated with the intrusion in anticipation of a search warrant for these records. In addition, we started collecting network traffic originating from the network block used by the intruder to gather evidence of ongoing intrusion activities.

Further investigation revealed that the intruder was using a stolen UUnet dialup account. Fortunately, the ISP maintained ANI records and was able to provide the phone number used to dial into the Internet. The FBI determined which house was assigned the phone number, obtained a search warrant, and seized the intruder's computers.

A forensic examination of the intruder's computer revealed substantial linkage with the victim systems. Information about stolen dialup accounts and victim systems were neatly organized in folders and files on the intruder's computer:

```
+-□ isps
 +-□ isp's.txt
 +-□ isp's2.txt
 +-□ pws.txt
 +-□ infected.txt

+-□ scan logs
 +-□ com
  +-□ ecommerce.com

  +-□ CorpX.com
  +-□ BankN.com
```

Sniffer logs from the compromised systems containing captured usernames and passwords were found on one of the intruder's hard drives. These sniffer files were accompanied by a file created by the intruder that listed the servers and associated usernames and passwords to which he had gained administrative access on various networks around the world. In addition, a tar file on the intruder's hard drive containing the rootkit found on the compromised systems

*(Continued)*

had metadata in the header of the tar files that showed it was created on one of the compromised systems. A keyword search of unallocated space found partial home directory listings from compromised servers, further demonstrating that the intruder's computer was used to gain unauthorized access to those systems. Furthermore, chat logs recovered from the computers showed the intruder exchanging information about compromised servers with his cohorts on Internet Relay Chat (IRC).

Records provided by UUnet, as a result of an FBI subpoena, indicated several dates and times, as well as ranges of times, that the stolen dialup account was used by the intruder to connect to the Internet from the intruder's home when gaining unauthorized access to victim systems. These time ranges correlated with unauthorized activities on the victim systems as well as with IRC chat logs recovered from the intruder's computer.

Although this chapter concentrates on servers, network devices, and network traffic, keep in mind that personal computers often have traces of network activities that can be preserved and examined using the techniques for examining hosts covered in previous chapters. Locard's Exchange Principle states that, when an offender comes in contact with a location or another person, an exchange of evidence occurs (Saferstein, 1998). As a result of this exchange, offenders leave something of themselves behind and take something of that person or place away with them. Locard was talking about the physical world, but his maxim holds for the human-engineered world of information technology as well. Sometimes the evidence transfer is intentionally designed into a system (as with logs). Sometimes, the transfer is an incidental (and perhaps temporary) by-product of the system design. To understand more clearly the application of this principle to forensic investigation of computer networks, suppose an individual uses his home computer to gain unauthorized access to a remote server via a network. Some transfer of digital data occurs. Something as simple as a listing of a directory on the server may remain on the intruder's hard drive for some time, providing a connection between the suspect and the crime scene. Examples of evidence transfer exist for almost every service provided over the Internet.

To provide practical examples of how logs are interpreted and used in digital investigations, data associated with the intrusion investigation scenario introduced in Chapter 4 are examined in further detail.

## OVERVIEW OF ENTERPRISE NETWORKS

Digital investigators must be sufficiently familiar with network components found in a typical organization to identify, preserve, and interpret the key sources of digital evidence in an Enterprise. This chapter concentrates on digital evidence associated with routers, firewalls, authentication servers, network sniffers, Virtual Private Networks (VPNs), and Intrusion Detection Systems (IDS). This section

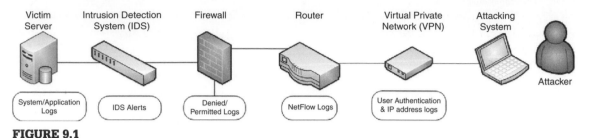

**FIGURE 9.1**

Simplified depiction of components and associated logs on Enterprise networks.

provides an overview of how logs from these various components of an Enterprise network can be useful in an investigation. Consider the simplified scenario in Figure 9.1 involving a secure server that is being misused in some way.

Logs generated by network security devices like firewalls and IDSs can be a valuable source of data in a network investigation. Access attempts blocked by a firewall or malicious activities detected by an IDS may be the first indication of a problem, alarming system administrators enough to report the activity to digital investigators. As discussed in Chapter 4, "Intrusion Investigation," configuring firewalls to record successful access as well as denied connection attempts gives digital investigators more information about how the system was accessed and possibly misused. By design, IDS devices only record events of interest, including known attack signatures like buffer overflows and potentially malicious activities like shell code execution. However, some IDSs can be configured to capture the full contents of network traffic associated with a particular event, enabling digital forensic analysts to recover valuable details like the commands that were executed, files that were taken, and the malicious payload that was uploaded as demonstrated later in this chapter.

Routers form the core of any large network, directing packets to their destinations. As discussed in the NetFlow section later in this chapter, routers can be configured to log summary information about every network connection that passes through them, providing a bird's eye view of activities on a network. For example, suppose you find a keylogger on a Windows server and you can determine when the program was installed. Examining the NetFlow logs relating to the compromised server for the time of interest can reveal the remote IP address used to download the keylogger. Furthermore, NetFlow logs could be searched for that remote IP address to determine which other systems in the Enterprise were accessed and may also contain the keylogger. As more organizations and ISPs collect NetFlow records from internal routers as well as those at their Internet borders, digital investigators will find it easier to reconstruct what occurred in a particular case.

Digital investigators may be able to obtain full network traffic captures, which are sometimes referred to as logging or packet capture, but are less like a log of activities than like a complete videotape of them—recorded network traffic is live, complete, and compelling. Replaying an individual's online activities as recorded in a full packet capture can give an otherwise intangible sequence of events a very tangible feel.

Authentication servers form the heart of most enterprise environments, associating activities with particular virtual identities. Logs from RADIUS and TACACS servers, as well as Windows Security Event logs on Domain Controllers, can help digital investigators attribute activities to a particular user account, which may lead us to the person responsible.

## PRACTITIONER'S TIP: VIRTUAL IDENTITIES

Because user accounts may be shared or stolen, it is not safe to assume that the owner of the user account is the culprit. Therefore, you are *never* going to identify a physical, flesh-and-blood individual from information logs. The universe of digital forensics deals with virtual identities only. You can never truly say that John Smith logged in at 9:00 AM, only that John Smith's account was authenticated at 9:00 AM. It is common, when pursuing an investigation, to conflate the physical people with the virtual identities

in your mind and in casual speech with colleagues. *Be careful.* When you are presenting your findings or even when evaluating them for your own purposes, remember that *your* evidence trail will stop and start at the keyboard, not at the fingers on the keys. Even if you have digital images from a camera, the image may be consistent with the appearance of a particular individual, but *as a digital investigator* you cannot take your conclusions any farther.

As discussed later in this chapter, VPNs are often configured to authenticate via RADIUS or Active Directory, enabling digital investigators to determine which account was used to connect. In addition, VPNs generally record the remote IP address of the computer being used to connect into the network, as well as the internal IP address assigned by the VPN to create a virtual presence on the enterprise network. These VPN logs are often critical for attributing events of concern within an organization to a particular user account and remote computer.

## PRACTITIONER'S TIP: TRACKING DOWN COMPUTERS WITHIN A NETWORK

When a computer is connected to a network it needs to know several things before it can communicate with a remote server: its own IP address, the IP address of its default router, the MAC address of its default router, and the IP address of the remote server. Many networks use the Dynamic Host Configuration Protocol (DHCP) to assign IP addresses to computers. When a networked system that uses DHCP is booted, it sends its MAC address to the DHCP server as a part

of its request for an IP address. Depending on its configuration, the server will either assign a random IP address or a specific address that has been set aside for the MAC address in question. In any event, DHCP servers maintain a table of the IP addresses currently assigned.

DHCP servers can retain logs to enable digital investigators to determine which computer was assigned an IP address during a time of interest, and potentially the associated user

*(Continued)*

**PRACTITIONER'S TIP: TRACKING DOWN COMPUTERS WITHIN A NETWORK—CONT'D**

account. For instance, the DHCP lease in Table 9.1 shows that the computer with hardware address 00:e0:98:82:4c:6b was assigned IP address 192.168.43.12 starting at 20:44 on April 1, 2001 (the date format is weekday yyy/mm/dd hh:mm:ss where 0 is Sunday).

Some DHCP servers can be configured to keep an archive of IP address assignments, but this practice is far from universal. Unless you are certain that archives are maintained, assume that the DHCP history is volatile and collect it as quickly as possible.

A DHCP lease does not guarantee that a particular computer was using an IP address at a given time. An individual could configure another computer with this same IP address at the same time, accidentally conflicting with the DHCP assignment or purposefully masquerading as the computer that originally was assigned this IP address via DHCP. The bright side is that such a conflict is often detected and leaves log records on the systems involved.

The same general process occurs when an individual connects to an Internet Service Provider (ISP) via a modem. Some ISPs record the originating phone number in addition to the IP address assigned, thus enabling investigators to track connections back to a particular phone line in a house or other building.

| **Table 9.1** DHCP Lease |
| --- |
| lease **192.168.43.12** { |
|    starts 0 2001/04/01 20:44:03; |
|    ends 1 2001/04/02 00:44:03; |
|    hardware ethernet **00:e0:98:82:4c:6b**; |
|    uid 01:00:e0:98:82:4c:6b; |
|    client-hostname "oisin"; |
| } |

Obtaining additional information about systems on the Internet is beyond the scope of this chapter. See Nikkel (2006) for a detailed methodology on documenting Internet name registry entries, Domain name records, and other information relating to remote systems.

## OVERVIEW OF PROTOCOLS

To communicate on a network, computers must use the same protocol. For example TCP/IP is the standard for computers to communicate across the Internet. The principle is fairly straightforward. Information is transmitted from a networked system in chunks called packets or datagrams. The chunks contain the data to be transferred along with the information needed to deliver them to their destination and to reconstruct the chunks into the original data. The extra information is added in layers when transmitted and stripped off in layers at the destination. This layering effectively wraps or encapsulates control details around the data before they are sent to the next layer, providing modular functionality at each layer. One layer, for instance, is used to specify the IP address of the destination system, and another layer is used to specify the destination application on that system by specifying the port being used by that application (there may be several ports on a server willing to receive data, and you don't want your request for a web page to end up in an SSH server). Both

**Table 9.2** Abstraction Layers of the TCP/IP Model

| TCP/IP Layer | Encapsulating Data Unit | Purpose of the Layer |
|---|---|---|
| Application | Data | Functions as a process to process communication |
| Transport | Segment | Functions as a virtual circuit creating a session between two hosts |
| Internet | Packet | Functions include sending and receiving packets of data from the other layers |
| Data Link | Frame | Functions to interconnect hosts on the local network |

of these layers will contain instructions for reconstructing the separated chunks, how to deal with delayed or out-of-order deliveries, and so forth. The TCP/IP model consists of four layers: data link, Internet, transport, and application layers, summarized in Table 9.2 and discussed further later.

At the data link layer, many computers run standard Ethernet (IEEE 802.3) to communicate with other computers on the same local area network. Ethernet provides a method for conveying bits of data over network cables, using the unique hardware identifiers associated with network cards (MAC addresses or physical addresses) to direct data to their destination. The format of a standard Ethernet frame is shown in Figure 9.2.

| 7 bytes | 1 byte | 6 bytes | 6 bytes | 2 bytes | 0-1500 bytes | 0-46 bytes | 4 bytes |
|---|---|---|---|---|---|---|---|
| Preamble | Start of Frame | Destination Address | Source Address | Length | Data | Padding | CRC |

**FIGURE 9.2**
Classic Ethernet frame.

The preamble and start-of-frame fields are functional components of the protocol, and are of little interest from an investigative or evidentiary standpoint. The source and destination Ethernet addresses are six bytes that are associated with the network cards on each computer. The length field contains the number of bytes in the data field—each frame must be at least 64 bytes long to allow network cards to detect collisions accurately (Held, 1994). The padding in the Ethernet frame ensures that each datagram is at least 64 bytes long and the cyclic redundancy check (CRC) is used to verify the integrity of the datagram at the time it is received.

**FIGURE 9.3**

Ethernet frame viewed using Wireshark.

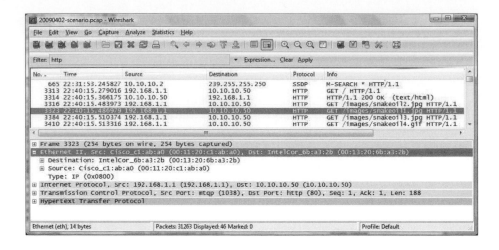

In Figure 9.3, there is an example of an Ethernet frame from the intrusion investigation scenario; it shows the source and destination Ethernet (MAC) address and the next layer protocol, IP. The Wireshark application displays the chunks of information that have been transmitted and captured over a network. The display parses the information into the various layers dictated by the protocols used for transmission and into any further protocol layers required by the type of service being used at the destination. In the second frame of the display, Wireshark has parsed four layers of delivery information (e.g., the third layer specifies the addresses of the source and destination systems and the fourth layer defines the source and destination ports) and then further parsed the protocol being used for the particular service being used in the transaction.

To communicate with machines on different networks, computers must run higher-level protocols such as Internet Protocol (IP) at the network layer and Transport Control Protocol (TCP) at the transport layer. TCP/IP provides a method for conveying packets of data over many physically distant and dissimilar networks, using Internet Protocol (IP) addresses to direct traffic to their destination. The format of a standard TCP/IP datagram is shown in Figure 9.4.

In Figure 9.5, there is an example of an IP packet in Wireshark from the intrusion investigation scenario; it shows the source and destination IP address and the next layer protocol, TCP.

The Transmission Control Protocol (TCP) is a connection-mode service, often called a virtual-circuit service that enables transmission in a reliable, sequenced manner that is analogous to a telephone call. TCP differs from the User Datagram Protocol (UDP), which is connectionless, meaning that each datagram is treated as a self-contained unit rather than part of a continuous transmission, and

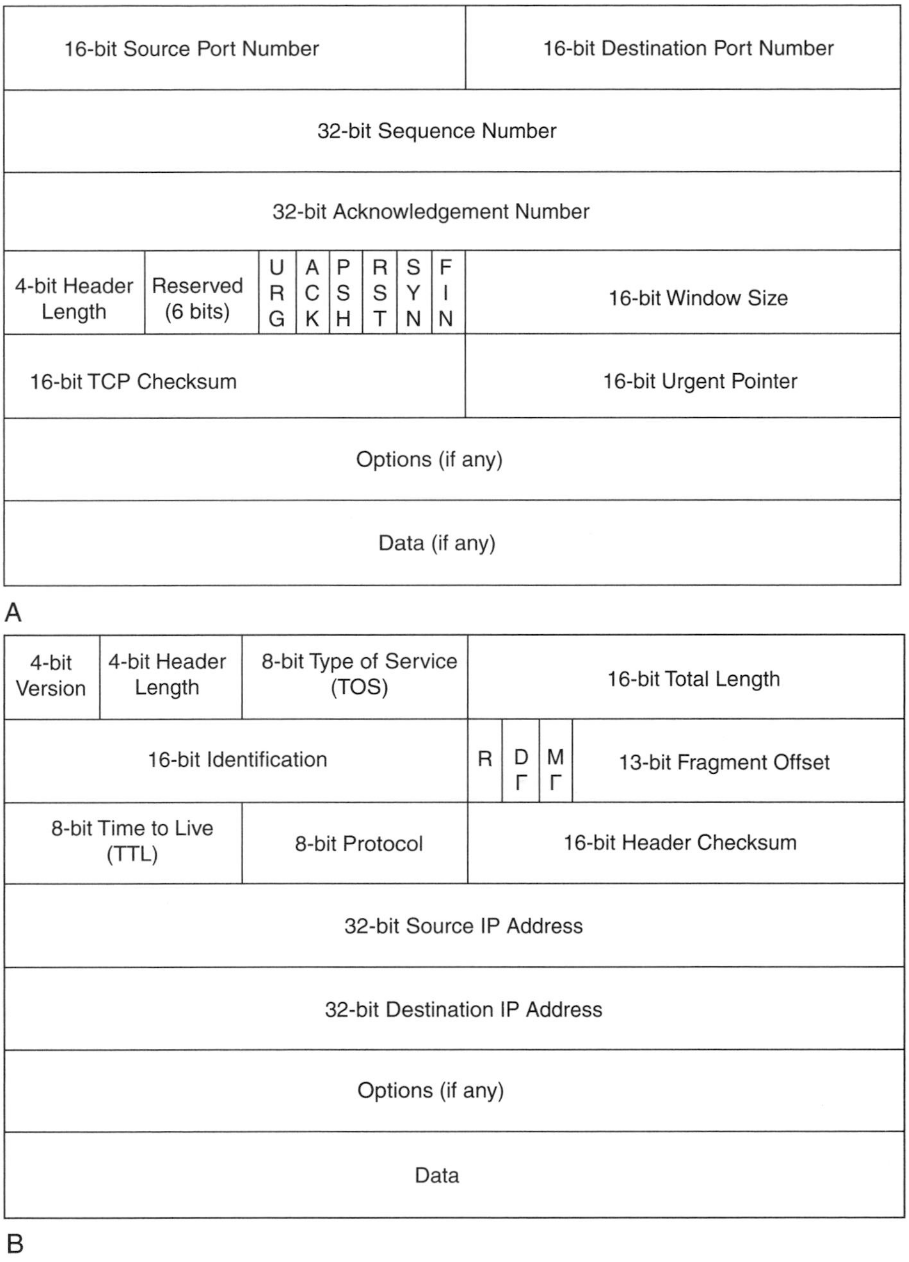

| 16-bit Source Port Number | | | | | | | | 16-bit Destination Port Number |
|---|---|---|---|---|---|---|---|---|
| 32-bit Sequence Number | | | | | | | | |
| 32-bit Acknowledgement Number | | | | | | | | |
| 4-bit Header Length | Reserved (6 bits) | U R G | A C K | P S H | R S T | S Y N | F I N | 16-bit Window Size |
| 16-bit TCP Checksum | | | | | | | | 16-bit Urgent Pointer |
| Options (if any) | | | | | | | | |
| Data (if any) | | | | | | | | |

A

| 4-bit Version | 4-bit Header Length | 8-bit Type of Service (TOS) | | | | 16-bit Total Length |
|---|---|---|---|---|---|---|
| 16-bit Identification | | | R | DГ | MГ | 13-bit Fragment Offset |
| 8-bit Time to Live (TTL) | | 8-bit Protocol | | | | 16-bit Header Checksum |
| 32-bit Source IP Address | | | | | | |
| 32-bit Destination IP Address | | | | | | |
| Options (if any) | | | | | | |
| Data | | | | | | |

B

**FIGURE 9.4(A), (B)**
Format of standard TCP/IP headers.

delivery of each unit is not guaranteed—analogous to a postal letter. Both TCP and UDP use ports to keep track of the communication session. By accepted convention, most ports used by most server applications are standardized. World Wide Web servers listen on port 80, FTP servers on port 21, DNS servers

**FIGURE 9.5**

IP packet in Wireshark Protocol Analyzer.

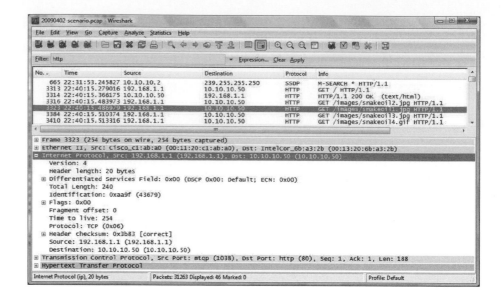

on port 53, SMB on port 445, and so forth. Clients are not normally so restricted since they can tell the server what client port they are using when they make their initial request to the server. A complete list of all TCP and UDP ports and services are defined in RFC 1700, which can be found at the following resource: www.ietf.org/rfc/rfc1700.txt. From an investigative standpoint, it is important to know that services can run on alternative ports; this reference is just a guideline for administrators to follow when configuring the server.

A TCP virtual-circuit is initiated using a process known as the *three-way hand shake*, illustrated in Figure 9.6.

The client informs the server that it wants to initiate a connection by sending a packet that is known commonly as a SYN packet—a packet containing the special SYN bit. This SYN packet also contains a sequence number that will be

**FIGURE 9.6**

Client server communication showing the establishment of flows using packets with SYN, SYN/ACK, and ACK bits set (reading arrows from top to bottom to establish chronology).

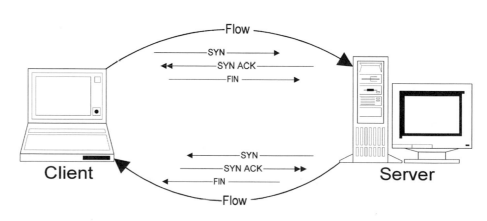

incremented in each subsequent packet that is sent, which enables the server to maintain the order of packets even if they are not received in their proper order.[1] When the server is ready to communicate, it responds with a packet that contains a SYN bit and an additional acknowledgement (ACK) bit. This packet also contains a sequence number that enables the client to maintain the order of packets as they are received from the server, and an ACK sequence number that informs the client of the next expected packet.

Once this acknowledgement packet is received, the client can begin sending data to the server in what is called a "flow", and will send as many packets as are necessary to convey its message. When the client has finished sending data, it closes the virtual-circuit by sending a packet containing a FIN bit. Significantly, whereas a flow is unidirectional, a TCP session is bidirectional, allowing data to be sent in both directions. Thus, a TCP connection is comprised of two flows, one from the client to the server, and another from the server to the client.[2]

In Figure 9.7, there is an example of a TCP segment in Wireshark from the intrusion investigation scenario; it shows the source and destination ports, the flags that were set and the sequence and acknowledgement numbers. For more

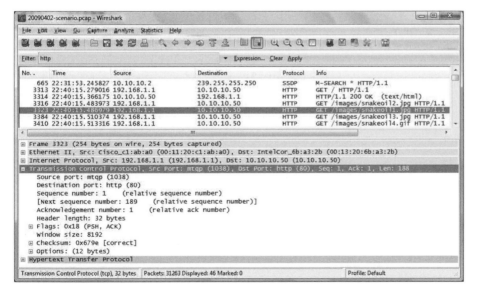

**FIGURE 9.7**

TCP Headers viewed in Wireshark

---

[1]Initial sequence numbers were originally obtained in a predictable manner but this allowed for a specific form of attack known as IP spoofing. Therefore, initial sequence numbers in more recent implementations of TCP are randomized so that an attacker cannot predict them.

[2]Both client and server use their own sequence numbers to enable full-duplex communication (Stevens, 1994).

details regarding the TCP/IP specification refer to Comer and RFC 768, RFC 791, RFC 792, and RFC 793.

In the displayed packet, the information inside the delivery layers is often formatted according to other protocols that are specific to the server being addressed on the destination system or to the type of transaction taking place between the source and the destination systems. Next we examine some of these higher-level protocols.

### HyperText Transfer Protocol (HTTP)

HTTP is an application layer protocol used for transferring information between computers on the World Wide Web. HTTP is based on a request/response standard between a client; usually the host and a server, a web site. The client initiates a request for a particular resource via a user agent and establishes a TCP connection usually on port 80 with a server. The server responds to the request with a status line and additional information that should include the resource requested. Resources to be accessed by HTTP are identified by Universal Resource Identifier (URI), which functions as a pathname to the resource. A resource can include all forms of data such as text, images, or multimedia shared on the Internet.

---

### PROTOCOL SPECIFICATIONS

HTTP is defined in RFC 1945 (HTTP/1.0) and RFC 2068 (HTTP/1.1). The RFC related to a protocol provides information that is helpful for understanding related log files. Another protocol, called the File Transfer Protocol or FTP (defined in RFC 0959), enables individuals to transfer files from one computer to another over the Internet.

---

As an investigator, it is important to understand the basic structure of HTTP because web browsing can be used for any online communication. Although HTTP is usually configured on TCP port 80, the administrator can configure the web server on any port. Furthermore, HTTP traffic can be encrypted with HTTP over TLS (Transport Layer Security), also called Secure HTTP (HTTPS). HTTPS typically uses TCP port 443, and though HTTPS still follows the HTTP standards, all the contents of the messages are encrypted, making it difficult to analyze the network traffic.

When conducting log analysis, it is important to understand the request method used by the client and the corresponding status code sent by the server. HTTP defines eight methods indicating the desired action to be performed on the requested resource. Table 9.3 summarizes the different actions that can be performed on the resource requested.

**Table 9.3** HTTP Request Methods

| Request Methods | Action Performed on the Resource |
| --- | --- |
| GET | Requests a representation of the specified resource |
| HEAD | This is identical to GET except that the server must not respond with a message body |
| POST | Submits data to be processed by the specified resource |
| PUT | Upload or update data to the specified resource |
| DELETE | Requests that the server deletes the resource identified |
| TRACE | Is a diagnostic "loopback" feature that includes the original request in the response |
| OPTIONS | Represents a request for the methods that the server supports |
| CONNECT | According to RFC 2616: "Reserves the method name CONNECT for use with a proxy that can dynamically switch to being a secure tunnel" |

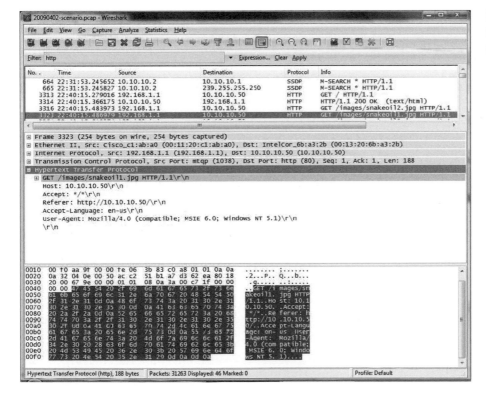

**FIGURE 9.8**

Wireshark packet analysis of an HTTP GET request.

As an example of an HTTP request, Figure 9.8 shows a GET request for the `snakeoil1.jpg` image on the intranet server (10.10.10.50) from the intrusion investigation scenario.

The server status line is the initial line of the server response and it includes the HTTP version, the status code, and the status message. It is important to understand that the status code and status message indicates how the server is responding to the specific request. Table 9.4 summarizes the different categories of responses that the server might send.

**Table 9.4(a)** HTTP Response Status Codes

| Response Status Code Category | Meaning |
|---|---|
| 100–199 | Reserved for informational messages. |
| 200–299 | Reserved for successful responses. For example, the 200 (ok) code indicates the request was successful and information was returned. |
| 300–399 | Indicates the resource is no longer at the URI. Redirection to the new URI may occur. |
| 400–499 | Indicates a client error. For example, the 404 code indicates that the resource cannot be found. |
| 500–599 | Indicates a server error. |

**Table 9.4(b)** Meaning of Common HTTP Request Codes

| Success | | Redirection | | Client Errors | | Server Error | |
|---|---|---|---|---|---|---|---|
| 200 | Success | 300 | Data requested has moved | 404 | File not found | 500 | Internal error |
| 201 | Okay post | 301 | Found data, has a temp URL | 400 | Bad request | 501 | Method not |
| 202 | Okay processing | 302 | Try another location | 401 | Unauthorized access | | Implemented |
| 203 | Partial information | 303 | Not modified | 402 | External redirect error | 502[8] | Server overloaded |
| 204 | Okay no response | 304 | Success/not modified | 403 | Forbidden | 503 | Gateway timeout |

[8] A 502 HTTP response code does not necessarily mean that the request failed. The requestor may have obtained some information.

For instance, Figure 9.9 shows the HTTP success code (200) returned in response to the GET request for the `snakeoil1.jpg` image in Figure 9.8.

Each time a resource on a web server is accessed over the Internet, an entry is made in an *access log* on the server detailing which computer on the Internet

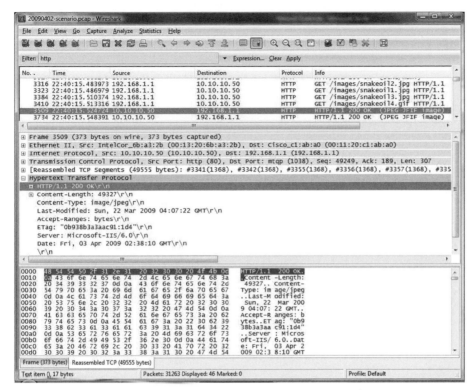

**FIGURE 9.9**
HTTP Status Code response.

was used to access which files at a certain time, as well as the HTTP return status code. Although the format of access log files depends on the web server and its configuration, they all resemble the Common Log Format (CLF) or extended CLF:

CLF: remote host, userID, date, time, request, status code, # bytes returned

Extended: remote host, userID, date, time, request, status code, # bytes returned, referring URL, browser

On Microsoft web services, these logs are generally located in `%systemroot%\system32\logfiles\` in a subdirectory associated with the server in question (e.g., W3SVC, FTPSVC) and have a slightly different format from the CLF. The following IIS web server log associated with the request for the snakeoil1.jpg image in Figure 9.9 is shown here:

```
2009-04-03 22:38:10 W3SVC1 10.10.10.50 GET /images/snakeoil1.jpg
 - 80 - 192.168.1.1 Mozilla/4.0+(compatible;+MSIE+6.0;+Windows+
 NT+5.1) 200 0 0
```

## FROM THE CASE FILES: CREDIT CARD THEFT

We were called in to investigate suspected theft of credit cards from an e-commerce site. Forensic examination of the MSSQL database server used to store the credit cards showed no signs of compromise. However, the primary web server used to fulfill e-commerce functions did contain evidence of intrusion. Specifically, the web server access logs showed repeated SQL injection attacks that enabled the intruder to bypass the e-commerce application on the web server and directly access records in the backend SQL database. The log entries resembled the following, showing the IP address used by the intruder (changed to 192.168.14.24 here for sanitization purposes) as well as the customer record and associated credit card number that was obtained by the intruder.

```
2009-03-07 04:22:51 W3SVC WWWSRV1 10.1.0.12 GET
/ecommerce/purchase.aspItemID=35745'%20=convert(int,(select
%20top%201%20convert(varchar,isnull(convert(varchar,CreditCardExpires),'
NULL'))%2b'/'%2bconvert(varchar,isnull(convert(varchar,CreditCardName),'
NULL'))%2b'/'%2bconvert(varchar,isnull(convert(varchar,CreditCardNumber),'
NULL'))%2b'/'%2bconvert(varchar,isnull(convert(varchar,CreditCardType),'
NULL'))%2b'/'%2bconvert(varchar,isnull(convert(varchar,CustomerID),'
NULL'))%2b'/'%2bconvert(varchar,isnull(convert(varchar,payID),'
NULL'))%20from%20EPayment%20where%20right(CreditCardExpires,2)%20not%20in%20
('01','05','04','03','02')%20and%20CreditCardExpires%20not%20in%20
('01/2006','02/2006','03/2006','04/2006','05/2006','06/2006','07/2006','
08/2006')%20and%20CustomerID%3E'0000000'%20order%20by%20CustomerID))--
sp_password|230|80040e07|Syntax_error_converting_the_varchar_value_'04/2010/
Joe_Blow/1234567891011121314/1/20/27981'_to_a_column_of_data_type_int.
80 - 192.168.14.24 HTTP/1.1
Mozilla/5.0+(Windows;+U;+Windows+NT+5.1;+en-
US;+rv:1.8.0.6)+Gecko/20060728+Firefox/1.5.0.6 - www.ecommerce1.com 500
0 0 2613 1341 312
```

Searching the web access logs further revealed the initial vulnerability scan the intruder launched against the system from a different IP address, and all subsequent exploration and unauthorized access events. The log entries showed that, over a period of days, the intruder was able to extract every credit card from the customer database.

## Server Message Block (SMB)

Server Message Block (SMB) is an application layer protocol originally developed by Microsoft that runs on top of other protocols to provide remote access to files, printers, and other network resources. SMB uses a client/server approach where the client initiates a request for resources and the server responds accordingly. Also, the server side service port will depend on the underlying transport protocol; SMB over TCP/IP commonly uses port 445 but the older NetBIOS API uses TCP port 139. While SMB is primarily a Windows file sharing protocol, it allows non-Windows machines to share resources in a fashion similar to that of native NetBIOS (see www.samba.org). As the protocol has evolved there are other implementations called Common Internet File System (CIFS).

The SMB protocol has many different commands, and a complete list is documented in SNIA (2002). The command sequence outlined in Table 9.5 is a typical message exchange for a client connecting to a server communicating with the SMB protocol.

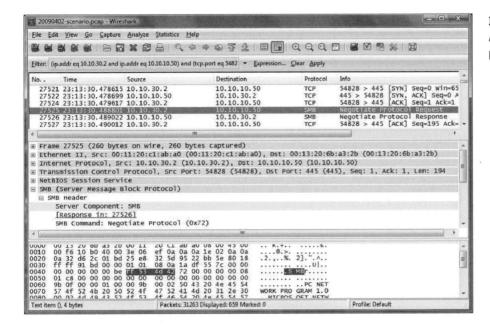

**FIGURE 9.10**
An SMB_COM_NEGOTIATE
packet viewed in Wireshark.

The SMB packet header contains significant information about the protocol in various header fields. Figure 9.10 shows the header and command code for an SMB_COM_NEGOTIATE packet that initiates an SMB session. Notice the protocol identifier \xff\x53\x4d\x42 in hexadecimal at the beginning of the packet that is common to all SMB packets. This hexadecimal value could be useful when an investigator needs to search, filter, or create a custom signature for SMB packets.

The next byte in an SMB packet contains the *command code*, indicating the type of SMB traffic such as in Table 9.5. Table 9.6 provides the hexadecimal values for some common SMB command codes.

Digital investigators can extract various details about a specific SMB session, like the username involved and resources accessed, by understanding the relationship of the process id (PID), multiplex id (MID), user id (UID), and tree id (TID) fields in the protocol header. The PID is set by the client to identify the specific request made to the server, and the MID field is used to keep track of multiple requests made by the same process. The UID field is set by the server once the user has authenticated, and the TID field identifies connections to shares once the connection has been established.

**Table 9.5** A Typical SMB Message Exchange Taken from the (SNIA, 2002)

| Client Command | Server Response |
| --- | --- |
| SMB_COM_NEGOTIATE | Must be the first message sent by a client to the server. Includes a list of SMB dialects supported by the client. Server response indicates which SMB dialect should be used. |
| SMB_COM_SESSION_SETUP_ANDX | Transmits the user's name and credentials to the server for verification. Successful server response has UID field set in SMB header used for subsequent SMBs on behalf of this user. |
| SMB_COM_TREE_CONNECT_ANDX | Transmits the name of the disk share (exported disk resource) the client wants to access. Successful server response has TID field set in SMB header used for subsequent SMBs referring to this resource. |
| SMB_COM_OPEN_ANDX | Transmits the name of the file, relative to TID, the client wants to open. Successful server response includes a file id (FID) the client should supply for subsequent operations on this file. |
| SMB_COM_READ | Client supplies TID, FID, file offset, and number of bytes to read. Successful server response includes the requested file data. |
| SMB_COM_CLOSE | Client closes the file represented by TID and FID. Server responds with success code. |
| SMB_COM_TREE_DISCONNECT | Client disconnects from resource represented by TID. |

**Table 9.6** Common SMB Command Codes

| SMB Command | Code Value |
| --- | --- |
| SMB_COM_READ_ANDX | 0 X 2E |
| SMB_COM_WRITE_ANDX | 0 X 2F |
| SMB_COM_NT_CREATE_ANDX | 0 X A2 |
| SMB_COM_TREE_CONNECT | 0 X 70 |
| SMB_COM_TREE_DISCONNECT | 0 X 71 |
| SMB_COM_NEGOTIATE | 0 X 72 |
| SMB_COM_SESSION_SETUP_ANDX | 0 X 73 |
| SMB_COM_LOGOFF_ANDX | 0 X 74 |
| SMB_COM_TREE_CONNECT_ANDX | 0 X 75 |

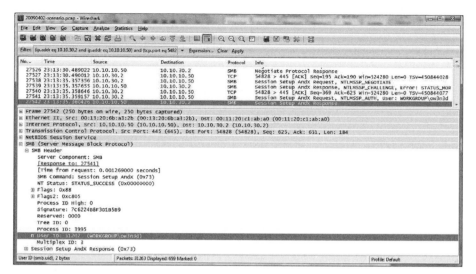

**FIGURE 9.11**

An SMB_COM_SESSION_SETUP_ANDX packet showing authentication of the ow3n3d user account from the intrusion investigation scenario and the associated UID (51202) assigned to this SMB session viewed using Wireshark.

Figure 9.11 shows the PID, MID and UID fields for an SMB_COM_SESSION_SETUP_ANDX packet from the intrusion investigation scenario. All communications associated with a particular SMB session will have the same UID, providing digital forensic examiners with a useful value for searching and filtering as discussed in "Forensic Examination of Network Traffic," later in this chapter.

Figure 9.12 shows an SMB_COM_TREE_CONNECT_ANDX packet from the intrusion investigation scenario containing the associated TID field and name

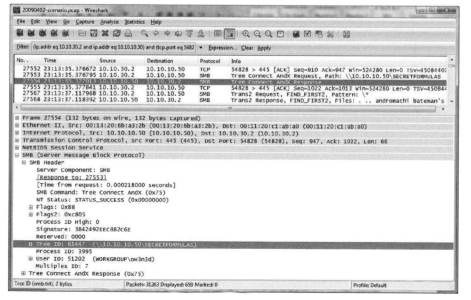

**FIGURE 9.12**

An SMB_COM_TREE_CONNECT_ANDX command showing access to the Secret Formulas network share on the intranet server (10.10.10.50) by the user account ow3n3d with the associated TID (61447) viewed using Wireshark.

**FIGURE 9.13**

SMB packet showing user account ow3n3d transferring data from Secret Formulas share on intranet server (10.10.10.50).

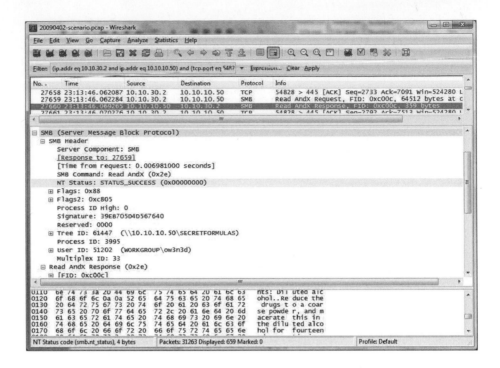

of the disk share (SECRETFORMULAS) being accessed. Searching the network traffic for a specific TID field will produce all packets associated with access to the specific resource on the server.

Finally, Figure 9.13 shows another packet with the TID 61447, revealing the ow3n3d user transferring data from the Secret Formulas network share.

## FROM THE CASE FILES: DATA THEFT

An intruder had gained unauthorized access to the core network of a major retailer and had obtained the password to a domain-level administrator account. The intruder was using this account to access NetBIOS shares on many Windows systems on the victim organization's internal network. Digital investigators captured network traffic of the intruder's activities and, by interpreting information in the SMB protocol, were able to determine which files were taken from particular systems and provided the resulting list of stolen assets to the client.

Security Event Logs on the server may contain log entries associated with SMB connections like account names used to authenticate, and the name and IP address of the client computer. For instance, a log entry associated with the preceding SMB connections from the intrusion investigation scenario is shown in Figure 4.5 of Chapter 4, "Intrusion Investigation."

> ## FROM THE CASE FILES: ANONYMOUS SMB CONNECTIONS
>
> An organization discovered that an intruder had gained unauthorized access to its internal network and was looking for open network shares on Windows systems. We were asked to determine whether the intruder could have taken files from any of the systems that were targeted via SMB. An examination of Security Event logs on the systems of concern revealed that the intruder only had anonymous access to many of the systems. Anonymous access is the default connection type that SMB creates when a username is not provided, and Windows systems can be configured to prevent anonymous access to resources. Further examination of the systems of concern confirmed that the intruder would not have had access to files on the disk with just anonymous access.

As this section begins to demonstrate, investigating criminal activity that involves computer networks requires a familiarity with a variety of different protocols. For the investigator to understand the network traffic and the resulting network log entries, it will require some research on the part of the analyst to learn the different aspects of each protocol. Practical applications of interpreting network traffic using Wireshark and other utilities are covered in "Forensic Examination of Network Traffic," later in this chapter.

## EVIDENCE PRESERVATION ON NETWORKS

There are some unique forensic challenges associated with preserving digital evidence on networks. Although some network-related data are stored on hard drives, more information is stored in volatile memory of network devices for a short time or in network cables for an instant. Even when collecting relatively static information such as firewall log files, it may not be feasible to shut down the system that contains these logs and then make a bitstream copy of the hard drive. The system may be a part of an organization's critical infrastructure and removing it from the network may cause more disruption or loss than the crime. Alternately, the storage capacity of the system may be prohibitively large to copy. So, how can evidence on a network be collected and documented in a way that demonstrates its authenticity, preserves its integrity, and maintains chain of custody?

In the case of log files, it is relatively straightforward to make copies of the files, calculate their message digest values (or digitally sign them), and document their characteristics (e.g., name, location, size, MAC times). All this information can be useful for establishing the integrity of the data at a later date and digitally signing files is a good method of establishing chain of custody, provided only a few people have access to the signing key. A failure to take these basic precautions can compromise an investigation. In 2000, for example, an individual known as Maxus stole credit card numbers from the Internet retailer CD Universe and demanded a $100,000 ransom. When denied the money, he posted 25,000 numbers on a web site. Apparently, employees from one or more of the computer security companies that handled the break-in inadvertently altered log files from the day of the attack—this failure to preserve the digital evidence eliminated the possibility of a prosecution (Bunker & Sullivan, 2000; Vilano, 2001).

Networked systems can also contain crucial evidence in volatile memory, evidence that can be lost if the network cable is disconnected or the computer is turned off. For instance, active network connections can be used to determine the IP address of an attacker. Methods and tools for preserving volatile data on Windows and UNIX systems are covered in *Malware Forensics* (Malin, Casey & Aquilina, 2008).

In addition to preserving the integrity of digital evidence, it is advisable to seek and collect corroborating information from multiple, independent sources. Last but not least, when collecting evidence from a network, it is important to keep an inventory of all the evidence with as much information describing the evidence as possible (e.g., filenames, origin, creation times/dates, modification times/dates, summary of contents). Although time-consuming, this process facilitates the pin-pointing of important items in the large volume of data common to investigations involving networks.

For detailed discussions about preserving various forms of data on a network, see Casey (2004a).

## COLLECTING AND INTERPRETING NETWORK DEVICE CONFIGURATION

Network devices are generally configured with minimal internal logging to conserve storage space and for optimal performance. Some network device functions are so thoroughly engineered to optimize performance that they are not normally logged at all. Although these devices can be configured to generate records of various kinds, the logs must be sent to a remote server for safekeeping because these devices do not contain permanent storage. Central syslog servers are commonly used to collect the log data.

In addition to generating useful logs, network devices can contain crucial evidence in volatile memory, evidence that can be lost if the network cable is disconnected or the device is shut down or rebooted. Routers are a prime example of this. Most routers are specialized devices with a CPU; ROM containing power on self-test and bootstrap code; flash memory containing the operating system; nonvolatile RAM containing configuration information; and volatile RAM containing the routing tables, ARP cache, limited log information, and buffered packets when traffic is heavy (Held & Hundley, 1999).

Routers are responsible for directing packets through a network to their destination and can be configured using Access Control Lists (ACLs) to make basic security-related decisions, blocking or allowing packets based on simple criteria. For instance, some organizations implement simple egress and ingress filtering in their border routers (blocking outgoing packets that have source addresses other than their own, and blocking incoming packets that contain source addresses belonging to them). This simple concept—only data addressed from the organization should be allowed out—greatly limits a malicious individual's ability to conceal his location. In some cases, digital investigators must document how a router is configured and other data stored in memory.

When detailed information contained in RAM is required, it may be necessary to connect to the network device and query it via its command interpreter. The most feasible way to examine the contents of RAM is to connect to the Cisco device via a console or over the network and query the router for the desired information. From a forensic standpoint, it is better to connect to the device locally using a console cable, but due to time and location the investigator may have to connect to the device across the network. When connecting across the network, the investigator should always use an SSH connection (secure) if available, in preference to a telnet session. Usually on a Cisco device, there are passwords protecting the console-line mode and the privilege exec mode in the CLI of the Cisco IOS. For additional information on how to connect to a Cisco device via a console cable check the following reference at www.cisco.com/en/US/products/hw/switches/ps700/products_tech_note09186a008010ff7a.shtml.

## MODES OF CISCO IOS COMMAND LINE INTERFACE

Cisco routers have different command line modes for executing different types of commands. User Exec Mode is the basic level of access presented when connecting to a router, and provides limited viewing of configuration settings as shown here.

```
cmdLabs> show users
Line  User  Host(s)  Idle     Location
*2 vty 0 idle        00:00    pool-70-22-11-200.balt.verizon.net
```

Privileged Exec Mode generally requires a password and is accessed by typing *enable* at the User Exec Mode. This level of access provides full configuration information but cannot change settings on the device as shown here.

```
cmdLabs# show ip interface brief
Interface          IP-Address        OK?    Method      Status    Protocol
FastEthernet0/0    10.10.10.1        YES    NVRAM       up        up
FastEthernet0/1    192.168.1.2       YES    NVRAM       up        up
Loopback0          10.1.1.1          YES    NVRAM       up
```

Global Configuration Mode is accessed by typing *configure terminal* (config t) at the Privileged Exec Mode. This level of access allows the user to change the settings on the device, for example, with the following command:

```
cmdLabs(config)# exception core-file DFI2/cmdLab_router
```

Much of the information collected from Cisco network devices can be obtained by running the `show` commands at the privileged exec mode on the command line interface of the Cisco IOS. The collection process can be documented by saving the HyperTerminal session and hashing the resulting file so that its integrity can be verified later. For example, the following output from a Cisco router shows portions of the results of the `show clock details` and `show running-config` commands.

**cmdLabs_router#show clock detail**
15:50:15.869 EST Wed May 13 2009
Time source is user configuration

**cmdLabs_router#show running-config**
Building configuration…

Current configuration : 2593 bytes
!
! Last configuration change at 15:45:38 EST Wed May 13 2009
! NVRAM config last updated at 15:45:46 EST Wed May 13 2009
!
version 12.3
service timestamps debug datetime msec
service timestamps log datetime msec
service password-encryption
!
hostname cmdLabs_router
!
boot-start-marker
boot-end-marker
!
logging buffered 51200 warnings
enable secret 5 $1$FU94$vZKrjHD75AkECB4IrMTdW1
!
username cmdlabs privilege 15 secret 5 $1$.g2n$7JBa2JiOWDb4ZppSYT40G/
clock timezone EST -5
!
ip ftp username anonymous
ip ftp password 7 151305030A33262B3D20
no ip domain lookup
ip domain name yourdomain.com
ip http server
ip http authentication local
ip flow-export source Loopback0

```
ip flow-export version 5
ip flow-export destination 10.10.10.10 9990
ip flow-aggregation cache as
   export destination 10.10.10.10 9991
   enabled
!
ip classless
ip route 0.0.0.0 0.0.0.0 192.168.1.1
!
!
banner motd ^C This is the cmdLab Router Authorized Access Only ^C
!
exception core-file cmdLabs_router
exception protocol ftp
exception region-size 65536
exception dump 10.10.10.100
!
!
end
```

Table 9.7 shows other Cisco commands that can be run to collect configuration information from the device.

**Table 9.7** Cisco ISO Commands

| Cisco ISO Command | Result |
| --- | --- |
| show clock detail | Displays the time set on the device and the status of a SNTP server |
| show reload | Displays when the device was last rebooted |
| show version | Displays information about the current Cisco IOS |
| show running-config | Displays configuration running in RAM |
| show startup-config | Displays configuration stored in NVRAM |
| show logging | Displays the logging information on the device |
| show ip route | Displays contents of the IP routing table |
| show users | Displays all users connected to the device |
| show interfaces | Displays statistics for all the interfaces |
| show ip interface brief | Displays a summary of all interfaces including IP addresses assigned |
| show access-list | Displays contents of all access control lists on the router |
| show ip nat translations verbose | Displays the NAT translation table |
| show monitor | Displays all SPAN/mirrored ports on a switch |
| exit | Moves back to User Exec Mode |

---

**PRACTITIONER'S TIP: CISCO COMMANDS CONDENSED**

As of the Cisco IOS release 11.2 the command `show tech-support` will allow for the collection of multiple sources of configuration information from the Cisco device. From a forensic standpoint, this is done by limiting the number of commands issued, and simplifying the collection process. This single command will contain the same output as:

```
show version
show running -config
```

```
show stacks
show interface
show controller
show process cpu
show process memory
show buffers
```

---

### Cisco Core Dumps

A core dump is a full copy of your router's memory. A router can be configured to write a core dump when the device crashes, and an investigator can manually create a core dump without rebooting the device by running the `write core` command in Privileged Exec Mode. The Cisco IOS can store or transfer the core dump file using various methods, but Cisco recommends using File Transfer Protocol (FTP) to a server attached to the router (Cisco, 2009). The following commands configure the FTP server authentication for the location to save the core dump:

```
cmdLabs# conf t
cmdLabs(conf)# exception core-file ROUTERNAME
cmdLabs(conf)# exception dump FTPSERVER
cmdLabs(conf)# exception protocol ftp
cmdLabs(conf)# exception region-size 65536
```

If the FTP server requires authentication, the correct username and password must be specified as follows:

```
cmdLabs(conf)# ip ftp username USERNAME
cmdLabs(conf)# ip ftp password PASSWORD
```

Then, to dump the contents of memory and send it to the FTP server, type `write core` in Privileged Exec Mode and you should see something like the following:

```
cmdLabs_router#write core
Remote host [10.10.10.100]?
Base name of core files to write [temp/cmdLab_router]?
Writing temp/cmdLab_routeriomem
!!!!!!!!!!!!!!!!!!!!!!!!!!!!!!!!!!!!!!!!!!!!!!!!!!!!!!!!!!!!!!!!
!!!!!!!!!!!!!!!!!!!!!!!!!!!!!!!!!!!!!!!!!!!!!!!!!!!!!!
Writing temp/cmdLab_router
!!!!!!!!!!!!!!!!!!!!!!!!!!!!!!!!!!!!!!!!!!!!!!!!!!!!!!!!!!!!!!!!
!!!!!!!!!!!!!!!!!!!!!!!!!!!!!!!!!!!!!!!!!!!!!!!!!!!!!!.
cmdLabs_router#
```

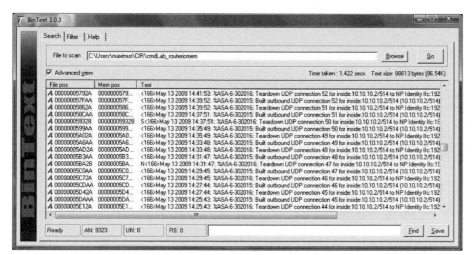

**FIGURE 9.14**
Contents of Router Memory Dump viewed using BinText showing cached contents of network traffic being handled by the router (firewall logs being sent to syslog server).

Analysis of the core dump file can be difficult, although the core dump can be viewed in a hex editor to extract some information as shown in Figure 9.14.

Core dump files can be submitted to Security Labs for basic analysis through its web site (http://cir.recurity.com/cir/), and it sells a tool with additional functionality, including extraction of packet headers into file in packet capture, or pcap, format that can be viewed using network traffic analysis tools.

## Firewalls

A firewall is a device that filters network traffic, restricting access to protected computer systems. Like a router, a firewall usually sends its logs to another computer for easy management and long-term storage but can also keep a list of recent log entries in its memory. Firewall logs generally show attempts to contact secured systems that were not permitted by the firewall configuration, and are not always specific about the reason the attempts were blocked. Typically, the computer attempting to access a machine behind the firewall without authorization will generate firewall activities as illustrated by the following Cisco Private Internet eXchange (PIX) firewall log segment.

```
Jun 14 10:00:07 firewall.secure.net %PIX-2-106001: Inbound TCP
  connection denied from 10.14.21.57/41371 to 10.14.42.6/113
  flags SYN

Jun 14 10:00:07 firewall.secure.net %PIX-2-106001: Inbound TCP
  connection denied from 10.14.43.23/2525 to 10.14.40.26/139
  flags SYN
```

The format of these log entries is similar to those of a router, starting with the date and time, followed by the name of the firewall, the PIX alert information (facility, severity, and message ID), the action, source, and destination. Additional information about PIX alerts is available at Cisco PIX (2000).

Firewall logs can be even more useful in an investigation when logging is enabled to record successful connections as shown here with a Cisco ASA device.

```
Apr 02 2009 23:12:23: %ASA-6-302013: Built inbound TCP
  connection 18 for dmz:10.10.30.2/54828 (10.10.30.2/54828) to
  inside:10.10.10.50/445 (10.10.10.50/445) (10.10.10.50/445)
Apr 02 2009 23:27:17: %ASA-6-302014: Teardown TCP connection
  18 for dmz:10.10.30.2/54828 to inside:10.10.10.50/445
  duration 0:14:54 bytes 33114 TCP FINs FINs
```

These two log entries are from the intrusion investigation scenario and show the SSH server (10.10.30.2 in the DMZ) connected to port 445 on the intranet server (10.10.10.50 on the secure network). The first log entry shows a TCP connection being established at 23:12 and the second log entry shows the session being ended at 23:27, which corresponds to the theft of trade secrets from a network file share.

## Virtual Private Networks

Many organizations use Virtual Private Networks (VPN) to allow authorized individuals to connect securely to restricted network resources from a remote location using the public Internet infrastructure. For instance, an organization might use a VPN to enable traveling sales representatives to connect to financial systems that are not generally available from the Internet. Using a VPN, sales representatives could dial into the Internet as usual (using low cost, commodity Internet service providers) and then establish a secure, encrypted connection the organization's network. A VPN essentially provides an encrypted tunnel through the public Internet, protecting all data that travels between the organization's network and the sales representative's computer.

Newer operating systems, including Windows 2000/XP/Vista have integrated VPN capabilities, implementing protocols like Point to Point Tunneling Protocol (PPTP) and IPsec to establish VPN. Newer network security devices like the Cisco ASA and Juniper SA Series also support VPN services via SSL, enabling users to establish a virtual connection simply using a web browser.

Digital investigators most commonly encounter VPN logs as a source of evidence associated with remote users accessing secured resources within the network from the Internet. The following logs from the Intrusion Investigation scenario for this chapter shows the ow3n3d user account authenticating with the VPN from a computer on the Internet with IP address 130.132.1.26.

```
Apr 02 2009 23:11:07: %ASA-6-113004: AAA user authentication
  Successful : server = 10.10.10.50 : user = ow3n3d ow3n3d
Apr 02 2009 23:11:07: %ASA-6-113009: AAA retrieved default
  group policy (DfltGrpPolicy) for user = ow3n3d ow3n3d
Apr 02 2009 23:11:07: %ASA-6-113008: AAA transaction status
  ACCEPT : user = ow3n3d ow3n3d
```

```
Apr 02 2009 23:11:07: %ASA-6-734001: DAP: User ow3n3d, Addr
  130.132.1.26, Connection Clientless: The following DAP
  records were selected for this connection: DfltAccessPolicy
  DfltAccessPolicy
Apr 02 2009 23:11:07: %ASA-6-716001: Group <DfltGrpPolicy>
  User <ow3n3d> IP <130.132.1.26> WebVPN session started.
  started.
Apr 02 2009 23:11:07: %ASA-6-716038: Group <DfltGrpPolicy>
  User <ow3n3d> IP <130.132.1.26> Authentication: successful,
  Session Type: WebVPN. WebVPN.
Apr 02 2009 23:11:07: %ASA-6-302013: Built inbound TCP
  connection 4 for outside:130.132.1.26/1484 (130.132.1.26/1484)
  to NP Identity Ifc:130.132.1.25/443 (130.132.1.25/443)
  (130.132.1.25/443)
Apr 02 2009 23:11:07: %ASA-6-725001: Starting SSL handshake
  with client outside:130.132.1.26/1484 for TLSv1 session.
<cut for brevity>
Apr 02 2009 23:29:20: %ASA-6-302014: Teardown TCP connection 19
  for outside:130.132.1.26/1495 to NP Identity Ifc:130.132.1.25/443
  duration 0:02:12 bytes 2591 TCP Reset-O Reset-O
```

Dedicated VPN network devices are available that implement protocols such as Layer 2 Tunneling Protocol (L2TP) and IPsec. One such device is used in the following case example to demonstrate how information from a VPN server can be useful in an investigation. The following case example demonstrates how to investigate an attack against a firewall coming from the Internet via a VPN.

## CASE EXAMPLE: INTRUDER CONNECTED TO A FIREWALL THROUGH VPN

This case example demonstrates how information gathered from running systems may be useful in an investigation, provided the information is documented thoroughly. However, we rarely catch intruders in the act, which emphasizes the importance of establishing reliable logging on all critical networked systems to support investigations after the fact as discussed in Chapter 4, "Intrusion Investigation."

A system administrator notices that an intruder is actively connected to the organization's main PIX firewall (Figure 9.15) and immediately contacts the Computer Incident Response Team. Knowing that a direct connection to the PIX using SSH does not show up in the list of connected users in PIX software version 5.2(3), investigators connect without fear of alerting the intruder of their presence.[3] The who command shows that the intruder is connected through the organization's VPN.

> pix# who
>     1:192.168.120.4(pc4.vpn.corpX.com)

The investigators then examine the active connections through the firewall to determine which protected servers the intruder is accessing. Using the show conn command to list all connections from 192.168.120.4 indicates that the intruder is connected to two servers using SSH (port 22).[4]

*(Continued)*

---

[3]Investigators could alternately connect via the console to achieve the same effect.

[4]The UIO flags indicate that the connection is Up and that data is being transmitted In, through and Out of the PIX.

## CASE EXAMPLE: INTRUDER CONNECTED TO A FIREWALL THROUGH VPN—CONT'D

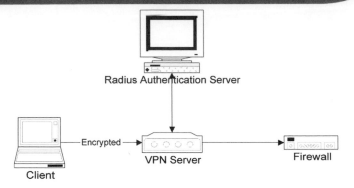

**FIGURE 9.15**

Attacker connected to router via dialup terminal server.

```
pix# show conn foreign 192.168.120.4 255.255.255.255
5947 in use, 31940 most used
TCP out 192.168.120.4:2189 in 192.168.50.5:22 idle
   0:14:06 Bytes 6649925 flags UIO
TCP out 192.168.120.4:2382 in 192.168.50.22:22 idle
   0:00:01 Bytes 5061 flags UIO
```

Whenever an examination must be performed on an active computer, the investigators perform analysis and collection tasks simultaneously. For instance, while listing the active connections through a firewall, investigators determine which connections are of interest and narrow their search accordingly. Similarly, to determine if the intruder changed the configuration and is connecting through the firewall via a newly opened hole, the investigators list the current configuration and compare it with a backup copy of the original configuration. This comparison indicates that a new rule was inserted to permit access from the VPN to server that contained highly sensitive, proprietary information.[5] Note that printing the command history can be used to document actions—the following listing shows that more commands were executed than were just presented:

```
pix# show history
   enable
   show version
   show clock
```

```
who
show config
show logging
show arp
show conn
show conn foreign
show conn foreign 192.168.120.4 255.255.255.255
show conn lport 10-100
show conn lport 22
show conn state
show history
```

In this case, to determine the user account used to connect through the VPN server, investigators connect to the server via its web interface and obtain a list of active sessions. This list indicates that user4 is assigned 192.168.120.4 by the VPN server.

```
VPN Concentrator Type: 3030
Bootcode Rev: Cisco Systems, Inc./VPN 3000
   Concentrator Series Version 2.5.Rel Jun 21 2000
   18:57:52
Software Rev: Cisco Systems, Inc./VPN 3000
   Concentrator Series Version 2.5.2 (D) Oct 26 2000
   15:18:42
Up Since: 12/18/2000 07:45:27
RAM Size: 128 MB
```

[5]This reconfiguration suggests that the intruder is highly skilled and knows which systems have information of interest.

| User Name | Public IP Address | Assigned IP Address | Protocol | Encryption | Login Time | Duration | Bytes Tx | Bytes Rx |
|---|---|---|---|---|---|---|---|---|
| user1 | 64.252.34.247 | 192.168.120.1 | PPTP | RC4-40 Stateless | Feb 19 07:16:11 | 9:27:59 | 173066 | 81634 |
| user2 | 205.167.18.179 | 192.168.120.2 | PPTP | RC4-128 Stateless | Feb 19 08:42:08 | 8:02:02 | 2651367 | 409564 |
| user3 | 64.252.65.193 | 192.168.120.3 | PPTP | RC4-40 Stateless | Feb 19 08:46:16 | 7:57:54 | 307537 | 90636 |
| user4 | 64.252.7.79 | 192.168.120.4 | PPTP | RC4-40 Stateless | Feb 19 13:58:35 | 2:45:35 | 1146346 | 258365 |
| user5 | 65.2.201.230 | 192.168.120.5 | PPTP | RC4-40 Stateless | Feb 17 08:03:33 | 56:40:37 | 88055544 | 37564000 |
| user6 | 63.22.219.90 | 192.168.120.6 | PPTP | RC4-128 Stateless | Feb 19 10:21:18 | 6:22:52 | 88556 | 9861816 |
| user7 | 64.252.36.212 | 192.168.120.7 | PPTP | RC4-40 Stateless | Feb 19 15:35:47 | 1:08:23 | 13430 | 14978 |
| user8 | 24.50.21.175 | 192.168.120.8 | PPTP | RC4-128 Stateless | Feb 19 11:02:00 | 5:42:10 | 2323577 | 469812 |
| user9 | 64.252.97.103 | 192.168.120.9 | PPTP | RC4-40 Stateless | Feb 18 20:51:41 | 19:52:29 | 9858730 | 4715345 |

The individual responsible for this account is connected from her home computer. A search of her home computer shows that she gained unauthorized access to many of the organization's most important systems and had stolen a significant amount of proprietary information. The individual had been recently hired and had used her position within the organization to steal valuable information and sell it to competitors.

## NetFlow

A growing number of routers (e.g., Cisco, Juniper, Extreme Networks) have a logging feature called NetFlow (Juniper calls it J-Flow data) that is invaluable in network investigations. NetFlow logs provide detailed information about network activities without capturing network content, thus providing high fidelity network visibility while avoiding the cost and privacy concerns of capturing full packet contents. Security-conscious organizations take full advantage of the power and lightweight nature of NetFlow logs (to say nothing of the price), collecting NetFlow logs from both internal and border routers to obtain greater visibility and situational awareness of their network activities.

When the NetFlow feature is enabled, routers record information about each flow, including the start and end times for the flow, source and destination IP addresses and port numbers, and the number of packets and octets in the flow. In the case of Internet Control Message Protocol (ICMP) traffic, the ICMP type and subtype are recorded in the destination port field of the NetFlow records.

Routers export flow information in a datagram called a Protocol Data Unit (PDU), which records one direction of the connection. The exact content of a PDU depends on the version of NetFlow being used but they all contain the current time according to the router, start and end times of the flow, source and destination IP addresses and ports of the flow, and the number of packets and bytes in the flow (NetFlow Export, 1998). NetFlow datagrams are sent to a system with a specialized NetFlow collector program listening on the specified port (8880). The `flow-tools` package is a free set of utilities for collecting and analyzing NetFlow logs as demonstrated further in this section.

Seeing all of the flows to and from a machine can be very useful in an investigation (Plonka, 2000). For instance, if a computer is compromised, the related NetFlow logs will show the source of the attack, the protocols used, ports accessed, amount of data transferred, and more. Once the source of the attack is known, the NetFlow logs can be searched for other machines on the network that were targeted by the attacker. As mentioned at the beginning of this chapter, looking at connections to compromised hosts at the time of attack can help pinpoint the attacker, as well as other hosts that were targeted by the same IP address. Of course, a detailed analysis of the compromised host is required to determine the results of each action observed using NetFlow (e.g., which files were downloaded via FTP). Also, the contents of each packet can be important (e.g., identifying a buffer overflow exploit), in which case you would need to analyze the contents of network traffic as discussed in detail later in this chapter.

## FROM THE CASE FILES: BIRD'S EYE VIEW OF THE INTRUSION

System administrators received an alert from their host-based IDS that a server had been compromised in the middle of the previous night. A preliminary forensic examination of the system revealed that system logs had been deleted, and recovered logs were incomplete. Intrusion detection system logs showed some activities relating to the attack, but not enough to gain a full understanding of the intruder's activities. NetFlow logs not only showed the connection associated with the remote exploitation of the compromised system, they also showed earlier reconnaissance activities (the intruder methodically scanning hosts on the network for vulnerable hosts), but also subsequent connections the intruder initiated from the compromised system, including obtaining rootkit files from a remote storage location on the Internet, and installing patches to prevent other malicious individuals from gaining unauthorized access to the system.

The maximum duration of a NetFlow record is 30 minutes, so longer TCP sessions will have multiple flow records spread over time. In addition, when no traffic for the flow has been seen in 15 seconds, the NetFlow record will be exported, requiring a new record to be initiated if additional traffic is transferred for that flow. Other events can cause a new NetFlow record to be started, like the flow table on the router reaching its maximum capacity and needing to export and flush older logs to make space for new ones. Therefore, it is often necessary to combine multiple flow records to get all information about a particular TCP session. In these cases, the TCP flags field can be used to determine whether a flow represents data from the start, middle, or end of the TCP session. Flows from the start of a session will have the SYN (but not FIN or RST) bit set, flows from the middle of the session will typically have no flag bits set, and flows from the end of the session will have the FIN or RST bits set (but not SYN).

## TOOL FEATURE: FLOW-TOOLS

The flow-tools package is a free, open source collection of utilities for processing and analyzing NetFlow logs (www.splintered.net). When responding to an incident it can be informative to obtain a high-level overview of activities before drilling down into specifics. When the source or target of an attack is not known, the utility named `flow-stat` can be employed to extract useful patterns from NetFlow logs. For instance, to determine which hosts on the network are sending the most data out of the network, use `flow-stat` as shown below to generate a report of source IP addresses (`-f9`), with a descending sort of the third field; octets (`-S3`). This command output shows that IP address 10.10.10.50 is sending the most data out of the network. The `flow-cat` program simply reads one or more flow logs and concatenates their contents and send their results to standard out.

```
$ flow-cat -p /var/flow/insiderouter/2009/
  2009-04/2009-04-02/ | flow-stat -f9 -p
  -S3 -T "High Exfiltration"
# --- ---- ---- Report Information
  --- --- ---
#
# Title:       High Exfiltration
# Fields:      Total
# Symbols:     Disabled
# Sorting:     Descending Field 3
# Name:        Source IP
#
# Args:        flow-stat -f9 -p -S3 -T High
               Exfiltration
#
#
# mode:               streaming
# capture start:      Thu Apr 2 21:30:24 2009
# capture end:        Sun Apr 5 16:45:28 2009
# capture period:     242104 seconds
```

```
# compress:         off
# byte order:       little
# stream version:   3
# export version:   5
# lost flows:       0
# corrupt packets:  0
# capture flows:    789
#
#
# IPaddr        flows      octets      packets
#
10.10.10.50     43         3328629     6858
10.10.10.10     621        85828       1111
10.10.10.2      125        45048       554
```

The `-p` option in the preceding command instructs `flow-stat` to include a summary of NetFlow metadata in the report, including the time period covered by the logs, the total number of flows, and any lost flows or corrupt packets.

NetFlow logs are most valuable to a network investigator when they are used to obtain an overview of transactions between attacker and victim hosts. As shown in Figure 9.16, the `flow-stat` source-destination IP address report format (`-f10`) reveals which source and destination hosts account for the bulk of traffic on the network, with results shown as a percentage of the total.

```
$ flow-cat /var/flow/insiderouter/2009/
  2009-04/2009-04-02/ | flow-stat -f10 -p
  -P -S3
<cut for brevity>
# src IPaddr dst IPaddr    flows  octets
  packets
#
10.10.10.50  192.168.1.1   3.549  95.086 77.344
10.10.10.50  10.10.30.2    0.760  1.063  3.004
10.10.10.10  68.237.161.12 30.418 0.995  5.632
```

*(Continued)*

## TOOL FEATURE: FLOW-TOOLS—CONT'D

This NetFlow output shows that most traffic is being sent to the Internet via the border gateway (192.168.1.1), and the next highest exchange of data was with a host on the DMZ (10.10.30.2). Further review of the detailed NetFlow records for these high exfiltration systems is warranted.

The flow-print utility simply takes the binary NetFlow files and converts them to plain text, displaying different fields depending on the report format specified. One of the more useful report formats for network investigations (–f5) is shown here, with NetFlow logs sorted by end time:

```
$ flow-cat /var/flow/insiderouter/2009/2009-04/2009-04-02/ | flow-filter -f test -Dattacker -Svictim | flow-print -f5
Start               End               Sif   SrcIPaddress   SrcP  DIf   DstIPaddress   DstP   P  Fl  Pkts   Octets
0402.21:56:03.666   0402.21:56:09.772  1    10.10.10.50    445   2     10.10.30.2     54823  6  3   6      987
0402.22:12:51.699   0402.22:12:51.711  1    10.10.10.50    139   2     10.10.30.2     54825  6  3   3      173
0402.22:12:51.711   0402.22:12:51.723  1    10.10.10.50    139   2     10.10.30.2     54826  6  3   3      173
0402.22:12:47.432   0402.22:12:52.184  1    10.10.10.50    445   2     10.10.30.2     54824  6  3   12     2421
0402.22:12:51.723   0402.22:12:52.292  1    10.10.10.50    139   2     10.10.30.2     54827  6  3   11     1700
0402.22:13:09.035   0402.22:28:03.157  1    10.10.10.50    445   2     10.10.30.2     54828  6  3   221    31304
```

This output includes the start and end time of the flow, source, and destination IP address and TCP or UDP ports, IP protocol type, the input and output interface numbers for the device where the NetFlow record was created, TCP flags, and a count of the number of octets and packets for each flow. In the preceding example we have removed several of the output fields to make it more readable. The column labeled "P" is the IP protocol type (6 is TCP, 17 is UDP). The column labeled "Fl" is the logical OR of all the TCP header flags seen (except for the ACK flag). The last two columns, labeled "Pkts" and "Octets" show the total number of packets and octets for

each flow. The date-time stamps in the preceding NetFlow logs are printed as MMDD.HH:MM:SS.SSS, so a timestamp of 0402.22:13:09.035 represents the time 22:13:09.035 on April 2. Observe that the year is not present in the date-time stamp. Therefore, NetFlow logs could be incorrect by a factor of years if the router clock is not set correctly, which can be troublesome from an investigative standpoint unless the clock of the router was checked for accuracy.

In some investigations it can be convenient to import this information into a spreadsheet for examination as shown in Figure 9.16. The spreadsheet filter can be used just to display

**FIGURE 9.16**

NetFlow records printed using flow-tools and imported into a spreadsheet.

| | A | B | C | D | E | F | G | H | I | J | K | L |
|---|---|---|---|---|---|---|---|---|---|---|---|---|
| 1 | Start | End | Sif | SrcIPaddress | SrcP | DIf | DstIPaddress | DstP | P | Fl | Pkts | Octets |
| 2 | | | | | | | | | | | | |
| 3 | 0402.22:29:39.477 | 0402.22:29:39.477 | 1 | 10.10.10.2 | 123 | 2 | 17.151.16.22 | 123 | 17 | 0 | 1 | 76 |
| 4 | 0402.22:29:44.097 | 0402.22:29:44.097 | 1 | 10.10.10.10 | 0 | 0 | 10.10.10.1 | 2048 | 1 | 0 | 1 | 84 |
| 5 | 0402.22:29:44.598 | 0402.22:29:44.598 | 1 | 10.10.10.10 | 0 | 0 | 10.1.1.1 | 771 | 1 | 0 | 1 | 112 |
| 6 | 0402.22:30:01.625 | 0402.22:30:07.635 | 1 | 10.10.10.10 | 0 | 2 | 10.10.30.2 | 2048 | 1 | 0 | 7 | 588 |
| 7 | 0402.22:30:19.655 | 0402.22:30:19.655 | 1 | 10.10.10.10 | 0 | 0 | 10.1.1.1 | 771 | 1 | 0 | 1 | 140 |
| 8 | 0402.22:30:42.477 | 0402.22:30:42.477 | 1 | 10.10.10.2 | 123 | 2 | 17.151.16.22 | 123 | 17 | 0 | 1 | 76 |
| 9 | 0402.22:30:47.702 | 0402.22:30:59.722 | 1 | 10.10.10.10 | 0 | 0 | 10.1.1.1 | 771 | 1 | 0 | 2 | 224 |
| 10 | 0402.22:30:49.781 | 0402.22:30:59.778 | 1 | 10.10.10.10 | 32769 | 2 | 71.242.0.12 | 53 | 17 | 0 | 2 | 134 |
| 11 | 0402.22:30:49.781 | 0402.22:30:59.778 | 1 | 10.10.10.10 | 32770 | 2 | 71.242.0.12 | 53 | 17 | 0 | 2 | 120 |
| 12 | 0402.22:30:49.781 | 0402.22:30:59.778 | 1 | 10.10.10.10 | 32771 | 2 | 71.242.0.12 | 53 | 17 | 0 | 2 | 130 |
| 13 | 0402.22:30:54.782 | 0402.22:31:04.774 | 1 | 10.10.10.10 | 32772 | 2 | 68.237.161.12 | 53 | 17 | 0 | 2 | 134 |
| 14 | 0402.22:30:54.782 | 0402.22:31:04.778 | 1 | 10.10.10.10 | 32773 | 2 | 68.237.161.12 | 53 | 17 | 0 | 2 | 120 |
| 15 | 0402.22:30:54.782 | 0402.22:31:04.778 | 1 | 10.10.10.10 | 32775 | 2 | 68.237.161.12 | 53 | 17 | 0 | 2 | 130 |
| 16 | 0402.22:31:15.338 | 0402.22:31:15.338 | 1 | 10.10.10.50 | 138 | 0 | 10.10.10.255 | 138 | 17 | 0 | 1 | 229 |
| 17 | 0402.22:31:09.773 | 0402.22:31:19.770 | 1 | 10.10.10.10 | 32776 | 2 | 71.242.0.12 | 53 | 17 | 0 | 2 | 158 |
| 18 | 0402.22:31:09.773 | 0402.22:31:19.770 | 1 | 10.10.10.10 | 32777 | 2 | 71.242.0.12 | 53 | 17 | 0 | 2 | 144 |
| 19 | 0402.22:31:09.773 | 0402.22:31:19.770 | 1 | 10.10.10.10 | 32778 | 2 | 71.242.0.12 | 53 | 17 | 0 | 2 | 154 |
| 20 | 0402.22:31:22.758 | 0402.22:31:22.758 | 1 | 10.10.10.10 | 0 | 0 | 10.1.1.1 | 771 | 1 | 0 | 1 | 112 |
| 21 | 0402.22:31:14.769 | 0402.22:31:24.766 | 1 | 10.10.10.10 | 32779 | 2 | 68.237.161.12 | 53 | 17 | 0 | 2 | 158 |
| 22 | 0402.22:31:14.769 | 0402.22:31:24.766 | 1 | 10.10.10.10 | 32780 | 2 | 68.237.161.12 | 53 | 17 | 0 | 2 | 144 |
| 23 | 0402.22:31:14.769 | 0402.22:31:24.766 | 1 | 10.10.10.10 | 32781 | 2 | 68.237.161.12 | 53 | 17 | 0 | 2 | 154 |

*(Continued)*

## TOOL FEATURE: FLOW-TOOLS—CONT'D

certain NetFlow records, like those containing IP address 10.10.10.50, or just traffic to or from port 80.

Alternately, the `flow-filter` utility can be used to extract NetFlow records meeting specific criteria. The following command lists all NetFlow records with a source port 80, revealing that all the connections to port 80 on 10.10.10.50 came via the VPN (192.168.1.1).

```
$ flow-cat /var/flow/insiderouter/2009/2009-04/2009-04-02/ | flow-filter -p80 | flow-print -f5
Start              End                 Sif  SrcIPaddress   SrcP  DIf  DstIPaddress   DstP  P  Fl  Pkts  Octets
0402.21:39:54.001  0402.22:39:56.044  1    10.10.10.50    80    2    192.168.1.1    1040  6  3   94    127167
0402.21:39:53.768  0402.22:39:54.177  1    10.10.10.50    80    2    192.168.1.1    1037  6  2   139   193506
0402.21:39:53.977  0402.22:39:54.201  1    10.10.10.50    80    2    192.168.1.1    1038  6  2   114   156792
0402.21:39:53.997  0402.22:39:54.201  1    10.10.10.50    80    2    192.168.1.1    1039  6  2   171   237835
0402.21:40:56.251  0402.22:41:00.526  1    10.10.10.50    80    2    192.168.1.1    1037  6  1   3     156
0402.21:40:56.255  0402.22:41:00.526  1    10.10.10.50    80    2    192.168.1.1    1038  6  1   3     156
0402.21:40:56.255  0402.22:40:56.255  1    10.10.10.50    80    2    192.168.1.1    1039  6  0   1     52
0402.21:41:34.854  0402.22:41:34.854  1    10.10.10.50    80    2    192.168.1.1    1039  6  1   2     104
```

To list just the flows between 10.10.10.50 and 10.10.30.2, use `flow-filter` with a configuration file (flow.acl) containing the following access lists:

ip access-list standard attacker permit host 10.10.30.2
ip access-list standard victim permit host 10.10.10.50

The `flow-filter` utility uses Cisco standard Access Control Lists (ACLs) to determine which records to extract from NetFlow logs. In this scenario, the preceding ACLs set the attacker IP address to 10.10.30.2 and the victim IP address to 10.10.10.50. The following command reads these ACLs from the `flow.acl file` and extracts NetFlow records with a destination IP address matching the attacker and source IP address matching the victim IP address. In more complex investigations, multiple IP addresses could be specified in the attacker and victim ACLs, providing powerful and comprehensive log extraction capabilities.

```
$ flow-cat /var/flow/insiderouter/2009/2009-04/2009-04-02/ | flow-filter -f flow.acl
  -Dattacker -Svictim | flow-print
srcIP          dstIP          prot    srcPort     dstPort     octets      packets
10.10.10.50    10.10.30.2     6       445         54823       987         6
10.10.10.50    10.10.30.2     6       139         54825       173         3
10.10.10.50    10.10.30.2     6       139         54826       173         3
10.10.10.50    10.10.30.2     6       445         54824       2421        12
10.10.10.50    10.10.30.2     6       139         54827       1700        11
10.10.10.50    10.10.30.2     6       445         54828       31304       221
```

The power of `flow-filter` becomes more apparent when there are multiple attacker or victim systems. By simply adding an ACL line to the attacker group in the `flow.acl` file for each attacking IP address as shown here, you can instruct `flow-filter` to provide a single, comprehensive list of malicious flows:

ip access-list standard attacker permit host 10.10.30.2
ip access-list standard attacker permit host 192.168.1.1
ip access-list standard victim permit host 10.10.10.50
In addition to the flow-filter utility, flow-tools includes the flow-nfilter and flow-report utilities, which permit the use of more detailed specifications for data selection and output.

---

**PRACTITIONER'S TIP: NETFLOW MISINTERPRETATION**

There are several ways that error can be introduced when dealing with NetFlow logs. First, NetFlow PDUs are exported when a flow ends, resulting in a log file with entries sorted by flow end times. This unusual ordering of events can be very confusing and can cause examiners to reach incorrect conclusions. Therefore, it is advisable to sort NetFlow logs using the start time of each flow before attempting to interpret them. Tools such as `flow-sort` are designed specifically for this purpose, and many NetFlow utilities include sort options specified using –s and –S arguments. Second, a NetFlow record does not indicate which host initiated the connection, only that one host sent data to another host. Therefore, it is necessary to infer which host initiated the connection, for example, by sorting the relevant flows using their start times to determine which flow was initiated first.

---

Other available tools for processing NetFlow data include SiLK (http://tools. netsa.cert.org/silk/), NfSen (http://nfsen.sourceforge.net), and Orion NetFlow Traffic Analyzer (NTA) from Solarwinds (www.solarwinds.com/ products/orion/nta).

When dealing with NetFlow as a source of evidence, digital investigators need to be cognizant of the fact that flow records exported from a router are encapsulated in a UDP datagram and may not reach the intended logging server. Therefore, like syslog, NetFlow logs may not be complete. Fortunately, newer versions of NetFlow records contain a sequence number that can be used to determine if any records are missing or if forged records have been inserted.

---

**FROM THE CASE FILES: NETFLOW LOSSES**

A server that contained PII was compromised and used to store and disseminate pirated movies. Digital investigators were asked to ascertain whether the intruders had taken the PII. A forensic examination of the server itself was inconclusive, but the organization provided NetFlow data that had the potential to show whether or not the intruders had accessed the SQL database that contained the data of concern. Unfortunately, a preliminary inspection of the NetFlow logs revealed that a substantial number of records were missing, most likely due to NetFlow UDP packets never reaching the collection server. The incomplete NetFlow logs contained very limited information relating to the compromised server during the time of interest. As a result, it was not possible to determine whether the PII had been stolen.

---

## Authentication Servers

Networks with large numbers of users must maintain a central repository of usernames and passwords, although the mechanism used to authenticate users may vary. For instance, when a home user connects to the Internet using a dial-up or DSL modem, the Internet Service Provider requires a username and password. These credentials are then passed on to an authentication server for validation. After users are authenticated successfully, they are assigned an IP address and a connection is established. A similar process occurs when an individual establishes a VPN connection into an organization's network.

The most common authentication protocols in this context are RADIUS (Remote Authentication Dial In User Service) and TACACS, and both routinely log information that can be useful in an investigation, including the IP address that was assigned to a given user account during a particular time period.

### RADIUS

RADIUS logs are generally difficult to read because a single event generates multiple log entries, and the multirecord entry format varies somewhat with the type of event recorded, as shown in Table 9.8.

---

**Table 9.8** Example RADIUS Log Showing Authentication Events Relating to jack and jill User Accounts

```
Fri May   1 00:00:03 2009
          User-Name = "jack"
          NAS-Port = 29
          NAS-IP-Address = 10.30.15.133
          Framed-IP-Address = 10.20.172.67
          NAS-Identifier = "Controller4"
          Airespace-Wlan-Id = 2
          Acct-Session-Id = "49fa5e88/00:13:02:83:40:
          b3/31898"
          Acct-Authentic = RADIUS
          Tunnel-Type:0 = VLAN
          Tunnel-Medium-Type:0 = IEEE-802
          Tunnel-Private-Group-Id:0 = "7"
          Acct-Status-Type = Interim-Update
          Acct-Input-Octets = 8229760
          Acct-Output-Octets = 185405776
          Acct-Input-Packets = 91214
          Acct-Output-Packets = 131982
          Acct-Session-Time = 5435
          Acct-Delay-Time = 0
          Calling-Station-Id = "10.20.172.67"
          Called-Station-Id = "10.30.15.133"
          Client-IP-Address = 10.30.15.133
          Acct-Unique-Session-Id = "a635af4c1429c174"
          Timestamp = 1241150403
```

*(Continued)*

**Table 9.8** Example RADIUS Log Showing Authentication Events Relating to jack and jill User Accounts—Cont'd

```
Fri May  1 00:00:05 2009
          User-Name = "jill"
          NAS-Port = 29
          NAS-IP-Address = 10.30.15.133
          Framed-IP-Address = 10.20.31.148
          NAS-Identifier = "Controller4"
          Airespace-Wlan-Id = 2
          Acct-Session-Id = "49fa4142/00:1f:3a:03:24:
          95/31472"
          Acct-Authentic = RADIUS
          Tunnel-Type:0 = VLAN
          Tunnel-Medium-Type:0 = IEEE-802
          Tunnel-Private-Group-Id:0 = "7"
          Acct-Status-Type = Stop
          Acct-Input-Octets = 2246601
          Acct-Output-Octets = 26698929
          Acct-Input-Packets = 29463
          Acct-Output-Packets = 19547
          Acct-Terminate-Cause = Idle-Timeout
          Acct-Session-Time = 12931
          Acct-Delay-Time = 0
          Calling-Station-Id = "10.20.31.148"
          Called-Station-Id = "10.30.15.133"
          Client-IP-Address = 10.30.15.133
          Acct-Unique-Session-Id = "1ae71829a07b3e5e"
          Timestamp = 1241150405
```

In order to simplify correlation of RADIUS logs with other formats (or just to read them at all), it's very helpful to select the fields you consider important and then write those fields from each logical record into a corresponding, one line, physical record.

## PRACTITIONER'S TIP: DEFINE THE NORM

When correlating logs from different sources, recorded in different formats, the first thing to do is to determine what information in each type of log record is worth extracting. In the case of RADIUS logs, there is a lot of information of interest to the network and RADIUS administrators that may not be particularly useful for event reconstruction. The key to correlating logs is to identify what you will need every log record to have in common (a timestamp, at least) and then what extra information specific to each type of log you wish to preserve as well.

What you are really doing is establishing your own log format for that investigation and then converting records from those different sources to that format. Correlating the records is then a very straightforward process.

The following Perl script will convert the multiline RADIUS records in Table 9.8 into short, one-line, summary records:

```perl
#!/usr/bin/perl
$/ = ''; # set paragraph mode on input record separator
my @fields = qw/User-Name Acct-Status-Type Framed-IP-Address/;
while ( <> )
{
    chomp;
    my @records = split /\s*[=\n]\s*/;
    $timestamp = shift @records;
    s/^\s+// for @records;
    s/"//g for @records;
    my %hash = @records;
    print join(',',$timestamp,"RADIUS",@hash{@fields}),"\n";
}
```

The script begins by defining the end-of-record character as a blank line, instead of the default newline character. It then reads each logical record one at a time, parses it, stores it in a hash, then prints out the fields of interest. The timestamp is represented somewhat differently than the other fields, so that is simply pulled out and printed. The other fields selected represent the authenticated userid, the type of RADIUS event logged (e.g., Start, Stop, Interim-Update, etc.), and the IP address from which the session originated. The resulting record is well-defined, compact, and in comma-separated format ready to be correlated with records from other sources.

```
$ radiuslogparser.pl < samplelog
Fri May 1 00:00:03 2009,RADIUS,jack,Interim-Update,10.20.172.67
Fri May 1 00:00:05 2009,RADIUS,jill,Stop,10.20.31.148
```

Inserting the field RADIUS in each record to define the type of log file can be very helpful when correlating with other log types, which often contain a server name or can be labeled to distinguish them (e.g., WEBACCESS, SYSLOG).

## TACACS

When an individual dials into the Internet, there are usually two forms of evidence at the ISP—the contents of the terminal server's memory and the logs from the associated authentication server. For instance, the TACACS log file in Table 9.9 shows two users (John and Mary) dialing into a dialup terminal server named ppp.corpX.com, authenticating against a TACACS server named tacacs-server, and being assigned IP addresses. For the sake of clarity, these IP addresses have been resolved to their associated canonical names (e.g., static2.corpX. com).

As defined in RFC 1492, TACACS assigns codes to certain requests when dealing with SLIP connections, including LOGIN (Type=1), LOGOUT (Type=7), SLIPON

**Table 9.9** TACACS Log Example

Jul 13 04:35:30 tacacs server tacacsd[18144]: validation request from ppp.corpX.com [Type=1]

Jul 13 04:35:30 tacacs-server tacacsd[18144]: login query from ppp.corpX.com TTY26 for john accepted

Jul 13 04:35:30 tacacs-server tacacsd[18145]: validation request from ppp.corpX.com [Type=7]

Jul 13 04:35:30 tacacs-server tacacsd[18145]: logout from ppp.corpX.com TTY26, user john(0)

**Jul 13 04:35:30 tacacs-server tacacsd[18146]: validation request from ppp.corpX.com [Type=9]**

**Jul 13 04:35:30 tacacs-server tacacsd[18146]: slipon from ppp.corpX.com SLIP26 for user**

**Jul 13 04:35:30 tacacs-server tacacsd[18146]: john(0) address static2.corpX.com**

Jul 13 04:36:17 tacacs-server tacacsd[18147]: validation request from ppp.corpX.com [Type=1]

Jul 13 04:36:17 tacacs-server tacacsd[18147]: login query from ppp-03.corpX.com TTY23 for mary accepted

Jul 13 04:36:17 tacacs-server tacacsd[18148]: validation request from ppp.corpX.com [Type=7]

Jul 13 04:36:17 tacacs-server tacacsd[18148]: logout from ppp.corpX.com TTY23, user mary(0)

Jul 13 04:36:17 tacacs-server tacacsd[18149]: validation request from ppp.corpX.com [Type=9]

Jul 13 04:36:17 tacacs-server tacacsd[18149]: slipon from ppp.corpX.com SLIP23 for user

Jul 13 04:36:17 tacacs-server tacacsd[18149]: mary(0) address static3.corpX.com

**Jul 13 04:38:24 tacacs-server tacacsd[18150]: validation request from ppp.corpX.com [Type=10]**

**Jul 13 04:38:24 tacacs-server tacacsd[18150]: slipoff from ppp.corpX.com SLIP26 for**

**Jul 13 04:38:24 tacacs-server tacacsd[18150]: john(0) address static2.corpX.com**

Jul 13 04:40:27 tacacs-server tacacsd[18151]: validation request from ppp.corpX.com [Type=10]

Jul 13 04:40:27 tacacs-server tacacsd[18151]: slipoff from ppp.corpX.com SLIP20 for

Jul 13 04:40:27 tacacs-server tacacsd[18151]: mary(0) address static3.corpX.com

(Type=9), and SLIPOFF (Type=10).[6] So, Table 9.9 shows that John made a SLIPON request at 04:35 and was assigned static2.corpX.com. Later, at 04:38, John requested a SLIPOFF when he disconnected from the terminal server and relinquished the IP address. Notably, the LOGOUT request does not indicate that the user disconnected, only that the user was authenticated against the TACACS server.

The following case example demonstrates how data from a router, terminal server, and authentication server can be used in an investigation.

---

[6] These logs may not show when someone logged out if the dialup connection was not terminated cleanly.

## CASE EXAMPLE: INTRUDER CONNECTED TO ROUTER THROUGH DIALUP

After repeated network disruptions, an organization determines that a malicious individual is repeatedly connecting to routers and reconfiguring them, causing large-scale disruption (Figure 9.17). Investigators monitor the routers and detect the intruder connecting to a router to reconfigure it. After noting the system time, router configuration, and other system information, the show users command is used to display the IP address of the computer that is actively connected to the router. In this case, the intruder was logged in via the organization's dialup terminal server and was assigned IP address 192.168.1.106.[7]

```
router> show users
  Line    User    Host(s)Idle    Location
* 2 vty   0       idle00:00:00   192.168.1.106
```

To document what actions the intruder took on the router, investigators collect the logs from RAM using the show logging command. The investigators later compare these logs with those stored remotely on the logging host (192.168.60.21).

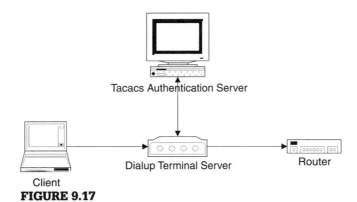

Tacacs Authentication Server

Client

Dialup Terminal Server

Router

**FIGURE 9.17**

Attacker connected to router via dialup terminal server.

```
router> show logging
Syslog logging: enabled (0 messages dropped, 0 flushes, 0 overruns)
   Console logging: level debugging, 38 messages logged
   Monitor logging: level debugging, 0 messages logged
   Buffer logging: level debugging, 38 messages logged
   Logging Exception size (8192 bytes)
   Trap logging: level debugging, 32 message lines logged
      Logging to 192.168.60.21, 32 message lines logged

Log Buffer (16384 bytes):

00:00:05: %LINK-3-UPDOWN: Interface FastEthernet0/0, changed state to up
00:00:07: %LINEPROTO-5-UPDOWN: Line protocol on Interface FastEthernet0/0, changed state to up
*Jul 19 10:30:54 PDT: %SYS-5-CONFIG_I: Configured from memory by console
*Jul 19 10:30:55 PDT: %SYS-5-RESTART: System restarted --
```

*(Continued)*

---

[7] The same results can be obtained using the who command.

## CASE EXAMPLE: INTRUDER CONNECTED TO ROUTER THROUGH DIALUP—CONT'D

Cisco Internetwork Operating System Software
IOS (tm) 7200 Software (C7200-K4P-M), Version 12.0(11.6)S, EARLY DEPLOYMENT MAIN
TENANCE INTERIM SOFTWARE
Copyright (c) 1986-2000 by cisco Systems, Inc.
Compiled Wed 12-Jul-00 23:10 by ccai
*Jul 19 10:30:56 PDT: %SSH-5-ENABLED: SSH 1.5 has been enabled
.Jul 19 10:30:59 PDT: %BGP-6-NLRI_MISMATCH: Mismatch NLRI negotiation with peer 206.251.0.252

Each log entry begins with the date and time, followed by the facility code (e.g., SEC, SYS, SSH, BGP), severity, and message. These codes and messages are detailed at Cisco IOS (2000). These router logs show the router being reconfigured and restarted, confirming that the intruder reconfigured the router. A comparison of the maliciously modified configuration with a backup of the original configuration shows that the intruder instructed the router to block all traffic, effectively creating a roadblock on the network.

Note that the `show history` command can be used to list the commands executed during the examination.

```
router> show history
       show clock
       show version
       show config
       show users
       show logging
       show history
```

TACACS authentication logs associated with the dialup server are examined to determine which account is being used to access the router via the dialup server. The logs show that user26 was assigned the IP address in question.

### LOGIN
Jul 19 10:25:34 tacacs-server tacacsd[25440]: validation request from ppp.corpX.com [Type=1]
Jul 19 10:25:34 tacacs-server tacacsd[25440]: login query from ppp.corpX.com TTY13 for user26 accepted

### LOGOUT
Jul 19 10:25:34 tacacs-server tacacsd[25441]: validation request from staffppp-01.net.yale.edu [Type=7]
Jul 19 10:25:34 tacacs-server tacacsd[25441]: logout from staffppp-01.net.yale.edu TTY13, user user26(0)

### SLIPON (192.168.1.106 assigned to user26)
Jul 19 10:25:34 tacacs-server tacacsd[25442]: validation request from ppp.corpX.com [Type=9]
Jul 19 10:25:34 tacacs-server tacacsd[25442]: slipon from ppp.corpX.com SLIP13 for user
Jul 19 10:25:34 tacacs-server tacacsd[25442]: user26(0) address 192.168.1.106

### SLIPOFF (user26 disconnects from dialup terminal server)
Jul 19 10:31:34 tacacs-server tacacsd[25443]: validation request from ppp.corpX.com [Type=10]
Jul 19 10:31:34 tacacs-server tacacsd[25443]: slip off from ppp.corpX.com SLIP13 for
Jul 19 10:31:34 tacacs-server tacacsd[25443]: user26(0) address 192.168.1.106

To document that user26 is connected to the dialup server and is assigned 192.168.1.106, investigators connect to the dialup server directly and obtain the following information.

*(Continued)*

## CASE EXAMPLE: INTRUDER CONNECTED TO ROUTER THROUGH DIALUP—CONT'D

```
pppsrv> who
Line    User     Host(s)            Idle Location
1 tty 1   user1    Async interface    02:25:20
2 tty 2   user2    Async interface    00:00:37
3 tty 3   user3    Async interface    00:00:06
4 tty 4   user4    Async interface    00:00:02
5 tty 5   user5    Async interface    00:00:06
6 tty 6   user6    Async interface    00:01:17
7 tty 7   user7    Async interface    00:03:43
8 tty 8   user8    Async interface    00:00:05
9 tty 9   user9    Async interface    00:05:24
10 tty 10 user10   Async interface    02:26:10
11 tty 11 user11   Async interface    00:00:05
14 tty 14 user14   Async interface    00:00:31
16 tty 16 user16   Async interface    00:04:38
17 tty 17 user17   Async interface    00:00:00
18 tty 18 user18   Async interface    00:00:03
19 tty 19 user19   Async interface    00:06:43
20 tty 20 user20   Async interface    00:00:45
21 tty 21 user21   Async interface    00:05:09
22 tty 22 user22   Async interface    00:00:03
26 tty 26 user26   Async interface    00.26.35
27 tty 27 user27   Async interface    00:00:00

pppsrvshow ip inter async26
Async26 is up, line protocol is up

    Interface is unnumbered. Using address of Ethernet0
      (192.168.1.10)
    Broadcast address is 255.255.255.255
```

```
    Peer address is 192.168.1.106    MTU is 1500 bytes
    Helper address is not set
    Directed broadcast forwarding is enabled
    Multicast reserved groups joined: 224.0.0.5 224.0.0.6
    Outgoing access list is not set
    Inbound access list is not set
    Proxy ARP is enabled
    Security level is default
    Split horizon is enabled
    ICMP redirects are always sent
    ICMP unreachables are always sent
    ICMP mask replies are never sent
    IP fast switching is disabled
    IP fast switching on the same interface is disabled
    IP multicast fast switching is disabled
    Router Discovery is disabled
    IP output datagram accounting is disabled
    IP access violation accounting is disabled
```

When the individual responsible for the user26 account is interviewed, it is determined that the account has been stolen and is being used by an unauthorized individual. Fortunately, the terminal server is configured to record the origination information for each call using Automatic Number Identification (ANI). This feature is used to trace the connection back to a local house. A warrant is obtained for the intruder's home and computer and an examination of this computer confirms that the offender had planned and launched an attack against the organization.

# FORENSIC EXAMINATION OF NETWORK TRAFFIC

The contents of network traffic can be invaluable in a network investigation, because some evidence exists only inside packet captures. Many host-based applications do not keep detailed records of network transmissions, and so capturing network traffic may provide you with information that is not recorded on a host. Furthermore, captured network traffic can contain full packet contents, whereas devices like firewalls and routers will not. Even an IDS, which may record some packet contents, typically only does so for packets that specifically trigger a rule, whereas a sniffer can be used to capture all traffic based upon the requirements of the investigator.

This section covers basic tools and techniques for extracting useful information from network traffic and is divided into three major areas: obtaining an overview of network activities, methods for filtering and searching network traffic for items of interest, and techniques for extracting data from network traffic so that it can be analyzed in a view that is more natural or intuitive than raw packet contents.

---

### PRACTITIONER'S TIP: CAUGHT IN THE ACT!

Sometimes you can find capture files on a host, as was the situation in the case in the Introduction of this chapter. This happens in several different situations. The most fun is when an attacker runs a sniffer, and leaves the output on the compromised system. You can extract this sniffer log when you do your examination and see exactly what the attacker was able to see during their reconnaissance of the target organization's internal network. There are also some host-based defenses that keep capture files, such as BlackICE. You can also extract these capture files and view the full contents of any packets that were alerted upon by this software.

---

## Tool Descriptions and Basic Usage

The focus of this chapter is on free tools that provide powerful search, filtering, and examination features: tcpdump, ngrep, Wireshark, and Network Miner. Commercial applications that can process larger volumes of network traffic and have more advanced features are also available like NetIntercept, NetDetector, and NetWitness Investigator (Casey, 2004b).

### *tcpdump*

Tcpdump is a network capture and protocol analysis tool (www.tcpdump.org). This program is based on the libpcap interface, a portable system-independent interface for user-level network datagram capture. Despite the name, tcpdump can also be used to capture non-TCP traffic, including UDP and ICMP. One of this tool's primary benefits is its wide availability, making it the de facto standard format for captured network traffic. The tcpdump program ships with many distributions of BSD, Linux, and Mac OS X, and there is a version that can be installed on Windows systems. Its long history also insures that there is a plethora of references available on the Internet and in text form for people that want to learn the tool. Usage and important options are shown in Table 9.10. Common filter expressions will be described later.

```
$ tcpdump [options] [filter expression]
```

**Table 9.10** Description of Select tcpdump Options

`$ tcpdump [options] [filter expression]`

| Command Options | Command |
| --- | --- |
| -r [file name] | Read in a capture file instead of capture from an interface. |
| -w [file name] | Output to a capture file rather than print to standard out. |
| -n | Do not resolve numbers into names. We do not want tcpdump to interpret things like port numbers into service names for us. As the investigator, it's our job to interpret the data. |
| -tttt | Four ts. Display the date, followed by the time—just the way we like to see it to support detailed analysis and reconstruction. |

For example, to use tcpdump to read in a capture file called `traffic.cap`, avoid the interpretation of port numbers, and display time in the appropriate format, you could issue the following command:

    $ tcpdump -ntttt -r traffic.cap

By default tcpdump extracts only the first 68 bytes of a datagram. Therefore, when the full content of network traffic is needed, it may be necessary to set a larger snaplen value using the -s option.

### ngrep

The ngrep program is a network capture tool and protocol analyzer that includes the ability to execute searches within packets for ASCII strings, hex values, and regular expressions (http://ngrep.sourceforge.net/). The basic syntax for ngrep is:

    $ ngrep [search expression] [options] [network filter]

Important options for ngrep are shown in Table 9.11. For additional instructions check the main page.

## REGULAR EXPRESSION SEARCHING

There are times when you will need to represent a range of values instead of something specific. For example, instead of the specific e-mail address example@example.net, you might need to search for any and all e-mail addresses. Regular expressions are a method for doing this type of flexible searching that is commonly used in forensics applications. There are many resources online and in print that detail the rich syntax of regular expressions.

**Table 9.11** Description of `ngrep` Options

| Search Target | Command |
| --- | --- |
| -X [hex value] | Specify a hex value as the search target. |
| -I [filename] | That's a dash "eye". Read in a capture file instead of capture from an interface. |
| -O [filename] | Output to a capture file rather than print to standard out. |
| -i | Perform a case insensitive regular expression search. This is not valid for hex searches and will produce an error. |
| -q | Don't print hash marks in the output. (These are extremely annoying.) |
| -v | Do an inverse search (i.e., search for packets that do *not* contain your search expression). |
| -t | Display the date, followed by the time—just the way we like to see it. |

## Wireshark

Wireshark is a network capture and protocol analyzer tool. Unlike tcpdump and ngrep, this tool has a graphical user interface and has the ability to interpret (a.k.a. decode) some application layer protocols that are encapsulated within TCP sessions. Its primary strengths include the ability to easily navigate through packet captures, an easy to use interface that provides a granular view of each packet in a capture file, and a robust set of protocol definitions that allow it to decode a wide variety of traffic types. However it does not handle extremely large sets of traffic very well, so if you are dealing with a large capture file, you will need to trim it down using other tools before viewing it in Wireshark.

By decoding protocols, more information can be obtained and more filtering and searching functions can be performed to locate important items. For instance, by decoding Domain Name Service (DNS) traffic, it is possible to create a filter that focuses on DNS-related traffic, making it easier to focus on activities relevant to an investigation and extract items of interest. Importantly, Wireshark makes assumptions about the expected behavior of protocols that prevent it from automatically classifying traffic that does not meet these basic assumptions. Therefore, when traffic of a known type is not identified correctly by Wireshark, it is necessary for an individual to inspect packets manually, identify the type of traffic, and instruct Wireshark to decode it correctly.

## Extracting Statistical Information from Network Traffic

Whether you are approaching network traffic without any leads or you have some items like IP addresses that you can use to filter or search, you should examine the set of packets in a methodical manner to extract data of interest for your investigation. Examples of data you might want to extract include:

- Statistics
- Alert data
- Web pages
- E-mails
- Chat records
- Files being transferred
- Voice conversations

### Extracting Statistics

You can easily generate a set of statistics regarding a set of network traffic that may help to guide your investigation. Common statistics that you will find useful include:

- Protocol usage
- Network endpoints
- Conversations
- Traffic volumes

There are many tools that will extract statistics from a network capture. The `capinfos` and `tshark` utilities are part of the Wireshark package, and `tshark` uses the same Display Filter syntax as shown in Table 9.12.

**Table 9.12** Commands for Extracting Statistics from Network Capture Files

| Desired Statistics | Command |
|---|---|
| Basic statistics about a capture file | `$ capinfos smb.cap` |
| Conversations by unique IP pairs | `$ tshark –nq –r smb.cap –z conv,ip` |
| Conversations by TCP/UDP ports | `$ tshark –nq –r smb.cap –z conv,tcp` |
| Protocol usage | `$ tshark –nq –r smb.cap –z io,phs` |

### TOOL FEATURE: PROFILING YOUR CAPTURE FILE

The output from the `capinfos` command used against the traffic capture log from the intrusion investigation scenario is shown here: Although this summary does not include details about packet contents, it does list information that will help you determine how to proceed. Most importantly, the `capinfos` output lists the date-time stamp of the first and last packets. This will tell you if the capture file even covers the date/time period in which you are interested. It

(Continued)

## TOOL FEATURE: PROFILING YOUR CAPTURE FILE—CONT'D

would be unpleasant to spend time analyzing a capture file that does not even occur near the date of your events of interest. The `capinfos` output also tells you the file type. In this case it is a libpcap capture file, which is fairly universal, and accepted by most applications. However if the file was not in libpcap format, you may have to convert it to a different type before using some of your analysis tools of choice.

```
[prompt]$ /tools/wireshark/Command\
  Line/capinfos scenario.pcap
File name: 20090402-scenario.pcap
File type: Wireshark/tcpdump/... - libpcap
File encapsulation: Ethernet
Number of packets: 31263
```

```
File size: 6337357 bytes
Data size: 5837125 bytes
Capture duration: 3764.043587 seconds
Start time: Thu Apr 2 22:28:42 2009
End time: Thu Apr 2 23:31:26 2009
Data rate: 1550.76 bytes/s
Data rate: 12406.07 bits/s
Average packet size: 186.71 bytes
```

The NetWitness Investigator application provides an overview screen of captured network traffic as shown in Figure 9.18.

This overview includes the duration of the packet capture, protocols and IP addresses in the captured traffic, and other details like user accounts and filenames observed in the data.

**FIGURE 9.18**

NetWitness Investigator summary of data in packet capture file from intrusion investigation scenario.

## IP Conversations

The `tshark` utility can be useful for extracting a list of unique IP pairs engaged in conversation in a single capture file as shown in Table 9.13. This extremely useful statistical data shows all IP address pairs that are communicating in a given capture file, and also the number of frames and bytes of data transferred between them. This overview can reveal something suspicious, such as a workstation system transferring large amounts of data outbound to an unknown system on the Internet.

The information in Table 9.13 is similar to that provided by NetFlow data (see the `flow-stat` example in the NetFlow section earlier in this chapter). Specifically, Table 9.13 shows the most traffic coming between the VPN (192.168.1.1) and intranet server (10.10.10.50), followed closely by traffic between the SSH server (10.10.30.2) and intranet server (10.10.10.50).

## Protocol Hierarchy

The `tshark` utility can be useful for extracting a list of basic protocols in use as shown on page 486 using network traffic from the intrusion investigation scenario. Some data has been cut from this display due to the volume. This type of statistic gives you a quick snapshot of the type of protocols in use in a given

**Table 9.13** Session Information Extracted from Network Capture Using `tshark`

| | | | <- | | -> | | Total | |
|---|---|---|---|---|---|---|---|---|
| | | | Frames | Bytes | Frames | Bytes | Frames | Bytes |
| 192.168.1.1 | <-> | 10.10.10.50 | 6592 | 3381827 | 10419 | 1130925 | 17011 | 4512752 |
| 10.10.10.50 | <-> | 10.10.10.2 | 1088 | 110500 | 646 | 71332 | 1734 | 181832 |
| 192.168.1.1 | <-> | 10.10.10.2 | 0 | 0 | 1208 | 215270 | 1208 | 215270 |
| 10.10.30.2 | <-> | 10.10.10.2 | 411 | 39417 | 411 | 44017 | 822 | 83434 |
| 10.10.30.2 | <-> | 10.10.10.50 | 256 | 40342 | 500 | 49555 | 756 | 89897 |
| 10.10.10.10 | <-> | 10.1.1.1 | 481 | 81866 | 131 | 16758 | 612 | 98624 |
| 68.237.161.12 | <-> | 10.10.10.10 | 480 | 41136 | 0 | 0 | 480 | 41136 |
| 71.242.0.12 | <-> | 10.10.10.10 | 480 | 41136 | 0 | 0 | 480 | 41136 |
| 10.10.10.255 | <-> | 10.10.10.2 | 73 | 6716 | 0 | 0 | 73 | 6716 |
| 17.151.16.22 | <-> | 10.10.10.2 | 59 | 5310 | 0 | 0 | 59 | 5310 |
| 10.10.10.2 | <-> | 10.10.10.1 | 9 | 630 | 26 | 2645 | 35 | 3275 |
| 10.10.10.255 | <-> | 10.10.10.245 | 25 | 3870 | 0 | 0 | 25 | 3870 |
| 10.10.10.255 | <-> | 10.10.10.50 | 10 | 2505 | 0 | 0 | 10 | 2505 |
| 239.255.255.250 | <-> | 10.10.10.2 | 9 | 1535 | 0 | 0 | 9 | 1535 |
| 224.0.0.251 | <-> | 10.10.10.10 | 8 | 1342 | 0 | 0 | 8 | 1342 |
| 10.10.30.2 | <-> | 10.10.10.10 | 7 | 686 | 0 | 0 | 7 | 686 |
| 10.10.10.10 | <-> | 10.10.10.1 | 2 | 196 | 2 | 196 | 4 | 392 |
| 224.0.0.251 | <-> | 10.10.10.2 | 3 | 396 | 0 | 0 | 3 | 396 |

capture file, and how much data has been transferred using those protocols. This is useful for discerning whether there is some blatantly abnormal activity in the network traffic, or if a protocol that you were trying to monitor is or is not present. The following example shows a variety of protocols are present, with large amounts of data being transferred via SMB as well as a moderate amount of SSH traffic.

```
================================================================
Protocol Hierarchy Statistics
Filter: frame
frame                    frames:31263 bytes:5837125
  ip                     frames:23196 bytes:5272720
    udp                  frames:2756 bytes:389875
      nbdgm              frames:20 bytes:4995
        smb              frames:20 bytes:4995
          mailslot       frames:20 bytes:4995
            browser      frames:20 bytes:4995
      ntp                frames:59 bytes:5310
      syslog             frames:1208 bytes:215270
      data               frames:350 bytes:65108
      nbns               frames:122 bytes:11632
      dns                frames:974 bytes:84190
        malformed        frames:3 bytes:180
      malformed          frames:5 bytes:300
      http               frames:18 bytes:3070
    tcp                  frames:20289 bytes:4864379
      nbss               frames:1225 bytes:182524
        smb              frames:1015 bytes:160614
        pipe             frames:178 bytes:32657
          lanman         frames:174 bytes:31321
          dcerpc         frames:4 bytes:1336
            srvsvc       frames:2 bytes:918
      ssh                frames:399 bytes:55444
      ldap               frames:172 bytes:41935
        ldap             frames:42 bytes:14719
          ldap           frames:2 bytes:880
      tcp.segments       frames:450 bytes:385838
        ldap             frames:9 bytes:3494
          ldap           frames:9 bytes:3494
        http             frames:13 bytes:6639
          image-jfif     frames:11 bytes:4763
          image-gif      frames:1 bytes:1406
          data-text-lines frames:1 bytes:470
        tpkt             frames:427 bytes:375176
          x224           frames:427 bytes:375176
            t125         frames:427 bytes:375176
        nbss             frames:1 bytes:529
```

```
        smb                 frames:1 bytes:529
      http                  frames:15 bytes:4916
        data-text-lines     frames:1 bytes:1353
      tpkt                  frames:7999 bytes:1195050
       x224                 frames:7999 bytes:1195050
         t125               frames:7989 bytes:1194181
     icmp                   frames:151 bytes:18466
    arp                     frames:284 bytes:16644
   ipv6                     frames:9 bytes:924
     udp                    frames:3 bytes:456
       dns                  frames:3 bytes:456
    icmpv6                  frames:6 bytes:468
==================================================================
```

## Filtering and Searching

Because they contain everything that traverses a network, packet capture files can easily become very large. This is especially true if the initial placement of network monitoring systems and capture expressions were not highly targeted. Even with a targeted capture, a small 10 MB capture file could contain tens of thousands of packets. As with any type of digital evidence, to examine a traffic capture log we must be able to search and filter that data to focus in on information that is relevant to our case. This section will focus on tools and techniques used to search network capture logs, and filtering your viewpoint for data of interest.

## Searching for Specific Hosts

One of the most common and basic searches you will have to perform is the search for systems of interest to your investigation. You will most likely be searching for these systems based upon an IP address, but in some situations you may know only a different identifier such as a Windows host name or MAC address. So you will need to be able to search for all of these items.

### Searching for Specific Hosts Using tcpdump
The commands in Table 9.14 can be used to search for specific hosts using tcpdump.

### Searching for Specific Hosts Using Wireshark or `tshark`
Filtering expressions can be entered into Wireshark in several ways. First, you can simply enter an expression into the Filter box shown in Figure 9.19. To do this you have to know the exact syntax of the filter expression (some of which will be defined for you on the following pages). Or, you can click the Expression button, also shown in Figure 9.19, and peruse a list of protocols and possible filter expressions available for them within the tool. As an example, Figure 9.19

**Table 9.14** Search Expressions to Find Specific Hosts Using tcpdump

| Search Target | Command |
|---|---|
| Searching for a specific MAC address | $ tcpdump –r file.cap –nntttt ether host 00:FE:AD:E8:B8:DC |
| Searching for a specific IP | $ tcpdump –r file.cap –nntttt host 192.168.1.5 |
| Searching for a specific IP network | $ tcpdump –r file.cap –nntttt net 192.168.1 |
| Searching for a specific Windows host name | $ |
| Searching for a specific DNS host name in DNS traffic | $ tcpdump –r file.cap –nntttt port 53 \| egrep google.com |
| Searching all networks in the range 192.168.50.0 to 192.168.100.0 | $ tcpdump –r file.cap –nntttt 'dst net 192 and (ip[17] > 49) and (ip[17] < 101)' |

**FIGURE 9.19**

Using Wireshark to perform a simple filter for just DNS traffic.

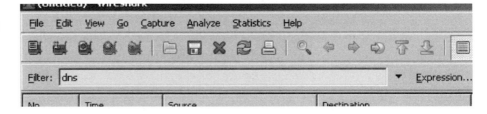

shows a simple dns filter in Wireshark for the DNS protocol. You will know that the filter expression is valid because the background color for the filter box will be green, as opposed to red if it is invalid. This expression will cause Wireshark to display only packets that it believes include the DNS protocol.

As a third method of filtering, you can expand the protocol descriptions in the Packet Detail pane (by default in the middle), highlight a value, then choose the Apply as Filter option from the Analyze menu in the menu bar as shown in Figure 9.20.

The commands in Table 9.15 can be used to search for specific hosts using Wireshark. Remember that these can be entered directly into the Filter box toward the top of the window.

## Searching for Specific Ports and Protocols

Another search you will need to perform frequently is for specific protocols and TCP/UDP ports. This will help you to narrow down a capture file onto a traffic type of interest.

**Table 9.15** Search Expressions to Find Specific Hosts Using Wireshark

| Search Target | Expression |
|---|---|
| Searching for a specific MAC address | eth.addr == 00:fe:ad:e8:b8:dc |
| Searching for a specific IP | ip.addr == 192.168.1.5 |
| Searching for a specific IP network | ip.addr == 192.168.1.0/24 |
| Searching for a specific Windows host name | |
| Searching for a specific DNS host name in DNS traffic | dns.qry.name == "www.google.com" or dns.resp.name == "www.google.com" |

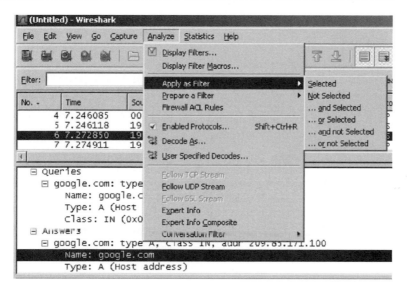

**FIGURE 9.20**

Using the Wireshark Apply as Filter option to select google.com from a packet and apply it to the entire network capture as a filter.

## Searching for Specific Protocols or Ports Using tcpdump

The commands in Table 9.16 can be used to search for specific protocols or port numbers using tcpdump.

**Table 9.16** Search Expressions to Find Protocols or Ports Using tcpdump

| Search Target | Command |
|---|---|
| Searching for a specific protocol | $ tcpdump –r file.cap –nntttt tcp |
| Searching for a specific port number | $ tcpdump –r file.cap –nntttt port 80 |
| Searching for a specific TCP or UDP port number | $ tcpdump –r file.cap –nntttt tcp port 53 |
| Searching for a specific TCP or UDP port number specifically as the source or destination port | $ tcpdump –r file.cap –nntttt tcp dst port 53 |

## Searching for Specific Protocols or Ports Using Wireshark

The filter expressions in Table 9.17 can be used to search for specific protocols or port numbers using Wireshark.

**Table 9.17** Search Expressions to Find Protocols or Ports Using Wireshark

| Search Target | Expression |
| --- | --- |
| Searching for a specific protocol | tcp |
| Searching for a specific TCP port number | tcp.port == 80 |
| Searching for a specific UDP port number | udp.port == 53 |
| Searching for a specific TCP or UDP port number specifically as the source or destination port | tcp.srcport == 80 udp.dstport == 53 |

## EXAMPLE: FILTERING A CAPTURE FILE TO REDUCE SIZE

In an earlier example, we used the `capinfos` command to footprint a capture file. According to the `capinfos` output, this capture file had over 31,623 frames. We can verify this by reading the network capture and sending the text output to the command wc –l, which will provide a line count. Since tcpdump outputs one packet per line of text output by default, this should give us the number of packets.

```
[prompt]$ tcpdump -r scenario.pcap | wc -l
reading from file scenario.pcap, link-type EN10MB (Ethernet)
31263
```

As expected, we see the output 31263, confirming the `capinfos` output for number of frames. This is too many frames to simply scan through by hand, so it will need to be filtered down. For example, we may be interested in HTTP traffic between the IP addresses 192.168.1.1 and 10.10.10.50 from the intrusion investigation scenario. The next example shows how the packet number decreases as we successively add these requirements to a tcpdump filter expression.

```
[prompt]$ tcpdump -r scenario.pcap "host 192.168.1.1" | wc -l
reading from file scenario.pcap, link-type EN10MB (Ethernet)
18219
[prompt]$ tcpdump -r scenario.pcap "host 192.168.1.1 and host 10.10.10.50" | wc -l
reading from file scenario.pcap, link-type EN10MB (Ethernet)
17011
[prompt]$ tcpdump -r scenario.pcap "host 192.168.1.1 and host 10.10.10.50 and port
  80" | wc -l
reading from file scenario.pcap, link-type EN10MB (Ethernet)
1072
```

This example has shown a reduction in the number of packets to analyze from an original 31263 down to 1072 using tcpdump. This is a much smaller number of packets to analyze, and you may be ready at this point to save the resulting packets into a new capture file to load into a GUI analysis program such as Wireshark or Network Miner. The following example shows how to save packet output to a new capture file, instead of outputting to text.

```
[prompt]$ tcpdump -r scenario.pcap -w output.cap "host 192.168.1.1 and host
  10.10.10.50 and port 80"
reading from file scenario.pcap, link-type EN10MB (Ethernet)
[prompt]$
```

*(Continued)*

**EXAMPLE: FILTERING A CAPTURE FILE TO REDUCE SIZE—CONT'D**

This overall strategy of filtering a file and saving new output is very useful for trimming large network captures to a manageable size. The original size of the example capture file at over 31,000 frames was actually fairly small. But you may find yourself responsible for analyzing much larger amounts of network traffic, with file sizes ranging into hundreds of GBs. In these situations, you will often have no choice but to filter the files from the command line before you can import them into many tools. As useful as they are, tools such as Wireshark and Network Miner cannot open and handle hundreds of GB of log files.

The syntax of the command line tools, as shown, is fairly straightforward. Your main difficulty will be in choosing criteria on which to filter your logs. This will depend entirely upon your investigative approach, and the information that you have discovered at a given point in your case. Some tools, tshark especially, offer a wide array of filters that you can use, but when dealing with very large capture files it is simpler to begin with basic data types such as IP address and port numbers.

## Searching for Specific Hex or ASCII Values in Packet Contents

You will eventually need to search for some type of value that is not well defined in a protocol field that is understood by your tool. To do this, you will need the ability to simply search packets for some specific ASCII or hex values, or to apply regular expressions to define a range of values.

### Searching for Specific ASCII or Hex Values Using ngrep

You can search for specific ASCII keywords or hex values using ngrep. You can also search for regular expressions. The tool will display specific packets that match your expression and if you so choose, save them to a file. The ngrep program also understands BPF network filter syntax—the same syntax used by tcpdump, so you can simultaneously search for a specific value and perform a filter on packet header values.

Table 9.18 provides some useful examples of ngrep for finding specific values in network traffic.

| Table 9.18 Search Expressions for Finding Specific Values Using ngrep | |
| --- | --- |
| **Search Target** | **Command** |
| Searching for a specific ASCII string | $ ngrep "google\.com" –iqt –I file.cap |
| Searching for a specific hex string | $ ngrep –X 416c –qt –I file.cap |
| Searching for a specific ASCII string while also filtering for a specific port | $ ngrep "google.com" –iqt –I file.cap port 53 |
| Searching for a specific regular expression | $ ngrep "port\=[0–9]" |

### Searching for Specific ASCII or Hex Values Using Wireshark

You can search for specific ASCII or hex values with Wireshark by using the filter expressions in Table 9.19.

**Table 9.19** Search Expressions for Finding Specific Values Using Wireshark

| Search Target | Expression |
|---|---|
| Searching for a specific ASCII string | frame matches Secret |
| Searching for a specific ASCII string, case insensitive | frame matches "(?i)secret" |
| Searching for a specific hex value | frame matches "\x42\x42\x51" |

## INTRUSION INVESTIGATION SCENARIO: THEFT OF STANLEY'S SECRET RECIPE

In the intrusion investigation scenario, events were observed where various images named snakeoil*.jpg were observed. The screenshot in Figure 9.21 shows the capture file from the scenario loaded into Wireshark, with a "frame matches" expression being used to search for the word "stanley," case insensitive, using the syntax noted in one of the

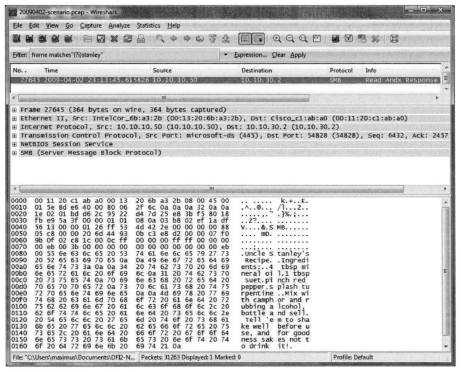

**FIGURE 9.21**
Searching network traffic for packets containing the word "stanley" or "Stanley" using Wireshark.

(Continued)

## INTRUSION INVESTIGATION SCENARIO: THEFT OF STANLEY'S SECRET RECIPE—CONT'D

tables earlier. This search is being done because one of the secret files from the scenario that was potentially stolen was named "stanley's," and included secret recipes. As you can see, this search turned up one packet that shows the secret recipe being moved from 10.10.10.50 to 10.10.30.2 via TCP 445, or SMB. Note that the case insensitive portion of this search was critical. Without it, this transmission would not have been discovered because inside the packet, the word "Stanley" begins with an uppercase S.

Is there anything else we can find out about the data theft based on the contents of network traffic? We certainly can! By searching for protocol specific data as described in "Overview of Protocols," earlier in this chapter, we may be able to learn more about what is happening behind the scenes. In this scenario, we can search for the username that was used to access the file. The Wireshark Follow TCP Stream

was used to focus on the TCP session containing the file as detailed later in this chapter, and the result was further filtered by adding the "and (ntlmssp.messagetype == 0x00000003)", which searches for a type of NTLM authentication. The result is shown in Figure 9.22, which shows the authentication request by the username ow3n3d, which relates to the SMB response shown in Figure 9.11 earlier in this chapter.

Now we know the name of the user account being used to access this file, in addition to the computer that issued the request. This information can now be correlated with other data from or about the device receiving this file to determine where it went from there, and who might have been accessing it. We could also roll this new piece of information back into our search of traffic captures, by doing a content search for the username ow3n3d in all packets.

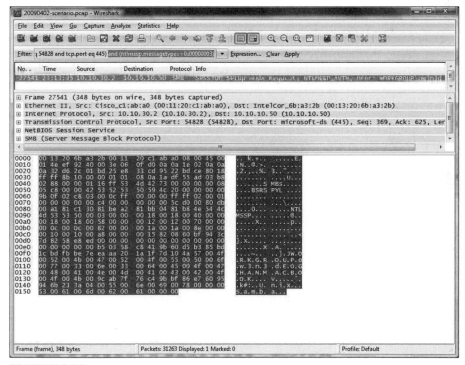

**FIGURE 9.22**

SMB authentication request by the ow3n3d account.

### Searching for an IP Address in Packet Contents

Is there a reason to search for an IP address in ASCII in packet contents instead of filtering for it? Absolutely. Check out the following example. In the next screenshot, an IP filter is being used to identify all packets that are to or from an IP of interest in the intrusion investigation scenario—130.132.1.26. As you can see in Figure 9.23, no packets were identified with this filter.

**FIGURE 9.23**

Using Wireshark to search for a specific IP address in header fields.

**FIGURE 9.24**

Using Wireshark to search for a specific IP address in packet data.

However, the next screenshot (Figure 9.24) shows a content filter being used to identify packets that contain the ASCII value 130.132.1.26. This filter does not reveal packets to or from this address, but it does show syslog entries in transit that contain records referencing the IP address. By conducting this simple content search for an IP, we now know:

- There is a syslog server somewhere in the network. If we didn't know this already, we now know of another valuable source of information.
- There are firewall and/or VPN logs being created that are logging traffic by this IP of interest (the syslog entries in Figure 9.24 are for a firewall/VPN device). If we were unaware of this, we now know of another valuable source of information.

## Automatically Extracting Files from a TCP Session

When it is necessary to extract many files from large quantities of network traffic, an automated method is required. One approach is to split the captured traffic into streams and then use a file carving tool to extract files from the individual streams. For instance, the open source tcpflow utility can be used to break network traffic into individual flows, placing data from each TCP stream in a separate file labeled with the source and destination IP addresses (Casey, 2004b). Running a file carving tool like foremost against the output from tcpflow will extract files of various types that were transferred over the network, including images and executables.

To reduce the amount of time and specialized knowledge required to examine network traffic, some commercial applications perform this type of file extraction

## PRACTITIONER'S TIP: ANTIVIRUS INTERFERENCE

When an application carves a file from a network capture log, that file will then be resident in memory, and possibly written to disk. Either of these actions may trigger a response from your antivirus software if it recognizes malicious or suspicious code in the output. If you wish to obtain these files for examination, you will need to either temporarily disable your real-time antivirus protection or set the tool's output folder as an exclusion from antivirus scans, or set the antivirus software to quarantine or perform no action upon detection as opposed to deleting the offending file.

automatically. For instance, Figure 9.25 shows all images extracted from network traffic in the intrusion investigation scenario using NetIntercept.

Given the complexity of network traffic, automated tools for analyzing network traffic may not always interpret data correctly. Therefore, it is advisable to analyze network traffic using multiple tools, and to verify important results at a low level using a tool like tcpdump or Wireshark.

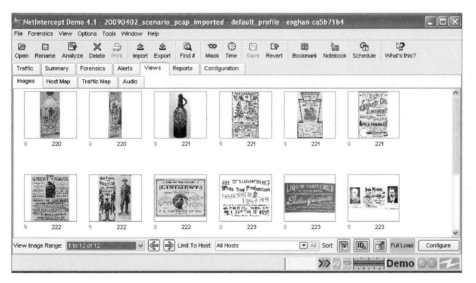

**FIGURE 9.25**
NetIntercept gallery showing all images transferred in network traffic.

## TOOL FEATURE: NETWORK MINER

When Network Miner opens a packet capture file, it automatically begins parsing the network traffic data for specific files, and it will list the file across its output tabs. Figure 9.26 shows Network Miner with the Files tab displaying each file that has been successfully carved from the network capture.

This tab includes information such as:

- The full path to the location on disk where Network Miner has stored the files that it has carved
- The source system that transmitted the file
- The destination system that received the file
- The port numbers used in the transaction—all HTTP in this example

(Continued)

| Fram... | Reconstructed file path | Source host | S. port | Destination ... | D. port | Protocol | Filen: |
|---|---|---|---|---|---|---|---|
| 3313 | C:\tools\NetworkMiner-0.87\assembledFiles\10.10.10.50\HTTP - TCP 80\index[1].html | 10.10.10.50 ... | TCP 80 | 192.168.1.1 | TCP 1037 | HttpGet... | index |
| 3323 | C:\tools\NetworkMiner-0.87\assembledFiles\10.10.10.50\HTTP - TCP 80\images\snakeoil1[1].jpg | 10.10.10.50 ... | TCP 80 | 192.168.1.1 | TCP 1038 | HttpGet... | snak |
| 3316 | C:\tools\NetworkMiner-0.87\assembledFiles\10.10.10.50\HTTP - TCP 80\images\snakeoil2[1].jpg | 10.10.10.50 ... | TCP 80 | 192.168.1.1 | TCP 1037 | HttpGet... | snak |
| 3384 | C:\tools\NetworkMiner-0.87\assembledFiles\10.10.10.50\HTTP - TCP 80\images\snakeoil3[1].jpg | 10.10.10.50 ... | TCP 80 | 192.168.1.1 | TCP 1039 | HttpGet... | snak |
| 3410 | C:\tools\NetworkMiner-0.87\assembledFiles\10.10.10.50\HTTP - TCP 80\images\snakeoil4[1].gif | 10.10.10.50 ... | TCP 80 | 192.168.1.1 | TCP 1040 | HttpGet... | snak |
| 3777 | C:\tools\NetworkMiner-0.87\assembledFiles\10.10.10.50\HTTP - TCP 80\images\snakeoil5[1].jpg | 10.10.10.50 | TCP 80 | 192.168.1.1 | TCP 1039 | HttpGet | snak |

**FIGURE 9.26**

Network Miner listing files extracted from network traffic.

## Manual Extraction of a File from a Single Packet

There will be times when an automated tool does not successfully identify and extract files in a network traffic capture, or when some other errors occur, such as the tool crashing when it attempts to read a specific capture file of interest. You will also sometimes encounter new or custom protocols for which a parser has not yet been written. In these situations, you will have two choices. You can manually extract the data from packets using a protocol analyzer such as Wireshark, or you can write your own script or plug-in to an existing tool that can parse the protocol after you determine how it works.

While investigating a large-scale network intrusion, network traffic showed the intruder connecting to a compromised system and placing an unknown executable on the system via SMB. Subsequent forensic examination of the compromised computer revealed that the intruder had deleted the unknown executable and it could not be recovered from the hard drive. Although available tools for examining network traffic could not extract the file automatically, we were able to recover the unknown executable manually and examine it to determine its functionality. The information obtained from this executable helped advance the investigation in a variety of ways.

It is relatively straightforward to extract a file contained in a single packet using the Wireshark protocol analyzer. Figure 9.27 shows a single packet in Wireshark that contains an executable file. Unless you have a full understanding of the protocol in use, you cannot be certain where the file being transferred begins or ends in the packet capture file. In this case, the Application Layer protocol in use is specific to communicate between the Metasploit Console and a compromised system in which the Meterpreter DLL was injected during an attack. This protocol is not well documented, and there are no parsers for it in common tools.

However, we can still make educated guesses using general knowledge of networking. Based upon the observation that this 898 byte frame is significantly smaller than the typical maximum frame size for an Ethernet network, we can surmise that the entire executable may be contained in this one frame. Were the executable to be much larger, then it would be split over multiple frames, that would each be at the maximum size for the network to move as much of the file as possible in each frame.

To extract a file contained within a single packet, first select the Data portion of the packet (which can be seen in the previous screen shot), then choose Export and Selected Packet

(Continued)

## EXAMPLE: EXTRACTING FILES FROM A PACKET CONTAINING AN UNKNOWN PROTOCOL—CONT'D

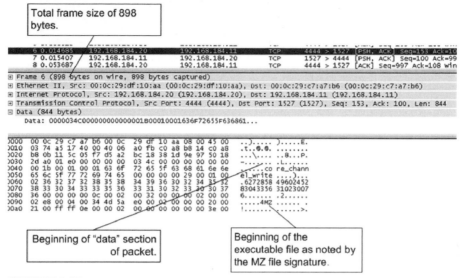

Total frame size of 898 bytes.

Beginning of "data" section of packet.

Beginning of the executable file as noted by the MZ file signature.

**FIGURE 9.27**

Packet containing an executable file.

Bytes from the File menu. You will then have the opportunity to save these bytes as a single file. At this point, you may not be done. As shown in the previous screenshot, there is data between the end of the TCP header and the beginning of the executable in the Data section of the frame. If that is the case, you can trim off the data that is not part of the file that you are trying to extract using a hex editor. In this example, everything prior to the executable file header is not part of the file

itself, and hence unnecessary. Figure 9.28 shows the exported packet bytes, saved as exe.dump, loaded into a hex editor. In Figure 9.28(a), the data before the executable header is highlighted. Figure 9.28(b) shows the file after this unrelated data has been cut from the dump file, and the executable file header is now at the front of the file where it should be. If there is nothing that needs to be removed at the end of the file as well, it would then be ready to be saved.

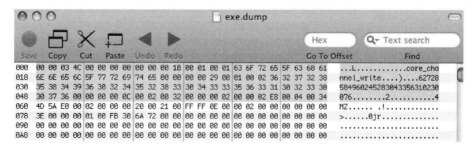

**FIGURE 9.28A**

Before removing unnecessary data.

(Continued)

uations

## EXAMPLE: EXTRACTING FILES FROM A PACKET CONTAINING AN UNKNOWN PROTOCOL—CONT'D

**FIGURE 9.28B**
After removing unnecessary data using the Cut button.

## Manually Extracting Files from a TCP Session

More often than not, files being sent through a network will be too large for a single packet. They will typically be transferred inside many packets in a session that will contain both the file itself, and Application Layer control data interspersed among the actual payload being transferred. You will need to extract and combine parts of the file contained within various packets in the TCP session. This can also be done with Wireshark and a hex editor.

## EXAMPLE: EXTRACTING FILES FROM A TCP SESSION CONTAINING AN UNKNOWN PROTOCOL

Figure 9.29 shows a packet in which an executable file transfer has started. As with the example in the previous section, this executable file transfer was initiated through communication between the Metasploit Console and the Meterpreter DLL injected into memory in an exploited system. As you look in the top pane of Wireshark, you see that multiple packets were transmitted that have the same size of 1460 bytes. This is the maximum size for the Data portion of the TCP segment for this communication session. This is a sign that the executable required multiple packets in order to be transferred as opposed to the previous example that required only one packet.

To extract the executable from these packets, we have to assemble them from the TCP session. This can be done with the Follow TCP Stream option of Wireshark. This option creates a display filter in Wireshark based on the source and destination IP address and source and destination port. As a result, only the packets contained within the TCP session are displayed. Second, it will open another window where it will display the aggregate Data contents of all TCP segments in the session. To use this feature, right-click on any packet in the session, and choose Follow TCP Stream from the drop-down menu.

Figure 9.30 shows the window that opens when you use the Follow TCP Stream feature of Wireshark. As noted in the callouts, it is important to have the Raw radio button selected, before you choose to save the raw data. This will ensure that you save off the entire executable. For example, if you chose the Hex Dump radio button instead, you would be saving off a text document with hexadecimal values from the TCP session instead of the raw binary data.

Also note that in Figure 9.30, data is mixed combining data from both the computer that initiated the session, as well as data from the other system. This illustrates not only that

*(Continued)*

## EXAMPLE: EXTRACTING FILES FROM A TCP SESSION CONTAINING AN UNKNOWN PROTOCOL—CONT'D

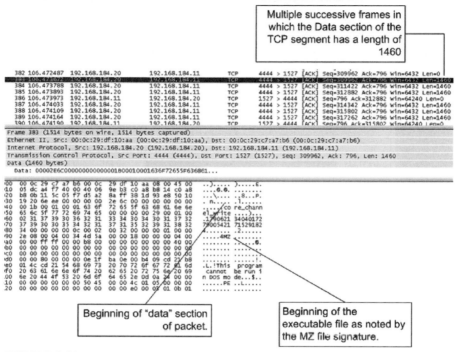

Multiple successive frames in which the Data section of the TCP segment has a length of 1460

Beginning of "data" section of packet.

Beginning of the executable file as noted by the MZ file signature.

**FIGURE 9.29**
Executable file split between multiple packets.

there is information from both systems in this raw session data, but that there will typically be data that is not part of the file that you are trying to extract. As with the single packet example shown previously, you will have to remove this extra data using a hex editor. This window does offer the ability to show only data from one of the two systems in the session, however this still may include more than the file being transferred, or even more than one file.

This brings up the following question. In the aggregated data from an entire TCP session, how do you know when the target file begins and ends, if you do not fully understand the protocol in use? You have several options:

- If the protocol is public, you can find online references for that protocol to learn how to identify protocol control data vs. actual data being transmitted.

- If the protocol is not public, but you have the server and client software used to create the captured network transmissions, or the source code for those programs, then you can reverse engineer those programs to determine how their communication works. This takes a great deal of effort and considerable skill.

- If you have access to the client and server software, you can use them to transfer files for which you know the exact content, and then find it in the network traffic to determine where it begins and ends. You can compare the known file with the other data in the network traffic to see if you can find out more about the protocol.

- You can make a best guess as to the beginning and end of the file based upon general observations of the network traffic.

*(Continued)*

## EXAMPLE: EXTRACTING FILES FROM A TCP SESSION CONTAINING AN UNKNOWN PROTOCOL—CONT'D

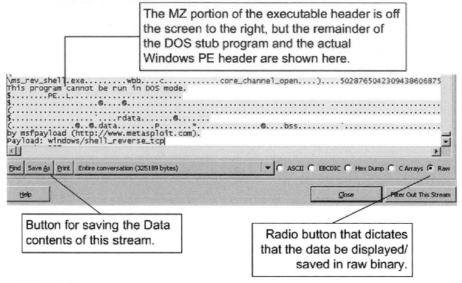

The MZ portion of the executable header is off the screen to the right, but the remainder of the DOS stub program and the actual Windows PE header are shown here.

Button for saving the Data contents of this stream.

Radio button that dictates that the data be displayed/saved in raw binary.

**FIGURE 9.30**

The Follow TCP Stream feature in Wireshark provides the content of conversation and provides an option to save the output to a file.

As mentioned previously, this example is not of a documented protocol. We can make some judgments by observing the network traffic. The following screenshot shows that the transfer of the executable file begins in the top packet. That packet is then followed by a series of additional TCP segments from the same source to the same destination that include the maximum amount of data. This series of transmissions is then followed by another packet in the same direction, with only 204 bytes of data, and then a packet in the reverse direction containing 8 bytes of data. This traffic was interspersed with empty TCP acknowledgement segments as is normal for TCP sessions.

What does this mean? Well the transfer of any file that spans multiple packets will invariably end with a TCP segment that does not contain the maximum amount of data, unless that file is of an exact size divisible by the maximum amount of data allowed in TCP segments for the session. So in Figure 9.31, we observe a series of segments with 1460 bytes of data until the

transmission nears an end, and sends the remainder of the file at 204 bytes. Remember that we are making some assumptions here. Without access to a protocol reference or reverse engineering of the software or source code, you cannot be absolutely sure of the data contents of a TCP session. If you have a protocol reference you should use it, but if you do not, a best guess is better than no data, and requires considerably less time than reverse engineering an unknown application.

Based on Figure 9.31 and the associated discussion in the previous paragraph, we can examine the packets more closely to determine what the end of the file looks like so that we can find it inside a hex editor. First, we need to choose the packets that we are interested in examining more closely to find the end of the file. Figure 9.32 shows these packets. We are interested in the packet that most probably contains the end of the file, and the next packet to contain data, as this will be present in the raw session dump and may mark the end of the file.

*(Continued)*

## EXAMPLE: EXTRACTING FILES FROM A TCP SESSION CONTAINING AN UNKNOWN PROTOCOL—CONT'D

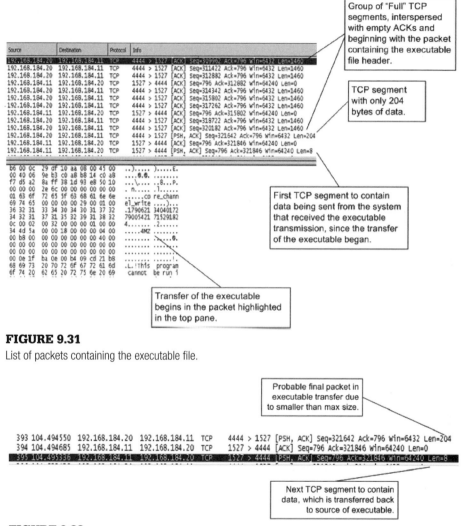

Group of "Full" TCP segments, interspersed with empty ACKs and beginning with the packet containing the executable file header.

TCP segment with only 204 bytes of data.

First TCP segment to contain data being sent from the system that received the executable transmission, since the transfer of the executable began.

Transfer of the executable begins in the packet highlighted in the top pane.

**FIGURE 9.31**

List of packets containing the executable file.

Probable final packet in executable transfer due to smaller than max size.

```
393 104.494550  192.168.184.20  192.168.184.11  TCP    4444 > 1527 [PSH, ACK] Seq=321642 Ack=796 Win=6432 Len=204
394 104.494685  192.168.184.11  192.168.184.20  TCP    1527 > 4444 [ACK] Seq=796 Ack=321846 Win=64240 Len=0
395 104.495336  192.168.184.11  192.168.184.20  TCP    1527 > 4444 [PSH, ACK] Seq=796 Ack=321846 Win=64240 Len=8
```

Next TCP segment to contain data, which is transferred back to source of executable.

**FIGURE 9.32**

Packet that more likely contains the end of the executable file.

Next we need to look inside each of these packets to determine their contents. First we examine the packet that we believe to be the end of the file. The Data section of the TCP segment shows a large block of zeros terminating with a hex string shown in Figure 9.33. At this point, we do not know for sure what that hex string is. It could be the end of the file, or it could be an end-of-file marker specific to the protocol. Again, without a protocol reference, reverse

*(Continued)*

## EXAMPLE: EXTRACTING FILES FROM A TCP SESSION CONTAINING AN UNKNOWN PROTOCOL—CONT'D

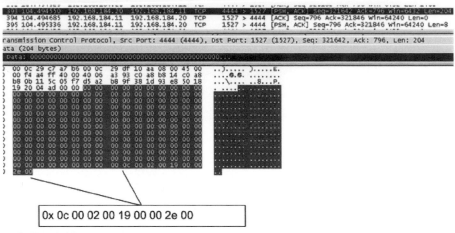

**FIGURE 9.33**

Possible end of file in packet payload.

engineering the software or performing tests with the software, we do not know what it is.

Next we look at the first packet to contain data after the one shown in Figure 9.33. It contains 8 bytes, shown in Figure 9.34. These bytes are most certainly not part of the file, as they are being sent back to the system that sent the file from the receiving machine.

If our assessment of this traffic is correct, in the raw dump of all data in the TCP session, we should see the final bytes of the file transfer immediately followed by the next set of data

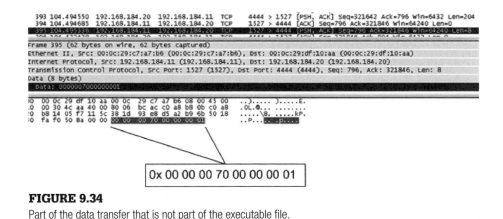

**FIGURE 9.34**

Part of the data transfer that is not part of the executable file.

*(Continued)*

## EXAMPLE: EXTRACTING FILES FROM A TCP SESSION CONTAINING AN UNKNOWN PROTOCOL—CONT'D

that is being transferred back from the system that received the file. So all together, there should be a row of hex in the dump that is:

```
0x 0c 00 02 00 19 00 00 2e 00 00 00 00 00 70
   00 00 00 01
```

Viewing the raw dump of data for this TCP session, we do indeed see that hex string. It is shown in Figure 9.35, highlighted in the hex editor. This confirms for us that the end of

the file transfer seems to occur at the location we have highlighted. However we still have been unable to determine whether or not the data at the end of the last segment in the file transfer is part of the file or some type of protocol control message such as an end of file marker. If we are dealing with an unknown protocol and if we do not have the software with which to conduct tests, we can no longer have any grounds to make a precise assessment. We basically have the two options shown in the callouts in the figure.

> Option: Cut here at the beginning of short hex string at the end of the file, trailing a block of zeros.

> Option: Cut here after the very end of the last data transferred with the file, and before the first set of data transferred back from the system that received the file.

**FIGURE 9.35**

Final bytes of executable file transfer.

## Intrusion Detection Systems

In addition to programs that simply capture and display network traffic based on general rules, there are programs that monitor network traffic and bring attention only to suspicious activity. These programs are called Intrusion Detection Systems (IDS). Some of these systems such as Bro (www.bro-ids.org) can be configured to store all traffic and then examine it for known attacks, and to archive significant features of network traffic for later analysis. Other systems such as Snort (www.snort.org) inspect the traffic and store only data that appear to be suspicious, ignoring anything that appears to be acceptable. These systems are not primarily concerned with preserving the authenticity and integrity of the data they collect, so additional measures must be taken when using these tools.

Although they are not designed specifically for gathering evidence, logs from an IDS can be useful in the instance of an offender breaking into a computer. Criminals who break into computers often destroy evidence contained in log files on the compromised machine to make an investigator's job more difficult. However, an IDS keeps a log of attacks at the network level that investigators can use to determine the offender's IP address. For example, if fraud is committed using a networked computer and investigators find that the computer was compromised and then scrubbed of all evidence, they may be able to determine which IP address was used by examining the log file from an IDS on the network.

Snort is a libpcap-based datagram sniffer that can be used as an Intrusion Detection System. Unlike tcpdump, Snort can perform datagram payload inspection, decoding the application layer of a datagram and comparing the contents with a list of rules. So, in addition to capturing network traffic, Snort can be configured with rules to detect certain types of datagrams, including hostile activity such as port scans, buffer overflows, and web server attacks. Additionally, Snort can be configured to reassemble fragmented packets before checking them against known attack signatures, thus foiling attempts to fly under the radar by fragmenting packets.

A sample of output from Snort is shown here, listing potentially malicious activity that was detected on the network.

```
[**] IDS188/trojan-probe-back-orifice  [**]
04/28-01:16:03.564474 0:D0:B7:C0:86:43 -> 0:E0:98:82:4C:6B type:0x800
    len:0xC3 192.168.1.100:1060 -> 192.168.1.104:31337 UDP TTL:128
    TOS:0x0 ID:1783 IpLen:20 DgmLen:181 Len: 161

[**] IDS189/trojan-active-back-orifice [**]
04/28-01:16:03.611368 0:E0:98:82:4C:6B -> 0:D0:B7:C0:86:43 type:0x800
    len:0xC9 192.168.1.104:31337 -> 192.168.1.100:1060 UDP TTL:128
    TOS:0x0 ID:16128 IpLen:20 DgmLen:187 Len: 167
```

The type of attack is provided on the first line of each entry, followed by a summary of the information in each datagram. In this case, the first alert indicates that an attacker at 192.168.1.100 is probing the target 192.168.1.104 for Back Orifice. The second attack shows the target responding to the Back Orifice probe, establishing a successful connection. In addition to generating alerts, Snort can capture the entire binary datagram and store it in a file in tcpdump format. Collecting the raw packet can be useful from both an investigative and evidentiary perspective as discussed in the following sections.

## FROM THE CASE FILES: CUSTOMIZED IDS SIGNATURES

In a network intrusion investigation, the intruders were using customized tools to command and control compromised systems. We learned enough about the intruders' tools to develop customized rules for the victim organization's IDS, enabling us to detect further malicious activities. The alerts generated by these customized signatures led to the discovery of additional compromised systems on the network.

# NETWORK LOG CORRELATION—A TECHNICAL PERSPECTIVE

As mentioned in Chapter 4, "Intrusion Investigation," care must be taken when importing logs into tools like Splunk to insure that the records and date-time stamps are interpreted correctly. NetFlow logs provide a good example because each record contains two date-time stamps (flow start and end times), and the date format (mmdd.hh:mm:ss) is not readily interpreted by Splunk. Loading NetFlow logs into Splunk without any reformatting results in all entries being associated with the date they were imported into the correlation tool as shown in Figure 9.36.

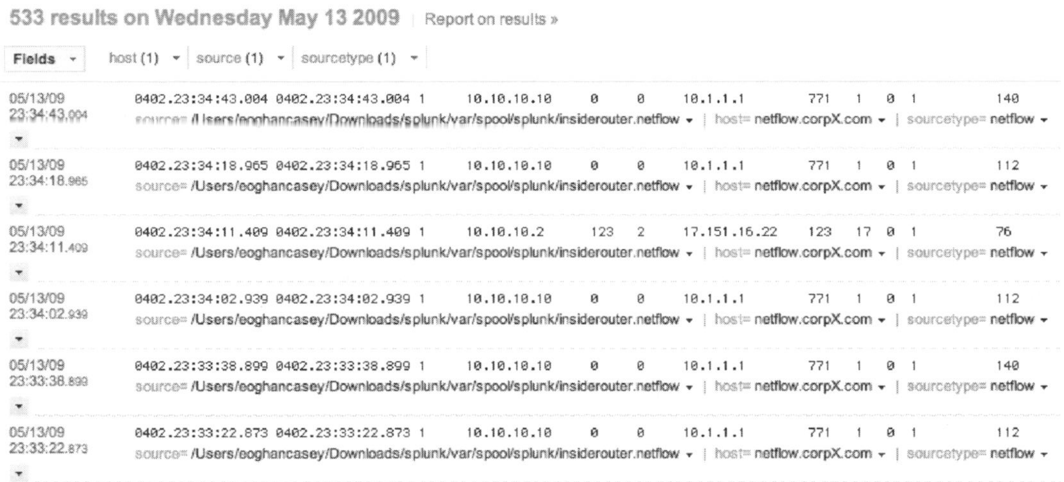


**FIGURE 9.36**
Splunk unable to interpret default date-time stamp format of NetFlow logs require reformatting of dates to enable correlation with other logs.

In order to correlate logs with each other, it is often necessary to reformat the date-time stamps in a way that log correlation tools recognize. Alternately, when a particular log is encountered on a large scale, it may be more efficient to create a template for the log format or use a tool that supports the particular type of log.

Once all data is loaded correctly into a correlation tool, the next challenge is to perform data reduction. The more data that is available, the more difficult this can be, particularly when network traffic is included in the correlation. The fine-grained detail can create so much noise that other logs can become difficult to discern. Filtering out the majority of irrelevant packets can provide a comprehensive correlation of logs showing sequences of interest as shown in Figure 9.37.

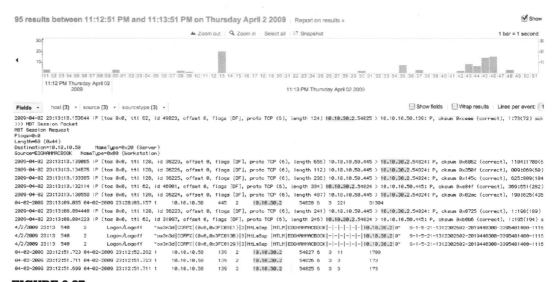

**FIGURE 9.37**
Splunk correlation and histogram.

Observe the tallest bar in the timeline histogram at the time of the data theft, caused by the large number of packets during data transfer.

Rather than filtering out noise to see what remains, it can be effective to use attributes gathered during the investigation to extract specific information from different logs. For instance, the following search in Splunk uses details gathered throughout the investigation of the intrusion investigation scenario to extract data from the various network logs around the time the trade secrets were stolen.

> (sourcetype="netflow" AND 10.10.30.2) OR
> (sourcetype="network-traffic" AND SMBtrans) OR
> (sourcetype="SecurityEvents" AND ow3n3d) OR
> (sourcetype="cisco_syslog" AND (ow3n3d OR jwiley)) OR
> (sourcetype="too_small" AND ow3n3d)

The results of this search are shown in Figure 9.38.

```
2009-04-02 23:13:53.806930 IP (tos 0x0, ttl 128, id 36342, offset 0, flags [DF], proto TCP (6), length 109) 10.10.10.50.445 > 10.10.30.2
2009-04-02 23:13:53.806847 IP (tos 0x0, ttl 62, id 54958, offset 0, flags [DF], proto TCP (6), length 109) 10.10.30.2.54828 > 10.10.10.50
04-02-2009 23:13:09.035 04-02-2009 23:28:03.157 1      10.10.10.50      445    2      10.10.30.2      54828 6    3   221     31304
4/2/2009 23:13  540      2        Logon/Logoff     "ow3n3d|CORPX|(0x0,0x3FC01E1 )|3|NtLmSsp  |NTLM|EOGHANMACBOOK|-|-|-|-|-|-|10.10.30.2|0"    S
4/2/2009 23:13  540      2        Logon/Logoff     "ow3n3d|CORPX|(0x0,0x3FC013B)|3|NtLmSsp  |NTLM|EOGHANMACBOOK|-|-|-|-|-|-|10.10.30.2|0"    S
4/2/2009 23:13  540      2        Logon/Logoff     "ow3n3d|CORPX|(0x0,0x3FC0129)|3|NtLmSsp  |NTLM|EOGHANMACBOOK|-|-|-|-|-|-|10.10.30.2|0"    S
04-02-2009 23:12:51.723 04-02-2009 23:12:52.292 1      10.10.10.50      139    2      10.10.30.2      54827 6    3   11      1700
04-02-2009 23:12:51.711 04-02-2009 23:12:51.723 1      10.10.10.50      139    2      10.10.30.2      54826 6    3   3       173
04-02-2009 23:12:51.699 04-02-2009 23:12:51.711 1      10.10.10.50      139    2      10.10.30.2      54825 6    3   3       173
04-02-2009 23:12:47.432 04-02-2009 23:12:52.184 1      10.10.10.50      445    2      10.10.30.2      54824 6    3   12      2421
Apr  2 23:12:46 Shell.CorpX.com sshd[3976]: Accepted keyboard-interactive/pam for jwiley from 10.10.20.1 port 1024 ssh2
Apr  2 23:12:46 Shell.CorpX.com sshd[3976]: Accepted keyboard-interactive/pam for jwiley from 10.10.20.1 port 1024 ssh2
Apr  2 23:12:46 Shell.CorpX.com com.apple.SecurityServer[22]: checkpw() succeeded, creating shared credential for user jwiley
Apr  2 23:12:46 Shell.CorpX.com com.apple.SecurityServer[22]: checkpw() succeeded, creating credential for user jwiley
4/2/2009 23:12  540      2        Logon/Logoff     "ow3n3d|CORPX|(0x0,0x3FBFF87)|3|Advapi  |Negotiate|JHL-IDNOLHYSVIA|-|JHL-IDNOLHYSVIA$|COI
Apr 02 2009 23:11:11: %ASA-6-716043: Group <DfltGrpPolicy> User <ow3n3d> IP <130.132.1.26> WebVPN Port Forwarding Java applet started. Cr
Apr 02 2009 23:11:07: %ASA-6-716038: Group <DfltGrpPolicy> User <ow3n3d> IP <130.132.1.26> Authentication: successful, Session Type: Web\
Apr 02 2009 23:11:07: %ASA-6-716001: Group <DfltGrpPolicy> User <ow3n3d> IP <130.132.1.26> WebVPN session started. started.
Apr 02 2009 23:11:07: %ASA-6-734001: DAP: User ow3n3d, Addr 130.132.1.26, Connection Clientless: The following DAP records were selected
Apr 02 2009 23:11:07: %ASA-6-113008: AAA transaction status ACCEPT : user = ow3n3d ow3n3d
Apr 02 2009 23:11:07: %ASA-6-113009: AAA retrieved default group policy (DfltGrpPolicy) for user = ow3n3d ow3n3d
Apr 02 2009 23:11:07: %ASA-6-113004: AAA user authentication Successful : server = 10.10.10.50 : user = ow3n3d ow3n3d
```

**FIGURE 9.38**

Splunk correlation combining logs from various sources, providing a reconstruction of events during the time of interest.

The combination of logs in Figure 9.38 tells a compelling story. Starting from the bottom, we can see an individual authenticated to the VPN using the ow3n3d account at 23:11 from the IP address 130.132.1.26. Because the VPN authenticates against the Domain Controller within CorpX, we see the same authentication event in the domain controller Security Event log at 23:12 (difference due to a clock offset). Next, the individual comes through the VPN and logs into the SSH server using the jwiley user account, which belongs to the disgruntled system administrator who is suspected of the data theft. Shortly thereafter, we see NetFlow logs recording SMB connections between the SSH Server (10.10.30.2) and intranet server (10.10.10.50) where the trade secrets are kept. These SMB connections are accompanied by entries in the Security Event logs on the intranet server, indicating that the ow3n3d user account was successfully authenticated from the SSH Server. The next line up in this correlation shows a single NetFlow record, corresponding to a transfer of 31304 bytes of data from 10.10.10.50 to 10.10.30.2 between 23:13 and 23:28. Some network traffic corresponding with some of this data theft is summarized at the top of the correlated logs, and there are many more packets relating to the transfer of stolen data. In brief, the involvement of the jwiley account in the middle of this reconstruction provides probable cause that the disgruntled system administrator was involved.

When multiple log entries or different log sources are needed to reconstruct events, it is easy to make mistakes and overlook relevant information. Such reconstructions can become quite complex and it is important to define the goal of the investigation at the start and to remain focused during the process. In addition to planning your investigative approach at the beginning, it is important to reevaluate the plan at each step in light of what has been found, and to perform periodic sanity checks on your results to ensure they are correct. The following case study illustrates the challenges of such an investigation.

Forensic log analysis is usually a reconstruction of activity over time. Since log records document events (even those that only mark time or report status can be considered events), activity can be viewed as a series of discrete events on a

## CASE STUDY

A financial services company offered customers personalized web service to monitor their own financial information, including credit ratings. Each customer had an account that could be verified for two levels of access, Tier 1 and Tier 2. The Tier 1 authentication would allow a customer to view commercially available information collected at the site. To view or to make

changes to their own financial data, they needed a Tier 2 authentication, which required a different password and answers to some challenge questions. A schematic of the systems and associated logs is provided in Figure 9.39.

Web administrators would authenticate to both servers as well, but at Tier 2 their accounts had administrative access to

**FIGURE 9.39**

Overview of the computer systems that provided customer access to financial details, showing the location of log files for web access and user authentication.

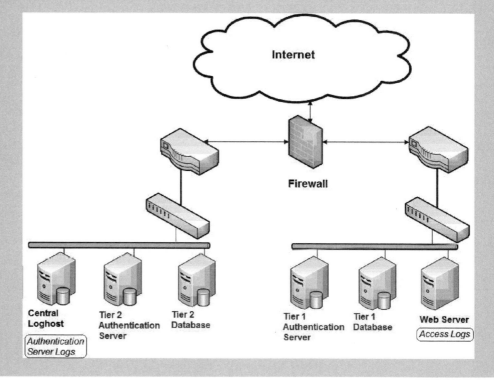

*(Continued)*

the web site and its databases and thus to everyone's financial information.

During routine maintenance, several fixes to minor problems were implemented simultaneously. As a result of the interactions of these fixes, every account on the system had full administrative access to all the accounts at Tier 2.

The problem went undetected for several months, until reported by one of the customers. The administrative access was not obvious and could be discovered only by trying to access someone else's financial information. It would not occur to most customers to try the experiment. Since it was one of the customers who discovered the problem, though, it obviously could happen.

Forensic investigators were asked to analyze available logs covering the vulnerable period to determine whether it was likely that any customers had exploited the information of others.

timeline. It may be important to identify activities that comprise more than one event, such as an entire user session. Such extended activities can be treated as a sequence of events with a defined start and end event.

In this case, we are interested in data-access events. More specifically, we are interested in access to data by an account that should not normally have access to the data.

This case does not involve sophisticated exploitation of technology, but the potential for almost casual exploitation of a maintenance error. Since every user was authorized, as far as the system was concerned, to access every other user's data, we will call an instance of a nonadministrative user accessing someone else's data "inappropriate."

We are dealing with two types of user. Customers, comprising the great majority of users, should not be accessing any data other than their own. Administrators will probably do so routinely. When we search for instances of inappropriate access, we should not include the administrators.

The next step is to determine how the events of interest will be represented in the log records. In particular, we need to determine how the events of interest will be represented *uniquely in order to distinguish them from all other events*. We begin by investigating the way that various authentication and access events are logged to see what information can be extracted from them. We are looking for instances in which an authenticated, nonadministrative user account was being used to access data belonging to another account. If the system logs held records of such access, we could simply examine those records. In this case, though, the system does not track that information explicitly. The only records logged by the system are the initial authentication, the subsequent access authentication (if any), and the web access records generated by the Apache web server.

Authentication to the initial server generates a record like this:

> 2009 08 17 03:09:36 +0000 tier1.yourmoolah.com authserver[28210]: [192.168.241.6] Authenticated user Jack Smollett

This record contains a timestamp, the name of the Tier 1 server, the process name and id of the authentication process, the IP address from which the authentication was made, the statement of a successful authentication, and the full name of the authenticated user.

This record shows that the user account belonging to Jack Smollett was authenticated to the Tier 1 server from IP address 192.168.241.6 on August 17 2009 at 03:09:36 GMT.

A user account authenticated to the Tier 2 server would generate a record like this one:

> 2009 08 17 03:09:39 +0000 tier2.yourmoolah.com accessserver[2940]: Authenticated user jsmollett

This record is similar to the one generated by the Tier 1 server except that it has no IP address and that it reports the system identifier of the user account (jsmollett) instead of the full name of the account holder. It is not unusual for different processes to log different types of information, particularly when the processes writing to the logs have been written specifically for an organization.

In this system, the only records of access to user data are in the access logs of the web server. The Apache access logs look like:

> 192.168.241.6 - - [17/Aug/2009:03:09:39 −0500] "GET / /User/data/content?accountdn=uid%3Djsmollett&targetobj=Yourmoo lah%3A%3AUser   %3A%3AProfile%3A%3ADisplay&format=Summary HTTP/1.1" 200 6229

This record, converted completely to ASCII text, reads:

> 192.168.241.6 - - [17/Aug/2009:03:09:39 −0500] "GET //User/data/content? accountdn=uid=jsmollett&targetobj=Yourmoolah::User::Profile:: Display&format=Summary HTTP/1.1" 200 6229

The web administrators can confirm that this is an HTTP request for the summary display of the information belonging to the account jsmollett. The summary display appears in response to a successful access authentication.

We have three relevant types of log record showing three different sets of information:

| Successful Tier 1 Authentication Record | Successful Tier 2 Authentication Record | Web Server Access Record |
|---|---|---|
| Timestamp | Timestamp | Timestamp |
| Server | Server | |
| Process Name | Process Name | |
| Process ID | Process ID | |
| Remote IP | | Remote IP |
| Success Confirmation | Success Confirmation | |
| Account Full Name | | |
| | Account ID | |
| | | HTTP GET Command |
| | | Account Summary Request for Account ID |

The actual access to data is recorded only in the Apache access log records. Unfortunately, those records do not record the account under which that access has been authorized. They do, however, report the IP address from which the access was made.

The authentication record also contains the IP address from which an authentication was made, as well as the full name of the account owner.

If a nonadministrative account is authenticated from a given IP address and then the data in some other account is accessed from the same IP address within a couple of minutes, the logs may well be recording the sort of event we are looking for.

Now consider the likelihood of false positives and false negatives. Could the log records described earlier be generated even when there was no inappropriate access? It could easily happen if two account holders accessed their own data in succession from the same IP address. They could be members of a family, or two people using wireless in a coffee shop behind a NAT. Could the log records described earlier fail to appear even when inappropriate access occurred? This could happen if there were a long time interval between the authentication and the access.

We can reduce the likelihood of both types of error by taking the Tier 2 server authentication records into account. The Tier 1 authentication alone does not permit anyone to access personal financial data. Even inappropriate access requires going through the Tier 2 server, and there is less likelihood of a long interval between the Tier 2 server authentication and the actual data access since Tier 2 authentication has no purpose other than the access of individual data.

Still, we need to tie the Tier 2 server record to the data access. The Tier 2 server record tells us which account has been granted access, but does not tie that account to the data being accessed through the IP address. It can, though, be tied to the Tier 1 server record (which must appear *before* the Tier 2 server record), which can then be associated with the data accessed using the IP address.

| Successful Tier 1 Authentication Record | Successful Tier 2 Authentication Record | Web Server Access Record |
|---|---|---|
| **Timestamp$_1$** | **Timestamp$_2$** | **Timestamp$_3$** |
| Server | Server | |
| Process Name | Process Name | |
| Process ID | Process ID | |
| **Remote IP$_1$** | | **Remote IP$_3$** |
| Success Confirmation | Success Confirmation | |
| **Account$_1$ Full Name** | | |
| | **Account$_2$ ID** | |
| | | HTTP GET Command |
| | | **Account$_3$ Summary Request for Account ID** |

We can make a working definition of our events of interest using the associations in the preceding table. We will say that an inappropriate access is defined by a triplet of records such as those in the table with the following relationships between the shaded fields:

$$\text{Timestamp}_1 < \text{Timestamp}_2 < \text{Timestamp}_3$$
$$\text{Remote IP}_1 = \text{Remote IP}_3$$
$$\text{Account}_1 = \text{Account}_2 \neq \text{Account}_3$$

Additionally, we impose reasonable constraints on the time intervals by the triplet by requiring:

$$\text{Timestamp}_3 - \text{Timestamp}_2 \leq 600 \text{ seconds}$$

This time interval allows 600 seconds to elapse between the authentication to the Tier 2 server and the access to data belonging to another account. The time interval helps to insure that the access really was related to the Tier 2 authentication. The value of 600 seconds (10 minutes) is arbitrary. If the working definition does not catch any inappropriate access events, we can relax or eliminate it to confirm that no such events appear in the log records.

Note that the Tier 1 server record identifies the account by the full name of the account holder, rather than the account ID. We will have to ask the system administrators to provide a mapping of one to the other.

Now that you have an initial framework on which to start analyzing the data, it's time to stop and question your assumptions. What assumptions have you built into the process thus far? It is just as important to record explicitly all assumptions that we are making in conducting the investigation as it is to record the data and data sources that we are using. We are assuming, for instance, that a user logs into the Tier 1 server and the Tier 2 server using the same account. Is it possible to authenticate to use different accounts for each? This can be addressed by asking the administrators to set up two test accounts and trying it ourselves. In any case, the assumption needs to be noted.

## Implementation

We have identified the log records to be investigated and the logs that contain them. We have also defined, at least for our first pass, the log profile of the events we are looking for. The next step is extracting the data we want and putting it in a format that will simplify data correlation.

This step can be executed in a number of ways. One of the most direct would be writing a script in a language such as Perl that used pattern matching to identify the records of interest, to extract the information that we are looking for, and to write it into a database that we could query for whatever information that interested us.

We should end up with a collection of data records that reflect the earlier tables:

| Tier1 | Tier2 | DataAccess |
|---|---|---|
| Tier1.Timestamp | Tier2.Timestamp | DataAccess.Timestamp |
| Tier1.RemoteIP | | DataAccess.RemoteIP |
| Tier1.AccountID | Tier2.AccountID | DataAccess.AccountID |

Note that the value for Tier1.AccountID is not taken directly from the record, but is found in the mapping of Account Full Names to Account IDs provided by CorpX. Note also that the accuracy of this mapping is one of our assumptions.

We can look for inappropriate access events using an algorithm like the following pseudo-code that can be written using any scripting language:

```
For every Tier2 record

    " " "
    Skip authentications by known administrative users (this test may be left out to
    test the algorithm)
    " " "

    If Tier2.AccountID is in list of valid administrative users, go to next iteration

    Locate the Tier1 record with

        The largest Tier1.Timestamp such that
    " " "
    Associate each Tier 2 authentication for an account with the most recent prior
    Tier1 authentication for that same account
    " " "
            Tier1.Timestamp < Tier2.Timestamp AND
            Tier1.AccountID = Tier2.AccountID

    Locate all DataAccess records with

    " " "
    Locate all access records from the IP of the Tier 1 authentication that were
    recorded within 30 seconds of the Tier 2 authentication and that are not for data
    belong to the ID used for the Tier 2 authentication
    " " "
        DataAccess.RemoteIP = Tier1.RemoteIP AND
        DataAccess.Timestamp - Tier2.Timestamp ≤ 600 seconds AND
        DataAccess.AccountID ≠ Tier2.AccountID

    Report DataAccess.Timestamp, Tier2.AccountID, Tier1.RemoteIP, DataAccess.AccountID
```

The constraint that data access events take place within 600-seconds of the Tier 2 authentication is included by false positives created by apparent correlations over unrealistic time intervals. It can be relaxed or eliminated in subsequent searches to ensure that nothing has been missed. It is also possible that a user would continue to access data in other accounts for more then 10 minutes, so any events we catch with the 600-second constraint should be examined more carefully to reconstruct all access activity.

Given a report like the one below, we would query our database for all details regarding the suspect accounts (in the Data Access ID column), such as the phenness account below.

| Possible Inappropriate Data Access Events | | | |
|---|---|---|---|
| Timestamp | Data Access ID | RemoteIP | Data Owner ID |
| 17aug2009:11:04:26 –0500 | phenness | 192.168.66.6 | jsmollett |
| 17aug2009:11:04:26 –0500 | phenness | 192.168.66.6 | jsmollett |
| 17aug2009:11:04:26 –0500 | phenness | 192.168.66.6 | jsmollett |
| 17aug2009:11:04:27 –0500 | phenness | 192.168.66.6 | jsmollett |
| 17aug2009:11:04:27 –0500 | phenness | 192.168.66.6 | jsmollett |
| 17aug2009:11:10:46 –0500 | phenness | 192.168.66.6 | tsnellin |
| 17aug2009:11:10:47 –0500 | phenness | 192.168.66.6 | tsnellin |
| 17aug2009:11:10:47 –0500 | phenness | 192.168.66.6 | tsnellin |
| 17aug2009:11:10:47 –0500 | phenness | 192.168.66.6 | tsnellin |
| 17aug2009:11:10:47 –0500 | phenness | 192.168.66.6 | tsnellin |
| 17aug2009:11:10:47 –0500 | phenness | 192.168.66.6 | tsnellin |
| 17aug2009:11:10:48 –0500 | phenness | 192.168.66.6 | tsnellin |
| 17aug2009:11:15:11 –0500 | phenness | 192.168.66.6 | sbloxham |
| 17aug2009:11:15:11 –0500 | phenness | 192.168.66.6 | sbloxham |
| 17aug2009:11:15:12 –0500 | phenness | 192.168.66.6 | sbloxham |
| 17aug2009:11:15:12 –0500 | phenness | 192.168.66.6 | sbloxham |
| 17aug2009:11:15:12 –0500 | phenness | 192.168.66.6 | sbloxham |
| 17aug2009:11:15:12 –0500 | phenness | 192.168.66.6 | sbloxham |
| . | | | |
| . | | | |
| . | | | |
| 06nov2009:05:59:30 –0500 | lwestenr | 192.168.77.7 | phenness |

Note the final event on 06 November 2009. We know that a customer reported the problem on that date. Assuming that customer reported the discovery promptly and that the access issue was dealt with immediately, we can expect the account ID lwestenr to belong to the reporting customer. At the very least, we would expect to find that customer linked to an inappropriate access somewhere in the records. Detecting that account would be another confirmation that our algorithm was working.

## CONCLUSION

In order to conduct an investigation involving computer networks, practitioners need to understand network architecture, be familiar with network devices and protocols, and have the ability to interpret the various network-level logs. Practitioners must also be able to search and combine large volumes of log data using search tools like Splunk or custom scripts. Perhaps most importantly, digital forensic analysts must be able to slice and dice network traffic using a variety of tools to extract the maximum information out of this valuable source of network-related digital evidence.

## REFERENCES

Bunker, M., & Sullivan, B. (2000). CD Universe Evidence Compromised. MSNBC, June 7.

Casey, E. (2004a). *Digital Evidence and Computer Crime: Forensic Science, Computers, and the Internet.* Academic Press.

Casey, E. (2004b). Network traffic as a source of evidence: tool strengths, weaknesses, and future needs. *Digital Investigation,* 1(1), 28–43.

Comer, D. E. (1995). Internetworking with TCP/IP Volume I: Principles, Protocols, and Architecture (Third Edition). Upper Saddle River, NJ: Prentice Hall.

Held, G., & Hundley, Kent (1999). In *Cisco Security Architecture.* New York: McGraw Hill. (p. 26).

Malin, C., Casey, E., & Aquilina, J. (2008). *Malware Forensics.* Syngress.

Plonka, D. (2000). *FlowScan: A Network Traffic Flow Reporting and Visualization Tool.* Usenix.

Saferstein, R. (1998). Criminalistics: An Introduction to Forensic Science. (6th edn). Upper Saddle River, NJ: Prentice Hall.

Stevens, S. W. (1994). In *TCP/IP Illustrated,* Volume 1: The Protocols. Addison Wesley.

Villano, M. (2001). Computer Forensics: IT Autopsy, CIO Magazine, March (http://www.cio.com/article/30022/Computer_Forensics_IT_Autopsy).

# CHAPTER 10

# Mobile Network Investigations

Dario Forte and Andrea de Donno

## INTRODUCTION

The use of mobile devices is increasing rapidly, with devices like the BlackBerry, iPhone, and G1 providing a wide variety of services, including communication (e.g., voice, SMS, e-mail), Internet access (web browsing), and satellite navigation (GPS). These technological advances create new opportunities for criminals while providing valuable sources of evidence. The bombs in the 2004 train bombings in Madrid apparently used cellular telephones as timers. The terrorists in the recent Mumbai attacks communicated using satellite telephones. Drug dealers and organized criminals are heavily dependent on inexpensive prepaid cellular telephones that are essentially anonymous and disposable.

Mobile network investigations are also commonly performed for "conventional crimes," often focusing on location information, logs of telephone calls, printouts of SMS messages, and associated metadata.

## CONTENTS

Introduction.....517

Mobile Network Technology......518

Investigations of Mobile Systems ...........522

Types of Evidence..........524

Where to Seek Data for Investigations .533

Interception of Digital Evidence on Mobile Networks.........537

References.......557

### FROM THE CASE FILES: EXONERATING SMS

The Criminal Court of Perugia examined data from mobile networks and devices while investigating the murder of Meredith Kercher, the English student killed between November 1 and 2, 2007. In this case, the specialized Police Unit made several technical investigations including mobile traffic and SMS analysis. In this particular case, only the analysis of the SMS enabled the police to determine the innocence of an unjustly accused suspect, Patrick Lumumba.

A *mobile device* is generally defined as any instrument that can connect to and operate on a mobile network, including cellular telephones, wireless modems, and pagers. Although a significant amount of useful digital evidence associated with mobile devices like cellular telephones is stored in embedded flash memory as detailed in Chapter 8, "Embedded System Analysis," the associated network is also a rich source of evidence. Compared with the wide variety of mobile devices, the supporting network technologies are reasonably consistent. The core mobile networks have similar components, the network service provider (NSP) will maintain usage logs and billing records, and investigators can intercept network traffic from mobile devices. Therefore, it is useful for investigators to understand the underlying network technologies, the types of data than can exist on mobile networks, and approaches to collecting and analyzing these sources of digital evidence.

This chapter begins with an overview of mobile networks and how they can be useful in digital investigations. This chapter concentrates on cellular and PCS technologies, but does not address satellite telephone networks. Methods of obtaining location information from mobile networks are described. The content and analysis of usage logs and billing records are covered, and the usefulness of text and multimedia messaging are demonstrated. The remainder of the chapter focuses on techniques and tools for capturing and analyzing traffic on mobile networks, culminating with a discussion of the legal and operational implication of interception.

# MOBILE NETWORK TECHNOLOGY

In the late 1980s, the mobile telephony system in Europe was based exclusively on the ETACS network created by various telephone companies and consisting of analog radio links operating at the frequency of 800 MHz. Although at the time it was considered to be the start of a revolution, few would have imagined how quickly the phenomenon would burgeon both into a fad and into a system for keeping close track of individuals.

The weak points of the ETACS network were the lack of coverage abroad, continuing interference with other users, and the ease of cloning. It often happened that some unknown party obtained possession of the serial number of a mobile device, combined it with a new account to elude the NSP and generated telephone traffic paid for by the unwitting victim. In the mid-1990s, the GSM network was introduced. It operated at a frequency of 900 MHz and later 1.8 GHz. GSM was introduced precisely to eliminate once and for all the problem of interference among radio links and, being digital, to make conversations more secure.

**Table 10.1** Telephony versus Telematic Services

| Telephony | Telematic |
|---|---|
| Telephone calls, including voice calls, voice messaging, conference calls, and data transmitted via telefax | Internet access<br>E-mail |
| Supplementary services, including call forwarding and call transfers | Fax, SMS and MMS messages via Internet |
| Messaging and multimedia services, including SMS services | Telephony via Internet (Voice over Internet Protocol–VoIP) |

The next revolution in mobile network technology came about in 2003 when the Japanese colossus Hutchinson Whampoa entered the European market with H3G, the third generation of mobile telephony. The telephone now became a video-telephone, using the 2.1 GHz band.

In the area of electronic communication services, it is necessary to distinguish between "telephony" and "telematic" services as shown in Table 10.1.

## Components of Mobile Networks

Mobile networks generally have the following components, as shown in Figure 10.1.

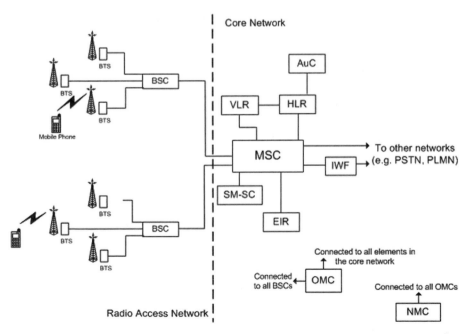

**FIGURE 10.1**

Common components of mobile networks (Gibbs & Clark, 2001).

The wireless portion of mobile networks uses Time Division Multiple Access (TDMA) or Code Division Multiple Access (CDMA) technology to transfer data via radio frequency. Fundamentally, CDMA is a spread-spectrum technology to enable data from multiple devices to be multiplexed on a single physical channel, whereas TDMA breaks the transmission signal into discrete timeslots for each device.

> TDMA is digital transmission technology that allows a number of users to access a single radio-frequency (RF) channel without interference by allocating unique time slots to each user within each channel. The TDMA digital transmission scheme multiplexes three signals over a single channel. The current TDMA standard for cellular divides a single channel into six time slots, with each signal using two slots, providing a 3 to 1 gain in capacity over advanced mobile-phone service (AMPS). Each caller is assigned a specific time slot for transmission. (IEC, 2007)

All the mobile network components in Figure 10.1 can be important in a digital investigation. Mobile devices connect to a base station (a.k.a. Base Transceiver Station) over a radio link using TDMA or CDMA technology. Each base station has at least one radio transceiver that provides radio coverage of a specific geographical region (a.k.a. cell).

Some mobile network technologies (including GSM but not IS-136) use base station controllers (BSC/CBSC) to control communication between base stations. For instance, the BSC coordinates the transfer of a device from one base station to another, enabling continuity of communication as a mobile device moves to different places within a given Location Area.[1] The wireless portion of mobile networks connect to a switching system, typically including a Mobile Switching Center (MSC), to perform call processing within the system and connect to other wireless networks and land lines. For instance, the MSC delivers call and SMS messages to mobile devices in its jurisdiction, and coordinates handovers of ongoing communications as a mobile device moves between Location Areas.

Because MSCs are the crux of communications between base stations and the core network, they generate a wealth of information about mobile network activities that can support digital investigations, including usage logs and charging detail records. Furthermore, all mobile devices that are currently being handled by a given MSC are listed in a Visitor Location Register (VLR) database associated with that MSC.

---

[1] A group of base stations and controllers in a given region is commonly referred to as a Location Area.

In addition to MSCs, mobile networks have systems called the Interworking Functions (IWF) that operate as a gateway to external data network like the Internet. An IWF is "essentially a bank of modems (ISDN, analog, etc.) and equipment to perform, if necessary, protocol conversions to connect the MSC to other data networks" (Gibbs & Clark, 2001).

Information about the individual subscriber, their billing details, and services they can use on the mobile network is contained in the Home Location Register (HLR) of their NSP. The current location of a given mobile device is also stored in the HLR. The HLR also contains the subscriber's encryption keys and supports billing. Information in the HLR is also used by an Authentication Center (AuC), which restricts access to the network and services to authorized subscribers, to provide security and prevent fraud.

At the heart of a mobile network, NSPs have one or more centers of operation to maintain and monitor their systems. These centers of operation provide access to data for billing or investigative purposes, and support interception of mobile traffic.

There are other service-specific systems in the core network that may contain data of relevance to an investigation. For instance, text messages are processed by a Short Message Service Center (SMSC). Although an SMSC may only retain messages for a short period, it can be a fruitful source of evidence depending on the policy of the operator. Voicemail stored on the provider network can be another useful source of evidence.

NSPs may also maintain additional information about activities relating to mobile devices and subscribers, including a blacklist of devices in their Equipment Identity Register (EIR) that have been reported stolen or have been flagged as bad for some other reason.

Another important aspect of mobile networks is the Signaling System 7 (SS7). This system provides the control link needed to support call establishment, routing, and information-exchange functions. For instance, SMS text messages can be transmitted over this link, thus providing communication services even when a call is not established. Investigators should be aware of SS7 because it releases information that is very useful as a correlation point.

Another number useful to obtain is the International Mobile Equipment Identifier (IMEI), which is a unique number associated with a particular device. The IMEI allows digital investigators to obtain valuable digital evidence associated with a particular mobile device even if a subject uses different NSPs or accounts with the same device. In addition to obtaining stored data from NSPs, digital investigators can use the IMEI to monitor telephone traffic associated with a particular device, obtaining voice communication, attempted calls, SMS, MMS, and video calls.

## PRACTITIONER'S TIP: IDLE TRACES

A mobile device begins to leave its traces on the mobile network the moment it is turned on. When a device is powered on it announces itself to the mobile network, generating a refresh of the authentication process. Like every technical device, a mobile device also releases technically sensitive information. For example, an International Mobile Subscriber Identity (IMSI) is essentially a unique number that is associated with a particular subscriber on a GSM or UMTS mobile network. The IMSI is stored on the SIM card in a mobile device and is used to authenticate the device on the mobile network and to control the other details such as HLR (Home Location Register) or copied locally in the VLR (Visitor Location Register). In order to avoid interception of this sensitive number, the IMSI is not directly sent over the network. It is substituted by a TMSI (Temporary Mobile Subscriber Identity), which is a temporary number, usually created for a single session. At the request of digital investigators, NSPs can use these unique identifiers to query their systems for all activities relating to a particular subscriber account, as detailed in Chapter 8, "Embedded Systems Analysis."

## INVESTIGATIONS OF MOBILE SYSTEMS

Investigations used to be carried out exclusively by people. In the pure spirit of investigation, you started from information obtained through an undercover agent followed by operations involving trailing suspects and intercepting ordinary mail. Without the help of technological systems, these investigations tended to last much longer than their more modern counterparts.

Today, the initiation of an investigation may involve, in addition to verbal information, an anomalous bank record, an image from a surveillance camera, or of course highly visible crimes such as theft or murder.

The first phase of the investigation involves interviewing people who may have relevant information and continues with monitoring the means of communication of suspects or others associated in some way with the case. In addition to the traditional telephone, there are other monitoring points such as electronic mailboxes, places visited by the suspect, Telepass accounts (devices used for automatic highway toll payment), credit card accounts, and other financial operations.

Nowadays, investigations are supported by software that is customized to meet different requirements. The investigator enters all the data available on a subject into the interception system and the server performs a thorough analysis, generating a series of connections via the mobile devices involved, the calls made or received, and so on, providing criminal police with a well-defined scheme on which to focus the investigation, and suggesting new hypotheses or avenues that might otherwise be hard to identify. Obviously, thanks to the support of the NSP, the data can be supplemented with historical information or other missing data such as other mobile devices connected to a given BTS on a given date and time. Data can also be provided for public payphones, which are often used to coordinate crimes. Again, thanks to a connection with the NSP, it is possible to obtain a historical record of telephone calls made and the location of the payphone with respect to other mobile devices. The same sort of record may also be obtained for *highway* travel using Telepass (conventional name for automatic wireless toll payment), including average speed and stops.

Having historical data of various kinds relating to an investigation accessible in a database can greatly assist the initial examination of a newly acquired mobile device. By extracting all telephone numbers in the phonebook of a mobile device seized during a search and entering names and numbers into the electronic system, digital investigators perform powerful analysis even in the initial phases of the investigation thanks to cross-referencing capabilities. For instance, investigative tools support advanced entity and relation searches, including the nicknames from phonebooks to locate additional related activities. In addition, some investigative tools enable digital investigators to perform traffic analysis, including georeferenced data and diagram generation as shown in Figure 10.2.

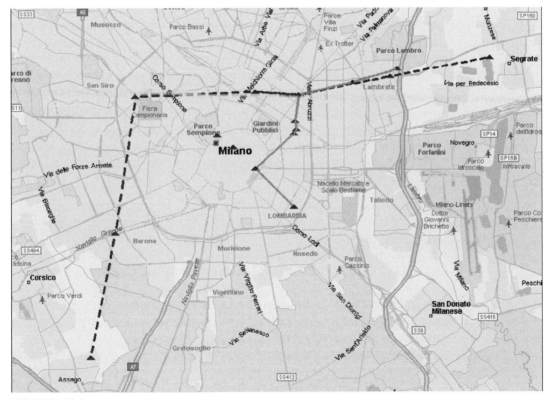

**FIGURE 10.2**
Cellular telephone tracking software, showing the relative movements of two mobile devices over a given period of time.

It is thus very important to have investigation software that can quickly import data online (secure and confidential connection with the MC) or from optical media, and that offers flexibility in subsequent processing.

# TYPES OF EVIDENCE

Mobile networks can provide information of relevance to an investigation, including the location of a mobile device, the past usage associated with a particular device or subscriber, as well as context of communications.

## Localization Parameters

The term *localization parameters* describes information that can be combined to localize an active mobile device and its related user. These localization parameters can be useful to track the position of a mobile device user, for several purposes, both for prosecution and defense.

### Determining the Position of a Given Mobile Device

The simple act of turning on a device and leaving it in an idle state will generate data on the network that can be used to determine its approximate location. As a mobile device is moved from one location to another, it updates the network. Basically speaking, there is a timeframe where the mobile device "announces" itself to the network. The possible alternatives are as follows:

- **Cell identification**: The mobile device can be reached by looking at the cell to which it is currently connected. There is a range of accuracy that starts from a few hundred meters in urban areas, up to 32 km in suburban areas and rural zones. The accuracy depends on the known range of the particular base station serving the mobile device at the time of positioning. The poor value of 32 km can be enhanced with the use of the so-called Enhanced Cell Identification (general accuracy of 550 meters).

- **Time difference of arrival** (TDOA): This method, also referred to as *multilateration*, measures the time it takes for a signal to travel from a mobile device to multiple base stations to estimate the device location. "It is a method commonly used in civil and military surveillance applications to accurately locate an aircraft, vehicle or stationary emitter by measuring the time difference of arrival (TDOA) of a signal from the emitter at three or more receiver sites." (Wang et al., 2008)

- **Time of arrival** (TOA): This approach is effectively the same as TDOA, but this technology uses the absolute time of arrival at a certain base station rather than the difference between multiple stations.

- **Enhanced Observed Time Difference** (E-OTD): This method is similar to TDOA, but in this case the position is calculated by the mobile device, not the base station. In essence, the mobile device receives signals from multiple base stations at the same time that a specially placed receiver receives the signals. The precision of this method can vary from 50 to 200 m.

- **Assisted-GPS**: A third-party service that generally relies on the Cell Identification.

Determining the location of a mobile device can be important for assessing alibis of suspects or the whereabouts of victims in the past, and ongoing tracking of the location can be useful in cases of abduction, missing persons, and other ongoing criminal activities.

### FROM THE CASE FILES: KIDNAPPING

In March 2006, Tommaso Onofri was kidnapped from his room during a robbery, under the eyes of the parents. After beginning as a mafia investigation, the real kidnappers have been traced and accused as a result of localization of their telephones and the related logs. Unfortunately, the digital evidence did not succeed in tracing the victim, who was found as a result of the confession of those arrested. However, at least the information from the mobile network helped apprehend the culprits.

From a practical perspective, there are tools that perform these techniques and display the results for digital investigators. Some of the information transmitted by the NSP to a monitoring center is the position on the basis of cell and the IMSI code. This is extremely important information in that it makes it possible to track the people responsible for serious crimes as they move.

The cell base looks like a truncated cone on an updated map in the interception server. This is a fundamentally important piece of information because it allows the suspects' position to be displayed on a single screen, giving the police an overall view of the group, possible interactions among its members, and logistics and operations sites, albeit with a large margin of error on the order of 100 to 200 meters if the monitored device is in a city, and 500 meters if it is in open country or sparsely inhabited areas. This difference derives from the fact that the position is determined by triangulation of the BTS. In a city, the GSM stations are located at a spacing of one every 100 to 150 meters (since there is a higher density of mobile devices and greater network demand for simultaneous calls), whereas in less populated areas there are fewer calls and no need for such density of coverage. Obviously, in situations where accuracy on the order of five meters is required, other types of localization systems are used, such as discrete satellite locators. However, we are leaving the realm of classic telephone interception here.

An example of mobile device tracking is provided in Figure 10.2. In this particular case, the investigative console shows two different mobile devices tracked both in terms of position and movements over a given period of time. Depending on the mobile devices and the related software, as many as 20 mobile devices can be tracked at the same time using this type of investigative system.

If the user identity is unknown, one of the ways to capture the IMSI code is to use the mobile GSM Interceptor device. Using new and innovative software, the GSM Interceptor can identify the target registered on the international level. The GSM Interceptor device allows investigators to receive and process digital GSM signals by standing in for the local BTS and "fooling" the mobile devices. Furthermore, via a sophisticated system of radio frequency triangulation, it localizes the position of the intercepted mobile phone. The location is accomplished by triangulation of the position of the GSM target and the BTS cells in the zone. In urban areas where the GSM cells are more numerous, the precision can reach an error margin of $\pm 2$ meters, whereas in rural areas it may be as wide as $\pm 250$ meters.

The device is managed by a Windows-based software and has a simple and intuitive user interface. The portable interceptor operates at the frequencies of 900 MHz and 1800 to 1900 MHz. It intercepts the conversation between two GSM users with the option of automatic or manual recording. The audio file is saved in standard formats that are compatible with WAV files.

### Remote Activation of Electronic Devices

Once, organized crime just used old-fashioned weapons. Now, with a mobile device and an Internet connection many more crimes can be committed. From the massacres of the 1990s to the latest terrorist attacks, mobile devices have played a fundamental role in the organization of crimes. With a ring or an SMS containing a code it is possible to activate or deactivate an electronic device in any part of the world. This is why the ability to trace an SMS or even a simple ring signal is particularly important, along with the refinement of technology for capturing any signal or use, even if apparently innocuous, of mobile phones.

Unfortunately, organized criminal groups, having considerable financial resources, enjoy various advantages in terms of budget and decision-making speed in undertaking countermeasures to thwart the various investigation and law-enforcement bodies. They hire experts in technology as well as researchers who spend their days seeking out the latest solutions in terms of protection.

When criminal figures meet for business, they often protect their privacy by jamming signals in the area around their meeting place. This prevents mobile devices from linking to the BTS and thus connecting to the network. This prevents investigators from connecting to the cell and getting an idea of the geographical location of the meeting. The jamming mechanism also temporarily interrupts the operation of mobile phones in the area that might represent a threat of interception.

A mobile device jamming system emits a signal to prevent the use of mobile phones within a certain radius. It emits a wide band radio signal at the same frequency range used for transmitting signals from the BTS to the mobile phones. This signal prevents the mobile device from decoding the network signal and thus causes the mobile device to disconnect from the network.

The transmission power can be regulated depending on need. Some of the technical specifications are listed in Table 10.2.

## Usage Logs/Billing Records

The logs maintained by an NSP can help digital investigators determine past usage of a mobile device, as well as communications between individuals. These logs are generated from Call Detail Records (CDR) maintained for billing

**Table 10.2** Technical Specification for Jamming Device

**Transmission**

Transmission power: up to 30 W
Signal source PLL synthesized
Input Power 110/220 VAC or 12/24 VDC regulated
Modules per unit single/dual/triple band
Remote control infrared
Internal antenna, internal directional antenna (s), 8 dBi gain
External antenna (opt.) via N-Type connectors

**Cellular Systems**

| | |
|---|---|
| Frequency bands | 851/869 – 894 MHz |
| | 925/935 – 960 MHz |
| | 1805 – 1880 MHz |
| | 1930 – 1990 MHz |
| | 2110 – 2170 MHz |
| Air interface standards | Analog: AMPS, N-AMPS, NMT, TACS |
| | Digital: GSM, CDMA, TDMA, iDEM, UMTS |

purposes. The data in the resulting logs that are commonly provided to investigators are summarized here:

- Telephone number of user
- Numbers called
- IMEI number of mobile device
- Information about the cell: provides information about the location of the calling phone on the basis of the BTS where the connection was made
- SMS sent: excluding the text, which is available only via decodification using a telephone signal interception system (discussed later in this chapter)
- Date, time, and duration of calls

Depending on the equipment used, the logs generated on a particular mobile network may include a variety of other details. To give digital investigators a better sense of what details these logs can contain, a generic example of a CDR from a GSM MSC is shown in Table 10.3.

The Oracle Communications Services Gatekeeper is used by many NSPs worldwide for service delivery platform (SDP) infrastructure in a controlled, optimized, and automated way. The data in Table 10.4 provide an example of the CDR information that is maintained by such a system.

Many external operators, including police units, have direct access to mobile network usage data via the Oracle Communications Services Gatekeeper solution, which is based on information technology, web and telecommunications industry standards such as Java Platform, Enterprise Edition (Java EE), web services, Session Initiation Protocol (SIP), IP Multimedia Subsystems (IMS), Simple Object Access Protocol (SOAP) and Representational State Transfer (REST). Investigators will find this data interesting for their activity.

Up to a few years ago, the analysis of usage logs was performed manually, reviewing the various elements present in the documentation sent by the NSP. Now this all happens in an almost completely automatic way using sophisticated software that can project all interrelations among a group of users and display the results on special maps. For example, these analysis tools could quickly show that mobile device number 330123456 called the number 331654321 a total of 23 times, of which 20 times were at the same time and from the same point (with a maximum error of 150 meters in an urban center). Using location data, digital investigators could then determine that another person of interest with the phone number 323555555 was also located in the same neighborhood one year ago. This type of linkage analysis can be very powerful in any investigation involving mobile devices.

**Table 10.3** Excerpts from a Generic CDR Collected from a GSM MSC (Gibbs and Clark, 2001)

```
Example: Mobile originated call (MOC)

CDR HEADER
CALL REFERENCE
NUMBER OF SUPPLEMENTARY SERVICE RECORDS
CALLING IMSI
CALLING IMEI
CALLING NUMBER
CALLING CATEGORY
CALLED IMSI
CALLED IMEI
CALLED NUMBER
DIALED DIGITS
CALLING SUBSCRIBER FIRST LOCATION AREA CODE
CALLING SUBSCRIBER FIRST CELL ID
CALLING SUBSCRIBER LAST LOCATION AREA CODE
CALLING SUBSCRIBER LAST CELL ID
OUT CIRCUIT GROUP
OUT CIRCUIT
BASIC SERVICE TYPE
CHARGING START TIME
CHARGING END TIME
CAUSE FOR TERMINATION
ORIGINATING CALL CHARGE TYPE
ORIGINATING CALL TARIFF CLASS
CONNECTED TO NUMBER
CHARGE NUMBER
CHARGE NATURE
CARRIER SELECTION
SPEECH VERSION
INTERMEDIATE CHARGE CAUSE
CLOSED USER GROUP INFORMATION
```

## Text/Multimedia Messages

A common use of mobile devices is to send messages in text or multimedia format. The Short Message Service (SMS) communication service, which has been in use for some fifteen years, allows transmission of a limited number of text characters using the telephony channel. The advantages of the service include the possibility of transmitting messages even in areas of very low GSM signal coverage, where a voice call would be disturbed or fail due to insufficient signal strength, and even when the voice channel is being used for a conversation.

**Table 10.4** CDR Data Stored in Oracle Communications Services Gatekeeper (http://download.oracle.com/docs/cd/E14148_01/wlcp/ocsg41_otn/tpref/edrcommon.html)

| Element | Represents |
|---|---|
| transaction_id | The Oracle Communications Services Gatekeeper transaction sequence number |
| service_name | The communication service whose use is being tracked |
| service_provider | The Service Provider ID |
| application_id | The Application ID |
| application_instance_id | The username of the Application Account; this is a string that is equivalent to the 2.2 value: Application Instance Group ID |
| container_transaction_id | The transaction ID from WebLogic Server, if available; this identifies the thread on which the request is executed |
| server_name | The name of the server in which the CDR was generated |
| Timestamp | The time at which the event was triggered (in milliseconds from midnight 1 January 1970) |
| service_correlation_ID | An identifier that allows the usage of multiple service types to be correlated into a single charging unit |
| charging_session_id | An ID correlating related transactions within a service capability module that belong to one charging session; for example, a call containing three call legs will produce three separate transactions within the same session |
| start_of_usage | The date and time the request began to use the services of the underlying network |
| connect_time | The date and time the destination party responded. Used for Call Control traffic only |
| end_of_usage | The date and time the request stopped using the services of the underlying network |
| duration_of_usage | The total time the request used the services of the underlying network |
| amount_of_usage | The used amount; used when charging is not time dependent, for example, as in flat-rate services |
| originating_party | The originating party's address |

**Table 10.4** CDR Data Stored in Oracle Communications Services Gatekeeper (http://download.oracle.com/docs/cd/E14148_01/wlcp/ocsg41_otn/tpref/edrcommon.html)—Cont'd

| Element | Represents |
| --- | --- |
| destination_party | The destination party's address; this is the first address in the case of send lists, with all additional addresses placed in the additional_info field |
| charging_info | A service code added by the application or by policy service |
| additional_info | If the communication service supports send lists, all destination addresses other than the first, under the key destination party; in addition any other information provided by the communication service |

SMS messages are intercepted using the same systems as used for intercepting voice calls. These systems not only record the telephone numbers of the originator and the recipient, but also the entire text of the message. On some networks, the SMS messages are archived for extended periods.

## FROM THE CASE FILES

Although network service providers generally only store text messages for weeks to ensure proper delivery, the case of the former mayor of Detroit demonstrates that some services archive text messages indefinitely. Kilpatrick resigned as part of a plea agreement in the perjury case against him that relied heavily on tens of thousands of text messages between him and his chief of staff that were archived by Skytel's SkyWriter service that Detroit City had selected for official business mobile devices (Linebaugh, 2008).

The Multimedia Message Service (MMS) is a more evolved form of SMS, where it is possible to attach other multimedia content to a classic text message, such as an audio, video, or photo file. Current interception systems also capture the multimedia content, saving it to a special folder for display or listening.

Although these forms of communication can be important to an investigation, they are maintained on core network only for a limited time. Therefore, it is more effective to capture these in transit during an investigation as detailed in the next section. The structure of intercepted SMS/MMS is easy to understand. Generally, the intercepted SMS content is presented with the Sender, Receiver, time and date, and content (text). Some interception platforms are also able to provide the location of mobile devices. MMS also has the graphical content that has been intercepted. In an investigation involving mobile devices, these kinds of intercepted information are usually correlated with the contents of mobile devices that were collected during the investigation.

## Intercepted Data

Some investigations of mobile networks require the interception of data, including SMS, MMS, and voice signals. *Interception* is defined as the capture of transiting information, which may be part of a conversation or some other form of communication, by a covert third party using mechanical or electronic means and without the awareness of the parties engaged in a supposedly private exchange.

The term *interception* frequently connotes and is perceived as an infringement on personal liberty, a *vulnus* to privacy. Interceptions are permitted by law in some cases but there are many limits designed to protect the rights of the individual. Abuses such as those recently in the European news, where there was serious and widespread misuse of the information in one EU country, may have significant negative impacts in the private sphere of a suspect, and perhaps violate specific codes of secrecy proper to certain activities, relations, or professions. Although Italy is not the only country where such episodes occur, the recent case of the top Italian telephone carrier, Telecom Italia, demonstrates the privacy risks associated with interception. Flaws in its legitimate interception system, called Radar, allowed individuals within their organization to perform unauthorized surveillance without anyone knowing (Edri, 2006). Extensive evidence of misuse was apparently found on the computers of several key employees.

### FROM THE CASE FILE: ATHENS AFFAIR

In 2005, it was discovered that someone had compromised a BSC/MSC system on the Vodafone Greece network, and had been intercepting communications of the Greek prime minister and many other political figures for many months. The malicious eavesdroppers had altered the legitimate interception software used for performing authorized wiretaps, called remote-control equipment subsystem (RES), that was running on an Ericsson AXE system Vodafone used as a BSC and MSC. Investigators were ultimately unable to determine who was responsible (Prevelakis & Spinellis, 2007).

There are different methods, techniques, and positions of interception depending on the case, the country, or the purpose. The interception of electronic or telematic communications represents a particular case. In some nations, for example, the judicial authorities may also authorize operations being carried out using privately owned devices and/or systems. The involvement of private concerns opens up the possibility of nonstandard implementations, which does anything but make things simple. In telematic communications, for example, there are additional and more specific areas of criticality than in "traditional" telephone conversations, in that a factor apparently external to the communication (e.g., a web page or destination IP address) often identifies or reveals the *content* of the communication. It may be possible, therefore, not only to reconstruct personal and social relations, but also to support conclusions regarding the political orientation, ideological convictions, or habits of the interceptees.

## WHERE TO SEEK DATA FOR INVESTIGATIONS

An investigator working with mobile networks has to find pertinent information not only directly from the networks within his or her purview, but also from third parties. This is why the various NSPs have to be able to provide this information. Thus there exists an additional service provider that is obliged to retain traffic data. This provider makes electronic communications services available to the public on public communications networks. This is an extremely important distinction to understand, since the investigator may not always know where to look for these data.

In certain states, for example, the following are not included in the commonly accepted concept of service provider:

- Subjects offering electronic communications services directly to limited groups of people (e.g., public or private subjects that allow only their employees or collaborators to communicate using the subjects' telephone or telematic services). These services, while falling within the general definition of "electronic communications services," cannot be considered publicly available. However, when the communication is with a user outside of the private network, the traffic data generated for that communication are subject to retention.

- Subjects who, while offering publicly available electronic communications services, do not directly generate or process the related traffic data.

- Owners or managers of public enterprises or private associations of any type whose sole purpose is providing the public, their customers, or their partners with terminals that can be used for communications, telematic or otherwise. An example of this is an Internet access point using wireless technology; excluded are public pay telephones enabled exclusively for voice telephony.

- Administrators of search engines. The telematic traffic data processed by these administrators, allowing easy traceability of operations performed by the user on the network, may in any case be qualified as "content." The concept of content is a hotly debated theme and much depends on the national context. In the United States, for example, these data have to be rendered available, whereas certain countries in Europe, especially in the more conservative states, are far from affirming this principle.

## PRACTITIONER'S TIP: REQUESTING DATA FROM NSPs

Digital investigators with proper legal authorization may request information from NSPs using dedicated software on a shared platform, the *Request Type* and *Service Type*. In some situations, information can be obtained by authorities with dedicated user accounts and passwords that enable them to connect to the NSP's system directly and use special search software. Requests can be for localization information, historic usage logs, and complete traffic interception. The request may focus on a particular telephone number, equipment identifier (e.g., IMEI), or subscriber identifier (e.g., IMSI). When requesting traffic data, digital investigators can also specify a particular base station or geographical area (address, municipality, etc.) as indicated on the warrant. In such a case, the NSP must determine which base stations cover the geographical area in question and provide traffic

data from each of them. It is also possible to define, per the warrant, the type of calls to investigate (e.g., incoming and/ or outgoing), as well as whether digital investigators require addition personal information like subscriber details about users in the investigated traffic data report.

In all cases, the request must contain the report and interception register number (RTAB or RINT), and must specify the start date for authorized gathering of data as specified in the warrant (include end date when applicable), and whether the number to monitor is a national account or originated with a foreign NSP offering roaming capabilities. In addition, the request should contain contact information for digital investigations, including a telephone number and/or e-mail address where messages containing localization data can be sent.

## Traffic Data that Generally Must be Retained

The obligation to retain data about telephony traffic data, including unanswered calls and data regarding telematic traffic, excluding in any case the content of the communications. In particular, the obligation of retention extends to data that the NSPs process in order to transmit the communication and for billing purposes. Thus, the NSPs have to retain, for the exclusive purposes of detecting and prosecuting crime, only the traffic data that derive from technical operations serving the purposes of providing services and billing them.

## LICIT PURPOSES

A limitation stating that the data retained by law may be used exclusively for the investigation, detection, and prosecution of specified crimes is in force in many countries. It imposes precise obligations for NSPs in the event that they

receive requests serving other purposes. For example, the NSPs must not comply with requests for data if such requests are made within the context of civil, administrative, or financial litigation.

### How Data May Be Acquired

Various laws have been enacted to define how traffic data retained by NSPs may be acquired. Therefore, it is essential for investigators to be familiar with the legislation in force in the country or jurisdiction in which they are operating. In certain countries, for example, the defendant's counsel or suspect's lawyer has the right to request directly from the NSP only those traffic data that refer to the "accounts registered in the name of the client."

In other countries, on the other hand, there are authorities specifically assigned by law to identify measures for guaranteeing the rights of the parties involved in questions of telephone and telematic traffic data retention for the purposes of detecting, investigating, and prosecuting crime. Precisely for this reason, anyone accessing or processing these data must adhere to certain principles:

- The legislated requirement to provide specific safeguards regarding the type and quantity of data to protect and the risks correlated with said protection. Providers are already required to prevent said risks by upholding common security obligations that go beyond merely the minimum measures required by law or regulation. These risks are then assumed by those who receive the data.

- The advisability of identifying, given the current situation, protective measures to be implemented in the processing of data by all providers so that the integrity of said data can be verified in an inspection (and admissible in dealings with the suspect or defendant's counsel) to ensure more effective security for telephone and telematic traffic data.

- The need to keep in mind the costs deriving from the implementation of the measures in the various countries or jurisdictions, also regarding the different technical and financial capacities of the parties involved.

- The transnational legislative context, especially in light of the opinions expressed by the various groups working to protect personal privacy.

- The technological state of the art, meaning that the various measures have to be periodically updated.

These are important matters with which to be familiar, especially in the field of cross-border investigations and litigation.

### European Legislation

Although US legislation has been discussed many times in a variety of legal publications, the increase in cross-border litigation and investigations obliges us to be familiar with what goes on in the Old World as well.

*European Directive 2002/58/EC*, on privacy and electronic communications, obliges EU Member States to protect the privacy of electronic communications and prohibits the retention of traffic data generated during the communication, with the exception of what is expressly authorized for the purposes indicated in the Directive.

The Directive regards the processing of personal data in connection with the provision of publicly available electronic communications services on public communications networks in the Community (Art. 3). Traffic data are defined here as "any data processed for the purpose of the conveyance of a communication on an electronic communications network or for the billing thereof" (Cf. Article 2 and Premise 15 of Directive 2002/58/EC).

In obliging EU Member States to enact national laws to ensure the confidentiality of communications over a public communications network and publicly available electronic communications services, the Directive places the accent on traffic data generated by the same services (Art. 5). These data, processed and/or stored by the NSP for the public network or the public electronic communication service, must be deleted or rendered anonymous when they are no longer necessary for the purposes of transmission of communications, with only certain specific exceptions (Art. 6, Par. 2, 3 and 5, and Art. 15, Par. 1; see *Opinion no. 1/2003* on the storage of traffic data for billing purposes adopted on January 29, 2003 by the Working Party on the Protection of Individuals with regard to the Processing of Personal Data).

Article 15, Paragraph 1 of the Directive allows Member States to "adopt legislative measures to restrict the scope of the rights and obligations provided for in Article 5, Article 6, Article 8(1), (2), (3) and (4), and Article 9 of this Directive when such restriction constitutes a necessary, appropriate and proportionate measure within a democratic society to safeguard national security (i.e. State security), defense, public security, and the prevention, investigation, detection and prosecution of criminal offences or of unauthorized use of the electronic communication system." To this end, the Member States may, among other options, adopt legislative measures that provide for data being retained for a limited period of time.

### Another EU Regulation: Directive 2006/24/EC

European Directive 2006/24/EC was drawn up by the European Parliament and Council on 15 March 2006 with the goal of harmonizing the regulations and legislative measures of the Member States regarding retention of traffic data for the purposes of investigation, detection, and prosecution of serious crime. The Directive was to be transposed into national law no later than 15 September 2007.

The Directive contains specific indications on the result agreed at the Communitarian level regarding both traffic data retention time limits (from a minimum of six months to a maximum of two years) and the appropriate and uniform specification of the "categories of data to be retained" (listed in Article 5) in relation to the specified services: fixed network telephony, mobile telephony, Internet access, Internet e-mail and Internet telephony.

This necessitates specifying the field of application of the various measures regarding the obligation to retain data.

# INTERCEPTION OF DIGITAL EVIDENCE ON MOBILE NETWORKS

The remainder of this chapter delves into the complex world of traffic interception in mobile networks investigations, starting with privacy implications, progressing into the technical details, and concluding with related legal framework.

## Privacy and Mobile Network Interception

In general, the freedom and confidentiality of personal communications are inviolable rights that can be compromised only if authorized by judicial authorities and with all the guarantees provided by law. In enacting laws in this regard, the legal systems in different countries or jurisdictions are rushing to dictate a series of limitations regarding the admissibility of interceptions:

- Interceptions are allowable only in cases involving certain specific crimes.
- Interceptions must be authorized.

These requirements are softened somewhat, as may be obviously desirable, in investigations regarding organized crime or international terrorism. In responding to what may be considered society's greatest ills, the possibility is granted to intercept telephone and electronic communications with the sole aim of preventing the commission of certain types of crimes. These are known as preventive interceptions and are considered constitutionally illegitimate in much of legal doctrine. In any case, depending on the legal system from which we operate our investigation, information acquired during preventive interceptions cannot be admitted in court as evidence or kept as such, cannot be cited in investigation documents, and cannot be made public.

Because interception can expose the most private types of information on a mobile network, in certain countries, the regulatory authorities have required higher security levels for information exchange between MC and JA. These security measures generally include:

- Operator authentication systems for access to data
- Immediate deletion of data after they are transmitted to the JA
- Encryption of data while in MC databases
- Technologically secure channels for data transmission
- Limited selection of operators authorized to process sensitive data
- Separation between accounting data and those produced per JA request

The goals of this combination of technical controls, operational oversight, and auditing are to reduce the risk of abuse and increase the chance that any misuse will be detected quickly. The next sections describe a number of shared features of the various laws and regulations in force at the international level.

### Authentication Systems

Processing of telephone and telematic traffic data by NSPs must be allowed only by authorized persons who are granted access by means of specific IT-based authentication systems using *strong authentication* techniques, consisting of the simultaneous use of at least two different authentication technologies, regardless of whether access to data for processing purposes is gained locally or remotely. As a corollary, access must be prevented unless the person has met the requirements of such an IT-based authentication system.

Regarding traffic data retained for the exclusive purpose of detecting, investigating, and prosecuting crime (i.e., those existing for more than six months postgeneration, or all data processed for this purpose if they have been stored, from the moment they are generated, separately from data processed for other purposes), one of these authentication technologies must be based on biometric characterization of the person in question, so as to ensure the physical presence of this person at the workstation used for the processing of the data.

Such methods of authentication must also be applied to all technical personnel (system, network or database administrators) who may have access to the traffic data stored in the NSP's databases.

Regarding authorization systems, specific procedures must be implemented to guarantee the strict separation of technical functions for assigning authentication credentials and identifying authorization profiles from those for the technical management and operation of the systems and databases. These different functions cannot be assigned to the same person at the same time.

### Separate Data Storage

Traffic data retained for the exclusive purpose of detecting, investigating, and prosecuting crime must necessarily be processed using information systems that are physically distinct from those used to process or store traffic data for other purposes. This refers to both processing devices and storage devices.

More specifically, the information systems used to process traffic data retained for the exclusive purposes of law enforcement must be different from those used for other company functions such as billing, marketing, fraud prevention, and so on, and also must be protected against the threat of intrusion by means of appropriate perimeter protection devices and tools that protect the communications network and the storage resources involved in the processing.

Traffic data retained for six months or less from their generation (which is often greater than the average limit established by law in the various countries), on the other hand, may be processed for the purposes of law enforcement either by using the same processing and storage systems used for general data processing, or by duplicating said data and storing them separately from the traffic data processed for "ordinary" purposes, so that they can be processed using systems specifically dedicated to this type of processing.

This prescription leaves NSPs the faculty of choosing, on the basis of their specific organizational model and technological endowment, the most appropriate IT architecture to use for the obligatory retention of traffic data and for all other company purposes. It permits, in fact, that the traffic data retained for up to six months from their generation can be processed, for purposes of law enforcement, with information systems that are not exclusively reserved for that type of processing, or else, that the data may be duplicated for processing using distinct systems dedicated exclusively to purposes of law enforcement. This is a very important point in that both the investigators and the defense counsel may request and obtain information from various points on the network of NSPs.

Regarding chain of custody, keep in mind that the laws in force affirm the principle whereby information systems used to process traffic data for the exclusive purpose of law enforcement must be located within restricted access areas (i.e., reserved exclusively to specifically authorized personnel for the performance of specifically assigned tasks) and outfitted with electronic control devices or security procedures that involve the registration of identification data for all persons admitted, including the times and dates of access.

### Deletion of Data

This is important for the investigation timeline. In many countries, at the expiration of the terms provided for by the regulations in force, the traffic data are rendered unavailable for processing or consultation. They are deleted or otherwise rendered anonymous without delay (within a technically feasible timeframe) in the databases, processing systems, and in systems and media used to create backup or disaster recovery copies, even if these copies have been created by the provider as required by law or regulation. These deletion or ano-nymization operations must be documented within 30 days at the latest from the expiration as provided by law. This is a rule applied particularly in certain European countries.

## Forensic Considerations

As with any form of digital evidence, and particularly when dealing with complex interception systems, it is important to maintain information that supports the chain of custody and data integrity of the acquired data.

### Audit Logs

Information technology measures must be implemented that are appropriate for ensuring oversight of operations performed on traffic data by each person who processes them, regardless of the qualification, competencies, or sector of operations of this person or purpose of said processing. The oversight must be effective and produce detailed records or logs, even for the processing of single data elements located in the different databases used.

These measures entail the recording in a special audit log of all operations per-formed, directly or indirectly, on the traffic data or on other personal informa-tion related to them. This is true regardless of whether the data derive from system-user interaction or are generated automatically by computer programs.

The audit log systems must ensure the completeness, inalterability, and authenticity of the records contained in them, with reference to all processing operations and all events relating to information security and subjected to the auditing process. To this end, data storage systems recording data onto nonal-terable (i.e., read-only) media must be used for the conservation of auditing data. This may be done in a centralized way for each processing system or data-center. Before being written, the data or groups of data have to be subjected to procedures based on the use of cryptographic technologies to attest to their integrity (e.g., generation of hash values).

### Information System Documentation

The information system used for processing traffic data must be accompa-nied by appropriate documentation adhering to accepted principles of soft-ware engineering. Documents that do not meet broadly accepted standards of description are not acceptable.

The description has to include, for each system, the logical and functional architecture, the overall architecture and the structure of the systems used for data processing, the input/output flow of the traffic data from/to other sys-tems, the architecture of the communications network, and indications of the subjects or classes of subjects having legitimate access to the system.

The documentation must be accompanied by system and application diagrams, which must illustrate the exact position of the systems where data are processed for the purposes of detection, investigation, and prosecution of crime.

The technical documentation must be updated and made available to the authorities when and if requested, together with detailed information on subjects having legitimate access to the systems for the processing of traffic data.

### Encryption and Data Protection

Traffic data processed exclusively for purposes of law enforcement must be protected using cryptographic techniques, particularly against risk of fortuitous acquisition risks or accidental alteration during maintenance operations on information apparatuses or ordinary system administration operations. In particular, measures must be adopted to ensure that the information residing in the databases and used by processing systems is unintelligible to those lacking the proper access credentials or authorization profiles. This is done by using forms of encryption or obfuscation of portions of the database or indices or by other technical measures based on cryptographic technologies.

## Evolution of Interception on Mobile Networks

The earliest telephone interception systems comprised a briefcase-sized device known as *multicells*, which were fairly expensive, on the order of $15,000. They consisted of a high powered transceiver with an analog C7-format local recorder. This system permitted the user to monitor a mobile phone, obtain its telephone number, and eavesdrop on the conversation. It essentially replaced the local phone tower by broadcasting at higher power.

The advent of GSM ushered in a period in which interception systems, not yet updated to the new protocols and still using the old technology, were rendered ineffective, thus leaving criminals completely undisturbed in their telephone communications.

Similarly, with the emergence of H3G in Europe, in spite of the fact that it had been in use in the east for some time, there was another technological gap regarding interception technology. The new protocols had to be released by H3G before the private companies that produce interception systems could begin the process of updating their servers and testing out their telephone interception systems. So here as well, the more advanced segments of the criminal world were well aware of this temporary advantage and did not hesitate to exploit its potentials. Nowadays, any multimedia content for a telephone can be intercepted, from video to audio, but investigative systems will always lag technological advances.

## How Telephone Interception Works

This section provides detailed information on how telephone (and telematic) interception works. Protocols naturally change from country to country, but they all share some common features. It is important to be familiar with this information since there is much discussion in the legal arena about the methods used to acquire evidence.

It bears mentioning at the outset that each NSP has an office that handles all requests for interception for the purposes of investigation.

The NSP never gains knowledge of the contents of the tapped telephone calls. Its role is limited to duplicating a suspect's communication line and deviating it to a Telephone Interception Center (TIC) specified in a warrant by the Judicial Authorities (JA). The tapped line is then handled by means of equipment provided by the telephone company or by a private company authorized by the JA. These companies are specialized in telephone interception systems, which we will talk about later. The subject handling the intercepted line will be referred to as a Monitoring Center (MC).

The MCs gather and process a large amount of data on the suspects and third parties with whom the suspects communicate, including the identity of the intercepted subject, and telephone traffic data such as numbers called, date, time and duration of the conversation. Other collected data include calls received, attempted calls, SMS texts, MMS contents, and the geographical location of the intercepted subject.

The MC may also provide personal information, service logs and past traffic records for the suspect, and suspend service for a particular subscriber or device if necessary.

### Anatomy of an Interception System

Mobile network interception systems are powerful systems with database backends that provide digital investigators with flexible access to captured content. These systems enable digital investigators to eavesdrop on conversations directly, watch video calls, review and print G3 and Super G3 faxes (zoom and rotation), and display localization details. Telematic information like e-mail and Internet chat can also be monitored.

Intercepted calls of a specific target can be duplicated in real time, sending the conversation to a mobile phone used by digital investigators to eavesdrop on conversations. Digital investigators can also receive an SMS notification of call intercept of a specific target, and the SMS may be customized to include the caller location.

In addition to real-time monitoring, digital investigators can search through previously recorded traffic. For instance, digital investigators can obtain a list of recordings using multiple search filters like the telephone number (whole or partial), warrant number, originator/recipient, user/interlocutor, account owners, date and time, duration, draft or final transcription keyword, and geographic location.

A typical interception system is composed of a server and peripheral units known as clients, which display data and carry out subsequent processing steps (eavesdropping and transcription). The interception server is connected by fixed line to the network operator, which passes information between the MC's system and the TIC. The server may be the size of a desktop computer for installation at a single police station or the size of a cabinet for multiline interception systems installed at large law enforcement facilities, as shown in Figure 10.3. A server may handle up to 500 lines simultaneously and runs sophisticated antivirus systems.

The system is modular and thus custom installations are possible to provide a broad range of interception capabilities, including:

**FIGURE 10.3**
Interception system (hardware).

- Supported interception interfaces: Analog, E1, T1, PRI, SS7, CAS, POS STM-16/64, ATM, GPRS, UMTS, TIIT, and ETSI HI-1, 2, 3 interfaces
- Nonintrusive TE and high impedance interfaces: ETSI, CALEA, and HI 1, 2, 3
- Simultaneous support of multiple interception taps
- Multiswitching/producer support
- Monitoring of tap system
- Encrypted transmission of interceptions

The Monitoring Center processes are subdivided into separate software modules. These software modules can be installed on a single server, distributed over a plurality of servers, each may be given its own dedicated server, or it is possible to have a plurality of servers running the same module. The distribution of the software modules depends on the simultaneous interception capacity needed, and the levels of security desired to ensure total functionality in the event of a breakdown in any component of the system.

As an example of a Monitoring Center, the monitoring system shown in Figure 10.4 runs on a Windows server operating system and has the following features:

- SQL professional database backend
- Up to 100 voice channels per server (depending from the configuration)
- Connection between central database and multiple servers
- Remote operation of telecommunications servers and centralization of the database
- Remote eavesdropping stations
- Mobile eavesdropping stations via UMTS (currently under development)
- No limit to simultaneous targets

- Target activation via telephone number, IMSI, IMEI, MSISDN, IP address, or e-mail address
- Voice, fax, and SMS decoding
- Decoding of audio-video for UMTS video calls
- VoIP decoding
- Decoding of HTTP, POP3, SMTP, FTP, Chat, Skype, Peer-to-peer (E-Mule), and others
- Taps on RADIUS, DHCP, and other protocols
- Eavesdropping in real time
- Map location and tracing
- External deviation of intercepted calls
- Teleconferencing option
- Decoding of TIM, Vodafone, H3G, "Telecom" "Infostrada", Wind, Cable and Wireless, Wind Internazionale, Teleconomy Internazionale, and other carrier protocols
- Total compatibility with future ETSI protocols already in operation
- Voice library containing fragments of recordings of recognized voices
- Specification of language of intercepted conversation, used also as filtering criterion
- Automatic archiving of interceptions

**FIGURE 10.4**

A sample screenshot of the monitoring console.

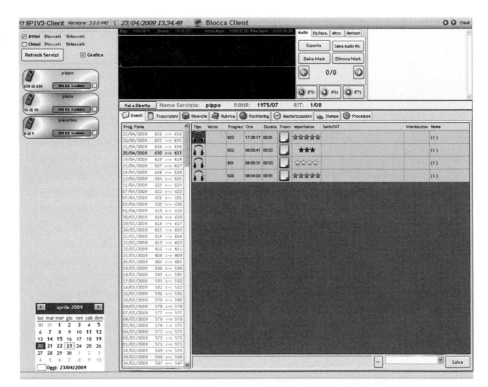

- Full backup on DLT tape for security and disaster recovery
- Multilingual operator interface

The system is able to simultaneously acquire voice, traffic, location, SMS, and fax data for all national and international landline and mobile telephone operators. The data may be stored in a single central database or in a distributed database with controlled access and credentials that can be configured for individual investigators or teams of investigators.

Additional features that may be available in interception systems include:

- **Interception Optimization**: IMEI number interception optimization on a single channel for movement from cell to cell (roaming); optimization of interception of international calls on a single channel even in the event of multiple telephone service providers.

- **Review Tools**: Automatic decoding and association of received logs and SMS. Transcription, summary, and note editor with graphic display of audio, and audio filters for equalization and removal of background noise, voice speed control, loop functions, fast forward, and rewind with complete keyboard and mouse control. Dedicated software for standalone review of data on storage media.

- **Voice Recognition**: Central database for storage of recognized voices complete with sample recordings and personal notes.

- **Archive/Integrity**: Centralized storage on a CD or DVD jukebox with data integrity control for the raw contents of the intercepted calls. Complete or partial copy to CD and DVD for police reports at each workstation and possibility to export individual recordings.

- **Technical Access Controls**: Management of single investigators or groups of investigators. Password access for recording of single lines and/or of single warrants, or for groups assigned to specific cases. Access credential assignment, modification, CD/DVD burning, and configuration of lines and warrants selected on the basis of preset (Administrator, Super User, Interpreter, Police Operator) or customized investigator classes.

- **Administration Features**: Automatic generation of interception request to NSPs. Generation of SMS messages with detailed reports in real time to the system administrator or technical support team in the event of failures or malfunctions.

- **Analysis of Target Behavior**: Predictive target behavior analysis, and graphic analysis for interactions among targets.

In addition, digital investigators can mark high priority recordings, possibly to specify which conversations to translate or transcribe. Furthermore, recordings that have been translated or transcribed can be classified by spoken language.

## Standard Item Report Layout

In response to an interception request, digital investigators may receive intercept related information (IRI) in a standard report format (a.k.a. item report). The IRI details can include data associated with successful and unsuccessful communications, as well as location information. All information in a report is transmitted to digital investigators along with the content of captured communications. Therefore, it is important that digital investigators understand the information in these standard reports. Generally, IRI item reports are formatted as shown in Table 10.5, with the monitored number (e.g., MSISDN, IMEI, IMSI) and time of the event.

Brief descriptions of the fields that may be present in an IRI record are described in Table 10.6. For further information, consult the ETSI and 3GPP specifications, available on www.etsi.org and www.3gpp.org.

The format of IRI records produced for older CS Network and ASN.1-Text networks are also described next. These report formats are still useful to know, because there are still "old" format report versions/schemes available. The data in these reports could be useful for international investigations in Africa and other parts of the developing world.

In an IRI record, the call types are categorized as Originating (the target originated a call or SMS) or Terminating (the target received a call or SMS). IRI records (a.k.a. item reports) having the same Communication Identity Number refer to the same interception event. The events are collected for single days and individual targets by means of the following format MSISDN/IMSI/IMEI_YYYYMMDD (e.g., 393291234567_20060101).

### Cell Information IRI Record Format (GSM/UMTS)

An algorithm has been implemented to analyze every IRI record passing through the formatting system. The algorithm looks at the globalCellID field

---

**Table 10.5** General Format of Intercept Related Information (IRI) Reports

##Monitored Number: 393291234567   Day: 2009–04–20

2008–04–19 03:53:65   &lt;Event type&gt;

&lt;Field(N-1)**1**_Name&gt;&lt;Field(N-1)**1**_Value&gt;
&lt;Field(N-1)**2**_Name&gt;&lt;Field(N-1)**2**_Value&gt;
&lt;Field(N-1)**3**_Name&gt;&lt;Field(N-1)**3**_Value&gt;
……………        ………………..
&lt;Field(**N**)**1**_Name&gt;&lt;Field(**N**)**1**_Value&gt;
&lt;Field(**N**)**2**_Name&gt;&lt;Field(**N**)**2**_Value&gt;

**Table 10.6** Description of Common Fields in an Intercept Related Information (IRI) Report

| Intercept Related Information Report Field | Meaning |
|---|---|
| IRIContent | IRI Record type. May contain: iRI-Begin-record iRI-Continue-record iRI-End-record iRI-Report-record |
| E164-Number | Identity of HLR. The field is formatted "xyz\<number>", where: 1   x   Number plan 1   y   Address type 1   z   Extension number   Node address |
| calledPartyNumber | Called party number |
| callingPartyNumber | Calling party number |
| cC-Link-Identifier | . |
| cCLink-State | Current state of Law Enforcement Monitoring Facility (LEMF) link |
| Communication-Identity-Number | Unambiguous ID number recorded at the monitoring center for the intercepted communication event; this number may be used to correlate different item reports referring to the same event |
| generalizedTime | Date and time of event |
| LEMF-Address | Law Enforcement Monitoring Facility (LEMF) address for target traffic |
| Imei | IMEI of target |
| Imsi | IMSI of target |
| msISDN | MSISDN of target |
| iRIversion | Set to value: version 2 |
| lawfulInterceptionIdentifier | Numerical or alphanumerical field representing the Lawful Interception Identifier (LIID) |
| Mnc | Mobile Network Code |

*(Continued)*

**Table 10.6** Description of Common Fields in an Intercept Related Information (IRI) Report—Cont'd

| Intercept Related Information Report Field | Meaning |
|---|---|
| network-Element-Identifier | Provides the identity of the network element |
| operator-Identifier | Provides the identity of the operator |
| winterSummerIndication | Daylight savings or standard time: "summertime" or "wintertime" |
| globalCellID | Target localization (see section) |
| intercepted-Call-Direct | Indicates whether the target made or received the call or SMS. Possible values: <br> originating-Target <br> terminating-Party |
| Content | Content of SMS message in ETSI format. |

(see Table 10.6) and correlates it with the information contained in the NSP systems where the cell is described. The information is saved in a separate file with the structure shown in Table 10.5. The field name is indicated on the left side of every IRI record and the value on the right. The "value" field may be delimited by the superscript character (ASCII 39). The fields found in an IRI record from the mobile network are summarized in Table 10.7.

The Communication-Identity-Number field is used to correlate cell information with interception events described earlier. The BTS localization field format is as follows:

- **Latitude** "AA<space>BB<space>CC.DD" referenced to geographic north—WGS84 reference
    AA (degrees)
    BB (minutes)
    CC (seconds)
    DD (hundredths of seconds)
- **Longitude** "AA<space>BB<space>CC.DD<space>T"—WGS84 reference
    AA (degrees)
    BB (minutes)
    CC (seconds)
    DD (hundredths of seconds)
    T (E or W)

If available, a file containing related cell information is added to data gathered for a given day.

**Table 10.7** Description of Fields in IRI Records for Mobile Networks (GSM/UTMS)

| Item Report Field | Meaning |
| --- | --- |
| CGI | Cell Global Identity |
| Communication-Identity-Number | Unambiguous ID number recorded at the monitoring center for the intercepted communication event; this number may be used to correlate different item reports referring to the same event |
| generalizedTime | Date and time of event |
| lawfulInterceptionIdentifier | Numerical or alphanumerical field representing the Lawful Interception Identifier (LIID) |
| winterSummerIndication | Daylight savings or standard time: "summertime" or "wintertime" |
| globalCellID | Target localization (see section) |
| Municipality | Municipality where the BTS or Node-B is located |
| Address | Address for the BTS or Node-B |
| Latitude | Latitude of the BTS/Node-B (Optional) |
| Longitude | Longitude of the BTS/Node-B (Optional) |
| Radial position | Radial position of the BTS/Node-B (Optional) 0–360 degrees |

## Packet Switched Network IRI Record Format (GSM/UMTS)

The IRI record format for ITI records associated with packet switched data networks is the same as shown in Table 10.5. Four types of events will generate IRI records that are sent to the Law Enforcement Monitoring Facility:

- **IRI-Begin:** Produced at the first attempt to initiate communication. It opens the transaction.
- **IRI-Continue:** Produced to indicate a further event in an attempt at communication.
- **IRI-End:** Produced at the end of the communication. It closes the transaction.
- **IRI-Report:** Generated for an event not related to a communication event.

The type of IRI records produced for each event type is provided in Table 10.8.

**Table 10.8** Type of IRI Record Generated for Events on GSM/UMTS Packet Switched Network

| Event | IRI Record Type |
|---|---|
| GPRS attach | REPORT |
| GPRS detach | REPORT |
| PDP context activation (successful) | BEGIN |
| PDP context modification | CONTINUE |
| PDP context activation (unsuccessful) | REPORT |
| Start of intercept with PDP context active | BEGIN |
| PDP context deactivation | END |
| Location update | REPORT |
| SMS | REPORT |

The meaning of fields found in every item report generated in a Monitoring Center are provided in Table 10.9.

## Mobile Encrypted Phone

A valid alternative to the use of normal GSM phones are encrypted telephones or "crypto phones." They use the normal telephone network but encrypt the transiting information.

The technical principle is based on breaking up the emitted voice message and recomposing it upon reception based on a particular encryption system. Practically speaking, each message is analyzed digitally and broken up into a certain number of packets of preset duration. The packets are then mixed up on the basis of a session key and transmitted to the recipient. An agent intercepting the call will hear only a sequence of disjointed frequencies that are completely incomprehensible to the human ear and completely undecipherable by any computerized voice analysis system. The recipient receives the call as an analog signal that is recomposed into comprehensible information by use of the same session key.

Security is further enhanced by continuous and automatic variation of the session key according to a specially designed algorithm. The session keys are varied automatically at the start of every conversation and at fixed intervals during the conversation itself.

A crypto phone has two separate channels, one for transmission and one for reception, and each is codified with a different sequence. In order to be able to communicate, the devices on either end of the communication have to know the session key. This key is never transmitted so interception is not

**Table 10.9** Definition of Fields in Interception GSM/UMTS Packet Switched Network

| Item Report Field | Meaning |
| --- | --- |
| APN | Access Point Name (APN) |
| GPRSevent | GPRS event (see Table 10.8) |
| GeneralizedTime | Date and time of event |
| globalCellID | Target localization |
| IMEI | IMEI of target |
| IMSI | IMSI of target |
| MSISDN | MSISDN of target |
| IRIversion | Set to value: version2 |
| MCC | Mobile Country Code |
| MNC | Mobile Network Code |
| Network-Element-Identifier | Provides the identity of the network element |
| Operator-Identifier | Provides the identity of the operator |
| WintorSummerIndication | Daylight savings or standard time: "summertime" or "wintertime" |
| TYPE | |
| IP-type | IP network type (IPv4, IPv6) |
| IP-value | IP address assigned to user at PDP-Context-Activation |

possible. Instead, the serial numbers are transmitted so that the session keys can be obtained from the onboard memories of each crypto phone. Certain phones allow the user to select the keys from a field of $10^{16}$ (10 quadrillion) possibilities.

A would-be interceptor, having an analogous device, or else via computerized analysis of the encrypted signal, would have to try out all possible combinations in order to decode just a fraction of the signals over the two channels. The time necessary to do that is estimated at approximately $3 \times 109$ seconds, or 34,700 days for every minute of conversation. Obviously decryption of an entire conversation is impossible. This currently represents a limit for investigations, and it will become increasingly difficult to overcome.

It is also possible for a group of users to create a private network in which a customized encryption algorithm will be used. Thus only those users who are part of the private network and thus possess the same customized session key will be able to use it.

The latest devices on the market have double encryption: software and hardware. The encryption method can be activated easily from the user menu. A powerful algorithm based on a 128-bit private key provides effective protection for communications, ensuring privacy and the authentication of the recipient. They use technology at 4800 bps for high-quality sound in encrypted communications.

Typical technical characteristics include:

- Normal or encrypted calls to other mobile or landline phones
- Proprietary (unpublished) symmetrical algorithm with 128-bit private keys
- Secure folder
- 100 traffic keys that allow the creation of responder groups
- BSO 900/1800/1900 tri-band
- High-resolution screen, QVGA, 256,000 colors, 240 × 320 pixels
- Integrated technologies: hi-fi ringer, MP3, SMS, MMS, WAP, GPRS, Bluetooth, MP3 player, and video camera, all with up to 40 MB of storage capacity

Figure 10.5 shows a common architecture for encrypted mobile/fixed phones. This figure shows that encrypted cellular telephones can perform a variety of

**FIGURE 10.5**

Encryption phone mixed network example.

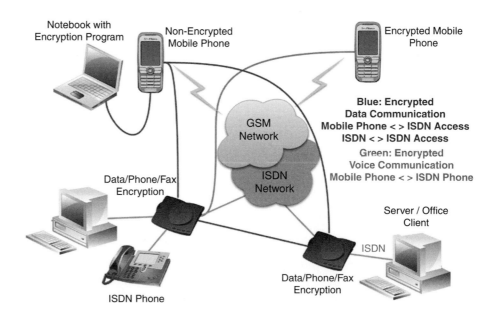

functions, not just encrypted voice communication. With the necessary software or hardware, encrypted mobile phones can exchange data with nonencrypted devices and computers.

The key exchange process for encrypted mobile devices can rely on standard public key infrastructures, to integrate with an enterprise environment. In such cases, as with any network investigation, it may be necessary to obtain logs from servers (e.g., RADIUS, key servers). However, encrypted mobile devices significantly hinder interception. Figure 10.6 represents the practical way the keys are exchanged between phones. Naturally, the illustrated situation is just a snapshot of a specific instant since the session keys are changed in every conversation. To decipher captured communications involving this type of system, it would be necessary to obtain all the private encryption keys.

## Analysis of Usage Logs

Usage logs represent information analytically and compactly, and contain a variety of attributes that can be useful in an investigation. This dense representation of information can often be difficult for digital investigators to read and interpret. Therefore it is generally useful to employ log analysis tools that can reorganize and cross-reference information on the basis of specific needs. A detailed analysis of the logs, known as "content analysis," allows the data to be classified according to specific criteria. The most important elaboration methods for processing logs are summed up:

- Data selection and project algorithms: Applied to a particular investigation. Only given data groups are selected.
- Targeted queries: Queries that cannot be defined as standard. They are targeted to particular investigative needs and are implemented by the investigators on a case-by-case basis.
- Cross-referenced data selection algorithms to classify the data according to complex criteria: Needed when particular correlations must be conducted.
- Statistical processing algorithms: Used, for example, when a particular amount of phone calls between mobile devices—for example before or after a homicide—must be demonstrated.

## Analysis of Mobile Phone Traffic

One of the current trends in this field is using a centralized platform for gathering and analyzing telephone traffic log files and other historical data for purposes of recording, storing, and analyzing telephone and Internet traffic data.

The system has been designed for ISPs, data centers, telecommunications operators, and companies using shared resources for telephone and Internet communications.

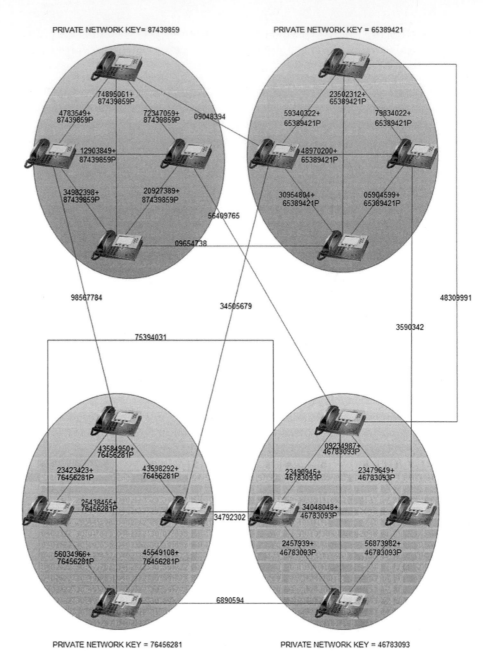

**FIGURE 10.6**

Encryption key exchange example.

Basically speaking, it is a product that allows users to monitor company resource use and easily manage different types of data (logs), whose analysis otherwise often entails long and complex operations.

One of the main features of this tool is that it should be capable of gathering data from a variety of different sources, including but not limited to:

- Telephone exchanges (PABX)
- Mail servers
- RADIUS servers
- Proxies

These data are then stored in a shared database to ensure homogeneous processing and aggregation and correlation operations for statistics, billing, auditing, or other purposes.

The system should be capable of processing large quantities of data by means of user-friendly search masks, thus facilitating the identification and correlation of important information that may derive from previous months or years.

Advanced analyses are usually performed on normalized data using data-mining applications. The identified data can easily be printed or exported in electronic format.

The data saved to the central database are confidential by nature and thus defined as "sensitive data," hence their secrecy must be ensured. System access and data processing protocols fully comply with laws and regulations in force regarding personal privacy.

This type of tool is a fundamental element in a complete security plan to protect the company network and all its shared resources. Its forensically compliant processes also ensure the validity of data for legal purposes. Its functions include:

- Manual or automatic file acquisition via standard or proprietary acquisition interfaces
- Normalization and storage of information contained in the files
- Archive management via data export and backup processes

Usually, a server includes the following modules, all of which are customizable:

- Acquisition
- Normalization
- Web application

### Acquisition

The tool should be able to interact with peripheral devices or systems that generate log files via local network or geographic connections using File Transfer (FTP, sFTP, etc.) or resource sharing (NFS, Microsoft network sharing, etc.) network protocols.

The system is also capable of acquiring files from optical media such as CDs and DVDs.

### Normalization

This type of module is usually equipped with a special process for synchronizing and scheduling the system analysis operations.

The main management issue is recognizing multiple log formats, including the proprietary formats of the principal telephone and network systems. Other formats can easily be added to meet specific needs.

The system produces preformatted reports, aggregating data on the basis of time intervals, originator of communication, type and quantity of traffic, and so on.

### Web Application

This module allows access to the system by web clients connected using the secure protocol (HTTPS) via Internet/intranet or standard browsers (Internet Explorer, Netscape Navigator, etc.).

A good system should be completely configured and operated via web interface.

With a common browser it is possible to:

- Configure and administrate the system
- Manage user profiles and privileges
- Generate normalized files
- Carry out filtered searches (username, telephone number, IP address, URL, etc.)
- Display the results and chronology of operations

## Semantic Intelligence

A further development in investigative software is represented by Semantic Intelligence. This is a particularly complex sort of software for analyzing unstructured data. Once everything available in electronic format (scanned documents, Word files, web documents, etc.) has been imported into the system, it permits keyword searches by definition and groups subjects present in different investigations (cases) even if they use aliases or nicknames.

Thanks to semantic searches, the law enforcement agents are able to obtain a significantly more complete picture, minimizing the likelihood of overlooking some historical detail due to human error. The prosecutor can also use it in an indictment, avoiding the need to leaf through paper documents to find the record needed in a specific moment or compare records for different years.

A drawback of this technology consists first of all in the high cost of use due to years of research and development on the part of some of the world's best software developers as well as the continual upgrading with new features and functions and translations into new languages (e.g., Arabic, Chinese). Another difficulty lies in the large and necessary job of transforming paper case documents into electronic documents needed to perform word searches.

## REFERENCES

EDRI (2006). Telecom Italia wiretapping scandal. Available on EDRI Online, www.edri.org/edrigram/number4.15/italy

Gibbs, K. E., & Clark, D. F. (2001). In E. Casey (Ed.), *Handbook of computer crime investigation*. Academic Press.

International Engineering Consortium. (2007). *Time Division Multiple Access (TDMA)*. Available online at www.iec.org/online/tutorials/tdma/index.asp

Linebaugh, K. (2008). Detroit mayor kilpatrick to resign in plea agreement. *The Wall Street Journal*. Available online at http://online.wsj.com/article/SB122053339750899459.html#printMode

Prevelakis, V., & Spinellis, D. (2007). *The Athens affair, IEEE spectrum*. Available at www.spectrum.ieee.org/jul07/5280

Wang, S., Min, J., & Yi, B. K. (2008). Location based services for mobiles: technologies and standards. In *IEEE International Conference on Communication (ICC)*. Beijing, China.

# Index

Note: Page numbers followed by *t* indicates tables; *f* indicates figures; *b* indicates boxes.

## A

ACK bit, 446–447
Address Book, Macintosh analysis, 379, 380*f*
Alibi, digital forensic analysis assessment, 28–29
AMX Corp, 1–2
Apple, *see* iPod; Macintosh
Attribution, digital forensic analysis applications, 27–28

## B

Back-door, embedded system access, 399–400, 400*b*
Backlog, management with limited resources, 33*b*
Backup tape, data preservation and collection, 105–106, 106*b*
Ball Grid Array (BGA) chip, removal and analysis, 410–411, 411*f*, 412*f*
BGA chip, *see* Ball Grid Array chip
Bind Torture Kill (BTK) case, 27–28
Bitlocker, analysis in Windows, 288–290
Boot loader
    data acquisition, 407–408
    features, 389
Boundary-scan/JTAG
    data acquisition, 408–410, 409*f*
    principles, 389
*Broccoli v. Echostar Communications*, 67–68
Brown, Josie Phyllis, 13*b*, 22*b*
Browsers, *see* Web browsers
BSD, *see* Unix, 302–303
BTK case, *see* Bind Torture Kill case

## C

Carr, Maxine, 28*b*
Carving, files, 36–37, 418

Catalog Node Identifier (CNID), Macintosh, 356
CDMA, *see* Code Division Multiple Access
Cell phones, *see* Embedded system; Mobile networks
Central processing unit (CPU), 386
Chapman, Jessica, 28*b*
Chat
    Unix analysis, 350–351
    Windows analysis, 282–283, 283*f*
Chief operating officer (COO), electronic discovery, 82*b*
Cisco routers
    IOS command line interface, 459*b*, 460
    ISO commands, 461*t*
    show tech-support command, 462*b*
    core dumps, 462–463, 463*f*
Cleaning
    chips, 411–412
    devices, 396
CLF, *see* Common Log Format
CNID, *see* Catalog Node Identifier
Code Division Multiple Access (CDMA), mobile networks, 520
*Coleman v. Morgan Stanley*, 64*b*
Command history, Unix, 332–334
Common Log Format (CLF), 451
Compression
    New Technology File System data compression, 222
    uncompressing files, 38*b*
COO, *see* Chief operating officer
Corrupted files, repair, 39
CPU, *see* Central processing unit
Creston Electronics, 1–2
Crime reconstruction, overview, 13–15

Custodian
    data preservation, 84*b*
    electronic discovery, 81–82, 82*b*

## D

Data abstraction, layers, 6–9
Data Attribute, New Technology File System, 225–226, 226*f*, 227*f*, 234*f*
Date-time stamp
    intrusions
        tampering, 180*b*
        temporal analysis, 180, 199*b*
        unsynchronized stamp resolution, 196–202, 198*t*
    Macintosh analysis, 355–356
    New Technology File System
        backdating, 231*b*
        features versus FAT, 224*b*
        tampering detection, 225*b*
        timestamp analysis in embedded systems, 424–426
    Unix analysis, 308*b*, 309–316
Deduplication, data reduction, 114–116, 115*b*
Defragmentation, Windows data destruction, 276–278, 276*f*
Deleted data salvaging
    file carving, 36–37
    files and folders, 32–48, 35*f*, 36*b*
    special files, 37–40
Desoldering, chips, 410–411
DHCP, *see* Dynamic Host Configuration Protocol
Digital camera, embedded metadata, 40–48, 41*b*
Digital clone, creation and use, 54*b*
Digital document, authentication, 31–32
Discover, *see* Electronic discovery

Disk image, Macintosh analysis, 369–370
Distributed Network Attack (DNA), 39–40
DNA, *see* Distributed Network Attack
DNS, *see* Domain name server
Documentation, importance, 25*b*, 76*b*, 77*t*
Domain name server (DNS), tracking in intrusion investigation, 165*b*
dtSearch, data reduction, 117*b*, 118*f*, 119*f*, 120*f*, 121*f*, 122*f*, 123*f*
Duncan, John Edward, III, 29*b*, 32*b*
Durall, Robert, 29–30
Dynamic Host Configuration Protocol (DHCP), lease, 441*b*

**E**

EEPROM, *see* Electrically erasable programmable read only memory
EFS, *see* Encrypted File System
Electrically erasable programmable read only memory (EEPROM), features, 387
Electronic discovery
  case management, 74–78, 74*b*
  costs, 75, 75*b*
  criminal procedure utilization for accentuation, 72–74
  data accessibility assessment, 71–72
  data preservation and collection
    backup tapes, 105–106, 106*b*
    cell phones, 104
    e-Mail
      Exmerge tool, 88*b*, 89*f*
      F-Response tool, 92*b*, 93*f*, 94*f*
      live servers, 85–86
      Lotus Domino server, 96–97, 96*b*
      Microsoft Exchange servers, 86–96, 91*f*, 92*b*, 95*b*
    evidence chain of custody and control, 104–105
    FTK Imager, 94*f*, 97–102, 97*b*, 98*f*
    Microsoft Backup, 101–102
    overview, 83–106, 84*b*
    Robocopy, 101–102, 102*f*
    transactional systems and databases, 102–104
    xxcopy, 100, 101*f*
  data processing

compressed or encrypted files, 109–110
  data reduction
    advanced analytics, 127–130
    case example, 108*b*
    deduplication, 114–116, 115*b*
    dtSearch, 117*b*, 118*f*, 119*f*, 120*f*, 121*f*, 122*f*, 123*f*
    keyword searching, 116–127, 126*b*
  data transformation and review, 130
  deleted file fragment recovery from unallocated space, 114–116
  deleted files and folders, 109
  e-mail, file servers, and backup tapes, 113–114
  forensic images, 108–113
  high-priority custodian computers, 110
  image files, 110
  indexing of documents, 120–124
  overview, 106–130
  personal data, 111–112
  Web usage exploration, 112–113
  data storage locations, 78
  documentation importance, 76*b*, 77*t*
  Electronic Discovery Reference Model, 64–65, 64*f*, 65*b*
  electronically stored information preservation obligations, 66–70, 67*b*
  initial meeting, disclosures, and agreements, 70–71
  international considerations, 66*b*
  interviews
    custodians, 81–82
    information technology personnel, 79–81
  legal basis, 66
  overview, 63–65
  presentation of data, 130–132
  quality assurance, 131*b*
E-Mail
  intrusion alerts, 171–172
  Macintosh analysis, 377–379, 378*f*
  preservation and collection

Exmerge tool, 88*b*, 89*f*
  F-Response tool, 92*b*, 93*f*, 94*f*
  live servers, 85–86
  Lotus Domino server, 96–97, 96*b*
  Microsoft Exchange servers, 86–96, 91*f*, 92*b*, 95*b*
  processing in electronic discovery, 113–114
  Unix analysis, 345–350
  Windows client analysis, 283–285, 284*b*
Embedded system
  acronyms, 431–433
  cell phones
    classification, 426–428
    file traces, 429
    improvised explosive devices, 412*f*, 426*b*
    multimedia data, 428–429
    video file system information and metadata, 428*t*
  central processing unit, 386
  data collection
    back-doors, 399–400, 400*b*
    brute force, 403–404
    correlation measurements, 402–403
    logical data acquisition, 405–406, 405*b*, 406*b*
    manual examination, 404–405
    physical data acquisition
      boot loaders, 407–408
      Boundary-scan/JTAG, 408–410, 409*f*
      chip cleaning, connecting, and reading, 411–413
      definition, 406–413
      desoldering, 410–411
      reballing of chips, 411
      software, 407
    procedural access, 398–399
  definition, 384–391
  devices, 385–386
  electrical diagram reconstruction, 430
  functionality determination, 429–430
  information recovery
    data carving, 418
    data records
      hex editors, 414–415, 415*f*
      IDA Pro, 415–417, 416*f*

file system recovery, 417–418
overview, 413–424
Samsung SGH-D500 phone
example
file system recovery, 422–424
flash translation layer,
421–422
overview, 419–424, 421*f*
tools, 418–419
memory
injection, 402
management, 389–390
measurement, 400–402, 401*f*
types, 387–389, 389*t*
overview, 383–384
prospects for analysis, 430–431
software reconstruction, 430
timestamp analysis, 424–426
trace preservation
cleaning, 396
live versus dead dilemmas,
392–396
network connectivity, 394–396
nondigital traces, 392
power maintenance, 393–394,
393*b*
repair, 396–397, 397*f*
security barriers, 394
EMF, *see* Enhanced Metafile
EnCase
Encrypted File System analysis,
291*f*, 292*b*
Macintosh inode file display, 358*f*
Windows Enhanced Metafile
conversion, 252*f*
Windows file permissions display,
220*b*
work flow, 112*b*
Encrypted File System (EFS), analysis
in Windows, 290–292, 291*f*,
292*b*
Encryption
mobile encrypted phones,
550–553, 552*f*, 554*f*
mobile network data protection,
541
overview, 33–37
Windows
Bitlocker, 288–290
Encrypted File System,
290–292, 291*f*, 292*b*
Enhanced Cell Identification,
positioning of mobile devices,
524

Enhanced Metafile (EMF), Windows
printer, 251–254, 252*f*
Enhanced Observed Time Difference
(E-OTD), positioning of
mobile devices, 525
Enron, 106*b*
Entwistle, Neil, 29
E-OTD, *see* Enhanced Observed Time
Difference
EPROM, *see* Erasable programmable
read only memory
Erasable programmable read only
memory (EPROM), features,
387
Ethernet, frame, 443*f*, 444*f*
Event Viewer, Windows, 242*f*
Evidence dynamics
causes, 9–10
minimization in intrusion
investigation, 160*b*
Exmerge tool, e-mail preservation
and collection, 88*b*, 89*f*

**F**
Fax, electronic, 38
FeRAM, *see* Ferro electric random
access memory
Ferro electric random access memory
(FeRAM), features, 389
Filename Attribute (FNA), New
Technology File System, 225
FileVault, accessing data, 370*b*
Firefox, Unix analysis, 339–344,
341*f*, 342*f*, 343*f*, 344*f*
Firewall
definition, 463–464
intruder connection through
virtual private network, 465*b*
logs, 463–464
Flash memory
features, 387–388
file systems, 390
Flow-tools, *see* NetFlow
FNA, *see* Filename Attribute
Forensic residue, identification, 49, 50*b*
Forensic soundness, 3–5
F-Response
e-mail preservation and
collection, 92*b*, 93*f*, 94*f*
intrusion investigation, 205
FTK Imager
data preservation and collection,
94*f*, 97–102, 97*b*, 98*f*

Windows file permissions display,
220*b*
Windows shadow copies, 268*f*
Functional analysis, overview, 14
Fuzzy hatching, intrusion
investigation, 185–186

**G**
Gaumer, John, 13*b*, 22*b*
GLBA. *see* Gramm-Leach-Bliley Act
Global Positioning System (GPS)
embedded information in mobile
devices, 12*b*
positioning of mobile devices,
524
SatNav artifact analysis, 54*b*
Globally Unique Identifier (GUID),
Office files, 30
Gmail, reconstruction of account
setup page, 47*f*
Goldenberg, David, 1–2
*The Good Practice Guide for
Computer-Based Electronic
Evidence*, 84–85
Google Maps, reconstruction of page,
52*f*
Google Spreadsheet, data extraction,
58*b*
GPS, *see* Global Positioning System
Gramm-Leach-Bliley Act (GLBA), 137
Grepmail, Unix analysis, 347–348
GUID, *see* Globally Unique Identifier
Guthrie, William, 29

**H**
Hash correlation, intrusion
investigation, 185
Header signatures, graphics files, 8*b*
Health Insurance Portability and
Accountability Act (HIPAA),
137
Hex editor, data record recovery from
embedded systems, 414–415,
415*f*
Heyne, Frank, 221*b*
Hiberfil.sys, 261–263
HIPAA, *see* Health Insurance
Portability and Accountability
Act
HLR, *see* Home Location Register
Home Location Register (HLR),
mobile networks, 521
HTTP, *see* Hypertext Transfer Protocol

Huntley, Ian, 28*b*
Hypertext Transfer Protocol (HTTP)
    overview, 448–452
    requests, 449*t*, 450*t*
    response status codes, 450*t*, 451*f*
    specifications, 448*b*
Hypothesis
    evaluation, 48
    formation, 48

# I

iCal, Macintosh analysis, 379–382,
    381*f*
IDA Pro, data record recovery from
    embedded systems, 415–417,
    416*f*
IDS, *see* Intrusion detection system
IMEI, *see* International Mobile
    Equipment Identifier
Inode
    Macintosh analysis, 357–359, 358*f*
    Unix, 322*f*, 325–326
*Integrated Service Solutions, Inc. v.
    Rodman*, 70*b*
Intent, digital forensic analysis
    determination, 29–30
Interception, mobile network data
    audit logs, 540
    authentication systems, 538
    data deletion, 539–540
    definition, 532–533
    encryption and data protection,
        541
    evolution, 541
    information system
        documentation, 540–541
    intercept related information
        report
        cell information IRI record
            format, 546–549
        layout, 546–550, 547*t*
        packet switched network IRI
            record format, 549–550,
            550*t*, 551*t*
    interception system features,
        542–546, 543*f*, 544*f*
    privacy concerns, 537–540
    separate data storage, 538–539
International Mobile Equipment
    Identifier (IMEI), 521–522, 522*b*
Internet Explorer, analysis in
    Windows, 280–282, 281*f*,
    00005:b0210

Interviews, *see* Electronic discovery
Intrusion detection system (IDS),
    503–505, 505*b*
Intrusions
    analysis examples, 180*b*,
        183*b*, 197*b*
    case management
        attributes
            account events, 167, 167*b*
            configuration settings, 166
            files of system, 166
            general event tracking, 167,
                168*t*
            host identity, 165–166,
                165*b*
            indicators of execution,
                166–167
            network transmissions and
                sessions, 167
            tracking, 164–165, 164*t*
        communication channels,
            162–163
        containment/remediation
            versus investigative success,
                163–164
        evidence dynamics
            minimization, 160*b*
        organizational structure,
            158–161, 159*f*
        project management
            comparison, 162*b*
        task tracking, 161–162, 161*t*,
            162*t*
    collection of evidence
        forensic acquisition of
            memory, 177–178
        live collection, 176–177
        log copying, 179*b*
        network packet capture,
            178–179
        overview, 175–179
    date-time stamp
        tampering, 180*b*
        temporal analysis, 180, 199*b*
        unsynchronized stamp
            resolution, 196–202, 198*t*
    domain/directory preparation,
        155–156
    evidence sources, 138*b*
    feeding analysis back into
        detection phase
        enterprise-wide visibility,
            203–204

        hardware load, 204
        host-based detection, 202–203
        network-based intrusion
            detection, 205–206
        rootkit interference
            circumvention for artificial
            sweeps, 204
    host-based analysis
        directory correlation, 186
        fuzzy hatching, 185–186
        hash correlation, 185
        keyword search, 186–187
        process structure correlation,
            186
        segmentation hashing,
            185–186
    incident response life cycle,
        139–140, 139*f*
    initial observations
        antivirus alerts, 170–171, 171*b*
        blacklist violations, 173
        crashes, 172–173
        e-mail with suspicious
            contents, 171–172
        external notifications,
            173–174, 173*b*
        intrusion detection system
            alert, 171
        network traffic abnormalities,
            173
    initial processing
        host analysis, 189–190
        log analysis, 173–174
        malicious code, 191
        overview, 188–191
    log correlation, 191*b*, 192*f*, 200*b*,
        200*f*, 201*f*
    network architecture, 154–155
    overview, 135–139, 136*b*
    preparation for security breach
        host preparation, 147–150
        infrastructure logging, 149*b*,
            150–153, 151*b*, 152*b*
        inventory of assets and data,
            145–146
        log retention, 147–150
        overview, 143–157, 144*b*,
            145*b*
        policies and procedures,
            146–147
        tools, 157*b*
        training and drills, 156–157
    reporting of investigations

audiences, 169–170
fact versus speculation,
168–169, 169b
interim reports, 170
scientific method for
investigation, 140–143, 183b
scope assessment, 141–143, 141f,
142b, 174–175
time synchronization, 156, 156b
tools
F-Response, 205
overview, 204–205
ProDiscoverIR, 184–185, 184f
trends, 135, 136t
written authorizations for
investigation, 143b
IP address, searching in packet
contents, 494, 494f
iPod, sharing analysis, 368b

**J**

Jamming device, technical
specification, 527t
*Johnson v. Wells Fargo*, 216b
JPG
deleted file recovery, 36b
header signatures, 8b
JTAG, *see* Boundary-scan/JTAG

**K**

Kercher, Meredith, 517b
Keyword search
data reduction
Boolean expressions, 126–127
dtSearch, 117b, 118f, 119f,
120f, 121f, 122f, 123f
field searching, 127
keyword completion, 126
keyword stemming, 127
overview, 116–127
phonic searching, 127
synonym searching, 127
targeted keywords, 124–126,
126b
intrusion investigation, 186–187

**L**

LADS, alternate data stream display,
221b
LDM, *see* Logical Disk Manager
*Leon v. IDX Systems Corp.*, 274b
Link file, analysis in Windows,
243–245, 244f, 245b

Linux, *see* Unix
$LogFile, 217–218, 217f
Logging
incomplete logs, 152b
infrastructure, 149b, 150–153,
151b, 152b
intrusion investigation
copying, 179b
log analysis, 173–174
log correlation, 191b, 192f,
200b, 200f, 201f
network-level logging, 151b
retention, 147–150
Logical Disk Manager (LDM),
analysis in Windows,
294–295, 295b
Lotus Domino server, e-mail
preservation and collection,
96–97, 96b
Lumumba, Patrick, 517b

**M**

Macintosh
Address Book, 379, 380f
application analysis, 364–365
disk images, 369–370
e-mail analysis, 377–379, 378f
external device connections,
368–369, 368b
file systems
data versus resource forks,
356, 357f
date-time stamps, 355–356
file attributes, 356, 356f
file deletion, 356–357
inodes, 357–359, 358f
partitioning, 355b
iCal, 379–382, 381f
imaging, 353–355
log on and off, 369
logs, 367–369
Notepad, 382f
property lists, 359, 360f
Safari use analysis, 374f,
375–377, 375t, 376f,
377b
system configuration files,
365–370
user accounts
overview, 359–364, 361f, 362b
passwords, 362–364
user folders
applications, 372–382, 374f

media files, 371–372
overview, 370–371
Mail, Macintosh analysis, 377–379,
378f
Mairix, Unix analysis, 348–350
Malware
digital forensic analysis rationale,
44
unknown code assessment
in intrusion investigation,
187–188
Master File Table (MFT), New
Technology File System
alternate data streams, 221b, 223
Data Attribute, 225–226, 226f,
227f, 234f
data access control, 219–221
data compression, 222
data runs with negative offsets,
228b
date-time stamp
backdating, 231b
features versus FAT, 224b
$LogFile, 217–218, 217f
tampering detection, 225b
Filename Attribute, 225
overview, 216–217
querying, 204
records, 223
reparse points, 222–223, 223f
$Secure, 219–221
Standard Information Attribute,
223–225
$Volume, 218–219, 218f, 219f
Memory management unit (MMU),
features, 389–390
Memory, *see* Embedded system
Metadata
extraction, 40–48, 41b
Unix, 318–322, 320f, 322f
Windows
application metadata,
232–235
extraction from Microsoft
Office, 233b, 234f
file system, 230–232
tampering, 235b
Metaviewer, output, 234f
MFT, *see* Master File Table
Microsoft Backup, data preservation
and collection, 101–102
Microsoft Exchange servers, e-mail
preservation and collection,
86–96, 91f, 92b, 95b

Microsoft Office, metadata
   extraction, 233b, 234f
Microsoft Windows, see Windows
MIME encoding, 38–39
MMS, see Multimedia Message Service
MMU, see Memory management unit
Mobile networks
   components, 519–522, 519f
   evidence types
      intercepted data, 532–533
      localization parameters,
         524–527
      positioning of mobile devices,
         524–526
      remote activation of electronic
         devices, 526–527
      text/multimedia messages,
         529–532
      usage logs and billing records,
         527–529
   interception
      audit logs, 540
      authentication systems, 538
      data deletion, 539–540
      definition, 532–533
      encryption and data
         protection, 541
      evolution, 541
      information system
         documentation, 540–541
      intercept related information
         report
            cell information IRI record
               format, 546–549
            layout, 546–550, 547t
            packet switched network
               IRI record format,
               549–550, 550t, 551t
      interception system features,
         542–546, 543f, 544f
      privacy concerns, 537–540
      separate data storage, 538–539
   investigation
      data collection, 535
      data sources, 533–537
      European regulations,
         535–537
      overview, 522–524, 523f
      service provider data types and
         request, 534–537, 534b
   mobile device definition, 518
   mobile encrypted phones,
      550–553, 552f, 554f

Semantic Intelligence, 556–557
telephony versus telematic
   services, 519t
traffic analysis, 553–556
usage log analysis, 553
Multimedia Message Service (MMS),
   evidence, 531

N
NAS, see Network-attached storage
NetFlow
   flow-tools package, 469b
   losses, 472b
   misinterpretation, 472b
   overview, 467–472
NetIntercept, intrusion investigation,
   495f
NetWitness, capture file profiling,
   483b
Network-attached storage (NAS),
   analysis in Windows, 298–299
Network-based intrusion
   detection (NIDS), intrusion
   investigation, 205–206
Network investigations
   authentication
      intruder connection to
         router through dialup,
         477b
      log correlation, 441b
      RADIUS, 473–475, 473t
      TACACS, 475–479, 476t
   challenges in evidence collection,
      15–16
   computer tracking within
      network, 441b
   credit card theft case, 452b
   cybertrail case example, 438b
   data theft case, 456b
   enterprise networks, 439–442,
      440f
   evidence preservation, 457–458
   firewalls, 463–464
   Hypertext Transfer Protocol,
      448–452, 449f, 450t, 451f
   log correlation, 505–516
   mobile networks, see Mobile
      networks
   NetFlow
      flow-tools package, 469b
      losses, 472b
      misinterpretation, 472b
      overview, 467–472

network device configuration,
   458–479, 459b, 461t, 462b, 463f
overview, 437–439
protocol types, 442–457
Server Message Block, 452–457,
   453f, 454t, 455f, 456f, 457b
traffic analysis
   capture files
      filtering to reduce size,
         490b
      profiling, 483b
   file extraction from TCP session
      automatic extraction,
         494–496, 495b, 495f,
         496f
      manual extraction,
         496–503, 496b, 498b
   hex or ASCII value searching,
      491–494, 491t, 492f, 492t
   host searching, 487–488, 488t
   intrusion detection systems,
      503–505
   IP address searching in packet
      contents, 494, 494f
   port and protocol searches,
      488–491
   protocol hierarchy, 485–487,
      486t
   tools
      ngrep, 481–482, 482t, 491,
         491t
      statistical information
         extraction, 483–487,
         483t
      tcpdump, 480–481, 481t,
         487, 489t
      tshark, 485, 485t, 487–488
      Wireshark, 482–483, 482t,
         487–488, 488f, 489f,
         490t, 491–494, 492b,
         492f, 492t, 494f, 498b
   virtual private network, 441–442,
      464–467, 465b
Network Miner, file extraction from
   TCP session, 495b, 496f
New Technology File System (NTFS)
   alternate data streams, 221b, 223
   data access control, 219–221
   data compression, 222
   date-time stamp
      backdating, 231b
      features versus FAT, 224b
      tampering detection, 225b

file deletion detection, 229–230
internal files, 215–216, 216*t*
$LogFile, 217–218, 217*f*
Master File Table
　Data Attribute, 225–226, 226*f*,
　　227*f*, 234*f*
　data runs with negative offsets,
　　228*b*
　Filename Attribute, 225
　overview, 216–217
　records, 223
　Standard Information
　　Attribute, 223–225
reparse points, 222–223, 223*f*
$Secure, 219–221
$Volume, 218–219, 218*f*, 219*f*
Ngrep, network traffic analysis
　ASCII and hex value searches,
　　491, 491*t*
　host searches, 488*t*
　options, 482*t*
　overview, 481–482
NIDS, *see* Network-based intrusion
　detection
Notepad, Macintosh analysis, 382*f*
NTFS, *see* New Technology File
　System

## O

Occam's razor, intrusion
　investigation, 182–184
OCR, *see* Optical character
　recognition
Office, *see* Microsoft Office
Operating system, configuration and
　usage, 42–48, 42*b*
Optical character recognition (OCR),
　38
OS X, *see* Macintosh
Outlook, analysis in Windows,
　283–285, 284*b*

## P

Pagefile, security risks, 149*b*
Pagefile.sys, 261–263
Passwords, Macintosh analysis,
　362–364
Payment Card Industry Data Security
　Standard (PCI DSS), 137
PCI DSS, *see* Payment Card Industry
　Data Security Standard
PDA, *see* Embedded system;
　Mobile networks

PDF, searching, 38
Power, maintenance in embedded
　systems, 393–394, 393*b*
Prefetch files, analysis in Windows,
　245–247, 246*f*, 275*f*
ProDiscoverIR
　intrusion investigation, 184–185,
　　184*f*
　$Volume file display, 219*f*
Programmable read only memory
　(PROM), features, 387
PROM, *see* Programmable read only
　memory
Proximity searching, caveats, 9*b*

## Q

*Qualcomm, Inc. v. Broadcom Corp.*, 69*b*

## R

RADIUS, *see* Remote Authentication
　Dial In User Service
RAID, *see* Redundant array of
　inexpensive disks
RAM, *see* Random access memory
Random access memory (RAM)
　features, 388–389
　Windows analysis, 285–287,
　　286*b*, 287*f*
Read only memory (ROM), features,
　387
Reballing, chips, 411
Recycle Bin, analysis in Windows,
　254–256, 254*f*, 255*f*, 256*f*
Redundant array of inexpensive disks
　(RAID)
　acquisition, 295–298
　creation, 293*f*
　levels, 293
　reconstruction, 297*b*, 298*b*
Registry, analysis in Windows, 270*b*,
　271–273, 272*f*, 273*b*
Relational analysis, overview, 14
Remote Authentication Dial In User
　Service (RADIUS), 473–475,
　473*t*
Repair, devices, 396–397, 397*f*
Reparse points, New Technology File
　System, 222–223, 223*f*
Resource fork, Macintosh analysis,
　356, 357*f*
Restore point (RP), analysis in
　Windows, 263–268, 263*f*,
　265*f*, 266*f*

Robocopy, data preservation and
　collection, 101–102, 102*f*
ROM, *see* Read only memory
Root directory, Unix, 316–318
RP, *see* Restore point

## S

Safari, Macintosh analysis, 374*f*,
　375–377, 375*t*, 376*f*, 377*b*
Salvaging, *see* Deleted data salvaging
Sarbanes-Oxley Act (SOX), 137
SatNav, artifact analysis, 54*b*
Scientific method
　application to digital forensics,
　　5–13, 10*b*
　intrusion investigation
　　overview, 140–143, 183*b*
　scope assessment, 141–143,
　　141*f*, 142*b*
$Secure, 219–221
Secure Shell, Unix, 339
Security breach, *see* Intrusions
Segmentation hashing, intrusion
　investigation, 185–186
Semantic Intelligence, mobile
　network analysis, 556–557
Server Message Block (SMB)
　anonymous connections, 457*b*
　command codes, 454*t*
　message exchange, 446*f*
　overview, 452–457
　packets, 453*f*, 455*f*, 456*f*
Shadow copies, analysis in Windows,
　266*f*, 267*f*, 268*f*
Short Message Service (SMS)
　analysis, 517*b*
　evidence, 529–532
SIA, *see* Standard Information
　Attribute
Skimming, magnetic cards, 392*b*
Skype, usage information extraction,
　55, 56*b*, 57*t*, 58*f*
SMB, *see* Server Message Block
SMS, *see* Short Message Service
Source
　digital forensic analysis, 30–31
　evidence relationship, 10–13
SOX, *see* Sarbanes-Oxley Act
Splunk
　log correlation, 200*b*
　network log correlation, 506*f*, 507*f*
Spoliation, *Leon v. IDX Systems
　Corp.*, 274*b*

SQLite, Firefox data in Unix, 339–344, 341*f*, 342*f*, 343*f*
Standard Information Attribute (SIA), New Technology File System, 223–225
Steganography, overview, 33–37
Storage area network, analysis in Windows, 298–299
Stroz Discovery, document categorization, 129, 129*f*
Superblock, Unix, 318–322, 320*f*
Swap space, Unix, 351
SYN bit, 446–447
SYN packet, 446–447
Syslog, Unix, 331*b*, 334–337
System V, Unix, 305–306

**T**

TACACS, 475–479, 476*t*
TCP/IP
    abstraction layers, 443*t*
    circuit initiation, 446*f*
    header format, 445*f*
    overview, 444–446
    TCP headers, 447*f*
Tcpdump, network traffic analysis overview, 480–481
    port and protocol searches, 481*t*, 487, 489*t*
TDMA, *see* Time Division Multiple Access
TDOA, *see* Time difference of arrival
Temporal analysis, overview, 14–15
Thin Small-Outline Package (TSOP) chip, removal and analysis, 410*f*, 411
Thumbs.db file, 236*b*, 249–251, 250*f*
Time difference of arrival (TDOA), positioning of mobile devices, 524
Time Division Multiple Access (TDMA), mobile networks, 520
Time of arrival (TOA), positioning of mobile devices, 524–525
Time synchronization, intrusion investigation, 156, 156*b*
Time zone, case complications, 51*b*
Timestamp, *see* Date-time stamp
TOA, *see* Time of arrival
Travis, Maury, 27*b*
Trojan horse, digital forensic analysis rationale, 44

Tshark, network traffic analysis host searching, 487–488
    IP conversation capture, 485, 485*t*
    protocol hierarchy, 485–487
TSOP chip, *see* Thin Small-Outline Package chip

**U**

Unallocated space
    deleted file fragment recovery, 114–116
    quantification, 37*b*
Unix
    boot process
        BSD, 306
        overview, 304–306
        System V, 305–306
    BSD programs, 302–303
    commercial operating systems, 303–304
    data deletion and recovery, 323–325, 325*b*
    definitions, 301–302
    file systems
        date-time stamp analysis, 308*b*, 309–316
        inodes out-of-place, 325–326
        metadata and file content, 318–322, 320*f*, 322*f*
        overview, 306–326, 308*f*
        root directory, 316–318
        useful features, 308–309
    forensic duplication, 306, 307*b*
    Linux, 302
    swap space, 351
    system configuration and scheduled tasks, 328–329
    user accounts, 326–328
    user activity artifacts
        application traces and recently opened files, 334–337, 335*f*, 336*f*
        command history, 332–334
        communications
            cache, 344, 345*f*
            chat, 350–351
            e-mail analysis, 345–350
            Firefox, 339–344, 341*f*, 342*f*, 343*f*, 344*f*
            Grepmail, 347–348
            Mairix, 348–350
            saved session, 344–345
            Secure Shell, 339

data deletion and destruction, 338–339
        log on and off, 329–330, 330*f*
        printers, 337–338, 337*b*, 337*f*
        removable media, 338
        Syslog, 331*b*, 334–337
USB device
    Macintosh traces, 368–369, 368*b*
    Unix traces, 338
    Windows traces, 256–261, 257*b*, 258*f*, 259*f*, 260*f*, 261*b*

**V**

Validation, tools, 26
Virginia Prescription Marketing Program (VPMP), 2
Virtual identity, versus actual identity, 441*b*
Virtual private network (VPN)
    firewall connection through virtual private network, 465*b*
    logs, 441–442, 464–467
Vista, *see* Windows
$Volume, 218–219, 218*f*, 219*f*
VPMP, *see* Virginia Prescription Marketing Program
VPN, *see* Virtual private network

**W**

Web browsers, *see also* specific browsers
    artifact interpretation, 52*b*
    page reconstruction, 52*f*, 53*b*
Wells, Holly, 28*b*
Windows
    autorun locations, 148*b*
    communications activity analysis
        chat, 282–283, 283*f*
        e-mail clients, 283–285, 284*b*
        Internet Explorer, 280–282, 281*f*, 282*b*
    data destruction
        defragmentation, 276–278, 276*f*
        deletion evidence, 278–279, 279*b*
        overview, 274–276, 275*f*
    emulators, 209
    encryption
        Bitlocker, 288–290
        Encrypted File System, 290–292, 291*f*, 292*b*

Event Viewer, 242*f*
Logical Disk Manager, 294–295, 295*b*
metadata
    application metadata, 232–235
        extraction from Microsoft Office, 233*b*, 234*f*
        file system, 230–232
        tampering, 235*b*
network-attached storage (NAS), 298–299
New Technology File System
    alternate data streams, 221*b*, 223
    data access control, 219–221
    data compression, 222
    date-time stamp
        backdating, 231*b*
        features versus FAT, 224*b*
        tampering detection, 225*b*
    file deletion detection, 229–230
    internal files, 215–216, 216*t*
    $LogFile, 217–218, 217*f*
    Master File Table
        Data Attribute, 225–226, 226*f*, 227*f*, 234*f*
        data runs with negative offsets, 228*b*
        Filename Attribute, 225
        overview, 216–217
        records, 223
        Standard Information Attribute, 223–225
    reparse points, 222–223, 223*f*
    $Secure, 219–221
    $Volume, 218–219, 218*f*, 219*f*
process memory, 285–287, 286*b*, 287*f*
redundant array of inexpensive disks

acquisition, 295–298
creation, 293*f*
levels, 293
reconstruction, 297*b*, 298*b*
startup process, 210–211, 211*f*, 212*f*, 213*f*
storage area network, 298–299
user activity artifacts
    event logging, 240–243, 241*f*, 242*b*, 242*f*, 243*b*
    external device connections, 256–261, 257*b*, 258*f*, 259*f*, 260*f*, 261*b*
    hiberfil.sys, 261–263
    installed programs, 247–249, 248*f*
    link file analysis, 243–245, 244*f*, 245*b*
    log on and log off, 235–273, 236*b*, 237*f*, 238*f*, 239*f*, 240*f*
    miscellaneous artifacts, 268–273, 270*b*, 270*t*
    pagefile.sys, 261–263
    prefetch files, 245–247, 246*f*, 275*f*
    printer files, 251–254, 252*f*, 253*f*
    Recycle Bin, 254–256, 254*f*, 255*f*, 256*f*
    registry analysis, 270*b*, 271–273, 272*f*, 273*b*
    restore points, 263–268, 263*f*, 265*f*, 266*f*
    shadow copies, 266*f*, 267*f*, 268*f*
    thumbs.db file, 236*b*, 249–251, 250*f*
versions, 210
Windows 7, 213–214
Windows Vista, 212–214, 213*f*

Windows XP, 211–212
WinFS, 214–215
Windows Mobile
    logical acquisition using .XRY, 8*f*
    physical acquisition using XACT, 7*f*
Winhex, data record recovery from embedded systems, 415*f*
Wireshark
    anonymous connections, 457*b*
    Ethernet frame display, 444*f*
    HTTP GET request, 449*f*
    Server Message Blocks, 453*f*, 455*f*
    TCP header display, 447*f*
Wireshark, network traffic analysis
    ASCII and hex value searches, 491–494, 492*b*, 492*f*, 492*t*
    file extraction from packet containing unknown protocol, 496*b*
    file extraction from TCP session containing unknown protocol, 498*b*
    host searches, 482*t*, 487–488, 488*f*, 489*f*
    IP address searches, 494*f*
    overview, 482–483
    port and protocol searches, 490*t*

**X**

XACT, information recovery from embedded systems, 418–419, 420*f*
XP, *see* Windows
xxcopy, data preservation and collection, 100, 101*f*

**Z**

*Zubulake v. UBS Warburg*, 67*b*, 75